# THE ENDURING VOICE

*Concerns in Literature Present and Past*

# THE ENDURING VOICE

## Concerns in Literature Present and Past

Margaret Ganz & Julia Ebel

*Brooklyn College*

The Macmillan Company, New York

## ACKNOWLEDGMENTS

City Lights Books. ALLEN GINSBERG, "America" from *Howl and Other Stories*. Copyright © 1956, 1959 by Allen Ginsberg. Reprinted by permission of City Lights Books.

Dodd, Mead & Company, Inc. GEORGE BERNARD SHAW, *Major Barbara* by George Bernard Shaw. Copyright 1907, 1913, 1930 by George Bernard Shaw; Copyright 1957, The Public Trustee as Executor of the Estate of George Bernard Shaw. Reprinted by permission of Dodd, Mead & Company, Inc., and The Society of Authors for the Estate of Bernard Shaw. MELVIN B. TOLSON, "Dark Symphony." Reprinted by permission of Dodd, Mead & Company, Inc., from *Rendezvous with America* by Melvin B. Tolson. Copyright 1944 by Dodd, Mead & Company, Inc.

Doubleday & Company, Inc. THEODORE ROETHKE, "In a Dark Time," copyright © 1960 by Beatrice Roethke, Administratrix of the Estate of Theodore Roethke. From the book *The Collected Poems of Theodore Roethke*. Reprinted by permission of Doubleday & Company, Inc.

Farrar, Straus & Giroux, Inc. ROBERT LOWELL, "The Voyage"; FLANNERY O'CONNOR, "Everything That Rises Must Converge"; TOM WOLFE, "Putting Daddy On." Reprinted with the permission of Farrar, Straus & Giroux, Inc., from *Imitations* by Robert Lowell, copyright © 1958, 1959, 1960, 1961 by Robert Lowell. From *Everything That Rises Must Converge* by Flannery O'Connor, copyright © 1961, 1965 by the Estate of Mary Flannery O'Connor. From *The Kandy Kolored Tangerine Flake Streamline Baby* by Tom Wolfe, copyright © 1964 by the New York Herald Tribune, Inc.

Grove Press, Inc. MALCOLM X, "Black Muslims" from *The Autobiography of Malcolm X*, with the assistance of Alex Haley. Reprinted by permission of Grove Press, Inc. Copyright © 1964 by Alex Haley and Malcolm X, Copyright © 1965 by Alex Haley and Betty Shabazz.

Harcourt Brace Jovanovich, Inc. E. E. CUMMINGS, "old age sticks" from *95 Poems* © 1958 by E. E. Cummings. Reprinted by permission of Harcourt Brace Jovanovich, Inc. "i sing of Olaf," Copyright, 1931, 1959 by E. E. Cummings. Reprinted from his volume, *Poems 1923–1954* by permission of Harcourt Brace Jovanovich, Inc. ROBERT LOWELL, "Children of Light" from *Lord Weary's Castle*, copyright, 1944, 1946, by Robert Lowell. Reprinted by permission of Harcourt Brace Jovanovich, Inc. GEORGE ORWELL, "Marrakech" from *Such, Such Were the Joys* by George Orwell, copyright 1945, 1952, 1953, by Sonia Brownell Orwell. Reprinted by permission of Harcourt Brace Jovanovich, Inc. VIRGINIA WOOLF, "Lord Chesterfield's Letters to His Son" from *The Second Common Reader* by Virginia Woolf, copyright, 1932, by Harcourt Brace Jovanovich, Inc.; copyright, 1960, by Leonard Woolf. Reprinted by permission of Harcourt Brace Jovanovich, Inc.

### ACKNOWLEDGMENTS

Harvard University Press. EMILY DICKINSON, "No rack can torture me". Reprinted by permission of the publishers and the Trustees of Amherst College from Thomas H. Johnson, Editor, *The Poems of Emily Dickinson*, Cambridge, Mass.: The Belknap Press of Harvard University Press, Copyright, 1951, 1955, by the President and Fellows of Harvard College.

The Macmillan Company. Free Press of Glencoe. WILLIAM BUTLER YEATS, "Easter 1916" and "The Second Coming." Reprinted with permission of The Macmillan Company from *Collected Poems* by William Butler Yeats. Copyright 1924 by The Macmillan Company, renewed 1952 by Bertha Georgie Yeats. "The Lake Isle of Innisfree." Reprinted with permission of The Macmillan Company from *Collected Poems* by William Butler Yeats. Copyright 1906 by the Macmillan Company, renewed 1934 by William Butler Yeats. "Sailing to Byzantium." Reprinted with permission of The Macmillan Company from *Collected Poems* by William Butler Yeats. Copyright 1928 by The Macmillan Company, renewed 1956 by Georgie Yeats.

The New York Times. Quotations from Walter Rugaber and J. Anthony Lukas, © 1968 by The New York Times Company. Reprinted by permission.

Random House, Inc. Alfred A. Knopf, Inc. D. H. LAWRENCE, "The Man Who Loved Islands" from *The Woman Who Rode Away*, by D. H. Lawrence. Copyright 1927 and renewed 1955 by Frieda Lawrence Ravagli. Reprinted by permission of Alfred A. Knopf, Inc. W. D. SNODGRASS, "April Inventory," Copyright © 1957 by W. D. Snodgrass. Reprinted from *Heart's Needle*, by W. D. Snodgrass, by permission of Alfred A. Knopf, Inc.

Charles Scribner's Sons. ERNEST HEMINGWAY, "Fathers and Sons" is reprinted with the permission of Charles Scribner's Sons from *Winner Take Nothing* by Ernest Hemingway. Copyright 1933 Charles Scribner's Sons; renewal copyright © 1961 Mary Hemingway.

The Society of Authors. GEORGE BERNARD SHAW, "Maxims for Revolutionists" from *The Revolutionist's Handbook and Pocket Companion* appended to *Man and Superman* by George Bernard Shaw. Reprinted by permission of The Society of Authors for the Bernard Shaw Estate.

The Viking Press, Inc. JAMES JOYCE, "A Portrait of the Artist as a Young Man" from *A Portrait of the Artist as a Young Man* by James Joyce. Copyright 1916 by B. W. Huebsch, Inc., renewed 1944 by Nora Joyce. Copyright © 1964 by the Estate of James Joyce. All rights reserved. Reprinted by permission of The Viking Press, Inc. JACK KEROUAC, "On the Road" from *On the Road* by Jack Kerouac. Reprinted by permission of The Viking Press, Inc.

The Village Voice, Inc. Quotations from "A Visit to Chicago: Blood, Sweat & Tears," by Steve Lerner, and "The Streets of Daleyland: A Riot by the Cops," by Jack Newfield. Reprinted by permission of *The Village Voice*. Copyrighted by The Village Voice, Inc., 1968.

Wesleyan University Press. DONALD DAVIE, "Remembering the Thirties," Copyright © 1955 by Donald Davie. Reprinted from *New and Selected Poems*, by Donald Davie, by permission of Wesleyan University Press. JAMES DICKEY, "In the Mountain Tent," Copyright © 1961 by James Dickey. Reprinted from *Drowning with Others*, by James Dickey, by permission of Wesleyan University Press. This poem was first published in *The New Yorker*. LOUIS SIMPSON, "My Father in the Night Commanding No," Copyright © 1963 by Louis Simpson. Reprinted from *At the End of the Open Road*, by Louis Simpson, by permission of Wesleyan University Press. This poem originally appeared in *The New Yorker*.

The World Publishing Company. NORMAN MAILER, "Miami and the Siege of Chicago." Reprinted by permission of the World Publishing Company from *Miami and the Siege of Chicago* by Norman Mailer. Copyright © 1968 by Norman Mailer. CHARLES WEBB, "The Graduate." Reprinted by permission of The World Publishing Company from *The Graduate* by Charles Webb. An NAL Book. Copyright © 1963 by Charles Webb.

# Preface

At the electronic pace of contemporary life the new and startling quickly grows obsolete and our memory span shortens. Various phrases and terms characterize our discourse and occupy our minds for a while. Although the words *protest, generation gap, confrontation, turning on* stirred our imaginations even as they helped us identify ourselves and our time, others may soon serve to define our obsessions and ideals.

The pressure and rapidity of change are so powerful that we not only discard language overnight but often overlook—in our eagerness for the relevant and expressive—the eternal nature of the problems which that language denotes. Proud of being the creators of change, we often fail to recognize that we are also its subjects—and its victims. As Kenneth Keniston points out in his study *The Uncommitted:*

> . . . as members of a society, we increasingly feel a . . . sense of unfamiliarity about the not-so-distant past: the Flaming Twenties, the depression, even the Second World War now seem slightly unreal and certainly old-fashioned—as when we comment on how "out-of-date" the films of those recent years now seem. This "out-of-datedness" of even the very recent social past signals the psychological loss of a sense of connection with it, the birth of a new sense of being stranded in the present.

And this feeling of "being stranded in the present" gives rise to the conviction that only the topical and the immediate can possibly be meaningful to us. Such a view confirms our isolation, sealing us off from the experiences of former ages on the assumption that since they did not share the *particulars* of our predicaments, they can offer no insight into the *general* questions that underlie them.

In denying the value of the past, man denies an essentially human desire, to which Keniston also refers, for a "sense of his own place in time, and of his place in a society and world located in history"; both are "central to his definition of himself." By a restricted taste for modernity, man also deprives himself of an understanding of art, which has a history of sustaining the burden of perennial human experience and sensation, and of supplying that needed "sense of . . . place in time" by giving enduring form to the mortal brevity of individual perception.

Even as art allows us to understand how the past has ordered the chaos of life into communicable forms, it helps us to deal with the experience of the present. Such a view of the continuum of art and its relation to the present is axiomatic to the organization of this book. Through the literature it contains, it seeks to display the antiquity and persistence of what may mistakenly be considered uniquely contemporary circumstances and preoccupations. Three such preoccupations are accordingly the focus of this collection of essays, short stories, poems, plays, and other prose: "The Generation Gap"; "Protest, Revolution, and Anarchy"; and "Dropping Out and Tuning In: Escape from the World and Transcendence of Self."

Even as the selections reflect the eternal nature of these concerns, they also implicitly display the variety of ways in which man has approached them. To emphasize the relation of past to present, strict chronological order has been modified to present roughly contemporary statements at the beginning of each section. This introductory unit is followed by a chronological sequence that moves from past centuries forward to the near present.

To underline the unique aspects of each age's attempt to describe and analyze enduring problems, the editors have raised questions on *language* intended to stress the individuality of each selection, its particular quality as an expression of thought and feeling, or as a mode of defining the self and of dealing with larger experiences. Questions that concern *theme, structure,* and *characterization* are also provided as well as introductory and explanatory notes. To prevent superficiality and vagueness in the answers, "Clues" have been included to direct the student to those key phrases (sometimes italicized for emphasis) that help him to avoid mere speculation and to forge a clear and concrete answer. Some questions and exercises are suited to a consideration of each reading separately, whereas others specifically emphasize thematic connections among the readings in a given section. Each thematic division concludes with extensive questions on all the works within it, and the final section unifies the examination of the three themes in a detailed study of Bernard Shaw's *Major Barbara*.

The specific organization of this text, far from being prescriptive, is intended to lead teachers and students to discover other modes of arrangement that can promote creative insights and syntheses. Our arrangement of this material is meant merely as one invitation to that fellowship in human experience which, as Joseph Conrad has told us, it is the artist's achievement to sustain:

> The changing wisdom of successive generations discards ideas, questions facts, demolishes theories. But the artist appeals to that part of our being which is not dependent on wisdom: to that in us which is a gift and not an acquisition—and, therefore, more permanently enduring. He speaks to our capacity for delight and wonder, to the sense of mystery surrounding our lives; to our sense of pity, and beauty and pain; to the latent feeling of fellowship with all creation—and to the subtle but invincible conviction of solidarity that knits together the loneliness of innumerable hearts, to the solidarity in dreams, in joy, in sorrow, in aspirations, in illusions, in hope, in fear, which binds men to each other, which binds together all humanity—the dead to the living and the living to the unborn.

M. G.<br>J. E.

# Contents

Section I: *The Generation Gap*

DONALD DAVIE, "Remembering the Thirties"     3
FLANNERY O'CONNOR, "Everything That Rises Must Converge"     6
LOUIS SIMPSON, "My Father in the Night Commanding No"     19
W. D. SNODGRASS, "April Inventory"     21
CHARLES WEBB, *The Graduate*, Chapters 1–4     24
TOM WOLFE, "Putting Daddy On"     91

GEOFFREY CHAUCER, "The Pardoner's Tale," lines 661–894     99
EDMUND SPENSER, *The Shepheardes Calender*, "Februarie," lines 51–247     105
FRANCIS BACON, "Of Parents and Children"; "Of Youth and Age"     114
RICHARD BRINSLEY SHERIDAN, *The Rivals*, from Act II, Scene 1; Act III, Scene 1     117
SAMUEL JOHNSON, *Rasselas*, Chapter XXVI     123
JOHN STUART MILL, *Autobiography*, Chapter II     126
SAMUEL BUTLER, *The Way of All Flesh*, Chapters 40–41     138
HENRY JAMES, "The Pupil"     149
JAMES JOYCE, *A Portrait of the Artist as a Young Man* (from Chapter II)     186
VIRGINIA WOOLF, "Lord Chesterfield's Letters to His Son"     193
E. E. CUMMINGS, "old age sticks"     198
ERNEST HEMINGWAY, "Fathers and Sons"     200

Section II: *Protest, Revolution, and Anarchy*

ALLEN GINSBERG, "America"     215
ROBERT LOWELL, "Children of Light"     219
NORMAN MAILER, "The Siege of Chicago," Chapters 14–16     220
MALCOLM X, *The Autobiography of Malcolm X*, Chapter 14     237
MELVIN B. TOLSON, "Dark Symphony"     263

WILLIAM SHAKESPEARE, *Troilus and Cressida*, from Act I, Scene 3     268
EDMUND BURKE, *Reflections on the Revolution in France* (Selections)     270
THOMAS PAINE, *Rights of Man* (Selections)     290
WILLIAM WORDSWORTH, "To Toussaint L'Ouverture"     313
PERCY BYSSHE SHELLEY, "Song to the Men of England"; "England in 1819"     314

THOMAS CARLYLE, *The French Revolution*, Volume I, Book VII, Chapter X ; from Chapter XI     317

RALPH WALDO EMERSON, "Speech at the Kansas Relief Meeting in Cambridge"     326

HENRY DAVID THOREAU, *Civil Disobedience*     331

MATTHEW ARNOLD, *Culture and Anarchy*, from Chapter II     349

GEORGE BERNARD SHAW, "Maxims for Revolutionists"     356

WILLIAM BUTLER YEATS, "Easter 1916"; "The Second Coming"     359

E. E. CUMMINGS, "i sing of Olaf"     365

GEORGE ORWELL, "Marrakech"     367

## Section III: *Dropping Out and Tuning In: Escape from the World and Transcendence of Self*

JAMES DICKEY, "In the Mountain Tent"     385

JACK KEROUAC, *On the Road*, Part Two, Chapter 6     386

THEODORE ROETHKE, "In a Dark Time"     398

ROBERT LOWELL, "The Voyage"     399

SIR WALTER RALEGH, "The Passionate Man's Pilgrimage"     405

SIR PHILIP SIDNEY, "Leave Me, O Love"     408

WILLIAM SHAKESPEARE, Sonnet 66     409

JOHN DONNE, "Holy Sonnet XIV"     410

GEORGE HERBERT, "Easter Wings"; "The Collar"     411

ANDREW MARVELL, "The Garden"     414

HENRY VAUGHAN, "The World"     417

WILLIAM BLAKE, "Ah, Sun-flower"     420

WILLIAM WORDSWORTH, "The World Is Too Much with Us"     420

SAMUEL TAYLOR COLERIDGE, *The Rime of the Ancient Mariner*     422

ALFRED, LORD TENNYSON, "The Lotos-Eaters"; "Ulysses"     442

HENRY DAVID THOREAU, *Walden*, Chapter II     452

WALT WHITMAN, "Song of Myself," Section 31     463

MATTHEW ARNOLD, "Dover Beach"     465

EMILY DICKINSON [No rack can torture me]     466

WILLIAM BUTLER YEATS, "The Lake Isle of Innisfree"; "Sailing to Byzantium"     467

JOHN MILLINGTON SYNGE, *In the Shadow of the Glen*     470

JAMES JOYCE, *A Portrait of the Artist as a Young Man*, Chapter IV     481

D. H. LAWRENCE, "The Man Who Loved Islands"     502

## Section IV: *Parents and Children; Revolution and Transcendence: A Gathering of Themes*

GEORGE BERNARD SHAW, *Major Barbara*     531

# Questions and Exercises

Section I: *The Generation Gap*

| | |
|---|---|
| DAVIE, "Remembering the Thirties" | 5 |
| O'CONNOR, "Everything That Rises Must Converge" | 18–19 |
| SIMPSON, "My Father in the Night Commanding No" | 21 |
| SNODGRASS, "April Inventory" | 23–24 |
| WEBB, *The Graduate* | 90 |
| WOLFE, "Putting Daddy On" | 97–98 |
| | |
| CHAUCER, "The Pardoner's Tale" | 104–105 |
| SPENSER, *The Shepheardes Calender* | 112–114 |
| BACON, "Of Parents and Children"; "Of Youth and Age" | 116 |
| SHERIDAN, *The Rivals* | 122–123 |
| JOHNSON, *Rasselas* | 125–126 |
| MILL, *Autobiography* | 137–138 |
| BUTLER, *The Way of All Flesh* | 148–149 |
| JAMES, "The Pupil" | 182–185 |
| JOYCE, *A Portrait of the Artist as a Young Man* | 192–193 |
| WOOLF, "Lord Chesterfield's Letters to His Son" | 197–198 |
| CUMMINGS, "old age sticks" | 199 |
| HEMINGWAY, "Fathers and Sons" | 208 |
| | |
| CROSS QUESTIONS | 208–212 |

Section II: *Protest, Revolution, and Anarchy*

| | |
|---|---|
| GINSBERG, "America" | 217–218 |
| LOWELL, "Children of Light" | 219 |
| MAILER, "The Siege of Chicago" | 235–236 |
| MALCOLM X, *The Autobiography of Malcolm X* | 260–263 |
| TOLSON, "Dark Symphony" | 267–268 |
| | |
| SHAKESPEARE, *Troilus and Cressida* | 269–270 |
| BURKE, *Reflections on the Revolution in France* | 288–290 |
| PAINE, *Rights of Man* | 311–313 |
| WORDSWORTH, "To Toussaint L'Ouverture" | 314 |
| SHELLEY, "Song to the Men of England"; "England in 1819" | 316–317 |
| CARLYLE, *The French Revolution* | 325–326 |

EMERSON, "Speech at the Kansas Relief Meeting in Cambridge"    330–331
THOREAU, *Civil Disobedience*    347–348
ARNOLD, *Culture and Anarchy*    354–356
SHAW, "Maxims for Revolutionists"    358–359
YEATS, "Easter 1916"; "The Second Coming"    362–364
CUMMINGS, "i sing of Olaf"    366–367
ORWELL, "Marrakech"    372–374

CROSS QUESTIONS    374–381

## Section III: *Dropping Out and Tuning In: Escape from the World and Transcendence of Self*

DICKEY, "In the Mountain Tent"    386
KEROUAC, *On the Road*    397–398
ROETHKE, "In a Dark Time"    399
LOWELL, "The Voyage"    404–405

RALEGH, "The Passionate Man's Pilgrimage"    407–408
SIDNEY, "Leave Me, O Love"    408
SHAKESPEARE, Sonnet 66    409–410
DONNE, "Holy Sonnet XIV"    410–411
HERBERT, "Easter Wings"; "The Collar"    412–414
MARVELL, "The Garden"    416–417
VAUGHAN, "The World"    419
BLAKE, "Ah, Sun-flower"    420
WORDSWORTH, "The World Is Too Much with Us"    421
COLERIDGE, *The Rime of the Ancient Mariner*    439–442
TENNYSON, "The Lotos-Eaters"; "Ulysses"    447–451
THOREAU, *Walden*    462–463
WHITMAN, "Song of Myself"    464
ARNOLD, "Dover Beach"    466
DICKINSON [No rack can torture me]    467
YEATS, "The Lake Isle of Innisfree"; "Sailing to Byzantium"    468–470
SYNGE, *In the Shadow of the Glen*    480–481
JOYCE, *A Portrait of the Artist as a Young Man*    500–502
LAWRENCE, "The Man Who Loved Islands"    521–524

CROSS QUESTIONS    524–527

## Section IV: *Parents and Children; Revolution and Transcendence: A Gathering of Themes*

SHAW, *Major Barbara*    600–607

# Section I

*The Generation Gap*

*Donald Davie (1922–    )*

# Remembering the Thirties

I

Hearing one saga, we enact the next.
We please our elders when we sit enthralled;
But then they're puzzled; and at last they're vexed
To have their youth so avidly recalled.

It dawns upon the veterans after all                    5
That what for them were agonies, for us
Are highbrow thrillers, though historical;
And all their feats quite strictly fabulous.

This novel written fifteen years ago,
Set in my boyhood and my boyhood home,                  10
These poems about "abandoned workings" show
Worlds more remote than Ithaca or Rome.

The Anschluss, Guernica[1]—all the names
At which those poets thrilled or were afraid
For me mean schools and schoolmasters and games;       15
And in the process some one is betrayed.

Ourselves perhaps. The Devil for a joke
Might carve his own initials on our desk,
And yet we'd miss the point because he spoke
An idiom too dated, Audenesque.                         20

Ralegh's Guiana[2] also killed his son.
A pretty pickle if we came to see
The tallest story really packed a gun,
The Telemachiad an Odyssey.

---

[1] Both the unification (*Anschluss*) of Germany and Austria, forced by Hitler in 1938, and the brutal destruction by German planes of a town in northern Spain (Guernica) during the Spanish Civil War—an event immortalized by Picasso—are significant themes in the politics of the late thirties.
[2] In 1595 Sir Walter Ralegh led an expedition part way up the Orinoco river in South America to search for gold. On a second expedition in 1617 his son was killed.

2

Even to them the tales were not so true                    25
As not to be ridiculous as well:
The ironmaster met his Waterloo,
But Rider Haggard[3] rode along the fell.


"Leave for Cape Wrath tonight!" They lounged away
On Fleming's trek[4] or Isherwood's[5] ascent.            30
England expected every man that day
To show his motives were ambivalent.


They played the fool, not to appear as fools
In time's long glass. A deprecating air
Disarmed, they thought, the jeers of later schools;       35
Yet irony itself is doctrinaire,


And, curiously, nothing now betrays
Their type to time's derision like this coy
Insistence on the quizzical, their craze
For showing Hector was a mother's boy.                    40


A neutral tone is nowadays preferred.
And yet it may be better, if we must,
To find the stance impressive and absurd
Than not to see the hero for the dust.


For courage is the vegetable king,                        45
The sprig of all ontologies, the weed
That beards the slag-heap with his hectoring,
Whose green adventure is to run to seed.

---

[3] Sir Henry Rider Haggard (1856–1925) wrote popular adventure novels such as *King Solomon's Mines* and *She*.

[4] The British writer Peter Fleming reported his voyages to remote areas in such travel books as *Brazilian Adventure* (1933) and *News from Tartary* (1936).

[5] In 1936 Christopher Isherwood (1904–    ) with his friend W. H. Auden (1907–    ) wrote the play *The Ascent of F6*, chronicling the career of an ambivalent hero and "mother's boy" such as Davie refers to.

*4*

## QUESTIONS: *Davie, "Remembering the Thirties"*

1. What basic difference in emotional response between generations is suggested in stanzas 1 and 2?
   *Clues:* • "enthralled" and "puzzled"
   • "agonies" and "thrillers"
   • "historical" and "fabulous"

2. What do the following words or phrases reveal about the meaning of one generation's experience to the next?
   *Clues:* • Hearing one *saga*, we *enact* the next.
   • highbrow *thrillers* . . .
   • This *novel* . . . /These *poems* . . .
   • An idiom too dated . . .

3. In what way does Davie suggest that the gap in perception between the generations is greater when the time span between them is smaller? (Note that in stanza 4 the same period of time is recalled by each.) How does the contrast between "poets" and "schoolmasters and games" underline this difference?

4. What words in the earlier stanzas anticipate the use of "tallest story" in stanza 6? What is the effect of "pretty pickle" in contrast with the preceding line? How does the line "The Telemachiad an Odyssey" amplify the point made in "Ralegh's Guiana also killed his son"?

5. How does Davie's treatment of the generation gap focus more directly on his immediate subject—the thirties—in the second section of the poem?
   *Clues:* • "Even to them"
   • "ridiculous as well"
   • "lounged away"
   What is the meaning of "England expected every man that day/ To show his motives were ambivalent"? Assess the effect of the statement as a witty variation of Nelson's original statement at the Battle of Trafalgar: "England expects every man to do his duty." In what way do Davie's lines anticipate his concern with "courage" in the last three stanzas?

6. When Davie warns of the dangers of not being able "to see the hero for the dust," in what way is he contrasting the general attitude of the thirties with the attitude of his own generation to the world?

7. In what way is the final tribute paid to the courage of the thirties, the reference to "the weed/ That beards the slag-heap with his hectoring," a vindication of "the stance" that is "impressive and absurd"? What earlier elements of the poem do the words *green adventure* and *run to seed* rehearse, and why this rehearsal of them? What is the ambiguity of the expression *run to seed?*

## EXERCISES

1. Write an essay on the following topic: "We shall perish if we see the past as fable instead of lesson."

2. Davie speaks of the "neutral tone" as preferred by his generation. Would you call that the characteristic tone of the present moment? You may use appropriate selections from this anthology to justify your answer.

*Flannery O'Connor (1925–1965)*

# Everything That Rises Must Converge

Her doctor had told Julian's mother that she must lose twenty pounds on account of her blood pressure, so on Wednesday nights Julian had to take her downtown on the bus for a reducing class at the Y. The reducing class was designed for working girls over fifty, who weighed from 165 to 200 pounds. His mother was one of the slimmer ones, but she said ladies did not tell their age or weight. She would not ride the buses by herself at night since they had been integrated, and because the reducing class was one of her few pleasures, necessary for her health, and *free*, she said Julian could at least put himself out to take her, considering all she did for him. Julian did not like to consider all she did for him, but every Wednesday night he braced himself and took her.

She was almost ready to go, standing before the hall mirror, putting on her hat, while he, his hands behind him, appeared pinned to the door frame, waiting like Saint Sebastian for the arrows to begin piercing him. The hat was new and had cost her seven dollars and a half. She kept saying, "Maybe I shouldn't have paid that for it. No, I shouldn't have. I'll take it off and return it tomorrow. I shouldn't have bought it."

Julian raised his eyes to heaven. "Yes, you should have bought it," he said "Put it on and let's go." It was a hideous hat. A purple velvet flap came down on one side of it and stood up on the other; the rest of it was green and looked like a cushion with the stuffing out. He decided it was less comical than jaunty and pathetic. Everything that gave her pleasure was small and depressed him.

She lifted the hat one more time and set it down slowly on top of her head. Two wings of gray hair protruded on either side of her florid face, but her eyes, sky-blue, were as innocent and untouched by experience as they must have been when she was ten. Were it not that she was a widow who had struggled fiercely to feed and clothe and put him through school and who was supporting him still, "until he got on his feet," she might have been a little girl that he had to take to town.

"It's all right, it's all right," he said. "Let's go." He opened the door himself and started down the walk to get her going. The sky was a dying violet and the houses stood out darkly against it, bulbous liver-colored monstrosities of a uniform ugliness though no two were alike. Since this had been a fashionable neighborhood forty years ago, his mother persisted in thinking they did well to have an apartment in it. Each house had a narrow collar of dirt around it in which sat usually a grubby child. Julian walked with his hands in his pockets, his head down and thrust forward and his eyes glazed with the determination to make himself completely numb during the time he would be sacrificed to her pleasure.

The door closed and he turned to find the dumpy figure, surmounted by the atrocious hat, coming toward him. "Well," she said, "you only live once and paying a little more for it, I at least won't meet myself coming and going."

"Some day I'll start making money," Julian said gloomily—he knew he never would—"and you can have one of those jokes whenever you take the fit." But first they would move. He visualized a place where the nearest neighbors would be three miles away on either side.

"I think you're doing fine," she said, drawing on her gloves. "You've only been out of school a year. Rome wasn't built in a day."

She was one of the few members of the Y reducing class who arrived in hat and gloves and who had a son who had been to college. "It takes time," she said, "and the world is in such a mess. This hat looked better on me than any of the others, though when she brought it out I said, 'Take that thing back. I wouldn't have it on my head,' and she said, 'Now wait till you see it on,' and when she put it on me, I said, 'We-ull,' and she said, 'If you ask me, that hat does something for you and you do something for the hat, and besides,' she said, 'with that hat, you won't meet yourself coming and going.'"

Julian thought he could have stood his lot better if she had been selfish, if she had been an old hag who drank and screamed at him. He walked along, saturated in depression, as if in the midst of his martyrdom he had lost his faith. Catching sight of his long, hopeless, irritated face, she stopped suddenly with a grief-stricken look, and pulled back on his arm. "Wait on me," she said. "I'm going back to the house and take this thing off and tomorrow I'm going to return it. I was out of my head. I can pay the gas bill with that seven-fifty."

He caught her arm in a vicious grip. "You are not going to take it back," he said. "I like it."

"Well," she said, "I don't think I ought . . ."

"Shut up and enjoy it," he muttered, more depressed than ever.

"With the world in the mess it's in," she said, "it's a wonder we can enjoy anything. I tell you, the bottom rail is on the top."

Julian sighed.

"Of course," she said, "if you know who you are, you can go anywhere." She said this every time he took her to the reducing class. "Most of them in it are not our kind of people," she said, "but I can be gracious to anybody. I know who I am."

"They don't give a damn for your graciousness," Julian said savagely. "Knowing who you are is good for one generation only. You haven't the foggiest idea where you stand now or who you are."

She stopped and allowed her eyes to flash at him. "I most certainly do know who I am," she said, "and if you don't know who you are, I'm ashamed of you."

"Oh hell," Julian said.

"Your great-grandfather was a former governor of this state," she said. "Your grandfather was a prosperous landowner. Your grandmother was a Godhigh."

"Will you look around you," he said tensely, "and see where you are now?" and he swept his arm jerkily out to indicate the neighborhood, which the growing darkness at least made less dingy.

"You remain what you are," she said. "Your great-grandfather had a plantation and two hundred slaves."

"There are no more slaves," he said irritably.

"They were better off when they were," she said. He groaned to see that she was off on that topic. She rolled onto it every few days like a train on an open track. He knew every stop, every junction, every swamp along the way, and knew the exact point at which her conclusion would roll majestically into the station: "It's ridiculous. It's simply not realistic. They should rise, yes, but on their own side of the fence."

"Let's skip it," Julian said.

"The ones I feel sorry for," she said, "are the ones that are half white. They're tragic."

"Will you skip it?"

"Suppose we were half white. We would certainly have mixed feelings."

"I have mixed feelings now," he groaned.

"Well let's talk about something pleasant," she said. "I remember going to Grandpa's when I was a little girl. Then the house had double stairways that went up to what was really the second floor—all the cooking was done on the first. I used to like to stay down in the kitchen on account of the way the walls smelled. I would sit with my nose pressed against the plaster and take deep breaths. Actually the place belonged to the Godhighs but your grandfather Chestny paid the mortgage and saved it for them. They were in reduced circumstances," she said, "but reduced or not, they never forgot who they were."

"Doubtless that decayed mansion reminded them," Julian muttered. He never spoke of it without contempt or thought of it without longing. He had seen it once when he was a child before it had been sold. The double stairways had rotted and been torn down. Negroes were living in it. But it remained in his mind as his mother had known it. It appeared in his dreams regularly. He would stand on the wide porch, listening to the rustle of oak leaves, then wander through the high-ceilinged hall into the parlor that opened onto it and gaze at the worn rugs and faded draperies. It occurred to him that it was he, not she, who could have appreciated it. He preferred its threadbare elegance to anything he could name and it was because of it that all the neighborhoods they had lived in had been a torment to him—whereas she had hardly known the difference. She called her insensitivity "being adjustable."

"And I remember the old darky who was my nurse, Caroline. There was no better person in the world. I've always had a great respect for my colored friends," she said. "I'd do anything in the world for them and they'd . . ."

"Will you for God's sake get off the subject?" Julian said. When he got on a bus by himself, he made it a point to sit down beside a Negro, in reparation as it were for his mother's sins.

"You're mighty touchy tonight," she said. "Do you feel all right?"

"Yes I feel all right," he said. "Now lay off."

She pursed her lips. "Well, you certainly are in a vile humor," she observed. "I just won't speak to you at all."

They had reached the bus stop. There was no bus in sight and Julian, his hands still jammed in his pockets and his head thrust forward, scowled down the empty street. The frustration of having to wait on the bus as well as ride on it began to creep up his neck like a hot hand. The presence of his mother was borne in upon him as she gave a pained sigh. He looked at her bleakly. She was holding herself very erect under the preposterous hat, wearing it like a banner of her imaginary dignity. There was in him an evil urge to break her spirit. He suddenly unloosened his tie and pulled it off and put it in his pocket.

She stiffened. "Why must you look like *that* when you take me to town?" she said. "Why must you deliberately embarrass me?"

"If you'll never learn where you are," he said, "you can at least learn where I am."

"You look like a—thug," she said.

"Then I must be one," he murmured.

"I'll just go home," she said. "I will not bother you. If you can't do a little thing like that for me . . ."

Rolling his eyes upward, he put his tie back on. "Restored to my class," he muttered. He thrust his face toward her and hissed, "True culture is in the mind, the *mind*," he said, and tapped his head, "the mind."

"It's in the heart," she said, "and in how you do things and how you do things is because of who you *are*."

"Nobody in the damn bus cares who you are."

"I care who I am," she said icily.

The lighted bus appeared on top of the next hill and as it approached, they moved out into the street to meet it. He put his hand under her elbow and hoisted her up on the creaking step. She entered with a little smile, as if she were going into a drawing room where everyone had been waiting for her. While he put in the tokens, she sat down on one of the broad front seats for three which faced the aisle. A thin woman with protruding teeth and long yellow hair was sitting on the end of it. His mother moved up beside her and left room for Julian beside herself. He sat down and looked at the floor across the aisle where a pair of thin feet in red and white canvas sandals were planted.

His mother immediately began a general conversation meant to attract anyone who felt like talking. "Can it get any hotter?" she said and removed from her purse a folding fan, black with a Japanese scene on it, which she began to flutter before her.

"I reckon it might could," the woman with the protruding teeth said, "but I know for a fact my apartment couldn't get no hotter."

"It must get the afternoon sun," his mother said. She sat forward and looked up and down the bus. It was half filled. Everybody was white. "I see we have the bus to ourselves," she said. Julian cringed.

"For a change," said the woman across the aisle, the owner of the red and white canvas sandals. "I come on one the other day and they were thick as fleas—up front and all through."

"The world is in a mess everywhere," his mother said. "I don't know how we've let it get in this fix."

"What gets my goat is all those boys from good families stealing automobile tires," the woman with the protruding teeth said. "I told my boy, I said you may not be rich but you been raised right and if I ever catch you in any such mess, they can send you on to the reformatory. Be exactly where you belong."

"Training tells," his mother said. "Is your boy in high school?"

"Ninth grade," the woman said.

"My son just finished college last year. He wants to write but he's selling typewriters until he gets started," his mother said.

The woman leaned forward and peered at Julian. He threw her such a malevolent look that she subsided against the seat. On the floor across the aisle there was an abandoned newspaper. He got up and got it and opened it out in front of him. His mother discreetly continued the conversation in a lower tone but the woman across the aisle said in a loud voice, "Well that's nice. Selling typewriters is close to writing. He can go right from one to the other."

"I tell him," his mother said, "that Rome wasn't built in a day."

Behind the newspaper Julian was withdrawing into the inner compartment of his mind where he spent most of his time. This was a kind of mental bubble in which he established himself when he could not bear to be a part of what was going on around him. From it he could see out and judge but in it he was safe from any kind of penetration from without. It was the only place where he felt free of the general idiocy of his fellows. His mother had never entered it but from it he could see her with absolute clarity.

The old lady was clever enough and he thought that if she had started from any of the right premises, more might have been expected of her. She lived according to the laws of her own fantasy world, outside of which he had never seen her set foot. The law of it was to sacrifice herself for him after she had first created the necessity to do so by making a mess of things. If he had permitted her sacrifices, it was only because her lack of foresight had made them necessary. All of her life had been a struggle to act like a Chestny without the Chestny goods, and to give him everything she thought a Chestny ought to have; but since, said she, it was fun to struggle, why complain? And when you had won, as she had won, what fun to look back on the hard times! He could not forgive her that she had enjoyed the struggle and that she thought *she* had won.

What she meant when she said she had won was that she had brought him up successfully and had sent him to college and that he had turned out so well—good looking (her teeth had gone unfilled so that his could be straightened), intelligent (he realized he was too intelligent to be a success), and with a future ahead of him (there was of course no future ahead of him). She excused his gloominess on the grounds that he was still growing up and his radical ideas on his lack of practical experience. She said he didn't yet know a thing about "life," that he hadn't even entered the real world—when already he was as disenchanted with it as a man of fifty.

The further irony of all this was that in spite of her, he had turned out so well. In spite of going to only a third-rate college, he had, on his own initiative, come out with a first-rate education; in spite of growing up dominated by a small mind, he had ended up with a large one; in spite of all her foolish views, he was free of prejudice and unafraid to face facts. Most miraculous of all, instead of being blinded by love for her as she was for him, he had cut himself emotionally free of her and could see her with complete objectivity. He was not dominated by his mother.

The bus stopped with a sudden jerk and shook him from his meditation. A woman from the back lurched forward with little steps and barely escaped falling in his newspaper as she righted herself. She got off and a large Negro got on. Julian kept his paper lowered to watch. It gave him a certain satisfaction to see injustice in daily operation. It confirmed his view that with a few exceptions there was no one worth knowing within a radius of three hundred miles. The Negro was well dressed and carried a briefcase. He looked around and then sat down on the other end of the seat where the woman with the red and white canvas sandals was sitting. He immediately unfolded a newspaper and obscured himself behind it. Julian's mother's elbow at once prodded insistently into his ribs. "Now you see why I won't ride on these buses by myself," she whispered.

The woman with the red and white canvas sandals had risen at the same time the Negro sat down and had gone further back in the bus and taken the seat of the woman who had got off. His mother leaned forward and cast her an approving look.

Julian rose, crossed the aisle, and sat down in the place of the woman with the canvas sandals. From this position, he looked serenely across at his mother. Her face had turned an angry red. He stared at her, making his eyes the eyes of a stranger. He felt his tension suddenly lift as if he had openly declared war on her.

He would have liked to get in conversation with the Negro and to talk with him about art or politics or any subject that would be above the comprehension of those around them, but the man remained entrenched behind his paper. He was either ignoring the change of seating or had never noticed it. There was no way for Julian to convey his sympathy.

His mother kept her eyes fixed reproachfully on his face. The woman with the protruding teeth was looking at him avidly as if he were a type of monster new to her.

"Do you have a light?" he asked the Negro.

Without looking away from his paper, the man reached in his pocket and handed him a packet of matches.

"Thanks," Julian said. For a moment he held the matches foolishly. A NO SMOKING sign looked down upon him from over the door. This alone would not have deterred him; he had no cigarettes. He had quit smoking some months before because he could not afford it. "Sorry," he muttered and handed back the matches. The Negro lowered the paper and gave him an annoyed look. He took the matches and raised the paper again.

His mother continued to gaze at him but she did not take advantage of his momentary discomfort. Her eyes retained their battered look. Her face seemed to be unnaturally red, as if her blood pressure had risen. Julian allowed no glimmer of sympathy to show on his face. Having got the advantage, he wanted desperately to keep it and carry it through. He would have liked to teach her a lesson that would last her a while, but there seemed no way to continue the point. The Negro refused to come out from behind his paper.

Julian folded his arms and looked stolidly before him, facing her but as if he did not see her, as if he had ceased to recognize her existence. He visualized a scene in which, the bus having reached their stop, he would remain in his seat and when she said, "Aren't you going to get off?" he would look at her as at a stranger who had rashly addressed him. The corner they got off on was usually deserted, but it was well lighted and it would not hurt her to walk by herself the four blocks to the Y. He decided to wait until the time came and then decide whether or not he would let her get off by herself. He would have to be at the Y at ten to bring her back, but he could leave her wondering if he was going to show up. There was no reason for her to think she could always depend on him.

He retired again into the high-ceilinged room sparsely settled with large pieces of antique furniture. His soul expanded momentarily but then he became aware of his mother across from him and the vision shriveled. He studied her coldly. Her feet in little pumps dangled like a child's and did not quite reach the floor. She was training on him an exaggerated look of reproach. He felt completely detached from her. At that moment he could with pleasure have slapped her as he would have slapped a particularly obnoxious child in his charge.

He began to imagine various unlikely ways by which he could teach her a lesson. He might make friends with some distinguished Negro professor or lawyer and bring him home to spend the evening. He would be entirely justified but her blood pressure would rise to 300. He could not push her to the extent of making her have a stroke, and moreover, he had never been successful at making any Negro friends. He had tried to strike up an acquaintance on the bus with some of the better types, with ones that looked like professors or ministers or lawyers. One morning he had sat down next to a distinguished-looking brown man who had answered his questions with a sonorous solemnity but who had turned out to be an undertaker. Another day he had sat down beside a cigar-smoking Negro with a diamond ring on his finger, but after a few stilted pleasantries, the Negro had rung the buzzer and risen, slipping two lottery tickets into Julian's hand as he climbed over him to leave.

He imagined his mother lying desperately ill and his being able to secure only a Negro doctor for her. He toyed with that idea for a few minutes and then dropped it for a momentary vision of himself participating as a sympathizer in a sit-in demonstration. This was possible but he did not linger with it. Instead, he approached the ultimate horror. He brought home a beautiful suspiciously Negroid woman. Prepare yourself, he said. There is nothing you can do about it. This is the woman I've chosen. She's intelligent, dignified, even good, and she's suffered and she hasn't thought it *fun*. Now persecute us, go ahead and persecute us. Drive her out of here, but remember, you're driving me too. His eyes were narrowed and through the indignation he had generated, he saw his mother across the aisle, purple-faced, shrunken to the dwarf-like proportions of her moral nature, sitting like a mummy beneath the ridiculous banner of her hat.

He was tilted out of his fantasy again as the bus stopped. The door opened with a sucking hiss and out of the dark a large, gaily dressed, sullen-looking colored woman got on with a little boy. The child, who might have been four, had on a short plaid suit and a Tyrolean hat with a blue feather in it. Julian hoped that he would sit down beside him and that the woman would push in beside his mother. He could think of no better arrangement.

As she waited for her tokens, the woman was surveying the seating possibilities—he hoped with the idea of sitting where she was least wanted. There was something familiar-looking about her but Julian could not place what it was. She was a giant of a woman. Her face was set not only to meet opposition but to seek it out. The downward tilt of her large lower lip was like a warning sign: DON'T TAMPER WITH ME. Her bulging figure was encased in a green crepe dress and her feet overflowed in red shoes. She had on a hideous hat. A purple velvet flap came down on one side of it and stood up on the other; the rest of it was green and looked like a cushion with the stuffing out. She carried a mammoth red pocketbook that bulged throughout as if it were stuffed with rocks.

To Julian's disappointment, the little boy climbed up on the empty seat beside his mother. His mother lumped all children, black and white, into the common category, "cute," and she thought little Negroes were on the whole cuter than little white children. She smiled at the little boy as he climbed on the seat.

Meanwhile the woman was bearing down upon the empty seat beside Julian. To his annoyance, she squeezed herself into it. He saw his mother's face change as the woman settled herself next to him and he realized with satisfaction that this was more objectionable to her than it was to him. Her face seemed almost gray and there was a look of dull recognition in her eyes, as if suddenly she had sickened at some awful confrontation. Julian saw that it was because she and the woman had, in a sense, swapped sons. Though his mother would not realize the symbolic significance of this, she would feel it. His amusement showed plainly on his face.

The woman next to him muttered something unintelligible to herself. He was conscious of a kind of bristling next to him, a muted growling like that of an angry cat. He could not see anything but the red pocketbook upright on the bulging green thighs. He visualized the woman as she had stood waiting for her tokens—the ponderous figure, rising from the red shoes upward over the solid hips, the mammoth bosom, the haughty face, to the green and purple hat.

His eyes widened.

The vision of the two hats, identical, broke upon him with the radiance of a brilliant sunrise. His face was suddenly lit with joy. He could not believe that Fate had thrust upon his mother such a lesson. He gave a loud chuckle so that she would look at him and see that he saw. She turned her eyes on him slowly. The blue in them seemed to have turned a bruised purple. For a moment he had an uncomfortable sense of her innocence, but it lasted only a second before principle rescued him. Justice entitled him to laugh. His grin hardened until it said to her as plainly as if he were saying aloud: Your punishment exactly fits your pettiness. This should teach you a permanent lesson.

Her eyes shifted to the woman. She seemed unable to bear looking at him and to find the woman preferable. He became conscious again of the bristling presence at his side. The woman was rumbling like a volcano about to become active. His mother's mouth began to twitch slightly at one corner. With a sinking heart, he saw incipient signs of recovery on her face and realized that this was going to strike her suddenly as funny and was going to be no lesson at all. She kept her eyes on the woman and an amused smile came over her face as if the woman were a monkey that had stolen her hat. The little Negro was looking up at her with large fascinated eyes. He had been trying to attract her attention for some time.

"Carver!" the woman said suddenly. "Come heah!"

When he saw that the spotlight was on him at last, Carver drew his feet up and turned himself toward Julian's mother and giggled.

"Carver!" the woman said. "You heah me? Come heah!"

Carver slid down from the seat but remained squatting with his back against the base of it, his head turned slyly around toward Julian's mother, who was smiling at him. The woman reached a hand across the aisle and snatched him to her. He righted himself and hung backwards on her knees, grinning at Julian's mother. "Isn't he cute?" Julian's mother said to the woman with the protruding teeth.

"I reckon he is," the woman said without conviction.

The Negress yanked him upright but he eased out of her grip and shot across the aisle and scrambled, giggling wildly, onto the seat beside his love.

"I think he likes me," Julian's mother said, and smiled at the woman. It was the smile she used when she was being particularly gracious to an inferior. Julian saw everything lost. The lesson had rolled off her like rain on a roof.

The woman stood up and yanked the little boy off the seat as if she were snatching him from contagion. Julian could feel the rage in her at having no weapon like his mother's smile. She gave the child a sharp slap across his leg. He howled once and then thrust his head into her stomach and kicked his feet against her shins. "Be-have," she said vehemently.

The bus stopped and the Negro who had been reading the newspaper got off. The woman moved over and set the little boy down with a thump between herself and Julian. She held him firmly by the knee. In a moment he put his hands in front of his face and peeped at Julian's mother through his fingers.

"I see yoooooooo!" she said and put her hand in front of her face and peeped at him.

The woman slapped his hand down. "Quit yo' foolishness," she said, "before I knock the living Jesus out of you!"

Julian was thankful that the next stop was theirs. He reached up and pulled the cord. The woman reached up and pulled it at the same time. Oh my God, he thought. He had the terrible intuition that when they got off the bus together, his mother would open her purse and give the little boy a nickel. The gesture would be as natural to her as breathing. The bus stopped and the woman got up and lunged to the front, dragging the child, who wished to stay on, after her. Julian and his mother got up and followed. As they neared the door, Julian tried to relieve her of her pocketbook.

"No," she murmured, "I want to give the little boy a nickel."

"No!" Julian hissed. "No!"

She smiled down at the child and opened her bag. The bus door opened and the woman picked him up by the arm and descended with him, hanging at her hip. Once in the street she set him down and shook him.

Julian's mother had to close her purse while she got down the bus step but as soon as her feet were on the ground, she opened it again and began to rummage inside. "I can't find but a penny," she whispered, "but it looks like a new one."

"Don't do it!" Julian said fiercely between his teeth. There was a street-light on the corner and she hurried to get under it so she could better see into her pocketbook. The woman was heading off rapidly down the street with the child still hanging backward on her hand.

"Oh little boy!" Julian's mother called and took a few quick steps and caught up with them just beyond the lamppost. "Here's a bright new penny for you," and she held out the coin, which shone bronze in the dim light.

The huge woman turned and for a moment stood, her shoulders lifted and her face frozen with frustrated rage, and stared at Julian's mother. Then all at once she seemed to explode like a piece of machinery that had been given one ounce of pressure too much. Julian saw the black fist swing out with the red pocketbook. He shut his eyes and cringed as he heard the woman shout, "He don't take nobody's pennies!" When he opened his eyes, the woman was disappearing down the street with the little boy staring wide-eyed over her shoulder. Julian's mother was sitting on the side-walk.

"I told you not to do that," Julian said angrily. "I told you not to do that!"

He stood over her for a minute, gritting his teeth. Her legs were stretched out in front of her and her hat was on her lap. He squatted down and looked her in the face. It was totally expressionless. "You got exactly what you deserved," he said. "Now get up."

He picked up her pocketbook and put what had fallen out back in it. He picked the hat up off her lap. The penny caught his eye on the sidewalk and he picked that up and let it drop before her eyes into the purse. Then he stood up and leaned over and held his hands out to pull her up. She remained immobile. He sighed. Rising above them on either side were black apartment buildings, marked with irregular rectangles of light. At the end of the block a man came out of a door and walked off in the opposite direction. "All right," he said, "suppose somebody happens by and wants to know why you're sitting on the sidewalk?"

She took the hand and, breathing hard, pulled heavily up on it and then stood for a moment, swaying slightly as if the spots of light in the darkness were circling around her. Her eyes, shadowed and confused, finally settled on his face. He did not try to conceal his irritation. "I hope this teaches you a lesson," he said. She leaned forward and her eyes raked his face. She seemed trying to determine his identity. Then, as if she found nothing familiar about him, she started off with a headlong movement in the wrong direction.

"Aren't you going on to the Y?" he asked.

"Home," she muttered.

"Well, are we walking?"

For answer she kept going. Julian followed along, his hands behind him. He saw no reason to let the lesson she had had go without backing it up with an explanation of its meaning. She might as well be made to understand what had happened to her. "Don't think that was just an uppity Negro woman," he said. "That was the whole colored race which will no longer take your condescending pennies. That was your black double. She can wear the same hat as you, and to be sure," he added gratuitously (because he thought it was funny), "it looked better on her than it did on you. What all this means," he said, "is that the old world is gone. The old manners are obsolete and your graciousness is not worth a damn." He thought bitterly of the house that had been lost for him. "You aren't who you think you are," he said.

She continued to plow ahead, paying no attention to him. Her hair had come undone on one side. She dropped her pocketbook and took no notice. He stooped and picked it up and handed it to her but she did not take it.

"You needn't act as if the world had come to an end," he said, "because it hasn't. From now on you've got to live in a new world and face a few realities for a change. Buck up," he said, "it won't kill you."

She was breathing fast.

"Let's wait on the bus," he said.

"Home," she said thickly.

"I hate to see you behave like this," he said. "Just like a child. I should be able to expect more of you." He decided to stop where he was and make her stop and wait for a bus. "I'm not going any further," he said, stopping. "We're going on the bus."

She continued to go on as if she had not heard him. He took a few steps and caught her arm and stopped her. He looked into her face and caught his breath. He was looking into a face he had never seen before. "Tell Grandpa to come get me," she said.

He stared, stricken.

"Tell Caroline to come get me," she said.

Stunned, he let her go and she lurched forward again, walking as if one leg were shorter than the other. A tide of darkness seemed to be sweeping her from him. "Mother!" he cried. "Darling, sweetheart, wait!" Crumpling, she fell to the pavement. He dashed forward and fell at her side, crying, "Mamma, Mamma!" He turned her over. Her face was fiercely distorted. One eye, large and staring, moved slightly to the left as if it had become unmoored. The other remained fixed on him, raked his face again, found nothing and closed.

"Wait here, wait here!" he cried and jumped up and began to run for help toward a cluster of lights he saw in the distance ahead of him. "Help, help!" he shouted, but his voice was thin, scarcely a thread of sound. The lights drifted farther away the faster he ran and his feet moved numbly as if they carried him nowhere. The tide of darkness seemed to sweep him back to her, postponing from moment to moment his entry into the world of guilt and sorrow.

## QUESTIONS: *O'Connor, "Everything That Rises Must Converge"*

1. What does the author suggest about the nature of the generation gap in the different ways she approaches the suffering of Julian and of his mother? Note the *metaphor* of martyrdom associated with Julian and the kinds of *verbs* used to describe his mother's activities (while Julian is shown as "waiting like Saint Sebastian for the arrows to begin piercing him," his mother is described as "a widow who had struggled fiercely to feed and clothe and put him through school and who was supporting him still").

   *Clue:* • Julian did not like to *consider* all she *did* for him. . . .

   a. What support does the story give to Julian's feeling that he is enduring a martyrdom because of his mother's tendency "to sacrifice herself for him after she had first created the necessity to do so by making a mess of things"?

   *Clues:* • "Well," she said, "I don't think I ought . . ."

   "Shut up and enjoy it," he muttered, more depressed than ever.

   • "I'll just go home," she said. "I will not bother you. If you can't do a little thing like that for me . . ."

   b. What other evidence is there of Julian's tendency to believe that he alone is put upon? Do the facts justify his view "that in spite of her, he had turned out so well"?

2. In what way does the author imply that the central problem of Julian's relations with his mother is a *reversal* of the conventional roles of child and parent? What connection does the story establish between the Black woman and Julian and between the child and Julian's mother?

   *Clues:* • . . . her eyes . . . were as innocent and untouched by experience as they must have been when she was ten.

   • Her feet in little pumps dangled like a child's. . . .

   • "I see yoooooooo!" she said and put her hand in front of her face and peeped at him.

   • . . . he was as disenchanted with it [the real world] as a man of fifty.

   • At that moment he could with pleasure have slapped her as he would have slapped a particularly obnoxious child in his charge.

   What connection can you establish between this approach to the story and the author's handling of Julian's reactions in the last two paragraphs?

3. How does the sentence "'I have mixed feelings now,' he groaned" appropriately represent a focal problem in the story?

   Consider Julian's complex attitude to

   a. his past (and specifically the family house).

   b. his mother: her appearance, her behavior, her values (consider Julian's feeling that his mother's hat is "hideous" and his statement to her, "I like it").

   c. Blacks (consider to what extent Julian's reactions to Blacks is a direct function of his feelings toward his mother; note particularly the fantasies in which he imposes the presence of Blacks upon her).

   For most of the story Julian is described as gloomy, depressed, or irritable. What connection does O'Connor make between his mood and his ambivalent feelings?

4. Julian's mother expresses herself in *clichés*—outworn expressions—such as "Rome

wasn't built in a day," and relies on conventional assumptions: "they never forgot who they were." How does this mode of speaking and feeling characterize her resistance (a) to social change, (b) to Julian's own attitude, behavior, and values?

*Clue:* • His mother excused his gloominess on the grounds that he was still growing up and his radical ideas on his lack of practical experience.

Although the reliance on clichés and conventional wisdom is so often identified with the older generation, we can think of a subculture of clichés among the young, for example, "Never trust anyone over thirty." In what sense may Julian be said to rely on his own clichés? (Consider his views on Blacks, for example.) What monumental cliché is destroyed in the tragic conclusion?

5. Julian reproaches his mother for her *moral confusion*, "You haven't the foggiest idea where you stand now or who you are." Is that criticism justified? (Consider the statement that her whole life "had been a struggle to act like a Chestny without the Chestny goods.") Why can the same criticism be applied to Julian?

*Clues:* • . . . in spite of all her foolish views, he was free of prejudice and unafraid to face facts. . . . He was not dominated by his mother.

• . . . from his [mental bubble] he could see her with absolute clarity.

• He felt completely detached from her.

• He was tilted out of his fantasy again as the bus stopped.

6. What is the symbolic function of (a) the reducing class, (b) the hat, (c) the penny? How do the first two symbols, the metaphor of the railway ("She rolled onto it [the topic of the Black's social condition] every few days like a train on an open track") and the reference to the fence ("They should rise, yes, but on their own side of the fence") explain the story's title?

7. We are told that after the incident, as Julian does not "try to conceal his irritation," his mother "leaned forward and her eyes raked his face. She seemed trying to determine his identity." As for Julian, just before his mother's final collapse, "He was looking into a face he had never seen before." What light do these statements cast on the central problems of self-knowledge and the knowledge of others (particularly those of a different generation) raised by the story as a whole?

## EXERCISE

That this is a story of initiation is etched in by the last sentence. Discuss as fully as possible the nature of that initiation.

*Louis Simpson (1923–     )*

# My Father in the Night Commanding No

My father in the night commanding No
Has work to do. Smoke issues from his lips;
    He reads in silence.
The frogs are croaking and the streetlamps glow.

And then my mother winds the gramophone;        5
The Bride of Lammermoor begins to shriek—
    Or reads a story
About a prince, a castle, and a dragon.

The moon is glittering above the hill.
I stand before the gateposts of the King—        10
    So runs the story—
Of Thule, at midnight when the mice are still.

And I have been in Thule! It has come true—
The journey and the danger of the world,
    All that there is        15
To bear and to enjoy, endure and do.

Landscapes, seascapes . . . where have I been led?
The names of cities—Paris, Venice, Rome—
    Held out their arms.
A feathered god, seductive, went ahead.        20

Here is my house. Under a red rose tree
A child is swinging; another gravely plays.
    They are not surprised
That I am here; they were expecting me.

And yet my father sits and reads in silence,        25
My mother sheds a tear, the moon is still,
    And the dark wind
Is murmuring that nothing ever happens.

Beyond his jurisdiction as I move
Do I not prove him wrong? And yet, it's true        30
    *They* will not change
There, on the stage of terror and of love.

The actors in that playhouse always sit
In fixed positions—father, mother, child
    With painted eyes.        35
How sad it is to be a little puppet!

Their heads are wooden. And you once pretended
To understand them! Shake them as you will,
    They cannot speak.
Do what you will, the comedy is ended.        40

Father, why did you work? Why did you weep,
Mother? Was the story so important?
 *"Listen!"* the wind
Said to the children, and they fell asleep.

QUESTIONS: *Simpson, " My Father in the Night Commanding No"*

1.   How do the different activities which each parent pursues characterize his temperament and his role in the family?
2.   How does stanza 6 clarify the relationships between the generations? What do the rest of the stanzas following it suggest about (a) the *roles* of members of a family? (b) the *capacity for communication* among members of a family?
 *Clues:*  in answering the above, examine carefully the following lines:
   • He reads in silence.

   • Or reads a story

   • . . . they were expecting me.

   • Is murmuring that nothing ever happens.

   • How sad it is to be a little puppet!

   •   And you once pretended
   To understand them!

   •   *"Listen!"* the wind
   Said to the children, and they fell asleep.

### EXERCISE

Suggest in one paragraph the particular power of the poem's title.

## *W. D. Snodgrass (1926–  )*
# April Inventory

The green catalpa tree has turned
All white; the cherry blooms once more.
In one whole year I haven't learned
A blessed thing they pay you for.
The blossoms snow down in my hair;   5
The trees and I will soon be bare.

The trees have more than I to spare.
The sleek, expensive girls I teach,
Younger and pinker every year,
Bloom gradually out of reach.   10
The pear tree lets its petals drop
Like dandruff on a tabletop.

The girls have grown so young by now
I have to nudge myself to stare.
This year they smile and mind me how                    15
My teeth are falling with my hair.
In thirty years I may not get
Younger, shrewder, or out of debt.


The tenth time, just a year ago,
I made myself a little list                              20
Of all the things I'd ought to know;
Then told my parents, analyst,
And everyone who's trusted me
I'd be substantial, presently.


I haven't read one book about                           25
A book or memorized one plot.
Or found a mind I didn't doubt.
I learned one date. And then forgot.
And one by one the solid scholars
Get the degrees, the jobs, the dollars.                 30


And smile above their starchy collars.
I taught my classes Whitehead's notions;
One lovely girl, a song of Mahler's.
Lacking a source-book or promotions,
I showed one child the colors of                        35
A luna moth and how to love.


I taught myself to name my name,
To bark back, loosen love and crying;
To ease my woman so she came,
To ease an old man who was dying.                       40
I have not learned how often I
Can win, can love, but choose to die.


I have not learned there is a lie
Love shall be blonder, slimmer, younger;
That my equivocating eye                                45
Loves only by my body's hunger;
That I have poems, true to feel,
Or that the lovely world is real.

While scholars speak authority
And wear their ulcers on their sleeves,                    50
My eyes in spectacles shall see
These trees procure and spend their leaves.
There is a value underneath
The gold and silver in my teeth.


Though trees turn bare and girls turn wives,                55
We shall afford our costly seasons;
There is a gentleness survives
That will outspeak and has its reasons.
There is a loveliness exists,
Preserves us. Not for specialists.                         60


# QUESTIONS: Snodgrass, *"April Inventory"*

1.  What are the special connotations attached to the word *inventory* in the poem? Why is the spring the appropriate time for it? How does the academic situation in and of itself and the teacher-student relationship enhance the inventory taking?

2.  In what sense do positive attributes become omens of doom—is bloom proving a token of decay—from the vantage point of the speaker?
    *Clue:* • The pear tree lets its petals drop
          Like dandruff on a tabletop.

3.  How does this double vision suggest that contrasting points of view are a key to the generation gap? What are the emotions felt by the speaker? Is the existence of the generation gap perhaps made to seem inevitable?
    *Clue:* • This year they smile and mind me how
          My teeth are falling with my hair.

4.  How does the introduction of another generation ("my parents, analyst") add complexity to the inventory? Suggest the importance of the word *substantial* in this stanza.

5.  In the light of the speaker's present feelings, why are the accomplishments in stanzas 6 and 7 very meaningful to him? How do these accomplishments prepare one for the final affirmation? Determine the importance of the following contrasts:
    a. "starchy collars" and "a song of Mahler's"
    b. "source-book or promotions" and "the colors of/A luna moth"
    c. "Can win, can love" and "choose to die"

6.  What does the failure previously to recognize "there is a lie/ Love shall be blonder, slimmer, younger" suggest about the point of view toward which the speaker is now moving?

7.  What is the ultimate triumph over "trees" and "girls"? Can it be seen as the triumph of one generation over another?
    *Clues* (last two stanzas):
            • My eyes in spectacles shall see
            These trees procure and spend their leaves.

- There is a value underneath
  The gold and silver in my teeth.

- "afford"; "outspeak"; "Preserves"

## EXERCISE

Compare and contrast Spenser's and Snodgrass' use of nature imagery in dealing with youth and age. What significant contrasts are observable in their treatment of love?

<br>

## *Charles Webb (1939–    )*
# The Graduate

### CHAPTERS 1–4

*This novel, which was first published in 1963, was relatively unknown until a highly successful film version appeared in 1968. The direction of Mike Nichols, the performance of Dustin Hoffman in the title role, and a song written for the film by Simon and Garfunkel won* The Graduate *unprecedented popularity.*

## *Chapter 1*

Benjamin Braddock graduated from a small Eastern college on a day in June. Then he flew home. The following evening a party was given for him by his parents. By eight o'clock most of the guests had arrived but Benjamin had not yet come down from his room. His father called up from the foot of the stairs but there was no answer. Finally he hurried up the stairs and to the end of the hall.

"Ben?" he said, opening his son's door.

"I'll be down later," Benjamin said.

"Ben, the guests are all here," his father said. "They're all waiting."

"I said I'll be down later."

Mr. Braddock closed the door behind him. "What is it," he said.

Benjamin shook his head and walked to the window.

"What is it, Ben."

"Nothing."

"Then why don't you come on down and see your guests."

Benjamin didn't answer.

"Ben?"

"Dad," he said, turning around, "I have some things on my mind right now."

"What things."

"Just some things."

"Well can't you tell me what they are?"

"No."

Mr. Braddock continued frowning at his son a few more moments, glanced at his watch, then looked back at Benjamin. "Ben, these are our friends down there," he said. "My friends. Your mother's friends. You owe them a little courtesy."

"Tell them I have to be alone right now."

"Mr. Robinson's out in the garage looking at your new sports car. Now go on down and give him a ride in it."

Benjamin reached into his pocket for a pair of shiny keys on a small chain. "Here," he said.

"What?"

"Give him the keys. Let him drive it."

"But he wants to see you."

"Dad, I don't want to see him right now," Benjamin said. "I don't want to see the Robinsons, I don't want to see the Pearsons, I don't want to see the . . . the Terhunes."

"Ben, Mr. Robinson and I have been practicing law together in this town for seventeen years. He's the best friend I have."

"I realize that."

"He has a client over in Los Angeles that he's put off seeing so he could be here and welcome you home from college."

"Dad—"

"Do you appreciate that?"

"I'd appreciate it if I could be alone!"

His father shook his head. "I don't know what's got into you," he said, "but whatever it is I want you to snap out of it and march right on down there."

Suddenly the door opened and Benjamin's mother stepped into the room. "Aren't you ready yet?" she said.

"No."

"We'll be right down," his father said.

"Well what's wrong," she said, closing the door behind her.

"I am trying to think!"

"Come on, Ben," his father said. He took his arm and began leading him toward the door.

"Goddammit will you leave me alone!" Benjamin said. He pulled away and stood staring at him.

"Ben?" Mr. Braddock said quietly, staring back at him, "don't you ever swear at your mother or me again."

Benjamin shook his head. Then he walked between them and to the door. "I'm going for a walk," he said. He stepped out into the hall and closed the door behind him.

He hurried to the head of the stairs and down but just as he had gotten to the front door and was about to turn the knob Mr. Terhune appeared out of the living room.

"Ben?" he said. "I want to shake your hand."

Benjamin shook it.

"Goddammit I'm proud of you," Mr. Terhune said, still holding his hand.

Benjamin nodded. "Thank you," he said. "Now if you'll excuse me I'm going for a walk. I'll be back later."

Mrs. Pearson appeared at the end of the hall. "Oh Benjamin," she said, smiling at him. She hurried to where he was standing and reached up to pull his head down and kiss him. "Benjamin?" she said. "I'm just speechless."

Benjamin nodded.

"Golly you did a fine job back there."

"I'm sorry to seem rude," Benjamin said, "but I'm trying to go on a walk right now."

Mr. Robinson appeared at the end of the hall with a drink in his hand. He began grinning when he saw Benjamin and walked into the group of people surrounding him to shake his hand. "Ben, how in hell are you," he said. "You look swell."

"I'm fine."

"Say, that's something out in the garage. That little Italian job your old man gave you for graduation?"

"Oh how exciting," Mrs. Pearson said.

"Let's go for a spin," Mr. Robinson said.

Benjamin reached into his pocket and pulled out the keys. "Can you work a foreign gearshift?" he said, holding them out.

"What?"

"Do you know how to operate a foreign gearshift."

"Well sure," Mr. Robinson said. "But I thought you'd take me for a little spin yourself."

"I can't right now," Benjamin said. "Excuse me." He reached for the doorknob and turned it, then pulled open the door. Just as he was about to step outside Mr. and Mrs. Carlson walked up onto the front porch.

"Well here he is himself," Mrs. Carlson said. She wrapped her arms around Benjamin and hugged him. "Ben?" she said, patting one of his shoulders, "I hope you won't be embarrassed if I tell you I'm just awfully proud to know you."

"I won't," Benjamin said. "But I have some things on my mind at the moment and I'm—"

"Here's something for you," Mr. Carlson said. He handed Benjamin a bottle wrapped with a red ribbon. "I hope they taught you to hold your liquor back there." He threw his arm around Benjamin's shoulder and swept him back inside the house.

Benjamin ducked under his arm and set the bottle of liquor beside the door. "Look," he said. "Could you please let me go for my walk!"

"What?"

"I'm sorry not to be more sociable," Benjamin said. "I appreciate everybody coming over but—"

"Now Ben," Mrs. Carlson said as her husband removed her coat, "I want you to tell me all about this prize you won. It was for teaching, wasn't it?"

Benjamin grabbed the doorknob but before he could turn it his father appeared beside him and put his arm around him. "Let's get you fixed up with a drink," he said.

"Dad?"

"Come on, Ben," his father said quietly. "You're making kind of a scene here."

"Then let me out!"

"Here we go," Mr. Braddock said. He began leading him away from the door.

"All right!" Benjamin said. He walked ahead of his father and into the living room, shaking his head.

"Well Benjamin," a woman said.

Benjamin nodded.

"Aren't you just thrilled to death?"

He walked on through the room, nodding at several more guests, and into the dining room where there was a tray of bottles on the dining-room table and a bucket of ice and some glasses. He selected one of the largest and poured it full of bourbon. Then he took several swallows, closed his eyes a moment and took several more. He refilled the glass to the top and turned around to see his mother standing in front of him.

"What's that," she said, frowning at the glass in his hand.

"This?"

"Yes."

"I don't know," he said. "Maybe it's a drink."

His mother turned her frown up to his face. "Ben, what's the trouble," she said.

"The trouble is I'm trying to get out of this house!"

"But what's on your mind."

"Different things, Mother."

"Well, can't you worry about them another time?"

"No."

Mrs. Braddock reached for his drink. "Here," she said, taking it. "Come out to the kitchen for a minute."

Benjamin shook his head but followed her through the swinging door and into the kitchen. Mrs. Braddock walked to the sink and poured out most of the drink, then filled the glass with water. "Can't you tell me what you're worried about?" she said, drying off the glass with a dish towel beside the sink.

"Mother, I'm worried about different things. I'm a little worried about my future."

"About what you're going to do?"

"That's right."

She handed him back the glass. "Well you still plan to teach don't you," she said.

"No."

"You don't?" she said. "Well what about your award."

"I'm not taking it."

"You're not?"

"No."

"Well Ben," she said, "that doesn't sound very wise, to pass up something you've spent four years working for."

Mr. Terhune pushed into the kitchen carrying his drink. "I thought I saw you duck in here," he said. "Now let's have the lowdown on that prize of yours."

"I'm not—"

"Tell him about it, Ben," his mother said.

"It's called the Frank Halpingham Education Award," Benjamin said. "It's given by the college. It puts me through two years of graduate school if I decide to go into teaching."

"Well now why did they pick you," Mr. Terhune said.

Benjamin didn't answer.

"He did some practice teaching back there," his mother said. "He's been an assistant teacher for two years. Last term they let him take a junior seminar in American History."

Mr. Terhune sipped at his drink. "Well, have you got in any graduate schools yet?" he said.

"Yes."

"He's in Harvard and Yale," his mother said. "And what's that other one?"

"Columbia."

Mr. Terhune sipped at his drink again. "It sounds like you've got things pretty well sewed up," he said.

Benjamin turned and walked quickly across the room to the back door. He opened it and walked out and to the edge of the swimming pool in the back yard. He stood staring down at the blue light rising up through the water for several moments before hearing the door open and bang shut behind him and someone walk across to where he was standing.

"Ben?" Mrs. McQuire said. "I think your yearbook is just unbelievable."

Benjamin nodded.

"Was there anyone who got his picture in there more times than you did?"

"Abe Frankel did."

Mrs. McQuire shook her head. "What a fantastic record you made for yourself."

"Ben?" Mr. Calendar came out beside the pool and shook Benjamin's hand. "Congratulations to you," he said.

"Have you seen Ben's yearbook?" Mrs. McQuire said.

"Why no."

"Let's see if I can remember all the different things," she said. "Ben, you tell me if I miss any." She cleared her throat and counted them off on her fingers as she talked. "Captain of the cross-country team. Head of the debating club. First in his class."

"I wasn't first."

"Oh?"

"I tied Abe Frankel for first."

"Oh," she said. "Now let's see what else. One of the editors of the school newspaper. Student teacher. I'm running out of fingers. Social chairman of his house. And that wonderful teaching award."

"Could I ask you a question," Benjamin said, turning suddenly toward her.

"Of course."

"Why are you so impressed with all those things."

"All the things you did?"

"Excuse me," Mr. Calendar said, holding up his glass. "I think I'll find a refill." He turned around and walked back into the house.

"Could you tell me that, Mrs. McQuire?"

She was frowning down into the bright blue water beside them. "Well," she said, "aren't you awfully proud of yourself? Of all those things?"

"No."

"What?" she said, looking up. "You're not?"

"I want to know why you're so impressed, Mrs. McQuire."

"Well," she said, shaking her head. "I'm afraid—I'm afraid I don't quite see what you're driving at."

"You don't know what I'm talking about, do you."

"Well not exactly. No."

"Then why do you—why do you—" He shook his head. "Excuse me," he said. He turned around and walked back toward the house.

"Ben?" she called after him. "I'm afraid I haven't been much help, but if it makes any difference I just want to say I'm thrilled to pieces by all your wonderful achievements and I couldn't be prouder if you were my own son."

Benjamin opened the door leading into the living room. He walked through the room keeping his eyes ahead of him on the carpet until Mrs. Calendar took his elbow.

"Ben?" she said. "I just think it's too terrific for words."

He walked past her and into the hall. Just as he got to the foot of the stairs his father came up behind him.

"Leave me alone."

"Ben, for God's sake what is it."

"I don't know what it is."

"Come here," Mr. Braddock said. He took his arm and led him down the hall and into a bedroom. "Son?" he said, closing the door and locking it. "Now what is it."

"I don't know."

"Well something seems pretty wrong."

"Something is."

"Well what."

"I don't know!" Benjamin said. "But everything—everything is grotesque all of a sudden."

"Grotesque?"

"Those people in there are grotesque. You're grotesque."

"Ben."

"I'm grotesque. This house is grotesque. It's just this feeling I have all of a sudden. And I don't know why!"

"Ben, it's because you're all tied up in knots."

Benjamin shook his head.

"Now I want you to relax."

"I can't seem to."

"Ben, you've just had four of the most strenuous years of your life back there."

"They were nothing," Benjamin said.

"What?"

"The whole four years," he said, looking up at his father. "They were nothing. All the things I did are nothing. All the distinctions. The things I learned. All of a sudden none of it seems to be worth anything to me."

His father was frowning. "Why do you say that."

"I don't know," Benjamin said. He walked across the room to the door. "But I've got to be alone. I've got to think until I know what's been happening to me."

"Ben?"

"Dad, I've got to figure this thing out before I go crazy," he said, unlocking the door. "I'm not just joking around either." He stepped back out into the hall.

"Ben?" Mr. Robinson said, holding out his hand. "I've got a client waiting for me over in Los Angeles."

Benjamin nodded and shook his hand.

"Real proud of you boy," Mr. Robinson said.

Benjamin waited till he had gone out the door, then turned around and walked upstairs and into his room. He closed the door behind him and sat down at his desk. For a long time he sat looking down at the rug, then he got up and walked to the window. He was staring out at a light over the street when the door opened and Mrs. Robinson stepped inside, carrying a drink and her purse.

"Oh," she said, "I guess this isn't the bathroom is it."

"It's down the hall," Benjamin said.

She nodded but instead of leaving the room stood in the doorway looking at him.

"It's right at the end of the hall," Benjamin said.

Mrs. Robinson was wearing a shiny green dress cut very low across her chest, and over one of her breasts was a large gold pin.

"Don't I get to kiss the graduate?" she said.

"What?"

She smiled at him.

"Mrs. Robinson," Benjamin said, shaking his head. "I'm kind of distraught at the moment. Now I'm sorry to be rude but I have some things on my mind."

She walked across the room to where he was standing and kissed one of his cheeks.

"It's good to see you," Benjamin said. "The bathroom's at the end of the hall."

Mrs. Robinson stood looking at him a moment longer, then turned around and walked to his bed. She seated herself on the edge of it and sipped at her drink. "How are you," she said.

"Look," Benjamin said. "I'm sorry not to be more congenial but I'm trying to think."

Mrs. Robinson had set her glass down on the rug. She reached into her purse for a package of cigarettes and held it out to Benjamin.

"No."

She took one for herself.

"Is there an ash tray in here?"

"No."

"Oh," she said, "I forgot. The track star doesn't smoke." She blew out her match and set it down on the bedspread.

Benjamin walked to his desk for a wastebasket and carried it to the bed. He picked up the match and dropped it in.

"Thank you."

He walked back to the window.

"What are you upset about," she said.

"Some personal things."

"Don't you want to talk about them?"

"Well they wouldn't be of much interest to you, Mrs. Robinson."

She nodded and sat quietly on the bed smoking her cigarette and dropping ashes into the wastebasket beside her.

"Girl trouble?" she said.

"What?"

"Do you have girl trouble?"

"Look," Benjamin said. "Now I'm sorry to be this way but I can't help it. I'm just sort of disturbed about things."

"In general," she said.

"That's right," Benjamin said. "So please." He shook his head and looked back out through the glass of the window.

Mrs. Robinson picked up her drink to take a swallow from it, then set it down and sat quietly until she was finished with her cigarette.

"Shall I put this out in the wastebasket?"

Benjamin nodded.

Mrs. Robinson ground it out on the inside of the wastebasket, then sat back up and folded her hands in her lap. It was quiet for several moments.

"The bathroom's at the end of the hall," Benjamin said.

"I know."

She didn't move from the bed but sat watching him until finally Benjamin turned around and walked to the door. "Excuse me," he said. "I think I'll go on a walk."

"Benjamin?"

"What."

"Come here a minute."

"Look I'm sorry to be rude, Mrs. Robinson. But I'm . . ."

She held out her hands. "Just for a minute," she said.

Benjamin shook his head and walked back to the bed. She took both his hands in hers and looked up into his face for several moments.

"What do you want," he said.

"Will you take me home?"

"What?"

"My husband took the car. Will you drive me home?"

Benjamin reached into one of his pockets for the keys. "Here," he said. "You take the car."

"What?"

"Borrow the car. I'll come and get it tomorrow."

"Don't you want to take me home?" she said, raising her eyebrows.

"I want to be alone, Mrs. Robinson. Now do you know how to work a foreign shift?"

She shook her head.

"You don't?"

"No."

Benjamin waited a few moments, then returned the keys to his pocket. "Let's go," he said.

Mr. Braddock was standing in the front doorway saying goodbye to the Terhunes. "Mrs. Robinson needs a ride home," Benjamin said. "I'll be right back."

"Wonderful party," Mrs. Robinson said. She took her coat from a closet beside the front door, put it on and followed Benjamin back through the house and out to the garage. He got into the car and started the engine and she got in beside him.

"What kind of car is this," she said.

"I don't know."

He backed out the driveway and they drove without speaking the several miles between the Braddocks' home and the Robinsons'. Benjamin stopped by the curb in front of her house. Mrs. Robinson reached up to push some hair away from her forehead and turned in her seat to smile at him.

"Thank you," she said.

"Right."

She didn't move from her seat. Finally Benjamin turned off the engine, got out and walked around to open the door for her.

"Thank you," she said, getting out.

"You're welcome."

"Will you come in, please?"

"What?"

"I want you to come in till I get the lights on."

"What for."

"Because I don't feel safe until I get the lights on."

Benjamin frowned at her, then followed her up a flagstone walk to the front porch. She found a key in her purse. When the door was opened she reached up to the wall just inside and turned on a hall light.

"Would you mind walking ahead of me to the sun porch?" she said.

"Can't you see now?"

"I feel funny about coming into a dark house," she said.

"But it's light in there now."

"Please?"

Benjamin waited a moment but then walked ahead of her down the hall and toward the rear of the house.

"To your left," she said.

Benjamin walked to his left and down three steps leading to the sun porch. Mrs. Robinson came in behind him and turned on a lamp beside a long couch against one of the walls.

"Thank you," she said.

"You're welcome."

"What do you drink," she said, "bourbon?"

Benjamin shook his head. "Look," he said. "I drove you home. I was glad to do it. But for God's sake I have some things on my mind. Can you understand that?"

She nodded.

"All right then."

"What do you drink," she said.

"What?"

"Benjamin, I'm sorry to be this way," she said. "But I don't want to be alone in this house."

"Why not."

"Please wait till my husband gets home."

"Lock the doors," Benjamin said. "I'll wait till you have all the doors locked."

33

"I want you to sit down till Mr. Robinson comes back."

"But I want to be alone!" Benjamin said.

"Well I know you do," she said. "But I don't."

"Are you afraid to be alone in your own house?"

"Yes."

"Can't you just lock the doors?"

Mrs. Robinson nodded at a chair behind him.

"When's he coming back," Benjamin said.

"I don't know."

Benjamin sat down in the chair. "I'll sit here till he gets back," he said. "Then I'll go. Good night."

"Don't you want some company?"

"No."

"A drink?"

"No."

Mrs. Robinson turned and walked up the three stairs leading from the porch. Benjamin folded his hands in his lap and looked at his reflection in one of the large panels of glass enclosing the room. Several moments later music began playing in another part of the house. He turned and frowned at the doorway. Then Mrs. Robinson walked back into the room carrying two drinks.

"Look. I said I didn't want any."

She handed it to him, then went to the side of the room and pulled a cord. Two large curtains slid closed across the windows. Benjamin shook his head and looked at the drink. Mrs. Robinson seated herself on a couch beside his chair. Then it was quiet.

"Are you always this much afraid of being alone?"

She nodded.

"You are."

"Yes."

"Well why can't you just lock the doors and go to bed."

"I'm very neurotic," she said.

Benjamin frowned at her a few moments, then tasted his drink and set it down on the floor.

"May I ask you a question?" Mrs. Robinson said.

He nodded.

"What do you think of me."

"What?"

"What do you think of me."

He shook his head.

"You've known me nearly all your life," she said. "Haven't you formed any—"

"Look. This is kind of a strange conversation. Now I told my father I'd be right back."

"Don't you have any opinions at all?"

"No," he said. He glanced at his watch. "Look, I'm sure Mr. Robinson will be here any minute. So please lock your doors and let me go."

"Benjamin?"

"What."

"Did you know I was an alcoholic?"

Benjamin shook his head. "Mrs. Robinson," he said, "I don't want to talk about this."

"Did you know that?"

"No."

"You never suspected?"

"Mrs. Robinson, this is none of my business," Benjamin said, rising from the chair. "Now excuse me because I've got to go."

"You never suspected I was an alcoholic."

"Goodbye, Mrs. Robinson."

"Sit down," she said.

"I'm leaving now."

She stood and walked to where he was standing to put one of her hands on his shoulder. "Sit down," she said.

"I'm leaving, Mrs. Robinson."

"Why."

"Because I want to be alone."

"My husband will probably be back quite late," she said.

Benjamin frowned at her.

"Mr. Robinson probably won't be here for several hours."

Benjamin took a step backwards. "Oh my God," he said.

"What?"

"Oh no, Mrs. Robinson. Oh no."

"What's wrong."

Benjamin looked at her a few moments longer, then turned around and walked to one of the curtains. "Mrs. Robinson," he said, "you didn't—I mean you didn't expect . . ."

"What?"

"I mean you—you didn't really think I would do something like that."

"Like what?"

"What do you think!" he said.

"Well I don't know."

"Come on, Mrs. Robinson."

"What?"

"For God's sake, Mrs. Robinson. Here we are. You've got me in your house. You put on music. You give me a drink. We've both been drinking already. Now you start opening up your personal life to me and tell me your husband won't be home for hours."

"So?"

"Mrs. Robinson," he said, turning around, "you are trying to seduce me."

She frowned at him.

"Aren't you."

She seated herself again on the couch.

"Aren't you?"

"Why no," she said, smiling. "I hadn't thought of it. I feel rather flattered that you . . ."

Suddenly Benjamin put his hands up over his face. "Mrs. Robinson?" he said. "Will you forgive me?"

"What?"

"Will you forgive me for what I just said?"

"It's all right."

"It's not all right! That's the worst thing I've ever said! To anyone!"

"Sit down."

"Please forgive me. Because I like you. I don't think of you that way. But I'm mixed up!"

"All right," she said. "Now finish your drink."

Benjamin sat back down in his chair and lifted his drink up from the floor. "Mrs. Robinson, it makes me sick that I said that to you."

"I forgive you," she said.

"Can you? Can you ever forget that I said that?"

"We'll forget it right now," she said. "Finish your drink."

"What is wrong with me," Benjamin said. He took several large swallows from his drink and set it back on the floor.

"Benjamin?"

"What, Mrs. Robinson."

She cleared her throat. "Have you ever seen Elaine's portrait?"

"Her portrait?"

"Yes."

Benjamin shook his head. "No."

"We had it done last Christmas. Would you like to see it?"

Benjamin nodded. "Very much."

"It's upstairs," she said, standing.

Benjamin followed her back to the front of the house and then up the thickly carpeted stairs to the second story. Mrs. Robinson walked ahead of him along a hall and turned into a room. A moment later dim yellow light spread out the doorway and into the hall. Benjamin walked into the room.

The portrait was hanging by itself on one of the walls and the light was coming from a small tubular lamp fixed at the top of the heavy gold frame. Benjamin looked at it, then nodded. "She's a very good looking girl," he said.

Mrs. Robinson seated herself on the edge of a single bed in a corner of the room.

Benjamin folded his arms across his chest and stepped up closer to the portrait to study some of the detail of the face. "I didn't remember her as having brown eyes," he said. He stepped back again and tilted his head slightly to the side. "She's really—she's really a beautiful girl."

"Benjamin?"

"Yes?"

She didn't answer. Benjamin turned to smile at her.

"Come here," she said quietly.

"What?"

"Will you come over here a minute?"

"Over there?"

She nodded.

"Sure," Benjamin said. He walked over to the bed. Mrs. Robinson reached up to put one of her hands on his sleeve. Then she stood slowly until she was facing him.

"Benjamin?" she said.

"Yes?"

She turned around. "Will you unzip my dress?"

Benjamin unfolded his arms suddenly and took a step backwards.

"I think I'll go to bed," she said.

"Oh," Benjamin said. "Well. Good night." He walked to the door.

"Won't you unzip the dress?"

"I'd rather not, Mrs. Robinson."

She turned around again and frowned at him. "Do you still think I'm trying to . . ."

"No I don't. But I just feel a little funny."

"You still think I'm trying to seduce you."

"I don't," Benjamin said. "But I think I'd better get downstairs now."

"Benjamin," she said, smiling, "you've known me all your life."

"I know that. I know that. But I'm—"

"Come on," she said, turning her back to him. "It's hard for me to reach."

Benjamin waited a moment, then walked back to her. He reached for the zipper and pulled it down along her back. The dress split open.

"Thank you."

"Right," Benjamin said. He walked back to the doorway.

"What are you so scared of," she said, smiling at him again.

"I'm not scared, Mrs. Robinson."

"Then why do you keep running away."

"Because you're going to bed," he said. "I don't think I should be up here."

"Haven't you ever seen anybody in a slip before?" she said, letting the dress fall down around her and onto the floor.

"Yes I have," Benjamin said, glancing away from her and at the portrait of Elaine. "But I just—"

"You still think I'm trying to seduce you, don't you."

"No I do not!" He threw his hands down to his sides. "Now I told you I feel terrible about saying that. But I don't feel right up here."

"Why not," she said.

"Why do you think, Mrs. Robinson."

"Well I don't know," she said. "We're pretty good friends I think. I don't see why you should be embarrassed to see me in a slip."

"Look," Benjamin said, pointing in back of him out the door. "What if— what if Mr. Robinson walked in right now."

"What if he did," she said.

"Well it would look pretty funny, wouldn't it."

"Don't you think he trusts us together?"

"Of course he does. But he might get the wrong idea. Anyone might."

"I don't see why," she said. "I'm twice as old as you are. How could anyone think—"

"But they would! Don't you see?"

"Benjamin," she said, "I'm not trying to seduce you. I wish you'd—"

"I know that. But please, Mrs. Robinson. This is difficult for me."

"Why is it," she said.

"Because I am confused about things. I can't tell what I'm imagining. I can't tell what's real. I can't—"

"Would you like me to seduce you?"

"What?"

"Is that what you're trying to tell me?"

"I'm going home now. I apologize for what I said. I hope you can forget it. But I'm going home right now." He turned around and walked to the stairs and started down.

"Benjamin?" she called after him.

"What."

"Will you bring up my purse before you go?"

Benjamin shook his head.

"Please?" she said.

"I have to go now. I'm sorry."

Mrs. Robinson walked out to the railing holding her green dress across the front of her slip and looked down at Benjamin standing at the foot of the stairs. "I really don't want to put this on again," she said. "Won't you bring it up?"

"Where is it."

"On the sun porch."

Benjamin hurried through the hall and found the purse beside the couch on the sun porch. He returned with it to the foot of the stairs. "Mrs. Robinson?"

"I'm in the bathroom," she called from upstairs.

"Well here's the purse."

"Could you bring it up?"

"Well I'll hand it to you. Come to the railing and I'll hand it up."

"Benjamin?" she called. "I'm getting pretty tired of this."

"What?"

"I am getting pretty tired of all this suspicion. Now if you won't do me a simple favor I don't know what."

Benjamin waited a moment, then carried the purse up to the top of the stairs.

"I'm putting it on the top step," he said.

"For God's sake, Benjamin, will you stop acting this way and bring me the purse?"

He frowned down the hallway. A line of bright light was coming from under the bathroom door. Finally he walked slowly down the hall toward it. "Mrs Robinson?"

"Did you bring it up?"

"I did," he said. "I'm putting it here by the door."

"Won't you bring it in to me?"

"I'd rather not."

"All right," she said from the other side of the door. "Put it across the hall."

"Where?"

"Across the hall," she said. "In the room where we were."

"Oh," Benjamin said. "Right." He walked quickly back into the room where Elaine's portrait was and set the purse on the end of the bed. Then he turned around and was about to leave the room when Mrs. Robinson stepped in through the door. She was naked.

"Oh God."

She smiled at him.

"Let me out," Benjamin said. He rushed toward the door but she closed it behind her and turned the lock under the handle.

"Don't be nervous," she said.

Benjamin turned around.

"Benjamin?"

"Get away from that door!"

"I want to say something first."

"Jesus Christ!" Benjamin put his hands up over his face.

"Benjamin, I want you to know I'm available to you," she said. "If you won't sleep with me this time—"

"Oh my God."

"If you won't sleep with me this time, Benjamin, I want you to know you can call me up any time you want and we'll make some kind of arrangement."

"Let me out!"

"Do you understand what I said?"

"Yes! Yes! Let me out!"

"Because I find you very attractive and any time—"

Suddenly there was the sound of a car passing along the driveway underneath the window.

Benjamin turned and leaped at the door. He pushed Mrs. Robinson aside, fumbled for the lock, then ran out the door and downstairs. He opened the front door of the house but then stepped back inside and hurried back onto the porch. He sat down with his drink and tried to catch his breath. The back door of the house slammed shut.

"Is that Ben's car in front?" Mr. Robinson called.

"Yes sir!" Benjamin said, jumping up from the chair.

Mr. Robinson came into the room.

"I drove—I drove your wife home. She wanted me to drive her home so I—so I drove her home."

"Swell," Mr. Robinson said. "I appreciate it."

"She's upstairs. She wanted me to wait down here till you got home."

"Standing guard over the old castle, are you."

"Yes sir."

"Here," Mr. Robinson said, reaching for Benjamin's glass. "It looks like you need a refill."

"Oh no."

"What?"

"I've got to go."

Mr. Robinson was frowning at him. "Is anything wrong?" he said. "You look a little shaken up."

"No," Benjamin said. "No. I'm just—I'm just—I'm just a little worried about my future. I'm a little upset about my future."

"Come on," Mr. Robinson said, taking the glass. "Let's have a nightcap together. I didn't get much of a chance to talk to you at the party."

Benjamin waited till Mr. Robinson had left the room, then took several deep breaths. When he finished taking the deep breaths he put his hands in his pockets and walked quickly back and forth till Mr. Robinson brought him his drink.

"Thank you very much sir," he said as he took it.

"Not at all," Mr. Robinson said. He carried his drink to the chair beside Benjamin's and sat. "Well," he said. "I guess I already said congratulations."

"Thank you."

Mr. Robinson nodded and sipped at his drink. "Ben?" he said. "How old are you now."

"Twenty. I'll be twenty-one next week."

Again Mr. Robinson nodded. "I guess you skipped a grade or two back there in high school," he said. "I guess that's why you graduated so young."

"Yes sir."

Mr. Robinson reached into his pocket for a package of cigarettes and held them out to Benjamin. He took one and put it in his mouth. "Ben?" Mr. Robinson said, picking up a book of matches and lighting the cigarette for him. "That's a hell of a good age to be."

"Thank you."

Mr. Robinson lit a cigarette for himself and dropped the match in an ash tray. "I wish I was that age again," he said.

Benjamin nodded.

"Because Ben?"

"What."

"You'll never be young again."

"I know."

"And I think maybe—I think maybe you're a little too worried about things right now."

"That's possible."

"You seem all wrapped up about things," Mr. Robinson said. "You don't seem to be— Ben, can I say something to you?"

"What."

"How long have we known each other now."

Benjamin shook his head.

"How long have you and I known each other. How long have your dad and I been partners."

"Quite a while."

"I've watched you grow up, Ben."

"Yes sir."

"In many ways I feel almost as though you were my own son."

"Thank you."

"So I hope you won't mind my giving you a friendly piece of advice."

"I'd like to hear it."

"Ben?" Mr. Robinson said, settling back in his chair and frowning up over Benjamin's head. "I know as sure as I'm sitting here that you're going to do great things someday."

"I hope you're right."

"Well I am right," he said. "That's something I just know. But Ben?"

"What."

"I think—" He dropped an ash from his cigarette into the ash tray. "I think you ought to be taking it a little easier right now than you seem to."

Benjamin nodded.

"Sow a few wild oats," Mr. Robinson said. "Take things as they come. Have a good time with the girls and so forth."

Benjamin glanced at the door.

"Because Ben, you're going to spend most of your life worrying. That's just the way it is, I'm afraid. But right now you're young. Don't start worrying yet, for God's sake."

"No."

"Before you know it you'll find a nice little girl and settle down and have a damn fine life. But until then I wish you'd try and make up a little for my mistakes by—"

Mrs. Robinson, dressed again in the green dress and the gold pin she had worn to the party, stepped into the room.

"Don't get up," she said.

Benjamin sat back down in the chair. Mrs. Robinson seated herself on the couch and picked up her unfinished drink from the floor.

"I was just telling Ben here he ought to sow a few wild oats," Mr. Robinson said. "Have a good time while he can. You think that's sound advice?"

Mrs. Robinson nodded.

"Yes I sure do," her husband said.

Benjamin finished his drink quickly and set it down on the table beside him. "I've got to go," he said.

"Just hang on here, Ben," Mr. Robinson said. "Wait'll I finish my drink, then I'm going to have you spin me around the block in that new car out front."

"Maybe he's tired," Mrs. Robinson said.

"Tired, Ben?"

"Oh no. No." He picked up his glass and held it up to his mouth till the ice cubes clicked down against his teeth. Then he replaced it on the table.

"Do you want another?" Mrs. Robinson said.

"What? No."

"Sure," Mr. Robinson said. "You have yourself a few flings this summer. I bet you're quite the ladies' man."

"Oh no."

"What?" Mr. Robinson said, grinning at him. "You look like the kind of guy that has to fight them off."

Benjamin reached for his glass.

"Are you sure you won't have another?" Mrs. Robinson said.

"No. No."

Mr. Robinson turned to his wife. "Doesn't he look to you like the kind of guy who has trouble keeping the ladies at a distance?"

"Yes he does."

"Oh say," Mr. Robinson said. "When does Elaine get down from Berkeley."

"Saturday," she said.

"Ben, I want you to give her a call."

"I will."

"Because I just know you two would hit it off real well. She's a wonderful girl and I'm just awful sorry you two haven't got to know each other better over the years."

"I am too," Benjamin said. He watched Mr. Robinson until he had taken the last swallow from his glass, then stood. "I'll take you around the block," he said.

"Great."

Benjamin walked ahead of Mr. and Mrs. Robinson through the hall and to the front door and opened it. Mrs. Robinson stepped out onto the front porch after them.

"Benjamin?"

He put his hands in his pockets and walked down across the flagstone path without answering her.

"Benjamin?"

"What."

"Thank you for taking me home."

Benjamin nodded without turning around.

"I'll see you soon, I hope," she said.

"Hey Ben," Mr. Robinson said, opening the door of the car and getting in. "What do you say we hit the freeway with this thing and see what she does."

## Chapter 2

During the next week Benjamin spent most of his time walking. On his twenty-first birthday he ate breakfast, then went out the front door, walked around the block, walked around the block again, then walked downtown. He walked back and forth along the main street till it was time to eat lunch, then went into a cafeteria. All during the afternoon he walked, sometimes stopping in a park or on a bus bench to rest a few minutes, but usually walking slowly past houses and stores, looking down at the sidewalk ahead of him.

Late in the afternoon he returned to his own block and to his house. He walked up toward the front door but then stopped as he noticed several people sitting in the living room. He turned around and walked back toward the sidewalk but before he reached it the front door opened and his mother stepped out onto the porch.

"Ben?"

"What."

"Come on in."

"I'm going on a walk," Benjamin said.

Mrs. Braddock hurried down toward the sidewalk to where he was standing. "It's your birthday," she said.

"I know that. I'm going for a walk on my birthday."

"Well the Arnolds came over from next door," she said. "I said you'd fix Peter and Louise some fruit juice as soon as you got back."

Benjamin took a deep breath, then turned around and walked with his mother slowly back to the house.

"I invited the Robinsons over," she said, "but Elaine had to stay up in Berkeley for summer school and I—"

Benjamin had stopped and was staring at her. "Are they in there?" he said, pointing at the house.

"What?"

"Are Mr. and Mrs. Robinson in that house?"

"No."

"Are they coming?"

"No."

"Are you sure, Mother?"

"Of course I'm sure," she said. "Is anything wrong?"

"No," Benjamin said. He walked the rest of the way to the house and inside and to the living room.

Mrs. Arnold, seated in the middle of the sofa, began waving one of her hands back and forth through the air and singing the moment she saw him. "Happy birthday to you. Happy birthday to you. Happy birthday dear . . ."

"Benjamin, it's good to see you," Mr. Arnold said, standing up and shaking his hand.

Peter and Louise ran up to him and wrapped their arms around his legs.

Benjamin's father was sitting on one of the chairs beside the fireplace, a drink in his hand. "Go out and get the kids some fruit juice," he said. "Then come on back and we have a little surprise for you."

Benjamin walked slowly across the living room with Peter and Louise still hanging onto his legs and laughing. He pushed open the door of the kitchen and walked inside.

"Get off my legs," he said when the door was closed.

They smiled up into his face.

"Get off my legs, I said!"

They released his legs and walked slowly to one of the corners of the room. Benjamin shook his head and opened the door of the refrigerator and looked inside. "What do you want," he said. "Grape juice or orange juice."

They stared at him from the corner without answering.

"Grape juice or orange juice!" Benjamin said, clenching his fist.

"Grape juice."

"All right then." He reached into the refrigerator for a bottle of grape juice and filled two small glasses. Peter and Louise walked across the kitchen to take them.

"Thank you."

Benjamin poured himself a glass of grape juice and carried it back into the living rooom.

"Ben?" his father said, grinning at him. "I think you'll get a real big kick out of your present this year."

Benjamin nodded and sat down on the sofa beside Mrs. Arnold.

"We've been hearing all about it," Mrs. Arnold said. "I can't wait to see it."

"Shall I bring it in now?" his father said.

"What."

"Your present."

Benjamin nodded and took a sip of the grape juice.

Mr. Braddock stood and left the room. When he came back several moments later he was carrying a large square box wrapped in white paper. "Many happy returns," he said, placing it on the rug at Benjamin's feet.

"I can't wait," Mrs. Arnold said.

Benjamin looked at her a moment, then reached down to break two strips of Scotch tape holding the paper together. Inside was a brown cardboard box. Mr. Arnold crossed the room to stand over him and watch him open it. Benjamin pulled up the two flaps of the carton and looked down into it.

"What is it," he said.

"Well pull her on up," his father said.

Inside the box was something made of black rubber that looked like several uninflated inner tubes folded up on top of each other. Benjamin reached down and pulled it out.

"Now unfold it," his father said.

Benjamin held it up and let it unfold. It was a suit. There were two black arms and two legs and a zipper running up the front of it and a black hood.

"What is it," Benjamin said. "Some kind of rubber suit?"

Mr. Arnold laughed. "It's a diving suit," he said.

"Oh," Benjamin said. He looked at it a moment longer, then nodded and began returning it to the box. "Thanks."

"You're not through yet," his father said, pulling it back up and holding it. "Keep digging."

"Isn't this exciting," Mrs. Arnold said.

Peter and Louise came over to sit on the rug beside him and watch. Benjamin reached down into the box and drew out a rubber mask with a glass plate in it, and two hoses leading out from the side of it.

"That's your mask," his father said.

Peter Arnold took it from him to hold. Benjamin reached in again for a large silver cylinder with the words COMPRESSED AIR stenciled on it in orange letters.

"That's your oxygen supply."

"I can see that," Benjamin said. He dropped the tank on the rug and reached into the box a final time and pulled up two black rubber fins. He looked at them a moment, then dropped them back into the box and sat back on the couch. "Thanks," he said. He reached for his grape juice.

"Well now, let's have a show before it gets dark," Mr. Braddock said.

"What?"

"I'll be right back," his father said. He turned around and hurried out of the room.

"What did he say?"

"I think he wants you to give us an exhibition out in the swimming pool," Mrs. Braddock said.

"Oh no," Benjamin said, straightening up on the couch.

Mr. Braddock returned carrying a long metal spear and handed it to Benjamin.

"Listen," Benjamin said.

"Go on up and get your gear on," his father said. "I'll set up some chairs out by the pool."

"Look," Benjamin said, shaking his head. "This is a great gift, but if you don't mind—"

"Let's go," Mr. Braddock said. He began gathering up the equipment from the floor and handing it to Benjamin.

"Dad, it's just what I wanted and all that but I can't—"

"We want to be sure it's safe," his mother said.

"Safe? Sure it is. Look." He reached down into the floor of the box and pulled out a white slip of paper. "Here's the guarantee right here."

"Let's go," his father said, taking his arm and pulling him up from the couch.

"This is ludicrous, Dad."

"Come on," Mr. Arnold said, grinning at him. "Let's see a few under-water stunts."

"Oh my God."

"Let's get to it," Mr. Braddock said. He piled the equipment in Benjamin's arms and began pushing him toward the hall.

"Come on now, Dad."

His father left him standing in the hall and returned to the living room. Benjamin waited a moment, then walked back to the entrance of the room.

"Dad?"

"What're you still doing down here."

"Could I see you a minute, please?"

"Oh no. You get ready."

"Could I see you a minute in the hall, please!"

Mr. Braddock walked back into the hall.

"Now I refuse to make a goddamn ass of myself in front of the Arnolds."

"Here we go," Mr. Braddock said. He began pushing him toward the stairs.

"Goddammit Dad!"

"Here we go," he said, pushing him up the stairs. "Happy birthday. Happy birthday."

"Dad I don't—"

"I'll give you three minutes to get it on," Mr. Braddock said. He turned around and walked back into the living room. Benjamin stood a moment on the stairs with his arms wrapped around the equipment, then carried it up and into the bathroom. "Jesus Christ," he said, throwing it on the floor. He shook his head and kicked off his shoes. Then he removed the rest of his clothes and sat down on the toilet. He tugged the rubber legs up around his own legs and forced his arms into the rubber arms and pulled up the zipper across his chest. He fixed the black rubber hood over his head and was about to return downstairs when he happened to glance out the bathroom window and into the back yard.

"Oh my God," he said.

The Arnolds and his mother were seated in metal chairs at one side of the pool. The two children were running back and forth on the grass. Standing at the other side of the pool were the Lewises, the other next-door neighbors and their teenaged daughter, and a man and a woman whom Benjamin had never seen before, standing beside them on the lawn holding drinks. At the rear of the yard the neighbors from in back were at the fence with their son. Benjamin pushed up the window.

"Say Dad?" he said.

Mr. Braddock was pulling a final chair up beside the pool.

"Hey Dad! Could I see you a minute!"

Mr. Braddock looked up at the window and grinned. "There he is, folks," he said, pointing at him. "Right up in the window there. He'll be right down." He held his hands up in front of him and began to applaud. The other guests gathered around the pool laughed and clapped. The Lewises' daughter turned to whisper something to her mother and her mother laughed and whispered something to their guests.

"Dad, for God's sake!"

"Hurry it up! Hurry it up! Folks," Mr. Braddock said, "he's a little shy. This is his first public appearance so you'll have to—"

Benjamin slammed the window shut and stared down at the two fins and the air tank and the mask on the floor of the bathroom. Then he picked them up and carried them downstairs and out through the living room to the back. He stood looking out the door at the swimming pool and the guests until finally Mr. Braddock rushed inside.

"Let's go."

"Does this amuse you?"

Mr. Braddock leaned back out the door. "He's downstairs, folks! The suit's on! Give us half a minute!" He closed the door and stepped back inside. "I'll help you on with the mask," he said.

"Dad, this is sick."

"Here." He took the mask and fitted it onto Benjamin's face. Then he strapped the air cylinder onto his back and connected it to the hoses running out the side of the mask. "Can you breathe all right?" he said. "Good." He got down on his knees and fitted the fins over Benjamin's feet, then stood up, grinned at him and walked back outside.

"Folks," he said, "let's hear you bring him out! A big round of applause!" The guests began to applaud. "Here he comes! Here he comes!"

Benjamin stepped out the door and into the back yard. The neighbors continued to clap and laugh. Mr. Lewis pulled a handkerchief out of his pocket to dry his eyes. The Arnold children began jumping up and down on the lawn and screaming and pointing at him. After several moments of applause Mr. Braddock raised his hands. It was quiet.

"Now ladies and gentlemen? The boy is going to perform spectacular and amazing feats of skill and daring under water."

Mr. Arnold laughed. "Get your pennies ready, folks."

"Are you ready, boy?" Mr. Braddock said. "All right then. On with the show!"

"On with the show!" the Arnold children yelled, jumping up and down. "On with the show! On with the show!" Mrs. Arnold stood up and took their hands and then it was suddenly perfectly quiet in the yard.

Benjamin cleared his throat. He walked slowly toward the edge of the pool, keeping his chin down against his chest so he could see where he was going through the mask, but before he reached the water one of his flippers got caught under his foot and he nearly pitched forward onto his face. The children began to laugh again and leap up and down.

"Oh no," Mrs. Arnold said. "That wasn't funny."

"Hey Ben," Mr. Arnold called. "Be careful when you come up. You don't want to get the bends."

Benjamin placed his foot down onto the top step at the shallow end of the pool, then walked slowly down the steps to the pool's floor.

"Wait a minute," his father said. He hurried to the edge of the pool with the spear. Benjamin stared at him a moment through the glass, then grabbed the spear away from him, turned around and began walking slowly down the slope of the pool toward the deep end. The water rose up around his black suit to the level of his chest. Then to his neck. Just as the water level was at his chin the flippers began scraping against the bottom of the pool. He let all his breath out and tried to force himself under but the air tank kept him afloat. He began thrashing with his arms but his head would not go under. The Arnold children began to laugh. Finally he turned around and began moving slowly back up toward the shallow end. The neighbors in back began booing through the fence. By the time he reached the steps everyone in the yard was booing except for his father, who was standing at the head of the pool frowning at him.

Benjamin pulled the mask partially away from his face. "The show's over," he said quietly.

"What's wrong."

"He needs a weight!" Mr. Arnold called. "That'll get him under. If you had a big rock it would do it."

"Right," Mr. Braddock said. He straightened up. "Folks?" he said. "There will be a brief intermission. Hang on to your seats." He hurried past the pool and through a gate into the rear part of the yard, where the incinerator was.

Benjamin stood quietly at the shallow end of the pool resting the end of his spear on the pool's floor and staring through his mask at Peter Arnold. It was perfectly quiet. When Mr. Braddock returned he was carrying a large piece of concrete used to keep the lid of the incinerator closed. Benjamin took it from him and walked slowly back toward the deep end. Some of the guests began laughing and applauding as his head went under and then it was perfectly quiet beneath the water as he walked gradually down to the very bottom of the pool. He stood a moment looking at a wall of the pool, then sat down. Finally he eased himself down onto his side and balanced the heavy piece of concrete on his hip. Then he turned his head to look up at the shiny silver surface of the pool above. "Dad?" he said quietly into his mask.

In the morning Benjamin got up earlier than usual. He dressed himself in a pair of khaki pants and an old jacket he had bought in the East at an army surplus store, and went downstairs. Mrs. Braddock was in the kitchen. "You're up early," she said.

Benjamin walked past her and sat down at the table in front of his grapefruit. "I'm leaving home," he said.

"What?"

"I said I'm leaving home," he said, picking up his spoon. "I'm clearing out after breakfast."

Mrs. Braddock reached up to wipe her hands on a towel beside the sink. "You're going away?" she said.

"That's right."

She frowned and walked across the room to sit down beside him at the table. "You're taking a trip?" she said.

"That is right," Benjamin said. He dug into the grapefruit.

"Well where are you going," she said.

"I don't know."

"You don't know where you're going?"

"No."

She sat a moment looking at him. "I don't understand what you mean," she said.

"If you want the cliché," Benjamin said, looking up from his grapefruit, "I'm going on the road."

"What?"

"On the road. I believe that's the conventional terminology."

"Well Ben," his mother said.

"What."

"I still don't understand this. You aren't just planning to throw your things in the car and leave, I hope."

"No."

"Then what."

"I'm hitchhiking."

"What?"

"Mother, you haven't been on the road much, have you."

Mrs. Braddock began shaking her head.

"Don't get excited, Mother. I'll be all right."

"You mean you're just going to pack your bag and go?"

"I'm not taking any luggage."

"What?"

"I'm taking what I have on."

"Are you serious?"

"Yes."

"Well how much money are you taking."

"Ten dollars."

"Oh," she said. "Then you won't be gone more than a day or two."

Benjamin raised a section of grapefruit to his mouth.

"How long will you be gone," his mother said.

"I don't know."

"More than a day or two?"

"Yes."

"But not more than a week."

"Look, Benjamin said. "Maybe five years, maybe ten. I don't know."

"What?"

Mr. Braddock came into the kitchen carrying the morning newspaper. "You're up early," he said.

"Ben, tell your father. Because I know he won't let you do it."

"What's up," Mr. Braddock said, sitting down at the table.

"I'm going on a trip."

"He's not taking the sports car. He's not taking any clothes. He has ten dollars in his pocket and he's—"

"Excuse me," Benjamin said. He reached for a bowl of sugar in the center of the table.

"What's all this about?" Mr. Braddock said.

"I'm leaving after breakfast on a trip," Benjamin said, sprinkling sugar on his grapefruit. "I have no idea where I'm going. Maybe just around the country or the continent. Maybe if I can get papers I'll work around the world. So that's that."

"Well what's the point of it."

"The point is I'm getting the hell out of here."

Mr. Braddock frowned at him. "This doesn't sound too well thought out," he said.

Benjamin raised a sugared section of grapefruit to his mouth.

"You just plan to work around? Bum around?"

"That's right."

"Meet all kinds of interesting people I suppose."

"That's right."

"Well Ben," his father said. "I don't see anything wrong with taking a little trip. But this is the wrong way to go about it."

"I don't think so."

"Listen," his father said. "How's this for an idea."

"I don't like it."

"How's this for an idea, Ben. Spend the summer picking out a graduate school in the East, then throw your things in the car and take a week or two driving back."

"No."

"What's wrong with that."

"Because I'm finished with schools, Dad." A section of grapefruit fell off his spoon and onto the table. "I never want to see another school again. I never want to see another educated person again in my life."

"Come on, Ben."

"Come on!" Benjamin said, standing up. "Now I have wasted twenty-one years of my life. As of yesterday. And that is a hell of a lot to waste."

"Sit down."

"Dad," Benjamin said, "for twenty-one years I have been shuffling back and forth between classrooms and libraries. Now you tell me what the hell it's got me."

"A damn fine education."

"Are you kidding me?"

"No."

"You call me educated?"

"I do."

"Well I don't," Benjamin said, sitting down again. "Because if that's what it means to be educated then the hell with it."

"Ben?" his mother said. "What are you talking about."

"I am trying to tell you," Benjamin said, "I'm trying to tell you that I am through with all this."

"All what."

"All this!" he said, holding his arms out beside him. "I don't know what it is but I'm sick of it. I want something else."

"What do you want."

"I don't know."

"Well look, Ben."

"Do you know what I want," Benjamin said, tapping his finger against the table.

"What."

"Simple people. I want simple honest people that can't even read or write their own name. I want to spend the rest of my life with these people."

"Ben."

"Farmers," Benjamin said. "Truck drivers. Ordinary people who don't have big houses. Who don't have swimming pools."

"Ben, you're getting carried away."

"I'm not."

"Ben, you have a romantic idea of this."

"Real people, Dad. If you want the cliché, I am going out to spend the rest of my life with the real people of this world."

"Aren't we real?" Mrs. Braddock said.

"It's trite to talk about it," Benjamin said. "I know how I feel."

They finished breakfast quietly. When it was over, Mr. Braddock pulled a checkbook out of his pocket and began making out a check.

"Dad, look."

"I want you to take this," he said.

"I don't want it."

He signed it and tore it out of the book. "Here," he said.

"No."

"Take it."

"I won't."

Mr. Braddock reached over to stuff it in the pocket of Benjamin's coat. Benjamin removed it, read the amount, then returned it to his pocket.

"Cash it if you have to," his father said.

"I won't have to."

"All right. But Ben?"

"What."

"I don't know how long this is going to last. I have a feeling you'll be back here before you think you will."

"I won't."

"But if you feel you have to get out and rub elbows with the real people for a while, then . . ."

Benjamin stood. "Goodbye," he said, holding out his hand.

His father shook it. "Call collect if you get into any kind of trouble."

"Ben?" Mrs. Braddock said. "Do you think you might be back by Saturday?"

"Mother."

"Because I invited the Robinsons over for dinner. It would be so much more fun if you were here."

## Chapter 3

The trip lasted just less than three weeks. It was late one night when Benjamin returned and both his parents were asleep. He tried the front door and found it locked. Then he tried the kitchen door at the side of the house and the door at the rear but both were locked. He attempted opening several windows but most of them were covered with screens and the ones without screens were locked. Finally he walked back around to the front porch and banged on the door until a light was turned on in his parents' bedroom. He waited till the light was turned on in the front hall. Then his father, wearing a bathrobe, pulled open the door.

"Ben," he said.

Benjamin walked past him and into the house.

"Well you're back."

"I'm back," Benjamin said. He walked to the foot of the stairs.

"Hey," Mr. Braddock said, grinning at him, "it looks like you've got a little beard started there."

"It comes off tomorrow."

"Well," his father said. "How are you."

"Tired."

"You're all tired out."

"That's right."

"So how was the trip."

"Not too great," Benjamin said. He began slowly climbing up the stairs.

"Well Ben?"

Benjamin stopped and let his head sag down between his shoulders. "Dad," he said, "I'm so tired I can't think."

"Well can't you tell me where you went?"

Benjamin knelt down on the stairs, then lay down on his side. "North," he said, closing his eyes.

"How far north."

"I don't know. Redding. One of those towns."

"Well that's where the big fire is," his father said. "You must have seen it."

Mrs. Braddock, wearing her bathrobe and pushing some hair out of her face, appeared at the foot of the stairs. "Ben?" she said. "Is that you?"

"Hello Mother," he said without opening his eyes.

"Are you all right?"

"Yes."

"Well how was the trip."

"Mother, I have never been this tired in all my life."

"He got up to Redding, he thinks," Mr. Braddock said. "One of those towns up there."

"Dad, I haven't slept in several days. I haven't eaten since yesterday and I'm about to drop over."

"You haven't eaten?" his mother said.

"No."

"I'll fix you something right away."

"Look," Benjamin said, raising his head up off the stair. "I'm so tired I can't even . . ."

Mrs. Braddock had already hurried out of the front hall and toward the kitchen.

"Come on in the living room a minute," Mr. Braddock said. "You'll get to bed right after a little food."

Benjamin slid back down the stairs, stood and followed his father slowly into the living room. He dropped down onto the sofa.

"Well now," Mr. Braddock said. "Let's have the report."

Benjamin's head fell back and he closed his eyes again.

"What about money. Did you cash my check?"

"No."

"Well what happened. Did you get some work?"

"Yes."

"What kind of work was it."

"Dad?"

"Come on, Ben," he said. "I'm interested in this."

Benjamin took a deep breath. "I fought a fire," he said.

"That big fire up there?" his father said. "You fought it?"

"That's right."

"Well that's right up there by Shasta. You must have been right up there in the Shasta country. That's beautiful country."

Benjamin nodded.

"How did they pay you on a deal like that," his father said.

"Five an hour."

"Five dollars an hour?"

"That's right."

"They give you the equipment and you go in and try to put out the flames."

Benjamin nodded.

"Well what about the Indians. I was reading they transported some Indians up there from a tribe in Arizona. Professional fire fighters. Did you see some of them?"

"I saw some Indians. Yes."

Mr. Braddock shook his head. "That is real exciting," he said. "What else happened."

Benjamin didn't answer.

"You didn't have any trouble getting rides."

"No."

"Well tell me where you stayed."

"Hotels."

Mr. Braddock nodded. "Maybe this trip wasn't such a bad idea after all," he said. "Did you have any other jobs besides the fire?"

"Yes."

"Well what were they."

"Dad, I washed dishes. I cleaned along the road. Now I am so tired I am going to be sick."

"Talk to a lot of interesting people, did you?"

"No."

"You didn't?"

"Dad, I talked to a lot of people. None of them were particularly interesting."

"Oh," his father said. "Did you talk to some of the Indians?"

"Yes Dad."

"They speak English, do they?"

"They try."

"Well what else did you—"

"Dad, the trip was a waste of time and I'd rather not talk about it."

"Oh?" his father said. "Why do you say that."

"It was a bore."

"Well it doesn't sound too boring if you were up there throwing water on that fire."

"It was a boring fire."

It was quiet for a few moments. "Can't you tell me a little more about it?"

"Dad—"

"Let's hear about some of the people you bumped into."

"You want to?"

"Sure," his father said. "What kind of people stopped to give you rides."

"Queers."

"What?"

"Queers usually stopped," he said. "I averaged about five queers a day. One queer I had to slug in the face and jump out of his car."

"Homosexuals?"

"Have you ever seen a queer Indian, Dad?"

"What?"

"Have you ever had a queer Indian approach you while you're trying to keep your clothes from burning up?"

Mr. Braddock sat frowning at him from the chair. "Did that happen?" he said.

"Dad, for what it was worth I did the whole tour. I talked to farmers. I talked to—"

"What would you talk to them about."

"The farmers?"

"Yes."

"Their crops. What else do they know how to talk about."

"Who else did you talk to."

"I talked to tramps. I talked to drunks. I talked to whores."

"Whores?"

"Yes Dad, I talked to whores. One of them swiped my watch."

"A whore stole your wrist watch?"

"Yes."

"Not while you were talking to her."

"No."

Mr. Braddock looked down at the rug. "Then you—then you spent the night with a whore."

"There were a few whores included in the tour, yes."

"More than one?"

"It grows on you."

"How many then."

"I don't remember," Benjamin said, putting his hands up over his eyes. "There was one in a hotel. There was one at her house. There was one in the back of a bar."

"Is this true, Ben?"

"One in a field."

"A field?"

"A cow pasture, Dad, It was about three in the morning and there was ice in the grass and cows walking around us."

"Ben, this doesn't sound too good."

"It wasn't."

"I think you'd better go down and have yourself looked at."

"Dad, I'm tired."

"Is she the one who took your watch?"

"No. The one in the hotel took it."

"Ben," Mr. Braddock said, shaking his head, "I don't know quite what to say. Where did you find these girls."

"Bars."

"They came right up to you?"

"Please let me sleep."

"I suppose you did quite a bit of drinking on the trip," Mr. Braddock said.

Benjamin nodded.

"You did."

"Well it's not too likely I'd spend the night with a stinking whore in a field full of frozen manure if I was stone cold sober, now is it "

"Good God, Benjamin."

Mrs. Braddock returned to the room with a glass of milk and a plate with a sandwich on it. She set them down on the table in front of Benjamin.

"Now," she said. "Let's hear all about the trip."

Benjamin shook his head and reached for the sandwich.

"What did you do," his mother said.

"Not much."

"Well, can't you tell me about it?"

"Mother, I saw some pretty scenery and had a nice time and came home."

"And you're sure you're all right."

"Yes."

"Because you look awfully tired."

"Go on to bed," Mr. Braddock said. "I want to talk to Ben a few minutes."

Mrs. Braddock waited a moment, then walked out of the room.

"Ben, how do you feel about things now," his father said.

"What things."

"I mean are you—do you feel a little more ready to settle down and take life easy now?"

He nodded.

"You do."

"Yes."

"Well what are your plans. Do you think you'll go back to graduate school this fall?"

"No."

Mr. Braddock frowned. "Why not," he said.

"Dad, we've been through this."

"You still—you still feel the same way about teaching."

"That's right," Benjamin said. He reached for his milk.

"Well, do you have any plans?"

"I do."

"Can you tell me what they are?"

"I plan to take it easy," Benjamin said. "I plan to relax and take it easy."

"Good," his father said. "I'm glad to hear you say that. You plan to put in a little loafing time around home."

"That's exactly right."

"Sure," his father said. "Rest up. Call up some girl who'd like to see you."

"I plan to."

"Good," Mr. Braddock said. He sat in the chair across from him while Benjamin finished eating the sandwich and drank the glass of milk. Several times he glanced up at Benjamin, then back down at the floor. "Ben?" he said finally.

"What."

"You sound—you sound kind of disillusioned about things."

"I'm sorry."

"Are you disillusioned? Or are you just tired."

Benjamin stood up and wiped off his mouth with the back of his hand. "I don't know what I am, Dad, and I don't particularly care," he said. "Excuse me." He walked out of the room and up the stairs and went to bed.

Two days after he got home from the trip Benjamin decided to begin his affair with Mrs. Robinson. He ate dinner with his parents in the evening, then went up to his room to take a shower and shave. When he had shined his best pair of shoes and dressed in a suit and tie he returned downstairs and told his parents he was going to a concert in Los Angeles. He showed them the article in the morning newspaper announcing the concert. Then he climbed into his car and drove to the Hotel Taft.

The Hotel Taft was on a hill in one of the better sections of town. A wide street curved up past large expensive homes until it neared the top of the hill, then there was an archway over the street with a sign on the archway reading Taft Hotel and as it passed under the archway the street turned into the entranceway of the hotel. Benjamin drove slowly under the archway, then up the long driveway until he came to the building itself. He had to slow his car and wait in a line while other cars, most of them driven by chauffeurs, stopped by the entrance of the building for a doorman to open the door for their passengers. When Benjamin was beside the entrance an attendant appeared at his car and pulled open the door.

"Thank you," Benjamin said as he climbed out.

Others the same age as Benjamin were walking across a broad pavilion leading to the doors of the hotel. A few of the boys were wearing suits but most were wearing summer tuxedos with black pants and white coats. A girl who had on a shiny white dress and a white orchid on one of her wrists walked arm-in-arm with her escort up to the door and in. Benjamin followed. Just inside the door a man smiled at Benjamin and pointed across the lobby of the hotel.

"Main ballroom," he said.

"What?"

"Are you with the Singleman party?"

"No," Benjamin said.

"I beg your pardon."

He nodded at the man, then walked into the large lobby, looking around him at the main desk and at the telephone booths against one wall and at the several elevators standing open with their operators in front of them. He walked slowly across the thick white carpet of the lobby to the door where the others had gone and for a long time stood looking into the ballroom. There were tables around the sides of the room covered with white tablecloths and in the center of each table was a small sign with a number on it. Some of the couples were wandering around the room looking for their tables and others were already seated talking together or leaning over the backs of their chairs to talk to someone at the next table. Just inside the door of the ballroom two women and a man were standing in a line. Each time a girl and her escort walked through the door the two women and the man smiled and shook their hands. Then the man reached into his pocket for a sheet of paper and told them where to sit.

"I'm Mrs. Singleman," the woman closest to the door said to Benjamin after he had stood to watch several couples go in.

"Oh," Benjamin said. "Well I'm not—" She was holding out her hand to him. He looked at it a moment, then shook it. "I'm pleased to meet you," he said, "but I'm—"

"What is your name," she said.

"My name's Benjamin Braddock. But I'm—"

"Benjamin?" she said. "I'd like you to know my sister, Miss DeWitte."

Miss DeWitte, wearing a large purple corsage on one of her breasts, stepped forward smiling and extended her hand.

"Well I'm glad to meet you," Benjamin said, shaking it, "but I'm afraid—"

"And that's Mr. Singleman," Mrs. Singleman said, nodding at her husband.

"How are you, Ben," Mr. Singleman said, shaking his hand. "Let's see if we can't find you a table here."

"Well that's very kind of you," Benjamin said. "But I'm not with the party."

"What?"

"I'm—I'm here to meet a friend." He nodded and walked back past them and into the lobby.

Across from the ballroom was a bar with a sign over its door reading The Verandah Room. Benjamin walked across the lobby and under the sign and into the bar. He found an empty table in one of the corners of the room beside a large window that stretched across the entire length of the wall and overlooked the grounds of the hotel.

Although he seldom smoked Benjamin bought a package of cigarettes when he ordered his first drink and smoked several of them as he drank. He kept his face to the window, sometimes watching the reflection of people as they came in through the door of the bar and found tables, but usually looking through the glass at the lighted walks and the trees and the shrubbery outside.

After several drinks he gave the waitress a tip and left the bar for the telephone booths in the lobby. He looked up the Robinsons' telephone number, memorized it and closed himself into a booth. For a long time he sat with the receiver in one hand and a coin in the other but without dropping it into the machine. Finally he returned the receiver to its hook and lighted another cigarette. He sat smoking it inside the closed booth and frowning down at one of the booth's walls. Then he ground it out under his foot and walked out of the booth and into the one beside it to call Mrs. Robinson.

"I don't quite know how to put this," he said when she answered the phone.

"Benjamin?"

"I say I don't quite know how to put this," he said again, "but I've been thinking about that time after the party. After the graduation party."

"You have."

"Yes," he said. "And I wondered—I wondered if I could buy you a drink or something."

A boy wearing a summer tuxedo closed himself into the booth beside Benjamin. Benjamin listened to him drop his coin into the telephone and dial.

"Shall I meet you somewhere?" Mrs. Robinson said.

"Well," Benjamin said, "I don't know. I mean I hope you don't think I'm out of place or anything. Maybe I could—maybe I could buy you a drink and we could just talk. Maybe—"

"Where are you," she said.

"The Taft Hotel."

"Do you have a room there?"

"What?"

"Did you get a room?"

"Oh no," Benjamin said. "No. I mean—look, don't come if you—if you're busy. I don't want to—"

"Will you give me an hour?"

"What?"

"An hour?"

"Oh," Benjamin said. "Well. I mean don't feel you have to come if you don't—in fact maybe some other—"

"I'll be there in an hour," Mrs. Robinson said. She hung up the phone.

Exactly an hour later she arrived. She had on a neat brown suit and white gloves and a small brown hat. Benjamin was sitting at the corner table looking out the window at the grounds of the hotel and didn't see her until she was standing directly across the table from him.

"Hello Benjamin."

"Oh," Benjamin said. He rose quickly from the chair, jarring the table with his leg. "Hello. Hello."

"May I sit down?"

"Of course," Benjamin said. He hurried around the table and held the chair for her as she sat.

"Thank you."

Benjamin watched her remove the two white gloves and drop them into a handbag she had set on the floor. Then he cleared his throat and returned to his chair.

"How are you," Mrs. Robinson said.

"Very well. Thank you." He looked down at a point in the center of the table.

It was quiet for several moments.

"May I have a drink?" Mrs. Robinson said.

"A drink," he said. "Of course." He looked up for the waitress. She was on the other side of the room taking an order. Benjamin whistled softly and motioned to her but she turned and walked in the other direction. "She didn't see me," he said, rising from his chair and jarring the table. "I'll—"

Mrs. Robinson reached across the table and rested her hand on his wrist. "There's time," she said.

Benjamin nodded and sat down. He kept his eyes on the waitress as she made her way to the bar and placed an order with the bartender. As she turned around and waited for him to fill it Benjamin waved his arm through the air.

"She saw me," he said.

"Good," Mrs. Robinson said.

They drank quietly, Benjamin smoking cigarettes and looking out the window, sometimes drumming his fingers on the surface of the table.

"You've been away," Mrs. Robinson said.

"What?"

"Weren't you away for a while?"

"Oh," Benjamin said. "The trip. I took a trip."

"Where did you go," Mrs Robinson said, taking a sip of her martini.

"Where did I go?"

"Yes."

"Where did I go," Benjamin said. "Oh. North. I went north."

"Was it fun?"

Benjamin nodded. "It was," he said. "Yes."

Mrs. Robinson sat quietly a few moments, smiling across the table at him.

"Darling?" she said.

"Yes?"

"You don't have to be so nervous, you know."

"Nervous," Benjamin said. "Well I am a bit nervous. I mean it's—it's pretty hard to be suave when you're . . ." He shook his head.

Mrs. Robinson sat back in her chair and picked up her drink again. "Tell me about your trip," she said.

"Well," Benjamin said. "There's not much to tell."

"What did you do," she said.

"What did I do," Benjamin said. "Well I fought a fire."

"Oh?"

"Yes. The big forest fire up there. You might have—you might have read about it in the newspaper."

She nodded.

"It was quite exciting," Benjamin said. "It was quite exciting to be right up there in the middle of it. They had some Indians too."

"Did you put it out?"

"What?"

"Did you get the fire out all right?"

"Oh," Benjamin said. "Well there were some others fighting it too. There were—yes. It was under control when I left."

"Good," she said.

Benjamin picked up his glass and quickly finished the drink. "Well," he said. "I'll buy you another."

Mrs. Robinson held up her glass. It was still nearly full. "Oh," Benjamin said. He nodded.

"Benjamin?"

"What."

"Will you please try not to be so nervous?"

"I am trying!"

"All right," she said.

Benjamin shook his head and turned to look out the window again.

"Did you get us a room?" Mrs. Robinson said.

"What?"

"Have you gotten us a room yet?"

"I haven't. No."

"Do you want to?"

"Well," Benjamin said. "I don't—I mean I could. Or we could just talk. We could have another drink and just talk. I'd be perfectly happy to—"

"Do you want me to get it?"

"You?" he said, looking up at her. "Oh no. No. I'll get it." He began nodding.

"Do you want to get it now?" she said.

"Now?"

"Yes."

"Well," he said. "I don't know."

"Why don't you get it."

"Why don't I get it now? Right now?"

"Why don't you."

"Well," Benjamin said. "I will then." He rose from the table. "I'll get it right now then." He walked a few steps away, stopped, then turned around and came back. "Mrs. Robinson, I'm sorry to be so awkward about this but—"

"I know," she said.

Benjamin shook his head and walked across the Verandah Room. He stood for several moments in the doorway looking at the clerk behind the main desk, then finally pushed his hands down into his pockets and walked across the thick white carpet.

"Yes sir?" the clerk said.

"A room. I'd like a room, please."

"A single room or a double room," the clerk said.

"A single," Benjamin said. "Just for myself, please."

The clerk pushed a large book across the counter at him. "Will you sign the register please?" There was a pen on the counter beside the book. Benjamin picked it up and quickly wrote down his name. Then he stopped and continued to stare at the name he had written as the clerk slowly pulled the register back to his side.

"Is anything wrong, sir?"

"What? No. Nothing."

"Very good, sir," the clerk said. "We have a single room on the fifth floor. Twelve dollars. Would that be suitable?"

"Yes," Benjamin said, nodding. "That would be suitable." He reached for his wallet.

"You can pay when you check out, sir."

"Oh," Benjamin said. "Right. Excuse me."

The clerk's hand went under the counter and brought up a key. "Do you have any luggage?" he said.

"What?"

"Do you have any luggage?"

"Luggage," Benjamin said. "Yes. Yes I do."

"Where is it."

"What?"

"Where is your luggage."

"Well it's in the car," Benjamin said. He pointed across the lobby. "It's out there in the car."

"Very good, sir." the clerk said. He held the key up in the air and looked around the lobby. "I'll have a porter bring it in."

"Oh no," Benjamin said.

"Sir?"

"I mean I'd—I'd rather not go to the trouble of bringing it all in. I just have a toothbrush. I can get it myself. If that's all right."

"Of course."

Benjamin reached for the key.

"I'll have a porter show you the room."

"Oh," Benjamin said, withdrawing his hand. "Well actually I'd just as soon find it myself. I just have the toothbrush to carry up and I think I can handle it myself."

"Whatever you say, sir." The man handed him the key.

"Thank you."

Benjamin walked across the lobby and out through the front doors of the hotel. He watched the doorman open the doors of several cars and a taxi that drove up, then he turned around and went back inside. As he passed the clerk he stopped and patted one of the pockets of his coat.

"Got it," he said.

"Sir?"

"The toothbrush. I got the toothbrush all right."

"Oh. Very good, sir."

Benjamin nodded. "Well," he said. "I guess I'll stop in the bar a minute before going up."

"You do whatever you like, sir."

"Thank you."

Benjamin returned to the Verandah Room. Mrs. Robinson looked up to smile at him when he came to the table.

"Well," Benjamin said. "I did it. I got it."

"You got us a room."

"Yes."

He reached into his pocket for the key. "It's on the fifth floor," he said, squinting at the number on the key. "Five hundred and ten it is."

"Shall we go up?" Mrs. Robinson said.

"Oh," Benjamin said, frowning. "Well I'm afraid there's a little problem."

"Oh?"

"I got a single."

Mrs. Robinson nodded. "That's all right," she said.

"Well that's all right," Benjamin said. "But the man at the desk. The clerk. He seemed—he seemed like he might be a little suspicious."

"Oh," she said. "Well do you want to go up alone first?"

"I think I'd better," Benjamin said. "And also—also I was wondering if you could wait. Till he's talking to someone. So he—I mean I signed my own name by mistake and I—"

"I'll be careful," Mrs. Robinson said.

"I know," Benjamin said. "But I don't know what their policy is here. I wouldn't—"

"Benjamin?"

"What."

"Will you try and relax please?"

"Well I'm trying," Benjamin said. "It's just that this clerk—he gave me a funny look."

"I'll be up in ten minutes," Mrs. Robinson said.

"Ten minutes," Benjamin said. "Right. I mean—right." He nodded and hurried away from the table.

In ten minutes Mrs. Robinson knocked on the door of the room. Benjamin had just drawn two large curtains over the window. He hurried across the carpet and pulled open the door for her. They stood looking at each other for a moment, then Benjamin began nodding.

"I see—I see you found it all right," he said.

She smiled at him and walked into the room, looking at a television set in the corner, then at the bed. She removed the small round hat from the top of her head and set it down on a writing desk against one of the walls.

"Well," Benjamin said. He nodded but didn't say anything more.

Mrs. Robinson walked slowly back to where he was standing. "Well?" she said, looking up into his face.

Benjamin waited a few moments, then brought one of his hands up to her shoulder. He bent his face down, cleared his throat, and kissed her. Then he lifted his face back up and nodded again. "Well," he said again, removing his hand from her shoulder.

Mrs. Robinson returned to the writing table and looked down at her hat. "Benjamin?"

"Yes?"

"I'll get undressed now," she said, running one of her fingers around the edge of the hat. "Is that all right?"

"Sure," Benjamin said. "Fine. Do you—do you—"

"What?"

"I mean do you want me to just stand here?" he said. "I don't—I don't know what you want me to do."

"Why don't you watch," she said.

"Oh. Sure. Thank you."

He watched her unbutton the three buttons on the front of her suit, then reach up to unbutton the top button on her blouse. She smiled at him as she moved her hand slowly down the front of her blouse, then leaned for support on the writing table and reached down to remove her shoes.

"Will you bring me a hanger?" she said.

"What?"

She straightened up and frowned at him. "Benjamin, if you want another drink we'll go down and have one."

"Oh no," Benjamin said. "A hanger. I'll get a hanger." He hurried to the closet and opened its door. "A wood one?" he said.

"What?"

"Do you want a wood one?"

"A wood one would be fine," she said.

"Right," Benjamin said. He reached into the closet for a wooden hanger and carried it across the room to her.

"Thank you," she said, taking it.

"You're welcome," Benjamin said. He walked back to the door. He slid his hands into his pockets and watched her as she removed the jacket of her suit, then the blouse she was wearing and hung them on the hanger.

Suddenly Benjamin began shaking his head. He pulled his hands up out of his pockets and opened his mouth to say something but then closed it again. "Mrs. Robin—?"

"What?"

"Nothing."

She frowned at him.

"Nothing," Benjamin said. "Nothing. Do you need another hanger."

"No," she said. She looked at him a moment longer, then pushed her skirt down around her legs, stepped out of it and folded it. "Would it be easier for you in the dark?" she said, draping the skirt through the hanger and over the wooden bar.

"No."

"You're sure."

"I'm sure. Yes."

"Hang this up please?" she said. Benjamin walked across the room to take the hanger from her and carried it to the closet. When he had hung it up and turned around she had let a half-slip she was wearing drop to the floor and was stepping out of it. She slid a girdle and the stockings fastened to it down around her legs and onto the floor. "Will you undo my bra?" she said, turning around.

"Your—your—"

"Will you?"

Benjamin looked at her a moment longer, then suddenly began shaking his head. He rushed to one of the walls of the room. "No!" he said.

"What?"

"Mrs. Robinson! Please! I can't!"

"What?"

"I cannot do this!"

Mrs. Robinson watched him for a moment, then turned and walked slowly to the bed. She seated herself and moved back to sit with her back against the board at the head of the bed. She crossed her legs in front of her and reached behind her back to unhook the bra. "You don't want to do it," she said.

"I want to but I can't!" he said to the wall. "Now I'm just—I'm sorry I called you up but I—"

"Benjamin?"

"I mean don't you see?" he said, turning around. "Don't you see that this is the worst thing I could possibly do? The very worst thing in the world?"

"Is it?"

He shook his head. "Now I feel awful about this," he said. "About having you come up here like this. But I—I just—Mrs. Robinson, I like being with you. It's not that. I mean maybe we—maybe we could do something else together. Could we—could we go to a movie? Can I take you to a movie?"

She frowned at him. "Are you trying to be funny?" she said.

"No! No! But I don't know what to say! Because I've got you up here and I—"

"And you don't know what to do."

"Well I know I can't do this!"

"Why not."

"For God's sake why do you think, Mrs. Robinson."

She shrugged. "I suppose you don't find me particularly desirable," she said.

"Oh no," Benjamin said, taking a step toward the bed. "No. That has nothing to do with it."

"You don't have to—"

"Look," Benjamin said. "Mrs. Robinson. I think—I think you're the most attractive woman of all my parents' friends. I mean that. I find you desirable. But I— For God's sake can you imagine my parents?" He held his arms up beside him.

"What?"

"Can you imagine what they'd say if they just saw us here in this room right now?"

"What would they say," she said.

"I have no idea, Mrs. Robinson. But for God's sake. They've brought me up. They've made a good life for me. And I think they deserve better than this. I think they deserve a little better than jumping into bed with the partner's wife."

She nodded.

"So it's nothing to do with you. But I respect my parents. I appreciate what they've—"

"Benjamin?" she said, looking up at him.

"What."

"Would you think I was being forward if I asked you a rather personal question?"

"Oh no," Benjamin said. "You can ask me anything you want. I'd be happy to—"

"Are you a virgin?" she said.

"What?"

"You don't have to tell me if you don't want."

Benjamin frowned at her. "Am I a virgin," he said.

She nodded.

Benjamin continued to frown at her and finally she smiled. "All right," she said. "You don't have to tell me."

"Well what do you think," he said.

"I don't know," she said. "I guess you probably are."

"Come on," Benjamin said.

"Well aren't you?"

"Of course I'm not."

"It's nothing you should be ashamed of, Benjamin," she said, dropping her bra beside her on the bed.

"What?"

She folded her arms over her breasts and leaned her head back against the wall. "I mean I wish you'd just admit to me you're a little bit frightened of being with a woman instead of . . ."

"What?"

"I wish you'd just tell me you don't think you'd be able to go through with it rather than . . ."

Benjamin shook his head. "Look," he said. "You're missing the point."

"I don't think so."

"Well you are," he said. "The point is that I come from a family where we trust each other."

Mrs. Robinson brought her head up and smiled slightly. "Come on," she said.

"What?"

"Now look," she said. "I'm sure there isn't a man living who wasn't a little scared his first time."

"But it's not!"

"Benjamin there's no reason to be scared of me."

"Do you really believe that?" he said, taking another step toward the bed. "Do you really believe I've never done this thing before?"

"Well," she said, "I think it's pretty obvious you haven't. You don't have the slightest idea what to do. You're nervous and awkward. You can't even—"

"Oh my God," Benjamin said.

"I mean just because you might be inadequate in one way doesn't—"

"Inadequate?!"

She nodded, then it was quiet. Benjamin stared at her as she frowned down at one of her breasts. "Well," she said finally, straightening up and putting one foot down on the floor. "I guess I'd better be—"

"Stay on that bed," Benjamin said. He removed his coat quickly and dropped it on the floor. Then he began unbuttoning his shirt. He walked to the bed to sit down beside her, then reached behind her head to remove several bobby pins. Mrs. Robinson shook her head and her hair fell down around her shoulders. Benjamin finished taking off his shirt and dropped it on the floor. Then he put his arms around her and eased her down onto her back on the bed. He kissed her and kicked off his shoes at the same time. Mrs. Robinson put her hands up at the sides of his head and then moved her fingernails up through his hair and finally wrapped both her arms around him and pressed him down against her until he could feel her breasts flattening underneath his chest and the muscles trembling in her arms. She pulled her mouth away from his and pushed it against his neck, then pushed one of her hands down between them to the buckle of his belt.

"Please," she said.

Benjamin raised his head up several inches to look at her face. Her eyes were closed and her mouth was partly open.

"Please," she said again.

Benjamin reached for the lamp on the table beside them. "Inadequate," he said, turning it off. "That's good. That's really pretty—"

"Please!"

He let her unbuckle his belt and push his pants down around his legs, then climbed on top of her and started the affair.

## Chapter 4

The date after which Benjamin was no longer eligible for the Frank Halpingham Education Award fell sometime in mid-September. He celebrated the event quietly and by himself. When his parents had gone to bed he carried a bottle of bourbon from the liquor cabinet out to the pool and drank it slowly and smoked cigarettes, grinding the first ones out on the cement beside the pool and then flipping the rest up in the air and watching them fall and sputter out in the bright blue water. It was not till long after midnight that he tossed the empty bottle into the pool, stood from his chair and walked slowly inside and upstairs to bed.

He spent most of his time at home. He got up late in the morning or early in the afternoon and dressed in his bathing suit. He usually ate breakfast by himself. Sometimes, if she wasn't shopping or reading in her room, his mother came into the kitchen to sit with him while he ate. After breakfast he went out to the pool. He had found an old rubber raft in one of the cupboards of the garage which had not been used since before high school when the family had taken it on weekend trips to the beach. Benjamin inflated it and although the rubber was cracked where it had been folded and stored, it still held air.

After breakfast Benjamin usually kicked it into the water from the edge of the pool where he had left it the day before, then walked slowly down the steps of the shallow end. Sometimes he carried a can of beer down into the pool with him and sat on the raft while he drank it. Then he tossed the empty can off beside the pool and eased himself down onto the raft to float for the rest of the day. Sometimes he floated on his back with his hands folded across his stomach and sometimes he lay on his stomach with his arms hanging down into the water beside the raft. Unless it rained he floated all afternoon and right up until it was time for dinner, getting off the raft only once every hour or so to inflate it when he felt the water slowly rising up around his chest.

He ate dinner each evening with his parents. He put on a shirt and rolled up its sleeves around his elbows after his father insisted he wear more than his bathing suit to the table. After dinner, on the nights he didn't dress and drive to the Taft Hotel, he took a can of beer with him into the den and watched television. During the early part of the evening he usually drank only beer as he watched television and then when it was later and his parents had gone to bed he usually poured himself a glassful of bourbon to drink as he watched the movies that came on after the shorter plays and comedy programs had ended. Sometimes, if his drink was still not finished, he sat a long time after the last movie was over watching one of the test patterns or the photograph of an American flag that one of the channels always put on the screen after they had played the national anthem and signed off the air. Once or twice he fell asleep in his chair and woke up hours later just as it was beginning to get light outside to find that the can of beer or the drink he had been holding had fallen out of his hand and spilled into his lap or across the rug. But usually the movies kept him awake. After a while he was able to calculate just how much to drink so that the moment the last movie ended he could set down his empty glass, turn off the set and go upstairs and be asleep almost the moment he slid between the sheets of his bed.

One evening, an hour or so after dinner had been finished, Mr. Braddock came into the den where Benjamin was watching television. Benjamin glanced at him, then back at the screen. Mr. Braddock closed the door behind him and walked to the set to turn it off. Benjamin scowled at him. Mr. Braddock seated himself behind a desk in the room and looked for a long time without saying anything at an ash tray Benjamin had perched on the arm of his chair.

"Ben?" he said finally, quietly. "What's happening."

"What's happening," Benjamin said, grinding out a cigarette.

"Yes."

"Well up until a minute ago I was watching TV."

Mr. Braddock shook his head. "Ben, I don't know what to say to you."

"You don't."

"No."

"Well what's the problem then."

"You're asking *me* what the problem is?"

Benjamin shrugged and reached into the pocket of his shirt for a new cigarette. "I don't see that there is one," he said. "The only problem I see is that you came busting in here and turned off a program."

"Ben," his father said, shaking his head. "Can't you talk to me? Can't you try and tell me what's wrong?"

"Look," Benjamin said. "Nothing's wrong at all. I mean you—you walk in here, you turn off the TV, you start wringing your hands and crying and asking me what's the problem. Just what in the hell do you want."

"Have you just lost all hope?"

"Oh my God," Benjamin said. He lit his cigarette and dropped the match into the ash tray.

"Well what is it then," Mr. Braddock said, holding up his hands. "You sleep all day long. You drink and watch television all night. Sometimes you disappear after dinner and don't come home till the next day. And you're trying to tell me there's no problem? Ben, you're in a complete tailspin."

"I'm in a complete tailspin."

"Ben," Mr. Braddock said, "we are your parents."

"I'm aware of that."

"We want to know what you're doing. Ben, what do you do when you take off after dinner. Do you sit in bars? Do you go to the movies? Is there a girl you're meeting somewhere?"

"No."

"Well then what."

"I drive around."

"All that time?"

"That's right."

Mr. Braddock shook his head. "That's rather hard to believe," he said.

"So don't believe it." Benjamin reached down for the can of beer on the rug beside his chair.

"And what are your plans. Do you have any plans at all?"

Benjamin swallowed some beer and returned the can to the rug. He wiped his mouth with the back of his hand. "Look," he said. "I'm perfectly content. All summer long you nagged at me to have a good time So now I'm having one. So why not leave well enough alone."

"This is what you call having a good time?"

"This is what I call having a ball."

Benjamin finished his cigarette slowly. When he was done he ground it out in the ash tray and sat a few moments longer with his arms resting on the arms of the chair and staring ahead of him at the dark screen. Then he glanced up at his father. "Do I have your permission to turn on the television?"

"No."

"I don't."

"No."

Mr. Braddock stood and walked to the window of the den. He looked out into the dark back yard. "I want to talk about this," he said.

"Dad, we've got nothing to say to each other."

"But we've got to, Ben."

"We don't."

"Ben I—I want to talk about values. Something."

"You want to talk about values," Benjamin said.

"Do you have any left?"

Benjamin frowned. "Do I have any values," he said. "Values. Values." He shook his head. "I can't think of any at the moment. No."

"How can you say that, son."

"Dad, I don't see any value in anything I've ever done and I don't see any value in anything I could possibly ever do. Now I think we've exhausted the topic. How about some TV."

"You're twenty-one years old," his father said.

"Come on, Dad."

"You have a wonderful mind and you're a well-educated young man."

"Dad," Benjamin said, reaching into his shirt pocket for another cigarette, "let's not beat around the bush. If you're trying to tell me you're throwing me out of the house why not come out with it."

"I'm not, Ben."

"Excuse me then. It sounded like you might be leading up to something of that nature."

"I'm leading up to this, Ben. There are certain things you seem completely unaware of."

"Such as."

"Well," Mr. Braddock said, "such as a few economic facts of life if you want to put it that way."

"Economics."

"Yes."

"I think I'm aware of them."

"Are you?"

Benjamin nodded. "I seem to remember taking a course or two on that subject," he said.

"Well you don't seem to have gotten much out of it."

"As I recall," Benjamin said, lighting his cigarette, "I got the highest grade in the class."

Mr. Braddock remained standing with his back to his son, looking out the window. "Well Ben," he said, "for all your intellectuality you don't—"

"I am not an intellectual!" Benjamin said. He dropped his match in the ash tray. "If you want to stand there and insult me I'd appreciate it if you'd stop short of that."

"For all your education, Ben, you seem rather naive about certain things. One of them is that someday you are going to have to earn a living."

"Am I?"

"Of course."

"Are you going broke or something? You can't afford to feed me any more?"

Mr. Braddock turned around to face him.

Benjamin stood. "Now look!" he said, waving his arm through the air. "I have been a goddamn—a goddamn ivy-covered status symbol around here for four years. And I think I'm entitled to—"

"What did you say?"

"What?"

"A status symbol? Is that what you said?"

Benjamin stared at him a moment, then looked down at the rug. "I didn't mean that," he said.

"Is that how you feel, Ben?"

"No."

"That your mother and I think of you as—"

"No!"

"Because—"

"Be quiet a minute. Now Dad? I appreciate everything you've done for me. I'm grateful for the education. But let's face it. It didn't work out. It wasn't worth a damn. Not one single damn thing was it worth."

Mr. Braddock returned slowly to the desk and seated himself. "I don't know quite what to say," he said.

"I didn't mean that about the ivy-covered—"

"All right," he said. "But Ben?"

"What."

"Something has to be done. Maybe the education didn't work out, as you put it. Maybe it wasn't worth a damn. But you can't go on like this."

"I try not to bother anyone."

"Well that's hardly the point. Just the life you're leading is taking it out of both your mother and me. I'm afraid your mother's much more upset than she lets you know."

"I'm sorry about that."

"And let's be honest about this, Ben. Your mother and I are certainly as much to blame as you are for whatever is happening."

"No you aren't."

"Well we are. We've raised you. We've tried to instill certain values into your thinking."

"Dad, I'm not blaming you."

"Well I'm blaming me then."

"Well you shouldn't."

"Ben," Mr. Braddock said, "something is horribly wrong."

"Look Dad," Benjamin said. "This is getting kind of melodramatic. Why don't we—"

"Just that?"

"What?"

"This is just melodrama to you?"

"Dad, look," he said. "The graduate comes home. He gets disillusioned. He gets bitter. He sits around home and goes to pot. His parents wring their hands and blame his failings on themselves. I mean—yes." He nodded. "It has kind of a hearts and flowers ring to it."

Mr. Braddock was about to say something more when he was interrupted by a knock on the door. Mrs. Braddock opened it and looked into the room.

"Mr. and Mrs. Robinson are here," she said. "Will you come out and say hello?"

Benjamin took a step backward toward the other door. "I'll be in my room," he said.

"Ben?"

"Mother, I don't feel too well."

His father was frowning at him from the desk. "Ben?" he said.

"What."

"What's going on."

"I don't know," Benjamin said. "I get these cramps sometimes after dinner. It helps if I lie down."

Still frowning at him, his father rose from his chair. Benjamin glanced up at them a moment, then down at the floor. "There," he said. "There. It's better." He nodded.

"Will you come out and say hello to the Robinsons?"

"Sure. I'd like to."

Mrs. Robinson was standing with her back to the fireplace, wearing the same brown suit she had worn the first night Benjamin had met her at the hotel.

"Hi," Benjamin said.

"How are you."

"Fine thank you."

"Looks like you've been in for a swim," Mr. Robinson said, holding out his hand.

"Yes sir," Benjamin said, shaking it. "This afternoon. I guess—I guess I haven't gotten around to changing yet."

"Well," Mr. Robinson said. "Have a seat. I haven't seen you for a while."

Benjamin sat down on the sofa. Mr. Robinson sat beside him.

"What're you up to."

"Sir?"

"What're you doing with yourself these days."

"Oh," Benjamin said. "Not too much. Taking it easy."

Mr. Robinson nodded. "That's what I'd do if I could," he said. "Nothing wrong with that."

"Yes sir. Thank you."

"So what are your plans," Mr. Robinson said.

"Indefinite," Benjamin said.

"I guess you've pretty well given up this teaching idea you had."

"Don't speak too soon," Mrs. Braddock said.

"What?"

"I still think Ben's going to be a teacher someday."

"I might at that," Benjamin said. "I guess I can't—I guess it's pretty hard to say at this stage of the game."

"Sure it is," Mr. Robinson said. "You take it easy. How's the girl situation."

"What?"

"Have you dug up any of those old girls you used to go to high school with?"

Benjamin shook his head. "I haven't been doing much dating," he said.

"Well what's wrong with you."

"What?"

"Come on," Mr. Robinson said, winking at his mother. "You can't tell me you don't have somebody stashed away."

"Oh no. No. No."

"Where's the old college spirit."

"No. I mean I don't—I don't—"

"Excuse me," Mrs. Robinson said. "I'll find a glass of water." She left the room.

"Ben, you go help her," Mrs. Braddock said.

Benjamin stood up and hurried out to the kitchen with Mrs. Robinson. "The glasses are up here," he said. He reached up and handed her one.

"Benjamin?"

"Be quiet," he said.

"Benjamin, I think you'd better go up to your room or something."

Benjamin shook his head and walked quickly out of the kitchen and back into the living room. Mrs. Robinson filled her glass and followed him.

"Hey Ben," Mr. Robinson said.

"Yes?"

"Come on back and sit down a minute."

Benjamin returned to the sofa.

"Elaine's coming down for a few days at Thanksgiving. I want you to call her up this time."

"I will."

"I mean it."

"I know," Benjamin said. "I know you do."

"Because I just think you two would hit it off real well together."

Benjamin nodded. "When—I mean when does she get down," he said.

"I'm not sure of the exact date," Mr. Robinson said. "I'll let your father know when I find out."

For a long time it was quiet. Benjamin sat looking down at the rug. Once he glanced up at his mother, who was sitting in her chair watching him, then he looked for a moment at his father's shoes and quickly back at the rug in front of him. His mother cleared her throat. Mr. Robinson moved slightly on the couch beside him. Then it was perfectly quiet again.

"What—what's wrong," Benjamin said.

"I know what I wanted to ask you," Mrs. Robinson said, walking across the room. "Where did you find this lamp."

Everyone turned to watch her bend over and look at a lamp on the table in the corner of the room.

"Where did that come from," Mrs. Braddock said. "Wasn't that given to us?"

Mr. Braddock nodded. "It was a gift," he said. "We've had it for years."

"I was looking for one this size last week," she said. "But I don't think they make them any more."

"I'll keep my eye open," Mrs. Braddock said.

"Would you?"

"Surely."

Mrs. Robinson smiled at her, then turned to her husband and raised her eyebrows. "We really should run," she said.

Later in the evening Benjamin was standing in his room at the window when his mother opened the door and stepped inside. "Can I talk to you a minute?" she said.

"What? Sure."

She closed the door behind her. "Benjamin?" she said. "Can I ask you what's on your mind?"

He frowned at her.

"There's something on your mind," she said. "Can you tell me what it is?"

He shrugged his shoulders. "I don't know," he said.

"Is it something to do with the Robinsons?"

"What?"

"You seemed—you seemed awfully uncomfortable downstairs with the Robinsons."

Benjamin nodded. "I was," he said.

"Well is—is something wrong?"

He nodded again and walked to the window. "Mother," he said, "I feel guilty."

"What?"

"I feel guilty sitting around home like this. I'm afraid your friends think I'm just a bum."

"Oh no, Ben."

"Well I get that feeling," Benjamin said. "I got it the other night when the Terhunes were here. Then I got it tonight when the Robinsons came over."

"Ben, they think the world of you."

"They think I should be out working. They think I should be at school."

"Oh no, Ben," she said. She walked across the room to him and took his hand. He pulled it away and shook his head.

"I feel worthless, Mother. I feel rotten about what I'm doing."

"You'll get over this, Ben," she said. "It's just a stage you're in. You'll get over it."

"Well I hope so."

"You will," she said. "So don't worry about it. Our friends think you're one of the finest people they know."

Benjamin nodded. His mother turned around and walked back toward the door, then stopped. "Benjamin?"

"What."

"I'm going to ask you something but you don't have to tell me if you don't want."

"What," he said.

"Well I'm going to ask you what you do when you go off at night."

"When I go off?"

She nodded.

Benjamin frowned down at the rug and began shaking his head.

"You don't have to tell me if you don't want."

"No, I do," he said. "I want to tell you."

It was quiet for several moments.

"I drive around," he said.

"What else."

"Nothing else."

"Well you don't drive around from midnight till noon the next day, Benjamin."

"Oh no."

"Then what do you do. Do you meet someone?"

"Meet someone?"

She nodded.

"Why did you say that."

"Well this is your business, Benjamin," she said, turning back toward the door. "If you—"

"No wait. Wait."

She stopped.

"I don't meet anyone, Mother, but why did you say that."

She shook her head. "Because I can't imagine what else you'd do."

"But what do you mean by 'meet someone.'"

"Let's forget it."

"No."

"Benjamin, I'm not going to pry into your affairs," she said, "but I'd rather you didn't say anything at all than be dishonest."

"What?"

"Good night, Benjamin."

"Well wait."

She frowned at him.

"You think I'm being dishonest?"

She nodded.

"Well why do you—why do you think that."

"Because I know you don't drive around for twelve hours."

"Oh," Benjamin said. "Well I don't. Shall I tell you what I do?"

"Not if you don't want."

"I do."

"But I don't want you to make up something."

"I'm not," Benjamin said. "But I'm—I'm not very proud of what I do. I usually get kind of drunk. I usually drive over to Los Angeles and go to some bars and get kind of drunk. Then I take a hotel room. So I won't have to drive home on the freeway. I mean it kind of scares me to drive home after—"

"Good night, Benjamin."

"What?"

"I'll see you tomorrow."

"Well Mother?"

"What."

"You believe me, don't you."

"No."

"You don't?"

She shook her head.

"But I want you to," he said. "Please. Please will you believe me!"

"Good night," she said.

As soon as she had left the room Benjamin sat down at his desk and pulled out a sheet of stationery to write a letter to Mrs. Robinson.

Dear Mrs. Robinson,

I cannot go on seeing you. It is ruining me and it is ruining my parents and I am a nervous wreck. My life is going quickly down the drain and right now at this moment I have got to do something. I don't know what. I am in a complete tailspin. I am thoroughly despicable in everything I am doing with you. Please burn this letter as soon as you have read it.

I am going to teach. I will see if they might possibly give me the award back and if not I will either work my way through graduate school somehow or accept a position at one of the colleges that made offers while I was still at school. That is the only possible choice I have other than being a filthy degenerate all my life. I hope you will understand that this decision in no way reflects upon yourself insofar as your desirability etc. are concerned but I can't live with myself any longer as I am. When you and your husband were here tonight it was all I could do to keep from screaming and running out of the room. I don't know why I should feel that way because I do not think what we are doing is of much consequence but for some reason it is making a nervous wreck of me which is something I don't particularly want to be the rest of my life.

The door of Benjamin's room opened suddenly. His hand froze on the page.

"Ben?" his father said.

Benjamin looked quickly around the desk and then slid the stationery box over the letter and stood.

"Ben," his father said, "your mother tells me you're a little worried about what our friends think of you."

"Oh," Benjamin said. "Well. I hate—I hate for them to think I'm just loafing around."

"Well Ben, what's happening is a problem. It's a terribly serious problem. But don't worry about our friends because they know you're a wonderful person."

Benjamin nodded. "Well I feel—I feel a little uncomfortable with them sometimes."

"It's Mrs. Robinson, isn't it."

"What?"

"Mrs. Robinson makes you feel a little uncomfortable, doesn't she."

"Well no," Benjamin said, suddenly shaking his head. "She's—I mean I don't—"

"Ben, I've known that woman for nearly twenty years and I still don't know her."

"What?"

"She's a funny one, Ben."

"Oh," Benjamin said.

"There's something about her that makes anybody feel uncomfortable. I don't know what. But don't let it—don't let it throw you." Mr. Braddock folded his arms across his chest. "Ben," he said, "I'm afraid they're a pretty miserable couple."

"They are?"

"I think so," he said. "I think she gives him a pretty hard time. I've never spoken to him about it but I think he's pretty disappointed with her."

"Oh," Benjamin said. He sat back down in the chair.

"You won't let this go beyond you and me."

"Oh no."

"But she's—she's really not much of a person. She never says much. She never makes any effort socially or any other way." He shook his head. "I'd be interested to know how they ever got together in the first place."

"Well," Benjamin said. "She's—I think she's fairly good looking."

"She's damn attractive," his father said. He stood looking down at the rug a few moments. "But she's not honest, Ben."

"She's not."

"I don't think so. I think she's devious. I don't think she was ever taught the difference between right and wrong the way you and I were. It's just a feeling I get about her. I couldn't tell you why." He looked up to smile. "So," he said, "don't let her throw you."

"I won't."

"What are you doing there."

"What?"

"Writing a letter?"

"Oh yes. Yes I am. This boy I graduated with. We were going to keep in touch but we never did."

"Good," his father said, grinning at him. "Keep up the old contacts. You never know when they'll come in handy." He turned and walked out of the door.

Benjamin waited till he was downstairs, then closed the door and locked it. He returned to his desk and slid the stationery box off the letter and continued.

> I don't know if you were ever taught the difference between right and wrong or not, but since I was, I feel a certain obligation to it and cannot continue in as devious a fashion as I have been. Since we never exactly lose ourselves in conversation I'm not sure how you feel about things but obviously what we are doing can only lead to some kind of disaster if we go on, so I feel, and I hope you do, that this is a good place to stop. Please don't think I haven't enjoyed having an affair with an "older woman" as I have not only enjoyed it but consider it a worth-while part of my general education. But it will be much better, I know, to remember it as it has been rather than as something it might become.
>
> Best wishes,
> Benjamin

"I got your note," Mrs. Robinson said, several evenings later over their drinks in the Verandah Room.

"The note," Benjamin said. "I'm afraid I got a little carried away there for a moment."

"Devious?" she said.

"What?"

"Do you really think I'm devious?"

"I said I got carried away. Now let's forget about it."

The affair continued on into the fall. At first Mrs. Robinson had sent Benjamin a note in the mail whenever she wanted to see him and he had met her in the Verandah Room the next evening near midnight. During the first month the notes had arrived not more than once a week. Then they began to arrive more frequently and finally Benjamin asked her not to send them because his mother usually took in the mail before he got up and had asked him several times who was sending them. Instead it was arranged that Benjamin would call Mrs. Robinson each afternoon and she would tell him over the phone if she could be at the hotel that night. One week he met her five nights in a row.

On the days that he met her Benjamin would eat dinner with his parents as usual, watch television until nearly midnight, then dress in his suit and drive to the hotel. At the hotel he would buy Mrs. Robinson a martini, then take a room for them. In the beginning he had gone up ahead to wait for her but after the first few weeks he waved at her from the entrance of the bar when he had gotten the room and they rode up together in the elevator. When they got in the room Benjamin always called down to the desk and left word that they were to call up to his room before dawn. When the call came Mrs. Robinson would get up and dress and drive home to fix breakfast for Mr. Robinson. Benjamin usually would not wake up till late in the morning. Then he would take a shower, dress and pay for the room on his way out of the hotel.

They seldom spoke to each other after the first several times. Usually they sat at a table next to the window in the Verandah Room looking out the window at the grounds of the hotel.

"Mrs. Robinson?" Benjamin said one night when the drinks had been brought to the table.

"What."

"I don't want to interrupt your thoughts, but do you think we might do a little talking?"

"What?"

"I say we don't seem to have very lively conversations, do we."

"No we don't," she said.

Benjamin nodded and turned to look at a palm tree outside in the grounds. He finished his drink without saying anything more, then stood. "I'll get the room," he said. He walked into the lobby and to the desk.

"Give me a twelve-dollar single," he said.

"Yes sir," the clerk said. He pushed the register across the desk and Benjamin signed. "Any luggage tonight, Mr. Gladstone?" he said.

Benjamin shook his head and walked back into the Verandah Room and to the table and dangled the key in front of Mrs. Robinson's face. "Let's go," he said.

They rode up in the elevator without talking and walked quietly down the hall and Benjamin opened the door and they walked in and shut it, still without saying anything. Mrs. Robinson removed her coat and dropped it on one of the chairs. Then she smiled at Benjamin and walked across the room to him and reached up to untie the knot of his tie.

"Wait a minute," Benjamin said. He pushed her hand away. "Sit down a minute," he said.

Mrs. Robinson raised her eyebrows.

"Will you please sit down a minute," Benjamin said, pointing at the bed.

Mrs. Robinson waited a moment, then turned around and walked to the bed. She seated herself on the end of it and reached down to remove one of her shoes.

"No," Benjamin said.

"What?"

"Will you leave the shoe on for a minute. Please."

She nodded and straightened up.

"Now," Benjamin said. "Do you—do you think we could just say a few words to each other first this time?"

"If you want."

"Good," Benjamin said. He pushed her coat to the side of the chair and seated himself. Then for a long time he sat looking down at the rug in front of him. It was perfectly quiet. He glanced up at her, then back down at the carpet.

"I mean are we dead or something?" he said.

"Well I just don't think we have much to say to each other."

"But why not!"

She shrugged her shoulders.

"I mean we're not stupid people, are we?"

"I don't know."

"Well we aren't," he said. "But all we ever do is come up here and throw off the clothes and leap into bed together."

"Are you tired of it?"

"I'm not. No. But do you think we could liven it up with a few words now and then?"

She didn't answer him.

"Look," Benjamin said, standing up. "Now there is something wrong with two human beings who know each other as intimately as we do who can't even speak together."

"Well what do you want to talk about, darling."

"Anything," he said, shaking his head. "Anything at all."

"Do you want to tell me about some of your college experiences?"

"Oh my God."

"Well?"

"Mrs. Robinson. If that's the best we can do let's just get the goddamn clothes off and—"

She reached down for her shoe.

"Leave it on!" Benjamin said. "Now we are going to do this thing. We are going to have a conversation. Think of another topic."

"How about art."

"Art," Benjamin said. He nodded. "That's a good subject. You start it off."

"You start it off," she said. "I don't know anything about it."

"Oh."

"Don't you?"

"Yes I do," Benjamin said. "I know quite a bit about it."

"Go ahead then."

Benjamin nodded. "Art," he said. "Well what do you want to know about it."

She shrugged.

"Are you interested more in modern art or more in classical art."

"Neither," she said.

"You're not interested in art?"

"No."

"Then why do you want to talk about it."

"I don't."

Benjamin nodded and looked back down at the rug.

"Can I take off my clothes now?"

"No. Think of another topic."

Mrs. Robinson looked up at the ceiling a moment. "Why don't you tell me what you did today," she said.

Benjamin stood up and walked to one of the curtains. "Mrs. Robinson?" he said. "This is pathetic."

"You don't want to tell me about your day?"

"My day," Benjamin said.

"Let's go to bed."

"I got up."

"What?"

"I am telling you about my day, Mrs. Robinson."

"Oh."

"I got up in the morning. About twelve. I ate breakfast. After breakfast I had some beers. After the beers I went out to the pool. I blew air in the raft. I put the raft on the water. I got in the water myself. I floated on the raft."

"What are you talking about," Mrs. Robinson said.

"I have this raft I float on in the afternoons," he said.

"Oh."

"Then I ate dinner. After dinner I watched two quiz shows. Then I watched half a movie. Then I came here. Now. Tell me about your day."

"Do you want me to?"

"Yes I do."

"I got up," she said.

Benjamin began shaking his head.

"Do you want to hear it or not?"

"Yes," Benjamin said. "But you might try and spice it up with a little originality."

"I got up," Mrs. Robinson said again. "I ate breakfast and went shopping. During the afternoon I read a novel."

"What one."

"What?"

"What novel did you read."

"I don't remember."

Benjamin nodded.

"Then I fixed dinner for my husband and waited until—"

"There!" Benjamin said, whirling around and pointing at her.

"What?"

"Your husband! Mr. Robinson! There's something we could have a conversation about."

"Him?"

"I mean everything," Benjamin said. "I don't know anything about how you—how you work this. I don't know how you get out of the house at night. I don't know the risk involved."

"There isn't any," she said.

"There's no risk?"

She shook her head.

"But how do you work it. How do you get out of the house."

"I walk out."

"You walk right out the door?"

She nodded.

"But your husband. What do you say to him."

"He's asleep."

"Always?"

"Benjamin, this isn't a very interesting topic."

"Please," Benjamin said. "Now tell me. How do you know he won't wake up sometime and follow you."

"Because he takes sleeping pills."

"But what if he forgets."

"What?"

"What if he forgets to take them. What if they don't work one night."

"He takes three sleeping pills every night at ten o'clock. Now why don't we—"

"No wait," Benjamin said. "I want to know these things. I mean I can think about them. At ten o'clock I can think about Mr. Robinson taking his three pills." He cleared his throat. "So," he said. "He takes the pills. But what about the noise from the car. What if—"

"The driveway's on my side of the house."

"We're talking," Benjamin said, smiling suddenly.

"What?"

"We're talking, Mrs. Robinson. We're talking!"

"Calm down, Benjamin."

"Now let's keep going here," he said, seating himself again in the chair.

"Can I undress and talk at the same time?"

"Right."

"Thank you."

"Now," Benjamin said. "You say the driveway's on your side of the house."

She nodded and began unbuttoning her blouse.

"So I guess you don't sleep in the same room."

"We don't."

"So you don't . . . I mean I don't like to seem like I'm prying but I guess you don't sleep together or anything."

"No we don't," she said, unbuttoning the final button.

"Well how long has this been going on."

"What?"

"That you've been sleeping in different rooms. Different beds."

Mrs. Robinson looked up at the ceiling a moment. "About five years," she said.

"Oh no."

"What?"

"Are you kidding me?"

"No."

"You have not slept with your husband for five years?"

"Now and then," she said, removing the blouse. "He gets drunk a few times a year."

"How many times a year."

"On New Year's Eve," she said. "Sometimes on his birthday."

Benjamin shook his head. "Man, is this interesting," he said.

"Is it?"

"So you don't love him. You wouldn't say you—"

"We've talked enough, Benjamin."

"Wait a minute. So you wouldn't say you loved him."

"Not exactly," she said, slipping out of her skirt and putting it on the hanger.

"But you don't hate him," Benjamin said.

"No, Benjamin, I don't hate him. Undo my bra." She backed up to the chair.

"You don't hate him and you don't love him," Benjamin said, reaching up to unfasten the two straps of her bra.

"That's right."

"Well how do you feel about him then."

"I don't," she said. She dropped the bra on the bureau.

"Well that's kind of a bad situation then, isn't it."

"Is it?"

"I mean it doesn't sound like it could be much worse. If you hated him at least you'd hate him."

She nodded and removed her slip.

"Well you loved him once, I assume," Benjamin said.

"What?"

"I say I assume you loved your husband once. When you first knew him."

"No," she said.

"What?"

"I never did, Benjamin. Now let's—"

"Well wait a minute," he said. "You married him."

She nodded.

"Why did you do that."

"See if you can guess," she said. She unfastened her stockings from the clasps and began peeling them down over her legs.

"Well I can't," Benjamin said.

"Try."

"Because of his money?"

"Try again," she said. She began forcing the girdle down around her legs.

"You were just lonely or something?"

"No."

Benjamin frowned. "For his looks?" he said. "He's a pretty handsome guy, I guess."

"Think real hard, Benjamin."

Benjamin frowned down at one of her feet, then shook his head. "I can't see why you did," he said, "unless . . . you didn't *have* to marry him or anything, did you?"

"Don't tell Elaine," Mrs. Robinson said.

"Oh no."

She nodded.

"You had to marry him because you got pregnant?"

"Are you shocked?"

"Well," Benjamin said, "I never thought of you and Mr. Robinson as the kind of people who . . ." He shook his head.

"All right," she said. "Now let's go to bed."

"Wait a minute. Wait a minute. So how did it happen."

"What?"

"I mean do you feel like telling me what were the circumstances?"

"Not particularly."

"I mean what was the setup. Was he a law student at the time?"

She nodded.

"And you were a student also."

"Yes."

"At college."

"Yes."

"What was your major."

She frowned at him. "Why are you asking me all this."

"Because I'm interested, Mrs. Robinson. Now what was your major subject at college."

"Art."

"Art?"

She nodded.

"But I thought you—I guess you kind of lost interest in it over the years then."

"Kind of."

"So," Benjamin said. "You were an art major and he was a law student. And you met him. How did you meet him. At a party or at a dance or—"

"I don't remember, Benjamin," she said, removing her bobby pins and shaking her head to let the hair fall down around her shoulders, "and I am getting pretty tired of this conversation."

"Well how did it happen. How did you get pregnant."

"How do you think."

"I mean did he take you up to his room with him? Did you go to a hotel?"

"Benjamin, what does it possibly matter."

"I'm curious."

"We'd go to his car," she said.

"Oh no."

"What?"

"In the car you did it?"

"I don't think we were the first."

"Well no," Benjamin said. "But it's—it's kind of hard to conceive of you and Mr. Robinson going at it in the car." He sat down in the chair again and began to smile. "In the car?" he said. "You and him?"

"Me and him."

He shook his head, still smiling. "So that's where old Elaine—" He looked up. "What kind of car was it."

"What?"

"Do you remember the make of car?"

"Oh my God."

"Really," Benjamin said. "I want to know."

"It was a Ford, Benjamin."

"A Ford!" he said, jumping up from the chair. "A Ford!" He laughed aloud. "Goddammit, a Ford! That's great!"

"That's enough."

He shook his head and smiled down at the rug. "So old Elaine Robinson got started in a Ford."

"Benjamin?"

"That's great."

"Benjamin?"

"What."

"Don't talk about Elaine."

He stopped smiling suddenly. "Don't talk about Elaine?" he said.
"No."
"Why not."
"Because I don't want you to," she said. She turned around and walked to the bed.
"Well why don't you."
Mrs. Robinson pulled the bedspread down along the bed and dropped it on the floor.
"Is there some big secret about her I don't know?"
"No."
"Then what's the big mystery."
"Take off your clothes," she said.
Benjamin frowned and removed his coat. He dropped it behind him onto the chair, then began unbuttoning his shirt.
"I wish you'd tell me," he said.
"There's nothing to tell."
"Well why is she a big taboo subject all of a sudden."
Mrs. Robinson uncovered one of the pillows at the head of the bed.
"Well," Benjamin said, removing his shirt and dropping it on his coat, "I guess I'll have to ask her out on a date and find out what's—"
Mrs. Robinson straightened up suddenly. She turned around to stare at him. "Benjamin, don't you ever take that girl out," she said.
"What?"
"Do you understand that."
"Well look. I have no intention of taking her out."
"Good."
"I was just kidding around."
"Good."
"But why shouldn't I."
"Because you shouldn't."
"Well why are you getting so upset."
"Let's drop it," Mrs. Robinson said. She turned back to the bed and uncovered the other pillow.
"Are you jealous of her?" Benjamin said. "Are you afraid she might steal me away from you?"
"No."
"Well then what."
She shook her head.
"Mrs. Robinson," Benjamin said, taking a step toward her, "I want to know why you feel so strongly about this."
"I have my reasons."
"Then let's hear them."
"No."
"Let's hear your reasons, Mrs. Robinson. Because I think I know what they are."

She reached down to pull the covers part way back.

"Your daughter shouldn't associate with the likes of me, should she."

"Benjamin."

"I'm not good enough for her to associate with, am I. I'm not good enough to even talk about her, am I."

"Let's drop it."

"We're not dropping it, Mrs. Robinson," he said, walking across the room. "Now that's the reason, isn't it. I'm a dirty degenerate, aren't I. I'm not fit to—"

"Benjamin?"

He took her arm and pulled her around to face him. "I'm good enough for you but I'm too slimy to associate with your daughter. That's it, isn't it."

She nodded.

"Isn't it!"

"Yes."

He stood a moment longer holding her arm, then pushed her down on the bed. "You go to hell," he said. He shook his head and walked back to the chair to pick up his shirt. "You go straight to hell, Mrs. Robinson."

"Benjamin?"

"Do you think I'm proud of myself?" he said, throwing the shirt down on the rug and walking back to stand in front of her. "Do you think I'm proud of this?"

"I wouldn't know."

"Well, I am not."

"You're not."

"No sir," he said. "I am not proud that I spend my time in hotel rooms with a broken-down alcoholic!"

"I see."

"And if you think I come here for any reason besides pure boredom, then you're all wrong."

She nodded.

"Because—Mrs. Robinson?"

"What."

"You make me sick! I make myself sick! This is the sickest, most perverted thing that ever happened to me!" He stared down at her a moment. "And you do what you want but I'm getting the hell out."

"Are you?"

"You're goddamn right I am," he said. He turned around, picked up his shirt from the floor and slid his arms into its sleeves. Mrs. Robinson sat up on the edge of the bed and watched him as he buttoned it and tucked the shirttails into his pants.

"Benjamin?" she said.

He shook his head.

"Did you mean those things you said, Benjamin?"

"You are damn right I did."

"I'm sorry," she said.

"Well, I am too. But that's the way it is."

"That's how you feel about me."

He nodded.

"That I'm a sick and disgusting person," she said, looking down at the rug.

Benjamin finished tucking in his shirttails, then looked at her. "Now don't start this," he said.

"What?"

"Don't start acting hurt."

"Don't you expect me to be a little hurt?"

"Now Mrs. Robinson," he said, pointing at her. "You told me yourself that you were an alcoholic."

She nodded. "And sick and disgusting," she said.

"Now wait a minute," he said. "You stand there and call me trash. What do you expect me to say."

"Did I call you that?"

"You did."

"I don't think so," she said.

"Well in so many words, Mrs. Robinson. You stand there and tell me I'm not good enough for your daughter."

"Did I say that?"

"Of course you did."

She shook her head.

"What?"

"Benjamin," she said, "I want to apologize to you if that's the impression you got."

"Well Mrs. Robinson," he said. "Two minutes ago you told me I wasn't good enough for your daughter. Now you say you're sorry I got that impression."

"I didn't mean it," she said.

"What?"

"I don't think you'd be right for each other," she said. "But I would never say you weren't as good a person as she is."

"You wouldn't."

"Of course I wouldn't."

Mrs. Robinson waited a moment, then stood and walked to the closet to remove her hanger of clothes.

"What are you doing."

"Well it's pretty obvious you don't want me around any more," she said.

"Well look," Benjamin said. "I was kind of upset there. I'm sorry I said those things."

"Benjamin, if that's how you feel—"

"But it's not."

"That's all right," she said, smiling at him. "I think I can understand why I'm disgusting to you."

"Oh no," Benjamin said. He hurried across the room. "Look," he said, taking her arm. "I like you. I wouldn't keep coming here if I didn't like you."

"But if it's sickening for you—"

"It's not!" he said. "I enjoy it. I look forward to it. It's the one thing I have to look forward to."

"You don't have to say that."

"Well I wouldn't. I would never say it if it wasn't true."

"May I stay then?" she said.

"Yes. Please. I want you to."

"Thank you."

"Well don't thank me, because I want you to."

She lifted the hanger back into the closet. "But you won't ever take out Elaine, will you."

"What?"

"I want you to promise me that."

Benjamin shook his head. "Look," he said. "Let's not talk about that. Let's not talk at all."

"Promise me."

"But why should I! Because I'm not good enough for her?"

"Because you're different."

"How are we different."

"You just are."

"She's good and I'm bad. Look. Why the hell did you bring this up. It never occurred to me to take her out."

"Then give me your word you won't."

"But I don't like to give my word about things."

"Why not."

"Because you never know what's going to happen."

"Then you're thinking of taking her out, aren't you."

"No," Benjamin said. "I give you my word I have no intention of taking her out."

"Now give me your word that you never will."

"This is absurd."

"Promise me, Benjamin."

"All right, for Christ's sake! I promise I will never take out Elaine Robinson."

"You swear to it."

"Yes."

"Thank you."

"Now let's get the hell into bed."

## QUESTIONS: *Webb, The Graduate*

1. Why is the initial situation—a *party* given for the recent graduate by his *parents*—a particularly appropriate device to dramatize the generation gap?

2. To make his points, the author frequently reverses roles or contradicts expectations in a manner characteristic of *irony*. Explain the irony in the following attitudes and situations:

    a. The guests' enthusiasm for Benjamin's intellectual accomplishments ("Aren't you just thrilled to death?"; "I just think it's too terrific for words").

    b. Benjamin being asked upstairs by Mrs. Robinson ostensibly to see her daughter's portrait.

    c. Mr. Robinson's encouragement to Benjamin to "Take things as they come. Have a good time with the girls and so forth."

    d. Benjamin's fashioning of the story of his adventures on the road in response to his father's questions.

3. Is the absence of a stated justification for Benjamin's sense that his education "wasn't worth a damn," that he has no values, and that his future goals are not worth pursuing an artistic flaw or merit? To what extent are we to hold his parents' values responsible for his tendency to "float" (his literal action in the pool being a metaphor for his state of mind)? Can we in some way connect his sexual inexperience with his despondency and uncertainty? Can we account for that sexual inexperience?

4. Despite his denials, is Benjamin committed to any values? Justify your answer by reference to specific actions and statements.

5. What attributes of Benjamin's parents prevent them from being merely stereotypes of parental rigidity, ineptitude, and tyranny? Yet in what subtle way do they manage to fail Benjamin by (a) lack of empathy, (b) timidity, (c) disingenuousness, (d) materialism, (e) desire to manipulate?

6. In what way does Benjamin fail his parents? To what extent, for instance, is he victim or aggressor in the conversation with his father in Chapter 4?

7. Why does Webb *not* reveal Benjamin's disillusioning experiences on the road? Why is the account he gives his father both sad and *comic*?

8. How does the letter to Mrs. Robinson reveal the degree to which Benjamin lacks self-knowledge and is susceptible to parental influence? In what subtle ways do the paternal and maternal inquisitions differ?

9. How do both Benjamin and Mrs. Robinson function as victims and aggressors in the discussion at the end of Chapter 4? How can we account for Benjamin's curiosity with regard to Mrs. Robinson's past and present life?

10. Can we fully believe in the scope of Benjamin's intellectual accomplishments at college? Justify your answer.

## EXERCISES

1. Write an essay on the ways in which the conflicts and uncertainties of a high school graduate resemble or differ from those of the college graduate in Webb's novel.

2. Write an essay on the ways in which parents and children can betray each other.

# Tom Wolfe (1932–    )
# Putting Daddy On

Parker wants me to go down to the Lower East Side and help him retrieve his son from the hemp-smoking flipniks. He believes all newspaper reporters know their way around in the lower depths. "Come on down and ride shotgun for me," he says. Parker has a funny way of speaking, using a lot of ironic metonymy and metaphor. He picked it up at Yale twenty-five years ago and has nurtured it through many lunches in the East 50's. On the other hand, he doesn't want to appear to be too uneasy. "I just want you to size it up for me," he says. "The whole thing is ridiculous, except that it is just as pathetic as hell. I feel like I'm on my back with all four feet up in the air." Parker says his son, Ben, suddenly left Columbia in his junior year, without saying anything, and moved to the Lower East Side. Parker speaks of the Lower East Side as the caravansary for flipniks. Flipniks is his word for beatniks. As Parker pictures it, his son, Ben, now lies around on the floor in lofts and four-story walkups on the Lower East Side, eaten by lice and aphids, smoking pot and having visions of the Oneness of the hip life.

I think Parker is a casualty of the Information Crisis. The world has had a good seventy-five years of Freud, Darwin, Pavlov, Max Weber, Sir James Frazer, Dr. Spock, Vance Packard and Rose Franzblau, and everything they have had to say about human motivation has filtered through Parker and all of Parker's friends in college, at parties, at lunch, in the magazines and novels they read and the conversations they have at home with wives who share the same esoterica. As a result, Parker understands everybody's motives, including his own, which he has a tendency to talk about and revile.

He understands, for example, that he is now forty-six years old and close to becoming a vice-president of the agency and that at this particular age and status he now actually feels the *need* to go to the kind of barbershop where one makes an appointment and has the same barber each time and the jowls are anointed with tropical oils. It is as if Parker were looking through a microscope at a convulsive amoeba, himself, Parker. "I can't go into any other kind of barbershop," he says. "It has gotten so I have an *actual*, *physical* need to have my hair cut in that kind of barbershop." He can go on like this about the clothes he buys, about the clubs he joins, the music he listens to, the way he feels about Negroes, anything.

He understands why pot-smoking is sort of a religion. He understands Oneness, lofts, visions, the Lower East Side. He understands why Ben has given up everything. He understands why his wife, Regina, says he is a ____ ____ ____ and has to *do* something. Her flannel mouth is supposed to goad him into action. He understands everything, the whole thing, and he is in a hopeless funk.

So here are Parker and I walking along Avenue B on the Lower East Side.

Parker is wearing a brown Chesterfield and a Madison Avenue crash helmet. Madison Avenue crash helmet is another of Parker's terms. It refers to the kind of felt hat that is worn with a crease down the center and no dents in the sides, a sort of homburg without a flanged brim. He calls it a Madison Avenue crash helmet and then wears one. Inevitably, Parker is looking over his own shoulder, following his own progress down Avenue B. Here is Parker with his uptown clothes and his anointed jowls, walking past the old Avenue B Cinema, a great rotting building with lions' heads and shattered lepers' windows. Here is Parker walking past corner stores with posters for Kassel, Kaplan, Aldrich and the others, plastered, torn, one on top of the other, like scales. Here is Parker walking along narrow streets with buildings all overhung with fire escapes on both sides. Here is this ripening, forty-six-year-old agency executive walking along amid the melted store fronts. There are whole streets on the Lower East Side where it looks as if the place had been under intense heat and started melting and then was suddenly frozen in amber. Half the storefronts are empty and there is a gray film inside the windows. Pipes, bins, shafts of wood and paper are all sort of sliding down the walls. The ceilings are always covered with squares of sheet metal with quaint moldings on them to make an all-over design, and they are all buckling. The signs have all flaked down to metal the color of weathered creosote, even the ones that say *Bodega y Carneceria*. Everything is collapsing under New York moss, which is a combination of lint and soot. In a print shop window, under the soot and lint, is a sample of a wedding announcement. Mr. and Mrs. Benjamin Arnschmidt announce the marriage of their daughter, Lillian, to Mr. Aaron Kornilov, on October 20, 1951. This seems to deepen Parker's funk. He is no doubt asking himself what sort of hopeless amber fix Lillian Arnschmidt and Aaron Kornilov are frozen in today.

Parker sticks his head inside a doorway. Then he walks in. Then he turns around and says, "Are you sure?"

"You said 488," I tell him, "this is 488."

"Nifty," Parker says.

Here is Parker in the entryway of a slum tenement. Slum tenements are worse than they sound. The hallway is painted with a paint that looks exactly the color, thickness and lumpiness of real mud. Parker and I walk in, and there are three big cans of garbage by the stairway. Behind them are two doors, one to the basement apartment, one to the first-floor apartment, out of which two or three children have overflowed when the mother rises in the doorway like a moon reflecting a 25-watt light and yells something in Spanish. The children squeeze back, leaving us with the garbage and the interesting mud tableau. At some point they painted the mud color over everything, even over the doorbell-buzzer box. They didn't bother to pull the wiring out. They just cut the wires and painted over the stubs. And there they have it, the color called Landlord's Brown, immune to time, flood, tropic heat, arctic chill, punk rumbles, slops, blood, leprotic bugs, cockroaches the size of mice, mice the size of rats, rats the size of Airedales, and lumpenprole tenants.

On the way up there are so many turns amid the muddy gloom, I can't tell what floor we stop at. But Parker finds the door up there and knocks.

For a while we don't hear anything, but there is a light through the door. Then somebody inside says, "Who is it?"

"Ben!" says Parker. "It's me."

There is another long pause, and then the door opens. There in the doorway, lit up from behind by an ochre light, is a boy with a very thick head of hair and a kind of Rasputin beard. It is a strange combination, the hair and the beard. The hair is golden, a little red, but mostly golden and very thick, thatchy, matted down over his ears and his forehead. But the beard is one of those beards that come out a different color. It is red and stiff like a nylon brush.

"Ah," says Parker, "the whole scene."

Ben says nothing. He just stands there in a pair of white ducks and rubber Zorrie sandals. He has no shirt on. He looks as robust as a rice pudding.

"The whole scene," Parker says again and motions toward Ben's Rasputin beard.

Ben is obviously pained to hear his old man using hip talk. He gives a peeved twist to his mouth. He is rather startling to look at, a little chunk of rice pudding with all this ferocious hair. Parker, the understanding, understands, but he is embarrassed, which is his problem.

"When did all this happen?" says Parker. "The beaver. When did you grow the beaver?"

Ben still just stands there. Then he narrows his eyes and clamps his upper teeth over his lower lip in the Italian tough guy manner, after the fashion of Jack Palance in *Panic in the Streets*.

"Beaver is a very old expression," says Parker. "Before you were born. About 1803. I was using a very old expression, from my childhood. Did you ever hear a song that goes 'Alpha, beta, delta handa poker?' That was a very hip song."

Then he says, "I didn't mean that, Ben. I just want to talk to you a minute."

"All right," says Ben, and he opens the door wider and we walk in.

We walk into a sort of kitchen. There is a stove with all four gas burners turned up, apparently for heat. The apartment is all one room, of the sort that might be termed extremely crummy. The walls actually have big slags of plaster missing and the lathing showing, as in a caricature of an extremely crummy place. The floor is impacted with dirt and looks as if it has been chewed up by something. And off to one side is more of the day's gathering gaffe: two more kids.

They are both up against the wall as if they have been squashed there. One of them is slouched up against the wall in an upright position. He is a chubby boy with receding blond hair and a walrus mustache. The other, a thin, Latin-looking boy with miles of black hair, is right next to him, only he is sitting down on the floor, with his back propped against the wall. They are both looking at us like the tar baby or a couple of those hard-cheese mestizos on the road to Acapulco. There is a sweet smell in the room. The understanding Parker isn't going to start in on that, however. Parker looks a little as if he has just been poleaxed and the sympathetic nervous system is trying to decide whether to twitch or fold up. Here is Parker in the net of the flipniks, in the caravansary.

Nobody is saying a word. Finally Ben nods toward the chubby boy and says, "This is Jaywak." Then he nods toward the boy on the floor and says, "This is Aywak."

Jaywak stares at Parker a little longer with the tar-baby look, and then he fans his lips out very slowly, very archly, into a smile. After what seems about eight or ten seconds, he holds out his hand. Parker shakes his hand, and as soon as he starts to do that, the boy on the floor, Aywak, sticks his hand straight up in the air. He doesn't get up or even look at Parker. He just sticks his hand straight up in the air and waits for Parker. Parker is so flustered he shakes it. Then Parker introduces me. All this time Ben never introduces Parker. He never says this is my father. One's old man does not show up in a brown Chesterfield with ratchety pleas in his poor old voice, such as he wants to talk to you.

"Well, take off your coat," says Ben. But when he says something to Parker, he looks at Jaywak and Aywak.

Parker keeps his coat wrapped around him like a flag and a shield. Parker can't take his eyes off the place. Between the kitchen and the other part of the apartment is a low divider, like a half-wall, with two funny pillars between it and the ceiling. God knows what the room was for originally. In the back part there is another big craggy space on the wall, apparently where a mantelpiece has been ripped off. Some kind of ratty cloth is over the windows. It is not the decor that gets you. It is this kind of special flipnik litter. Practically every Lower East Side pad has it. Little objects are littered all over the floor, a sock, a Zorrie sandal, a T shirt, a leaflet from the Gospel Teachers, some kind of wool stuffing, a rubber door wedge, a toothbrush, cigarette butts, an old pair of blue wool bathing trunks with a white belt, a used Band-Aid, all littered around the chewed-up floor. There is almost no furniture, just a mattress in the corner with a very lumpy-looking blanket over it. There is also a table top, with no legs, propped up on some boxes. Parker keeps gawking.

"Very colorful," he says.

"It's not very colorful," Ben says. "It's a place."

Ben's voice tends to groan with pretentious simplicity.

Suddenly Aywak, the tar baby on the floor, speaks up.

"It has a lot of potential," he says. "It really has a lot of potential. Doesn't it? Or doesn't it?"

He looks straight at Parker with his eyes rolled up sadly.

"We're helping Bewak," he says. "We're helping Bewak put down the tiles. Bewak's going to do a lot with this place because it has a lot of potential. We talked it over. We're going to put all these tiles over he-e-e-ere, and then, over he-e-e-ere, on this wall, all these bricks. White bricks. We're going to paint them white. I kind of like the idea, all these white bricks and the tiles. I mean, it's not *much*. I'm not saying it's a *lot*. But the important thing is to know what you've got to do and then do something about it and *improve* on it, you know?"

"Cool it," says Ben.

This is all very bad for Parker. Suddenly Parker turns to Jaywak and says, "He's an interior decorator. What do you do?"

"I'm not an interior decorator," says Aywak, "I've got a trade."

"I'm a social worker," says Jaywak. Jaywak spreads his face out into the smile again.

"Who do you social work for?" says Parker.

"Well, it's sort of like the Big Brothers," says Jaywak. "You know the Big Brothers?"

Jaywak says this very seriously, looking at Parker with a very open look on his face, so that Parker has to nod.

"Yes," Parker says.

"Well, it's like them," says Jaywak, "only . . . only . . ."—his voice becomes very distant and he looks off to where the mantelpiece used to be— "only it's different. We work with older people. I can't tell you how different it is."

"I'm not an interior decorator," says Aywak. "I don't want you to think I'm an interior decorator. We're not going to do miracles in here. This is *not* the greatest building in the world. I mean, that's probably pretty obvious. But I mean, like I was going on about it—but that just happens to be the way I *feel* about it."

"What are you if you're not an interior decorator?" says Jaywak.

"You mean, what do I *do*?" says Aywak.

"I mean, what do you *do*," says Jaywak.

"That's a very important question," says Aywak, "and I think he's right about it."

" 'What do you do?' "

"Yes."

"Someone ask Aywak what he does," Jaywak says.

"I have a trade," says Aywak. "I'm a cooper. I make barrels. Barrels and barrels and barrels. You probably think I'm kidding."

So Parker turns on Ben. He speaks severely his only time. "Just what do *you* do?" he says to Ben. "I'd really like to know!"

"What do *you* do?" says Ben. "What are you doing right now?"

"Look," says Parker, "I don't care what you want to look like in front of these—"

Ben reaches into an old tin of tea and pulls out a string of dried figs. This is one of the Lower East Side's arty foods, along with Ukrainian sausages. Ben turns completely away from Parker and says to me, "Do you want a fig?"

I shake my head no, but even that much seems stupid.

"Are you going to listen?" says Parker.

"They're very good for you," says Aywak, "only they're filling. You know what I mean?"

"Yeah," Jaywak says to me, "sometimes you *want* to be hungry. You know? Suppose you want to be hungry, only you aren't hungry. Then you want to *get* hungry, you know? You're just waiting to get hungry again. You think about it. You want it. You want to get hungry again, but the time won't pass."

"A dried fig ruins it," says Aywak.

"Yeah!" says Jaywak.

I have the eerie feeling they're starting in on me.

"Are you going to listen?" Parker is saying to Ben.

"Sure," says Ben. "Let's have a talk. What's new? Is something new?"

Parker seems to be deflating inside his Chesterfield. Here is Parker amid the flipniks, adrift amid the litter while the gas jets burn.

Parker turns to me. "I'm sorry," he says. Then he turns to Ben. "O.K., we're going."

"O.K.," says Ben.

"Only one thing," says Parker. "What do you want me to . . ."

He doesn't finish. He turns around and walks toward the door  Then he wheels around again.

"What do you want me to tell your mother?"

"What do you mean?" Ben says.

"Do you have a message for her?"

"Such as what?"

"Well, she's been praying for you again."

"Are you being funny?"

"No, it's true," says Parker. "She has been praying for you again. I hear her in the bedroom. She has her eyes shut tight, like this, and she is on her knees. She says things like, 'O dear Lord, guide and protect my Ben wherever he may be tonight. Do you remember, O Lord, how my sweet Ben stood before me in the morning so that I might kiss him upon his forehead in the early brightness? Do you remember, O Lord, the golden promise of this child, my Ben?' Well, you know, Bewak, things like that. I don't want to embarrass you."

"That was extremely witty," Ben says.

"What do you want me to tell her?" says Parker.

"Why don't you just go?" Ben says.

"Well, we're all going to be on our knees praying tonight, Bewak," says Parker. "So long, Bewak."

Down in the hallway, in the muddy tableau, Parker begins chuckling.

"I know what I'm going to tell Regina," he says. "I'm going to tell her Ben has become a raving religious fanatic and was down on his knees in a catatonic trance when we got there."

"What is all this about kneeling in prayer?"

"I don't know," Parker says. "I just want everybody who is japping me to get down on their knees, locked in a battle of harmless zeal. I discovered something up there."

"Which was?"

"He's repulsive," says Parker. "The whole thing was repulsive. After a while I didn't see it from the inside. It wasn't me looking at my own son. I saw it from the outside. It repelled me, that was all. It repelled me."

At the corner of Avenue B and 2d Street Parker sticks out his hand and bygod there is a cab. It is amazing. There are no cabs cruising the Lower East Side. Parker looks all around before he gets in the cab. Up the street, up Avenue B, you can see the hulk of the Avenue B Cinema and the edge of the park.

"That is a good augury," he tells me. "If you can walk right out on the street and get a cab—any time, any place, just stick out your hand and a cab stops—if you can do that, that is the sign that you are on top of it in New York."

Parker doesn't say anything more until we're riding up Fourth Avenue, or Park Avenue South, as it now is, up around 23rd Street, by the Metropolitan Life Insurance Building.

"You tell me," he says. "What could I say to him? I couldn't say anything to him. I threw out everything I had. I couldn't make anything skip across the pond. None of them. Not one."

## QUESTIONS: *Wolfe, "Putting Daddy On"*

1. "... Parker understands everybody's motives, including his own, which he has a tendency to talk about and revile." What *conventional* and *contemporary* parental characteristics does this statement reveal?

   *Clues:* • ... and revile.

   • It is as if Parker were looking through a microscope at a convulsive amoeba, himself, Parker.

2. The narrator describes Parker as "a casualty of the Information Crisis." In what way is Parker a casualty? Consider the comments: "He understands everything, the whole thing, and he is in a hopeless funk" and "He calls it a Madison Avenue crash helmet and then wears one."

   a. What use does Parker make of the "authorities" he has at his disposal? Note (1) the list of writers from Freud to the columnist Rose Franzblau, (2) the repetition of the ironic "he understands" in paragraphs 2, 3, and 4.

   b. What connections can we make between the way Parker uses these authorities and the references to religion the story contains?

   *Clues:* • He understands why pot-smoking is sort of a religion.

   • "What's all this about kneeling in prayer?"

   "I don't know," Parker says. "I just want everybody who is japping me to get down on their knees, locked in a battle of harmless zeal. I discovered something up there."

    c. In what ways does Wolfe use language to suggest that Parker can only deal with experience through words, not action, and—more generally—to dramatize the generation gap?

*Clues:*  • "Come on down and ride shotgun for me," he says.

       • Parker speaks of the Lower East Side as the caravansary for flipniks.

       • "Nifty," Parker says.

       • "Ah," says Parker, "the whole scene."

       • "Beaver is a very old expression," says Parker. "Before you were born. About 1803. I was using a very old expression, from my childhood. Did you ever hear a song that goes 'Alpha, beta, delta handa poker?' That was a very hip song."

3. What evidence do we have that the younger generation may well be suffering from a different version of the self-consciousness which affects their elders? Note the appearance, behavior, and conversation of Ben and his friends. How much of it can we diagnose as a mode of "putting Daddy on"? Determine the extent to which the behavior of the young people is determined by that of the adults in their midst.

*Clues:*  • They are both looking at us like the tar baby. . . .

       • He just sticks his hand straight up in the air and waits for Parker.

       • "It's not very colorful. . . . It's a place."

       • "It has a lot of potential. . . . It really has a lot of potential. Doesn't it? Or doesn't it?"

       • ". . . This is *not* the greatest building in the world. I mean, that's probably pretty obvious. But I mean, like I was going on about it—but that just happens to be the way I *feel* about it."

       • ". . . You want to get hungry again, but the time won't pass."

4. Parker tells the narrator that he wants to "retrieve" his son, and tells Ben that he wants to "talk." What parental roles are implied in these words and what view of Parker's performance in these roles does the story provide?

*Clue:*  • All this time Ben never introduces Parker. . . . One's old man does not show up in a brown Chesterfield with ratchety pleas in his poor old voice. . . .

5. What feelings (aside from the repulsion he himself mentions) make up Parker's rejection of his son? Note the references to the cab, to Park Avenue South, and to the Metropolitan Life Insurance Building. Comment on the reverberations of the phrases "I threw out everything I had" and "I couldn't make anything skip across the pond."

6. What contribution does the narrator make to our understanding of the cultures of both generations?

## EXERCISE

Discuss why the title "Putting Daddy On" could also be appropriate for the second scene of *The Rivals*. Indicate the differences you can detect between the eighteenth-century version of the "put-on" and that of the twentieth century.

Geoffrey Chaucer (1340?–1400)

# The Pardoner's Tale (lines 661–894)

*The excerpt printed here represents only the Tale proper without those trimmings of sermonizing, absolution-offering, and relic selling that are the Pardoner's stock in trade. In the lines preceding the Tale he describes the sinful nature of his future protagonists—given to dancing, gambling, drinking, and swearing—and enthusiastically launches into a graphic description of these vices. At the conclusion of the Tale, having gotten the pilgrims primed for salvation, as it were, he tries to sell his pardons and relics. Only the Host's crudely honest denunciation checks the Pardoner, whose whole life repudiates the doctrine he preaches through his Tale: "Greed is the Root of all Evil."*

Thise riotoures thre of whiche I telle,
Longe erst er prime rong of any belle,
Were set hem in a taverne for to drynke,
And as they sat, they herde a belle clynke
Biforn a cors, was caried to his grave.      665
That oon of hem gan callen to his knave:
"Go bet,"[1] quod he, "and axe redily
What cors is this that passeth heer forby;
And looke that thou reporte his name weel."
   "Sire," quod this boy, "it nedeth never-a-deel;     670
It was me toold er ye cam heer two houres.
He was, pardee, an old felawe of youres;
And sodeynly he was yslayn to-nyght,
Fordronke, as he sat on his bench upright.
Ther cam a privee theef, men clepeth[2] Deeth,     675
That in this contree al the peple sleeth,
And with his spere he smoot his herte at wo,
And wente his wey withouten wordes mo.
He hath a thousand slayn this pestilence.
And, maister, er ye come in his presence,     680
Me thynketh that it were necessarie
For to be war of swich an adversarie.
Beth redy for to meete hym everemoore;
Thus taughte me my dame;[3] I sey namoore."
"By seinte Marie!" seyde this taverner     685
"The child seith sooth, for he hath slayn this yeer,

---

[1] *Go bet:* go better, faster.  [2] *clepeth:* call.  [3] *dame:* mother.

Henne over a mile, withinne a greet village,
Bothe man and womman, child, and hyne,[4] and page;
I trowe his habitacioun be there.
To been avysed greet wysdom it were,                                       690
Er that he dide a man a dishonour."
 "Ye, Goddes armes!" quod this riotour,
"Is it swich peril with hym for to meete?
I shal hym seke by wey and eek by strete,
I make avow to Goddes digne bones!                                         695
Herkneth, felawes, we thre been al ones;
Lat ech of us holde up his hand til oother,
And ech of us bicomen otheres brother,
And we wol sleen this false traytour Deeth.
He shal be slayn, he that so manye sleeth,                                  700
By Goddes dignitee, er it be nyght!"
 Togidres han thise thre hir trouthes plight
To lyve and dyen ech of hem for oother,
As though he were his owene ybore brother.
And up they stirte, al dronken in this rage,                               705
And forth they goon towardes that village
Of which the taverner hadde spoke biforn.
And many a grisly ooth thanne han they sworn,
And Cristes blessed body al torente—
Deeth shal be deed, if that they may hym hente![5]                          710
 Whan they han goon nat fully half a mile,
Right as they wolde han troden over a stile,
An oold man and a povre with hem mette.
This olde man ful mekely hem grette,
And seyde thus, "Now, lordes, God yow see!"                                715
 The proudeste of thise riotoures three
Answerde agayn, "What, carl,[6] with sory grace!
Why artow al forwrapped save thy face?
Why lyvestow so longe in so greet age?"
 This olde man gan looke in his visage,                              720
And seyde thus, "For I ne kan nat fynde
A man, though that I walked into Ynde,
Neither in citee ne in no village,
That wolde chaunge his youthe for myn age;
And therfore moot I han myn age stille,                                    725
As longe tyme as it is Goddes wille.
Ne Deeth, allas! ne wol nat han my lyf.
Thus walke I, lyk a restelees kaityf,
And on the ground, which is my moodres gate,

---

[4] *hyne:* hind, farm worker.   [5] *hente:* seize.   [6] *carl:* churl.

I knokke with my staf, bothe erly and late,        730
And seye 'Leeve[7] mooder, leet me in!
Lo how I vanysshe, flessh, and blood, and skyn!
Allas! whan shul my bones been at reste?
Mooder, with yow wolde I chaunge my cheste     735
That in my chambre longe tyme hath be,
Ye, for an heyre clowt to wrappe in me!'
But yet to me she wol nat do that grace,
For which ful pale and welked[8] is my face.
    But, sires, to yow it is no curteisye
To speken to an old man vileynye,         740
But he trespasse in word, or elles in dede.
In Hooly Writ ye may yourself wel rede:
'Agayns an oold man, hoor upon his heed,
Ye sholde arise;' wherfore I yeve yow reed,
Ne dooth unto an oold man noon harm now,   745
Namoore than that ye wolde men did to yow
In age, if that ye so longe abyde.
And God be with yow, where ye go or ryde!
I moot go thider as I have to go."
    "Nay, olde cherl, by God, thou shalt nat so,"   750
Seyde this oother hasardour anon;
"Thou partest nat so lightly, by Seint John!
Thou spak right now of thilke traytour Deeth,
That in this contree alle oure freendes sleeth.
Have heer my trouthe, as thou art his espye,   755
Telle where he is, or thou shalt it abye,
By God, and by the hooly sacrement!
For soothly thou art oon of his assent
To sleen us yonge folk, thou false theef!"
    "Now, sires," quod he, "if that ye be so leef   760
To fynde Deeth, turne up this croked wey,
For in that grove I lafte hym, by my fey,
Under a tree, and there he wole abyde;
Noght for youre boost he wole him no thyng hyde.
Se ye that ook? Right there ye shal hym fynde.   765
God save yow, that boghte agayn mankynde,
And yow amende!" Thus seyde this olde man;
And everich of thise riotoures ran
Til he cam to that tree, and ther they founde
Of floryns fyne of gold ycoyned rounde     770
Wel ny an eighte busshels, as hem thoughte.
No lenger thanne after Deeth they soughte,

---

[7] *leeve:* dear.   [8] *welked:* withered.

But ech of hem so glad was of that sighte,
For that the floryns been so faire and brighte,
That doun they sette hem by this precious hoord.      775
The worste of hem, he spak the firste word.
   "Bretheren," quod he, "taak kep⁹ what that I seye;
My wit is greet, though that I bourde¹⁰ and pleye.
This tresor hath Fortune unto us yiven,
In myrthe and jolitee oure lyf to lyven,      780
And lightly as it comth, so wol we spende.
Ey! Goddes precious dignitee! who wende
To-day that we sholde han so fair a grace?
But myghte this gold be caried fro this place
Hoom to myn hous, or elles unto youres—      785
For wel ye woot that al this gold is oures—
Thanne were we in heigh felicitee.
But trewely, by daye it may nat bee.
Men wolde seyn that we were theves stronge,
And for oure owene tresor doon us honge.      790
This tresor moste ycaried be by nyghte
As wisely and as slyly as it myghte.
Wherfore I rede that cut among us alle
Be drawe, and lat se wher the cut wol falle;
And he that hath the cut with herte blithe      795
Shal renne to the town, and that ful swithe,¹¹
And brynge us breed and wyn ful prively.
And two of us shul kepen subtilly
This tresor wel; and if he wol nat tarie,
Whan it is nyght, we wol this tresor carie,      800
By oon assent, where as us thynketh best."
That oon of hem the cut broghte in his fest,
And bad hem drawe, and looke where it wol falle;
And it fil on the yongeste of hem alle,
And forth toward the toun he wente anon.      805
And also soone as that he was gon,
That oon of hem spak thus unto that oother:
"Thow knowest wel thou art my sworen brother;
Thy profit wol I telle thee anon.
Thou woost wel that oure felawe is agon,      810
And heere is gold, and that ful greet plentee,
That shal departed been among us thre.
But nathelees, if I kan shape it so
That it departed were among us two,
Hadde I nat doon a freendes torn to thee?"      815
   That oother answerde, "I noot hou that may be.

⁹ *kep:* heed.  ¹⁰ *bourde:* jest.  ¹¹ *swithe:* swiftly.

He woot wel that the gold is with us tweye;
What shal we doon? What shal we to hym seye?"
    "Shal it be conseil?"[12] seyde the firste shrewe,
"And I shal tellen in a wordes fewe                              820
What we shal doon, and brynge it wel aboute."
    "I graunte," quod that oother, "out of doute,
That, by my trouthe, I wol thee nat biwreye."
    "Now," quod the firste, "thou woost wel we be tweye,
And two of us shul strenger be than oon.                          825
Looke whan that he is set, that right anoon
Arys as though thou woldest with hym pleye,
And I shal ryve hym thurgh the sydes tweye
Whil that thou strogelest with hym as in game,
And with thy daggere looke thou do the same;                     830
And thanne shal al this gold departed be,
My deere freend, bitwixen me and thee.
Thanne may we bothe oure lustes all fulfille,
And pleye at dees right at oure owene wille."
And thus acorded been thise shrewes tweye                        835
To sleen the thridde, as ye han herd me seye.
    This yongeste, which that wente to the toun,
Ful ofte in herte he rolleth up and doun
The beautee of thise floryns newe and brighte.
"O Lord!" quod he, "if so were that I myghte                      840
Have al this tresor to myself allone,
Ther is no man that lyveth under the trone
Of God that sholde lyve so murye as I!"
And atte laste the feend, oure enemy,
Putte in his thought that he sholde poyson beye,                 845
With which he myghte sleen his felawes tweye;
For-why the feend foond hym in swich lyvynge
That he hadde leve him to sorwe brynge.
For this was outrely his fulle entente,
To sleen hem bothe, and nevere to repente.                       850
And forth he gooth, no lenger wolde he tarie,
Into the toun, unto a pothecarie,
And preyde hym that he hym wolde selle
Som poyson, that he myghte his rattes quelle;
And eek ther was a polcat in his hawe,[13]                       855
That, as he seyde, his capouns hadde yslawe,
And fayn he wolde wreke hym, if he myghte,
On vermyn that destroyed hym by nyghte.
    The pothecarie answerde, "And thou shalt have
A thyng that, also God my soule save,                            860

---

[12] *conseil:* a secret.    [13] *hawe:* yard.

In al this world ther is no creature,
That eten or dronken hath of this confiture
Noght but the montance[14] of a corn of whete,
That he ne shal his lif anon forlete;
Ye, sterve[15] he shal, and that in lasse while          865
Than thou wolt goon a paas nat but a mile,
This poysoun is so strong and violent."
    This cursed man hath in his hond yhent
This poysoun in a box, and sith he ran
Into the nexte strete unto a man,                        870
And borwed hym large botelles thre;
And in the two his poyson poured he;
The thridde he kepte clene for his drynke.
For al the nyght he shoop hym for to swynke
In cariynge of the gold out of that place.               875
And whan this riotour, with sory grace,
Hadde filled with wyn his grete botels thre,
To his felawes agayn repaireth he.
    What nedeth it to sermone of it moore?
For right as they hadde cast his deeth bifoore,          880
Right so they han hym slayn, and that anon.
And whan that this was doon, thus spak that oon:
"Now lat us sitte and drynke, and make us merie,
And afterward we wol his body berie."
And with that word it happed hym, par cas,              885
To take the botel ther the poyson was,
And drank, and yaf his felawe drynke also,
For which anon they storven bothe two.
    But certes, I suppose that Avycen[16]
Wroot nevere in no canon, ne in no fen,                 890
Mo wonder signes of empoisonyng
Than hadde thise wrecches two, er hir endyng.
Thus ended been thise homycides two,
And eek the false empoysonere also.

## QUESTIONS: *Chaucer, "The Pardoner's Tale"*

1. Why is the early warning to the roisterers particularly effective when put in the mouth of a child?
2. What connection is there between the defiance of and disrespect toward old age and the young men's determination to defy and destroy death?

---

[14] *montance:* amount.     [15] *sterve:* perish.     [16] The eleventh-century Arabic philosopher Avicenna discusses poisons in one of the sections (called *fens*) of his work, *The Book of the Canon of Medicine.*

3.  Is there any evidence for the young man's claim in lines 758–759 that the old man wants to destroy the young men? If not, what assumptions about the older generation might account for their distrust?

4.  How does the attitude of the old man toward death differ from that of the young men? What does the difference tell us about the differences in values between the generations?

5.  How does the attitude of the old man toward material goods differ from that of the young men? What relationship does the story imply between attitudes toward material goods and attitudes toward death?

6.  What connection is there between the young men's defiance of the old man and their proceeding to gratify their need for pleasure and their craving for the means to secure it? What is the moral appropriateness of the old man's assurance to the roisterers that they will find Death under the tree?

7.  Does the story as a whole point to any positive precepts concerning the relationships between youth and age?

*Edmund Spenser (1552?–1599)*

# The Shepheardes Calender

## *Februarie* (lines 51–247)
### Ægloga Secunda.

### Argvment

*This Æglogue is rather morall and generall, then bent to any secrete or particular purpose. It specially conteyneth a discourse of old age, in the persone of Thenot an olde Shepheard, who for his crookednesse and vnlustinesse, is scorned of Cuddie an vnhappy Heardmans boye. The matter very well accordeth with the season of the moneth, the yeare now drouping, and as it were, drawing to his last age. For as in this time of yeare, so then in our bodies thereis a dry and withering cold, which congealeth the crudled blood, and frieseth the wether-beaten flesh, with stormes of Fortune, and hoare frosts of Care. To which purpose the olde man telleth a tale of the Oake and the Bryer, so liuely and so feelingly, as if the thing were set forth in some Picture before our eyes, more plainly could not appeare.*

Cvddie.   Ah foolish old man, I scorne thy skill,
That wouldest me, my springing youngth to spil.
I deeme, thy braine emperished bee
Through rusty elde, that hath rotted thee:
Or sicker thy head veray tottie is,                                    55
So on thy corbe shoulder it leanes amisse.
Now thy selfe hast lost both lopp and topp,
Als my budding braunch thou wouldest cropp:
But were thy yeares greene, as now bene myne,

To other delights they would encline. 60
Tho wouldest thou learne to caroll of Loue,
And hery with hymnes thy lasses gloue.
Tho wouldest thou pype of *Phyllis* prayse:
But *Phyllis* is myne for many dayes:
I wonne her with a gyrdle of gelt, 65
Embost with buegle about the belt.
Such an one shepeheards woulde make full faine:
Such an one would make thee younge againe.

THENOT.   Thou art a fon, of thy loue to boste,
All that is lent to loue, wyll be lost. 70

CVDDIE.   Seest, howe brag yond Bullocke beares,
So smirke, so smoothe, his pricked eares?
His hornes bene as broade, as Rainebowe bent,
His dewelap as lythe, as lasse of Kent.
See howe he venteth into the wynd. 75
Weenest of loue is not his mynd?
Seemeth thy flocke thy counsell can,
So lustlesse bene they, so weake so wan,
Clothed with cold, and hoary wyth frost.
Thy flocks father his corage hath lost: 80
Thy Ewes, that wont to haue blowen bags,
Like wailefull widdowes hangen their crags:
The rather Lambes bene starued with cold,
All for their Maister is lustlesse and old.

THENOT.   *Cuddie,* I wote thou kenst little good, 85
So vainely taduaunce thy headlesse hood.
For Youngth is a bubble blown vp with breath,
Whose witt is weakenesse, whose wage is death,
Whose way is wildernesse, whose ynne Penaunce,
And stoopegallaunt Age the hoste of Greeuaunce. 90
But shall I tel thee a tale of truth,
Which I cond of *Tityrus* in my youth,
Keeping his sheepe on the hils of Kent?

CVDDIE.   To nought more *Thenot,* my mind is bent,
Then to heare nouells of his deuise: 95
They bene so well thewed, and so wise,
What euer that good old man bespake.

THENOT.   Many meete tales of youth did he make,
And some of loue, and some of cheualrie:
But none fitter then this to applie. 100
Now listen a while, and hearken the end.

There grewe an aged Tree on the greene,
A goodly Oake sometime had it bene,

With armes full strong and largely displayd,
But of their leaues they were disarayde:                    105
The bodie bigge, and mightely pight,
Throughly rooted, and of wonderous hight:
Whilome had bene the King of the field,
And mochell mast to the husband did yielde,
And with his nuts larded many swine.                       110
But now the gray mosse marred his rine,
His bared boughes were beaten with stormes,
His toppe was bald, and wasted with wormes,
His honor decayed, his braunches sere.
  Hard by his side grewe a bragging brere,                 115
Which proudly thrust into Thelement,
And seemed to threat the Firmament.
Yt was embellisht with blossomes fayre,
And thereto aye wonned to repayre
The shepheards daughters, to gather flowres,               120
To peinct their girlonds with his colowres.
And in his small bushes vsed to shrowde
The sweete Nightingale singing so lowde:
Which made this foolish Brere wexe so bold,
That on a time he cast him to scold,                       125
And snobbe the good Oake, for he was old.
  Why standst there (quoth he) thou brutish blocke?
Nor for fruict, nor for shadowe serues thy stocke:
Seest, how fresh my flowers bene spredde,
Dyed in Lilly white, and Cremsin redde,                    130
With Leaues engrained in lusty greene,
Colours meete to clothe a mayden Queene.
Thy wast bignes but combers the grownd,
And dirks the beauty of my blossomes rownd.
The mouldie mosse, which thee accloieth,                   135
My Sinamon smell too much annoieth.
Wherefore soone I rede thee, hence remoue,
Least thou the price of my displeasure proue.
So spake this bold brere with great disdaine:
Little him answered the Oake againe,                       140
But yielded, with shame and greefe adawed,
That of a weede he was ouercrawed.
  Yt chaunced after vpon a day,
The Hus-bandman selfe to come that way,
Of custome for to seruewe his grownd,                      145
And his trees of state in compasse rownd.
Him when the spitefull brere had espyed,
Causlesse complained, and lowdly cryed

Vnto his Lord, stirring vp sterne strife:
O my liege Lord, the God of my life,            150
Pleaseth you ponder your Suppliants plaint,
Caused of wrong, and cruell constraint,
Which I your poore Vassall dayly endure
And but your goodnes the same recure,
Am like for desperate doole to dye,            155
Through felonous force of mine enemie.
  Greatly aghast with this piteous plea,
Him rested the goodman on the lea,
And badde the Brere in his plaint proceede.
With painted words tho gan this proude weede,    160
(As most vsen Ambitious folke:)
His colowred crime with craft to cloke.
  Ah my soueraigne, Lord of creatures all,
Thou placer of plants both humble and tall,
Was not I planted of thine owne hand,        165
To be the primrose of all thy land,
With flowring blossomes, to furnish the prime,
And scarlot berries in Sommer time?
How falls it then, that this faded Oake,
Whose bodie is sere, whose braunches broke,    170
Whose naked Armes stretch vnto the fyre,
Vnto such tyrannie doth aspire:
Hindering with his shade my louely light,
And robbing me of the swete sonnes sight?
So beate his old boughes my tender side,      175
That oft the bloud springeth from woundes wyde:
Vntimely my flowres forced to fall,
That bene the honor of your Coronall.
And oft he lets his cancker wormes light
Vpon my braunches, to worke me more spight:    180
And oft his hoarie locks downe doth cast,
Where with my fresh flowretts bene defast.
For this, and many more such outrage,
Crauing your goodlihead to aswage
The ranckorous rigour of his might,         185
Nought aske I, but onely to hold my right:
Submitting me to your good sufferance,
And praying to be garded from greeuance.
  To this the Oake cast him to replie
Well as he couth: but his enemie           190
Had kindled such coles of displeasure,
That the good man noulde stay his leasure,
But home him hasted with furious heate,

Encreasing his wrath with many a threate.
His harmefull Hatchet he hent in hand,                    195
(Alas, that it so ready should stand)
And to the field alone he speedeth.
(Ay little helpe to harme there needeth)
Anger nould let him speake to the tree,
Enaunter his rage mought cooled bee:                     200
But to the roote bent his sturdy stroke,
And made many wounds in the wast Oake.
The Axes edge did oft turne againe,
As halfe vnwilling to cutte the graine:
Semed, the sencelesse yron dyd feare,                    205
Or to wrong holy eld did forbeare.
For it had bene an auncient tree,
Sacred with many a mysteree,
And often crost with the priestes crewe,
And often halowed with holy water dewe.                  210
But sike fancies weren foolerie,
And broughten this Oake to this miserye.
For nought mought they quitten him from decay:
For fiercely the good man at him did laye.
The blocke oft groned vnder the blow,                    215
And sighed to see his neare ouerthrow.
In fine the steele had pierced his pitth,
Tho downe to the earth he fell forthwith:
His wonderous weight made the grounde to quake,
Thearth shronke vnder him, and seemed to shake.          220
There lyeth the Oake, pitied of none.
   Now stands the Brere like a Lord alone,
Puffed vp with pryde and vaine pleasaunce:
But all this glee had no continuaunce.
For eftsones Winter gan to approche,                     225
The blustring Boreas did encroche,
And beate vpon the solitarie Brere:
For nowe no succoure was seene him nere.
Now gan he repent his pryde to late:
For naked left and disconsolate,                         230
The byting frost nipt his stalke dead,
The watrie wette weighed downe his head,
And heaped snowe burdned him so sore,
That nowe vpright he can stand no more:
And being downe, is trodde in the durt                   235
Of cattell, and brouzed, and sorely hurt.
Such was thend of this Ambitious brere,
For scorning Eld

CVDDIE.  Now I pray thee shepheard, tel it not forth:
 Here is a long tale, and little worth.      240
 So longe haue I listened to thy speche,
 That graffed to the ground is my breche:
 My hartblood is welnigh frorne I feele,
 And my galage growne fast to my heele:
 But little ease of thy lewd tale I tasted.    245
 Hye thee home shepheard, the day is nigh wasted.
      Thenots Embleme.

*Iddio perche è vecchio,*
*Fa suoi al suo essempio.*

   Cuddies Embleme.       250

  *Niuno vecchio,*
  *Spaventa Iddio.*

## GLOSSE.

Sicker) sure.  Tottie) wauering.

Corbe) crooked.  Herie) worshippe.

Phyllis) the name of some mayde vnknowen, whom Cuddie, whose person is secrete,
 loued. The name is vsuall in Theocritus, Virgile, and Mantuane.

Belte) a girdle or wast band.  A fon) a foole.

lythe) soft and gentile.

Venteth) snuffeth in the wind.

Thy flocks Father) the Ramme.  Crags) neckes.

Rather Lambes) that be ewed early in the beginning of the yeare.

Youth is) A verye moral and pithy Allegorie of youth, and the lustes thereof, compared to a wearie wayfaring man.

Tityrus) I suppose he meane Chaucer, whose prayse for pleasaunt tales cannot dye,
 so long as the memorie of hys name shal liue, and the name of Poetrie shal endure.

Well thewed) that is, Bene moratæ, full of morall wisenesse.

There grew) This tale of the Oake and the Brere, he telleth as learned of Chaucer,
 but it is cleane in another kind, and rather like to Æsopes fables. It is very excellente
 for pleasaunt descriptions, being altogether a certaine Icon or Hypotyposis of
 disdainfull younkers.

Embellisht) beautified and adorned.

To wonne) to haunt or frequent.  Sneb) checke.

Why standst) The speach is scorneful and very presumptuous.

Engrained) dyed in grain.

Accloieth) encombreth.

Adawed) daunted and confounded.

Trees of state) taller trees fitte for timber wood.

Sterne strife) said Chaucer, .s. fell and sturdy.

O my liege) A maner of supplication, wherein is kindly coloured the affection and
 speache of Ambitious men.

Coronall) Garlande.  Flourets) young blossomes.

The Primrose) The chiefe and worthiest.

Naked armes) metaphorically ment of the bare boughes, spoyled of leaues. This colourably he speaketh, as adiudging hym to the fyre.

The blood) spoken of a blocke, as it were of a liuing creature, figuratiuely, and (as they saye) κατ· εἰκασμόν.

Hoarie lockes) metaphorically for withered leaues.

Hent) caught.    Nould) for would not.

Ay) euermore.    Wounds) gashes.

Enaunter) least that.

The priestes crewe) holy water pott, wherewith the popishe priest vsed to sprinckle and hallowe the trees from mischaunce. Such blindnesse was in those times, which the Poete supposeth, to haue bene the finall decay of this auncient Oake.

The blocke oft groned) A liuelye figure, whiche geueth sence and feeling to vnsensible creatures, as Virgile also sayeth: Saxa gemunt grauido &c.

Boreas) The Northerne wynd, that bringeth the moste stormie weather.

Glee) chere and iollitie.

For scorning Eld) And minding (as shoulde seme) to haue made ryme to the former verse, he is conningly cutte of by Cuddye, as disdayning to here any more.

Galage) a startuppe or clownish shoe.

### Embleme.

This embleme is spoken of Thenot, as a moral of his former tale: namelye, that God, which is himselfe most aged, being before al ages, and without beginninge, maketh those, whom he loueth like to himselfe, in heaping yeares vnto theyre dayes, and blessing them wyth longe lyfe. For the blessing of age is not giuen to all, but vnto those, whome God will so blesse: and albeit that many euil men reache vnto such fulnesse of yeares, and some also wexe olde in myserie and thraldome, yet therefore is not age euer the lesse blessing. For euen to such euill men such number of yeares is added, that they may in their last dayes repent, and come to their first home. So the old man checketh the rashheaded boy, for despysing his gray and frostye heares.

Whom Cuddye doth counterbuff with a byting and bitter prouerbe, spoken indeede at the first in contempt of old age generally. For it was an old opinion, and yet is continued in some mens conceipt, that men of yeares haue no feare of god at al, or not so much as younger folke. For that being rypened with long experience, and hauing passed many bitter brunts and blastes of vengeaunce, they dread no stormes of Fortune, nor wrathe of Gods, nor daunger of menne, as being eyther by longe and ripe wisedome armed against all mischaunces and aduersitie, or with much trouble hardened against all troublesome tydes: lyke vnto the Ape, of which is sayed in Æsops fables, that oftentimes meeting the Lyon, he was at first sore aghast and dismayed at the grimnes and austeritie of hys countenance, but at last being acquainted with his lookes, he was so furre from fearing him, that he would familiarly gybe and iest with him: Suche longe experience breedeth in some men securitie. Although it please Erasimus a great clerke and good old father, more fatherly and fauourablye to construe it in his Adages for his own behoofe, That by the prouerbe Nemo Senex metuit Iouem, is not meant, that old men haue no feare of God at al, but that they be furre from superstition and Idolatrous regard of false Gods, as is Iupiter. But his greate learning notwithstanding, it is to plaine, to be gainsayd, that olde men are muche more enclined to such fond fooleries, then younger heades.

## QUESTIONS: *Spenser, The Shepheardes Calender*

1. In the first fifty lines the argument between Cuddie and Thenot with regard to the cold winter weather pits the industry, adaptability, experience, and resignation of *age* against the impatience, inexperience, laziness, and forgetfulness of *youth*. What specific weaknesses in each generation are next attacked in the exchanges (lines 50–97) that precede the tale of the Oak and the Briar? Which of the two speakers in each of the dialogues seems to have the more convincing argument—Cuddie or Thenot? How do the images of *nature* and of *animals* reinforce the criticism? Why is it appropriate that the attack of youth on age should be the more personal one?
   *Clues:* • Als my budding braunch thou wouldest cropp:

   > • Thy Ewes, that wont to haue blowen bags,
   >   Like wailefull widdowes hangen their crags:

   > • For Youngth is a bubble blown vp with breath.
   >   Whose witt is weakenesse, whose wage is death,

2. In what ways is Thenot's fable of the Oak and the Briar a correct account of the relationship between Thenot and Cuddie? Consider (a) Cuddie's attitude to Thenot, (b) the way Thenot describes Cuddie in lines 51–69.

3. What characteristics of age and youth are suggested by the images of nature in the story of Oak and Briar (for example, "wasted with wormes" as against "embellisht with blossomes fayre")? What suspicions, angers, and fears of youth with regard to the older generation do the complaints of the Briar against the Oak indirectly suggest?
   *Clue:* • Hindering with his shade my louely light,
   And robbing me of the swete sonnes sight?

4. What evidence is there that the attack against age is to be viewed as a manifestation of *hybris* in the story? Note the particular choice of words.

5. Why is Cuddie's reaction to the story so appropriate a conclusion to what has gone on before?

## EXERCISES

1. In the two scenes from Sheridan's *The Rivals* in this section the moral triumph is accorded to youth. Assess as justly as you can Spenser's stand in this text on the question of the respective claims of youth and age. Take the mottoes—and the comments on them in the Gloss—into account.

2. Comment briefly on the pertinence to this text of the following maxims from Bernard Shaw's *The Revolutionist's Handbook*:
   > Every man over forty is a scoundrel.

   > Youth, which is forgiven everything, forgives itself nothing: age, which forgives itself everything, is forgiven nothing.

3. In the light of Spenser's dialogue between Thenot and Cuddie, examine the following poem and its parody, which are also exchanges between a young man and an old one on their respective conditions.

## *The Old Man's Comforts and How He Gained Them*

ROBERT SOUTHEY (1774–1843)

"You are old, Father William," the young man cried;
  "The few locks which are left you are gray;
You are hale, Father William—a hearty old man:
  Now tell me the reason, I pray."

"In the days of my youth," Father William replied,                    5
  "I remembered that youth would fly fast,
And abused not my health and my vigor at first,
  That I never might need them at last."

"You are old, Father William," the young man cried,
  "And pleasures with youth pass away;                               10
And yet you lament not the days that are gone:
  Now tell me the reason, I pray."

"In the days of my youth," Father William replied,
  "I remembered that youth could not last;
I thought of the future, whatever I did,                             15
  That I never might grieve for the past."

"You are old, Father William," the young man cried,
  "And life must be hastening away;
You are cheerful and love to converse upon death:
  Now tell me the reason, I pray."                                   20

"I am cheerful, young man," Father William replied;
  "Let the cause thy attention engage;
In the days of my youth, I remembered my God,
  And He hath not forgotten my age."

## *You Are Old, Father William*

LEWIS CARROLL [Charles Lutwidge Dodgson] (1832–1898)

"You are old, Father William," the young man said,
  "And your hair has become very white;
And yet you incessantly stand on your head—
  Do you think, at your age, it is right?"

"In my youth," Father William replied to his son,                    5
  "I feared it might injure the brain;
But now that I'm perfectly sure I have none,
  Why, I do it again and again."

"You are old," said the youth," as I mentioned before,
  And have grown most uncommonly fat;                                10
Yet you turned a back-somersault in at the door—
  Pray, what is the reason of that?"

"In my youth," said the sage, as he shook his grey locks,
  "I kept all my limbs very supple
By the use of this ointment—one shilling the box—        15
  Allow me to sell you a couple."

"You are old," said the youth, "and your jaws are too weak
  For anything tougher than suet;
Yet you finished the goose, with the bones and the beak—
  Pray how did you manage to do it?"        20

"In my youth," said his father, "I took to the law,
  And argued each case with my wife;
And the muscular strength, which it gave to my jaw,
  Has lasted the rest of my life."

"You are old," said the youth, "one would hardly suppose    25
  That your eye was as steady as ever;
Yet you balanced an eel on the end of your nose—
  What made you so awfully clever?"

"I have answered three questions, and that is enough,"
  Said his father; "don't give yourself airs!
Do you think I can listen all day to such stuff?        30
  Be off, or I'll kick you downstairs!"

a.  State the characteristics of Father William in the Southey poem and determine what changes they undergo in the Carroll parody. What essential assumptions does the Carroll poem undermine with regard to (1) the nature of authority, (2) the values held by age, (3) the quality of its behavior?

b.  Determine what makes Carroll's debunking an amusing rather than an unpleasant challenge to authority.

## *Francis Bacon (1561–1626)*
# Of Parents and Children *and* Of Youth and Age

*These two prose pieces come from Bacon's* The Essayes or Counsels, Civil and Morall, *1597–1625. The essays deal in random aspects of man's private and public life, and characteristically include examples of behavior taken as much from literary and historical sources as from personal experience.*

### OF PARENTS AND CHILDREN

The joys of parents are secret; and so are their griefs and fears. They cannot utter the one, nor they will not utter the other. Children sweeten labours, but they make misfortunes more bitter. They increase the cares of life, but they mitigate the remembrance of death. The perpetuity by generation is common to beasts, but memory, merit, and noble works are proper to men. And surely a man shall see the noblest works and foundations have proceeded from childless men, which have sought to express the images of their minds, where those of their bodies have failed. So the care of posterity is most in them that have no posterity. They that are the first raisers of their houses are most indulgent towards their children, beholding them as the continuance not only of their kind but of their work; and so both children and creatures.

The difference in affection of parents towards their several children is many times unequal and sometimes unworthy, especially in the mother; as Salomon saith, *A wise son rejoiceth the father, but an ungracious son shames the mother.* A man shall see, where there is a house full of children, one or two of the eldest respected, and the youngest made wantons, but in the midst some that are as it were forgotten, who many times nevertheless prove the best. The illiberality of parents in allowance towards their children is an harmful error; makes them base; acquaints them with shifts; makes them sort with mean company; and makes them surfeit more when they come to plenty. And therefore the proof is best, when men keep their authority towards their children, but not their purse. Men have a foolish manner (both parents and schoolmasters and servants) in creating and breeding an emulation between brothers during childhood, which many times sorteth to discord when they are men, and disturbeth families. The Italians make little difference between children and nephews or near kinsfolks; but so they be of the lump, they care not though they pass not through their own body. And, to say truth, in nature it is much a like matter; insomuch that we see a nephew sometimes resembleth an uncle or a kinsman more than his own parent, as the blood happens. Let parents choose betimes the vocations and courses they mean their children should take, for then they are most flexible; and let them not too much apply themselves to the disposition of their children, as thinking they will take best to that which they have most mind to. It is true that if the affection or aptness of the children be extraordinary, then it is good not to cross it; but generally the precept is good, *optimum elige, suave et facile illud faciet consuetudo.*[1] Younger brothers are commonly fortunate but seldom or never where the elder are disinherited.

## Of Youth and Age

A man that is young in years may be old in hours, if he have lost no time. But that happeneth rarely. Generally youth is like the first cogitations, not so wise as the second. For there is a youth in thoughts, as well as in ages. And yet the invention of young men is more lively than that of old; and imaginations stream into their minds better, and as it were more divinely. Natures that have much heat and great and violent desires and perturbations are not

---

[1] Select the best; habit will make it pleasant and easy.

ripe for action till they have passed the meridian of their years, as it was with Julius Cæsar and Septimius Severus. Of the latter of whom it is said, *Juventutem egit erroribus, imo furoribus, plenam.*[1] And yet he was the ablest emperor, almost, of all the list. But reposed natures may do well in youth. As it is seen in Augustus Cæsar, Cosmus, Duke of Florence, Gaston de Fois, and others. On the other side, heat and vivacity in age is an excellent composition for business. Young men are fitter to invent than to judge, fitter for execution than for counsel, and fitter for new projects than for settled business. For the experience of age, in things that fall within the compass of it, directeth them, but in new things abuseth them. The errors of young men are the ruin of business, but the errors of aged men amount but to this, that more might have been done, or sooner. Young men in the conduct and manage of actions embrace more than they can hold; stir more than they can quiet; fly to the end, without consideration of the means and degrees; pursue some few principles which they have chanced upon absurdly; care not[2] to innovate, which draws unknown inconveniences; use extreme remedies at first; and that which doubleth all errors, will not acknowledge or retract them, like an unready horse that will neither stop nor turn. Men of age object too much, consult too long, adventure too little, repent too soon, and seldom drive business home to the full period, but content themselves with a mediocrity of success. Certainly it is good to compound employments of both, for that will be good for the present, because the virtues of either age may correct the defects of both; and good for succession, that young men may be learners, while men in age are actors; and, lastly, good for extern accidents, because authority followeth old men, and favour and popularity youth. But for the moral part, perhaps youth will have the pre-eminence, as age hath for the politic. A certain rabbin, upon the text, *Your young men shall see visions, and your old men shall dream dreams*, inferreth that young men are admitted nearer to God than old, because vision is a clearer revelation than a dream. And certainly the more a man drinketh of the world, the more it intoxicateth, and age doth profit rather in the powers of understanding than in the virtues of the will and affections. There be some have an over-early ripeness in their years, which fadeth betimes. These are, first, such as have brittle wits, the edge whereof is soon turned, such as was Hermogenes the rhetorician, whose books are exceeding subtle, who afterwards waxed stupid. A second sort is of those that have some natural dispositions which have better grace in youth than in age, such as is a fluent and luxuriant speech, which becomes youth well, but not age; so Tully saith of Hortensius, *Idem manebat, neque idem decebat.*[3] The third is of such as take too high a strain at the first, and are magnanimous more than tract of years can uphold. As was Scipio Africanus, of whom Livy saith in effect, *Ultima primis cedebant.*[4]

---

[1] He spent a youth filled with errors, indeed madness.
[2] Are not careful.
[3] He remained the same, but the same was no longer appropriate.
[4] His latter days were inferior to his first.

## QUESTIONS: *Bacon, " Of Parents and Children"/ " Of Youth and Age"*

1. Bacon was a lawyer by profession and served as a judge for a substantial part of his career as public servant (most of which came after the composition of these essays). How does his vocation color his style?

2. Which of Bacon's assumptions concerning the relations between parents and children alienate us? Which of his assumptions appeal to us? Justify your answer with specific references to the text and with full references to modern circumstances.

   *Clues:*

   • "Of Parents and Children"

   Let parents choose betimes the vocations and courses they mean their children should take, for then they are most flexible . . .

   Younger brothers are commonly fortunate, but seldom or never where the elder are disinherited.

   • "Of Youth and Age"

   Young men are fitter to invent than to judge, fitter for execution than for counsel, and fitter for new projects than for settled business.

3. On the basis of Bacon's account of the generation gap, what would you imagine to be (a) his vision of the ideal child? (b) his vision of the ideal parent?


## *Richard Brinsley Sheridan (1751–1816)*
# The Rivals

### FROM ACT II, SCENE I

#### (*Enter* SIR ANTHONY ABSOLUTE)

Sir, I am delighted to see you here and looking so well! your sudden arrival at Bath made me apprehensive for your health.

SIR ANTHONY. Very apprehensive, I dare say, Jack.—What, you are recruiting here, hey?

ABSOLUTE. Yes, sir, I am on duty.

SIR ANTHONY. Well, Jack, I am glad to see you, though I did not expect it, for I was going to write to you on a little matter of business.—Jack, I have been considering that I grow old and infirm, and shall probably not trouble you long.

ABSOLUTE. Pardon, sir, I never saw you look more strong and hearty; and I pray frequently that you may continue so.

SIR ANTHONY. I hope your prayers may be heard, with all my heart. Well, then, Jack, I have been considering that I am so strong and hearty I may continue to plague you a long time. Now, Jack, I am sensible that the income of your commission, and what I have hitherto allowed you, is but a small pittance for a lad of your spirit.

ABSOLUTE.  Sir, you are very good.

SIR ANTHONY.  And it is my wish, while yet I live, to have my boy make some figure in the world. I have resolved, therefore, to fix you at once in a noble independence.

ABSOLUTE.  Sir, your kindness overpowers me—such generosity makes the gratitude of reason more lively than the sensations even of filial affection.

SIR ANTHONY.  I am glad you are so sensible of my attention—and you shall be master of a large estate in a few weeks.

ABSOLUTE.  Let my future life, sir, speak my gratitude; I cannot express the sense I have of your munificence.—Yet, sir, I presume you would not wish me to quit the army?

SIR ANTHONY.  Oh, that shall be as your wife chooses.

ABSOLUTE.  My wife, sir!

SIR ANTHONY.  Ay, ay, settle that between you—settle that between you.

ABSOLUTE.  A *wife*, sir, did you say?

SIR ANTHONY.  Ay, a wife—why, did not I mention her before?

ABSOLUTE.  Not a word of her, sir.

SIR ANTHONY.  Odd so!—I mus'n't forget *her* though.—Yes, Jack, the independence I was talking of is by marriage—the fortune is saddled with a wife—but I suppose that makes no difference.

ABSOLUTE.  Sir! sir!—you amaze me!

SIR ANTHONY.  Why, what the devil's the matter with the fool? Just now you were all gratitude and duty.

ABSOLUTE.  I was, sir—you talked to me of independence and a fortune, but not a word of a wife.

SIR ANTHONY.  Why—what difference does that make? Odds life, sir! if you have the estate, you must take it with the live stock on it, as it stands.

ABSOLUTE.  If my happiness is to be the price, I must beg leave to decline the purchase.—Pray, sir, who is the lady?

SIR ANTHONY.  What's that to you, sir?—Come, give me your promise to love, and to marry her directly.

ABSOLUTE.  Sure, sir, this is not very reasonable, to summon my affections for a lady I know nothing of!

SIR ANTHONY.  I am sure, sir, 'tis more unreasonable in you to *object* to a lady you know nothing of.

ABSOLUTE.  Then, sir, I must tell you plainly that my inclinations are fixed on another—my heart is engaged to an angel.

SIR ANTHONY.  Then pray let it send an excuse. It is very sorry—but business prevents its waiting on her.

ABSOLUTE.  But my vows are pledged to her.

SIR ANTHONY.  Let her foreclose, Jack; let her foreclose; they are not worth redeeming; besides, you have the angel's vows in exchange, I suppose; so there can be no loss there.

ABSOLUTE.  You must excuse me, sir, if I tell you, once for all, that in this point I cannot obey you.

SIR ANTHONY. Hark'ee, Jack;—I have heard you for some time with patience—I have been cool—quite cool; but take care—you know I am compliance itself—when I am not thwarted;—no one more easily led —when I have my own way;—but don't put me in a frenzy.

ABSOLUTE. Sir, I must repeat—in this I cannot obey you.

SIR ANTHONY. Now damn me! if ever I call you Jack again while I live!

ABSOLUTE. Nay, sir, but hear me.

SIR ANTHONY. Sir, I won't hear a word—not a word! not one word! so give me your promise by a nod—and I'll tell you what, Jack—I mean, you dog—if you don't, by——

ABSOLUTE. What, sir, promise to link myself to some mass of ugliness! to——

SIR ANTHONY. Zounds! sirrah! the lady shall be as ugly as I choose: she shall have a hump on each shoulder; she shall be as crooked as the crescent; her one eye shall roll like the bull's in Cox's Museum, she shall have a skin like a mummy, and the beard of a Jew—she shall be all this, sirrah!—yet I will make you ogle her all day, and sit up all night to write sonnets on her beauty.

ABSOLUTE. This is reason and moderation indeed!

SIR ANTHONY. None of your sneering, puppy! no grinning, jackanapes!

ABSOLUTE. Indeed, sir, I never was in a worse humour for mirth in my life.

SIR ANTHONY. 'Tis false, sir. I know you are laughing in your sleeve; I know you'll grin when I am gone, sirrah!

ABSOLUTE. Sir, I hope I know my duty better.

SIR ANTHONY. None of your passion, sir! none of your violence, if you please!—It won't do with me, I promise you.

ABSOLUTE. Indeed, sir, I never was cooler in my life.

SIR ANTHONY. 'Tis a confounded lie!—I know you are in a passion in your heart; I know you are, you hypocritical young dog! but it won't do.

ABSOLUTE. Nay, sir, upon my word——

SIR ANTHONY. So you will fly out! can't you be cool like me? What the devil good can passion do?—Passion is of no service, you impudent, insolent, overbearing reprobate!—There, you sneer again! don't provoke me!—but you rely upon the mildness of my temper—you do, you dog! you play upon the meekness of my disposition!—Yet take care—the patience of a saint may be overcome at last!—but mark! I give you six hours and a half to consider of this: if you then agree, without any condition, to do everything on earth that I choose, why—confound you! I may in time forgive you.—If not, zounds! don't enter the same hemisphere with me! don't dare to breathe the same air, or use the same light with me; but get an atmosphere and sun of your own! I'll strip you of your commission; I'll lodge a five-and-threepence in the hands of trustees, and you shall live on the interest.—I'll disown you, I'll disinherit you, I'll unget you! and damn me! if ever I call you Jack again!

(*Exit* SIR ANTHONY)

ACT III, SCENE I: *The North Parade*

(*Enter* CAPTAIN ABSOLUTE)

ABSOLUTE. 'Tis just as Fag told me, indeed. Whimsical enough, faith. My father wants to force me to marry the very girl I am plotting to run away with! He must not know of my connection with her yet awhile. He has too summary a method of proceeding in these matters. However, I'll read my recantation instantly. My conversion is something sudden, indeed —but I can assure him it is very *sincere*. So, so—here he comes. He looks plaguy gruff. (*Steps aside*)

(*Enter* SIR ANTHONY ABSOLUTE)

SIR ANTHONY. No—I'll die sooner than forgive him. Die, did I say? I'll live these fifty years to plague him. At our last meeting, his impudence had almost put me out of temper. An obstinate, passionate, self-willed boy! Who can he take after? This is my return for getting him before all his brothers and sisters!—for putting him, at twelve years old, into a marching regiment, and allowing him fifty pounds a year, besides his pay, ever since! But I have done with him; he's anybody's son for me. I never will see him more, never—never—never—never.

ABSOLUTE. (*Aside, coming forward*) Now for a penitential face.

SIR ANTHONY. Fellow, get out of my way.

ABSOLUTE. Sir, you see a penitent before you.

SIR ANTHONY. I see an impudent scoundrel before me.

ABSOLUTE. A sincere penitent. I am come, sir, to acknowledge my error, and to submit entirely to your will.

SIR ANTHONY. What's that?

ABSOLUTE. I have been revolving, and reflecting, and considering on your past goodness, and kindness, and condescension to me.

SIR ANTHONY. Well, sir?

ABSOLUTE. I have been likewise weighing and balancing what you were pleased to mention concerning duty, and obedience, and authority.

SIR ANTHONY. Well, puppy?

ABSOLUTE. Why, then, sir, the result of my reflections is—a resolution to sacrifice every inclination of my own to your satisfaction.

SIR ANTHONY. Why now you talk sense—absolute sense.—I never heard anything more sensible in my life. Confound you! you shall be Jack again.

ABSOLUTE. I am happy in the appellation.

SIR ANTHONY. Why, then, Jack, my dear Jack, I will now inform you who the lady really is. Nothing but your passion and violence, you silly fellow, prevented my telling you at first. Prepare, Jack, for wonder and rapture— prepare. What think you of Miss Lydia Languish?

ABSOLUTE. Languish! What, the Languishes of Worcestershire?

SIR ANTHONY. Worcestershire! no. Did you ever meet Mrs. Malaprop and her niece, Miss Languish, who came into our country just before you were last ordered to your regiment?

ABSOLUTE. Malaprop! Languish! I don't remember ever to have heard the names before. Yet stay—I think I do recollect something. Languish! Languish! She squints, don't she? A little red-haired girl?

SIR ANTHONY. Squints! A red-haired girl! Zounds! no.

ABSOLUTE. Then I must have forgot; it can't be the same person.

SIR ANTHONY. Jack! Jack! what think you of blooming, love-breathing seventeen?

ABSOLUTE. As to that, sir, I am quite indifferent. If I can please you in the matter, 'tis all I desire.

SIR ANTHONY. Nay, but, Jack, such eyes! such eyes! so innocently wild! so bashfully irresolute! not a glance but speaks and kindles some thought of love! Then, Jack, her cheeks! her cheeks, Jack! so deeply blushing at the insinuations of her tell-tale eyes! Then, Jack, her lips! O, Jack, lips smiling at their own discretion; and if not smiling, more sweetly pouting; more lovely in sullenness.

ABSOLUTE. That's she, indeed. Well done, old gentleman.        (*Aside*)

SIR ANTHONY. Then, Jack, her neck! O Jack! Jack!

ABSOLUTE. And which is to be mine, sir; the niece or the aunt?

SIR ANTHONY. Why, you unfeeling, insensible puppy, I despise you! When I was of your age, such a description would have made me fly like a rocket! The aunt, indeed! Odds life! when I ran away with your mother, I would not have touched anything old or ugly to gain an empire.

ABSOLUTE. Not to please your father, sir?

SIR ANTHONY. To please my father! zounds! not to please—Oh, my father —odd so!—yes—yes; if my father indeed had desired—that's quite another matter. Though he wa'n't the indulgent father that I am, Jack.

ABSOLUTE. I dare say not, sir.

SIR ANTHONY. But, Jack, you are not sorry to find your mistress is so beautiful?

ABSOLUTE. Sir, I repeat it—if I please you in this affair, 'tis all I desire. Not that I think a woman the worse for being handsome; but, sir, if you please to recollect, you before hinted something about a hump or two, one eye, and a few more graces of that kind—now, without being very nice, I own I should rather choose a wife of mine to have the usual number of limbs, and a limited quantity of back: and though one eye may be very agreeable, yet as the prejudice has always run in favour of two, I would not wish to affect a singularity in that article.

SIR ANTHONY. What a phlegmatic sot it is! Why, sirrah, you're an anchorite! —a vile, insensible stock. You a soldier!—you're a walking block, fit only to dust the company's regimentals on! Odds life! I have a great mind to marry the girl myself!

ABSOLUTE. I am entirely at your disposal, sir: if you should think of addressing Miss Languish yourself, I suppose you would have me marry the aunt; or if you should change your mind, and take the old lady—'tis the same to me—I'll marry the niece.

SIR ANTHONY. Upon my word, Jack, thou'rt either a very great hypocrite, or—but, come, I know your indifference on such a subject must be all a lie—I'm sure it must—come, now—damn your demure face!—come, confess, Jack—you have been lying, ha'n't you? You have been playing the hypocrite, hey!—I'll never forgive you, if you ha'n't been lying and playing the hypocrite.

ABSOLUTE. I'm sorry, sir, that the respect and duty which I bear to you should be so mistaken.

SIR ANTHONY. Hang your respect and duty! But come along with me, I'll write a note to Mrs. Malaprop, and you shall visit the lady directly. Her eyes shall be the Promethean torch to you—come along, I'll never forgive you, if you don't come back stark mad with rapture and impatience —if you don't, egad, I will marry the girl myself! *(Exeunt)*

## Sheridan, *The Rivals*

### Note

*The comic power of the two scenes depends on our conventional acceptance of certain values regarding the relationship between parents and children, more specifically on our expectation that certain moral attributes will inevitably govern it: self-control, good judgment, protectiveness, devotion on the one hand; exuberance, ingenuousness, humility, and unquestioning respect on the other. With the emphasis on words rather than action Sheridan uses certain comic devices (reversal, exaggeration, contradiction, anticlimax) to present us with the following, essentially serious, moral problems:*

*1. The frequency with which the ideal family relationship is betrayed in real life by both the parent and the child.*

*2. The existence of a genuine difference in the aims, roles, and assumptions of the two generations (note in the two scenes the successive attempts of each generation to manipulate the other).*

## QUESTIONS

1. In Act II, Scene 1, what reversal of the standards mentioned above does Sheridan suggest through Sir Anthony Absolute's (note the name) cryptic comment: "the fortune is saddled with a wife"? What other words and phrases in the exchanges that follow further illustrate Sir Anthony's values (as, for example, "Let her foreclose, Jack")?

2. What view of Sir Anthony's parental role does Sheridan give us in Act II, Scene 1, by using (a) exaggeration, (b) contradiction, (c) anticlimax, (d) irony? How does Sir Anthony (through Sheridan's comic treatment of him) violate the conventions of parental attributes referred to above?
   *Clues:* • not one word! so give me your promise by a nod—
   • get an atmosphere and sun of your own!

3. In Act III, Scene 1, a significant exchange of roles takes place: the victim-child turns against the tyrant-parent the very arguments at first used against him.

How does Jack's adoption of the world-wise role identified with the older generation and his father's adoption of supposedly youthful attitudes serve as an attack on the parent generation? What specific vices of that generation are uncovered here?

Clues: • . . . though one eye may be very agreeable, yet as the prejudice has always run in favour of two, I would not wish to affect a singularity in that article.

• I'll never forgive you, if you ha'n't been lying and playing the hypocrite.

4. Which of the vices suggested above is Jack himself guilty of? What depth does his fallibility give to Sheridan's conception of the generation gap?

Clues: • Mild, gentle, considerate father—I kiss your hands!— (II, 1)

• I am come, Sir, to acknowledge my error, and to submit entirely to your will. (III, 1)

Why do we both condone and enjoy Jack's failings?

5. How in Act III, Scene 1, does Sir Anthony's relish of Lydia's youth and beauty suggest that it is his *role* in life rather than his emotional inclinations that leads him to preach expediency to his son? (Note that in Act II we have been told that Sir Anthony "married himself for love!") What long-range view of the generation gap, suggested by the importance of role-playing, is dramatized in this scene?

## EXERCISE

Focusing on Act I, Scene 2, of *The Rivals*, compare and contrast the relationship between Mrs. Malaprop and Lydia with that of Sir Anthony and Captain Absolute. Observe the comic devices used in this scene to reveal aspects of the generation gap and determine how they resemble or differ from those in the preceding texts. Suggest whether the difference in the sexes affects the nature of the generation gap.

*Samuel Johnson (1709–1784)*

# Rasselas

*The following selection is from Johnson's fictitious biography of a young "Abyssinian" prince whose name gives the book its title. Rasselas lives in the Happy Valley, but it is a perplexing place since its inhabitants are forced to remain there (under penalty of death). Rasselas, his sister Nekayah, and two followers manage to escape and begin their quest for a "choice of life": they want to discover how to live. Their search brings them into contact with a wide range of people, vocations, and circumstances. In the following chapter the princess Nekayah reports to her brother her experiences of family life in many households.*

## CHAPTER XXVI

### THE PRINCESS CONTINUES HER REMARKS UPON PRIVATE LIFE

Nekayah, perceiving her brother's attention fixed, proceeded in her narrative.

"In families where there is or is not poverty, there is commonly discord. If a kingdom be, as Imlac tells us, a great family, a family likewise is a little kingdom, torn with factions and exposed to revolutions. An unpractised observer expects the love of parents and children to be constant and equal; but this kindness seldom continues beyond the years of infancy: in a short time the children become rivals to their parents. Benefits are allayed by reproaches, and gratitude debased by envy.

"Parents and children seldom act in concert; each child endeavours to appropriate the esteem or fondness of the parents, and the parents, with yet less temptation, betray each other to their children. Thus, some place their confidence in the father, and some in the mother, and by degrees the house is filled with artifices and feuds.

"The opinions of children and parents, of the young and the old, are naturally opposite, by the contrary effects of hope and despondence, of expectation and experience, without crime or folly on either side. The colours of life in youth and age appear different, as the face of nature in spring and winter. And how can children credit the assertions of parents, which their own eyes show them to be false?

"Few parents act in such a manner as much to enforce their maxims by the credit of their lives. The old man trusts wholly to slow contrivance[1] and gradual progression; the youth expects to force his way by genius,[2] vigour, and precipitance.[3] The old man pays regard to riches, and the youth reverences virtue. The old man deifies prudence; the youth commits himself to magnanimity and chance. The young man, who intends no ill, believes that none is intended, and therefore acts with openness and candour; but his father, having suffered the injuries of fraud, is impelled to suspect, and too often allured to practise it. Age looks with anger on the temerity of youth, and youth with contempt on the scrupulosity of age. Thus parents and children, for the greatest part, live on to love less and less; and, if those whom nature has thus closely united are the torments of each other, where shall we look for tenderness and consolation?"

"Surely," said the prince, "you must have been unfortunate in your choice of acquaintance: I am unwilling to believe that the most tender of all relations is thus impeded in its effects by natural necessity."

"Domestic discord," answered she, "is not inevitably and fatally necessary, but yet is not easily avoided. We seldom see that a whole family is virtuous; the good and evil cannot well agree, and the evil can yet less agree with one another. Even the virtuous fall sometimes to variance,[4] when their

---

[1] *slow contrivance:* careful planning.  [2] *genius:* native ability.  [3] *precipitance:* impetuousness.
[4] *variance:* dissension.

virtues are of different kinds, and tending to extremes. In general, those parents have most reverence who most deserve it; for he that lives well cannot be despised.

"Many other evils infest private life. Some are the slaves of servants whom they have trusted with their affairs. Some are kept in continual anxiety to the caprice of rich relations, whom they cannot please, and dare not offend. Some husbands are imperious, and some wives perverse; and, as it is always more easy to do evil than good, though the wisdom or virtue of one can very rarely make many happy, the folly or vice of one man often make many miserable."

"If such be the general effect of marriage," said the prince, "I shall for the future think it dangerous to connect my interest with that of another, lest I should be unhappy by my partner's fault."

"I have met," said the princess, "with many who live single for that reason; but I never found that their prudence ought to raise envy. They dream away their time without friendship, without fondness, and are driven to rid themselves of the day, for which they have no use, by childish amusements, or vicious delights. They act as beings under the constant sense of some known inferiority, that fills their minds with rancour, and their tongues with censure. They are peevish at home, and malevolent abroad; and, as the outlaws of human nature, make it their business and their pleasure to disturb that society which debars them from its privileges. To live without feeling or exciting sympathy, to be fortunate without adding to the felicity of others, or afflicted without tasting the balm of pity, is a state more gloomy than solitude; it is not retreat but exclusion from mankind. Marriage has many pains, but celibacy has no pleasures."

"What then is to be done?" said Rasselas; "the more we inquire, the less we can resolve. Surely he is most likely to please himself that has no other inclination to regard."


## QUESTIONS: *Johnson, Rasselas*

1.  Johnson's style, like Bacon's, is rich in *antithesis* (or balancing of a word or clause with another for purposes of contrast). How do Johnson's antitheses differ from Bacon's in scope and feeling? Justify your answer.

    *Clues:*  • Bacon: Children sweeten labours, but they make misfortunes more bitter. They increase the cares of life, but they mitigate the remembrance of death. The perpetuity by generation is common to beasts, but memory, merit, and noble works are proper to men.

    • Johnson: The old man pays regard to riches, and the youth reverences virtue. The old man deifies prudence; the youth commits himself to magnanimity and chance. . . . Age looks with anger on the temerity of youth, and youth with contempt on the scrupulosity of age.

2. Johnson's view of the "private life" places considerable emphasis on its bleaker aspects (for example, "a family . . . is a little kingdom, torn with factions and exposed to revolutions"). Does he show any sense of the more satisfying aspects of private life?

3. What in Johnson's estimation are the sources of domestic friction and personal discomfort?

## EXERCISE

Looking upon Bacon's and Johnson's respective reflections as signs of their personalities, attempt an imaginative portrait of either Bacon or Johnson.

## *John Stuart Mill (1806–1873)*

# Autobiography

## CHAPTER II

*In Chapter I, Mill describes his unusual education under the exclusive and very personal supervision of his father ("I have no remembrance of the time when I began to learn Greek, I have been told that it was when I was three years old . . . I learnt no Latin until my eighth year") which had allowed him by the age of seven a substantial acquaintance with Herodotus, Xenophon, and Plato. While much of Chapter I describes the course of study he undertook, and his reactions to it, it contains some more personal comments on his teacher in which both the strengths and the limitations of his father's method are suggested—very often through the author's choice of words. Mill's characteristic mode of expression seems, on the surface, to be wholly controlled and logical. But a careful reading reveals emotional ambiguities of which the author may not have been fully aware.*

*The following passage from Chapter I is an appropriate preparation for the reading of Chapter II. The italicized words are clues to some of Mill's feelings:*

[My father] was *often*, and *much beyond reason*, provoked by my failures in cases where success *could not have been expected*; but *in the main* his method was right, and it succeeded. . . . Striving, *even in an exaggerated degree*, to call forth the activity of my faculties, by making me find out everything for myself, he gave me his explanations not before, but after, I had felt *the full force of the difficulties*. . . .

## Moral Influences in Early Youth. My Father's Character and Opinions.

In my education, as in that of everyone, the moral influences, which are so much more important than all others, are also the most complicated, and the most difficult to specify with any approach to completeness. Without attempting the hopeless task of detailing the circumstances by which, in this respect, my early character may have been shaped, I shall confine myself to a few leading points, which form an indispensable part of any true account of my education.

I was brought up from the first without any religious belief, in the ordinary acceptation of the term. My father, educated in the creed of Scotch presbyterianism, had by his own studies and reflections been early led to reject not only the belief in revelation, but the foundations of what is commonly called Natural Religion. I have heard him say, that the turning point of his mind on the subject was reading Butler's Analogy. That work, of which he always continued to speak with respect, kept him, as he said, for some considerable time, a believer in the divine authority of Christianity; by proving to him, that whatever are the difficulties in believing that the Old and New Testaments proceed from, or record the acts of, a perfectly wise and good being, the same and still greater difficulties stand in the way of the belief, that a being of such a character can have been the Maker of the universe. He considered Butler's argument as conclusive against the only opponents for whom it was intended. Those who admit an omnipotent as well as perfectly just and benevolent maker and ruler of such a world as this, can say little against Christianity but what can, with at least equal force, be retorted against themselves. Finding, therefore, no halting place in Deism, he remained in a state of perplexity, until, doubtless after many struggles, he yielded to the conviction, that, concerning the origin of things nothing whatever can be known. This is the only correct statement of his opinion; for dogmatic atheism he looked upon as absurd; as most of those, whom the world has considered Atheists, have always done. These particulars are important, because they show that my father's rejection of all that is called religious belief, was not, as many might suppose, primarily a matter of logic and evidence: the grounds of it were moral, still more than intellectual. He found it impossible to believe that a world so full of evil was the work of an Author combining infinite power with perfect goodness and righteousness. His intellect spurned the subtleties by which men attempt to blind themselves to this open contradiction. The Sabæan, or Manichæan theory of a Good and Evil Principle, struggling against each other for the government of the universe, he would not have equally condemned; and I have heard him express surprise, that no one revived it in our time. He would have regarded it as a mere hypothesis; but he would have ascribed to it no depraving influence. As it was, his aversion to religion, in the sense usually attached to the term, was of the same kind with that of Lucretius: he regarded it with the feelings due not to a mere mental delusion, but to a great moral evil. He looked upon it as the greatest enemy of morality: first, by setting up factitious excellencies,—belief in creeds, devotional feelings, and ceremonies, not connected with the good of human kind,—and causing these to be accepted as substitutes for genuine virtues: but above all, by radically vitiating the standard of morals; making it consist in doing the will of a being, on whom it lavishes indeed all the phrases of adulation, but whom in sober truth it depicts as eminently hateful. I have a hundred times heard him say, that all ages and nations have represented their gods as wicked, in a constantly increasing progression, that mankind have gone on adding trait after trait till they reached the most perfect conception of wickedness which the human mind can devise, and have called this God, and prostrated themselves before it. This *ne plus ultra* of wickedness he considered to be embodied in what is commonly presented to mankind as the creed of Christianity. Think (he used to say) of a being who would make a Hell—who would create the human race with the infallible foreknowledge, and therefore with the intention, that the great majority of them were to be consigned to horrible and everlasting torment. The time, I believe, is drawing near when this dreadful conception of an object of worship will be no longer identified with Christianity; and when all persons, with any sense of moral good and evil, will look upon it with the same indignation with which my father regarded it. My father was as well aware as anyone that Christians do not, in general, undergo the demoralizing consequences which seem inherent in such a creed, in the manner or to the extent which might have been expected from it. The same slovenliness of thought, and subjection of the reason to fears, wishes, and affections, which enable them to accept a theory involving a contradiction in terms, prevents them from perceiving the logical consequences of the theory. Such is the facility with which mankind believe at one and the same time things inconsistent with one another, and so few are those who draw from what they receive as truths, any consequences but those recommended to them by their feelings, that multitudes have held the undoubting belief in an Omnipotent Author of Hell, and have nevertheless identified that being with the best conception they were able to form of perfect goodness. Their worship was not paid to the demon which such a being as they imagined would really be, but to their own idea of excellence. The evil is, that such a belief keeps the ideal wretchedly low; and opposes the most obstinate resistance to all thought which has a tendency to raise it higher. Believers shrink from every train of ideas which would lead the mind to a clear conception and an elevated standard of excellence, because they feel (even when they do not distinctly see) that such a standard would conflict with many of the dispensations of nature, and with much of what they are accustomed to consider as the Christian creed. And thus morality continues a matter of blind tradition, with no consistent principle, nor even any consistent feeling, to guide it.

It would have been wholly inconsistent with my father's ideas of duty, to allow me to acquire impressions contrary to his convictions and feelings respecting religion: and he impressed upon me from the first, that the manner in which the world came into existence was a subject on which nothing was known: that the question, "Who made me?" cannot be answered, because we have no experience or authentic information from which to answer it; and that any answer only throws the difficulty a step further back, since the question immediately presents itself, Who made God? He, at the same time, took care that I should be acquainted with what had been thought by mankind on these impenetrable problems. I have mentioned at how early an age he made me a reader of ecclesiastical history; and he taught me to take the strongest interest in the Reformation, as the great and decisive contest against priestly tyranny for liberty of thought.

I am thus one of the very few examples, in this country, of one who has, not thrown off religious belief, but never had it: I grew up in a negative state with regard to it. I looked upon the modern exactly as I did upon the ancient religion, as something which in no way concerned me. It did not seem to me more strange that English people should believe what I did not, than that the men I read of in Herodotus should have done so. History had made the variety of opinions among mankind a fact familiar to me, and this was but a prolongation of that fact. This point in my early education had, however, incidentally one bad consequence deserving notice. In giving me an opinion contrary to that of the world, my father thought it necessary to give it as one which could not prudently be avowed to the world. This lesson of keeping my thoughts to myself, at that early age, was attended with some moral disadvantages; though my limited intercourse with strangers, especially such as were likely to speak to me on religion, prevented me from being placed in the alternative of avowal or hypocrisy. I remember two occasions in my boyhood, on which I felt myself in this alternative, and in both cases I avowed my disbelief and defended it. My opponents were boys, considerably older than myself: one of them I certainly staggered at the time, but the subject was never renewed between us: the other who was surprised, and somewhat shocked, did his best to convince me for some time, without effect.

The great advance in liberty of discussion, which is one of the most important differences between the present time and that of my childhood, has greatly altered the moralities of this question; and I think that few men of my father's intellect and public spirit, holding with such intensity of moral conviction as he did, unpopular opinions on religion, or on any other of the great subjects of thought, would now either practise or inculcate the withholding of them from the world, unless in the cases, becoming fewer every day, in which frankness on these subjects would either risk the loss of means of subsistence, or would amount to exclusion from some sphere of usefulness peculiarly suitable to the capacities of the individual. On religion in particular the time appears to me to have come, when it is the duty of all who being qualified in point of knowledge, have on mature consideration satisfied themselves that the current opinions are not only false but hurtful, to make their dissent known; at least, if they are among those whose station or reputation, gives their opinion a chance of being attended to. Such an avowal would put an end, at once and for ever, to the vulgar prejudice, that what is called, very improperly, unbelief, is connected with any bad qualities either of mind or heart. The world would be astonished if it knew how great a proportion of its brightest ornaments—of those most distinguished even in popular estimation for wisdom and virtue—are complete sceptics in religion; many of them refraining from avowal, less from personal considerations, than from a conscientious, though now in my opinion a most mistaken apprehension, lest by speaking out what would tend to weaken existing beliefs, and by consequence (as they suppose) existing restraints, they should do harm instead of good.

Of unbelievers (so called) as well as of believers, there are many species, including almost every variety of moral type. But the best among them, as no one who has had opportunities of really knowing them will hesitate to affirm (believers rarely have that opportunity), are more genuinely religious, in the best sense of the word religion, than those who exclusively arrogate to themselves the title. The liberality of the age, or in other words the weakening of the obstinate prejudice which makes men unable to see what is before their eyes because it is contrary to their expectations, has caused it to be very commonly admitted that a Deist may be truly religious: but if religion stands for any graces of character and not for mere dogma, the assertion may equally be made of many whose belief is far short of Deism. Though they may think the proof incomplete that the universe is a work of design, and though they assuredly disbelieve that it can have an Author and Governor who is absolute in power as well as perfect in goodness, they have that which constitutes the principal worth of all religions whatever, an ideal conception of a Perfect Being, to which they habitually refer as the guide of their conscience; and this ideal of Good is usually far nearer to perfection than the objective Deity of those, who think themselves obliged to find absolute goodness in the author of a world so crowded with suffering and so deformed by injustice as ours.

My father's moral convictions, wholly dissevered from religion, were very much of the character of those of the Greek philosophers; and were delivered with the force and decision which characterized all that came from him. Even at the very early age at which I read with him the Memorabilia of Xenophon, I imbibed from that work and from his comments a deep respect for the character of Socrates; who stood in my mind as a model of ideal excellence: and I well remember how my father at that time impressed upon me the lesson of the "Choice of Hercules." At a somewhat later period the lofty moral standard exhibited in the writings of Plato operated upon me with great force. My father's moral inculcations were at all times mainly those of the "Socratici viri;" justice, temperance (to which he gave a very extended application), veracity, perseverance, readiness to encounter pain and especially labour; regard for the public good; estimation of persons according to their merits, and of things according to their intrinsic usefulness; a life of exertion in contradiction to one of self-indulgent sloth. These and other moralities he conveyed in brief sentences, uttered as occasion arose, of grave exhortation, or stern reprobation and contempt.

But though direct moral teaching does much, indirect does more; and the effect my father produced on my character, did not depend solely on what he said or did with that direct object, but also, and still more, on what manner of man he was.

In his views of life he partook of the character of the Stoic, the Epicurean, and the Cynic, not in the modern but the ancient sense of the word. In his personal qualities the Stoic predominated. His standard of morals was Epicurean, inasmuch as it was utilitarian, taking as the exclusive test of right and wrong, the tendency of actions to produce pleasure or pain. But he had (and this was the Cynic element) scarcely any belief in pleasure; at least in his later years, of which alone, on this point, I can speak confidently. He was not insensible to pleasures; but he deemed very few of them worth the price which, at least in the present state of society, must be paid for them. The greater number of miscarriages in life, he considered to be attributable to the overvaluing of pleasures. Accordingly, temperance, in the large sense intended by the Greek philosophers—stopping short at the point of moderation in all indulgences—was with him, as with them, almost the central point of educational precept. His inculcations of this virtue fill a large place in my childish remembrances. He thought human life a poor thing at best, after the freshness of youth and of unsatisfied curiosity had gone by. This was a topic on which he did not often speak, especially, it may be supposed, in the presence of young persons: but when he did, it was with an air of settled and profound conviction. He would sometimes say, that if life were made what it might be, by good government and good education, it would be worth having: but he never spoke with anything like enthusiasm even of that possibility. He never varied in rating intellectual enjoyments above all others, even in value as pleasures, independently of their ulterior benefits. The pleasures of the benevolent affections he placed high in the scale; and used to say, that he had never known a happy old man, except those who were able to live over again in the pleasures of the young. For passionate emotions of all sorts, and for everything which has been said or written in exaltation of them, he professed the greatest contempt. He regarded them as a form of madness. "The intense" was with him a bye-word of scornful disapprobation. He regarded as an aberration of the moral standard of modern times, compared with that of the ancients, the great stress laid upon feeling. Feelings, as such, he considered to be no proper subjects of praise or blame. Right and wrong, good and bad, he regarded as qualities solely of conduct—of acts and omissions; there being no feeling which may not lead, and does not frequently lead, either to good or to bad actions: conscience itself, the very desire to act right, often leading people to act wrong. Consistently carrying out the doctrine, that the object of praise and blame should be the discouragement of wrong conduct and the encouragement of right, he refused to let his praise or blame be influenced by the motive of the agent. He blamed as severely what he thought a bad action, when the motive was a feeling of duty, as if the agents had been consciously evil doers. He would not have accepted as a plea in mitigation for inquisitors, that they sincerely believed burning heretics to be an obligation of conscience. But though he did not allow honesty of purpose to soften his disapprobation of actions, it had its full effect on his estimation of characters. No one prized conscientiousness and rectitude of intention more highly, or was more incapable of valuing any person in whom he did not feel assurance of it. But he disliked people quite as much for any other deficiency, provided he thought it equally likely to make them act ill. He disliked, for instance, a fanatic in any bad cause, as much or more than one who adopted the same cause from self-interest, because he thought him even more likely to be practically mischievous. And thus, his aversion to many intellectual errors, or what he regarded as such, partook, in a certain sense, of the character of a moral feeling. All this is merely saying that he, in a degree once common, but now very unusual, threw his feelings into his opinions; which truly it is difficult to understand how any one who possesses much of both, can fail to do. None but those who do not care about opinions, will confound it with intolerance. Those, who having opinions which they hold to be immensely important, and their contraries to be prodigiously hurtful, have any deep regard for the general good, will necessarily dislike, as a class and in the abstract, those who think wrong what they think right, and right what they think wrong: though they need not therefore be, nor was my father, insensible to good qualities in an opponent, nor governed in their estimation of individuals by one general presumption, instead of by the whole of their character. I grant that an earnest person, being no more infallible than other men, is liable to dislike people on account of opinions which do not merit dislike; but if he neither himself does them any ill office, nor connives at its being done by others, he is not intolerant: and the forbearance which flows from a conscientious sense of the importance to mankind of the equal freedom of all opinions, is the only tolerance which is commendable, or, to the highest moral order of minds, possible.

It will be admitted, that a man of the opinions, and the character, above described, was likely to leave a strong moral impression on any mind principally formed by him, and that his moral teaching was not likely to err on the side of laxity or indulgence. The element which was chiefly deficient in his moral relation to his children was that of tenderness. I do not believe that this deficiency lay in his own nature. I believe him to have had much more feeling than he habitually showed, and much greater capacities of feeling than were ever developed. He resembled most Englishmen in being ashamed of the signs of feeling, and by the absence of demonstration, starving the feelings themselves. If we consider further that he was in the trying position of sole teacher, and add to this that his temper was constitutionally irritable, it is impossible not to feel true pity for a father who did, and strove to do, so much for his children, who would have so valued their affection, yet who must have been constantly feeling that fear of him was drying it up at its source. This was no longer the case later in life, and with his younger children. They loved him tenderly: and if I cannot say so much of myself, I was always loyally devoted to him. As regards my own education, I hesitate to pronounce whether I was more a loser or gainer by his severity. It was not such as to prevent me from having a happy childhood. And I do not believe that boys can be induced to apply themselves with vigour, and what is so much more difficult, perseverance, to dry and irksome studies, by the sole force of persuasion and soft words. Much must be done, and much must be learnt, by children, for which rigid discipline, and known liability to punishment, are indispensable as means. It is, no doubt, a very laudable effort, in modern teaching, to render as much as possible of what the young are required to learn, easy and interesting to them. But when this principle is pushed to the length of not requiring them to learn anything *but* what has been made easy and interesting, one of the chief objects of education is sacrificed. I rejoice in the decline of the old brutal and tyrannical system of teaching, which, however, did succeed in enforcing habits of application; but the new, as it seems to me, is training up a race of men who will be incapable of doing anything which is disagreeable to them. I do not, then, believe that fear, as an element in education, can be dispensed with; but I am sure that it ought not to be the main element; and when it predominates so much as to preclude love and confidence on the part of the child to those who should be the unreservedly trusted advisers of after years, and perhaps to seal up the fountains of frank and spontaneous communicativeness in the child's nature, it is an evil for which a large abatement must be made from the benefits, moral and intellectual, which may flow from any other part of the education.

During this first period of my life, the habitual frequenters of my father's house were limited to a very few persons, most of them little known to the world, but whom personal worth, and more or less of congeniality with at least his political opinions (not so frequently to be met with then as since) inclined him to cultivate; and his conversations with them I listened to with interest and instruction. My being an habitual inmate of my father's study made me acquainted with the dearest of his friends, David Ricardo, who by his benevolent countenance, and kindliness of manner, was very attractive to young persons, and who after I became a student of political economy, invited me to his house and to walk with him in order to converse on the subject. I was a more frequent visitor (from about 1817 or 1818) to Mr. Hume, who, born in the same part of Scotland as my father, and having been, I rather think, a younger schoolfellow or college companion of his, had on returning from India renewed their youthful acquaintance, and who coming like many others greatly under the influence of my father's intellect and energy of character, was induced partly by that influence to go into Parliament, and there adopt the line of conduct which has given him an honourable place in the history of his country. Of Mr. Bentham I saw much more, owing to the close intimacy which existed between him and my father. I do not know how soon after my father's first arrival in England they became acquainted. But my father was the earliest Englishman of any great mark who thoroughly understood, and in the main adopted, Bentham's general views of ethics, government and law: and this was a natural foundation for sympathy between them, and made them familiar companions in a period of Bentham's life during which he admitted much fewer visitors than was the case subsequently. At this time Mr. Bentham passed some part of every year at Barrow Green House, in a beautiful part of the Surrey hills, a few miles from Godstone, and there I each summer accompanied my father in a long visit. In 1813, Mr. Bentham, my father, and I made an excursion, which included Oxford, Bath and Bristol, Exeter, Plymouth, and Portsmouth. In this journey I saw many things which were instructive to me, and acquired my first taste for natural scenery, in the elementary form of fondness for a "view." In the succeeding winter we moved into a house very near Mr. Bentham's, which my father rented from him, in Queen Square, Westminster. From 1814 to 1817 Mr. Bentham lived during half of each year at Ford Abbey, in Somersetshire (or rather in a part of Devonshire surrounded by Somersetshire), which intervals I had the advantage of passing at that place. This sojourn was, I think, an important circumstance in my education. Nothing contributes more to nourish elevation of sentiments in a people, than the large and free character of their habitations. The middle-age architecture, the baronial hall, and the spacious and lofty rooms, of this fine old place, so unlike the mean and cramped externals of English middle class life, gave the sentiment of a large and freer existence, and were to me a sort of poetic cultivation, aided also by the character of the grounds in which the Abbey stood; which were riant and secluded, umbrageous, and full of the sound of falling waters.

I owed another of the fortunate circumstances in my education, a year's residence in France, to Mr. Bentham's brother, General Sir Samuel Bentham. I had seen Sir Samuel Bentham and his family at their house near Gosport in the course of the tour already mentioned (he being then Superintendent of the Dockyard at Portsmouth), and during a stay of a few days which they made at Ford Abbey shortly after the peace, before going to live on the Continent. In 1820 they invited me for a six months' visit to them in the South of France, which their kindness ultimately prolonged to nearly a twelvemonth. Sir Samuel Bentham, though of a character of mind different from that of his illustrious brother, was a man of very considerable attainments and general powers, with a decided genius for mechanical art. His wife, a daughter of the celebrated chemist, Dr. Fordyce, was a woman of strong will and decided character, much general knowledge, and great practical good sense of the Edgeworth kind: she was the ruling spirit of the household, as she deserved, and was well qualified, to be. Their family consisted of one son (the eminent botanist) and three daughters, the youngest about two years my senior. I am indebted to them for much and various instruction, and for an almost parental interest in my welfare. When I first joined them, in May 1820, they occupied the Château of Pompignan (still belonging to a descendant of Voltaire's enemy) on the heights overlooking the plain of the Garonne between Montauban and Toulouse. I accompanied them in an excursion to the Pyrenees, including a stay of some duration at Bagnères de Bigorre, a journey to Pau, Bayonne, and Bagnères de Luchon, and an ascent of the Pic du Midi de Bigorre.

This first introduction to the highest order of mountain scenery made the deepest impression on me, and gave a colour to my tastes through life. In October we proceeded by the beautiful mountain route of Castres and St. Pons, from Toulouse to Montpellier, in which last neighbourhood Sir Samuel had just bought the estate of Restinclière, near the foot of the singular mountain of St. Loup. During this residence in France I acquired a familiar knowledge of the French language, and acquaintance with the ordinary French literature; I took lessons in various bodily exercises, in none of which however I made any proficiency; and at Montpellier I attended the excellent winter courses of lectures at the Faculté des Sciences, those of M. Anglada on chemistry, of M. Provençal on zoology, and of a very accomplished representative of the eighteenth century metaphysics, M. Gergonne, on logic, under the name of Philosophy of the Sciences. I also went through a course of the higher mathematics under the private tuition of M. Lenthéric, a professor at the Lycée of Montpellier. But the greatest, perhaps, of the many advantages which I owed to this episode in my education, was that of having breathed for a whole year, the free and genial atmosphere of Continental life. This advantage was not the less real though I could not then estimate, nor even consciously feel it. Having so little experience of English life, and the few people I knew being mostly such as had public objects, of a large and personally disinterested kind, at heart, I was ignorant of the low moral tone of what, in England, is called society; the habit of, not indeed professing, but taking for granted in every mode of implication, that conduct is of course always directed towards low and petty objects; the absence of high feelings which manifests itself by sneering depreciation of all demonstrations of them, and by general abstinence (except among a few of the stricter religionists) from professing any high principles of action at all, except in those preordained cases in which such profession is put on as part of the costume and formalities of the occasion. I could not then know or estimate the difference between this manner of existence, and that of a people like the French, whose faults, if equally real, are at all events different; among whom sentiments, which by comparison at least may be called elevated, are the current coin of human intercourse, both in books and in private life; and though often evaporating in profession, are yet kept alive in the nation at large by constant exercise, and stimulated by sympathy, so as to form a living and active part of the existence of great numbers of persons, and to be recognized and understood by all. Neither could I then appreciate the general culture of the understanding, which results from the habitual exercise of the feelings, and is thus carried down into the most uneducated classes of several countries on the Continent, in a degree not equalled in England among the so-called educated, except where an unusual tenderness of conscience leads to a habitual exercise of the intellect on questions of right and wrong. I did not know the way in which, among the ordinary English, the absence of interest in things of an unselfish kind, except occasionally in a special thing here and there, and the habit of not speaking to others, nor much even to themselves, about the things in which they do feel interest, causes both their feelings and their intellectual faculties to remain undeveloped, or to develope themselves only in some single and very limited direction; reducing them, considered as spiritual beings, to a kind of negative existence. All these things I did not perceive till long afterwards; but I even then felt, though without stating it clearly to myself, the contrast between the frank sociability and amiability of French personal intercourse, and the English mode of existence in which everybody acts as if everybody else (with few, or no exceptions) was either an enemy or a bore. In France, it is true, the bad as well as the good points, both of individual and of national character, come more to the surface, and break out more fearlessly in ordinary inter-course, than in England: but the general habit of the people is to show, as well as to expect, friendly feeling in every one towards every other, wherever there is not some positive cause for the opposite. In England it is only of the best bred people, in the upper or upper middle ranks, that anything like this can be said.

In my way through Paris, both going and returning, I passed some time in the house of M. Say, the eminent political economist, who was a friend and correspondent of my father, having become acquainted with him on a visit to England a year or two after the peace. He was a man of the later period of the French Revolution, a fine specimen of the best kind of French Republican, one of those who had never bent the knee to Bonaparte though courted by him to do so; a truly upright, brave, and enlightened man. He lived a quiet and studious life, made happy by warm affections, public and private. He was acquainted with many of the chiefs of the Liberal party, and I saw various noteworthy persons while staying at his house; among whom I have pleasure in the recollection of having once seen Saint-Simon, not yet the founder either of a philosophy or a religion, and considered only as a clever *original*. The chief fruit which I carried away from the society I saw, was a strong and permanent interest in Continental Liberalism, of which I ever afterwards kept myself *au courant*, as much as of English politics: a thing not at all usual in those days with Englishmen, and which had a very salutary influence on my development, keeping me free from the error always prevalent in England, and from which even my father with all his superiority to prejudice was not exempt, of judging universal questions by a merely English standard. After passing a few weeks at Caen with an old friend of my father's, I returned to England in July 1821; and my education resumed its ordinary course.

## QUESTIONS: *Mill, Autobiography*

1. Mill had an *agnostic* upbringing. (A literal translation of the Greek root of *agnostic* would be "don't know.") Agnosticism maintains that the nature of God and the divine world, like that of anything else that cannot be seen or measured, is simply unknowable and unprovable. In your opinion, did Mill's upbringing spare him any of the spiritual and personal conflicts endured by children whose parents try to provide them with definite and affirmative beliefs?

2. Read carefully the third paragraph, beginning "It would have been wholly inconsistent . . ." How are the ambiguities in this paragraph similar to those discussed in the introduction to the selection? What do they reveal about Mill's feelings toward the moral upbringing his father gave him? What do they imply about one generation's conception of what it owes to another?

3. Mill declares that his early education in the matter of religion had "one bad consequence": "In giving me an opinion contrary to that of the world, my father thought it necessary to give it as one which could not prudently be avowed to the world." What moral options were thus left for Mill? What option did he choose? How does this choice prepare us for his ultimate attitude toward the "avowal" of religious disbelief? (See the fifth paragraph, beginning "The great advance in liberty of discussion . . .")

4. Compare Mill's discussion of his moral and religious upbringing with the common complaint that where ethical and theological principles are concerned parents don't practice what they preach.

5. At the age of 20, Mill underwent what he calls "a crisis in my mental history," a profound nervous disturbance triggered by his realization that his father's most cherished ideas could not move him emotionally. He felt then that even if his father could somehow be brought to understand what was ailing his son, "he was not the physician who could heal it." And Mill writes in Chapter V:

> All those to whom I *looked up*, were of *opinion* that the pleasure of sympathy with human beings, and the feelings which made the good of others, and especially of mankind *on a large scale*, the object of existence, were the greatest and surest sources of happiness. Of the truth of this I was convinced, but to *know* that a feeling would make me happy if I had it, *did not give me the feeling*. My education, I thought, had failed to create these *feelings* in sufficient strength to resist the dissolving influence of *analysis*, while the whole course of my intellectual cultivation had made precocious and premature analysis the inveterate *habit* of my mind. I was thus, as I said to myself, left stranded at the commencement of my voyage, with a well-equipped ship and a rudder, but no sail; without any real *desire* for the ends which I had been so carefully fitted out to work for: no *delight* in virtue, or the *general good*, but also just as little in anything else. . . . I had had . . . some gratification of vanity at too early an age . . . little as it was which I had attained, yet having been attained too early . . . it had made me *blasé* and indifferent to the pursuit. Thus neither *selfish* nor

*unselfish* pleasures were pleasures to me. And there seemed no power in nature sufficient to begin the formation of my character anew, and create in a mind now irretrievably analytic, *fresh* associations of *pleasure* with any of the objects of *human desire*. [Editors' italics].

In the chapter you have read, what aspects of the temperament and the teachings of the elder Mill shed light on his son's later "crisis"?

*Clues:* • The greater number of miscarriages in life, he considered to be attributable to the overvaluing of pleasures.

• He thought human life a *poor thing at best*, after the freshness of youth and of unsatisfied curiosity had gone by.

• "The intense" was with him a bye-word of *scornful* disapprobation.

• It will be admitted . . . that his teaching *was not likely to err* on the side of laxity or indulgence.

6. How does the later part of Chapter II, which introduces some of James Mill's friends and praises French life, suggest the limitations in John Stuart Mill's upbringing?

*Clues:* • . . . the dearest of his friends, David Ricardo, who by his *benevolent countenance*, and *kindliness of manner*, was *very attractive* to *young* persons . . .

• . . . the *free* and *genial* atmosphere of Continental life.

• . . . a people like the French . . . among whom *sentiments* . . . are the *current coin* of human intercourse, both in books and in private life . . .

7. What were the virtues that Mill saw in his upbringing? Do any of the attributes he praises suggest that he is, in the last analysis, his father's child?

## EXERCISE

Justify or refute the following statement: "A present-day 'Crisis in the Mental History' of a thoughtful and sensitive person is likely to be produced by an upbringing diametrically opposed to that of Mill, one which stresses an *emotional* rather than an analytic approach to learning and to life."

## Samuel Butler (1835–1902)
# The Way of All Flesh

### CHAPTERS 40–41

*The action immediately preceding Chapter 40 is the dismissal of a servant (because she is pregnant) from the household of Theobald and Christina Pontifex. Their adolescent son, Ernest, is outraged that the girl, of whom he is very fond—and of whose plight he is innocent—has been thrown out with almost no money and no prospects. He also knows " that she had said she should hang or drown herself, which the boy implicitly believed she would." He runs after the carriage and gives Ellen not only his knife and pocket money but also the watch he inherited from his aunt. Consider these three paragraphs in Chapter 39:*

In the first place he should be late for dinner—and this was one of the offences on which Theobald had no mercy. Also he should have to say where he had been, and there was danger of being found out if he did not speak the truth. Not only this, but sooner or later it must come out that he was no longer possessed of the beautiful watch which his dear aunt had given him—and what, pray, had he done with it? Or how had he lost it? The reader will know very well what he ought to have done. He should have gone straight home, and if questioned should have said, " I have been running after the carriage to catch our housemaid Ellen, whom I am very fond of; I have given her my watch, my knife and all my pocket money, so that I have now no pocket money at all and shall probably ask you for some more sooner than I otherwise might have done, and you will also have to buy me a new watch, and a knife." But then fancy the consternation which such an announcement would have occasioned. Fancy the scowl, and flashing eyes of the infuriate Theobald, "You unprincipled young scoundrel," he would exclaim, "do you mean to vilify your own parents, by implying that they have dealt harshly by one whose profligacy has disgraced their house?"

Or he might take it with one of those sallies of sarcastic calm, of which he believed himself to be a master. "Very well, Ernest, very well; I shall say nothing; you can please yourself; you are not yet twenty-one, but pray act as if you were your own master; your poor aunt doubtless gave you the watch that you might fling it away upon the first improper character you came across; I think I can now understand, however, why she did not leave you her money; and after all your godfather may just as well have it as the kind of people on whom you would lavish it, if you had had it."

Then his mother would burst into tears and implore him to repent and seek the things belonging to his peace while there was yet time, by falling on his knees to Theobald and assuring him of his unfailing love for him as the kindest and tenderest father in the universe. Ernest could do all this just as well as Theobald himself, and now as he lay on the grass, speeches, some one or other of which was as certain to come as the sun to set, kept running in his head till they confuted the idea of telling the truth by reducing it to an absurdity. Truth might be heroic, but it was not within the range of practical domestic politics.

*Preceding Ernest's decision " to tell a lie" ( that he has inadvertently dropped the watch on the road and so lost it), these paragraphs reveal the factors which lead to that decision and which provoke the reactions and events of our main text, Chapters 40 and 41.*

# Chapter 40

When Ernest got home and sneaked in through the back door, he heard his father's voice in its angriest tones, enquiring whether Master Ernest had already returned. He felt as Jack must have felt in the story of Jack and the bean stalk, when from the oven in which he was hidden he heard the ogre ask his wife what young children she had got for his supper. With much courage, and as the event proved, with not less courage than discretion, he took the bull by the horns, and announced himself at once as having just come in after having met with a terrible misfortune. Little by little he told his story, and though Theobald stormed somewhat at his "incredible folly and carelessness," he got off better than he expected. Theobald and Christina had indeed at first been inclined to connect his absence from dinner with Ellen's dismissal, but on finding it clear (as Theobald said—everything was always "clear" with Theobald) that Ernest had not been in the house all the morning, and could therefore have known nothing of what had happened, he was acquitted on this count—for once in a way, without a stain upon his character. Perhaps Theobald was in a good temper; he may have seen from the paper that morning that his stocks had been rising; it may have been this or twenty other things, but whatever it was he did not scold so much as Ernest had expected, and, seeing the boy look exhausted and believing him to be much grieved at the loss of his watch, Theobald actually prescribed him a glass of wine after his dinner, which, strange to say, did not choke him, but made him see things more cheerfully than was usual with him.

That night when he said his prayers, he inserted a few paragraphs to the effect that he might not be discovered, and that things might go well with Ellen, but he was anxious and ill at ease. His guilty conscience pointed out to him a score of weak places in his story through any one of which detection might even yet easily enter. Next day and for many days afterwards he fled when no man was pursuing, and trembled each time he heard his father's voice calling for him. He had already so many causes of anxiety that he could stand little more, and even in spite of all his endeavours to look cheerful, even his mother could see that something was preying upon his mind. Then the idea returned to her that after all her son might not be innocent in the Ellen matter—and this was so interesting that she felt bound to get as near the truth as she could.

"Come here, my poor pale-faced heavy-eyed boy," she said to him one day in her kindest manner, "come and sit down by me and we will have a little quiet confidential talk together, will we not?"

The boy went mechanically to the sofa. Whenever his mother wanted what she called a confidential talk with him she always selected the sofa as the most suitable ground on which to open her campaign. All mothers do this; the sofa is to them what the dining-room is to their husbands. In the present case the sofa was particularly well adapted for a strategic purpose, being an old-fashioned one with high back, mattress, bolsters and cushions. Once safely penned into one of its deep corners, it was, like a dentist's chair, not too easy to get out of again. Here she could get at him better to pull him about, if this should seem desirable, or if she thought fit to cry she could bury her head in the sofa cushion and abandon herself to an agony of grief which seldom failed of its effect. None of her favourite manœuvres were so easily adopted in her usual seat—the armchair on the right hand side [of] the fireplace, and so well did her son know from his mother's tone that this was going to be a sofa conversation that he took his place like a lamb as soon as she began to speak and before she could reach the sofa herself.

"My dearest boy," began his mother taking hold of his hand and placing it within her own, "promise me never to be afraid either of your dear papa or of me; promise me this, my dear, as you love me promise it to me," and she kissed him again and again and stroked his hair. But with her other hand she still kept hold of his; she had got him and she meant to keep him.

The lad hung down his head and promised. What else could he do? "You know there is no one, dear, dear Ernest, who loves you so much as your papa and I do; no one who watches so carefully over your interests or who is so anxious to enter into all your little joys and troubles as we are; but, my dearest boy, it grieves me to think sometimes that you have not that perfect love for and confidence in us which you ought to have. You know, my darling, that it would be as much our pleasure as our duty to watch over the development of your moral and spiritual nature, but alas! you will not let us see your moral and spiritual nature—at times we are almost inclined to doubt whether you have a moral and spiritual nature at all. Of your inner life, my dear, we know nothing beyond such scraps as we can glean in spite of you, from little things which escape you almost before you know that you have said them."

The boy winced at this. It made him feel hot and uncomfortable all over. He knew so well how careful he ought to be, and yet do what he could, from time to time his forgetfulness of the part betrayed him into unreserve. His mother saw that he winced, and enjoyed the scratch she had given him. Had she felt less confident of victory she had better have foregone the pleasure of touching as it were the eyes at the end of the snail's horns in order to enjoy seeing the snail draw them in again—but she knew that when she had got him well down into the sofa, and held his hand she had the enemy almost absolutely at her mercy, and could do pretty much what she liked.

"Papa does not feel," she continued, "that you love him with that fulness and unreserve which would prompt you to have no concealment from him, and to tell him everything freely and fearlessly as your most loving earthly friend next only to your Heavenly Father. Perfect love, as we know, casteth out fear: your father loves you perfectly, my darling, but he does not feel as though you loved him perfectly in return. If you fear him it is because you do not love him as he deserves, and I know it sometimes cuts him to the very heart to think that he has earned from you a deeper and more willing sympathy than you display towards him. Oh Ernest, Ernest, do not grieve one who is so good and noble-hearted by conduct which I can call by no other name than ingratitude."

Ernest could never stand being spoken to in this way by his mother: for he still believed that she loved him, and that he was fond of her and had a friend in her—up to a certain point. But his mother was beginning to come to the end of her tether; she had played the domestic confidence trick upon him times out of number already. Over and over again had she wheedled from him all she wanted to know, and afterwards got him into the most horrible scrape by telling the whole to Theobald. Ernest had remonstrated more than once upon these occasions, and had pointed out to his mother how disastrous to him his confidences had been, but Christina had always joined issue with him and shewn him in the clearest possible manner that in each case she had been right, and that he could not reasonably complain. Generally it was her conscience that forbade her to be silent, and against this there was no appeal, for we are all bound to follow the dictates of our conscience. Ernest used to have to recite a hymn about conscience. It was to the effect that if you did not pay attention to its voice it would soon leave off speaking. "My mamma's conscience has not left off speaking," said Ernest to one of his chums at Roughborough, "it's always jabbering."

When a boy has once spoken so disrespectfully as this about his mother's conscience it is practically all over between him and her; Ernest through sheer force of habit, of the sofa, and of the return of the associated ideas, was still so moved by the siren's voice as to yearn to sail towards her, and fling himself into her arms, but it would not do; there were other associated ideas that returned also, and the mangled bones of too many a murdered confession were lying whitening round the skirts of his mother's dress to allow him by any possibility to trust her further. So he hung his head and look sheepish, but kept his own counsel.

"I see my dearest," continued his mother, "either that I am mistaken, and that there is nothing on your mind, or that you will not unburden yourself to me; but, oh Ernest, tell me at least this much: is there nothing that you repent of, nothing which makes you unhappy in connection with that miserable girl Ellen?"

Ernest's heart failed him. "I am a dead boy now," he said to himself. He had not the faintest conception what his mother was driving at, and thought she suspected about the watch; but he held his ground.

I do not believe he was much more of a coward than his neighbours, only he did not know that all sensible people are cowards when they are off their beat, or when they think they are going to be roughly handled. I believe, if the truth were known, it would be found that even the valiant St. Michael himself tried hard to shirk his famous combat with the dragon: he pretended not to see all sorts of misconduct on the dragon's part; shut his eyes to the eating up of I do not know [how] many hundreds of men women and children whom he had promised to protect; allowed himself to be publicly insulted a dozen times over without resenting it; and in the end when even an angel could stand it no longer he shilly-shallied and temporised an unconscionable time before he would fix the day and hour for the encounter. As for the actual combat it was much such another wurrawurra as Mrs. Allaby had had with the young man who had in the end married her eldest daughter, till after a time, behold, there was the dragon lying dead, while he was himself alive and not very seriously hurt after all.

"I do not know what you mean, mamma," exclaimed Ernest anxiously and more or less hurriedly.

His mother construed his manner into indignation at being suspected, and being rather frightened herself she turned tail and scuttled off as fast as her tongue could carry her.

"Oh," she cried, "I see by your tone that you are innocent! Oh! oh! how I thank my heavenly father for this; may he for his dear son's sake keep you always *pure*. Your father, my dear" (here she spoke hurriedly but gave him a searching look) "was as pure as a spotless angel when he came to me—[so be] self-denying, truly truthful both in word and deed, never forgetful whose son and grandson you are, nor of the name we gave you, of the sacred stream in whose waters your sins were washed out of you through the blood and blessing of Christ, etc."

But Ernest cut this—I will not say short—but a great deal shorter than it would have been if Christina had had her say out—by extricating himself from his mamma's embrace and showing a clean pair of heels. As he got near the purlieus of the kitchen (where he was more at ease) he heard his father calling his mother, and again his guilty conscience rose against him. "He has found all out now," it cried, "and he is going to tell mamma—this time I am done for." But there was nothing in it; his father only wanted the key of the cellaret. Then Ernest slunk off into a coppice or spinney behind the rectory paddock, and consoled himself with a pipe of tobacco. Here in the wood with the summer's sun streaming through the trees, and a book, and his pipe, the boy forgot his cares, and had an interval of that rest without which I verily believe his life would have been insupportable.

Of course Ernest was made to look for his lost property, and a reward was offered for it; but it seemed he had wandered a good deal off the path, thinking to find a lark's nest, more than once, and looking for a watch and purse on Battersby pie-wipes was like looking for a needle in a bundle of hay: besides it might have been found and taken by some tramp, or by a magpie, of which there were many in the neighbourhood, so that after a week or ten days the search was discontinued, and the unpleasant fact had to be faced that Ernest must have another watch, another knife, and a small sum of pocket money.

It was only right, however, that Ernest should pay half the cost of the watch; this should be made easy for him, for it should be deducted from his pocket money in half-yearly instalments extending over two, or even it might be, three years. In Ernest's own interests, then, as well as those of his father and mother, it would be well the watch should cost as little as possible, so it was resolved to buy a second-hand one. Nothing was to be said to Ernest, but it was to be bought, and laid upon his plate as a surprise just before the holidays were over. Theobald would have to go to the county town in a few days and could then find some second-hand watch which would answer sufficiently well. In the course of time, therefore, Theobald went, furnished with a long list of household commissions, among which was the purchase of a watch for Ernest.

Those, as I have said, were always happy times, when Theobald was away for a whole day certain; the boy was beginning to feel easy in his mind as though God had heard his prayers, and he was not going to be found out. Altogether the day had proved an unusually tranquil one, but alas! it was not to close as it had begun; the fickle atmosphere in which he lived was never more likely to breed a storm than after such an interval of brilliant calm, and when Theobald returned Ernest had only to look in his face to see that a hurricane was approaching.

Christina too saw that something had gone very wrong, and was quite frightened lest Theobald should have heard of some serious money loss; he did not however at once unbosom himself, but rang the bell and said to the servant, "Tell Master Ernest I wish to speak to him in the dining-room."

## CHAPTER 41

Long before Ernest reached the dining-room his ill-divining soul had told him that his sin had found him out. What head of a family ever sends for any of its members into the dining-room, if his intentions are honourable?

When he reached it he found it empty—his father having been called away for a few minutes unexpectedly upon some parish business—and he was left in the same kind of suspense as people are in after they have been ushered into their dentist's anteroom.

Of all the rooms in the house he hated the dining-room worst. It was here that he had had to do his Latin and Greek lessons with his father. It had a smell of some particular kind of polish or varnish which was used in polishing the furniture, and neither I nor Ernest can even now come within range of the smell of this kind of varnish without our hearts failing us.

Over the chimney-piece there was a veritable old master, one of the few original pictures which Mr. George Pontifex had brought from Italy. It was supposed to be a Salvator Rosa and had been bought as a great bargain. The subject was Elijah or Elisha (whichever it was) being fed by the ravens in the desert. There were the ravens in the upper right-hand corner with bread and meat in their beaks and claws, and there was the prophet in question in the lower left-hand corner looking longingly up towards them. When Ernest was a very small boy it had been a constant matter of regret to him that the food which the ravens carried never actually reached the prophet; he did not understand the limitation of the painter's art, and wanted the meat and the prophet to be brought into direct contact. One day with the help of some steps which had been left in the room he had clambered up to the picture and with a piece of bread and butter traced a greasy line right across it from the ravens to Elisha's mouth, after which he had felt more comfortable.

Ernest's mind was drifting back to this youthful escapade when he heard his father's hand on the door, and in another second Theobald entered.

"Oh Ernest," said he, in an off-hand rather cheery manner, "there's a little matter which I should like you to explain to me, as I have no doubt you very easily can."

Thump, thump, thump, went Ernest's heart against his ribs; but his father's manner was so much nicer than usual that he began to think it might be all only another false alarm.

"It had occurred to your mother and myself that we should like to set you up with a watch again before you went back to school" ("Oh that's all," said Ernest to himself, quite relieved), "and I have been to-day to look out for a second-hand one which should answer every purpose so long as you are at school."

Theobald spoke as if watches had half a dozen purposes besides time-keeping, but he could hardly open his mouth without using one or other of his tags, and "answering every purpose" was one of them.

Ernest was breaking out into the usual expressions of gratitude, when Theobald continued, "You are interrupting me," and Ernest's heart thumped again.

"You are interrupting me, Ernest. I have not yet done." Ernest was instantly dumb.

"I passed several shops with second-hand watches for sale, but I saw none of a description and price which pleased me till at last I was shewn one which had, so the shopman said, been left with him recently for sale, and which I at once recognised as the one which had been given you by your Aunt Alethæa. Even if I had failed to recognise it, as perhaps I might have done, I should have identified it directly it reached my hands, inasmuch as it had 'E. P., a present from A. P.' engraved upon the inside.

"I need say no more to shew that this was the very watch which you told your mother and me that you had dropped out of your pocket"—up to this time Theobald's manner had been studiously calm, and his words had been uttered slowly; but here he suddenly quickened and flung off the mask as he added the words, "or some such cock and bull story, which your mother and I were too truthful to disbelieve. You can guess what must be our feelings now."

Ernest felt that this last home-thrust was just. In his less anxious moments he had thought his papa and mamma "green" for the readiness with which they had believed him, but he could not deny that their credulity was proof of their habitual truthfulness of mind. In common justice he must own that it was very dreadful for two such truthful people to have a son as untruthful as he knew himself to be.

"Believing that a son of your mother and myself would be incapable of falsehood, I at once assumed that some tramp had picked the watch up and was now trying to dispose of it."

This to the best of my belief was not accurate. Theobald's first assumption had been that it was Ernest who was trying to sell the watch, and it was an inspiration of the moment to say that his magnanimous mind had at once conceived the idea of a tramp.

"You may imagine how shocked I was when I discovered that the watch had been brought for sale by that miserable woman Ellen"—here Ernest's heart hardened a little, and he felt as near an approach to an instinct to turn as one so defenceless could be expected to feel; his father quickly perceived this and continued, "who was turned out of this house under circumstances which I will not pollute your ears by more particularly describing.

"I put aside the horrid conviction which was beginning to dawn upon me, and assumed that in the interval between her dismissal and her leaving this house, she had added theft to her other sin, and having found your watch in your bedroom had purloined it. It even occurred to me that you might have missed your watch after the woman was gone, and, suspecting who had taken it, had run after the carriage in order to recover it; but when I told the shopman of my suspicions he assured me that the person who left it with him had declared most solemnly that it had been given her by her master's son, whose property it was, and who had a perfect right to dispose of it.

"Determined to know the truth, I insisted that the shopkeeper should send for this woman, and interrogate her in my hearing, but without her seeing me. This was accordingly done, and from an inner room, I heard all that passed.

"At first—as women of that stamp invariably do—she tried prevarication, but on being threatened that she should at once be given into custody if she did not tell the whole truth, she described the way in which you had run after the carriage, till as she said you were black in the face, and insisted on giving her all your pocket money, your knife, and your watch. She added that my coachman John—whom I shall instantly discharge—was witness to the whole transaction. Now Ernest, be pleased to tell me whether this appalling story is true or false?"

It never occurred to Ernest to ask his father why he did not hit a man his own size, or to stop him midway in the story with a remonstrance against being kicked when he was down. The boy was too much shocked and shaken to be inventive; he could only drift, and stammer out that the tale was true.

"So I fear," said Theobald, "and now Ernest be good enough to ring the bell."

When the bell had been answered, Theobald desired that John should be sent for, and when John came Theobald calculated the wages due to him, and desired him at once to leave the house.

John's manner was quiet and respectful, and [he] took his dismissal as a matter of course, for Theobald had hinted enough to make him understand why he was being discharged; but when he saw Ernest sitting pale and awestruck on the edge of his chair against the dining-room wall, a sudden thought seemed to strike him, and turning to Theobald he said in a broad Northern accent which I will not attempt to reproduce—

"Look here master, I can guess what all this is about—now before I goes I want to have a word with you."

"Ernest," said Theobald, "leave the room."

"No Master Ernest, you shan't," said John planting himself against the door. "Now, master," he continued, "you may do as you please about me; I've been a good servant to you, and I don't mean to say as you've been a bad master to me; but I do say that if you bear hardly on Master Ernest here, I have those in the village as'll hear on't and let me know; and if I do hear on't I'll come back and break every bone in your skin—so there."

John's breath came and went quickly, as though he would have been well enough pleased to begin the bone-breaking business at once. Theobald turned of an ashen colour—not, as he explained afterwards, at the idle threats of a detected and angry ruffian, but at such atrocious insolence from one of his own servants.

"I shall leave Master Ernest, John," he rejoined proudly, "to the reproaches of his own conscience." ("Thank God and thank John," thought Ernest.) "As for yourself, I admit that you have been an excellent servant until this unfortunate business came on, and I shall have much pleasure in giving you a character, if you want one. Have you anything more to say?"

"No more nor what I have said," said John sullenly, "but what I've said I means and I'll stick to—character or no character."

"Oh you need not be afraid about your character, John," said Theobald kindly, "and as it is getting late, there can be no occasion for you to leave the house before tomorrow morning."

To this there was no reply from John, who retired, packed up his things, and left the house at once.

When Christina heard what had happened she said she could condone all except that Theobald should have been subjected to such insolence from one of his own servants through the misconduct of his son. Theobald was the bravest man in the whole world, and could easily have collared the wretch and turned him out of the room, but how far more dignified, how far nobler had been his reply. How it would tell in a novel or upon the stage —for though the stage as a whole was immoral, yet there were doubtless some plays which were improving spectacles—she could fancy the whole house hushed with excitement at hearing John's menace, and hardly breathing by reason of their interest and expectation of the coming answer. Then the actor—probably the great and good Mr. Macready—would say, "I shall leave Master Ernest, John, to the reproaches of his own conscience," oh it was sublime! What a roar of applause must follow—then she should enter herself, and fling her arms about her husband's neck, and call him her lion-hearted husband. When the curtain dropped, it would be buzzed about the house that the scene just witnessed had been drawn from real life, and had actually occurred in the household of the Rev. Theobald Pontifex, who had married a Miss Allaby, etc., etc.

As for Ernest the suspicions which had already crossed her mind were deepened; but she thought it better to leave the matter where it was. At present she was in a very strong position. Ernest's official purity was firmly established, but at the same time he had shewn himself so impressionable that she was able to fuse two contradictory impressions concerning him into a single idea, and consider him as a kind of Joseph and Don Juan in one. This was what she had wanted all along; but her vanity being gratified by the possession of such a son, there was an end of it; the son himself was naught.

Let me say in passing that this power of cutting logical Gordian knots and fusing two contradictory or conflicting statements into a harmonious whole—is one without which no living being whether animal or plant could continue to live for a single day, or indeed could ever have come into existence. This holds good concerning all things that have a reproductive system, but it is most easily seen in the case of those forms that are reproduced by parents of different sexes. The first thing which the male and female elements must do when they unite to form offspring is to fuse the conflicting memories and inconsistent renderings of their two parents into a single consistent story. But to return.

No doubt if John had not interfered Ernest would have had to expiate his offence with ache, penury and imprisonment. As it was, the boy was "to consider himself" as undergoing these punishments[1] and as suffering pangs of unavailing remorse inflicted on him by his conscience into the bargain; but beyond the fact that Theobald kept him more closely to his holiday task, and the continued coldness of his parents, no ostensible punishment was meted out to him. Ernest however tells me that he looks back upon this as the time when he began to know that he had a cordial and active dislike for both his parents, which I suppose means that he was now beginning to be aware that he was reaching man's estate.[2]

## QUESTIONS: *Butler, The Way of All Flesh*

1. How does the reference to Jack and the Beanstalk at the beginning of Chapter 40 clarify Ernest's attitude toward his father and explain his impulse to lie to him? Does the reference to Jack and the Beanstalk suggest an archetypal generational fear?

2. Butler, speaking of Christina's calling Ernest to the sofa, says "All mothers do this." What aspect of maternal behavior does Butler particularly attack when he details the "manoeuvres" characteristic of "the domestic confidence trick"? Is the sofa to be considered a more treacherous battleground than the dining room?

   *Clues:* • Note particularly the manner in which *tone* and *imagery* sustain the condemnation. Assess the significance of the references to the "dentist's chair" (the reference to the dentist reappears in Chapter 41), "the snail's horns," "the siren's voice."

3. How does the reference to St. Michael and the dragon amplify the effect of the earlier reference to Jack and the Beanstalk?

---

[1] As Jones heard of a small man sometimes telling a big one to consider himself horsewhipped, after the big one had horsewhipped him.

[2] But if he had not found it out already an event was now about to happen which could hardly fail to reveal it to him.

4. What does the manipulation of point of view in the account of the decision to purchase a watch for Ernest reveal about his parents?

   *Clues:* • It was only right . . .

   • . . . this should be made easy for him. . . .

   • In Ernest's own interests. . . .

   • . . . which would answer sufficiently well.

5. What central parental failure is highlighted in both the first and last paragraphs of Chapter 40 by the equation between emotional states and financial conditions?

6. In what way does the presence of the painting (of the prophet fed by the ravens) in the dining room represent an ironic criticism of the Pontifex household? What does Ernest's reaction to the painting when a child tell us about his nature? about his plight?

7. What similarity does the narrator imply between Theobald's treatment of his son and his treatment of his servant John in the confrontation scene about the watch?

8. In what way do the vanity and self-absorption demonstrated by Christina in her daydream about the stage and in her assumptions about Ernest fit in with the possessiveness and manipulativeness she has revealed earlier?

9. What does the last sentence of Chapter 41 suggest about Butler's view of the relationship between the generations?

### EXERCISES

1. Compare and contrast the relationship between Ernest and his parents in *The Way of All Flesh* and that of Benjamin and his parents in *The Graduate*, particularly with regard to the problems of (a) hostility and dissembling on the part of the offspring; (b) manipulativeness and materialism on the part of the parents.

2. Suggest the relevance to these chapters of Francis Bacon's statement: "The illiberality of parents in allowance towards their children is a harmful error."

*Henry James (1843–1916)*

# The Pupil

### I

The poor young man hesitated and procrastinated: it cost him such an effort to broach the subject of terms, to speak of money to a person who spoke only of feelings and, as it were, of the aristocracy. Yet he was unwilling to take leave, treating his engagement as settled, without some more conventional glance in that direction than he could find an opening for in the manner of the large affable lady who sat there drawing a pair of soiled *gants de Suède*[1] through a fat jewelled hand and, at once pressing and gliding,

[1] *gants de Suède:* suede gloves.

repeated over and over everything but the thing he would have liked to hear. He would have liked to hear the figure of his salary; but just as he was nervously about to sound that note the little boy came back—the little boy Mrs. Moreen had sent out of the room to fetch her fan. He came back without the fan, only with the casual observation that he couldn't find it. As he dropped this cynical confession he looked straight and hard at the candidate for the honour of taking his education in hand. This personage reflected somewhat grimly that the first thing he should have to teach his little charge would be to appear to address himself to his mother when he spoke to her— especially not to make her such an improper answer as that.

When Mrs. Moreen bethought herself of this pretext for getting rid of their companion Pemberton supposed it was precisely to approach the delicate subject of his remuneration. But it had been only to say some things about her son that it was better a boy of eleven shouldn't catch. They were extravagantly to his advantage save when she lowered her voice to sigh, tapping her left side familiarly, "And all overclouded by *this*, you know; all at the mercy of a weakness—!" Pemberton gathered that the weakness was in the region of the heart. He had known the poor child was not robust: this was the basis on which he had been invited to treat, through an English lady, an Oxford acquaintance, then at Nice, who happened to know both his needs and those of the amiable American family looking out for something really superior in the way of a resident tutor.

The young man's impression of his prospective pupil, who had come into the room as if to see for himself the moment Pemberton was admitted, was not quite the soft solicitation the visitor had taken for granted. Morgan Moreen was somehow sickly without being "delicate," and that he looked intelligent—it is true Pemberton wouldn't have enjoyed his being stupid— only added to the suggestion that, as with his big mouth and big ears he really couldn't be called pretty, he might too utterly fail to please. Pemberton was modest, was even timid; and the chance that his small scholar would prove cleverer than himself had quite figured, to his anxiety, among the dangers of an untried experiment. He reflected, however, that these were risks one had to run when one accepted a position, as it was called, in a private family; when as yet one's university honours had, pecuniarily speaking, remained barren. At any rate when Mrs. Moreen got up as to intimate that, since it was understood he would enter upon his duties within the week she would let him off now, he succeeded, in spite of the presence of the child, in squeezing out a phrase about the rate of payment. It was not the fault of the conscious smile which seemed a reference to the lady's expensive identity, it was not the fault of this demonstration, which had, in a sort, both vagueness and point, if the allusion didn't sound rather vulgar. This was exactly because she became still more gracious to reply: "Oh I can assure you that all that will be quite regular."

Pemberton only wondered, while he took up his hat, what "all that" was to amount to—people had such different ideas. Mrs. Moreen's words, however, seemed to commit the family to a pledge definite enough to elicit from the child a strange little comment in the shape of the mocking foreign ejaculation "Oh la-la!"

Pemberton, in some confusion, glanced at him as he walked slowly to the window with his back turned, his hands in his pockets and the air in his elderly shoulders of a boy who didn't play. The young man wondered if he should be able to teach him to play, though his mother had said it would never do and that this was why school was impossible. Mrs. Moreen exhibited no discomfiture; she only continued blandly: "Mr. Moreen will be delighted to meet your wishes. As I told you, he has been called to London for a week. As soon as he comes back you shall have it out with him."

This was so frank and friendly that the young man could only reply, laughing as his hostess laughed: "Oh I don't imagine we shall have much of a battle."

"They'll give you anything you like," the boy remarked unexpectedly, returning from the window. "We don't mind what anything costs—we live awfully well."

"My darling, you're too quaint!" his mother exclaimed, putting out to caress him a practised but ineffectual hand. He slipped out of it, but looked with intelligent innocent eyes at Pemberton, who had already had time to notice that from one moment to the other his small satiric face seemed to change its time of life. At this moment it was infantine, yet it appeared also to be under the influence of curious intuitions and knowledges. Pemberton rather disliked precocity and was disappointed to find gleams of it in a disciple not yet in his teens. Nevertheless he divined on the spot that Morgan wouldn't prove a bore. He would prove on the contrary a source of agitation. This idea held the young man, in spite of a certain repulsion.

"You pompous little person! We're not extravagant!" Mrs. Moreen gaily protested, making another unsuccessful attempt to draw the boy to her side. "You must know what to expect," she went on to Pemberton.

"The less you expect the better!" her companion interposed. "But we *are* people of fashion."

"Only so far as *you* make us so!" Mrs. Moreen tenderly mocked. "Well then, on Friday—don't tell me you're superstitious—and mind you don't fail us. Then you'll see us all. I'm so sorry the girls are out. I guess you'll like the girls. And, you know, I've another son, quite different from this one."

"He tries to imitate me," Morgan said to their friend.

"He tries? Why he's twenty years old!" cried Mrs. Moreen.

"You're very witty," Pemberton remarked to the child—a proposition his mother echoed with enthusiasm, declaring Morgan's sallies to be the delight of the house.

The boy paid no heed to this; he only enquired abruptly of the visitor, who was surprised afterwards that he hadn't struck him as offensibly forward: "Do you *want* very much to come?"

"Can you doubt it after such a description of what I shall hear?"

Pemberton replied. Yet he didn't want to come at all; he was coming because he had to go somewhere, thanks to the collapse of his fortune at the end of a year abroad spent on the system of putting his scant patrimony into a single full wave of experience. He had had his full wave but couldn't pay the score at his inn. Moreover he had caught in the boy's eyes the glimpse of a far-off appeal.

"Well, I'll do the best I can for you," said Morgan; with which he turned away again. He passed out of one of the long windows; Pemberton saw him go and lean on the parapet of the terrace. He remained there while the young man took leave of his mother, who, on Pemberton's looking as if he expected a farewell from him, interposed with: "Leave him, leave him; he's so strange!" Pemberton supposed her to fear something he might say. "He's a genius—you'll love him," she added. "He's much the most interesting person in the family." And before he could invent some civility to oppose to this she wound up with: "But we're all good, you know!"

"He's a genius—you'll love him!" were words that recurred to our aspirant before the Friday, suggesting among many things that geniuses were not invariably loveable. However, it was all the better if there was an element that would make tutorship absorbing: he had perhaps taken too much for granted it would only disgust him. As he left the villa after his interview he looked up at the balcony and saw the child leaning over it. "We shall have great larks!" he called up.

Morgan hung fire a moment and then gaily returned: "By the time you come back I shall have thought of something witty!"

This made Pemberton say to himself "After all he's rather nice."

## II

On the Friday he saw them all, as Mrs. Moreen had promised, for her husband had come back and the girls and the other son were at home. Mr. Moreen had a white moustache, a confiding manner and, in his buttonhole, the ribbon of a foreign order—bestowed, as Pemberton eventually learned, for services. For what services he never clearly ascertained: this was a point—one of a large number—that Mr. Moreen's manner never confided. What it emphatically did confide was that he was even more a man of the world than you might first make out. Ulick, the firstborn, was in visible training for the same profession—under the disadvantage as yet, however, of a buttonhole but feebly floral and a moustache with no pretensions to type. The girls had hair and figures and manners and small fat feet, but had never been out alone. As for Mrs. Moreen Pemberton saw on a nearer view that her elegance was intermittent and her parts didn't always match. Her husband, as she had promised, met with enthusiasm Pemberton's ideas in regard to a salary. The young man had endeavoured to keep these stammerings modest, and Mr. Moreen made it no secret that *he* found them wanting in "style." He further mentioned that he aspired to be intimate with his children, to be their best friend, and that he was always looking out for them.

That was what he went off for, to London and other places—to look out; and this vigilance was the theory of life, as well as the real occupation, of the whole family. They all looked out, for they were very frank on the subject of its being necessary. They desired it to be understood that they were earnest people, and also that their fortune, though quite adequate for earnest people, required the most careful administration. Mr. Moreen, as the parent bird, sought sustenance for the nest. Ulick invoked support mainly at the club, where Pemberton guessed that it was usually served on green cloth. The girls used to do up their hair and their frocks themselves, and our young man felt appealed to to be glad, in regard to Morgan's education, that, though it must naturally be of the best, it didn't cost too much. After a little he *was* glad, forgetting at times his own needs in the interest inspired by the child's character and culture and the pleasure of making easy terms for him.

During the first weeks of their acquaintance Morgan had been as puzzling as a page in an unknown language—altogether different from the obvious little Anglo-Saxons who had misrepresented childhood to Pemberton. Indeed the whole mystic volume in which the boy had been amateurishly bound demanded some practice in translation. Today, after a considerable interval, there is something phantasmagoric, like a prismatic reflexion or a serial novel, in Pemberton's memory of the queerness of the Moreens. If it were not for a few tangible tokens—a lock of Morgan's hair cut by his own hand, and the half-dozen letters received from him when they were disjoined—the whole episode and the figures peopling it would seem too inconsequent for anything but dreamland. Their supreme quaintness was their success—as it appeared to him for a while at the time; since he had never seen a family so brilliantly equipped for failure. Wasn't it success to have kept him so hatefully long? Wasn't it success to have drawn him in that first morning at déjeuner,[2] the Friday he came—it was enough to *make* one superstitious—so that he utterly committed himself, and this not by calculation or on a signal, but from a happy instinct which made them, like a band of gipsies, work so neatly together? They amused him as much as if they had really been a band of gipsies. He was still young and had not seen much of the world—his English years had been properly arid; therefore the reversed conventions of the Moreens—for they had *their* desperate proprieties —struck him as topsy-turvy. He had encountered nothing like them at Oxford; still less had any such note been struck to his younger American ear during the four years at Yale in which he had richly supposed himself to be reacting against a Puritan strain. The reaction of the Moreens, at any rate, went ever so much further. He had thought himself very sharp that first day in hitting them all off in his mind with the "cosmopolite" label. Later it seemed feeble and colourless—confessedly helplessly provisional.

He yet when he first applied it felt a glow of joy—for an instructor he was still empirical—rise from the apprehension that living with them would

2 *déjeuner:* breakfast.

really be to see life. Their sociable strangeness was an intimation of that—
their chatter of tongues, their gaiety and good humour, their infinite daw-
dling (they were always getting themselves up, but it took for ever, and
Pemberton had once found Mr. Moreen shaving in the drawing-room), their
French, their Italian and, cropping up in the foreign fluencies, their cold
tough slices of American. They lived on maccaroni and coffee—they had
these articles prepared in perfection—but they knew recipes for a hundred
other dishes. They overflowed with music and song, were always humming
and catching each other up, and had a sort of professional acquaintance
with Continental cities. They talked of "good places" as if they had been
pickpockets or strolling players. They had at Nice a villa, a carriage, a piano
and a banjo, and they went to official parties. They were a perfect calendar
of the "days" of their friends, which Pemberton knew them, when they
were indisposed, to get out of bed to go to, and which made the week larger
than life when Mrs. Moreen talked of them with Paula and Amy. Their
initiations gave their new inmate at first an almost dazzling sense of culture.
Mrs. Moreen had translated something at some former period—an author
whom it made Pemberton feel *borné*[3] never to have heard of. They could
imitate Venetian and sing Neapolitan, and when they wanted to say something very particular communicated with each other in an ingenious dialect
of their own, an elastic spoken cipher which Pemberton at first took for some
*patois*[4] of one of their countries, but which he "caught on to" as he would
not have grasped provincial development of Spanish or German.

"It's the family language—Ultramoreen," Morgan explained to him
drolly enough; but the boy rarely condescended to use it himself, though he
dealt in colloquial Latin as if he had been a little prelate.

Among all the "days" with which Mrs. Moreen's memory was taxed she
managed to squeeze in one of her own, which her friends sometimes forgot.
But the house drew a frequented air from the number of fine people who were
freely named there and from several mysterious men with foreign titles and
English clothes whom Morgan called the Princes and who, on sofas with the
girls, talked French very loud—though sometimes with some oddity of accent
—as if to show they were saying nothing improper. Pemberton wondered
how the Princes could ever propose in that tone and so publicly: he took for
granted cynically that this was what was desired of them. Then he recognised
that even for the chance of such an advantage Mrs. Moreen would never
allow Paula and Amy to receive alone. These young ladies were not at all
timid, but it was just the safeguards that made them so candidly free. It was
a houseful of Bohemians who wanted tremendously to be Philistines.

In one respect, however, certainly, they achieved no rigour—they were
wonderfully amiable and ecstatic about Morgan. It was a genuine tenderness,
an artless admiration, equally strong in each. They even praised his beauty,
which was small, and were as afraid of him as if they felt him of finer clay.

[3] *borné*: limited.  [4] *patois*: jargon.

They spoke of him as a little angel and a prodigy—they touched on his want of health with long, vague faces. Pemberton feared at first an extravagance that might make him hate the boy, but before this happened he had become extravagant himself. Later, when he had grown rather to hate the others, it was a bribe to patience for him that they were at any rate nice about Morgan, going on tiptoe if they fancied he was showing symptoms, and even giving up somebody's "day" to procure him a pleasure. Mixed with this too was the oddest wish to make him independent, as if they had felt themselves not good enough for him. They passed him over to the new member of their circle very much as if wishing to force some charity of adoption on so free an agent and get rid of their own charge. They were delighted when they saw Morgan take so to his kind playfellow, and could think of no higher praise for the young man. It was strange how they contrived to reconcile the appearance, and indeed the essential fact, of adoring the child with their eagerness to wash their hands of him. Did they want to get rid of him before he should find them out? Pemberton was finding them out month by month. The boy's fond family, however this might be, turned their backs with exaggerated delicacy, as if to avoid the reproach of interfering. Seeing in time how little he had in common with them—it was by *them* he first observed it; they proclaimed it with complete humility—his companion was moved to speculate on the mysteries of transmission, the far jumps of heredity. Where his detachment from most of the things they represented had come from was more than an observer could say—it certainly had burrowed under two or three generations.

As for Pemberton's own estimate of his pupil, it was a good while before he got the point of view, so little had he been prepared for it by the smug young barbarians to whom the tradition of tutorship, as hitherto revealed to him, had been adjusted. Morgan was scrappy and surprising, deficient in many properties supposed common to the *genus* and abounding in others that were the portion only of the supernaturally clever. One day his friend made a great stride: it cleared up the question to perceive that Morgan *was* supernaturally clever and that, though the formula was temporarily meagre, this would be the only assumption on which one could successfully deal with him. He had the general quality of a child for whom life had not been simplified by school, a kind of homebred sensibility which might have been bad for himself but was charming for others, and a whole range of refinement and perception—little musical vibrations as taking as picked-up airs— begotten by wandering about Europe at the tail of his migratory tribe. This might not have been an education to recommend in advance, but its results with so special a subject were as appreciable as the marks on a piece of fine porcelain. There was at the same time in him a small strain of stoicism, doubtless the fruit of having had to begin early to bear pain, which counted for pluck and made it of less consequence that he might have been thought at school rather a polyglot little beast. Pemberton indeed quickly found himself rejoicing that school was out of the question: in any million of boys it was probably good for all but one, and Morgan was that millionth. It would have made him comparative and superior—it might have made him really require kicking. Pemberton would try to be school himself—a bigger seminary than five hundred grazing donkeys, so that, winning no prizes, the boy would remain unconscious and irresponsible and amusing—amusing, because, though life was already intense in his childish nature, freshness still made there a strong draught for jokes. It turned out that even in the still air of Morgan's various disabilities jokes flourished greatly. He was a pale lean acute undeveloped little cosmopolite, who liked intellectual gymnastics and who also, as regards the behaviour of mankind, had noticed more things than you might suppose, but who nevertheless had his proper playroom of superstitions, where he smashed a dozen toys a day.

## III

At Nice once, toward evening, as the pair rested in the open air after a walk, and looked over the sea at the pink western lights, he said suddenly to his comrade: "Do you like it, you know—being with us all in this intimate way?"

"My dear fellow, why should I stay if I didn't?"

"How do I know you'll stay? I'm almost sure you won't, very long."

"I hope you don't mean to dismiss me," said Pemberton.

Morgan debated, looking at the sunset. "I think if I did right I ought to."

"Well, I know I'm supposed to instruct you in virtue; but in that case don't do right."

"You're very young—fortunately," Morgan went on, turning to him again.

"Oh yes, compared with you!"

"Therefore it won't matter so much if you do lose a lot of time."

"That's the way to look at it," said Pemberton accommodatingly.

They were silent a minute; after which the boy asked: "Do you like my father and my mother very much?"

"Dear me, yes. Charming people."

Morgan received this with another silence; then unexpectedly, familiarly, but at the same time affectionately, he remarked: "You're a jolly old humbug!"

For a particular reason the words made our young man change colour. The boy noticed in an instant that he had turned red, whereupon he turned red himself and pupil and master exchanged a longish glance in which there was a consciousness of many more things than are usually touched upon, even tacitly, in such a relation. It produced for Pemberton an embarrassment; it raised in a shadowy form a question—this was the first glimpse of it—destined to play a singular and, as he imagined, owing to the altogether peculiar conditions, an unprecedented part in his intercourse with his little companion. Later, when he found himself talking with the youngster in a way in which few youngsters could ever have been talked with, he thought of that clumsy moment on the bench at Nice as the dawn of an understanding that had broadened. What had added to the clumsiness then was that he thought it his duty to declare to Morgan that he might abuse him, Pemberton, as much as he liked, but must never abuse his parents. To this Morgan had the easy report that he hadn't dreamed of abusing them; which appeared to be true: it put Pemberton in the wrong.

"Then why am I a humbug for saying *I* think them charming?" the young man asked, conscious of a certain rashness.

"Well—they're not your parents."

"They love you better than anything in the world—never forget that," said Pemberton.

"Is that why you like them so much?"

"They're very kind to me," Pemberton replied evasively.

"You *are* a humbug!" laughed Morgan, passing an arm into his tutor's. He leaned against him looking off at the sea again and swinging his long thin legs.

"Don't kick my shins," said Pemberton while he reflected "Hang it, I can't complain of them to the child!"

"There's another reason too," Morgan went on, keeping his legs still.

"Another reason for what?"

"Besides their not being your parents."

"I don't understand you," said Pemberton.

"Well, you will before long. All right!"

He did understand fully before long, but he made a fight even with himself before he confessed it. He thought it the oddest thing to have a struggle with the child about. He wondered he didn't hate the hope of the Moreens for bringing the struggle on. But by the time it began any such sentiment for that scion was closed to him. Morgan was a special case, and to know him was to accept him on his own odd terms. Pemberton had spent his aversion to special cases before arriving at knowledge. When at last he did arrive his quandary was great. Against every interest he had attached himself. They would have to meet things together. Before they went home that evening at Nice the boy had said, clinging to his arm:

"Well, at any rate you'll hang on to the last."

"To the last?"

"Till you're fairly beaten."

"*You* ought to be fairly beaten!" cried the young man, drawing him closer.

## IV

A year after he had come to live with them Mr. and Mrs. Moreen suddenly gave up the villa at Nice. Pemberton had got used to suddenness, having seen it practised on a considerable scale during two jerky little tours—one in Switzerland the first summer, and the other late in the winter, when they all ran down to Florence and then, at the end of ten days, liking it much less than they had intended, straggled back in mysterious depression. They had returned to Nice "for ever," as they said; but this didn't prevent their squeezing, one rainy muggy May night, into a second-class railway-carriage —you could never tell by which class they would travel—where Pemberton helped them to stow away a wonderful collection of bundles and bags. The explanation of this manœuvre was that they had determined to spend the summer "in some bracing place"; but in Paris they dropped into a small furnished apartment—a fourth floor in a third-rate avenue, where there was a smell on the staircase and the *portier*[5] was hateful—and passed the next four months in blank indigence.

The better part of this baffled sojourn was for the preceptor and his pupil, who, visiting the Invalides and Notre Dame, the Conciergerie and all the museums, took a hundred remunerative rambles. They learned to know their Paris, which was useful, for they came back another year for a longer stay, the general character of which in Pemberton's memory today mixes pitiably and confusedly with that of the first. He sees Morgan's shabby knicker-bockers—the everlasting pair that didn't match his blouse and that as he grew longer could only grow faded. He remembers the particular holes in his three or four pair of coloured stockings.

Morgan was dear to his mother, but he never was better dressed than was absolutely necessary—partly, no doubt, by his own fault, for he was as indifferent to his appearance as a German philosopher. "My dear fellow, you *are* coming to pieces," Pemberton would say to him in sceptical remonstrance; to which the child would reply, looking at him serenely up and down: "My dear fellow, so are you! I don't want to cast you in the shade." Pemberton could have no rejoinder for this—the assertion so closely represented the fact. If however the deficiencies of his own wardrobe were a chapter by themselves he didn't like his little charge to look too poor. Later he used to say "Well, if we're poor, why, after all, shouldn't we look it?" and he consoled himself with thinking there was something rather elderly and gentlemanly in Morgan's disrepair—it differed from the untidiness of the urchin who plays and spoils his things. He could trace perfectly the degrees by which, in proportion as her little son confined himself to his tutor for society, Mrs. Moreen shrewdly forbore to renew his garments. She did nothing that didn't show, neglected him because he escaped notice, and then, as he illustrated this clever policy, discouraged at home his public appearances. Her position was logical enough—those members of her family who did show had to be showy.

During this period and several others Pemberton was quite aware of how he and his comrade might strike people; wandering languidly through the Jardin des Plantes as if they had nowhere to go, sitting on the winter days in the galleries of the Louvre, so splendidly ironical to the homeless, as if for the advantage of the *calorifère*.[6] They joked about it sometimes: it was the

[5] *portier:* doorman.
[6] *calorifère:* radiator.

sort of joke that was perfectly within the boy's compass. They figured them-selves as part of the vast vague hand-to-mouth multitude of the enormous city and pretended they were proud of their position in it—it showed them "such a lot of life" and made them conscious of a democratic brotherhood. If Pemberton couldn't feel a sympathy in destitution with his small com-panion—for after all Morgan's fond parents would never have let him really suffer—the boy would at least feel it with him, so it came to the same thing. He used sometimes to wonder what people would think they were—to fancy they were looked askance at, as if it might be a suspected case of kidnapping. Morgan wouldn't be taken for a young patrician with a preceptor—he wasn't smart enough; though he might pass for his companion's sickly little brother. Now and then he had a five-franc piece, and except once, when they bought a couple of lovely neckties, one of which he made Pemberton accept, they laid it out scientifically in old books. This was sure to be a great day, always spent on the quays, in a rummage of the dusty boxes that garnish the parapets. Such occasions helped them to live, for their books ran low very soon after the beginning of their acquaintance. Pemberton had a good many in England, but he was obliged to write to a friend and ask him kindly to get some fellow to give him something for them.

If they had to relinquish that summer the advantage of the bracing climate the young man couldn't but suspect this failure of the cup when at their very lips to have been the effect of a rude jostle of his own. This had represented his first blow-out, as he called it, with his patrons; his first successful attempt—though there was little other success about it—to bring them to a consideration of his impossible position. As the ostensible eve of a costly journey the moment had struck him as favourable to an earnest protest, the presentation of an ultimatum. Ridiculous as it sounded, he had never yet been able to compass an uninterrupted private interview with the elder pair or with either of them singly. They were always flanked by their elder children, and poor Pemberton usually had his own little charge at his side. He was conscious of its being a house in which the surface of one's deli-cacy got rather smudged; nevertheless he had preserved the bloom of his scruple against announcing to Mr. and Mrs. Moreen with publicity that he shouldn't be able to go on longer without a little money. He was still simple enough to suppose Ulick and Paula and Amy might not know that since his arrival he had only had a hundred and forty francs; and he was magnanimous enough to wish not to compromise their parents in their eyes. Mr. Moreen now listened to him, as he listened to every one and to every thing, like a man of the world, and seemed to appeal to him—though not of course too grossly —to try and be a little more of one himself. Pemberton recognised in fact the importance of the character—from the advantage it gave Mr. Moreen. He was not even confused or embarrassed, whereas the young man in his service was more so than there was any reason for. Neither was he surprised —at least any more than a gentleman had to be who freely confessed himself a little shocked—though not perhaps strictly at Pemberton.

"We must go into this, musn't we, dear?" he said to his wife. He assured his young friend that the matter should have his very best attention; and he melted into space as elusively as if, at the door, he were taking an inevitable but deprecatory precedence. When, the next moment, Pemberton found himself alone with Mrs. Moreen it was to hear her say "I see, I see"—stroking the roundness of her chin and looking as if she were only hesitating between a dozen easy remedies. If they didn't make their push Mr. Moreen could at least disappear for several days. During his absence his wife took up the subject again spontaneously, but her contribution to it was merely that she had thought all the while they were getting on so beautifully. Pemberton's reply to this revelation was that unless they immediately put down something on account he would leave them on the spot and for ever. He knew she would wonder how he would get away, and for a moment expected her to enquire. She didn't, for which he was almost grateful to her, so little was he in a position to tell.

"You won't, you *know* you won't—you're too interested," she said. "You *are* interested, you know you are, you dear kind man!" She laughed with almost condemnatory archness, as if it were a reproach—though she wouldn't insist; and flirted a soiled pocket-handkerchief at him.

Pemberton's mind was fully made up to take his step the following week. This would give him time to get an answer to a letter he had dispatched to England. If he did in the event nothing of the sort—that is if he stayed another year and then went away only for three months—it was not merely because before the answer to his letter came (most unsatisfactory when it did arrive) Mr. Moreen generously counted out to him, and again with the sacrifice to "form" of a marked man of the world, three hundred francs in elegant ringing gold. He was irritated to find that Mrs. Moreen was right, that he couldn't at the pinch bear to leave the child. This stood out clearer for the very reason that, the night of his desperate appeal to his patrons, he had seen fully for the first time where he was. Wasn't it another proof of the success with which those patrons practised their arts that they had managed to avert for so long the illuminating flash? It descended on our friend with a breadth of effect which perhaps would have struck a spectator as comical, after he had returned to his little servile room, which looked into a close court where a bare dirty opposite wall took, with the sound of shrill clatter, the reflexion of lighted back windows. He had simply given himself away to a band of adventurers. The idea, the word itself, wore a romantic horror for him—he had always lived on such safe lines. Later it assumed a more interesting, almost a soothing, sense: it pointed a moral, and Pemberton could enjoy a moral. The Moreens were adventurers not merely because they didn't pay their debts, because they lived on society, but because their whole view of life, dim and confused and instinctive, like that of clever colour-blind animals, was speculative and rapacious and mean. Oh they were "respectable," and that only made them more *immondes!*[7] The young man's analysis, while he brooded, put it at last very simply—they were adventurers because they were toadies and snobs. That was the completest account of them—it was the law of their being. Even when this truth became vivid to their ingenious inmate he remained unconscious of how much his mind had been prepared for it by the extraordinary little boy who had now become such a complication in his life. Much less could he then calculate on the information he was still to owe the extraordinary little boy.

## V

But it was during the ensuing time that the real problem came up—the problem of how far it was excusable to discuss the turpitude of parents with a child of twelve, of thirteen, of fourteen. Absolutely inexcusable and quite impossible it of course at first appeared; and indeed the question didn't press for some time after Pemberton had received his three hundred francs. They produced a temporary lull, a relief from the sharpest pressure. The young man frugally amended his wardrobe and even had a few francs in his pocket. He thought the Moreens looked at him as if he were almost too smart, as if they ought to take care not to spoil him. If Mr. Moreen hadn't been such a man of the world he would perhaps have spoken of the freedom of such neckties on the part of a subordinate. But Mr. Moreen was always enough a man of the world to let things pass—he had certainly shown that. It was singular how Pemberton guessed that Morgan, though saying nothing about it, knew something had happened. But three hundred francs, especially when one owed money, couldn't last for ever; and when the treasure was gone— the boy knew when it had failed—Morgan did break ground. The party had returned to Nice at the beginning of the winter, but not to the charming villa. They went to an hotel, where they stayed three months, and then moved to another establishment, explaining that they had left the first because, after waiting and waiting, they couldn't get the rooms they wanted. These apartments, the rooms they wanted, were generally very splendid; but fortunately they never *could* get them—fortunately, I mean, for Pemberton, who reflected always that if they had got them there would have been a still scanter educational fund. What Morgan said at last was said suddenly, irrelevantly, when the moment came, in the middle of a lesson, and consisted of the apparently unfeeling words: "You ought to *filer*,[8] you know—you really ought."

Pemberton stared. He had learnt enough French slang from Morgan to know that to *filer* meant to cut sticks. "Ah my dear fellow, don't turn me off!"

Morgan pulled a Greek lexicon toward him—he used a Greek-German— to look out a word, instead of asking it of Pemberton. "You can't go on like this, you know."

[7] *immondes:* vile.

[8] *filer:* cut and run (present American slang equivalent: split).

"Like what, my boy?"

"You know they don't pay you up," said Morgan, blushing and turning his leaves.

"Don't pay me?" Pemberton stared again and feigned amazement. "What on earth put that into your head?"

"It has been there a long time," the boy replied rummaging his book.

Pemberton was silent, then he went on: "I say, what are you hunting for? They pay me beautifully."

"I'm hunting for the Greek for awful whopper," Morgan dropped.

"Find that rather for gross impertinence and disabuse your mind. What do I want of money?"

"Oh that's another question!"

Pemberton wavered—he was drawn in different ways. The severely correct thing would have been to tell the boy that such a matter was none of his business and bid him go on with his lines. But they were really too intimate for that; it was not the way he was in the habit of treating him; there had been no reason it should be. On the other hand Morgah had quite lighted on the truth—he really shouldn't be able to keep it up much longer; therefore why not let him know one's real motive for forsaking him? At the same time it wasn't decent to abuse to one's pupil the family of one's pupil; it was better to misrepresent than to do that. So in reply to his comrade's last exclamation he just declared, to dismiss the subject, that he had received several payments.

"I say—I say!" the boy ejaculated, laughing.

"That's all right," Pemberton insisted. "Give me your written rendering."

Morgan pushed a copybook across the table, and he began to read the page, but with something running in his head that made it no sense. Looking up after a minute or two he found the child's eyes fixed on him and felt in them something strange. Then Morgan said: "I'm not afraid of the stern reality."

"I haven't yet seen the thing you *are* afraid of—I'll do you that justice!"

This came out with a jump—it was perfectly true—and evidently gave Morgan pleasure. "I've thought of it a long time," he presently resumed.

"Well, don't think of it any more."

The boy appeared to comply, and they had a comfortable and even an amusing hour. They had a theory that they were very thorough, and yet they seemed always to be in the amusing part of lessons, the intervals between the dull dark tunnels, where there were waysides and jolly views. Yet the morning was brought to a violent end by Morgan's suddenly leaning his arms on the table, burying his head in them and bursting into tears: at which Pemberton was the more startled that, as it then came over him, it was the first time he had ever seen the boy cry and that the impression was consequently quite awful.

The next day, after much thought, he took a decision and, believing it to be just, immediately acted on it. He cornered Mr. and Mrs. Moreen again and let them know that if on the spot they didn't pay him all they owed him he wouldn't only leave their house but would tell Morgan exactly what had brought him to it.

"Oh you *haven't* told him?" cried Mrs. Moreen with a pacifying hand on her well-dressed bosom.

"Without warning you? For what do you take me?" the young man returned.

Mr. and Mrs. Moreen looked at each other; he could see that they appreciated, as tending to their security, his superstition of delicacy, and yet that there was a certain alarm in their relief. "My dear fellow," Mr. Moreen demanded, "what use *can* you have, leading the quiet life we all do, for such a lot of money?"—a question to which Pemberton made no answer, occupied as he was in noting that what passed in the mind of his patrons was something like: "Oh then, if we've felt that the child, dear little angel, has judged us and how he regards us, and we haven't been betrayed, he must have guessed—and in short it's *general!*" an inference that rather stirred up Mr. and Mrs. Moreen, as Pemberton had desired it should. At the same time, if he had supposed his threat would do something towards bringing them round, he was disappointed to find them taking for granted —how vulgar their perception *had* been!—that he had already given them away. There was a mystic uneasiness in their parental breasts, and that had been the inferior sense of it. None the less, however, his threat did touch them; for if they had escaped it was only to meet a new danger. Mr. Moreen appealed to him, on every precedent, as a man of the world; but his wife had recourse, for the first time since his domestication with them, to a fine *hauteur*,[9] reminding him that a devoted mother, with her child, had arts that protected her against gross misrepresentation.

"I should misrepresent you grossly if I accused you of common honesty!" our friend replied; but as he closed the door behind him sharply, thinking he had not done himself much good, while Mr. Moreen lighted another cigarette, he heard his hostess shout after him more touchingly:

"Oh you do, you *do*, put the knife to one's throat!"

The next morning, very early, she came to his room. He recognised her knock, but had no hope she brought him money; as to which he was wrong, for she had fifty francs in her hand. She squeezed forward in her dressing-gown, and he received her in his own, between his bath-tub and his bed. He had been tolerably schooled by this time to the "foreign ways" of his hosts. Mrs. Moreen was ardent, and when she was ardent she didn't care what she did; so she now sat down on his bed, his clothes being on the chairs, and, in her preoccupation, forgot, as she glanced round, to be ashamed of giving him such a horrid room. What Mrs. Moreen's ardour now bore upon was the design of persuading him that in the first place she was very good-natured to bring him fifty francs, and that in the second, if he would only see

[9] *hauteur:* haughtiness.

it, he was really too absurd to expect to be *paid*. Wasn't he paid enough without perpetual money—wasn't he paid by the comfortable luxurious home he enjoyed with them all, without a care, an anxiety, a solitary want? Wasn't he sure of his position, and wasn't that everything to a young man like him, quite unknown, with singularly little to show, the ground of whose exorbitant pretensions it had never been easy to discover? Wasn't he paid above all by the sweet relation he had established with Morgan—quite ideal as from master to pupil—and by the simple privilege of knowing and living with so amazingly gifted a child; than whom really (and she meant literally what she said) there was no better company in Europe? Mrs. Moreen herself took to appealing to him as a man of the world; she said "Voyons, mon cher,"[10] and "My dear man, look here now"; and urged him to be reasonable, putting it before him that it was truly a chance for him. She spoke as if, according as he *should* be reasonable, he would prove himself worthy to be her son's tutor and of the extraordinary confidence they had placed in him.

After all, Pemberton reflected, it was only a difference of theory and the theory didn't matter much. They had hitherto gone on that of remunerated, as now they would go on that of gratuitous, service; but why should they have so many words about it? Mrs. Moreen at all events continued to be convincing; sitting there with her fifty francs she talked and reiterated as women reiterate, and bored and irritated him, while he leaned against the wall with his hands in the pockets of his wrapper, drawing it together round his legs and looking over the head of his visitor at the grey negations of his window. She wound up with saying: "You see I bring you a definite proposal."

"A definite proposal?"

"To make our relations regular, as it were—to put them on a comfortable footing."

"I see—it's a system," said Pemberton. "A kind of organised blackmail."

Mrs. Moreen bounded up, which was exactly what he wanted. "What do you mean by that?"

"You practise on one's fears—one's fears about the child if one should go away."

"And pray what would happen to him in that event?" she demanded with majesty.

"Why he'd be alone with *you*."

"And pray with whom *should* a child be but with those whom he loves most?"

"If you think that, why don't you dismiss me?"

"Do you pretend he loves you more than he loves *us*?" cried Mrs. Moreen.

"I think he ought to. I make sacrifices for him. Though I've heard of those *you* make I don't see them."

---

[10] "*Voyons, mon cher*": translated in the expression that follows.

Mrs. Moreen stared a moment; then with emotion she grasped her inmate's hand. "*Will* you make it—the sacrifice?"

He burst out laughing. "I'll see. I'll do what I can. I'll stay a little longer. Your calculation's just—I *do* hate intensely to give him up; I'm fond of him and he thoroughly interests me, in spite of the inconvenience I suffer. You know my situation perfectly. I haven't a penny in the world and, occupied as you see me with Morgan, am unable to earn money."

Mrs. Moreen tapped her undressed arm with her folded banknote. "Can't you write articles? Can't you translate as *I* do?"

"I don't know about translating; it's wretchedly paid."

"I'm glad to earn what I can," said Mrs. Moreen with prodigious virtue.

"You ought to tell me who you do it for." Pemberton paused a moment, and she said nothing; so he added: "I've tried to turn off some little sketches, but the magazines won't have them—they're declined with thanks."

"You see then you're not such a phœnix," his visitor pointedly smiled—"to pretend to abilities you're sacrificing for our sake."

"I haven't time to do things properly," he ruefully went on. Then as it came over him that he was almost abjectly good-natured to give these explanations he added: "If I stay on longer it must be on one condition—that Morgan shall know distinctly on what footing I am."

Mrs. Moreen demurred. "Surely you don't want to show off to a child?"

"To show *you* off, do you mean?"

Again she cast about, but this time it was to produce a still finer flower. "And *you* talk of blackmail!"

"You can easily prevent it," said Pemberton.

"And *you* talk of practising on fears?" she bravely pushed on.

"Yes, there's no doubt I'm a great scoundrel."

His patroness met his eyes—it was clear she was in straits. Then she thrust out her money at him. "Mr. Moreen desired me to give you this on account."

"I'm much obliged to Mr. Moreen, but we *have* no account."

"You won't take it?"

"That leaves me more free," said Pemberton.

"To poison my darling's mind?" groaned Mrs. Moreen.

"Oh your darling's mind—!" the young man laughed.

She fixed him a moment, and he thought she was going to break out tormentedly, pleadingly: "For God's sake, tell me what *is* in it!" But she checked this impulse—another was stronger. She pocketed the money—the crudity of the alternative was comical—and swept out of the room with the desperate concession: "You may tell him any horror you like!"

## VI

A couple of days after this, during which he had failed to profit by so free a permission, he had been for a quarter of an hour walking with his charge in silence when the boy became sociable again with the remark: "I'll tell you how I know it; I know it through Zénobie."

"Zénobie? Who in the world is *she?*"

"A nurse I used to have—ever so many years ago. A charming woman. I liked her awfully, and she liked me."

"There's no accounting for tastes. What is it you know through her?"

"Why what their idea is. She went away because they didn't fork out. She did like me awfully, and she stayed two years. She told me all about it— that at last she could never get her wages. As soon as they saw how much she liked me they stopped giving her anything. They thought she'd stay for nothing—just *because*, don't you know?" And Morgan had a queer little conscious lucid look. "She did stay ever so long—as long as she could. She was only a poor girl. She used to send money to her mother. At last she couldn't afford it any longer, and went away in a fearful rage one night—I mean of course in a rage against *them*. She cried over me tremendously, she hugged me nearly to death. She told me all about it," the boy repeated. "She told me it was their idea. So I guessed, ever so long ago, that they have had the same idea with you."

"Zénobie was very sharp," said Pemberton. "And she made you so."

"Oh that wasn't Zénobie; that was nature. And experience!" Morgan laughed.

"Well, Zénobie was a part of your experience."

"Certainly I was a part of hers, poor dear!" the boy wisely sighed. "And I'm part of yours."

"A very important part. But I don't see how you know I've been treated like Zénobie."

"Do you take me for the biggest dunce you've known?" Morgan asked. "Haven't I been conscious of what we've been through together?"

"What we've been through?"

"Our privations—our dark days."

"Oh our days have been bright enough."

Morgan went on in silence for a moment. Then he said: "My dear chap, you're a hero!"

"Well, you're another!" Pemberton retorted.

"No I'm not, but I ain't a baby. I won't stand it any longer. You must get some occupation that pays. I'm ashamed, I'm ashamed!" quavered the boy with a ring of passion, like some high silver note from a small cathedral chorister, that deeply touched his friend.

"We ought to go off and live somewhere together," the young man said.

"I'll go like a shot if you'll take me."

"I'd get some work that would keep us both afloat," Pemberton continued.

"So would I. Why shouldn't *I* work? I ain't such a beastly little muff as *that* comes to."

"The difficulty is that your parents wouldn't hear of it. They'd never part with you; they worship the ground you tread on. Don't you see the proof of it?" Pemberton developed. "They don't dislike me; they wish me no harm; they're very amiable people, but they're perfectly ready to expose me to any awkwardness in life for your sake."

The silence in which Morgan received his fond sophistry struck Pemberton somehow as expressive. After a moment the child repeated: "You *are* a hero!" Then he added: "They leave me with you altogether. You've all the responsibility. They put me off on you from morning till night. Why then should they object to my taking up with you completely? I'd help you."

"They're not particularly keen about my being helped, and they delight in thinking of you as *theirs*. They're tremendously proud of you."

"I'm not proud of *them*. But you know that," Morgan returned.

"Except for the little matter we speak of they're charming people," said Pemberton, not taking up the point made for his intelligence, but wondering greatly at the boy's own, and especially at this fresh reminder of something he had been conscious of from the first—the strangest thing in his friend's large little composition, a temper, a sensibility, even a private ideal, which made him as privately disown the stuff his people were made of. Morgan had in secret a small loftiness which made him acute about betrayed meanness; as well as a critical sense for the manners immediately surrounding him that was quite without precedent in a juvenile nature, especially when one noted that it had not made this nature "old-fashioned," as the word is of children —quaint or wizened or offensive. It was as if he had been a little gentleman and had paid the penalty by discovering that he was the only such person in his family. This comparison didn't make him vain, but it could make him melancholy and a trifle austere. While Pemberton guessed at these dim young things, shadows of shadows, he was partly drawn on and partly checked, as for a scruple, by the charm of attempting to sound the little cool shallows that were so quickly growing deeper. When he tried to figure to himself the morning twilight of childhood, so as to deal with it safely, he saw it was never fixed, never arrested, that ignorance, at the instant he touched it, was already flushing faintly into knowledge, that there was nothing that at a given moment you could say an intelligent child didn't know. It seemed to him that he himself knew too much to imagine Morgan's simplicity and too little to disembroil his tangle.

The boy paid no heed to his last remark; he only went on: "I'd have spoken to them about their idea, as I call it, long ago if I hadn't been sure what they'd say."

"And what would they say?"

"Just what they said about what poor Zénobie told me—that it was a horrid dreadful story, that they had paid her every penny they owed her."

"Well, perhaps they had," said Pemberton.

"Perhaps they've paid you!"

"Let us pretend they have, and *n'en parlons plus.*"[11]

---

[11] *n'en parlons plus:* let's not speak of it any more.

"They accused her of lying and cheating"—Morgan stuck to historic truth. "That's why I don't want to speak to them."

"Lest they should accuse me too?" To this Morgan made no answer, and his companion, looking down at him—the boy turned away his eyes, which had filled—saw that he couldn't have trusted himself to utter. "You're right. Don't worry them," Pemberton pursued. "Except for that, they *are* charming people."

"Except for *their* lying and *their* cheating?"

"I say—I say!" cried Pemberton, imitating a little tone of the lad's which was itself an imitation.

"We must be frank, at the last; we *must* come to an understanding," said Morgan with the importance of the small boy who lets himself think he is arranging great affairs—almost playing at shipwreck or at Indians. "I know all about everything."

"I dare say your father has his reasons," Pemberton replied, but too vaguely, as he was aware.

"For lying and cheating?"

"For saving and managing and turning his means to the best account. He has plenty to do with his money. You're an expensive family."

"Yes, I'm very expensive," Morgan concurred in a manner that made his preceptor burst out laughing.

"He's saving for *you*," said Pemberton. "They think of you in everything they do."

"He might, while he's about it, save a little—" The boy paused, and his friend waited to hear what. Then Morgan brought out oddly: "A little reputation."

"Oh there's plenty of that. That's all right!"

"Enough of it for the people they know, no doubt. The people they know are awful."

"Do you mean the princes? We mustn't abuse the princes."

"Why not? They haven't married Paula—they haven't married Amy. They only clean out Ulick."

"You *do* know everything!" Pemberton declared.

"No I don't after all. I don't know what they live on, or how they live, or *why* they live! What have they got and how did they get it? Are they rich, are they poor, or have they a *modeste aisance?*[12] Why are they always chiveying me about—living one year like ambassadors and the next like paupers? Who are they, anyway, and what are they? I've thought of all that—I've thought of a lot of things. They're so beastly worldly. That's what I hate most—oh I've *seen* it! All they care about is to make an appearance and to pass for something or other. What the dickens do they want to pass for? What *do* they, Mr. Pemberton?"

"You pause for a reply," said Pemberton, treating the question as a joke,

[12] *modeste aisance:* modest competence (means of life adequate for necessities).

yet wondering too and greatly struck with his mate's intense if imperfect vision. "I haven't the least idea."

"And what good does it do? Haven't I seen the way people treat them—the 'nice' people, the ones they want to know? They'll take anything from them—they'll lie down and be trampled on. The nice ones hate that—they just sicken them. You're the only really nice person we know."

"Are you sure? They don't lie down for me!"

"Well, you shan't lie down for them. You've got to go—that's what you've got to do," said Morgan.

"And what will become of you?"

"Oh I'm growing up. I shall get off before long. I'll see you later."

"You had better let me finish you," Pemberton urged, lending himself to the child's strange superiority.

Morgan stopped in their walk, looking up at him. He had to look up much less than a couple of years before—he had grown, in his loose leanness, so long and high. "Finish me?" he echoed.

"There are such a lot of jolly things we can do together yet. I want to turn you out—I want you to do me credit."

Morgan continued to look at him. "To give you credit—do you mean?"

"My dear fellow, you're too clever to live."

"That's just what I'm afraid you think. No, no, it isn't fair—I can't endure it. We'll separate next week. The sooner it's over the sooner to sleep."

"If I hear of anything—any other chance—I promise to go," Pemberton said.

Morgan consented to consider this. "But you'll be honest," he demanded; "you won't pretend you haven't heard?".

"I'm much more likely to pretend I have."

"But what can you hear of, this way, stuck in a hole with us? You ought to be on the spot, to go to England—you ought to go to America."

"One would think you were *my* tutor!" said Pemberton.

Morgan walked on and after a little had begun again: "Well, now that you know I know and that we look at the facts and keep nothing back—it's much more comfortable, isn't it?"

"My dear boy, it's so amusing, so interesting, that it will surely be quite impossible for me to forego such hours as these."

This made Morgan stop once more. "You *do* keep something back. Oh you're not straight—*I* am!"

"How am I not straight?"

"Oh you've got your idea!"

"My idea?"

"Why that I probably shan't make old—make older—bones, and that you can stick it out till I'm removed."

"You *are* too clever to live!" Pemberton repeated.

"I call it a mean idea," Morgan pursued. "But I shall punish you by the way I hang on."

"Look out or I'll poison you!" Pemberton laughed.

"I'm stronger and better every year. Haven't you noticed that there hasn't been a doctor near me since you came?"

"*I'm* your doctor," said the young man, taking his arm and drawing him tenderly on again.

Morgan proceeded and after a few steps gave a sigh of mingled weariness and relief. "Ah now that we look at the facts it's all right!"

## VII

They looked at the facts a good deal after this; and one of the first consequences of their doing so was that Pemberton stuck it out, in his friend's parlance, for the purpose. Morgan made the facts so vivid and so droll, and at the same time so bald and so ugly, that there was fascination in talking them over with him, just as there would have been heartlessness in leaving him alone with them. Now that the pair had such perceptions in common it was useless for them to pretend they didn't judge such people; but the very judgement and the exchange of perceptions created another tie. Morgan had never been so interesting as now that he himself was made plainer by the sidelight of these confidences. What came out in it most was the small fine passion of his pride. He had plenty of that, Pemberton felt—so much that one might perhaps wisely wish for it some early bruises. He would have liked his people to have a spirit and had waked up to the sense of their perpetually eating humble-pie. His mother would consume any amount, and his father would consume even more than his mother. He had a theory that Ulick had wriggled out of an "affair" at Nice: there had once been a flurry at home, a regular panic, after which they all went to bed and took medicine, not to be accounted for on any other supposition. Morgan had a romantic imagination, fed by poetry and history, and he would have liked those who "bore his name"—as he used to say to Pemberton with the humour that made his queer delicacies manly—to carry themselves with an air. But their one idea was to get in with people who didn't want them and to take snubs as if they were honourable scars. Why people didn't want them more he didn't know—that was people's own affair; after all they weren't superficially repulsive, they were a hundred times cleverer than most of the dreary grandees, the "poor swells" they rushed about Europe to catch up with. "After all they *are* amusing—they are!" he used to pronounce with the wisdom of the ages. To which Pemberton always replied: "Amusing—the great Moreen troupe? Why they're altogether delightful; and if it weren't for the hitch that you and I (feeble performers!) make in the *ensemble* they'd carry everything before them."

What the boy couldn't get over was the fact that this particular blight seemed, in a tradition of self-respect, so undeserved and so arbitrary. No doubt people had a right to take the line they liked, but why should *his* people have liked the line of pushing and toadying and lying and cheating? What had their forefathers—all decent folk, so far as he knew—done to them, or what had *he* done to them? Who had poisoned their blood with the fifth-rate social ideal, the fixed idea of making smart acquaintances and getting into the *monde chic*,[13] especially when it was foredoomed to failure and exposure? They showed so what they were after; that was what made the people they wanted not want *them*. And never a wince for dignity, never a throb of shame at looking each other in the face, never any independence or resentment or disgust. If his father or his brother would only knock some one down once or twice a year! Clever as they were they never guessed the impression they made. They were good-natured, yes—as good-natured as Jews at the doors of clothing-shops! But was that the model one wanted one's family to follow? Morgan had dim memories of an old grandfather, the maternal, in New York, whom he had been taken across the ocean at the age of five to see: a gentleman with a high neck-cloth and a good deal of pronunciation, who wore a dress-coat in the morning, which made one wonder what he wore in the evening, and had, or was supposed to have, "property" and something to do with the Bible Society. It couldn't have been but that *he* was a good type. Pemberton himself remembered Mrs. Clancy, a widowed sister of Mr. Moreen's, who was as irritating as a moral tale and had paid a fortnight's visit to the family at Nice shortly after he came to live with them. She was "pure and refined," as Amy said over the banjo, and had the air of not knowing what they meant when they talked, and of keeping something rather important back. Pemberton judged that what she kept back was an approval of many of their ways; therefore it was to be supposed that she too was of a good type, and that Mr. and Mrs. Moreen and Ulick and Paula and Amy might easily have been of a better one if they would.

But that they wouldn't was more and more perceptible from day to day. They continued to "chivey," as Morgan called it, and in due time became aware of a variety of reasons for proceeding to Venice. They mentioned a great many of them—they were always strikingly frank and had the brightest friendly chatter, at the late foreign breakfast in especial, before the ladies had made up their faces, when they leaned their arms on the table, had something to follow the *demi-tasse*, and, in the heat of familiar discussion as to what they "really ought" to do, fell inevitably into the languages in which they could *tutoyer*.[14] Even Pemberton liked them then; he could endure even Ulick when he heard him give his little flat voice for the "sweet sea-city." That was what made him have a sneaking kindness for them—that they were so out of the workaday world and kept him so out of it. The summer had waned when, with cries of ecstasy, they all passed out on the balcony that overhung the Grand Canal. The sunsets then were splendid and the Dorringtons had arrived. The Dorringtons were the only reason they hadn't talked of at breakfast; but the reasons they didn't talk of at breakfast always came out in the end. The Dorringtons on the other hand

---

[13] *monde chic:* fashionable world.
[14] *tutoyer:* use the familiar *tu* ("you") as a sign of intimacy instead of the formal *vous*.

came out very little; or else when they did they stayed—as was natural—for hours, during which periods Mrs. Moreen and the girls sometimes called at their hotel (to see if they had returned) as many as three times running. The gondola was for the ladies, as in Venice too there were "days," which Mrs. Moreen knew in their order an hour after she arrived. She immediately took one herself, to which the Dorringtons never came, though on a certain occasion when Pemberton and his pupil were together at Saint Mark's— where, taking the best walks they had ever had and haunting a hundred churches, they spent a great deal of time—they saw the old lord turn up with Mr. Moreen and Ulick, who showed him the dim basilica as if it belonged to them. Pemberton noted how much less, among its curiosities, Lord Dorrington carried himself as a man of the world; wondering too whether, for such services, his companions took a fee from him. The autumn at any rate waned, the Dorringtons departed, and Lord Verschoyle, the eldest son, had proposed neither for Amy nor for Paula.

One sad November day, while the wind roared round the old palace and the rain lashed the lagoon, Pemberton, for exercise and even somewhat for warmth—the Moreens were horribly frugal about fires; it was a cause of suffering to their inmate—walked up and down the big bare *sala*[15] with his pupil. The scagliola floor was cold, the high battered casements shook in the storm, and the stately decay of the place was unrelieved by a particle of furniture. Pemberton's spirits were low, and it came over him that the fortune of the Moreens was now even lower. A blast of desolation, a portent of disgrace and disaster, seemed to draw through the comfortless hall. Mr. Moreen and Ulick were in the Piazza, looking out for something, strolling drearily, in mackintoshes, under the arcades; but still, in spite of mackintoshes, unmistakeable men of the world. Paula and Amy were in bed—it might have been thought they were staying there to keep warm. Pemberton looked askance at the boy at his side, to see to what extent he was conscious of these dark omens. But Morgan, luckily for him, was now mainly conscious of growing taller and stronger and indeed of being in his fifteenth year. This fact was intensely interesting to him and the basis of a private theory—which, however, he had imparted to his tutor—that in a little while he should stand on his own feet. He considered that the situation would change—that in short he should be "finished," grown up, producible in the world of affairs and ready to prove himself of sterling ability. Sharply as he was capable at times of analysing, as he called it, his life, there were happy hours when he remained, as he also called it—and as the name, really, of their right ideal—"jolly" superficial; the proof of which was his fundamental assumption that he should presently go to Oxford, to Pemberton's college, and aided and abetted by Pemberton, do the most wonderful things. It depressed the young man to see how little in such a project he took account of ways and means: in other connexions he mostly kept to the measure.

---

[15] *sala:* room, hall.

Pemberton tried to imagine the Moreens at Oxford and fortunately failed; yet unless they were to adopt it as a residence there would be no *modus vivendi* for Morgan. How could he live without an allowance, and where was the allowance to come from? He, Pemberton, might live on Morgan; but how could Morgan live on *him?* What was to become of him anyhow? Somehow the fact that he was a big boy now, with better prospects of health, made the question of his future more difficult. So long as he was markedly frail the great consideration he inspired seemed enough of an answer to it. But at the bottom of Pemberton's heart was the recognition of his probably being strong enough to live and not yet strong enough to struggle or to thrive. Morgan himself at any rate was in the first flush of the rosiest consciousness of adolescence, so that the beating of the tempest seemed to him after all but the voice of life and the challenge of fate. He had on his shabby little overcoat, with the collar up, but was enjoying his walk.

It was interrupted at last by the appearance of his mother at the end of the *sala.* She beckoned him to come to her, and while Pemberton saw him, complaisant, pass down the long vista and over the damp false marble, he wondered what was in the air. Mrs. Moreen said a word to the boy and made him go into the room she had quitted. Then, having closed the door after him, she directed her steps swiftly to Pemberton. There *was* something in the air, but his wildest flight of fancy wouldn't have suggested what it proved to be. She signified that she had made a pretext to get Morgan out of the way, and then she enquired—without hesitation—if the young man could favour her with the loan of three louis. While, before bursting into a laugh, he stared at her with surprise, she declared that she was awfully pressed for the money; she was desperate for it—it would save her life.

"Dear lady, *c'est trop fort!*"[16] Pemberton laughed in the manner and with the borrowed grace of idiom that marked the best colloquial, the best anecdotic, moments of his friends themselves. "Where in the world do you suppose I should get three louis, *du train dont vous allez?*"[17]

"I thought you worked—wrote things. Don't they pay you?"

"Not a penny."

"Are you such a fool as to work for nothing?"

"You ought surely to know that."

Mrs. Moreen stared, then she coloured a little. Pemberton saw she had quite forgotten the terms—if "terms" they could be called—that he had ended by accepting from herself; they had burdened her memory as little as her conscience. "Oh yes, I see what you mean—you've been very nice about that; but why drag it in so often?" She had been perfectly urbane with him ever since the rough scene of explanation in his room the morning he made her accept *his* "terms"—the necessity of his making his case known to Morgan. She had felt no resentment after seeing there was no danger Morgan would take the matter up with her. Indeed, attributing this immunity to the

<hr/>

[16] *c'est trop fort:* it's too much.   [17] *du train dont vous allez:* at the rate you are going.

good taste of his influence with the boy, she had once said to Pemberton "My dear fellow, it's an immense comfort you're a gentleman." She repeated this in substance now. "Of course you're a gentleman—that's a bother the less!" Pemberton reminded her that he had not "dragged in" anything that wasn't already in as much as his foot was in his shoe; and she also repeated her prayer that, somewhere and somehow, he would find her sixty francs. He took the liberty of hinting that if he could find them it wouldn't be to lend them to *her*—as to which he consciously did himself injustice, knowing that if he had them he would certainly put them at her disposal. He accused himself, at bottom and not unveraciously, of a fantastic, a demoralised sympathy with her. If misery made strange bedfellows it also made strange sympathies. It was moreover a part of the abasement of living with such people that one had to make vulgar retorts, quite out of one's own tradition of good manners. "Morgan, Morgan, to what pass have I come for you?" he groaned while Mrs. Moreen floated voluminously down the *sala* again to liberate the boy, wailing as she went that everything was too odious.

Before their young friend was liberated there came a thump at the door communicating with the staircase, followed by the apparition of a dripping youth who poked in his head. Pemberton recognised him as the bearer of a telegram and recognised the telegram as addressed to himself. Morgan came back as, after glancing at the signature—that of a relative in London—he was reading the words: "Found jolly job for you, engagement to coach opulent youth on own terms. Come at once." The answer happily was paid and the messenger waited. Morgan, who had drawn near, waited too and looked hard at Pemberton; and Pemberton, after a moment, having met his look, handed him the telegram. It was really by wise looks—they knew each other so well now—that, while the telegraph-boy, in his waterproof cape, made a great puddle on the floor, the thing was settled between them. Pemberton wrote the answer with a pencil against the frescoed wall, and the messenger departed. When he had gone the young man explained himself.

"I'll make a tremendous charge; I'll earn a lot of money in a short time, and we'll live on it."

"Well, I hope the opulent youth will be a dismal dunce—he probably will," Morgan parenthesised—"and keep you a long time a-hammering of it in."

"Of course the longer he keeps me the more we shall have for our old age."

"But suppose *they* don't pay you!" Morgan awfully suggested.

"Oh there are not two such—!" but Pemberton pulled up; he had been on the point of using too invidious a term. Instead of this he said "Two such fatalities."

Morgan flushed—the tears came to his eyes. "*Dites toujours*[18] two such rascally crews!" Then in a different tone he added: "Happy opulent youth."

"Not if he's a dismal dunce."

"Oh they're happier then. But you can't have everything, can you?" the boy smiled.

[18] *Dites toujours:* Go on—say it.

Pemberton held him fast, hands on his shoulders—he had never loved him so. "What will become of *you*, what will you do?" He thought of Mrs. Moreen, desperate for sixty francs.

"I shall become an *homme fait*."[19] And then as if he recognised all the bearings of Pemberton's allusion: "I shall get on with them better when you're not here."

"Ah don't say that—it sounds as if I set you against them!"

"You do—the sight of you. It's all right; you know what I mean. I shall be beautiful. I'll take their affairs in hand; I'll marry my sisters."

"You'll marry yourself!" joked Pemberton; as high, rather tense pleasantry would evidently be the right, or the safest, tone for their separation.

It was, however, not purely in this strain that Morgan suddenly asked: "But I say—how will you get to your jolly job? You'll have to telegraph to the opulent youth for money to come on."

Pemberton bethought himself. "They won't like that, will they?"

"Oh look out for them!"

Then Pemberton brought out his remedy. "I'll go to the American Consul; I'll borrow some money of him—just for the few days, on the strength of the telegram."

Morgan was hilarious. "Show him the telegram—then collar the money and stay!"

Pemberton entered into the joke sufficiently to reply that for Morgan he was really capable of that; but the boy, growing more serious, and to prove he hadn't meant what he said, not only hurried him off to the Consulate— since he was to start that evening, as he had wired to his friend—but made sure of their affair by going with him. They splashed through the tortuous perforations and over the humpbacked bridges, and they passed through the Piazza, where they saw Mr. Moreen and Ulick go into a jeweller's shop. The Consul proved accommodating—Pemberton said it wasn't the letter, but Morgan's grand air—and on their way back they went into Saint Mark's for a hushed ten minutes. Later they took up and kept up the fun of it to the very end; and it seemed to Pemberton a part of that fun that Mrs. Moreen, who was very angry when he had announced her his intention, should charge him, grotesquely and vulgarly and in reference to the loan she had vainly endeavoured to effect, with bolting lest they should "get something out" of him. On the other hand he had to do Mr. Moreen and Ulick the justice to recognise that when on coming in *they* heard the cruel news they took it like perfect men of the world.

## VIII

When he got at work with the opulent youth, who was to be taken in hand for Balliol, he found himself unable to say if this aspirant had really such poor parts or if the appearance were only begotten of his own long association

---

[19] *homme fait:* man of experience.

with an intensely living little mind. From Morgan he heard half a dozen times: the boy wrote charming young letters, a patchwork of tongues, with indulgent postscripts in the family Volapuk and, in little squares and rounds and crannies of the text, the drollest illustrations—letters that he was divided between the impulse to show his present charge as a vain, a wasted incentive, and the sense of something in them that publicity would profane. The opulent youth went up in due course and failed to pass; but it seemed to add to the presumption that brilliancy was not expected of him all at once that his parents, condoning the lapse, which they good-naturedly treated as little as possible as if it were Pemberton's, should have sounded the rally again, begged the young coach to renew the siege.

The young coach was now in a position to lend Mrs. Moreen three louis, and he sent her a post-office order even for a larger amount. In return for this favour he received a frantic scribbled line from her: "Implore you to come back instantly—Morgan dreadfully ill." They were on the rebound, once more in Paris—often as Pemberton had seen them depressed he had never seen them crushed—and communication was therefore rapid. He wrote to the boy to ascertain the state of his health, but awaited the answer in vain. He accordingly, after three days, took an abrupt leave of the opulent youth and, crossing the Channel, alighted at the small hotel, in the quarter of the Champs Elysées, of which Mrs. Moreen had given him the address. A deep if dumb dissatisfaction with this lady and her companions bore him company: they couldn't be vulgarly honest, but they could live at hotels, in velvety *entresols*,[20] amid a smell of burnt pastilles, surrounded by the most expensive city in Europe. When he had left them in Venice it was with an irrepressible suspicion that something was going to happen; but the only thing that could have taken place was again their masterly retreat. "How is he? where is he?" he asked of Mrs. Moreen; but before she could speak these questions were answered by the pressure round his neck of a pair of arms, in shrunken sleeves, which still were perfectly capable of an effusive young foreign squeeze.

"Dreadfully ill—I don't see it!" the young man cried. And then to Morgan: "Why on earth didn't you relieve me? Why didn't you answer my letter?"

Mrs. Moreen declared that when she wrote he was very bad, and Pemberton learned at the same time from the boy that he had answered every letter he had received. This led to the clear inference that Pemberton's note had been kept from him so that the game to be practised should not be interfered with. Mrs. Moreen was prepared to see the fact exposed, as Pemberton saw the moment he faced her that she was prepared for a good many other things. She was prepared above all to maintain that she had acted from a sense of duty, that she was enchanted she had got him over, whatever they might say, and that it was useless of him to pretend he didn't know in all his bones

[20] *entresol:* mezzanine floor.

that his place at such a time was with Morgan. He had taken the boy away from them and now had no right to abandon him. He had created for himself the gravest responsibilities and must at least abide by what he had done.

"Taken him away from you?" Pemberton exclaimed indignantly.

"Do it—do it for pity's sake; that's just what I want. I can't stand *this*—and such scenes. They're awful frauds—poor dears!" These words broke from Morgan, who had intermitted his embrace, in a key which made Pemberton turn quickly to him and see that he had suddenly seated himself, was breathing in great pain and was very pale.

"*Now* do you say he's not in a state, my precious pet?" shouted his mother, dropping on her knees before him with clasped hands, but touching him no more than if he had been a gilded idol. "It will pass—it's only for an instant; but don't say such dreadful things!"

"I'm all right—all right," Morgan panted to Pemberton, whom he sat looking up at with a strange smile, his hands resting on either side on the sofa.

"Now do you pretend I've been dishonest, that I've deceived?" Mrs. Moreen flashed at Pemberton as she got up.

"It isn't *he* says it, it's I!" the boy returned, apparently easier but sinking back against the wall; while his restored friend, who had sat down beside him, took his hand and bent over him.

"Darling child, one does what one can; there are so many things to consider," urged Mrs. Moreen. "It's his *place*—his only place. You see *you* think it is now."

"Take me away—take me away," Morgan went on, smiling to Pemberton with his white face.

"Where shall I take you, and how—oh *how*, my boy?" the young man stammered, thinking of the rude way in which his friends in London held that, for his convenience, with no assurance of prompt return, he had thrown them over; of the just resentment with which they would already have called in a successor, and of the scant help to finding fresh employment that resided for him in the grossness of his having failed to pass his pupil.

"Oh we'll settle that. You used to talk about it," said Morgan. "If we can only go all the rest's a detail."

"Talk about it as much as you like, but don't think you can attempt it. Mr. Moreen would never consent—it would be so *very* hand-to-mouth," Pemberton's hostess beautifully explained to him. Then to Morgan she made it clearer: "It would destroy our peace, it would break our hearts. Now that he's back it will be all the same again. You'll have your life, your work and your freedom, and we'll all be happy as we used to be. You'll bloom and grow perfectly well, and we won't have any more silly experiments, will we? They're too absurd. It's Mr. Pemberton's place—every one in his place. You in yours, your papa in his, me in mine—*n'est-ce pas, chéri?* We'll all forget how foolish we've been and have lovely times."

She continued to talk and to surge vaguely about the little draped stuffy salon while Pemberton sat with the boy, whose colour gradually came back;

and she mixed up her reasons, hinting that there were going to be changes, that the other children might scatter (who knew?—Paula had her ideas) and that then it might be fancied how much the poor old parent-birds would want the little nestling. Morgan looked at Pemberton, who wouldn't let him move; and Pemberton knew exactly how he felt at hearing himself called a little nestling. He admitted that he had had one or two bad days, but he protested afresh against the wrong of his mother's having made them the ground of an appeal to poor Pemberton. Poor Pemberton could laugh now, apart from the comicality of Mrs. Moreen's mustering so much philosophy for her defence—she seemed to shake it out of her agitated petticoats, which knocked over the light gilt chairs—so little did their young companion, *marked*, unmistakeably marked at the best, strike him as qualified to repudiate any advantage.

He himself was in for it at any rate. He should have Morgan on his hands again indefinitely; though indeed he saw the lad had a private theory to produce which would be intended to smooth this down. He was obliged to him for it in advance; but the suggested amendment didn't keep his heart rather from sinking, any more than it prevented him from accepting the prospect on the spot, with some confidence moreover that he should do so even better if he could have a little supper. Mrs. Moreen threw out more hints about the changes that were to be looked for, but she was such a mixture of smiles and shudders—she confessed she was very nervous—that he couldn't tell if she were in high feather or only in hysterics. If the family was really at last going to pieces why shouldn't she recognise the necessity of pitching Morgan into some sort of lifeboat? This presumption was fostered by the fact that they were established in luxurious quarters in the capital of pleasure; that was exactly where they naturally *would* be established in view of going to pieces. Moreover didn't she mention that Mr. Moreen and the others were enjoying themselves at the opera with Mr. Granger, and wasn't *that* also precisely where one would look for them on the eve of a smash? Pemberton gathered that Mr. Granger was a rich vacant American—a big bill with a flourishy heading and no items; so that one of Paula's "ideas" was probably that this time she hadn't missed fire—by which straight shot indeed she would have shattered the general cohesion. And if the cohesion was to crumble what would become of poor Pemberton? He felt quite enough bound up with them to figure to his alarm as a dislodged block in the edifice.

It was Morgan who eventually asked if no supper had been ordered for him; sitting with him below, later, at the dim delayed meal, in the presence of a great deal of corded green plush, a plate of ornamental biscuit and an aloofness marked on the part of the waiter. Mrs. Moreen had explained that they had been obliged to secure a room for the visitor out of the house; and Morgan's consolation—he offered it while Pemberton reflected on the nastiness of luke-warm sauces—proved to be, largely, that this circumstance would facilitate their escape. He talked of their escape—recurring to it often afterwards—as if they were making up a "boy's book" together. But he likewise expressed his sense that there was something in the air, that the Moreens couldn't keep it up much longer. In point of fact, as Pemberton was to see, they kept it up for five or six months. All the while, however, Morgan's contention was designed to cheer him. Mr. Moreen and Ulick, whom he had met the day after his return, accepted that return like perfect men of the world. If Paula and Amy treated it even with less formality an allowance was to be made for them, inasmuch as Mr. Granger hadn't come to the opera after all. He had only placed his box at their service, with a bouquet for each of the party; there was even one apiece, embittering the thought of his profusion, for Mr. Moreen and Ulick. "They're all like that," was Morgan's comment; "at the very last, just when we think we've landed them they're back in the deep sea!"

Morgan's comments in these days were more and more free; they even included a large recognition of the extraordinary tenderness with which he had been treated while Pemberton was away. Oh yes, they couldn't do enough to be nice to him, to show him they had him on their mind and make up for his loss. That was just what made the whole thing so sad and caused him to rejoice after all in Pemberton's return—he had to keep thinking of their affection less, had less sense of obligation. Pemberton laughed out at this last reason, and Morgan blushed and said "Well, dash it, you know what I mean." Pemberton knew perfectly what he meant; but there were a good many things that—dash it too!—it didn't make any clearer. This episode of his second sojourn in Paris stretched itself out wearily, with their resumed readings and wanderings and maunderings, their potterings on the quays, their hauntings of the museums, their occasional lingerings in the Palais Royal when the first sharp weather came on and there was a comfort in warm emanations, before Chevet's wonderful succulent window. Morgan wanted to hear all about the opulent youth—he took an immense interest in him. Some of the details of his opulence—Pemberton could spare him none of them—evidently fed the boy's appreciation of all his friend had given up to come back to him; but in addition to the greater reciprocity established by that heroism he had always his little brooding theory, in which there was a frivolous gaiety too, that their long probation was drawing to a close. Morgan's conviction that the Moreens couldn't go on much longer kept pace with the unexpended impetus with which, from month to month, they did go on. Three weeks after Pemberton had rejoined them they went on to another hotel, a dingier one than the first; but Morgan rejoiced that his tutor had at least still not sacrificed the advantage of a room outside. He clung to the romantic utility of this when the day, or rather the night, should arrive for their escape.

For the first time, in this complicated connexion, our friend felt his collar gall him. It was, as he had said to Mrs. Moreen in Venice, *trop fort*—everything was *trop fort*. He could neither really throw off his blighting burden nor find in it the benefit of a pacified conscience or of a rewarded affection. He had spent all the money accruing to him in England, and he saw his youth

going and that he was getting nothing back for it. It was all very well of
Morgan to count it for reparation that he should now settle on him permanently—there was an irritating flaw in such a view. He saw what the boy had
in his mind; the conception that as his friend had had the generosity to come
back he must show his gratitude by giving him his life. But the poor friend
didn't desire the gift—what could he do with Morgan's dreadful little life?
Of course at the same time that Pemberton was irritated he remembered
the reason, which was very honourable to Morgan and which dwelt simply in
his making one so forget that he was no more than a patched urchin. If one
dealt with him on a different basis one's misadventures were one's own fault.
So Pemberton waited in a queer confusion of yearning and alarm for the
catastrophe which was held to hang over the house of Moreen, of which he
certainly at moments felt the symptoms brush his cheek and as to which he
wondered much in what form it would find its liveliest effect.

Perhaps it would take the form of sudden dispersal—a frightened *sauve qui
peut*,[21] a scuttling into selfish corners. Certainly they were less elastic than
of yore; they were evidently looking for something they didn't find. The
Dorringtons hadn't re-appeared, the princes had scattered; wasn't that the
beginning of the end? Mrs. Moreen had lost her reckoning of the famous
"days"; her social calendar was blurred—it had turned its face to the wall.
Pemberton suspected that the great, the cruel discomfiture had been the
unspeakable behaviour of Mr. Granger, who seemed not to know what he
wanted, or, what was much worse, what *they* wanted. He kept sending flowers,
as if to bestrew the path of his retreat, which was never the path of a return.
Flowers were all very well, but—Pemberton could complete the proposition.
It was now positively conspicuous that in the long run the Moreens were
a social failure; so that the young man was almost grateful the run had not
been short. Mr. Moreen indeed was still occasionally able to get away on
business and, what was more surprising, was likewise able to get back.
Ulick had no club, but you couldn't have discovered it from his appearance,
which was as much as ever that of a person looking at life from the window
of such an institution; therefore Pemberton was doubly surprised at an answer
he once heard him make his mother in the desperate tone of a man familiar
with the worst privations. Her question Pemberton had not quite caught;
it appeared to be an appeal for a suggestion as to whom they might get to
take Amy. "Let the Devil take her!" Ulick snapped; so that Pemberton
would see that they had not only lost their amiability but had ceased to
believe in themselves. He could also see that if Mrs. Moreen was trying to
get people to take her children she might be regarded as closing the hatches
for the storm. But Morgan would be the last she would part with.

One winter afternoon—it was a Sunday—he and the boy walked far
together in the Bois de Boulogne. The evening was so splendid, the cold
lemon-coloured sunset so clear, the stream of carriages and pedestrians so

---

[21] *sauve qui peut*: every man for himself.

amusing and the fascination of Paris so great, that they stayed out later than usual and became aware that they should have to hurry home to arrive in time for dinner. They hurried accordingly, arm-in-arm, good-humoured and hungry, agreeing that there was nothing like Paris after all and that after everything too that had come and gone they were not yet sated with innocent pleasures. When they reached the hotel they found that, though scandalously late, they were in time for all the dinner they were likely to sit down to. Confusion reigned in the apartments of the Moreens—very shabby ones this time, but the best in the house—and before the interrupted service of the table, with objects displaced almost as if there had been a scuffle and a great wine-stain from an overturned bottle, Pemberton couldn't blink the fact that there had been a scene of the last proprietary firmness. The storm had come—they were all seeking refuge. The hatches were down, Paula and Amy were invisible—they had never tried the most casual art upon Pemberton, but he felt they had enough of an eye to him not to wish to meet him as young ladies whose frocks had been confiscated—and Ulick appeared to have jumped overboard. The host and his staff, in a word, had ceased to "go on" at the pace of their guests, and the air of embarrassed detention, thanks to a pile of gaping trunks in the passage, was strangely commingled with the air of indignant withdrawal.

When Morgan took all this in—and he took it in very quickly—he coloured to the roots of his hair. He had walked from his infancy among difficulties and dangers, but he had never seen a public exposure. Pemberton noticed in a second glance at him that the tears had rushed into his eyes and that they were tears of a new and untasted bitterness. He wondered an instant, for the boy's sake, whether he might successfully pretend not to understand. Not successfully, he felt, as Mr. and Mrs. Moreen, dinnerless by their extinguished hearth, rose before him in their little dishonoured salon, casting about with glassy eyes for the nearest port in such a storm. They were not prostrate but were horribly white, and Mrs. Moreen had evidently been crying. Pemberton quickly learned however that her grief was not for the loss of her dinner, much as she usually enjoyed it, but the fruit of a blow that struck even deeper, as she made all haste to explain. He would see for himself, so far as that went, how the great change had come, the dreadful bolt had fallen, and how they would now all have to turn themselves about. Therefore cruel as it was to them to part with their darling she must look to him to carry a little further the influence he had so fortunately acquired with the boy—to induce his young charge to follow him into some modest retreat. They depended on him—that was the fact—to take their delightful child temporarily under his protection: it would leave Mr. Moreen and herself so much more free to give the proper attention (too little, alas! had been given) to the readjustment of their affairs.

"We trust you—we feel we *can*," said Mrs. Moreen, slowly rubbing her plump white hands and looking with compunction hard at Morgan, whose chin, not to take liberties, her husband stroked with a tentative paternal forefinger.

"Oh yes—we feel that we *can*. We trust Mr. Pemberton fully, Morgan," Mr. Moreen pursued.

Pemberton wondered again if he might pretend not to understand; but everything good gave way to the intensity of Morgan's understanding. "Do you mean he may take me to live with him for ever and ever?" cried the boy. "May take me away, away, anywhere he likes?"

"For ever and ever? *Comme vous-y-allez!*"[22] Mr. Moreen laughed indulgently. "For as long as Mr. Pemberton may be so good."

"We've struggled, we've suffered," his wife went on; "but you've made him so your own that we've already been through the worst of the sacrifice."

Morgan had turned away from his father—he stood looking at Pemberton with a light in his face. His sense of shame for their common humiliated state had dropped; the case had another side—the thing was to clutch at *that*. He had a moment of boyish joy, scarcely mitigated by the reflexion that with this unexpected consecration of his hope—too sudden and too violent; the turn taken was away from a *good* boy's book—the "escape" was left on their hands. The boyish joy was there an instant, and Pemberton was almost scared at the rush of gratitude and affection that broke through his first abasement. When he stammered "My dear fellow, what do you say to *that?*" how could one not say something enthusiastic? But there was more need for courage at something else that immediately followed and that made the lad sit down quickly on the nearest chair. He had turned quite livid and had raised his hand to his left side. They were all three looking at him, but Mrs. Moreen suddenly bounded forward. "Ah his darling little heart!" she broke out; and this time, on her knees before him and without respect for the idol, she caught him ardently in her arms. "You walked him too far, you hurried him too fast!" she hurled over her shoulder at Pemberton. Her son made no protest, and the next instant, still holding him, she sprang up with her face convulsed and with the terrified cry "Help, help! he's going, he's gone!" Pemberton saw with equal horror, by Morgan's own stricken face, that he was beyond their wildest recall. He pulled him half out of his mother's hands, and for a moment, while they held him together, they looked all their dismay into each other's eyes. "He couldn't stand it with his weak organ," said Pemberton—"the shock, the whole scene, the violent emotion."

"But I thought he *wanted* to go to you!" wailed Mrs. Moreen.

"I *told* you he didn't, my dear," her husband made answer. Mr. Moreen was trembling all over and was in his way as deeply affected as his wife. But after the very first he took his bereavement as a man of the world.

## QUESTIONS: *James, " The Pupil "*

1. What meaningful contrast is revealed in the very first scene between the parent and the child, preparing us for an understanding of the larger gap between them?

---

[22] *Comme vous-y-allez :* how you do go on.

*Clues:* • ... the large *affable* lady who sat there drawing a pair of *soiled gants de Suède* through a fat jewelled hand and, at once *pressing* and *gliding*, repeated over and over *everything* but the thing he would have liked to hear.

• He came back without the fan, only with the *casual* observation that he couldn't find it. As he dropped this *cynical confession* he looked *straight* and *hard* at the candidate for the honour of taking his education in hand.

2. Examine the suggestions of *asceticism* in the statements referring to Morgan. What is their significance in the light of Morgan's indictment of his parents as "so beastly worldly"?

*Clues:* • "It's the family language—Ultramoreen," Morgan explained to him drolly enough; but the boy rarely condescended to use it himself, though he dealt in colloquial Latin as if he had been a little prelate.

• Morgan was dear to his mother, but he never was better dressed than was absolutely necessary—partly, no doubt, by his own fault, for he was as indifferent to his appearance as a German philosopher.

• "I'm ashamed, I'm ashamed!" quavered the boy with a ring of passion, like some high silver note from a small cathedral chorister, that deeply touched his friend.

3. Which traditional *parental* responsibilities are assumed by Morgan? Which traditional parental responsibilities are assumed by Pemberton? Which are relinquished by Morgan's parents? How does this reversal of roles convey the pathological state of the family?

*Clues:* • Pemberton had got used to suddenness, having seen it practised on a considerable scale during two jerky little tours. ... They had returned to Nice "for ever," as they said; but this didn't prevent their squeezing, one rainy muggy May night, into a second-class railway-carriage ... where Pemberton helped them to stow away a wonderful collection of bundles and bags.

• Mrs. Moreen shrewdly forbore to renew his garments. She did nothing that didn't show, neglected him because he escaped notice, and then, as he illustrated this clever policy, discouraged at home his public appearances.

• Wasn't he paid enough without perpetual money—wasn't he paid by the comfortable luxurious home he enjoyed with them all, without a care, an anxiety, a solitary want. ... Wasn't he paid above all by the sweet relation he had established with Morgan—quite ideal as from master to pupil—and by the simple privilege of knowing and living with so amazingly gifted a child. ...

• "You've all the responsibility. They put me off on you from morning till night. Why then should they object to my taking up with you completely? I'd help you."

• "He might, while he's about it, save a little—" The boy paused, and his friend waited to hear what. Then Morgan brought out oddly: "A little reputation."

• "I shall be beautiful. I'll take their affairs in hand; I'll marry my sisters."

a. How do the suggestions of *age* rather than *youth* in Morgan amplify the reversal?

   *Clues:* • . . . the air in his elderly shoulders of a boy who didn't play.

   "You're very young—fortunately," Morgan went on, turning to him again.

b. How do the suggestions that Morgan functions as *teacher* rather than *student* also amplify the reversal? Consider the ironic nature of the title.

   *Clues:* • "I hope you don't mean to dismiss me," said Pemberton.

   Morgan debated, looking at the sunset. "I think if I did right I ought to."

   "Well, I know I'm supposed to instruct you in virtue; but in that case *don't do right.*"

   "You're *very young—fortunately,*" Morgan went on, turning to him again.

   "Oh yes, compared with you!"

   "Therefore it won't matter so much if you do *lose a lot of time.*"

   • What Morgan said at last was said suddenly, irrelevantly, when the moment came, in the middle of a lesson, and consisted of the apparently unfeeling words: "You ought to *filer,* you know—you really ought."

4. What distinction is made between the failure of Morgan's mother and that of his father?

   *Clues:* • "He's a genius—you'll love him!" she added.

   • He further mentioned that he aspired to be intimate with his children, to be their best friend, and that he was always looking out for them.

   • . . . a tentative paternal forefinger.

   • "Ah his darling little heart!" she broke out; and this time, on her knees before him and without respect for the idol, she caught him ardently in her arms.

   • . . . he took his bereavement as a man of the world.

5. Examine closely the third paragraph in Section II, beginning "He yet when he first applied it felt a glow of joy" and ending "he would not have grasped provincial development of Spanish or German." What characteristics of the Moreen way of life does James reveal in this paragraph through metaphors of *language and nationality*?

6. Explain the significance of *money* in the story as (a) an integral part of the plot and (b) as a metaphor used to characterize the Moreens' way of life as well as their treatment of Pemberton and Morgan. How is money used as a metaphor to describe the relationship between Pemberton and Morgan?

   *Clues:* • "They'll give you anything you like," the boy remarked unexpectedly, returning from the window. "We don't mind what anything costs—we *live awfully well.*"

   • "You know they don't pay you up," said Morgan, blushing and turning his leaves.

   "Don't pay me?" Pemberton stared again and feigned amazement. "What on earth put that into your head?"

"It has been there a long time," the boy replied rummaging his book.

   • "There are such a lot of jolly things we can do together yet. I want to turn you out—I want you to do me credit."

Morgan continued to look at him. "To *give you credit*—do you mean?"

7. What is the metaphorical significance of Morgan's *heart* condition? How are the reactions to Morgan's health a touchstone of his parents' values?

8. What is the precise nature of the *twofold* betrayal of Morgan at the conclusion? Consider carefully Pemberton's assumptions and their interaction with those of Morgan as they are revealed in the following passages (and others you may find). Also note the function of *language* (particularly the use of *irony*) in anticipating the ultimate victimization of Morgan.

*Clues:* • He had had his full wave [of experience] but *couldn't pay the score* at his inn.

   • He could neither really throw off his *blighting burden* nor find in it the benefit of a pacified conscience or of a rewarded affection. He had spent all the money accruing to him in England, and he saw his youth going and that he was *getting nothing back* for it. It was all very well of Morgan to count it for *reparation* that he should now settle on him *permanently*—there was an *irritating flaw* in such a view. He saw what the boy had in his mind; the conception that as his friend had had the generosity to come back he must show his gratitude by *giving him his life*.

   • "I haven't yet seen the thing you *are* afraid of—I'll do you that justice!"

This came out with a jump—it was perfectly true—and evidently gave Morgan pleasure. "I've thought of it a long time," he presently resumed.

"Well, don't think of it any more."

   • "You had better *let me finish you*," Pemberton urged, lending himself to the child's strange superiority.

Morgan stopped in their walk, looking up at him. . . . "Finish me?" he echoed.

"There are such a lot of jolly things we can do together yet. I want to *turn you out*—I want you *to do me credit*."

Morgan continued to look at him. "To *give you* credit—do you mean?"

"My dear fellow, you're *too clever to live*."

   • ". . . But I shall punish you by the way I hang on."

"Look out or I'll poison you!" Pemberton laughed.

   • "I'm stronger and better every year. Haven't you noticed that there hasn't been a doctor near me since you came?"

"*I'm* your doctor," said the young man, taking his arm and drawing him tenderly on again.

• When he stammered "My dear fellow, what do you say to *that*?" *how could one not say* something enthusiastic?

# A Portrait of the Artist as a Young Man

## FROM CHAPTER II

Stephen was once again seated beside his father in the corner of a railway carriage at Kingsbridge. He was travelling with his father by the night mail to Cork. As the train steamed out of the station he recalled his childish wonder of years before and every event of his first day at Clongowes. But he felt no wonder now. He saw the darkening lands slipping past him, the silent telegraphpoles passing his window swiftly every four seconds, the little glimmering stations, manned by a few silent sentries, flung by the mail behind her and twinkling for a moment in the darkness like fiery grains flung backwards by a runner.

He listened without sympathy to his father's evocation of Cork and of scenes of his youth, a tale broken by sighs or draughts from his pocketflask whenever the image of some dead friend appeared in it or whenever the evoker remembered suddenly the purpose of his actual visit. Stephen heard but could feel no pity. The images of the dead were all strange to him save that of uncle Charles, an image which had lately been fading out of memory. He knew, however, that his father's property was going to be sold by auction and in the manner of his own dispossession he felt the world give the lie rudely to his phantasy.

At Maryborough he fell asleep. When he awoke the train had passed out of Mallow and his father was stretched asleep on the other seat. The cold light of the dawn lay over the country, over the unpeopled fields and the closed cottages. The terror of sleep fascinated his mind as he watched the silent country or heard from time to time his father's deep breath or sudden sleepy movement. The neighbourhood of unseen sleepers filled him with strange dread as though they could harm him; and he prayed that the day might come quickly. His prayer, addressed neither to God nor saint, began with a shiver, as the chilly morning breeze crept through the chink of the carriage door to his feet, and ended in a trail of foolish words which he made to fit the insistent rhythm of the train; and silently, at intervals of four seconds, the telegraphpoles held the galloping notes of the music between punctual bars. This furious music allayed his dread and, leaning against the window-ledge, he let his eyelids close again.

They drove in a jingle across Cork while it was still early morning and Stephen finished his sleep in a bedroom of the Victoria Hotel. The bright warm sunlight was streaming through the window and he could hear the din of traffic. His father was standing before the dressingtable, examining his hair and face and moustache with great care, craning his neck across the waterjug and drawing it back sideways to see the better. While he did so he sang softly to himself with quaint accent and phrasing:

> 'Tis youth and folly
> Makes young men marry,
> So here, my love, I'll
>       No longer stay.
> What can't be cured, sure,
> Must be injured, sure,
>       So I'll go to
>       Amerikay.

> My love she's handsome,
> My love she's bonny:
> She's like good whisky
>       When it is new;
> But when 'tis old
> And growing cold
> It fades and dies like
>       The mountain dew.

The consciousness of the warm sunny city outside his window and the tender tremors with which his father's voice festooned the strange sad happy air, drove off all the mists of the night's ill humour from Stephen's brain. He got up quickly to dress and, when the song had ended, said:

—That's much prettier than any of your other *come-all-yous*.[1]

—Do you think so? asked Mr Dedalus.

—I like it, said Stephen.

—It's a pretty old air, said Mr Dedalus, twirling the points of his moustache. Ah, but you should have heard Mick Lacy sing it! Poor Mick Lacy! He had little turns for it, grace notes he used to put in that I haven't got. That was the boy who could sing a *come-all-you*, if you like.

Mr Dedalus had ordered drisheens[2] for breakfast and during the meal he crossexamined the waiter for local news. For the most part they spoke at crosspurposes when a name was mentioned, the waiter having in mind the present holder and Mr Dedalus his father or perhaps his grandfather.

—Well, I hope they haven't moved the Queen's College anyhow, said Mr Dedalus, for I want to show it to this youngster of mine.

Along the Mardyke the trees were in bloom. They entered the grounds of the college and were led by the garrulous porter across the quadrangle. But their progress across the gravel was brought to a halt after every dozen or so paces by some reply of the porter's.

—Ah, do you tell me so? And is poor Pottlebelly dead?

—Yes, sir. Dead, sir.

During these halts Stephen stood awkwardly behind the two men, weary

---

[1] *come-all-yous*: popular songs associated with street singers.
[2] *drisheens*: white pudding made of meat and oatmeal.

of the subject and waiting restlessly for the slow march to begin again. By the time they had crossed the quadrangle his restlessness had risen to fever. He wondered how his father, whom he knew for a shrewd suspicious man, could be duped by the servile manners of the porter; and the lively southern speech which had entertained him all the morning now irritated his ears.

They passed into the anatomy theatre where Mr Dedalus, the porter aiding him, searched the desks for his initials. Stephen remained in the background, depressed more than ever by the darkness and silence of the theatre and by the air it wore of jaded and formal study. On the desk before him he read the word *Fœtus* cut several times in the dark stained wood. The sudden legend startled his blood: he seemed to feel the absent students of the college about him and to shrink from their company. A vision of their life, which his father's words had been powerless to evoke, sprang up before him out of the word cut in the desk. A broadshouldered student with a moustache was cutting in the letters with a jackknife, seriously. Other students stood or sat near him laughing at his handiwork. One jogged his elbow. The big student turned on him, frowning. He was dressed in loose grey clothes and had tan boots.

Stephen's name was called. He hurried down the steps of the theatre so as to be as far away from the vision as he could be and, peering closely at his father's initials, hid his flushed face.

But the word and the vision capered before his eyes as he walked back across the quadrangle and towards the college gate. It shocked him to find in the outer world a trace of what he had deemed till then a brutish and individual malady of his own mind. His recent monstrous reveries came thronging into his memory. They too had sprung up before him, suddenly and furiously, out of mere words. He had soon given in to them and allowed them to sweep across and abase his intellect, wondering always where they came from, from what den of monstrous images, and always weak and humble towards others, restless and sickened of himself when they had swept over him.

—Ay, bedad! And there's the Groceries[3] sure enough! cried Mr Dedalus. You often heard me speak of the Groceries, didn't you, Stephen. Many's the time we went down there when our names had been marked, a crowd of us, Harry Peard and little Jack Mountain and Bob Dyas and Maurice Moriarty, the Frenchman, and Tom O'Grady and Mick Lacy that I told you of this morning and Joey Corbet and poor little good hearted Johnny Keevers of the Tantiles.

The leaves of the trees along the Mardyke were astir and whispering in the sunlight. A team of cricketers passed, agile young men in flannels and blazers, one of them carrying the long green wicketbag. In a quiet bystreet a German band of five players in faded uniforms and with battered brass instruments was playing to an audience of street arabs and leisurely messenger

---

[3] *Groceries:* a pub.

boys. A maid in a white cap and apron was watering a box of plants on a sill which shone like a slab of limestone in the warm glare. From another window open to the air came the sound of a piano, scale after scale rising into the treble.

Stephen walked on at his father's side, listening to stories he had heard before, hearing again the names of the scattered and dead revellers who had been the companions of his father's youth. And a faint sickness sighed in his heart. He recalled his own equivocal position in Belvedere,[4] a free boy, a leader afraid of his own authority, proud and sensitive and suspicious, battling against the squalor of his life and against the riot of his mind. The letters cut in the stained wood of the desk stared upon him, mocking his bodily weakness and futile enthusiasms and making him loathe himself for his own mad and filthy orgies. The spittle in his throat grew bitter and foul to swallow and the faint sickness climbed to his brain so that for a moment he closed his eyes and walked on in darkness.

He could still hear his father's voice.

—When you kick out for yourself, Stephen—as I daresay you will one of those days—remember, whatever you do, to mix with gentlemen. When I was a young fellow I tell you I enjoyed myself. I mixed with fine decent fellows. Everyone of us could do something. One fellow had a good voice, another fellow was a good actor, another could sing a good comic song, another was a good oarsman or a good racketplayer, another could tell a good story and so on. We kept the ball rolling anyhow and enjoyed ourselves and saw a bit of life and we were none the worse of it either. But we were all gentlemen, Stephen—at least I hope we were—and bloody good honest Irishmen too. That's the kind of fellows I want you to associate with, fellows of the right kidney. I'm talking to you as a friend, Stephen. I don't believe in playing the stern father. I don't believe a son should be afraid of his father. No, I treat you as your grandfather treated me when I was a young chap. We were more like brothers than father and son. I'll never forget the first day he caught me smoking. I was standing at the end of the South Terrace one day with some maneens like myself and sure we thought we were grand fellows because we had pipes stuck in the corners of our mouths. Suddenly the governor passed. He didn't say a word, or stop even. But the next day, Sunday, we were out for a walk together and when we were coming home he took out his cigar case and said: *By the bye, Simon, I didn't know you smoked:* or something like that. Of course I tried to carry it off as best I could. *If you want a good smoke,* he said, *try one of these cigars. An American captain made me a present of them last night in Queenstown.*

Stephen heard his father's voice break into a laugh which was almost a sob.

—He was the handsomest man in Cork at that time, by God he was! The women used to stand to look after him in the street.

He heard the sob passing loudly down his father's throat and opened his

---

[4] *Belvedere:* the Jesuit school Stephen is now attending.

eyes with a nervous impulse. The sunlight breaking suddenly on his sight turned the sky and clouds into a fantastic world of sombre masses with lake-like spaces of dark rosy light. His very brain was sick and powerless. He could scarcely interpret the letters of the signboards of the shops. By his monstrous way of life he seemed to have put himself beyond the limits of reality. Nothing moved him or spoke to him from the real world unless he heard in it an echo of the infuriated cries within him. He could respond to no earthly or human appeal, dumb and insensible to the call of summer and gladness and companionship, wearied and dejected by his father's voice. He could scarcely recognise as his his own thoughts, and repeated slowly to himself:

—I am Stephen Dedalus. I am walking beside my father whose name is Simon Dedalus. We are in Cork, in Ireland. Cork is a city. Our room is in the Victoria Hotel. Victoria and Stephen and Simon. Simon and Stephen and Victoria. Names.

The memory of his childhood suddenly grew dim. He tried to call forth some of its vivid moments but could not. He recalled only names: Dante,[5] Parnell,[6] Clane, Clongowes.[7] A little boy had been taught geography by an old woman who kept two brushes in her wardrobe. Then he had been sent away from home to a college. In the college he had made his first communion and eaten slim jim out of his cricketcap and watched the firelight leaping and dancing on the wall of a little bedroom in the infirmary and dreamed of being dead, of mass being said for him by the rector in a black and gold cope, of being buried then in the little graveyard of the community off the main avenue of limes. But he had not died then. Parnell had died. There had been no mass for the dead in the chapel and no procession. He had not died but he had faded out like a film in the sun. He had been lost or had wandered out of existence for he no longer existed. How strange to think of him passing out of existence in such a way, not by death but by fading out in the sun or by being lost and forgotten somewhere in the universe! It was strange to see his small body appear again for a moment: a little boy in a grey belted suit. His hands were in his sidepockets and his trousers were tucked in at the knees by elastic bands.

On the evening of the day on which the property was sold Stephen followed his father meekly about the city from bar to bar. To the sellers in the market, to the barmen and barmaids, to the beggars who importuned him for a lob Mr Dedalus told the same tale, that he was an old Corkonian, that he had been trying for thirty years to get rid of his Cork accent up in Dublin and that Peter Pickackafax beside him was his eldest son but that he was only a Dublin jackeen.

---

[5] *Dante:* a maiden lady, one-time governess to the Dedalus children.

[6] *Parnell:* Charles Stewart Parnell (1846–1891), parliamentary leader of the Irish independence movement, was disowned by his followers when named as correspondent in a divorce suit. He died soon after his loss of power.

[7] *Clane, Clongowes:* Clane, a village near Clongowes, the Jesuit school Stephen attended as a young boy.

They had set out early in the morning from Newcombe's coffeehouse where Mr Dedalus' cup had rattled noisily against its saucer, and Stephen had tried to cover that shameful sign of his father's drinkingbout of the night before by moving his chair and coughing. One humiliation had succeeded another: the false smiles of the market sellers, the curvettings and oglings of the barmaids with whom his father flirted, the compliments and encouraging words of his father's friends. They had told him that he had a great look of his grandfather and Mr Dedalus had agreed that he was an ugly likeness. They had unearthed traces of a Cork accent in his speech and made him admit that the Lee was a much finer river than the Liffey. One of them in order to put his Latin to the proof had made him translate short passages from Dilectus and asked him whether it was correct to say: *Tempora mutantur nos et mutamur in illis* or *Tempora mutantur et nos mutamur in illis*.[8] Another, a brisk old man, whom Mr Dedalus called Johnny Cashman, had covered him with confusion by asking him to say which were prettier, the Dublin girls or the Cork girls.

—He's not that way built, said Mr Dedalus. Leave him alone. He's a levelheaded thinking boy who doesn't bother his head about that kind of nonsense.

—Then he's not his father's son, said the little old man.

—I don't know, I'm sure, said Mr Dedalus, smiling complacently.

—Your father, said the little old man to Stephen, was the boldest flirt in the city of Cork in his day. Do you know that?

Stephen looked down and studied the tiled floor of the bar into which they had drifted.

—Now don't be putting ideas into his head, said Mr Dedalus. Leave him to his Maker.

—Yerra, sure I wouldn't put any ideas into his head. I'm old enough to be his grandfather. And I am a grandfather, said the little old man to Stephen. Do you know that?

—Are you? asked Stephen.

—Bedad I am, said the little old man. I have two bouncing grandchildren out at Sunday's Well. Now then! What age do you think I am? And I remember seeing your grandfather in his red coat riding out to hounds. That was before you were born.

—Ay, or thought of, said Mr Dedalus.

—Bedad I did, repeated the little old man. And, more than that, I can remember even your greatgrandfather, old John Stephen Dedalus, and a fierce old fireeater he was. Now then! There's a memory for you!

—That's three generations—four generations, said another of the company. Why, Johnny Cashman, you must be nearing the century.

—Well, I'll tell you the truth, said the little old man. I'm just twentyseven years of age.

---

[8] *Tempora mutantur nos et mutamur in illis* or *Tempora mutantur et nos mutamur in illis*. The times change and we change with them (the second version is the correct one metrically).

—We're as old as we feel, Johnny, said Mr Dedalus. And just finish what you have there, and we'll have another. Here, Tim or Tom or whatever your name is, give us the same again here. By God, I don't feel more than eighteen myself. There's that son of mine there not half my age and I'm a better man than he is any day of the week.

—Draw it mild now, Dedalus. I think it's time for you to take a back seat, said the gentleman who had spoken before.

—No, by God! asserted Mr Dedalus. I'll sing a tenor song against him or I'll vault a fivebarred gate against him or I'll run with him after the hounds across the country as I did thirty years ago along with the Kerry Boy and the best man for it.

—But he'll beat you here, said the little old man, tapping his forehead and raising his glass to drain it.

—Well, I hope he'll be as good a man as his father. That's all I can say, said Mr Dedalus.

—If he is, he'll do, said the little old man.

—And thanks be to God, Johnny, said Mr Dedalus, that we lived so long and did so little harm.

—But did so much good, Simon, said the little old man gravely. Thanks be to God we lived so long and did so much good.

Stephen watched the three glasses being raised from the counter as his father and his two cronies drank to the memory of their past. An abyss of fortune or of temperament sundered him from them. His mind seemed older than theirs: it shone coldly on their strifes and happiness and regrets like a moon upon a younger earth. No life or youth stirred in him as it had stirred in them. He had known neither the pleasure of companionship with others nor the vigour of rude male health nor filial piety. Nothing stirred within his soul but a cold and cruel and loveless lust. His childhood was dead or lost and with it his soul capable of simple joys, and he was drifting amid life like the barren shell of the moon.

> Art thou pale for weariness
> Of climbing heaven and gazing on the earth,
> Wandering companionless . . . ?

He repeated to himself the lines of Shelley's fragment. Its alternation of sad human ineffectualness with vast inhuman cycles of activity chilled him, and he forgot his own human and ineffectual grieving.

## QUESTIONS: *Joyce, A Portrait of the Artist as a Young Man*

1. Why are the words "he felt no wonder now" an appropriate introduction to this selection? What connection is there between the state of mind in which Stephen is and the statement in the second paragraph suggesting Stephen's reaction to his father: "Stephen heard but could feel no pity"?

2. What indications are there in the first few paragraphs that the natures of father and son differ? Do they have something in common?

3. In what way is the prayer uttered in the train an anticipation of Stephen's later moods and a clue to his nature?

4. Why does the word *foetus* allow Stephen to bridge the generation gap and get "a vision of [the students'] life, which his father's words had been powerless to evoke"? What does he discover about the unconscious life of the older generations? How does the lack of recognition by one generation of another generation's unconscious life promote the generation gap? What part in this process is played by the pride of the young and the insensitivity of the old?

5. Examine the passage which begins with "Stephen walked on at his father's side," and ends with "fellows of the right kidney." How does the contrast between Mr. Dedalus' *spoken* reminiscences about the past and Stephen's *silent* broodings about his present mental and emotional life dramatize the contrast in their temperaments and values? How does that contrast exemplify a generation gap?

   Clues: • The letters . . . stared upon him, mocking his bodily weakness and futile enthusiasms. . . .

   • We kept the ball rolling anyhow and enjoyed ourselves and saw a bit of life and we were none the worse of it either.

6. What contrast does the narrator establish between the reminiscences of Mr. Dedalus and Stephen's memories of his own childhood? What role might this contrast play in defining the gap between Stephen and his father?

   Clue: • . . . he had made his first communion and eaten slim jim out of his cricketcap and watched the firelight leaping and dancing on the wall of a little bedroom in the infirmary and dreamed of being dead. . . .

7. How does *dramatic* and *verbal irony* operate in Mr. Dedalus'
   a. assertion that he is talking to Stephen "as a friend"?
   b. reference to Stephen's grandfather: "The women used to stand to look after him in the street"?
   c. conviction that Stephen is "a levelheaded thinking boy who doesn't bother his head about that kind of nonsense" (the relative prettiness of Dublin and Cork girls) and that others should not "be putting ideas into his head"?
   d. claim that, with regard to his son, "I'm a better man than he is any day of the week" and expressed hope that "he'll be as good a man as his father"?

8. What is the effect of the reference to "four generations" in dramatizing Stephen's alienation?

9. What is the dramatic relevance to what precedes of Stephen's realization that "His mind seemed older than theirs: it shone coldly on their strifes and happiness and regrets like a moon upon a younger earth"?

10. How does the last sentence of the selection lead us back to the train scene?

# *Virginia Woolf (1882–1941)*
# Lord Chesterfield's Letters to His Son

When Lord Mahon edited the letters of Lord Chesterfield he thought it necessary to warn the intending reader that they are "by no means fitted for early or indiscriminate perusal". Only "those people whose understandings are fixed and whose principles are matured" can, so his Lordship said, read them with impunity. But that was in 1845. And 1845 looks a little distant now. It seems to us now the age of enormous houses without any bathrooms. Men smoke in the kitchen after the cook has gone to bed. Albums lie upon drawing-room tables. The curtains are very thick and the women are very pure. But the eighteenth century also has undergone a change. To us in 1930 it looks less strange, less remote than those early Victorian years. Its civilisation seems more rational and more complete than the civilisation of Lord Mahon and his contemporaries. Then at any rate a small group of highly educated people lived up to their ideals. If the world was smaller it was also more compact; it knew its own mind; it had its own standards. Its poetry is affected by the same security. When we read the *Rape of the Lock* we seem to find ourselves in an age so settled and so circumscribed that masterpieces were possible. Then, we say to ourselves, a poet could address himself whole-heartedly to his task and keep his mind upon it, so that the little boxes on a lady's dressing-table are fixed among the solid possessions of our imaginations. A game at cards or a summer's boating party upon the Thames has power to suggest the same beauty and the same sense of things vanishing that we receive from poems aimed directly at our deepest emotions. And just as the poet could spend all his powers upon a pair of scissors and a lock of hair, so too, secure in his world and its values, the aristocrat could lay down precise laws for the education of his son. In that world also there was a certainty, a security that we are now without. What with one thing and another times have changed. We can now read Lord Chesterfield's letters without blushing, or, if we do blush, we blush in the twentieth century at passages that caused Lord Mahon no discomfort whatever.

When the letters begin, Philip Stanhope, Lord Chesterfield's natural son by a Dutch governess, was a little boy of seven. And if we are to make any complaint against the father's moral teaching, it is that the standard is too high for such tender years. "Let us return to oratory, or the art of speaking well; which should never be entirely out of our thoughts", he writes to the boy of seven. "A man can make no figure without it in Parliament, or the Church, or in the law", he continues, as if the little boy were already considering his career. It seems, indeed, that the father's fault, if fault it be, is one common to distinguished men who have not themselves succeeded as they should have done and are determined to give their children—and Philip was an only child—the chances that they have lacked. Indeed, as the letters go on one may suppose that Lord Chesterfield wrote as much to amuse himself by turning over the stores of his experience, his reading, his knowledge of the world, as to instruct his son. The letters show an eagerness, an animation which prove that to write to Philip was not a task, but a delight. Tired, perhaps, with the duties of office and disillusioned with its disappointments, he takes up his pen and, in the relief of free communication at last, forgets that his correspondent is, after all, only a schoolboy who cannot understand half the things that his father says to him. But, even so, there is nothing to repel us in Lord Chesterfield's preliminary sketch of the unknown world. He is all on the side of moderation, toleration, ratiocination. Never abuse whole bodies of people, he counsels; frequent all churches, laugh at none; inform yourself about all things. Devote your mornings to study, your evenings to good society. Dress as the best people dress, behave as they behave, never be eccentric, egotistical, or absent-minded. Observe the laws of proportion, and live every moment to the full.

So, step by step, he builds up the figure of the perfect man—the man that Philip may become, he is persuaded, if he will only—and here Lord Chesterfield lets fall the words which are to colour his teaching through and through —cultivate the Graces. These ladies are, at first, kept discreetly in the background. It is well that the boy should be indulged in fine sentiments about women and poets to begin with. Lord Chesterfield adjures him to respect them both. "For my own part, I used to think myself in company as much above me when I was with Mr. Addison and Mr. Pope, as if I had been with all the Princes in Europe", he writes. But as time goes on the Virtues are more and more taken for granted. They can be left to take care of themselves. But the Graces assume tremendous proportions. The Graces dominate the life of man in this world. Their service cannot for an instant be neglected. And the service is certainly exacting. For consider what it implies, this art of pleasing. To begin with, one must know how to come into a room and then how to go out again. As human arms and legs are notoriously perverse, this by itself is a matter needing considerable dexterity. Then one must be dressed so that one's clothes seem perfectly fashionable without being new or striking; one's teeth must be perfect; one's wig beyond reproach; one's finger-nails cut in the segment of a circle; one must be able to carve, able to dance, and, what is almost as great an art, able to sit gracefully in a chair. These things are the alphabet of the art of pleasing. We now come to speech. It is necessary to speak at least three languages to perfection. But before we open our lips we must take a further precaution—we must be on our guard never to laugh. Lord Chesterfield himself never laughed. He always smiled. When at length the young man is pronounced capable of speech he must avoid all proverbs and vulgar expressions; he must enunciate clearly and use perfect grammar; he must not argue; he must not tell stories; he must not talk about himself. Then, at last, the young man may begin to practise the finest of the arts of pleasing—the art of flattery. For every man and every woman has some prevailing vanity. Watch, wait, pry, seek out their weakness "and you will then know what to bait your hook with to catch them". For that is the secret of success in the world.

It is at this point, such is the idiosyncrasy of our age, that we begin to feel uneasy. Lord Chesterfield's views upon success are far more questionable than his views upon love. For what is to be the prize of this endless effort and self-abnegation? What do we gain when we have learnt to come into rooms and to go out again; to pry into people's secrets; to hold our tongues and to flatter, to forsake the society of low-born people which corrupts and the society of clever people which perverts? What is the prize which is to reward us? It is simply that we shall rise in the world. Press for a further definition, and it amounts perhaps to this: one will be popular with the best people. But if we are so exacting as to demand who the best people are we become involved in a labyrinth from which there is no returning. Nothing exists in itself. What is good society? It is the society that the best people believe to be good. What is wit? It is what the best people think to be witty. All value depends upon somebody else's opinion. For it is the essence of this philosophy that things have no independent existence, but live only in the eyes of other people. It is a looking-glass world, this, to which we climb so slowly; and its prizes are all reflections. That may account for our baffled feeling as we shuffle, and shuffle vainly, among these urbane pages for something hard to lay our hands upon. Hardness is the last thing we shall find. But, granted the deficiency, how much that is ignored by sterner moralists is here seized upon, and who shall deny, at least while Lord Chesterfield's enchantment is upon him, that these imponderable qualities have their value and these shining Graces have their radiance? Consider for a moment what the Graces have done for their devoted servant, the Earl.

Here is a disillusioned politician, who is prematurely aged, who has lost his office, who is losing his teeth, who, worst fate of all, is growing deafer day by day. Yet he never allows a groan to escape him. He is never dull; he is never boring; he is never slovenly. His mind is as well groomed as his body. Never for a second does he "welter in an easy-chair". Private though these letters are, and apparently spontaneous, they play with such ease in and about the single subject which absorbs them that it never becomes tedious or, what is still more remarkable, never becomes ridiculous. It may be that the art of pleasing has some connection with the art of writing. To be polite, considerate, controlled, to sink one's egotism, to conceal rather than to obtrude one's personality may profit the writer even as they profit the man of fashion.

Certainly there is much to be said in favour of the training, however we define it, which helped Lord Chesterfield to write his Characters. The little papers have the precision and formality of some old-fashioned minuet. Yet the symmetry is so natural to the artist that he can break it where he likes; it never becomes pinched and formal, as it would in the hands of an imitator. He can be sly; he can be witty; he can be sententious, but never for an instant does he lose his sense of time, and when the tune is over he calls a halt. "Some succeeded, and others burst" he says of George the First's mistresses: the King liked them fat. Again, "He was fixed in the house of lords, that hospital of incurables". He smiles: he does not laugh. Here the eighteenth century, of course, came to his help. Lord Chesterfield, though he was polite to everything, even to the stars and Bishop Berkeley's philosophy, firmly refused, as became a son of his age, to dally with infinity or to suppose that things are not quite as solid as they seem. The world was good enough and the world was big enough as it was. This prosaic temper, while it keeps him within the bounds of impeccable common sense, limits his outlook. No single phrase of his reverberates or penetrates as so many of La Bruyère's do. But he would have been the first to deprecate any comparison with that great writer; besides, to write as La Bruyère wrote, one must perhaps believe in something, and then how difficult to observe the Graces! One might perhaps laugh; one might perhaps cry. Both are equally deplorable.

But while we amuse ourselves with this brilliant nobleman and his views on life we are aware, and the letters owe much of their fascination to this consciousness, of a dumb yet substantial figure on the farther side of the page. Philip Stanhope is always there. It is true that he says nothing, but we feel his presence in Dresden, in Berlin, in Paris, opening the letters and poring over them and looking dolefully at the thick packets which have been accumulating year after year since he was a child of seven. He had grown into a rather serious, rather stout, rather short young man. He had a taste for foreign politics. A little serious reading was rather to his liking. And by every post the letters came—urbane, polished, brilliant, imploring and commanding him to learn to dance, to learn to carve, to consider the management of his legs, and to seduce a lady of fashion. He did his best. He worked very hard in the school of the Graces, but their service was too exacting. He sat down half-way up the steep stairs which lead to the glittering hall with all the mirrors. He could not do it. He failed in the House of Commons; he subsided into some small post in Ratisbon; he died untimely. He left it to his widow to break the news which he had lacked the heart or the courage to tell his father—that he had been married all these years to a lady of low birth, who had borne him children.

The Earl took the blow like a gentleman. His letter to his daughter-in-law is a model of urbanity. He began the education of his grandsons. But he seems to have become a little indifferent to what happened to himself after that. He did not care greatly if he lived or died. But still to the very end he cared for the Graces. His last words were a tribute of respect to those goddesses. Some one came into the room when he was dying; he roused himself: "Give Dayrolles a chair", he said, and said no more.

## QUESTIONS: *Woolf, "Lord Chesterfield's Letters to His Son"*

1. Consider the passage in the first paragraph beginning "And 1845 looks a little distant now" and ending "so circumscribed that masterpieces were possible." What distinctions does Virginia Woolf draw in this passage between the mode of life and assumptions of the eighteenth century and those of the nineteenth century? What do her comments about these two centuries reveal about her attitude to the twentieth century?

2. What truths about the generation gap (also dealt with in Donald Davie's "Remembering the Thirties") are suggested by the following?
   a. In the statement about the eighteenth century: "To us in 1930 it looks less strange, less remote than those early Victorian years."

    b. In the suggestion that if we feel any unease, we would "blush in the twentieth century at passages that caused Lord Mahon no discomfort whatever."

3. How does the suggestion that Lord Chesterfield's interest in his son is in part vicarious, making him unaware "that his correspondent is, after all, only a schoolboy," prepare us for the criticism of his values which follows?

4. What is the effect of using the terms *the Virtues* and *the Graces* for what we might ordinarily call "moral virtues" and "social accomplishments"? What judgment of Lord Chesterfield is revealed in the author's statement, as a summary of Chesterfield's attitudes, that the Virtues "can be left to take care of themselves"?

5. What connection does Virginia Woolf imply between Lord Chesterfield's desire to provide "an only child" with "the chances [he had] lacked" and his forgetfulness of his correspondent's inability to "understand half the things that his father says to him"? How representative is this situation of the relationship between the generations?

6. What shift in tone and approach to her subject become apparent with the sentence, "It is at this point, such is the idiosyncrasy of our age, that we begin to feel uneasy"? What ironic criticism of the values of Lord Chesterfield is implied by "the idiosyncrasy of our age" and by the following:

    a. The later statement that Lord Chesterfield "firmly refused, as became a son of his age, to dally with infinity or to suppose that things are not quite as solid as they seem. The world was good enough and the world was big enough as it was."

    b. The author's suggestion that from Lord Chesterfield's point of view laughing and crying would be "equally deplorable," and a great obstacle to observing the Graces.

## E. E. Cummings (1894–1962)
## "old age sticks"

old age sticks
up Keep
Off
signs) &

youth yanks them         5
down (old
age
cries No

Tres) & (pas)
youth laughs         10
(sing
old age

scolds Forbid
den Stop
Must                                                          15
n't Don't

&) youth goes
right on
gr
owing old                                                    20

## QUESTIONS: *Cummings, "old age sticks"*

1. How does this poem establish that it is the function of age to preserve values?
   *Clues:*    • up Keep
                Off
                signs) &

              • den Stop
                Must
                n't Don't

   What in the performance of this function provokes youthful rebellion?

2. What contrasting characteristics of youth and age are suggested by "sticks/up" and "yanks . . . down"? In what way is their behavior similar?

3. Cummings specifies *old* age in this poem. What is the purpose or effect of this qualification?

4. The dramatic highlight of the poem occurs in the last stanza. What is its tone? What view of the generation gap does it imply?

5. What contribution to Cummings' theme is made by the physical appearance of the poem?
   *Clues:*    • Off

              • cries No

              • Tres) & (pas)

              • n't Don't

              • gr
                owing old

## EXERCISE

Compare Cummings' view of the progress of youth with that expressed by Spenser in the lines:

> For Youngth is a bubble blown vp with breath,
> Whose witt is weakenesse, whose wage is death,

*Clue:*    • Compare "yanks . . . down" with "blown vp with breath" and "youth laughs" with "Whose witt is weakenesse."

# Ernest Hemingway (1899–1961)
# Fathers and Sons

*This story from the collection* Winner Take Nothing *is the last of the semi-autobiographical stories dealing with Nick Adams. Others appear in* In Our Time *and* Men Without Women.

There had been a sign to detour in the center of the main street of this town, but cars had obviously gone through, so, believing it was some repair which had been completed, Nicholas Adams drove on through the town along the empty, brick-paved street, stopped by traffic lights that flashed on and off on this traffic-less Sunday, and would be gone next year when the payments on the system were not met; on under the heavy trees of the small town that are a part of your heart if it is your town and you have walked under them, but that are only too heavy, that shut out the sun and that dampen the houses for a stranger; out past the last house and onto the highway that rose and fell straight away ahead with banks of red dirt sliced cleanly away and the second-growth timber on both sides. It was not his country but it was the middle of fall and all of this country was good to drive through and to see. The cotton was picked and in the clearings there were patches of corn, some cut with streaks of red sorghum, and, driving easily, his son asleep on the seat by his side, the day's run made, knowing the town he would reach for the night, Nick noticed which corn fields had soy beans or peas in them, how the thickets and the cut-over land lay, where the cabins and houses were in relation to the fields and the thickets; hunting the country in his mind as he went by; sizing up each clearing as to feed and cover and figuring where you would find a covey and which way they would fly.

In shooting quail you must not get between them and their habitual cover, once the dogs have found them, or when they flush they will come pouring at you, some rising steep, some skimming by your ears, whirring into a size you have never seen them in the air as they pass, the only way being to turn and take them over your shoulder as they go, before they set their wings and angle down into the thicket. Hunting this country for quail as his father had taught him, Nicholas Adams started thinking about his father. When he first thought about him it was always the eyes. The big frame, the quick movements, the wide shoulders, the hooked, hawk nose, the beard that covered the weak chin, you never thought about—it was always the eyes. They were protected in his head by the formation of the brows; set deep as though a special protection had been devised for some very valuable instrument. They saw much farther and much quicker than the human eye sees and they were the great gift his father had. His father saw as a big-horn ram or as an eagle sees, literally.

He would be standing with his father on one shore of the lake, his own eyes were very good then, and his father would say, "They've run up the flag." Nick could not see the flag or the flag pole. "There," his father would say, "it's your sister Dorothy. She's got the flag up and she's walking out onto the dock."

Nick would look across the lake and he could see the long wooded shore-line, the higher timber behind, the point that guarded the bay, the clear hills of the farm and the white of their cottage in the trees but he could not see any flag pole, or any dock, only the white of the beach and the curve of the shore.

"Can you see the sheep on the hillside toward the point?"

"Yes."

They were a whitish patch on the gray-green of the hill.

"I can count them," his father said.

Like all men with a faculty that surpasses human requirements, his father was very nervous. Then, too, he was sentimental, and, like most sentimental people, he was both cruel and abused. Also, he had much bad luck, and it was not all of it his own. He had died in a trap that he had helped only a little to set, and they had all betrayed him in their various ways before he died. All sentimental people are betrayed so many times. Nick could not write about him yet, although he would, later, but the quail country made him remember him as he was when Nick was a boy and he was very grateful to him for two things; fishing and shooting. His father was as sound on those two things as he was unsound on sex, for instance, and Nick was glad that it had been that way; for some one has to give you your first gun or the opportunity to get it and use it, and you have to live where there is game or fish if you are to learn about them, and now, at thirty-eight, he loved to fish and to shoot exactly as much as when he first had gone with his father. It was a passion that had never slackened and he was very grateful to his father for bringing him to know it.

While for the other, that his father was not sound about, all the equipment you will ever have is provided and each man learns all there is for him to know about it without advice; and it makes no difference where you live. He remembered very clearly the only two pieces of information his father had given him about that. Once when they were out shooting together Nick shot a red squirrel out of a hemlock tree. The squirrel fell, wounded, and when Nick picked him up bit the boy clean through the ball of the thumb.

"The dirty little bugger," Nick said and smacked the squirrel's head against the tree. "Look how he bit me."

His father looked and said, "Suck it out clean and put some iodine on when you get home."

"The little bugger," Nick said.

"Do you know what a bugger is?" his father asked him.

"We call anything a bugger," Nick said.

"A bugger is a man who has intercourse with animals."

"Why?" Nick said.

"I don't know," his father said. "But it is a heinous crime."

Nick's imagination was both stirred and horrified by this and he thought of various animals but none seemed attractive or practical and that was the sum total of direct sexual knowledge bequeathed him by his father except on one other subject. One morning he read in the paper that Enrico Caruso had been arrested for mashing.

"What is mashing?"

"It is one of the most heinous of crimes," his father answered. Nick's imagination pictured the great tenor doing something strange, bizarre, and heinous with a potato masher to a beautiful lady who looked like the pictures of Anna Held on the inside of cigar boxes. He resolved, with considerable horror, that when he was old enough he would try mashing at least once.

His father had summed up the whole matter by stating that masturbation produced blindness, insanity, and death, while a man who went with prostitutes would contract hideous venereal diseases and that the thing to do was to keep your hands off of people. On the other hand his father had the finest pair of eyes he had ever seen and Nick had loved him very much and for a long time. Now, knowing how it had all been, even remembering the earliest times before things had gone badly was not good remembering. If he wrote it he could get rid of it. He had gotten rid of many things by writing them. But it was still too early for that. There were still too many people. So he decided to think of something else. There was nothing to do about his father and he had thought it all through many times. The handsome job the undertaker had done on his father's face had not blurred in his mind and all the rest of it was quite clear, including the responsibilities. He had complimented the undertaker. The undertaker had been both proud and smugly pleased. But it was not the undertaker that had given him that last face. The undertaker had only made certain dashingly executed repairs of doubtful artistic merit. The face had been making itself and being made for a long time. It had modelled fast in the last three years. It was a good story but there were still too many people alive for him to write it.

Nick's own education in those earlier matters had been acquired in the hemlock woods behind the Indian camp. This was reached by a trail which ran from the cottage through the woods to the farm and then by a road which wound through the slashings to the camp. Now if he could still feel all of that trail with bare feet. First there was the pine-needle loam through the hemlock woods behind the cottage where the fallen logs crumbled into wood dust and long splintered pieces of wood hung like javelins in the tree that had been struck by lightning. You crossed the creek on a log and if you stepped off there was the black muck of the swamp. You climbed a fence out of the woods and the trail was hard in the sun across the field with cropped grass and sheep sorrel and mullen growing and to the left the quaky bog of the creek bottom where the killdeer plover fed. The spring house was in that creek. Below the barn there was fresh warm manure and the other older manure that was caked dry on top. Then there was another fence and the hard, hot trail from the barn to the house and the hot sandy road that ran down to the woods, crossing the creek, on a bridge this time, where the cat-tails grew that you soaked in kerosene to make jack-lights with for spearing fish at night.

Then the main road went off to the left, skirting the woods and climbing the hill, while you went into the woods on the wide clay and shale road, cool under the trees, and broadened for them to skid out the hemlock bark the Indians cut. The hemlock bark was piled in long rows of stacks, roofed over with more bark, like houses, and the peeled logs lay huge and yellow where the trees had been felled. They left the logs in the woods to rot, they did not even clear away or burn the tops. It was only the bark they wanted for the tannery at Boyne City; hauling it across the lake on the ice in winter, and each year there was less forest and more open, hot, shadeless, weed-grown slashing.

But there was still much forest then, virgin forest where the trees grew high before there were any branches and you walked on the brown, clean, springy-needled ground with no undergrowth and it was cool on the hottest days and they three lay against the trunk of a hemlock wider than two beds are long, with the breeze high in the tops and the cool light that came in patches, and Billy said:

"You want Trudy again?"

"You want to?"

"Uh Huh."

"Come on."

"No, here."

"But Billy—"

"I no mind Billy. He my brother."

Then afterwards they sat, the three of them, listening for a black squirrel that was in the top branches where they could not see him. They were waiting for him to bark again because when he barked he would jerk his tail and Nick would shoot where he saw any movement. His father gave him only three cartridges a day to hunt with and he had a single-barrel twenty-gauge shotgun with a very long barrel.

"Son of a bitch never move," Billy said.

"You shoot, Nickie. Scare him. We see him jump. Shoot him again," Trudy said. It was a long speech for her.

"I've only got two shells," Nick said.

"Son of a bitch," said Billy.

They sat against the tree and were quiet. Nick was feeling hollow and happy.

"Eddie says he going to come some night sleep in bed with you sister Dorothy."

"What?"

"He said."

Trudy nodded.

"That's all he want do," she said. Eddie was their older half-brother. He was seventeen.

"If Eddie Gilby ever comes at night and even speaks to Dorothy you know what I'd do to him? I'd kill him like this." Nick cocked the gun and hardly taking aim pulled the trigger, blowing a hole as big as your hand in the head or belly of that half-breed bastard Eddie Gilby. "Like that. I'd kill him like that."

"He better not come then," Trudy said. She put her hand in Nick's pocket.

"He better watch out plenty," said Billy.

"He's big bluff," Trudy was exploring with her hand in Nick's pocket. "But don't you kill him. You get plenty trouble."

"I'd kill him like that," Nick said. Eddie Gilby lay on the ground with all his chest shot away. Nick put his foot on him proudly.

"I'd scalp him," he said happily.

"No," said Trudy. "That's dirty."

"I'd scalp him and send it to his mother."

"His mother dead," Trudy said. "Don't you kill him, Nickie. Don't you kill him for me."

"After I scalped him I'd throw him to the dogs."

Billy was very depressed. "He better watch out," he said gloomily.

"They'd tear him to pieces," Nick said, pleased with the picture. Then, having scalped that half-breed renegade and standing, watching the dogs tear him, his face unchanging, he fell backward against the tree, held tight around the neck, Trudy holding, choking him, and crying, "No kill him! No kill him! No kill him! No. No. No. Nickie. Nickie. Nickie!"

"What's the matter with you?"

"No kill him."

"I got to kill him."

"He just a big bluff."

"All right," Nickie said. "I won't kill him unless he comes around the house. Let go of me."

"That's good," Trudy said. "You want to do anything now? I feel good now."

"If Billy goes away." Nick had killed Eddie Gilby, then pardoned him his life, and he was a man now.

"You go, Billy. You hang around all the time. Go on."

"Son a bitch," Billy said. "I get tired this. What we come? Hunt or what?"

"You can take the gun. There's one shell."

"All right. I get a big black one all right."

"I'll holler," Nick said.

Then, later, it was a long time after and Billy was still away.

"You think we make a baby?" Trudy folded her brown legs together happily and rubbed against him. Something inside Nick had gone a long way away.

"I don't think so," he said.

"Make plenty baby what the hell."

They heard Billy shoot.

"I wonder if he got one."

"Don't care," said Trudy.

Billy came through the trees. He had the gun over his shoulder and he held a black squirrel by the front paws.

"Look," he said. "Bigger than a cat. You all through?"

"Where'd you get him?"

"Over there. Saw him jump first."

"Got to go home," Nick said.

"No," said Trudy.

"I got to get there for supper."

"All right."

"Want to hunt tomorrow?"

"All right."

"You can have the squirrel."

"All right."

"Come out after supper?"

"No."

"How you feel?"

"Good."

"All right."

"Give me kiss on the face," said Trudy.

Now, as he rode along the highway in the car and it was getting dark, Nick was all through thinking about his father. The end of the day never made him think of him. The end of the day had always belonged to Nick alone and he never felt right unless he was alone at it. His father came back to him in the fall of the year, or in the early spring when there had been jacksnipe on the prairie, or when he saw shocks of corn, or when he saw a lake, or if he ever saw a horse and buggy, or when he saw, or heard, wild geese, or in a duck blind; remembering the time an eagle dropped through the whirling snow to strike a canvas-covered decoy, rising his wings beating, the talons caught in the canvas. His father was with him, suddenly, in deserted orchards and in new-plowed fields, in thickets, on small hills, or when going through dead grass, whenever splitting wood or hauling water, by grist mills, cider mills and dams and always with open fires. The towns he lived in were not towns his father knew. After he was fifteen he had shared nothing with him.

His father had frost in his beard in cold weather and in hot weather he sweated very much. He liked to work in the sun on the farm because he did not have to and he loved manual work, which Nick did not. Nick loved his father but hated the smell of him and once when he had to wear a suit of his father's underwear that had gotten too small for his father it made him feel sick and he took it off and put it under two stones in the creek and said that he had lost it. He had told his father how it was when his father had made him put it on but his father had said it was freshly washed. It had been, too. When Nick had asked him to smell of it his father sniffed at it indignantly and said that it was clean and fresh. When Nick came home from fishing without it and said he lost it he was whipped for lying.

Afterwards he had sat inside the woodshed with the door open, his shotgun loaded and cocked, looking across at his father sitting on the screen porch reading the paper, and thought, "I can blow him to hell. I can kill him." Finally he felt his anger go out of him and he felt a little sick about it being the gun that his father had given him. Then he had gone to the Indian camp, walking there in the dark, to get rid of the smell. There was only one person in his family that he liked the smell of; one sister. All the others he avoided all contact with. That sense blunted when he started to smoke. It was a good thing. It was good for a bird dog but it did not help a man.

"What was it like, Papa, when you were a little boy and used to hunt with the Indians?"

"I don't know," Nick was startled. He had not even noticed the boy was awake. He looked at him sitting beside him on the seat. He had felt quite alone but this boy had been with him. He wondered for how long. "We used to go all day to hunt black squirrels," he said. "My father only gave me three shells a day because he said that would teach me to hunt and it wasn't good for a boy to go banging around. I went with a boy named Billy Gilby and his sister Trudy. We used to go out nearly every day all one summer."

"Those are funny names for Indians."

"Yes, aren't they," Nick said.

"But tell me what they were like."

"They were Ojibways," Nick said. "And they were very nice."

"But what were they like to be with?"

"It's hard to say," Nick Adams said. Could you say she did first what no one has ever done better and mention plump brown legs, flat belly, hard little breasts, well holding arms, quick searching tongue, the flat eyes, the good taste of mouth, then uncomfortably, tightly, sweetly, moistly, lovely, tightly, achingly, fully, finally, unendingly, never-endingly, never-to-end-ingly, suddenly ended, the great bird flown like an owl in the twilight, only it daylight in the woods and hemlock needles stuck against your belly. So that when you go in a place where Indians have lived you smell them gone and all the empty pain killer bottles and the flies that buzz do not kill the sweetgrass smell, the smoke smell and that other like a fresh cased marten skin. Nor any jokes about them nor old squaws take that away. Nor the sick sweet smell they get to have. Nor what they did finally. It wasn't how they ended. They all ended the same. Long time ago good. Now no good.

And about the other. When you have shot one bird flying you have shot all birds flying. They are all different and they fly in different ways but the sensation is the same and the last one is as good as the first. He could thank his father for that.

"You might not like them," Nick said to the boy. "But I think you would."

"And my grandfather lived with them too when he was a boy, didn't he?"

"Yes. When I asked him what they were like he said that he had many friends among them."

"Will I ever live with them?"

"I don't know," Nick said. "That's up to you."

"How old will I be when I get a shotgun and can hunt by myself?"

"Twelve years old if I see you are careful."

"I wish I was twelve now."

"You will be, soon enough."

"What was my grandfather like? I can't remember him except that he gave me an air rifle and an American flag when I came over from France that time. What was he like?"

"He's hard to describe. He was a great hunter and fisherman and he had wonderful eyes."

"Was he greater than you?"

"He was a much better shot and his father was a great wing shot too."

"I'll bet he wasn't better than you."

"Oh, yes he was. He shot very quickly and beautifully. I'd rather see him shoot than any man I ever knew. He was always very disappointed in the way I shot."

"Why do we never go to pray at the tomb of my grandfather?"

"We live in a different part of the country. It's a long way from here."

"In France that wouldn't make any difference. In France we'd go. I think I ought to go to pray at the tomb of my grandfather."

"Sometime we'll go."

"I hope we won't live somewhere so that I can never go to pray at your tomb when you are dead."

"We'll have to arrange it."

"Don't you think we might all be buried at a convenient place? We could all be buried in France. That would be fine."

"I don't want to be buried in France," Nick said.

"Well, then, we'll have to get some convenient place in America. Couldn't we all be buried out at the ranch?"

"That's an idea."

"Then I could stop and pray at the tomb of my grandfather on the way to the ranch."

"You're awfully practical."

"Well, I don't feel good never to have even visited the tomb of my grandfather."

"We'll have to go," Nick said. "I can see we'll have to go."

## QUESTIONS: *Hemingway, "Fathers and Sons"*

1. How do the particular circumstances of the story (the protagonist's presence in a countryside not familiar to him and in the company of his son) dramatize the theme of the ambiguous relation between the generations?
2. How does Nick Adams in retrospect evaluate his father's advice on (a) hunting and fishing, (b) sexual matters? How just is Nick's contention that it is more important to be instructed in the first than in the second? Could he be subconsciously rationalizing? Could the author be doing so?
3. Why are Nick's fantasies, brought on by his father's warnings, amusing? What later scene suggests that the protagonist has come to a certain understanding of parental predicaments?
4. How characteristic of Nick's nature is hostility? When is it heightened by prejudice? What, in regard to his father, is the climactic evidence of that hostility?
5. In what way are the values suggested by the relationship between the Indian brother and sister different from those which seem to govern Nick's family?
6. What may be the function of Nick's son in clarifying the relationships that prevail between generations? Does the last scene give you a sense of completion? Justify your answer.

## EXERCISES

Write an essay on
1. The limits of possible truthfulness between parents and children (not just on sexual matters but on other aspects of life).
2. Parental advice-giving as a source of friction in the family.

# Cross Questions

## *Chaucer, Spenser, Bacon, Johnson, James, Cummings, Davie, Snodgrass*

These authors have dealt with the relationships between generations of persons who have *no kinship* to each other. What light do the tensions and conflicts between them shed on the reasons for the generation gap *within families?*

*Clues:*    Spenser:   Ah foolish old man, I scorne thy skill,
That wouldest me, my springing youngth to spil.

      Johnson:  Age looks with anger on the temerity of youth, and youth with contempt on the scrupulosity of age.

  Snodgrass:  The sleek, expensive girls I teach,
Younger and pinker every year,
Bloom gradually out of reach.

## *Bacon, Johnson, Hemingway, Simpson, Webb*

1. What to each of these authors are the most important *characteristics* of the generation gap? What variations can you detect among the writers in their *attitudes* toward the existence of such a gap?

Clues: Johnson: ... in a short time the children become rivals to their parents. Benefits are allayed by reproaches, and gratitude debased by envy. [Johnson gives the symptoms of this rivalry. What do you think might be its causes?]

Bacon: The illiberality [i.e., stinginess] of parents in allowance towards their children is an harmful error. .... And therefore the proof is best, when men keep their authority towards their children, but not their purse.

Hemingway: Nick loved his father but hated the smell of him and once when he had to wear a suit of his father's underwear that had gotten too small for his father it made him feel sick. ...

Webb: "Dad, look. ... The graduate comes home. He gets disillusioned. He gets bitter. He sits around home and goes to pot. His parents wring their hands and blame his failings on themselves. ... It has kind of a hearts and flowers ring to it."

2. Bacon and Johnson make direct statements about conflicts between generations. What do Hemingway, Simpson, and Webb, who do not make such statements but rather suggest tensions by other means, tell us about the generation gap through (a) *narration* and *description?* (b) *dialogue*: What topics are the subject of conversation between parents and children? What topics are not discussed? What conclusions do these dialogues allow one to make about the relationships between the generations? (c) *imagery* and *symbolism?*

Clues: Hemingway: The big frame ... the beard that covered the weak chin, you never thought about—it was always the eyes.

His father saw as a big-horn ram or as an eagle sees, literally.

His father came back to him in the fall ... remembering the time an eagle dropped through the whirling snow to strike a canvas-covered decoy, rising his wings beating, the talons caught in the canvas.

Simpson: The actors in that playhouse always sit
In fixed positions—father, mother, child
  With painted eyes.
How sad it is to be a little puppet!

Webb: Sometimes ... he sat a long time after the last movie was over watching one of the test patterns or the photograph of an American flag that one of the channels always put on the screen after they had played the national anthem and signed off the air.

## Sheridan, Mill, Butler, Woolf

1. What *threat to the emotional life* of the younger generation do these authors detect in the exercise of authority by the older generation? Take into account the particular parental values which determine the exercise of that authority. What

qualitative difference is there between Mill's view of the dangers and that of the other three authors?

Clues:  Sheridan: "A sincere penitent. I am come, sir, to acknowledge my error, and to submit entirely to your will."

> Mill: . . . it is impossible not to feel true pity for a father . . . who could have so valued their [his children's] affection, yet who must have been constantly feeling that fear of him was drying it up at its source.

> Butler: . . . he hung his head and looked sheepish, but kept his own counsel.

> Woolf: He left it to his widow to break the news which he had lacked the heart or the courage to tell his father. . . .

2. How does the difference in *point of view* of the four writers affect the treatment of the subject? Note that although Mill's is the only personal account, the personal presence of the other writers is felt—to a lesser or greater degree. Whose presence is felt most? Whose least? Justify your answer.

Clues:  • The presence of the narrator in Butler.
       • The use of the third person plural in Woolf.

3. What *stylistic* devices enhance the treatment of the generation gap in these four authors and give each treatment its particular flavor? Note any resemblances in the use of language.

Clues:  Sheridan: ". . . she shall be crooked as the crescent; her one eye shall roll like the bull's at Cox's Museum, she shall have a skin like a mummy, and the beard of a Jew. . . . Yet I will make you ogle her all day. . . ."

> Mill: . . . his moral teaching was not likely to err on the side of laxity or indulgence.

> Butler: . . . the mangled bones of too many a murdered confession were lying whitening round the skirts of his mother's dress. . . .

> Woolf: He sat down half-way up the steep stairs which lead to the glittering hall with all the mirrors.

## Sheridan, James, Joyce, O'Connor, Wolfe, Webb

In each of the works by these authors, children, adolescents, or young men consciously live *very private* or *fantasy* lives or assume *disguises* in order to deal with parental authority. Explain in each case what aspect of parental authority motivates the younger generation to a form of escape. What mode of parental behavior is implicitly criticized in each case by the form of the "put-on"?

Clues:  Sheridan: Captain Absolute's ironic self-abasement.

> Joyce: The inappropriateness of Mr. Dedalus' advice to Stephen on how to live ("remember, whatever you do, to mix with gentlemen").

> James: The pupil's early remark to his tutor about his family: "We don't mind what anything costs—we live awfully well."

Webb: The inappropriateness of the Braddocks' party for Benjamin. Consider also what other forms of *betrayal of parents by children* are explored by some of these authors. On what grounds are acts of rebellion, defiance, and negation made to seem justifiable and appealing? Which author least condones the betrayal? Which makes it most acceptable? Consider with which of the above authors Butler might most have identified himself in the treatment of this theme.

## Butler, James, Webb, Wolfe

1. Simpson in "My Father in the Night Commanding No" writes "And yet my father sits and reads in silence,/ My mother sheds a tear . . ." What light do these descriptions cast on the *respective roles* of the parent figures in the works of the above authors? Are the contributions that the fathers make to the generation gap qualitatively different from those of the mothers? If so, how?

   *Clues:* Butler: The dining room and the sofa as respective domains of the father and mother.

   James: "We trust you, we feel we *can*," said Mrs. Moreen, slowly rubbing her plump white hands and looking with compunction hard at Morgan, whose chin, not to take liberties, her husband stroked with a tentative paternal forefinger.

   Webb: The respective attempts by Mr. and Mrs. Braddock to find out what troubles Benjamin.

2. How does the generational drama differ in the works of those authors who deal exclusively in the relations of children with *only one parent*, namely O'Connor (mother and son), Sheridan, Mill, Virginia Woolf, and Hemingway (father and son)?

## Hemingway, Joyce, O'Connor, Wolfe, Webb

1. Given the fact that certain flaws in character (pride, arrogance, willfulness, hypocrisy) are associated with the older generation in its authoritative position by earlier writers like Bacon, Sheridan, and Butler, with what *moral flaws* in the older generation are modern writers like Hemingway, Joyce, O'Connor, Webb, and Wolfe concerned?

   *Clues:* Hemingway: Nick loved his father but hated the smell of him. . . .

   Joyce: . . . Stephen had tried to cover that shameful sign of his father's drinkingbout of the night before. . . .

   O'Connor: At that moment he could with pleasure have slapped her as he would have slapped a particularly obnoxious child in his charge.

   Wolfe: "What do *you* do?" . . . "What are you doing right now?"

2. In *The Revolutionist's Handbook* of *Man and Superman* Shaw says "The best brought-up children are those who have seen their parents as they are. Hypocrisy is not the parent's first duty." In the light of the above question on the weaknesses of the older generation as seen by the modern writers, what new burdens, perhaps

unsuspected by Shaw, has the view of parents "as they are" in fact imposed upon the children? Since the major modern complaint against parents is still that of hypocrisy, has the term undergone a modification of meaning?

3. What part in the treatment of the generation gap by the five writers above does the conflict between *intellect* and *emotion*, pride and love play in determining the younger generation's attitude toward the older?

    a. Note in particular the intellectual tendencies of Stephen, Julian, and Benjamin.

    b. Consider that the threat to the emotional life of the younger generation has become qualitatively different in modern times, that it now faces the reverse of Mill's problem.

4. All the five writers use *description* for symbolic purposes. Compare and contrast their efforts, suggesting what each of them achieves through style. (Consider, for example, the treatment of neighborhoods by Joyce, O'Connor, and Wolfe, and of a natural setting by Hemingway.)

# Section II

*Protest, Revolution, and Anarchy*

## Allen Ginsberg (1926– )

# America

America I've given you all and now I'm nothing.
America two dollars and twentyseven cents January 17, 1956.
I can't stand my own mind.
America when will we end the human war?
Go fuck yourself with your atom bomb.                                              5
I don't feel good don't bother me.
I won't write my poem till I'm in my right mind.
America when will you be angelic?
When will you take off your clothes?
When will you look at yourself through the grave?                                  10
When will you be worthy of your million Trotskyites?
America why are your libraries full of tears?
America when will you send your eggs to India?
I'm sick of your insane demands.
When can I go into the supermarket and buy what I need with my good
     looks?                                                                        15
America after all it is you and I who are perfect not the next world.
Your machinery is too much for me.
You made me want to be a saint.
There must be some other way to settle this argument.
Burroughs is in Tangiers I don't think he'll come back it's sinister.               20
Are you being sinister or is this some form of practical joke?
I'm trying to come to the point.
I refuse to give up my obsession.
America stop pushing I know what I'm doing.
America the plum blossoms are falling.                                             25
I haven't read the newspapers for months, everyday somebody goes on
     trial for murder.
America I feel sentimental about the Wobblies.
America I used to be a communist when I was a kid I'm not sorry.
I smoke marijuana every chance I get.
I sit in my house for days on end and stare at the roses in the closet.             30
When I go to Chinatown I get drunk and never get laid.
My mind is made up there's going to be trouble.
You should have seen me reading Marx.
My psychoanalyst thinks I'm perfectly right.
I won't say the Lord's Prayer.                                                     35
I have mystical visions and cosmic vibrations.
America I still haven't told you what you did to Uncle Max after he came
     over from Russia.

I'm addressing you.
Are you going to let your emotional life be run by Time Magazine?
I'm obsessed by Time Magazine.                                        40
I read it every week.
Its cover stares at me every time I slink past the corner candystore.
I read it in the basement of the Berkeley Public Library.
It's always telling me about responsibility. Businessmen are serious. Movie
    producers are serious. Everybody's serious but me.
It occurs to me that I am America.                                    45
I am talking to myself again.


Asia is rising against me.
I haven't got a chinaman's chance.
I'd better consider my national resources.
My national resources consist of two joints of marijuana millions of genitals
    an unpublishable private literature that goes 1400 miles an hour and
    twentyfive-thousand mental institutions.                          50
I say nothing about my prisons nor the millions of underprivileged who live
    in my flowerpots under the light of five hundred suns.
I have abolished the whorehouses of France, Tangiers is the next to go.
My ambition is to be President despite the fact that I'm a Catholic.


America how can I write a holy litany in your silly mood?
I will continue like Henry Ford my strophes are as individual as his auto-
    mobiles more so they're all different sexes.                       55
America I will sell you strophes $2500 apiece $500 down on your old
    strophe
America free Tom Mooney
America save the Spanish Loyalists
America Sacco & Vanzetti must not die
America I am the Scottsboro boys.                                      60
America when I was seven momma took me to Communist Cell meetings
    they sold us garbanzos a handful per ticket a ticket costs a nickel and the
    speeches were free everybody was angelic and sentimental about the
    workers it was all so sincere you have no idea what a good thing the
    party was in 1835 Scott Nearing was a grand old man a real mensch
    Mother Bloor made me cry I once saw Israel Amter plain. Everybody
    must have been a spy.
America you don't really want to go to war.
America it's them bad Russians.
Them Russians them Russians and them Chinamen. And them Russians.
The Russia wants to eat us alive. The Russia's power mad. She wants to
    take our cars from out our garages.                               65
Her wants to grab Chicago. Her needs a Red Readers' Digest. Her wants

our auto plants in Siberia. Him big bureaucracy running our filling-
stations.
That no good. Ugh. Him make Indians learn read. Him need big black
niggers. Hah. Her make us all work sixteen hours a day. Help.
America this is quite serious.
America this is the impression I get from looking in the television set.
America is this correct? 70
I'd better get right down to the job.
It's true I don't want to join the Army or turn lathes in precision parts
factories, I'm nearsighted and psychopathic anyway.
America I'm putting my queer shoulder to the wheel.

## Ginsberg, *"America"*

### Note

*The references to such figures as the Wobblies, the Spanish Loyalists, Sacco and Vanzetti,
and the Scottsboro boys evoke radical political and social causes before World War II.
There is an echo of Browning's line in "Memorabilia": "Ah! did you once see Shelley
plain."*

### QUESTIONS

1. In a lyric poem like Louis Simpson's "My Father in the Night Commanding
No" or W. D. Snodgrass' "April Inventory," a speaker (the "I" and "me"
of the poem) is revealing to us his identity, his real self. To what extent does
Ginsberg do the same thing in "America"? What elements in his presentation
work against the sense of a clearly delineated identity? What vision of modern
American man does this approach reflect?
    *Clues:* • I can't stand my own mind.
    • I don't feel good don't bother me.
      I won't write my poem till I'm in my right mind.
    • There must be some other way to settle this argument.
    • I'm trying to come to the point.
    • It occurs to me that I am America.
      I am talking to myself again.
    • America how can I write a holy litany in your silly mood?
    • America this is quite serious.

2. In an eighteenth-century poem the reader might find an address by such personi-
fied abstractions as Poverty, or Britannia, or Chaos. Are the personifications
in this poem and their voices clearly set off from the sections of the poem that
are in Ginsberg's own voice? Can we, in fact, be certain who the speakers are?
What does this blurring of distinctions do to the poem?
    *Clues:* • Asia is rising against me.
      I haven't got a chinaman's chance.
      I'd better consider my national resources.

*217*

My national resources consist of two joints of marijuana millions of genitals an unpublishable private literature that goes 1400 miles an hour and twentyfive-thousand mental institutions.

- My ambition is to be President despite the fact that I'm a Catholic.
- The Russia wants to eat us alive.
- That no good. Ugh. Him make Indians learn read.

3. The speaker declares at one point in the poem: "America after all it is you and I who are perfect not the next world." Does this comment represent a sudden reversal of his general negative attitude toward America? Does the later statement "When I go to Chinatown I get drunk and never get laid" represent a concession to American morality, and therefore an admission that it is not all bad? Consider tone carefully.

4. What central American attitudes and institutions is Ginsberg attacking? Does his declaration "It occurs to me that I am America" destroy the impact of his criticism? If not, what dimension does it give to the poem as a whole?

5. In what way does the poem seek to reverse our conventional attitudes toward mental illness (and sexual inversion)? What connection is there between this attempted reversal and the negation of materialistic values in the poem?

Clues:  • I don't feel good don't bother me.
   I won't write my poem till I'm in my right mind.

  • I refuse to give up my obsession.

  • I have mystical visions and cosmic vibrations.

  • I'm obsessed by Time Magazine.

  • I'm talking to myself again.

  • My national resources consist of . . . twentyfive-thousand mental institutions.

  • . . . I'm nearsighted and psychopathic anyway.

  • America I'm putting my queer shoulder to the wheel.

What connection do you see between Ginsberg's vision of himself as mentally unstable and his assumption of the role of the artist, whose *occupation* may be said to be to "stare at the roses in the closet"?

# EXERCISES

1. Discuss the ways in which the state of mind of Ginsberg's speaker resembles that of (a) the Ancient Mariner in Coleridge's poem, (b) the protagonist in Lawrence's "The Man Who Loved Islands," (c) the young in Mailer's "The Siege of Chicago" who "would try every idea, every drug, every action . . ." Are these resemblances merely superficial or do they suggest a common agony or alienation?

2. Ginsberg frankly concedes in interviews that his poetic style is derived from Walt Whitman. Discuss the significant differences between Whitman's use of this style in the excerpt from "Song of Myself" in Section III and Ginsberg's in "America."

*Robert Lowell (1917–     )*

# Children of Light

Our fathers wrung their bread from stocks and stones
And fenced their gardens with the Redman's bones;
Embarking from the Nether Land of Holland,
Pilgrims unhoused[1] by Geneva's[2] night,
They planted here the Serpent's seeds of light;                    5
And here the pivoting searchlights probe to shock
The riotous glass houses built on rock,
And candles gutter by an empty altar,
And light is where the landless blood of Cain
Is burning, burning the unburied grain.                            10

QUESTIONS: *Lowell, "Children of Light"*

1.  Is this poem only a protest against the values of modern America? What connection do you see between the *failings* suggested in the latter part of the poem and the *hardships* referred to in the beginning?

    *Clue:*   • Our fathers wrung their bread from *stocks* and stones
              And *fenced* their *gardens* with the *Redman's bones;*

2.  By the division and capitalization of "Nether Land" in line 3, Lowell not only refers to the Pilgrims' emigration from the Lowlands but ironically exploits the negative connotations of "Nether" to suggest moral failings. How is irony used as a tool of protest in the references to the following:

    a.  Light: Consider the significance of the "*Serpent's* seeds of light," "*pivoting* searchlights," "*riotous* glass houses," "candles" that "gutter," "*burning* . . . grain."

    b.  The Scriptures: "Children of Light" (Luke 16:1–13), "wrung their bread," "the Serpent's" (Genesis 3), "built on rock" (Matthew 16:18), "blood of Cain" (Genesis 4:1–16).

    c.  Cultivation: "wrung their bread," "planted here," "landless blood," "unburied grain" (surplus grain destroyed to maintain prices).

3.  The poet is himself a descendant of the Puritans whose values he deals with here. What aspect of their spirit is apparent in his criticism? He is also a convert to Catholicism. Does this information seem to you significant in your comprehension of the poem? Why or why not?

---

[1] *unhoused :* without receiving the last sacrament.
[2] *Geneva :* associated with John Calvin and the doctrine of Puritanism.

# The Siege of Chicago

## CHAPTERS 14–16

### *Chapter 14*

They were young men who were not going to Vietnam. So they would show every lover of war in Vietnam that the reason they did not go was not for lack of the courage to fight: no, they would carry the fight over every street in Old Town and the Loop where the opportunity presented itself. If they had been gassed and beaten, their leaders arrested on fake charges (Hayden, picked up while sitting under a tree in daylight in Lincoln Park, naturally protested; the resulting charge was "resisting arrest") they were going to demonstrate that they would not give up, that they were the stuff out of which the very best soldiers were made. Sunday, they had been driven out of the park, Monday as well, now Tuesday. The centers where they slept in bedrolls on the floor near Lincoln Park had been broken into by the police, informers and provocateurs were everywhere; tonight tear-gas trucks had been used. They were still not ready to give up. Indeed their militancy may have increased. They took care of the worst of their injured and headed for the Loop, picking up fellow demonstrators as they went. Perhaps the tear gas was a kind of catharsis for some of them, a letting of tears, a purging of old middle-class weakness. Some were turning from college boys to revolutionaries. It seemed as if the more they were beaten and tear-gassed, the more they rallied back. Now, with the facility for underground communication which seemed so instinctive a tool in their generation's equipment, they were on their way to Grant Park, en masse, a thousand of them, two thousand of them, there were conceivably as many as five thousand boys and girls massed in Grant Park at three in the morning, listening to speakers, cheering, chanting, calling across Michigan Avenue to the huge brooding façade of the Hilton, a block wide, over twenty-five stories high, with huge wings and deep courts (the better to multiply the number of windows with a view of the street and a view of Grant Park). The lights were on in hundreds of bedrooms in the Hilton, indeed people were sleeping and dreaming all over the hotel with the sound of young orators declaiming in the night below, voices rising twenty, twenty-five stories high, the voices clear in the spell of sound which hung over the Hilton. The Humphrey headquarters were here, and the McCarthy headquarters. Half the Press was quartered here, and Marvin Watson as well. Postmaster General and Presidential troubleshooter, he had come to bring some of Johnson's messages to Humphrey. His suite had a view of the park. Indeed two-thirds of the principals at the convention must have had a view early this morning, two and three and four A.M. of this Tuesday night, no, this Wednesday morning, of Grant Park filled across the street with a revolutionary army of dissenters and demonstrators and college children and McCarthy workers and tourists ready to take a crack on the head, all night they could hear the demonstrators chanting, "Join us, join us," and the college bellow of utter contempt, "Dump the Hump! Dump the Hump!" all the fury of the beatings and the tear-gassings, all the bitter disappointments of that recently elapsed bright spring when the only critical problem was who would make a better President, Kennedy or McCarthy (now all the dread of a future with Humphrey or Nixon). There was also the sense that police had now entered their lives, become an element pervasive as drugs and books and sex and music and family. So they shouted up to the windows of the Hilton, to the delegates and the campaign workers who were sleeping, or shuddering by the side of their bed, or cheering by their open window; they called up through the night on a stage as vast and towering as one of Wagner's visions and the screams of police cars joined them, pulling up, gliding away, blue lights revolving, lines of police hundreds long in their sky-blue shirts and sky-blue crash helmets, penning the demonstrators back of barriers across Michigan Avenue from the Hilton, and other lines of police and police fences on the Hilton's side of the street. The police had obviously been given orders not to attack the demonstrators here, not in front of the Hilton with half the Democratic Party watching them, not now at three in the morning—would anyone ever discover for certain what was to change their mind in sixteen hours?

Now, a great cheer went up. The police were being relieved by the National Guard. The Guard was being brought in! It was like a certificate of merit for the demonstrators to see the police march off and new hundreds of Guardsmen in khaki uniforms, helmets, and rifles take up post in place, army trucks coughing and barking and filing back and forth on Michigan Avenue, and on the side streets now surrounding the Hilton, evil-looking jeeps with barbed-wire gratings in front of their bumpers drove forward in echelons and parked behind the crowd. Portable barbed-wire fences were now riding on Jeeps.

Earlier in the week, it had been relatively simple to get into the Hilton. Mobs of McCarthy workers and excited adolescents had jammed the stairs and the main entrance room of the lobby chanting all day, singing campaign songs, mocking every Humphrey worker they could recognize, holding station for hours in the hope, or on the rumor, that McCarthy would be passing through, and the cheers had the good nature and concerted rhythmic steam of a football rally. That had been Saturday and Sunday and Monday, but the police finally had barricaded the kids out of the lobby, and now at night covered the entrances to the Hilton, and demanded press passes, and room keys, as warrants of entry. The Hilton heaved and staggered through a variety of attacks and breakdowns. Like an old fort, like the old fort of the old Democratic Party, about to fall forever beneath the ministrations of its high shaman, its excruciated warlock, derided by the young, held in contempt by its own soldiers—the very delegates who would be loyal to

Humphrey in the nomination and loyal to nothing in their heart—this spiritual fort of the Democratic Party was now housed in the literal fort of the Hilton staggering in place, all boilers working, all motors vibrating, yet seeming to come apart from the pressures on the street outside, as if the old Hilton had become artifact of the party and the nation.

Nothing worked well in the hotel, and much didn't work at all. There was no laundry because of the bus strike, and the house phones usually did not function; the room phones were tapped so completely, and the devices so over-adjacent, that separate conversations lapped upon one another in the same earpiece, or went jolting by in all directions like three handballs at play at once in a four-wall handball court. Sometimes the phone was dead, sometimes it emitted hideous squawks, or squeals, or the harsh electronic displeasure of a steady well-pulsed static. Sometimes one got long distance by taking it through the operator, sometimes one got an outside line only by ringing the desk and demanding it, sometimes one could get the hotel operator only by dialing the outside line. All the while, a photograph of Mayor Daley the size of a postage stamp was pasted on the cradle of the phone. "Welcome to the 1968 National Democratic Convention," it said. Often, one could not even extract a whimper from the room phone. It had succumbed. Sometimes the phone stayed dead for hours. Success in a convention is reduced to success in communications, as the reporter was yet to learn; communications in the headquarters of the largest party in the nation most renowned for the technology of its communications was breaking apart under strikes, pressure, sabotage, security, security over-check, over-development and insufficient testing of advanced technical devices: at the base of the pyramid, sheer human inefficiencies before the combined on-slaught of pressure and street war.

The elevators worked abominably. On certain floors the signal did not seem to ring. One could wait a half hour for an elevator to stop on the way down. After a time everybody went up to the top in order to be able to go down. Yet one could not use the stairs, for Secret Servicemen were guarding them. It could, at worst, demand an hour to go to one's room and go down again. So it might have been better to live in a hotel across the Loop; but then there were traffic jams and police lines and demonstrators every night, demonstrators marching along with handkerchiefs to their noses.

This night with the demonstrators up and aroused in Grant Park, tear gas was blowing right into the hotel. The police had tried to gas the kids out of the park when they first arrived in numbers from Lincoln Park, but the wind blew the wrong way, blew the tears across the street into the air conditioning of the Hilton lobby, and delegates and Press and officials walked about with smarting eyes, burning throats, and the presentiment that they were going to catch a cold. The lobby stunk. Not from the tear gas, but from stink bombs, or some advanced variety of them, for the source of the odor was either mysterious, or unremovable, or had gotten into the very entrails of the air-conditioning since it got worse from day to day and drenched the coffee shop and the bars and the lobby with a stench not easily forgettable. Standing near someone the odor of vomit always prevailed from the bombs— no, it was worse than vomit, rather like a truly atrocious body odor which spoke of the potential for sour vomit in every joint of a bad piece of psychic work. So personal relations were curious. One met attractive men or women, shook hands with them, chatted for a time, said good-bye. One's memory of the occasion was how awful it had smelled. Delegates, powerful political figures, old friends, and strangers all smelled awful.

So nothing worked well in the hotel, and everything stank, and crowds— those who could get in—milled about, and police guarded the entrance, and across the street as the reporter moved through the tight press of children sitting packed together on the grass, cheering the speakers, chanting "Join us! Join us!" and "Dump the Hump" the smell of the stink bombs was still present, but different now, equally evil and vomitous but from a faded odor of Mace. The nation divided was going to war with stinks; each side would inflict a stink upon the other. The years of sabotage were ahead—a fearful perspective: they would be giving engineering students tests in loyalty before they were done; the F.B.I. would come to question whoever took a mail order course in radio. It was possible that one was at the edge of that water- shed year from which the country might never function well again, and service in American hotels would yet be reminiscent of service in Mexican motels. Whatever! the children were alive with revolutionary fire on this fine Tuesday night, this early Wednesday morning, and the National Guard policing them was wide-awake as well. Incidents occurred. Flare-ups. A small Negro soldier started pushing a demonstrator with his rifle, pushing him in sudden fury as at the wild kickoff of a wild street fight; the demonstrator— who looked to be a kindly divinity student—aghast at what he had set off; he had not comprehended the Negro wished no special conversation from him. And a National Guard officer came running up to pull the Negro back. (On the next night, there would be no Negroes in the line of National Guards.)

The kids were singing. There were two old standards which were sung all the time. An hour could not go by without both songs. So they sang "We Shall Overcome" and they sang "This Land Is Your Land," and a speaker cried up to the twenty-five stories of the Hilton, "We have the votes, you have the guns," a reference to the polls which had shown McCarthy to be more popular than Hubert Humphrey (yes, if only Rockefeller had run for the Democrats and McCarthy for the Republicans this would have been an ideal contest between a spender and a conservative) and then another speaker, referring to the projected march on the Amphitheatre next day, shouted, "We're going to march without a permit—the Russians demand a permit to have a meeting in Prague," and the crowd cheered this. They cheered with wild enthusiasm when one speaker, a delegate, had the inspira- tion to call out to the delegates and workers listening in the hundreds of rooms at the Hilton with a view of the park, "Turn on your lights, and blink them if you are with us. If you are with us, if you are sympathetic to us, blink your lights, blink your lights." And to the delight of the crowd, lights began to blink in the Hilton, ten, then twenty, perhaps so many as fifty lights were blinking at once, and a whole bank of lights on the fifteenth floor and the twenty-third floor went off and on at once, off and on at once. The McCarthy headquarters on the fifteenth and the twenty-third were blinking, and the crowd cheered. Now they had become an audience to watch the actors in the hotel. So two audiences regarded each other, like ships signalling across a gulf of water in the night, and delegates came down from the hotel; a mood of new beauty was in the air, there present through all the dirty bandaged kids, the sour vomit odor of the Mace, the sighing and whining of the army trucks moving in and out all the time, the adenoids, larynxes, wheezes and growls of the speakers, the blinking of lights in the Hilton, yes, there was the breath of this incredible crusade where fear was in every breath you took, and so breath was tender, it came into the lungs as a manifest of value, as a gift, and the children's faces were shining in the glow of the headlights of the National Guard trucks and the searchlights of the police in front of the Hilton across Michigan Avenue. And the Hilton, sinking in its foundations, twinkled like a birthday cake. Horrors were coming tomorrow. No, it is today. It is Wednesday already.

## Chapter 15

If Wednesday was nominating day, it was also the afternoon when the debate on the Vietnam peace plank took place. Indeed, it was also the evening when the Massacre of Michigan Avenue occurred, an extraordinary event: a massacre, equal on balance to some of the old Indian raids, yet no one was killed. Of course, a great many people were hurt. And several hundred delegates started to march back from the stockyards, early Thursday morning after the nomination, carrying lit candles in protest. It was obviously one of the more active days in the history of any convention.

Worn out by his portentous Southern sense of things to come, Lester Maddox, the fourth candidate, Governor of Georgia, even resigned his candidacy Wednesday morning. We quote from Walter Rugaber of the *New York Times*:

> His wife, Virginia, sat beside him weeping softly as Mr. Maddox ended his 11-day fling with a last news conference in the brightly lit Grand Ballroom of the Conrad Hilton Hotel.
>
> He talked about misinformed socialist and power-mad politicians. He assailed the Democrats as the party of "looting, burning, killing and draft-card burning. What's more," he said, "I denounce them all."

Then he caught a plane back to Atlanta. Who would declare that the chanting in Grant Park through the long hours of Tuesday night and the semi-obscene shouts—Dump the Hump!—had done nothing to accelerate his decision?

Originally, the debate on the Vietnam plank had been scheduled for

Tuesday night, but the convention went on past midnight, so the hawks attempted to have it early in the morning. It was their hope to begin at I A.M. New York time, and thus obtain the pleasure of denying the doves a large television audience. But the doves raised a post-midnight demonstration on the floor which became progressively more obstreperous until Mayor Daley made the mistake of rising to remonstrate with the gallery, warning that they would be cleared out of their seats if they did not quiet down. "Let's act like ladies and gentlemen, and let people be heard," said Daley to the convention and to millions on television, looking for all the world like the best b.o. ever to come out of *Guys and Dolls*. But it was obvious the greater share of the noise came from behind Daley on the floor, from the rear where McCarthy and McGovern delegates from New York, California, South Dakota, Massachusetts, Wisconsin and Oregon were placed far from the podium. At any rate, the Administration forces lost their play. It was one thing for them to cut off a discussion—that was simply accomplished. One had only to give a signal, then make a quick motion which could as quickly be recognized by the Chairman who would whip in a lightning move for a voice-vote. "The ayes . . . the nays . . . The ayes have it," he would say, and rap his gavel, walk off the podium, close the session. But here, after midnight, the hawks were not trying to cut off a discussion, rather they wished to begin one; the doves had nothing to lose by a noisy non-stop protest. Moves for silence, whacks of the gavel by Carl Albert looking poisonous for being ignored, loud music of the band to drown out the rear delegation. Nothing worked. The television cameras were focussed on the doves who were protesting the lateness of the hour. The hawks could insist on their move, but they would look like the worst of the cattle gang on television. So a signal was passed to Daley by an Administration spokesman who drew his finger across his throat, an unmistakable sign to cut off conversation for the night. Daley, looking like he had just been stuffed with a catfish, stood up, got the floor, made a move to adjourn. Immediately recognized by Carl Albert. The little Chairman was now sufficiently excited to start to say Mayor Daley of the Great State of Chicago. He recovered quickly, however, quick enough to rap his gavel, and declare that the Chair accepted the motion, snapping it through with a slick haste, as if it had been his idea all along! The debate was postponed until Wednesday afternoon.

The debate, however, proved anti-climactic. There had been hopes that McCarthy would speak, idle dreams he might make a great speech; but it was rumored that the Senator, weighing the imponderable protocol of these profoundly established convention manners, had decided he would not enter debate unless Lyndon Johnson came to the Amphitheatre for his birthday party. Johnson, however, was not in the hall; he was still in Texas where he would remain (on the advice of his best wise men since they could not guarantee the character of his reception in the Amphitheatre, nor the nature of the stimulation it might give the streets). Therefore, McCarthy, respecting the balance, was not present either.

The hawks had first proposed fifteen minutes for the debate, then thirty. An hour was the maximum obtainable by the doves. On the greatest national issue any convention had faced since the second world war, debate would provide an hour of speech for each side. Moreover, the sides would make alternate speeches. Thus, no massive presentation of argument nor avalanche of emotion would ever result.

These restrictions having limited the outcome before they began, Rep. Philip Burton of California spoke first for the minority, then Senator Muskie of Maine for the majority. Burton asked that we "heed the voices of men and women of good will who across the land call for peace," Muskie went through the differences in the majority and minority planks, and the similarities, and then concluded that the majority protected our soldiers, whereas the minority was too quick to desire peace at any price.

The speakers came on. They seemed careful to abstain from rich, extravagant, or passionate language. No one got up to say that one million men on our side could not dominate a quarter million men on the other, for that would have been unpatriotic (which for a politician is sacrilege equal to burning money or flooding property) no, the best of the majority roamed mean and keen over the legalities, the technicalities of commitment, the safety of American soldiers, the tempo for establishing representative government; they spoke in styles sometimes reminiscent of the eminent sanity of Dean Rusk; he was always a model of sanity on every detail but one: he had a delusion that the war was not bottomless in its lunacy. Of course, words like lunacy were not for the floor of the convention. Muskie; Sen. McGee of Wyoming; Governor Hearnes of Missouri; Mrs. Geri Joseph of Minnesota; David Pryor of Arkansas; Rep. Ed Edmondson of Oklahoma; Mayor Wilson Wyatt of Louisville; Rep. Zablocki of Wisconsin, and Rep. Hale Boggs of Louisiana, Chairman of the Platform Committee, spoke for the majority long enough to put in nitpicking points and intone against Communism. The whine in one American's nasal passages obviously stimulated something in the inner canal of other American ears when Communism was given its licks. The hawks then extolled the dove-like nature of the majority plank. The doves, however, came back by way of Senator Morse to reply that the "majority report stripped of its semantics is nothing but a naked proposal to continue the failures of our policy in Vietnam." Also speaking for the doves: Paul O'Dwyer of New York; Ken O'Donnell of Massachusetts; John Gilligan of Ohio; Senator Gore of Tennessee; Ted Sorensen of New York, and Pierre Salinger of California.

For those who are curious let us give excerpts of a few speeches.

*Senator Edmund Muskie:* "The choice is this: A negotiated settlement with, or a negotiated settlement without safeguards to protect free elections. . . . A bombing halt with, or a bombing halt without consideration of the air protection for our troops against military risks arising north of the demilitarized zone. . . . Mr. Chairman, I urge the adoption of the majority plank." (Muskie was obviously a contented rooster.)

*Theodore Sorensen:* "We call for an end to the bombing now—they call for an end if and when and maybe.

"Second, we call for a mutual withdrawal of all U.S. and North Vietnamese troops now. . . . The majority plank says maybe, sometime, if all Vietcong hostilities can somehow cease first.

"Third, we call, as Ted Kennedy called, for letting the South Vietnamese decide for themselves the shape of their own future. They call for the United States to stay and conform the Vietnamese to our political and economic standards.

"Fourth, we call for a reduction of American troops now. . . . They call for a reduction in troops only when the South Vietnamese Army can take over. . . ."

*Governor Warren Hearnes:* ". . . many of the decisions that are being made here in this convention hall by we politicians have been dictated by the prospects of victory or defeat. Victory or defeat in November.

". . . For God's sake, if you adopt the minority report, you are going to jeopardize the lives of the servicemen in Vietnam."

*Kenneth O'Donnell:* ". . . we were forced to watch a Congress of the United States . . . cut the budget $6-billion in the last Congress, and they cut it out of all the programs affecting the lives of every single American, out of the programs of health, in education and the problems that face our children . . . we will not have the money unless we are able in some fashion to disengage ourselves from the expenditures not only of our best treasure, the young men, but the fact that we are spending $30-billion a year in a foreign adventure in South Vietnam. It must end."

*Representative Hale Boggs:* "Can General Abrams supply an answer to me on this question, and I pose the question:

"Is there any possibility of your providing even an approximate estimate of the additional casualties we would take if we stopped the bombing of North Vietnam unilaterally and unconditionally?

"And the answer came back and here I read it to you—these are not my words, these are the words of General Abrams: 'If the bombing in North Vietnam now authorized were to be suspended unilaterally, the enemy in ten days to two weeks could develop a capability in the DMZ area in terms of scale, intensity, and duration of combat on the order of five times what he now has.'

"I cannot agree. I cannot agree to place our forces at the risk which the enemy's capability would then pose. That, my friends, concludes our debate." (Hale Boggs was the hawk's own tern.)

The Administration was taking no chances on birds. A confidential White House briefing had been thrown into the shot-load for this debate, and by the time the last speaker had his word, the military were concluding the debate, that same military which had been giving expert guesses for years on just how many troops and just how many bombs would be necessary to guarantee victory in exactly so many weeks or exactly so many months; the party was still buying just such expert advice. "Scale, intensity, and duration of combat on the order of five times." The Texas delegation up front cheered. Put a big man in a big uniform, let him recite big figures, and they would take the word of no priest or pope. In America the uniform always finished first, the production expert second, and Christ was welcome to come in third. So the vote came out as $1,567\frac{3}{4}$ to $1,041\frac{1}{2}$—the majority plank was passed. Lyndon Johnson was vindicated by the same poor arguments which had originally implicated him. Politics was property, and the gravitational power of massive holdings was sufficient to pull you out of your own soup.

But the floor would not rest. The New York and California delegations began to sing "We Shall Overcome." Quickly, the Platform was passed; still the New York delegation sang. Now Wisconsin stood on its seats. The rear of the floor booed the front of the floor. A few hundred posters, STOP THE WAR, quickly printed a couple of hours earlier for this occasion, were held up. Defeated delegates yelled, "Stop the War," in the fierce frustration of knowing that the plank was Lyndon Johnson's and the party was still his. The convention recessed. Still the New York delegation sang, "We Shall Overcome," standing on their seats. The convention band across the way tried to drown them out. It played in ever-increasing volume "We Got a Lot of Living to Do."

The managers of the convention turned the New York microphones down, and amplified the public address system for the band. So on the floor of the convention, the doves were drowned in hostile sound, but on the television sets, the reception was opposite, for the networks had put their own microphones under the voices of the delegates, and they sang in force across the continent. Thus a few thousand people on the floor and the gallery heard little of the doves—all the rest of America heard them well. Politics-is-property had come to the point of fission. He who controlled the floor no longer controlled the power of public opinion. Small wonder the old party hands hated the networks—it was agitating to have mastered the locks and keys in the house of politics and discover that there was a new door they could not quite shut. In disgust the hawk delegations left the floor. The doves continued to sing "We Shall Overcome." Now, the orchestra played "Happy Days Are Here Again."

The demonstrators chanted, "We want peace! We want peace!" "I'm Looking Over a Four-Leaf Clover," the orchestra offered, then rejected, then switched over to "If You Knew Suzy," then they gave up. The demonstrators began to sing the "Battle Hymn of the Republic." New York, California, Oregon, Wisconsin, South Dakota and other delegations marched around the empty floor. It was half an hour after the convention had recessed. Still they sang. It had been a long war to lose.

## Chapter 16

Meanwhile, a mass meeting was taking place about the bandshell in Grant Park, perhaps a quarter of a mile east of Michigan Avenue and the Conrad Hilton. The meeting was under the auspices of the Mobilization, and a crowd of ten or fifteen thousand appeared. The Mayor had granted a permit to assemble, but had refused to allow a march. Since the Mobilization had announced that it would attempt, no matter how, the march to the Amphitheatre that was the first purpose of their visit to Chicago, the police were out in force to surround the meeting.

An episode occurred during the speeches. Three demonstrators climbed a flag pole to cut down the American flag and put up a rebel flag. A squad of police charged to beat them up, but got into trouble themselves, for when they threw tear gas, the demonstrators lobbed the canisters back, and the police, choking on their own gas, had to fight their way clear through a barrage of rocks. Then came a much larger force of police charging the area, overturning benches, busting up members of the audience, then heading for Rennie Davis at the bullhorn. He was one of the coordinators of the Mobilization, his face was known, he had been fingered and fingered again by plainclothesmen. Now urging the crowd to sit down and be calm, he was attacked from behind by the police, his head laid open in a three-inch cut, and he was unconscious for a period. Furious at the attack, Tom Hayden, who had been in disguise these last two days to avoid any more arrests for himself, spoke to the crowd, said he was leaving to perform certain special tasks, and suggested that others break up into small groups and go out into the streets of the Loop "to do what they have to do." A few left with him; the majority remained. While it was a People's Army and therefore utterly unorganized by uniform or unity, it had a variety of special troops and regular troops; everything from a few qualified Kamikaze who were ready to charge police lines in a Japanese snake dance and dare on the consequence, some vicious beatings, to various kinds of small saboteurs, rock-throwers, gauntlet-runners—some of the speediest of the kids were adept at taunting cops while keeping barely out of range of their clubs—not altogether alien to running the bulls at Pamplona. Many of those who remained, however, were still nominally pacifists, protesters, Gandhians—they believed in non-violence, in the mystical interposition of their body to the attack, as if the violence of the enemy might be drained by the spiritual act of passive resistance over the years, over the thousands, tens of thousands, hundreds of thousands of beatings over the years. So Allen Ginsberg was speaking now to them.

The police looking through the plexiglass face shields they had flipped down from their helmets were then obliged to watch the poet with his bald head, soft eyes magnified by horn-rimmed eyeglasses, and massive dark beard, utter his words in a croaking speech. He had been gassed Monday night and Tuesday night, and had gone to the beach at dawn to read Hindu Tantras to some of the Yippies, the combination of the chants and the gassings had all but burned out his voice, his beautiful speaking voice, one of the most powerful and hypnotic instruments of the Western world was down to the scrapings of the throat now, raw as flesh after a curettage.

"The best strategy for you," said Ginsberg, "in cases of hysteria, over-excitement or fear, is still to chant 'OM' together. It helps to quell flutterings of butterflies in the belly. Join me now as I try to lead you."

The crowd chanted with Ginsberg. They were of a generation which would try every idea, every drug, every action—it was even possible a few of them had made out with freaky kicks on tear gas these last few days—so they would chant OM. There were Hindu fanatics in the crowd, children who loved India and scorned everything in the West; there were cynics who thought the best thing to be said for a country which allowed its excess population to die by the millions in famine-ridden fields was that it would not be ready soon to try to dominate the rest of the world. There were also militants who were ready to march. And the police there to prevent them, busy now in communication with other detachments of police, by way of radios whose aerials were attached to their helmets, thereby giving them the look of giant insects.

A confused hour began. Lincoln Park was irregular in shape with curving foot walks; but Grant Park was indeed not so much a park as a set of belts of greenery cut into files by major parallel avenues between Michigan Avenue and Lake Michigan half a mile away. Since there were also cross streets cutting the belts of green perpendicularly, a variety of bridges and pedestrian overpasses gave egress to the city. The park was in this sense an alternation of lawn with superhighways. So the police were able to pen the crowd. But not completely. There were too many bridges, too many choices, in effect, for the police to anticipate. To this confusion was added the fact that every confrontation of demonstrators with police, now buttressed by the National Guard, attracted hundreds of newsmen, and hence began a set of attempted negotiations between spokesmen for the demonstrators and troops, the demonstrators finally tried to force a bridge and get back to the city. Repelled by tear gas, they went to other bridges, still other bridges, finally found a bridge lightly guarded, broke through a passage and were loose in the city at six-thirty in the evening. They milled about in the Loop for a few minutes, only to encounter the mules and three wagons of the Poor People's Campaign. City officials, afraid of provoking the Negroes on the South Side, had given a permit to the Reverend Abernathy, and he was going to march the mules and wagons down Michigan Avenue and over to the convention. An impromptu march of the demonstrators formed behind the wagons immediately on encountering them and ranks of marchers, sixty, eighty, a hundred in line across the width of Michigan Avenue began to move forward in the gray early twilight of 7 p.m.; Michigan Avenue was now suddenly jammed with people in the march, perhaps so many as four or five thousand people, including onlookers on the sidewalk who jumped in. The streets of the Loop were also reeking with tear gas—the wind had blown some of the gas west over Michigan Avenue from the drops on the bridges, some gas still was penetrated into the clothing of the marchers. In broken ranks, half a march, half a happy mob, eyes red from gas, faces excited by the tension of the afternoon, and the excitement of the escape from Grant

Park, now pushing down Michigan Avenue toward the Hilton Hotel with dreams of a march on to the Amphitheatre four miles beyond, and in the full pleasure of being led by the wagons of the Poor People's March, the demonstrators shouted to everyone on the sidewalk, "Join us, join us, join us," and the sidewalk kept disgorging more people ready to march.

But at Balbo Avenue, just before Michigan Avenue reached the Hilton, the marchers were halted by the police. It was a long halt. Perhaps thirty minutes. Time for people who had been walking on the sidewalk to join the march, proceed for a few steps, halt with the others, wait, get bored, and leave. It was time for someone in command of the hundreds of police in the neighborhood to communicate with his headquarters, explain the problem, time for the dilemma to be relayed, alternatives examined, and orders conceivably sent back to attack and disperse the crowd. If so, a trap was first set. The mules were allowed to cross Balbo Avenue, then were separated by a line of police from the marchers, who now, several thousand compressed in this one place, filled the intersection of Michigan Avenue and Balbo. There, dammed by police on three sides, and cut off from the wagons of the Poor People's March, there, right beneath the windows of the Hilton which looked down on Grant Park and Michigan Avenue, the stationary march was abruptly attacked. The police attacked with tear gas, with Mace, and with clubs, they attacked like a chain saw cutting into wood, the teeth of the saw the edge of their clubs, they attacked like a scythe through grass, lines of twenty and thirty policemen striking out in an arc, their clubs beating, demonstrators fleeing. Seen from overhead, from the nineteenth floor, it was like a wind blowing dust, or the edge of waves riding foam on the shore.

The police cut through the crowd one way, then cut through them another. They chased people into the park, ran them down, beat them up; they cut through the intersection at Michigan and Balbo like a razor cutting a channel through a head of hair, and then drove columns of new police into the channel who in turn pushed out, clubs flailing, on each side, to cut new channels, and new ones again. As demonstrators ran, they reformed in new groups only to be chased by the police again. The action went on for ten minutes, fifteen minutes, with the absolute ferocity of a tropical storm, and watching it from a window on the nineteenth floor, there was something of the detachment of studying a storm at evening through a glass, the light was a lovely gray-blue, the police had uniforms of sky-blue, even the ferocity had an abstract elemental play of forces of nature at battle with other forces, as if sheets of tropical rain were driving across the street in patterns, in curving patterns which curved upon each other again. Police cars rolled up, prisoners were beaten, shoved into wagons, driven away. The rain of police, maddened by the uncoiling of their own storm, pushed against their own barricades of tourists pressed on the street against the Hilton Hotel, then pressed them so hard—but here is a quotation from J. Anthony Lukas in *The New York Times*:

Even elderly bystanders were caught in the police onslaught. At one point, the police turned on several dozen persons standing quietly behind police barriers in front of the Conrad Hilton Hotel watching the demonstrators across the street.

For no reason that could be immediately determined, the blue-helmeted policemen charged the barriers, crushing the spectators against the windows of the Haymarket Inn, a restaurant in the hotel. Finally the window gave way, sending screaming middle-aged women and children backward through the broken shards of glass.

The police then ran into the restaurant and beat some of the victims who had fallen through the windows and arrested them.

Now another quote from Steve Lerner in *The Village Voice*:

When the charge came, there was a stampede toward the sidelines. People piled into each other, humped over each other's bodies like coupling dogs. To fall down in the crush was just as terrifying as facing the police. Suddenly I realized my feet weren't touching the ground as the crowd pushed up onto the sidewalk. I was grabbing at the army jacket of the boy in front of me; the girl behind me had a stranglehold on my neck and was screaming incoherently in my ear.

Now, a longer quotation from Jack Newfield in *The Village Voice*. (The accounts in *The Voice* of September 5 were superior to any others encountered that week.)

At the southwest entrance to the Hilton, a skinny, long-haired kid of about seventeen skidded down on the sidewalk, and four overweight cops leaped on him, chopping strokes on his head. His hair flew from the force of the blows. A dozen small rivulets of blood began to cascade down the kid's temple and onto the sidewalk. He was not crying or screaming, but crawling in a stupor toward the gutter. When he saw a photographer take a picture, he made a V sign with his fingers.

A doctor in a white uniform and Red Cross arm band began to run toward the kid, but two other cops caught him from behind and knocked him down. One of them jammed his knee into the doctor's throat and began clubbing his rib cage. The doctor squirmed away, but the cops followed him, swinging hard, sometimes missing.

A few feet away a phalanx of police charged into a group of women, reporters, and young McCarthy activists standing idly against the window of the Hilton Hotel's Haymarket Inn. The terrified people began to go down under the unexpected police charge when the plate glass window shattered, and the people tumbled backward through the glass. The police then climbed through the broken window and began to beat people, some of whom had been drinking quietly in the hotel bar.

At the side entrance of the Hilton Hotel four cops were chasing one frightened kid of about seventeen. Suddenly, Fred Dutton, a former aide to Robert Kennedy, moved out from under the marquee and interposed his body between the kid and the police.

"He's my guest in this hotel," Dutton told the cops.

The police started to club the kid.

Dutton screamed for the first cop's name and badge number. The cop grabbed Dutton and began to arrest him, until a Washington *Post* reporter identified Dutton as a former RFK aide.

Demonstrators, reporters, McCarthy workers, doctors, all began to stagger into the Hilton lobby, blood streaming from face and head wounds. The lobby smelled from tear gas, and stink bombs dropped by the Yippies. A few people began to direct the wounded to a makeshift hospital on the fifteenth floor, the McCarthy staff headquarters.

Fred Dutton was screaming at the police, and at the journalists to report all the "sadism and brutality." Richard Goodwin, the ashen nub of a cigar sticking out of his fatigued face, mumbled, "This is just the beginning. There'll be four years of this."

The defiant kids began a slow, orderly retreat back up Michigan Avenue. They did not run. They did not panic. They did not fight back. As they fell back they helped pick up fallen comrades who were beaten or gassed. Suddenly, a plain-clothesman dressed as a soldier moved out of the shadows and knocked one kid down with an overhand punch. The kid squatted on the pavement of Michigan Avenue, trying to cover his face, while the Chicago plainclothesman punched him with savage accuracy. Thud, thud, thud. Blotches of blood spread over the kid's face. Two photographers moved in. Several police formed a closed circle around the beating to prevent pictures. One of the policemen then squirted Chemical Mace at the photographers, who dispersed. The plainclothesman melted into the line of police.

Let us escape to the street. The reporter, watching in safety from the nineteenth floor, could understand now how Mussolini's son-in-law had once been able to find the bombs he dropped from his airplane beautiful as they burst, yes, children, and youths, and middle-aged men and women were being pounded and clubbed and gassed and beaten, hunted and driven, sent scattering in all directions by teams of policemen who had exploded out of their restraints like the bursting of a boil, and nonetheless he felt a sense of calm and beauty, void even of the desire to be down there, as if in years to come there would be beatings enough, some chosen, some from nowhere, but it was as if the war had finally begun, and this was therefore a great and solemn moment, as if indeed even the gods of history had come together from each side to choose the very front of the Hilton Hotel before the television cameras of the world and the eyes of the campaign workers and the delegates' wives, yes, there before the eyes of half the principals at the convention was this drama played, as if the military spine of a great liberal party had finally separated itself from the skin, as if, no metaphor large enough to suffice, the Democratic Party had here broken in two before the eyes of a nation like Melville's whale charging right out of the sea.

A great stillness rose up from the street through all the small noise of clubbing and cries, small sirens, sigh of loaded arrest vans as off they pulled, shouts of police as they wheeled in larger circles, the intersection clearing further, then further, a stillness rose through the steel and stone of the hotel, congregating in the shocked centers of every room where delegates and wives and Press and campaign workers innocent until now of the intimate working of social force, looked down now into the murderous paradigm of Vietnam there beneath them at this huge intersection of this great city. Look—a boy was running through the park, and a cop was chasing. There he caught him on the back of the neck with his club! There! The cop is returning to his own! And the boy stumbling to his feet is helped off the ground by a girl who has come running up.

Yes, it could only have happened in a meeting of the Gods, that history for once should take place not on some back street, or some inaccessible grand room, not in some laboratory indistinguishable from others, or in the sly undiscoverable hypocrisies of a committee of experts, but rather on the center of the stage, as if each side had said, "Here we will have our battle. Here we will win."

The demontsrators were afterwards delighted to have been manhandled before the public eye, delighted to have pushed and prodded, antagonized and provoked the cops over these days with rocks and bottles and cries of "Pig" to the point where police had charged in a blind rage and made a stage at the one place in the city (besides the Amphitheatre) where audience, actors, and cameras could all convene, yes, the rebels thought they had had a great victory, and perhaps they did; but the reporter wondered, even as he saw it, if the police in that half hour of waiting had not had time to receive instructions from the power of the city, perhaps the power of the land, and the power had decided, "No, do not let them march another ten blocks and there disperse them on some quiet street, no, let it happen before all the land, let everybody see that their dissent will soon be equal to their own blood; let them realize that the power is implacable, and will beat and crush and imprison and yet kill before it will ever relinquish the power. So let them see before their own eyes what it will cost to continue to mock us, defy us, and resist. There are more millions behind us than behind them, more millions who wish to weed out, poison, gas, and obliterate every flower whose power they do not comprehend than heroes for their side who will view our brute determination and still be ready to resist. There are more cowards alive than the brave. Otherwise we would not be where we are," said the Prince of Greed.

Who knew. One could thank the city of Chicago where drama was still a property of the open stage. It was quiet now, there was nothing to stare down on but the mules, and the police guarding them. The mules had not moved through the entire fray. Isolated from the battle, they had stood there in harness waiting to be told to go on. Only once in a while did they turn their heads. Their role as actors in the Poor People's March was to wait and to serve. Finally they moved on. The night had come. It was dark. The intersection was now empty. Shoes, ladies' handbags, and pieces of clothing lay on the street outside the hotel.

234

# QUESTIONS: *Mailer, "The Siege of Chicago"*

1. Examine carefully the effects which Mailer achieves in the following passage through the use of figurative language (particularly similes):

> The police attacked with tear gas, with Mace, and with clubs, they attacked like a chain saw cutting into wood ... they attacked like a scythe through grass. ... Seen from overhead, from the nineteenth floor, it was like a wind blowing dust, or the edge of waves riding foam on the shore ... they cut through the intersection at Michigan and Balbo like a razor cutting a channel through a head of hair. ... The action went on for ten minutes, fifteen minutes, with the absolute ferocity of a tropical storm ... even the ferocity had an abstract elemental play of forces of nature at battle with other forces, as if sheets of tropical rain were driving across the street in patterns, in curving patterns which curved upon each other again.

2. How do images of *warfare* and *theater* heighten the meaning of events, lending them epic or cosmic significance?

   *Clues:* • ... they called up through the night on a *stage* as vast and towering as one of *Wagner's* visions. ...

   • The *nation divided* was going to *war* with stinks ....

   • ... an extraordinary event: a *massacre*, equal on balance to some of the old *Indian raids*. ...

   • The hawks could insist on their move, but they would look like the worst of the *cattle gang* on *television*.

   • Yes, it could have happened in a meeting of *the Gods*, that *history* for once should take place ... on the center of the stage, as if each side had said, "Here we will have our *battle*. Here we will *win*."

3. "The Siege of Chicago" is basically a description of *collective* action and the clash of *collective* entities. Some of the nouns and pronouns that predominate are "the young men," "they," "the police," "the kids," "the demonstrators," "the children," "the crowd," "the majority," "the power of the city," "the power of the land." Mailer even depersonalizes the individual "I" into "the reporter." What does this approach suggest about Mailer's vision of the modern world? Does this vision seem to you justified? Why?

4. Offhand the reader would probably feel that Mailer powerfully sympathizes with "the demonstrators" and shares their feelings of loathing for the government and police of Chicago and for the President of the United States. But Mailer, like Orwell in the essay "Marrakech," maintains an unusually dispassionate tone toward much of what he describes. At one point he writes of the crowd: "They were of a generation which would try every idea, every drug, every action. ..." Here the distance between narrator and crowd is very clear. When the police attack, Mailer writes of himself: "The reporter, watching in safety from the nineteenth floor, could understand now how Mussolini's son-in-law had once been able to find the bombs he dropped from his airplane beautiful as they burst. ..." At the same time, as in "Marrakech," we have a sense that Mailer *is* powerfully involved in what he is describing. How can we resolve this seeming contradiction?

5. Some writers have suggested that the modern communications media—notably radio and television—have revolutionized our view of the world. Above all, they maintain, the media have made it possible for thousands or even millions of people to have a simultaneous or collective emotional experience, and the result is to "retribalize" mankind by tying us very closely to each other. The images and sounds we receive from the media thus take the place of the collective myths that bind a primitive tribe together. What evidence does "The Siege of Chicago" offer to substantiate this view?

Clues:   • Now, with the facility for *underground communication* which seemed so instinctive a tool in their generation's equipment, they were on their way to Grant Park, en masse, a thousand of them, two thousand of them, there were conceivably as many as five thousand boys and girls. . . .

• So on the floor of the convention, the doves were drowned in hostile sound, but on the television sets, the reception was opposite. . . . Thus *a few thousand* people on the floor and the gallery heard little of the doves—*all the rest of America* heard them well. . . . He who controlled the floor no longer controlled the power of public opinion.

• . . . every confrontation of demonstrators with police . . . attracted hundreds of newsmen. . . .

• . . . but the reporter wondered . . . if the police in that half hour of waiting had not had time to receive instructions from the power of the city, perhaps the power of the land, and the power had decided, "No . . . let it happen *before all the land*, let *everybody* see that their dissent will soon be equal to their own blood. . . . There are more millions behind us than behind them . . ." said the Prince of Greed.

6. Can one reconcile Mailer's vision of a public-opinion victory by the doves on the floor of the convention with the conviction that he attributes to "the power of the land," that "there are more millions behind us than behind them"? Most polls after the convention showed that a majority of Americans sympathized with the Chicago police rather than the demonstrators. Does this majority reaction negate Mailer's interpretation of the events at Chicago, and particularly of the relationship between doves, demonstrators, and the media? If not, why not?

## EXERCISES

1. Compare the vision of America offered by "The Siege of Chicago" and the one in Allen Ginsberg's poem "America" and indicate the similarities in these writers' vision of themselves and of their roles as artists.

2. Compare Mailer's attitude toward and stylistic treatment of rebellion with those of Carlyle in the selection *The French Revolution* in this section.

3. Compare Mailer's use of epic language and motifs with that of E. E. Cummings in "i sing of Olaf."

## Malcolm X *(1925–1965)*

# The Autobiography of Malcolm X

## CHAPTER 14

### *Black Muslims*

*The reference to Brother Johnson Hinton's case (in paragraph 1) is to a successful demonstration of peaceful protest against "police brutality"—the unwarranted beating by police of a Muslim brother—which calls attention to the Black Muslims (the details are in the last few paragraphs of the preceding chapter). The term* two-edged sword *is clarified by Malcom X's earlier reference to the "sharp truth" of Elijah Muhammad in addressing an audience: "It is like a two-edged sword. It cuts into you. It causes you great pain, but if you can take the truth, it will cure you and save you from what otherwise would be certain death." Of the "Fruit of Islam," the author says earlier: "Our moral laws were policed by our Fruit of Islam—able, dedicated, and trained Muslim men." As for the meaning of "X," Malcolm X explains it as follows in Chapter 12: "The Muslim's 'X' symbolized the true African family name that he never could know. For me, my 'X' replaced the white slave-master name of 'Little' which some blue-eyed devil named Little had imposed upon my paternal forebears."*

In the spring of nineteen fifty-nine—some months before Brother Johnson Hinton's case had awakened the Harlem black ghetto to us—a Negro journalist, Louis Lomax, then living in New York, asked me one morning whether our Nation of Islam would cooperate in being filmed as a television documentary program for the Mike Wallace Show, which featured controversial subjects. I told Lomax that, naturally, anything like that would have to be referred to The Honorable Elijah Muhammad. And Lomax did fly to Chicago to consult Mr. Muhammad. After questioning Lomax, then cautioning him against some things he did not desire, Mr. Muhammad gave his consent.

Cameramen began filming Nation of Islam scenes around our mosques in New York, Chicago, and Washington, D.C. Sound recordings were made of Mr. Muhammad and some ministers, including me, teaching black audiences the truths about the brainwashed black man and the devil white man.

At Boston University around the same time, C. Eric Lincoln, a Negro scholar then working for his doctorate, had selected for his thesis subject the Nation of Islam. Lincoln's interest had been aroused the previous year when, teaching at Clark College in Atlanta, Georgia, he received from one of his Religion students a term paper whose introduction I can now quote from

Lincoln's book. It was the plainspoken convictions of one of Atlanta's numerous young black collegians who often visited our local Temple Fifteen.

"The Christian religion is incompatible with the Negro's aspirations for dignity and equality in America," the student had written. "It has hindered where it might have helped; it has been evasive when it was morally bound to be forthright; it has separated believers on the basis of color, although it has declared its mission to be a universal brotherhood under Jesus Christ. Christian love is the white man's love for himself and for his race. For the man who is not white, Islam is the hope for justice and equality in the world we must build tomorrow."

After some preliminary research showed Professor Lincoln what a subject he had hold of, he had been able to obtain several grants, and a publisher's encouragement to expand his thesis into a book.

On the wire of our relatively small Nation, these two big developments—a television show, and a book about us—naturally were big news. Every Muslim happily anticipated that now, through the white man's powerful communications media, our brainwashed black brothers and sisters across the United States, and devils, too, were going to see, hear, and read Mr. Muhammad's teachings which cut back and forth like a two-edged sword.

We had made our own very limited efforts to employ the power of print. First, some time back, I had made an appointment to see editor James Hicks of the *Amsterdam News*, published in Harlem. Editor Hicks said he felt every voice in the community deserved to be heard. Soon, each week's *Amsterdam News* carried a little column that I wrote. Then, Mr. Muhammad agreed to write a column for that valuable *Amsterdam News* space, and my column was transferred to another black newspaper, the Los Angeles *Herald Dispatch*.

But I kept wanting to start, somehow, our own newspaper, that would be filled with Nation of Islam news.

Mr. Muhammad in 1957 sent me to organize a Temple in Los Angeles. When I had done that, being in that city where the *Herald Dispatch* was, I went visiting and I worked in their office; they let me observe how a newspaper was put together. I've always been blessed in that if I can once watch something being done, generally I can catch onto how to do it myself. Quick "picking up" was probably the number one survival rule when I'd been out there in the streets as a hustler.

Back in New York, I bought a second-hand camera. I don't know how many rolls of film I shot until I could take usable pictures. Every chance I had, I wrote some little news about interesting Nation of Islam happenings. One day every month, I'd lock up in a room and assemble my material and pictures for a printer that I found. I named the newspaper *Muhammad Speaks* and Muslim brothers sold it on the ghetto sidewalks. Little did I dream that later on, when jealousy set in among the hierarchy, nothing about me would be printed in the paper I had founded.

Anyway, national publicity was in the offing for the Nation of Islam when

Mr. Muhammad sent me on a three-week trip to Africa. Even as small as we then were, some of the African and Asian personages had sent Mr. Muhammad private word that they liked his efforts to awaken and lift up the American black people. Sometimes, the messages had been sent through me. As Mr. Muhammad's emissary, I went to Egypt, Arabia, to the Sudan, to Nigeria, and Ghana.

You will often hear today a lot of the Negro leaders complaining that what thrust the Muslims into international prominence was the white man's press, radio, television, and other media. I have no shred of argument with that. They are absolutely correct. Why, none of us in the Nation of Islam remotely anticipated what was about to happen.

In late 1959, the television program was aired, "The Hate That Hate Produced"—the title—was edited tightly into a kaleidoscope of "shocker" images ... Mr. Muhammad, me, and others speaking ... strong-looking, set-faced black men, our Fruit of Islam ... white-scarved, white-gowned Muslim sisters of all ages ... Muslims in our restaurants, and other businesses ... Muslims and other black people entering and leaving our mosques. ...

Every phrase was edited to increase the shock mood. As the producers intended, I think people sat just about limp when the program went off.

In a way, the public reaction was like what happened back in the 1930's when Orson Welles frightened America with a radio program describing, as though it was actually happening, an invasion by "men from Mars."

No one now jumped from any windows, but in New York City there was an instant avalanche of public reaction. It's my personal opinion that the "Hate ... Hate ..." title was primarily responsible for the reaction. Hundreds of thousands of New Yorkers, black and white, were exclaiming "Did you hear it? Did you see it? Preaching *hate* of white people!"

Here was one of the white man's most characteristic behavior patterns— where black men are concerned. He loves himself so much that he is startled if he discovers that his victims don't share his vainglorious self-opinion. In America for centuries it had been just fine as long as the victimized, brutalized and exploited black people had been grinning and begging and "Yessa, Massa" and Uncle Tomming. But now, things were different. First came the white newspapers—feature writers and columnists: "Alarming" ... "hate-messengers" ... "threat to the good relations between the races" ... "black segregationists" ... "black supremacists," and the like.

And the newspapers' ink wasn't dry before the big national weekly news magazines started: "Hate-teachers" ... "violence-seekers" ... "black racists" ... "black fascists" ... "anti-Christian" ... "possibly Communist-inspired. ..."

It rolled out of the presses of the biggest devil in the history of mankind. And then the aroused white man made his next move.

Since slavery, the American white man has always kept some handpicked Negroes who fared much better than the black masses suffering and slaving out in the hot fields. The white man had these "house" and "yard" Negroes for his special servants. He threw them more crumbs from his rich table, he even let them eat in his kitchen. He knew that he could always count on them to keep "good massa" happy in his self-image of being so "good" and "righteous." "Good massa" always heard just what he wanted to hear from "these house" and "yard" blacks. "You're such a good, *fine* massa!" Or, "Oh, massa, those old black nigger fieldhands out there, they're happy just like they are; why, massa, they're not intelligent enough for you to try and do any better for them, massa—"

Well, slavery time's "house" and "yard" Negroes had become more sophisticated, that was all. When now the white man picked up his telephone and dialed his "house" and "yard" Negroes—why, he didn't even need to instruct the trained black puppets. They had seen the television program: had read the newspapers. They were already composing their lines. They knew what to do.

I'm not going to call any names. But if you make a list of the biggest Negro "leaders," so-called, in 1960, then you've named the ones who began to attack us "field" Negroes who were sounding *insane*, talking that way about "good massa."

"By no means do these Muslims represent the Negro masses—" That was the first worry, to reassure "good massa" that he had no reason to be concerned about his fieldhands in the ghettoes. "An irresponsible hate cult" . . . "an unfortunate Negro image, just when the racial picture is improving—"

They were stumbling over each other to get quoted. "A deplorable reverse-racism" . . . "Ridiculous pretenders to the ancient Islamic doctrine" . . . "Heretic anti-Christianity—"

The telephone in our then small Temple Seven restaurant nearly jumped off the wall. I had a receiver against my ear five hours a day. I was listening, and jotting in my notebook, as press, radio, and television people called, all of them wanting the Muslim reaction to the quoted attacks of these black "leaders." Or I was on long-distance to Mr. Muhammad in Chicago, reading from my notebook and asking for Mr. Muhammad's instructions.

I couldn't understand how Mr. Muhammad could maintain his calm and patience, hearing the things I told him. I could scarcely contain myself.

My unlisted home telephone number somehow got out. My wife Betty put down the phone after taking one message, and it was ringing again. It seemed that wherever I went, telephones were ringing.

The calls naturally were directed to me, New York City being the major news-media headquarters, and I was the New York minister of Mr. Muhammad. Calls came, long-distance from San Francisco to Maine . . . from even London, Stockholm, Paris. I would see a Muslim brother at our restaurant, or Betty at home, trying to keep cool; they'd hand me the receiver, and I couldn't believe it, either. One funny thing—in all that hectic period, something quickly struck my notice: the Europeans never pressed the "hate" question. Only the American white man was so plagued and obsessed with being "hated." He was so guilty, it was clear to me, of hating Negroes.

"Mr. Malcolm X, why do you teach black supremacy, and hate?" A red flag waved for me, something chemical happened inside me, every time I heard that. When we Muslims had talked about "the devil white man" he had been relatively abstract, someone we Muslims rarely actually came into contact with, but now here was that devil-in-the-flesh on the phone—with all of his calculating, cold-eyed, self-righteous tricks and nerve and gall. The voices questioning me became to me as breathing, living devils.

And I tried to pour on pure fire in return. "The white man so guilty of white supremacy can't hide *his* guilt by trying to accuse The Honorable Elijah Muhammad of teaching black supremacy and hate! All Mr. Muhammad is doing is trying to uplift the black man's mentality and the black man's social and economic condition in this country.

"The guilty, two-faced white man can't decide *what* he wants. Our slave foreparents would have been put to death for advocating so-called 'integration' with the white man. Now when Mr. Muhammad speaks of 'separation,' the white man calls us 'hate-teachers' and 'fascists'!

"The white man doesn't *want* the blacks! He doesn't *want* the blacks that are a parasite upon him! He doesn't *want* this black man whose presence and condition in this country expose the white man to the world for what he is! So why do you attack Mr. Muhammad?"

I'd have *scathing* in my voice; I *felt* it.

"For the white man to ask the black man if he hates him is just like the rapist asking the *raped*, or the wolf asking the *sheep*, 'Do you hate me?' The white man is in no moral *position* to accuse anyone else of hate!

"Why, when all of my ancestors are snake-bitten, and I'm snake-bitten, and I want my children to avoid snakes, what does that *snake* sound like accusing *me* of hate-teaching?"

"Mr. Malcolm X," those devils would ask, "why is your Fruit of Islam being trained in judo and karate?" An image of black men learning anything suggesting self-defense seemed to terrify the white man. I'd turn their question around: "Why does judo or karate suddenly get so ominous because black men study it? Across America, the Boy Scouts, the YMCA, even the YWCA, the CYP, PAL—they *all* teach judo! It's all right, it's fine—until *black men* teach it! Even little grammar school classes, little girls, are taught to defend themselves—"

"How many of you are in your organization, Mr. Malcolm X? Right Reverend Bishop T. Chickenwing says you have only a handful of members—"

"Whoever tells you how many Muslims there are doesn't know, and whoever does know will never tell you—"

The Bishop Chickenwings were also often quoted about our "anti-Christianity." I'd fire right back on that:

"Christianity is the white man's religion. The Holy Bible in the white man's hands and his interpretations of it have been the greatest single ideological weapon for enslaving millions of non-white human beings. Every country the white man has conquered with his guns, he has always paved the way, and salved his conscience, by carrying the Bible and interpreting it to call the people 'heathens' and 'pagans'; then he sends his guns, then his missionaries behind the guns to mop up—"

White reporters, anger in their voices, would call us "demagogues," and I would try to be ready after I had been asked the same question two or three times.

"Well, let's go back to the Greek, and maybe you will learn the first thing you need to know about the word 'demagogue.' 'Demagogue' means, actually, 'teacher of the people.' And let's examine some demagogues. The greatest of all Greeks, Socrates, was killed as a 'demagogue.' Jesus Christ died on the cross because the Pharisees of His day were upholding their law, not the spirit. The modern Pharisees are trying to heap destruction upon Mr. Muhammad, calling him a demagogue, a crackpot, and fanatic. What about Gandhi? The man that Churchill called 'a naked little fakir,' refusing food in a British jail? But then a quarter of a billion people, a whole sub-continent, rallied behind Gandhi—and they twisted the British Lion's tail! What about Galileo, standing before his inquisitors, saying 'The earth *does* move!' What about Martin Luther, nailing on a door his thesis against the all-powerful Catholic church which called him 'heretic'? We, the followers of The Honorable Elijah Muhammad, are today in the ghettoes as once the sect of Christianity's followers were like termites in the catacombs and the grottoes—and they were preparing the grave of the mighty Roman Empire!"

I can remember those hot telephone sessions with those reporters as if it were yesterday. The reporters were angry. I was angry. When I'd reach into history, they'd try to pull me back to the present. They would quit interviewing, quit their work, trying to defend their personal white devil selves. They would unearth Lincoln and his freeing of the slaves. I'd tell them things Lincoln said in speeches, *against* the blacks. They would drag up the 1954 Supreme Court decision on school integration.

"That was one of the greatest magical feats ever performed in America," I'd tell them. "Do you mean to tell me that nine Supreme Court judges, who are past masters of legal phraseology, couldn't have worked their decision to make it stick as *law*? No! It was trickery and magic that told Negroes they were desegregated—Hooray! Hooray!—and at the same time it told whites 'Here are your loopholes.'"

The reporters would try their utmost to raise some "good" white man whom I couldn't refute as such. I'll never forget how one practically lost his voice. He asked me did I feel *any* white men had ever done anything for the black man in America. I told him, "Yes, I can think of two. Hitler, and Stalin. The black man in America couldn't get a decent factory job until

Hitler put so much pressure on the white man. And then Stalin kept up the pressure—"

But I don't care what points I made in the interviews, it practically never got printed the way I said it. I was learning under fire how the press, when it wants to, can twist, and slant. If I had said "Mary had a little lamb," what probably would have appeared was "Malcolm X Lampoons Mary."

Even so, my bitterness was less against the white press than it was against those Negro "leaders" who kept attacking us. Mr. Muhammad said he wanted us to try our best not to publicly counterattack the black "leaders" because one of the white man's tricks was keeping the black race divided and fighting against each other. Mr. Muhammad said that this had traditionally kept the black people from achieving the unity which was the worst need of the black race in America.

But instead of abating, the black puppets continued ripping and tearing at Mr. Muhammad and the Nation of Islam—until it began to appear as though we were afraid to speak out against these "important" Negroes. That's when Mr. Muhammad's patience wore thin. And with his nod, I began returning their fire.

"Today's Uncle Tom doesn't wear a handkerchief on his head. This modern, twentieth-century Uncle Thomas now often wears a top hat. He's usually well-dressed and well-educated. He's often the personification of culture and refinement. The twentieth-century Uncle Thomas sometimes speaks with a Yale or Harvard accent. Sometimes he is known as Professor, Doctor, Judge, and Reverend, even Right Reverend Doctor. This twentieth-century Uncle Thomas is a *professional* Negro . . . by that I mean his profession is being a Negro for the white man."

Never before in America had these hand-picked so-called "leaders" been publicly blasted in this way. They reacted to the truth about themselves even more hotly than the devilish white man. Now their "institutional" indictments of us began. Instead of "leaders" speaking as themselves, for themselves, now their weighty name organizations attacked Mr. Muhammad.

"Black bodies with white heads!" I called them what they were. Every one of those "Negro progress" organizations had the same composition. Black "leaders" were out in the public eye—to be seen by the Negroes for whom they were supposed to be fighting the white man. But obscurely, behind the scenes, was a white boss—a president, or board chairman, or some other title, pulling the real strings.

It was hot, hot copy, both in the white and the black press. *Life, Look, Newsweek* and *Time* reported us. Some newspaper chains began to run not one story, but a series of three, four, or five "exposures" of the Nation of Islam. The *Reader's Digest* with its worldwide circulation of twenty-four million copies in thirteen languages carried an article titled "Mr. Muhammad Speaks," by the writer to whom I am telling this book; and that led off other major monthly magazines' coverage of us.

Before very long, radio and television people began asking me to defend our Nation of Islam in panel discussions and debates. I was to be confronted by handpicked scholars, both whites and some of those Ph.D. "house" and "yard" Negroes who had been attacking us. Every day, I was more incensed with the general misrepresentation and distortion of Mr. Muhammad's teachings; I truly think that not once did it cross my mind that previously I never had been *inside* a radio or television station—let alone faced a microphone to audiences of millions of people. Prison debating had been my only experience speaking to anyone but Muslims.

From the old hustling days I knew that there were tricks to everything. In the prison debating, I had learned tricks to upset my opponents, to catch them where they didn't expect to be caught. I knew there were bound to be tricks I didn't know anything about in arguing on the air.

I knew that if I closely studied what the others did, I could learn things in a hurry to help me to defend Mr. Muhammad and his teachings.

I'd walk into those studios. The devils and black Ph.D. puppets would be acting so friendly and "integrated" with each other—laughing and calling each other by first names, and all that; it was such a big lie it made me sick in my stomach. They would even be trying to act friendly toward me—we all knowing they had asked me there to try and beat out my brains. They would offer me coffee. I would tell them "No, thanks," to please just tell me where was I supposed to sit. Sometimes the microphone sat on the table before you, at other times a smaller, cylindrical microphone was hung on a cord around your neck. From the start, I liked those microphones better; I didn't have to keep constantly aware of my distance from a microphone on the table.

The program hosts would start with some kind of dice-loading, non-religious introduction for me. It would be something like "—and we have with us today the fiery, angry chief Malcolm X of the New York Muslims. . . ." I made up my own introduction. At home, or driving my car, I practiced until I could interrupt a radio or television host and introduce myself.

"I represent Mr. Elijah Muhammad, the spiritual head of the fastest-growing group of Muslims in the Western Hemisphere. We who follow him know that he has been divinely taught and sent to us by God Himself. We believe that the miserable plight of America's twenty million black people is the fulfillment of divine prophecy. We also believe the presence today in America of The Honorable Elijah Muhammad, his teachings among the so-called Negroes, and his naked warning to America concerning her treatment of these so-called Negroes, is all the fulfillment of divine prophecy. I am privileged to be the minister of our Temple Number Seven here in New York City which is a part of the Nation of Islam, under the divine leadership of The Honorable Elijah Muhammad—"

I would look around at those devils and their trained black parrots staring at me, while I was catching my breath—and I had set my tone.

They would outdo each other, leaping in on me, hammering at Mr. Muhammad, at me, and at the Nation of Islam. Those "integration"-mad Negroes—you know what they jumped on. *Why* couldn't Muslims *see* that "integration" was the answer to American Negroes' problems? I'd try to rip that to pieces.

"No *sane* black man really wants integration! No *sane* white man really wants integration! No sane black man really believes that the white man ever will give the black man anything more than token integration. No! The Honorable Elijah Muhammad teaches that for the black man in America the only solution is complete *separation* from the white man!"

Anyone who has ever heard me on radio or television programs knows that my technique is non-stop, until what I want to get said is said. I was developing the technique then.

"The Honorable Elijah Muhammad teaches us that since Western society is deteriorating, it has become overrun with immorality, and God is going to judge it, and destroy it. And the only way the black people caught up in this society can be saved is not to *integrate* into this corrupt society, but to *separate* from it, to a land of our *own*, where we can reform ourselves, lift up our moral standards, and try to be godly. The Western world's most learned diplomats have failed to solve this grave race problem. Her learned legal experts have failed. Her sociologists have failed. Her civil leaders have failed. Her fraternal leaders have failed. Since all of these have *failed* to solve this race problem, it is time for us to sit down and *reason*! I am certain that we will be forced to agree that it takes *God Himself* to solve this grave racial dilemma."

Every time I mentioned "separation," some of them would cry that we Muslims were standing for the same thing that white racists and demagogues stood for. I would explain the difference. "No! We reject *segregation* even more militantly than you say you do! We want *separation*, which is not the same! The Honorable Elijah Muhammad teaches us that *segregation* is when your life and liberty are controlled, regulated, *by someone else*. To *segregate* means to control. Segregation is that which is forced upon inferiors by superiors. But *separation* is that which is done voluntarily, by two equals— for the good of both! The Honorable Elijah Muhammad teaches us that as long as our people here in America are dependent upon the white man, we will always be begging him for jobs, food, clothing, and housing. And he will always control our lives, regulate our lives, and have the power to segregate us. The Negro here in America has been treated like a child. A child stays within the mother until the time of birth! When the time of birth arrives, the child must be separated, or it will *destroy* its mother and itself. The mother can't carry that child after its time. The child cries for and needs its own world!"

Anyone who has listened to me will have to agree that I believed in Elijah Muhammad and represented him one hundred per cent. I never tried to take any credit for myself.

I was never in one of those panel discussions without some of them just waiting their chance to accuse me of "inciting Negroes to violence." I didn't even have to do any special studying to prepare for that one.

"The greatest miracle Christianity has achieved in America is that the black man in white Christian hands has not grown violent. It *is* a miracle that 22 million black people have not *risen up* against their oppressors—in which they would have been justified by all moral criteria, and even by the democratic tradition! It is a miracle that a nation of black people has so fervently continued to believe in a turn-the-other cheek and heaven-for-you-after-you-die philosophy! It *is a miracle* that the American black people have remained a peaceful people, while catching all the centuries of hell that they have caught, here in white man's heaven! The *miracle* is that the white man's puppet Negro 'leaders,' his preachers and the educated Negroes laden with degrees, and others who have been allowed to wax fat off their black poor brothers, have been able to hold the black masses quiet until now."

I guarantee you one thing—every time I was mixed up in those studios with those brainwashed, "integration-mad" black puppets, and those tricky devils trying to rip and tear me down, as long as the little red light glowed "on the air," I tried to represent Elijah Muhammad and the Nation of Islam to the utmost.

Dr. C. Eric Lincoln's book was published amid widening controversy about us Muslims, at just about the time we were starting to put on our first big mass rallies.

Just as the television "Hate That Hate Produced" title had projected that "hate-teaching" image on us, now Dr. Lincoln's book was titled *The Black Muslims in America*. The press snatched at that name. "Black Muslims" was in all the book reviews, which quoted from the book only what was critical of us, and generally praised Dr. Lincoln's writing.

The public mind fixed on "Black Muslims." From Mr. Muhammad on down, the name "Black Muslims" distressed everyone in the Nation of Islam. I tried for at least two years to kill off that "*Black* Muslims." Every newspaper and magazine writer and microphone I got close to: "*No!* We are black *people* here in America. Our *religion* is Islam. We are properly called 'Muslims'!" But that "Black Muslims" name never got dislodged.

Our mass rallies, from their very beginning, were astounding successes. Where once Detroit's struggling little Temple One proudly sent a ten-automobile caravan to Chicago to hear Mr. Muhammad, now, from East Coast Temples—the older Temples as well as the new ones that all of the massive publicity had helped to bring into being—as many as 150, 200 and even as many as 300 big, chartered buses rolled the highways to wherever Mr. Muhammad was going to speak. On each bus, two Fruit of Islam men were in charge. Big three-by-nine-foot painted canvas banners hung on the buses' sides, to be read by the highway traffic and thousands of people at home and on the sidewalks of the towns the buses passed through.

Hundreds more Muslims and curious Negroes drove their own cars. And

Mr. Muhammad with his personal jet plane from Chicago. From the airport to the rally hall, Mr. Muhammad's motorcade had a siren-screaming police escort. Law agencies once had scoffed at our Nation as "black crackpots"; now they took special pains to safeguard against some "white crackpots" causing any "incidents" or "accidents."

America had never seen such fantastic all-black meetings! To hear Elijah Muhammad, up to ten thousand and more black people poured from public and private transportation to overflow the big halls we rented, such as the St. Nicholas Arena in New York City, Chicago's Coliseum, and Washington, D.C.'s Uline Arena.

The white man was barred from attendance—the first time the American black man had ever dreamed of such a thing. And that brought us new attacks from the white man and his black puppets. "Black segregationists . . . racists!" Accusing *us* of segregation! Across America, whites barring blacks was standard.

Many hundreds arrived too late for us to seat them. We always had to wire up outside loudspeakers. An electric atmosphere excited the great, shifting masses of black people. The long lines, three and four abreast, funneling to the meeting hall, were kept in strict order by Fruit of Islam men communicating by walkie-talkie. In anterooms just inside the halls, more Fruit of Islam men and white-gowned, veiled mature Muslim sisters thoroughly searched every man, woman, and child seeking to enter. Any alcohol and tobacco had to be checked, and any objects which could possibly be used to attempt to harm Mr. Muhammad. He always seemed deathly afraid that some one would harm him, and he insisted that everyone be searched to forestall this. Today I understand better, why.

The hundreds of Fruit of Islam men represented contingents which had arrived early that morning, from their Temples in the nearest cities. Some were detailed as ushers, who seated the people by designated sections. The balconies and the rear half of the main floor were filled with black people of the general public. Ahead of them were the all-Muslim seating sections—the white-garbed beautiful black sisters, and the dark-suited, white-shirted brothers. A special section near the front was for black so-called "dignitaries." Many of these had been invited. Among them were our black puppet and parrot attackers, the intellectuals and professional Negroes over whom Mr. Muhammad grieved so much, for these were the educated ones who should have been foremost in leading their poor black brothers out of the maze of misery and want. We wanted them to miss not a single syllable of the truths from Mr. Muhammad in person.

The front two or three press rows were filled with the black reporters and cameramen representing the Negro press, or those who had been hired by the white man's newspapers, magazines, radio, and television. America's black writers should hold a banquet for Mr. Muhammad. Writing about the Nation of Islam was the path to success for most of the black writers who now are recognized.

Up on the speaker's platform, we ministers and other officials of the Nation, entering from backstage, found ourselves chairs in the five or six rows behind the big chair reserved for Mr. Muhammad. Some of the ministers had come hundreds of miles to be present. We would be turning about in our chairs, beaming with smiles, wringing each other's hands, and exchanging "As-Salaam-Alaikum" and "Wa-Alaikum-Salaam" in our genuine deep rejoicing to see each other again.

Always, meeting us older hands in Mr. Muhammad's service for the first time, there were several new ministers of small new Temples. My brothers Wilfred and Philbert were respectively now the ministers of the Detroit and Lansing Temples. Minister Jeremiah X headed Atlanta's Temple. Minister John X had Los Angeles' Temple. The Messenger's son, Minister Wallace Muhammad, had the Philadelphia Temple. Minister Woodrow X had the Atlantic City Temple. Some of our ministers had unusual backgrounds. The Washington, D.C., Temple Minister Lucius X was previously a Seventh Day Adventist and a 32nd degree Mason. Minister George X of the Camden, New Jersey, Temple was a pathologist. Minister David X was previously the minister of a Richmond, Virginia, Christian church; he and enough of his congregation had become Muslims so that the congregation split and the majority turned the church into our Richmond Temple. The Boston Temple's outstanding young Minister Louis X, previously a well-known and rising popular singer called "The Charmer," had written our Nation's popular first song, titled "White Man's Heaven Is Black Man's Hell." Minister Louis X had also authored our first play, "Orgena" ("A Negro" spelled backwards); its theme was the all-black trial of a symbolic white man for his world crimes against non-whites; found guilty, sentenced to death, he was dragged off shouting about all he had done "for the nigra people."

Younger even than our talented Louis X were some newer ministers. Minister Thomas J. X of the Hartford Temple being one example, and another the Buffalo Temple's Minister Robert J. X.

I had either originally established or organized for Mr. Muhammad most of the represented temples. Greeting each of these Temples' brother ministers would bring back into my mind images of "fishing" for converts along the streets and from door-to-door wherever the black people were congregated. I remembered the countless meetings in living rooms where maybe seven would be a crowd; the gradually building, building—on up to renting folding chairs for dingy little storefronts which Muslims scrubbed to spot-lessness.

We together on a huge hall's speaking platform, and that vast audience before us, miraculously manifested, as far as I was concerned, the incomprehensible power of Allah. For the first time, I truly understood something Mr. Muhammad had told me: he claimed that when he was going through the sacrificial trials of fleeing the black hypocrites from city to city, Allah had often sent him visions of great audiences who would one day hear the teachings; and Mr. Muhammad said the visions also buoyed him when he was locked up for years in the white man's prison.

The great audience's restless whisperings would cease. . . .

At the microphone would be the Nation's National Secretary John Ali, or the Boston Temple Minister Louis X. They enlivened the all-black atmosphere, speaking of the new world open to the black man through the Nation of Islam. Sister Tynetta Dynear would speak beautifully of the Muslim women's powerful, vital contributions, of the Muslim women's roles in our Nation's efforts to raise the physical, mental, moral, social, and political condition of America's black people.

Next, I would come to the microphone, specifically to condition the audience to hear Mr. Muhammad who had flown from Chicago to teach us all in person.

I would raise up my hand, "*As-Salaikum-Salaam—*"

"*Wa-Alaikum-Salaam!*" It was a roared response from the great audience's Muslim seating section.

There was a general pattern that I would follow on these occasions:

"My black brothers and sisters—of all religious beliefs, or of no religious beliefs—we all have in common the greatest binding tie we could have . . . we all are *black* people!

"I'm not going to take all day telling you some of the greatnesses of The Honorable Elijah Muhammad. I'm just going to tell you now his *greatest* greatness! He is the *first*, the *only* black leader to identify, to you and me, *who* is our enemy!

"The Honorable Elijah Muhammad is the first black leader among us with the *courage* to tell us—out here in public—something which when you begin to think of it back in your homes, you will realize we black people have been *living* with, we have been *seeing*, we have been *suffering*, all of our lives!

"Our *enemy* is the *white man*!

"And why is Mr. Muhammad's teaching us this such a great thing? Because when you know *who* your enemy is, he can no longer keep you divided, and fighting, one brother against the other! Because when you *recognize* who your enemy is, he can no longer use trickery, promises, lies, hypocrisy, and his evil acts to keep you deaf, dumb, and blinded!

"When you recognize *who* your enemy is, he can no longer brainwash you, he can no longer pull wool over your eyes so that you never stop to see that you are living in pure *hell* on this earth, while *he* lives in pure *heaven* on this same earth!—This enemy who tells you that you are both supposed to be worshiping the same white Christian God that—you are told—stands for the *same* things for *all* men!

"Oh, *yes*, that devil is our enemy. I'll *prove* it! Pick up any daily newspaper! Read the false charges leveled against our beloved religious leader. It only points up the fact that the Caucasian race never wants any black man who is not their puppet or parrot to speak for our people. This Caucasian devil slavemaster does not want or trust us to leave him—yet when we stay here among him, he continues to keep us at the very *lowest level* of his society!

"The white man has always *loved* it when he could keep us black men tucked away somewhere, always out of sight, around the corner! The white man has always *loved* the kind of black leaders whom he could ask, 'Well, how's things with your people up there?' But because Mr. Elijah Muhammad takes an uncompromising stand with the white man, the white man *hates* him! When you hear the *white man* hate him, you, too, because you don't understand Biblical prophecy, wrongly label Mr. Muhammad—as a racist, a hate-teacher, or of being anti-white and teaching black supremacy—"

The audience suddenly would begin a rustling of turning. . . .

Mr. Muhammad would be rapidly moving along up a center aisle from the rear—as once he had entered our humble little mosques—this man whom we regarded as Islam's gentle, meek, brown-skinned Lamb. Stalwart, striding, close-cropped, handpicked Fruit of Islam guards were a circle surrounding him. He carried his Holy Bible, his holy Quran. The small, dark pillbox atop his head was gold-embroidered with Islam's flag, the sun, moon, and stars. The Muslims were crying out their adoration and their welcome. "Little Lamb!" "As-Salaikum-Salaam!" "Praise be to Allah!"

Tears would be in more eyes than mine. He had rescued me when I was a convict; Mr. Muhammad had trained me in his home, as if I was his son. I think that my life's peaks of emotion, until recently, at least, were when, suddenly, the Fruit of Islam guards would stop stiffly at attention, and the platform's several steps would be mounted alone by Mr. Muhammad, and his ministers, including me, sprang around him, embracing him, wringing both his hands. . . .

I would turn right back to the microphone, not to keep waiting those world's biggest black audiences who had come to hear him.

"My black brothers and sisters—*no* one will know *who* we are . . . until *we* know who we are! We never will be able to *go* anywhere until we know *where* we are! The Honorable Elijah Muhammad is giving us a true identity, and a true position—the first time they have ever been *known* to the American black man!

"You can be around this man and never *dream* from his actions the power and the authority he has—" (Behind me, believe me when I tell you, I could *feel* Mr. Muhammad's *power*.)

"He does not *display*, and *parade*, his *power*! But no other black leader in America has followers who will lay down their lives if he says so! And I don't mean all of this non-violent, begging-the-white-man kind of dying . . . all of this sitting-in, sliding-in, wading-in, eating-in, diving-in, and all the rest—

"My black brothers and sisters, you have come from your homes to hear— now you are *going* to hear—America's *wisest* black man! America's *boldest* black man! America's most *fearless* black man! This wilderness of North America's most *powerful* black man!"

Mr. Muhammad would come quickly to the stand, looking out over the vacuum-quiet audience, his gentle-looking face set, for just a fleeting moment. Then, "As-Salaikum-Salaam—"

"WA-ALAIKUM-SALAAM!"

The Muslims roared it, as they settled to listen. From experience, they knew that for the next two hours Mr. Muhammad would wield his two-edged sword of truth. In fact, every Muslim worried that he overtaxed himself in the length of his speeches, considering his bronchial asthmatic condition.

"I don't have a degree like many of you out there before me have. But history don't care anything about your degrees.

"The white man, he has filled you with a fear of him from ever since you were little black babies. So over you is the greatest enemy a man can have— and that is fear. I know some of you are afraid to listen to the truth—you have been raised on fear and lies. But I am going to preach to you the truth until you are free of that fear. . . .

"Your slavemaster, he brought you over here, and of your past everything was destroyed. Today, you do not know your true language. What tribe are you from? You would not recognize your tribe's name if you heard it. You don't know nothing about your true culture. You don't even know your family's real name. You are wearing a *white man's* name! The white slave-master, who *hates* you!

"You are a people who think you know all about the Bible, and all about Christianity. You even are foolish enough to believe that nothing is *right* but Christianity!

"You are the planet Earth's only group of people ignorant of yourself, ignorant of your own kind, of your true history, ignorant of your enemy! You know nothing at *all* but what your white slavemaster has chosen to tell you. And he has told you only that which will benefit himself, and his own kind He has taught you, for *his* benefit, that you are a neutral, shiftless, helpless so-called 'Negro.'

"I say '*so-called*' because you are *not* a '*Negro*.' There is no such thing as a race of '*Negroes*.' You are members of the Asiatic nation, from the tribe of *Shabazz*! 'Negro' is a false label forced on you by your slavemaster! He has been pushing things onto you and me and our kind ever since he brought the first slave shipload of us black people here—"

When Mr. Muhammad paused, the Muslims before him cried out, "Little Lamb!" . . . "All praise is due to Allah!" . . . "*Teach*, Messenger!" He would continue.

"The *ignorance* we of the black race here in America have, and the *self-hatred* we have, they are fine examples of what the white slavemaster has seen fit to teach to us. Do we show the plain common sense, like every other people on this planet Earth, to unite among ourselves? No! We are humbling ourselves, sitting-in, and begging-in, trying to *unite* with the slavemaster! I don't seem able to imagine any more ridiculous sight. A thousand ways every day, the white man is telling you 'You can't live here, you can't enter here, you can't eat here, drink here, walk here, work here, you can't ride here, you can't play here, you can't study here.' Haven't we yet seen enough to see that he has no plan to *unite* with you?

"You have tilled his fields! Cooked his food! Washed his clothes! You have cared for his wife and children when he was away. In many cases, you have even suckled him at your *breast*! You have been far and away better Christians than this slavemaster who *taught* you his Christianity!

"You have sweated blood to help him build a country so rich that he can today afford to give away millions—even to his *enemies*! And when those enemies have gotten enough from him to then be able to attack him, you have been his brave soldiers, *dying* for him. And you have been always his most faithful servant during the so-called 'peaceful' times—

"And, *still*, this Christian American white man has not got it in him to find the human *decency*, and enough sense of *justice*, to recognize us, and accept us, the black people who have done so much for him, as fellow human beings!"

"YAH, Man!" . . . "*Um-huh!*" "*Teach,* Messenger!" . . . "*Yah!*" . . . "*Tell 'em!*" . . . "You *right!*" . . . "Take your *time* up there, little Messenger!" . . . "Oh, *yes!*"

Others besides the Muslims would be shouting now. We Muslims were less extroverted than Christian Negroes. It would sound now like an old-fashioned camp meeting.

"So let us, the black people, *separate* ourselves from this white man slavemaster, who despises us so much! You are out here begging him for some so-called '*integration*!' But what is this slavemaster white, *rapist*, going about saying! He is saying *he* won't integrate because black blood will *mongrelize* his race! *He* says that—and look at *us*! Turn around in your seats and look at each other! This slavemaster white man already has '*integrated*' us until you can hardly find among us today any more than a very few who are the black color of our foreparents!"

"God-a-mighty, the man's right!" . . . " *Teach,* Messenger—" "*Hear* him! *Hear* him!"

"He has left such a little black in us," Mr. Muhammad would go on, "that now he despises us so bad—meaning he despises *himself,* for what he has *done* to us—that he tells us that *legally* if we have got *one* drop of black blood in us, that means you are all-black as far as his laws are concerned! Well, if that's all we've got left, we want to *reclaim* that one drop!"

Mr. Muhammad's frail strength could be seen to be waning. But he would teach on:

"So let us *separate* from this white man, and for the same reason *he* says— in time to save ourselves from any more '*integration*!'

"Why *shouldn't* this white man who likes to think and call himself so good, and so generous, this white man who finances even his enemies—why *shouldn't* he subsidize a separate state, a separate territory, for we black people who have been such faithful slaves and servants? A separate territory on which we can lift *ourselves* out of these white man's *slums* for us, and his *breadlines* for us. And even for *those* he is complaining that we cost him too much! We can do something for *ourselves*! We never have done what we *could*—because we have been brainwashed so well by the slavemaster white man that we must come to him, begging him, for everything we want, and need—"

After perhaps ninety minutes, behind Mr. Muhammad, every minister would have to restrain himself from bolting up to his side, to urge him that it was enough. He would be pressing his hands tightly against the edges of the speaker's stand, to support himself.

"We black people don't *know* what we can do. You never can know what *anything* can do—until it is set *free*, to act by itself! If you have a cat in your house that you pamper and pet, you have to free that cat, set it on its *own*, in the woods, before you can see that the cat had it *in* him to shelter and feed itself!

"We, the black people here in America, we never have been *free* to find *out* what we really can *do*! We have knowledge and experience to pool to do for ourselves! All of our lives we have farmed—we can grow our own food. We can set up factories to manufacture our own necessities! We can build other kinds of businesses, to establish trade, and commerce—and become independent, as other civilized people are—

"We can *throw off* our brainwashing, and our self-hate, and live as *brothers* together . . .

". . . some land of our *own*! . . . Something for *ourselves*! . . . leave this white slavemaster to *himself*. . . ."

Mr. Muhammad always stopped abruptly when he was unable to speak any longer.

The standing ovation, a solid wall of sound, would go on unabating.

Standing up there, flailing my arms, finally I could quiet the audiences as Fruit of Islam ushers began to pass along the seating rows the large, waxed paper buckets we used to take up the collection. I would speak.

"You *know*, from what you have just heard, that no white money finances The Honorable Elijah Muhammad and his program—to 'advise' him and 'contain' him! Mr. Muhammad's program, and his followers, are not 'integrated.' Mr. Muhammad's program and organization are *all*-black!

"We are the *only* black organization that *only* black people support! These so-called 'Negro progress' organizations—Why, they insult your intelligence, claiming they are fighting in your behalf, to get you the equal rights you are asking for . . . claiming they are *fighting* the white man who refuses to give you your rights. Why, the white man *supports* those organizations! If you belong, you pay your two, or three, or five dollars a year—but *who* gives those organizations those two, and three, and five *thousand* dollar donations? The *white* man! He *feeds* those organizations! So he controls those organizations! He *advises* them—so he *contains* them! Use your common sense—aren't you going to advise and control and contain anyone that you support, like your child?

"The white man would love to support Mr. Elijah Muhammad. Because if Mr. Muhammad had to rely on his support, he could *advise* Mr. Muhammad. My black brothers and sisters, it is *only* because *your* money, *black* money, supports Mr. Muhammad, that he can hold these all-black meetings from city to city, telling us black men the *truth*! That's why we are asking for your all-black *support*!"

Nearly all bills—and far from all one-dollar bills, either, filled the waxed buckets. The buckets were swiftly emptied, then refilled, as the Fruit of Islam ushers covered the entire audience.

The audience atmosphere was almost as if the people had gone limp. The collections always covered the rally expenses, and anything beyond that helped to continue building the Nation of Islam.

After several big rallies, Mr. Muhammad directed that we would admit the white press. Fruit of Islam men thoroughly searched them, as everyone else was searched—their notebooks, their cameras, camera cases, and whatever else they carried. Later, Mr. Muhammad said that *any* whites who wanted to hear the truth could attend our public rallies, until a small separate section for whites was filled.

Most whites who came were students and scholars. I would watch their congealed and reddened faces staring up at Mr. Muhammad. "The white man *knows* that his acts have been those of a devil!" I would watch also the faces of the professional black men, the so-called intellectuals who attacked us. They possessed the academic know-how, they possessed the technical and the scientific skills that could help to lead their mass of poor, black brothers out of our condition. But all these intellectual and professional black men could seem to think of was humbling themselves, and begging, trying to "integrate" with the so-called "liberal" white man who was telling them, "In time . . . everything's going to work out one day . . . just wait and have patience." These intellectual and professional Negroes couldn't use what they knew for the benefit of their own black kind simply because even among themselves they were disunited. United among themselves, united with their own kind, they could have benefited black people all over the world!

I would watch the faces of those intellectual and professional Negroes growing grave, and set—as the truth hit home to them.

We were watched. Our telephones were tapped. Still right today, on my home telephone, if I said, "I'm going to bomb the Empire State Building," I guarantee you in five minutes it would be surrounded. When I was speaking publicly sometimes I'd guess which were F.B.I. faces in the audience, or other types of agents. Both the police and the F.B.I. intently and persistently visited and questioned us. "I do not fear them," Mr. Muhammad said. "I have all that I need—the truth."

Many a night, I drifted off to sleep, filled with wonder at how the two-edged-sword teachings so hurt, confused, concerned, and upset the government full of men trained highly in all of the modern sciences. I felt that it never could have been unless The Most Learned One, Allah Himself, had given the little fourth-grade-trained Messenger something.

Black agents were sent to infiltrate us. But the white man's "secret" spy often proved, first of all, a black man. I can't say *all* of them, of course, there's no way to know—but some of them, after joining us, and hearing, seeing and *feeling* the truth for every black man, revealed their roles to us. Some resigned from the white man's agencies and came to work in the Nation of Islam. A few kept their jobs to counterspy, telling us the white man's statements and plans about our Nation. This was how we learned that after wanting to know what happened within our Temples, the white law agencies' second major concern was the thing that I believe still ranks today as a big worry among America's penologists: the steadily increasing rate at which black convicts embrace Islam.

Generally, while still in prison, our convict-converts pre-conditioned themselves to meet our Nation's moral laws. As it had happened with me, when they left prison, they entered a Temple fully qualified to become registered Muslims. In fact, convict-converts usually were better prepared than were numerous prospective Muslims who never had been inside a prison.

We were not nearly so easy to enter as a Christian church. One did not merely declare himself a follower of Mr. Muhammad, then continue leading the same old, sinful, immoral life. The Muslim first had to change his physical and moral self to meet our strict rules. To remain a Muslim he had to maintain those rules.

Few temple meetings were held, for instance, without the minister looking down upon some freshly shaved bald domes of new Muslim brothers in the audience. They had just banished from their lives forever that phony, lye-conked, metallic-looking hair, or "the process," as some call it these days. It grieves me that I don't care where you go, you see this symbol of ignorance and self-hate on so many Negroes' heads. I know it's bound to hurt the feelings of some of my good conked non-Muslim friends—but if you study closely any conked or "processed" Negro, you usually find he is an ignorant Negro. Whatever "show" or "front" he affects, his hair lye-cooked to be "white-looking" fairly shouts to everyone who looks at his head, "I'm ashamed to be a Negro." He will discover, just as I did, that he will be much-improved mentally whenever he discovers enough black self-pride to have that mess clipped off, and then wear the natural hair that God gives black men to wear.

No Muslim smokes—that was another of our rules. Some prospective Muslims found it more difficult to quit tobacco than others found quitting the dope habit. But black men and women quit more easily when we got them to consider seriously how the white man's government cared less about the public's health than about continuing the tobacco industry's *billions* in tax revenue. "What does a serviceman pay for a carton of cigarettes?"

a prospective Muslim convert would be asked. It helped him to see that every regularly priced carton he bought meant that the white man's government took around two dollars of a black man's hard-earned money for taxes, not for tobacco.

You may have read somewhere—a lot has been written concerning it— about the Nation of Islam's phenomenal record of dope-addiction cures of longtime junkies. In fact, the *New York Times* carried a story about how some of the social agencies have asked representatives of the Muslim program for clinical suggestions.

The Muslim program began with recognizing that color and addiction have a distinct connection. It is no accident that in the entire Western Hemisphere, the greatest localized concentration of addicts is in *Harlem*.

Our cure program's first major ingredient was the painfully patient work of Muslims who previously were junkies themselves.

In the ghetto's dope jungle, the Muslim ex-junkies would fish out addicts who knew them back in those days. Then with an agonizing patience that might span anywhere from a few months to a year, our ex-junky Muslims would conduct the addicts through the Muslim six-point therapeutic process.

The addict first was brought to admit to himself that he was an addict. Secondly, he was taught *why* he used narcotics. Third, he was shown that there was a *way* to stop addiction. Fourth, the addict's shattered self-image, and ego, were built up until the addict realized that he had, *within*, the self-power to end his addiction. Fifth, the addict voluntarily underwent a cold turkey break with drugs. Sixth, finally cured, now an ex-addict completes the cycle by "fishing" up other addicts whom he knows, and supervising their salvaging.

This sixth stage always instantly eliminated what so often defeats the average social agencies—the characteristic addict's hostility and suspicion. The addict who is "fished" up knew personally that the Muslim approaching him very recently had the same fifteen to thirty dollar a day habit. The Muslim may be this addict's buddy; they had plied the same dope jungle. They even may have been thieves together. The addict had *seen* the Muslim drifting off to sleep leaning against a building, or stepping as high over a matchstick as if it were a dog. And the Muslim, approaching the addict, uses the same old junkie jungle language.

Like the alcoholic, the junkie can never start to cure himself until he recognizes and accepts his true condition. The Muslim sticks like a leech, drumming at his old junkie buddy, "You're hooked, man!" It might take months before the addict comes to grips with this. The curative program is never really underway until this happens.

The next cure-phase is the addict's realization of *why* he takes dope. Still working on his man, right in the old jungle locale, in dives that you wouldn't believe existed, the Muslim often collects audiences of a dozen junkies. They listen only because they know the clean-cut proud Muslim had earlier been like them.

Every addict takes junk to escape something, the Muslim explains. He explains that most black junkies really are trying to narcotize themselves against being a black man in the white man's America. But, actually, the Muslim says, the black man taking dope is only helping the white man to "prove" that the black man is nothing.

The Muslim talks confidentially, and straight. "Daddy, you know I know how you feel. Wasn't I right out here with you? Scratching like a monkey, smelling all bad, living mad, hungry, stealing and running and hiding from Whitey. Man, what's a black man buying Whitey's dope for but to make Whitey richer—killing yourself!"

The Muslim can tell when his quarry is ready to be shown that the way for him to quit dope is through joining the Nation of Islam. The addict is brought into the local Muslim restaurant, he may occasionally be exposed to some other social situations—among proud, clean Muslims who show each other mutual affection and respect instead of the familiar hostility of the ghetto streets. For the first time in years, the addict hears himself called, genuinely, "Brother," "Sir" and "Mr." No one cares about his past. His addiction may casually be mentioned, but if so, it is spoken of as merely an especially tough challenge that he must face. Everyone whom this addict meets is confident that he will kick the habit.

As the addict's new image of himself builds, inevitably he begins thinking that he can break the habit. For the first time he is feeling the effects of black self-pride.

That's a powerful combination for a man who has been existing in the mud of society. In fact, once he is motivated no one can change more completely than the man who has been at the bottom. I call myself the best example of that.

Finally, vitally, this addict will decide for himself that he wants to go on cold turkey. This means to endure the physical agonies of abruptly quitting dope.

When this time comes, ex-addict Muslims will arrange to spend the necessary days in around-the-clock shifts, attending the addict who intends to purge himself, on the way to becoming a Muslim.

When the addict's withdrawal sets in, and he is screaming, cursing, and begging, "Just one shot, man!" the Muslims are right there talking junkie jargon to him. "Baby, knock that monkey off your back! Kick that habit! Kick Whitey off your back!" The addict, writhing in pain, his nose and eyes running, is pouring sweat from head to foot. He's trying to knock his head against the wall, flailing his arms, trying to fight his attendants, he is vomiting, suffering diarrhea. "Don't hold nothing back! Let Whitey go, baby! You're going to stand tall, man! I can see you now in the Fruit of Islam!"

When the awful ordeal is ended, when the grip of dope is broken, the Muslims comfort the weak ex-addict, feeding him soups and broths, to get him on his feet again. He will never forget these brothers who stood by him during this time. He will never forget that it was the Nation of Islam's program which rescued him from the special hell of dope. And that black brother (or the sister, whom Muslim sisters attend) rarely ever will return to the use of narcotics. Instead, the ex-addict when he is proud, clean, renewed, can scarcely wait to hit the same junkie jungle he was in, to "fish" out some buddy and salvage *him*!

If some white man, or "approved" black man, created a narcotics cure program as successful as the one conducted under the aegis of the Muslims, why, there would be government subsidy, and praise and spotlights, and headlines. But we were attacked instead. Why shouldn't the Muslims be subsidized to save millions of dollars a year for the government and the cities? I don't know what addicts' crimes cost nationally, but it is said to be *billions* a year in New York City. An estimated $12 million a year is lost to thieves in Harlem alone.

An addict doesn't work to supply his habit, which may cost anywhere from ten to fifty dollars a day. How could he earn that much? No! The addict steals, he hustles in other ways; he preys upon other human beings like a hawk or a vulture—as I did. Very likely, he is a school drop-out, the same as I was, an Army reject, psychologically unsuited to a job even if he was offered one, the same as I was.

Women addicts "boost" (shoplift), or they prostitute themselves. Muslim sisters talk hard to black prostitutes who are struggling to quit using dope in order to qualify morally to become registered Muslims. "You are helping the white man to regard your body as a garbage can—"

Numerous "exposés" of the Nation of Islam have implied that Mr. Muhammad's followers were chiefly ex-cons and junkies. In the early years, yes, the converts from society's lowest levels were a sizable part of the Nation's broad base of membership. Always Mr. Muhammad instructed us, "Go after the black man in the mud." Often, he said, those converted made the best Muslims.

But gradually we recruited other black people—the "good Christians" whom we "fished" from their churches. Then, an increase began in the membership percentage of educated and trained Negroes. For each rally attracted to the local temple a few more of that particular city's so-called "middle-class" Negroes, the type who previously had scoffed at us "Black Muslims" as "demagogues," and "hate-teachers," "black racists" and all the rest of the names. The Muslim truths—listened to, thought about— reaped for us a growing quota of young black men and women. For those with training and talents, the Nation of Islam had plenty of positions where those abilities were needed.

There were some registered Muslims who would never reveal their membership, except to other Muslims, because of their positions in the white man's world. There were, I know, a few, who because of their positions were known only to their ministers and to Mr. Elijah Muhammad.

In 1961, our Nation flourished. Our newspaper *Muhammad Speaks'* full back page carried an architect's drawing of a $20 million Islamic Center proposed to be built in Chicago. Every Muslim was making personal financial contribution toward the Center. It would include a beautiful mosque, school, library, and hospital, and a museum documenting the black man's glorious history.

Mr. Muhammad visited the Muslim countries, and upon his return he directed that we would begin calling our temples "mosques."

There was a sharp climb now, too, in the number of Muslim-owned small businesses. Our businesses sought to demonstrate to the black people what black people could do for themselves—if they would only unify, trade with each other—exclusively where possible—and hire each other, and in so doing, keep black money within the black communities, just as other minorities did.

Recordings of Mr. Muhammad's speeches were now regularly being broadcast across America over small radio stations. In Detroit and Chicago, school-age Muslim children attended our two Universities of Islam—through high school in Chicago, and through junior high in Detroit. Starting from kindergarten, they learned of the black man's glorious history and from the third grade they studied the black man's original language, Arabic.

Mr. Muhammad's eight children now were all deeply involved in key capacities in the Nation of Islam. I took a deep personal pride in having had something to do with that—at least in some cases, years before. When Mr. Muhammad had sent me out in his service as a minister, I began to feel it was a shame that his children worked as some of them then did for the white man, in factories, construction work, driving taxis, things like that. I felt that I should work for Mr. Muhammad's family as sincerely as I worked for him. I urged Mr. Muhammad to let me put on a special drive within our few small mosques, to raise funds which would enable those of his children working for the white man to be instead employed within our Nation. Mr. Muhammad agreed, the special fund drive did prove successful, and his children gradually did begin working for the Nation. Emanuel, the oldest, today runs the dry-cleaning plant. Sister Ethel (Muhammad) Sharrieff is the Muslim Sisters' Supreme Instructor. (Her husband, Raymond Sharrieff, is Supreme Captain of the Fruit of Islam.) Sister Lottie Muhammad supervises the two Universities of Islam. Nathaniel Muhammad assists Emanuel in the dry-cleaning plant. Herbert Muhammad now publishes *Muhammad Speaks*, the Nation's newspaper that I began. Elijah Muhammad. Jr., is the Fruit of Islam Assistant Supreme Captain. Wallace Muhammad was the Philadelphia Mosque Minister, until finally he was suspended from the Nation along with me—for reasons I will go into. The youngest child, Akbar Muhammad, the family student, attends the University of Cairo at El-Azhar. Akbar also has broken with his father.

I believe that it was too strenuous a marathon of long speeches that Mr. Muhammad made at our big rallies which, abruptly, badly aggravated his long-bothersome bronchial asthmatic condition.

Just in conversation, Mr. Muhammad would suddenly begin coughing, and the coughing tempo would increase until it racked his slight body.

Mr. Muhammad almost doubled up sometimes. Soon, he had to take to his bed. As hard as he tried not to, as deeply as it grieved him, he had to cancel several long-scheduled appearances at big-city rallies. Thousands were disappointed to have to hear me instead, or other poor substitutes for Mr. Muhammad in person.

Members of the Nation were deeply concerned. Doctors recommended a dry climate. The Nation bought Mr. Muhammad a home in Phoenix, Arizona. One of the first times I visited Mr. Muhammad there, I stepped off a plane into flashing and whirring cameras until I wondered who was behind me. Then I saw the cameramen's guns; they were from the Arizona Intelligence Division.

The wire of our Nation of Islam brought all Muslims the joyful news that the Arizona climate did vastly relieve the Messenger's suffering. Since then he has spent most of each year in Phoenix.

Despite the fact that Mr. Muhammad, convalescing, could no longer work the daily hours he had previously worked in Chicago, he was now more than ever burdened with heavy decision-making and administrative duties. In every respect, the Nation was expanded both internally and externally. Mr. Muhammad simply could no longer allot as much time as previously to considering and deciding which public-speaking, radio, and television requests he felt I should accept—as well as to some organizational matters which I had always brought to him for advice or decision.

Mr. Muhammad evidenced the depth of his trust in me. In those areas I've described, he told me to make the decisions myself. He said that my guideline should be whatever I felt was wise—whatever was in the general good interests of our Nation of Islam.

"Brother Malcolm, I want you to become well known," Mr. Muhammad told me one day. "Because if you are well known, it will make *me* better known," he went on.

"But, Brother Malcolm, there is something you need to know. You will grow to be hated when you become well known. Because usually people get jealous of public figures."

Nothing that Mr. Muhammad ever said to me was more prophetic.

## QUESTIONS: *Malcolm X, The Autobiography of Malcolm X*

1. The following are two interpretations of *The Autobiography of Malcolm X*. In the light of the chapter you have read, which do you feel to be most justified? Can they be reconciled in any way?
   a. The leading quality of Malcolm's prose is total, impassioned honesty, firmness of belief, straightforwardness of expression. Compare his work to Norman Mailer's, or even George Orwell's, and the striking thing is the total absence of the *striving for effect* that often betrays writers into artiness and false clever-

ness. There are few metaphors or similes, and those which do occur tend to be conventional: teachings "which cut back and forth like a two-edged sword," "the maze of misery and want." In place of fancy metaphors we have a complete lack of self-consciousness in expression. Malcolm isn't ashamed to confess his religious faith and dependence on Allah or his trust in Elijah Muhammad. It's typical of him that he should describe the sight of "devils and black Ph.D. puppets" in a network studio as "such a big lie it made me sick in my stomach," a statement which has only a single word with more than one syllable. Words of this kind cut "like a two-edged sword" through most of the involuted, convoluted trash that is published by our newspapers, journals, and literary quarterlies. The naked truths that Malcolm first brought to the world's attention—truths about oppression, degradation, self-hate— tell us that other writers aren't talking *about anything at all except themselves*. They are just confirming what Malcolm calls "the white man's love for himself," which includes a love of hearing yourself talk and talk and talk and talk . . .

b. The enslavement and deportation of Africans deserves a high place in the Chamber of Horrors of civilized man; and the treatment of the black man since the so-called "Emancipation" has continued the horror down into our own time. A civilization that could do these things and at the same time *conceal them from itself by pretense* and euphemism was and is a civilization in an advanced state of psychosis, a condition that includes, according to the dictionary, a "partial or complete withdrawal from reality." In the world of Malcolm X and the Nation of Islam, we see the psychosis confronted point-for-point by a counter-psychosis. Just as slaveholders were able to deal "firmly" with their Blacks only by suppressing a knowledge of their humanity, so Malcolm's "firmness," "straightforwardness," "elemental power," and "burning conviction" are attained only by refusing to grant non-Blacks their full and varied humanity. In place of the shuffling, shiftless, yet somehow dangerous Negro, we have the forging of a monolithic entity called "the white man" or "the white devil," a process that we might call the collectiviza-tion of social vision and that is one of the most hateful and murderous of human fantasies ("*the* Negro," "*the* Jew," "*the* Sicilian," "*the* Oriental"). It is one of the classic forms of hatred that simply *has* to be discharged, at any cost; and the non-Blacks who are exhilarated by its "power" tend to be those who powerfully hate themselves, bad allies for anyone, bad allies for the Black.

2. Section II concerns "Protest, Revolution, and Anarchy," social phenomena that we often oppose to order, stability, structure. We think of the latter as "con-servative" values. Are there any respects in which the ideas of Malcolm X and the Nation of Islam would have to be called conservative? If so, how can such conservatism be reconciled with the image of Malcolm X as a "revolutionary"?

Clues: • "All Mr. Muhammad is doing is trying to uplift the black man's mentality and the black man's social and economic condition in this country."

• . . . the white-garbed beautiful black sisters, and the dark-suited, white-shirted brothers.

- "Do we show the plain common sense, *like every other people on this planet Earth*, to unite among ourselves? No!"

- ... proud, *clean* Muslims who show each other mutual affection and *respect* instead of the familiar hostility of the ghetto streets. For the first time in years, the addict hears himself called, genuinely, "*Brother*," "*Sir*" and "*Mr.*"

3. Malcolm X tends to excite his readers precisely because he seems free from the ironies, hesitations, perplexities, ambivalences that often paralyze other thinkers. Is it arguable that there is still some ambivalence in his vision of the "white devil"? If so, what form does it take and what are its political implications?

   *Clues:* • "We, the followers of The Honorable Elijah Muhammad, are today in the ghettoes as once the sect of Christianity's followers were like *termites* in the catacombs and the grottoes—and they were *preparing the grave of the mighty Roman Empire!*"

   • "No *sane* black man really wants integration! No *sane* white man really wants integration!"

   • "We want *separation.* . . . Segregation is that which is forced upon inferiors by superiors. But *separation* is that which is done voluntarily, by two equals—*for the good of both!*"

   • "The Negro here in America has been treated like a child. A child stays *within the mother* until the time of birth! When the time of birth arrives, the child must be separated, or it will *destroy its mother and itself.* The *mother* can't *carry* that child after its time."

   • "The white slavemaster, who *hates* you!"

   • "Use your common sense—aren't you going to advise and control and contain anyone that you support, *like your child?*"

   • Most whites who came were students and scholars. I would watch their *congealed and reddened faces* staring up at Mr. Muhammad. "The white man *knows* that his acts have been those of a devil!"

   • Many a night, I drifted off to sleep, filled with wonder at how the two-edged-sword teachings so *hurt, confused, concerned,* and upset the government full of men trained highly in all of the modern sciences.

4. Malcolm X searingly expresses his contempt for the "Uncle Thomas" with "a Yale or Harvard accent," "those Ph.D. 'house' and 'yard' Negroes who had been attacking us," "black Ph.D. puppets," "trained black parrots." To what extent does this attitude reflect (a) a general dislike of pretensions to learning and superiority? (b) a genuine acknowledgment of superior skill combined with anger at the failure to use it for the benefit of fellow Blacks? (c) a largely repressed feeling of envy for an achievement which one has been denied the opportunity even to strive for? Is there a parallel between the attitude of Malcolm X toward education and a general American inclination to distrust professionals with degrees?

   *Clues:* • Well, slavery time's "house" and "yard" Negroes had become more sophisticated, that was all. When now the white man picked up his telephone and dialed his "house" and "yard" Negroes—why he didn't even need to instruct the trained black puppets. . . . They were already composing their lines. They knew what to do.

- "Sometimes he is known as Professor, Doctor, Judge, and Reverend. . . . This twentieth century Uncle Thomas is a *professional* Negro . . . by that I mean his profession is *being a Negro for the white man.*"
- Black "*leaders*" were out in the public eye. . . . But obscurely, behind the scenes, was a *white boss*—a president, or board chairman, *pulling the real strings.*
- "I don't have a degree like many of you out there before me have. *But history don't care anything about your degrees.*"
- I would watch also the faces of the professional black men, the *so-called* intellectuals who attacked us. They possessed the *academic know-how, they possessed the technical and the scientific skills* that could help to lead their mass of poor, black brothers out of our condition. But all these intellectual and professional black men could seem to think of *was humbling themselves, and begging, trying* to "integrate" with the so-called "liberal" white man. . . .

## EXERCISES

1. Malcolm X's assumption "that color and addiction have a distinct connection" has since been invalidated. Taking into account more recent social reactions to black activism, comment on the validity of his assumption in this chapter that the white man is essentially self-loving and self-satisfied.
2. Compare and contrast the vision of themselves in relation to American values and institutions that Malcolm X and Allen Ginsberg project.
3. Compare the black visions of America in this chapter and in Melvin Tolson's poem "Dark Symphony."
4. Discuss the reservations and qualifications a sympathetically disposed white reader might have toward this chapter of *The Autobiography of Malcolm X.*

## *Melvin B. Tolson (1898–1966)*

# Dark Symphony

I

ALLEGRO MODERATO[1]
Black Crispus Attucks taught
　　　　Us how to die
Before white Patrick Henry's bugle breath
Uttered the vertical
　　　　Transmitting cry:
"Yea, give me liberty or give me death."

---

[1] *Allegro Moderato:* moderately fast.

Waifs of the auction block,
                Men black and strong        5
The juggernauts of despotism withstood,
Loin-girt with faith that worms
                Equate the wrong
And dust is purged to create brotherhood.

No Banquo's ghost can rise
                Against us now,
Aver we hobnailed Man beneath the brute,    10
Squeezed down the thorns of greed
                On Labor's brow,
Garroted lands and carted off the loot.

2

LENTO GRAVE[2]

The centuries-old pathos in our voices
Saddens the great white world,
And the wizardry of our dusky rhythms    15
Conjures up shadow-shapes of ante-bellum years:

Black slaves singing *One More River to Cross*
In the torture tombs of slave-ships,
Black slaves singing *Steal Away to Jesus*
In jungle swamps,    20
Black slaves singing *The Crucifixion*
In slave-pens at midnight,
Black slaves singing *Swing Low, Sweet Chariot*
In cabins of death,
Black slaves singing *Go Down, Moses*    25
In the canebrakes of the Southern Pharaohs.

3

ANDANTE SOSTENUTO[3]

They tell us to forget
The Golgotha we tread . . .
We who are scourged with hate,
A price upon our head.    30
They who have shackled us
Require of us a song,
They who have wasted us
Bid us condone the wrong.

[2] *Lento Grave:* very slow, solemn, sad.  [3] *Andante Sostenuto:* sustained or prolonged, and moderately slow.

They tell us to forget                                    35
Democracy is spurned.
They tell us to forget
The Bill of Rights is burned.
Three hundred years we slaved,
We slave and suffer yet:                                  40
Though flesh and bone rebel,
They tell us to forget!

Oh, how can we forget
Our human rights denied?
Oh, how can we forget                                     45
Our manhood crucified?
When Justice is profaned
And plea with curse is met,
When Freedom's gates are barred,
Oh, how can we forget?                                    50

4

TEMPO PRIMO[4]

The New Negro strides upon the continent
In seven-league boots . . .
The New Negro
Who sprang from the vigor-stout loins
Of Nat Turner, gallows-martyr for Freedom,               55
Of Joseph Cinquez, Black Moses of the Amistad Mutiny,
Of Frederick Douglass, oracle of the Catholic Man,
Of Sojourner Truth, eye and ear of Lincoln's legions,
Of Harriet Tubman, Saint Bernard of the Underground Railroad.

The New Negro                                             60
Breaks the icons of his detractors,
Wipes out the conspiracy of silence,
Speaks to *his* America:

"My history-moulding ancestors
Planted the first crops of wheat on these shores,        65
Built ships to conquer the seven seas,
Erected the Cotton Empire,
Flung railroads across a hemisphere,
Disemboweled the earth's iron and coal,
Tunneled the mountains and bridged rivers,               70
Harvested the grain and hewed forests,
Sentineled the Thirteen Colonies,

[4] *Tempo Primo:* the same tempo as the first movement (i.e., *allegro moderato*).

Unfurled Old Glory at the North Pole,
Fought a hundred battles for the Republic."

The New Negro:                                     75
His giant hands fling murals upon high chambers,
His drama teaches a world to laugh and weep,
His music leads continents captive,
His voice thunders the Brotherhood of Labor,
His science creates seven wonders,                    80
His Republic of Letters challenges the Negro-baiters.

The New Negro,
Hard-muscled, Fascist-hating, Democracy-ensouled,
Strides in seven-league boots
Along the Highway of Today                          85
Toward the Promised Land of Tomorrow!

### 5

#### LARGHETTO[5]

None in the Land can say
To us black men Today:
You send the tractors on their bloody path,
And create Okies for *The Grapes of Wrath*.          90
You breed the slum that breeds a *Native Son*
To damn the good earth Pilgrim Fathers won.

None in the Land can say
To us black men Today:
You dupe the poor with rags-to-riches tales,      95
And leave the workers empty dinner pails.
You stuff the ballot box, and honest men
Are muzzled by your demagogic din.

None in the Land can say
To us black men Today:                            100
You smash stock markets with your coined blitzkriegs,
And make a hundred million guinea pigs.
You counterfeit our Christianity,
And bring contempt upon Democracy.

None in the Land can say                      105
To us black men Today:
You prowl when citizens are fast asleep,
And hatch Fifth Column plots to blast the deep
Foundations of the State and leave the Land
A vast Sahara with a Fascist brand.                110

[5] *Larghetto:* moderately slow.

6

TEMPO DI MARCIA[6]
Out of abysses of Illiteracy,
Through labyrinths of Lies,
Across waste lands of Disease . . .
We advance!

Out of dead-ends of Poverty,                                    115
Through wildernesses of Superstition,
Across barricades of Jim Crowism . . .
We advance!

With the Peoples of the World . . .
We advance!                                                    120

## QUESTIONS: *Tolson, "Dark Symphony"*

1.  What successive visions of *the black man* does the poem offer us? What movement
    or development do these visions suggest? How does each vision coincide with the
    musical notation at the head of the section in which it appears?
    *Clues:*  • Black Crispus Attucks taught
                            Us how to die
              *Before* white Patrick Henry's bugle breath
              Uttered the vertical
                            Transmitting cry;
          • The centuries-old *pathos* in our voices
            *Saddens* the great white world,
          • In the canebrakes of the *Southern Pharaohs.*
          • They tell us to forget
            The *Golgotha* we tread . . .
            We who are scourged with hate,
            A *price* upon our head.
          • The *New Negro* strides upon the continent
            In *seven-league* boots . . .
            The New Negro
            Who sprang from the *vigor-stout loins*
          • To us *black men* Today:
          • With *the Peoples of the World* . . .
            We advance!
    What vision of *the white man* is developed throughout this work? Why does Tolson
    focus his attack on the white man in section 5 of the poem?
2.  There is a profound difference between the black slaves sadly singing amid
    degradation in the second "movement" and the heroes in the fourth from whose
    "vigour-stout loins" the "New Negro" has sprung. What other elements in the

---

[6] *Tempo di Marcia:* march time.

fourth movement help bridge the gap between these opposed portraits of the Black? Why have these elements been made much of by modern black activists?

3. The fifth movement of the poem is filled with powerful metaphors (some of them deliberately mixed), such as "muzzled by your demagogic din," "coined blitzkriegs," "A vast Sahara with a Fascist brand." Do all the metaphors work equally well? Are some more skillful than others? Discuss.

4. The verse pattern of the six movements differs very considerably. Various forms of rhyme are used in the first, third, and fifth; the second, fourth, and sixth are in blank and free verse. What relation can you detect between these patterns and the content of the passages?

5. Who are "the Peoples of the World"? Why are the words capitalized? Is the capitalization an effective device?

## EXERCISE

Discuss the extent to which Tolson's vision of America coincides with that of Ginsberg in "America" and that of Cummings in "i sing of Olaf." Comment on the significance attached in each work to *alienation* and to the power of negative achievement (what one accomplishes by *not doing*).

## *William Shakespeare (1564–1616)*
# Troilus and Cressida

*In Act I, Scene 3, Agamemnon and Nestor first address the council of Greek chieftains, who have been unsuccessfully besieging Troy for seven years, and speak in praise of the valor and determination that adversity can produce. Ulysses then suggests that the Greeks have failed to conquer Troy because proper order, or "degree," has not been observed in their army.*

### FROM ACT I, SCENE 3

.... Degree being vizarded,[1]
Th' unworthiest shows as fairly in the mask.[2]
The heavens themselves, the planets, and this centre[3]
Observe degree, priority, and place,
Insisture,[4] course, proportion, season, form,                    5
Office, and custom, in all line of order.
And therefore is the glorious planet Sol
In noble eminence enthroned and sphered
Amidst the other, whose med'cinable eye

[1] *vizarded:* masked.
[2] *mask:* masquerade.  [3] *centre:* earth.  [4] *insisture:* duty, service.

Corrects the influence of evil planets,     10
And posts, like the commandment of a king,
Sans check, to good and bad. But when the planets
In evil mixture to disorder wander,
What plagues, and what portents, what mutiny,
What raging of the sea, shaking of earth,     15
Commotion in the winds, frights, changes, horrors,
Divert and crack, rend and deracinate
The unity and married calm of states
Quite from their fixture? O, when degree is shaked,
Which is the ladder of all high designs,     20
The enterprise is sick. How could communities,
Degrees in schools, and brotherhoods in cities,
Peaceful commerce from dividable shores,
The primogenity and due of birth,
Prerogative of age, crowns, sceptres, laurels,     25
But by degree stand in authentic place?
Take but degree away, untune that string,
And hark what discord follows. Each thing meets
In mere oppugnancy.[5] The bounded waters
Should lift their bosoms higher than the shores     30
And make a sop of all this solid globe.
Strength should be lord of imbecility,
And the rude son should strike his father dead.
Force should be right, or rather right and wrong,
Between whose endless jar[6] justice resides,     35
Should lose their names, and so should justice too.
Then everything includes itself in power,
Power into will, will into appetite,
And appetite, an universal wolf,
So doubly seconded with will and power,     40
Must make perforce an universal prey
And last eat up himself. . . .

## QUESTIONS: *Shakespeare, Troilus and Cressida*

1.  "Degree" in the sense used by Ulysses is defined by the *American Heritage Dictionary* as "relative social or official rank, dignity, or position." In other words, Ulysses argues that any upheaval in the established hierarchy of society— what we now call the "power structure"—brings catastrophic results in its train. In what ways does his position resemble that of a modern reactionary who is totally opposed to social change? In what ways is it different? Consider the assumptions about the world which underlie it.

---

[5] *oppugnancy:* antagonism.   [6] *jar:* jarring, collision.

Clues:  • And therefore is the glorious *planet Sol*
      In noble eminence enthroned and sphered
      Amidst the other, whose *medicinable eye*
      *Corrects* the influence of evil planets,

     • Take but degree away, *untune* that *string*
      And hark what discord follows. *Each thing* meets
      In mere oppugnancy. The *bounded waters*
      Should lift their bosoms higher than the shores
      And *make a sop* of all this *solid globe*.

2. Ulysses' view has some obvious weaknesses. It refuses even to *consider* the possibility of injustice occurring within the established patterns of authority and hierarchy, or of a justifiable rebellion. What are its strengths?
   *Clue:*  • Then everything includes itself in power,
      Power into will, will into appetite,
      And appetite, an universal wolf,
      So doubly seconded with will and power,
      Must make perforce an universal prey
      And last eat up himself.

## EXERCISES

1. Suggest the manner in which a modern revolutionary might take exception to the way in which *degree* in this speech sustains the institutions of *government, education, commerce,* and *the family.*

2. Discuss whether a modern conservative would be justified in finding the closing section of the speech, with its vision of "appetite" as "an universal wolf" turning finally to self-destruction, an appropriate description of the modern revolutionary nihilist.

# Burke's Reflections on the Revolution in France and Paine's Rights of Man

*The material selected here relates to one significant incident in the early days of the French Revolution: the return of Louis XVI and Marie Antoinette to Paris from Versailles on October 6, 1789, at the instigation of a Paris mob. (The same event is depicted by Carlyle in the selection from his* The French Revolution *reprinted in this anthology.) Because* Rights of Man *was intended by Paine as a rebuttal of Burke's views in the* Reflections, *and the Paine selection here directly addresses itself to pertinent arguments and criticisms in the Burke selection, the two works are most profitably read together. It is important to remember that the date of Burke's work is 1790, that of Paine 1791, a time prior to the worst excesses of the French Revolution. (Paine himself, later imprisoned for his moderate views, barely managed to escape execution.) The account of the incident of the king and queen's return to Paris by a modern historian, Georges Lefebvre in* The French Revolution *(which precedes the Carlyle selection), confirms the essential facts in Paine's version, and in Burke's for that matter. Indeed, Burke and Paine do not so much present different events as very different temperamental reactions to them. It is the striking contrasts in attitudes and assumptions which makes these two men such interesting representatives of opposing political views on the nature and significance of revolution.*

## Edmund Burke (1729–1797)

# Reflections on the Revolution in France

*The form of Burke's essay is that of, in the words of the subtitle, "A Letter Intended to Have Been Sent to a Gentleman in Paris." The "famous sermon of the Old Jewry" which provoked Burke's indignation was preached by the Reverend Richard Price on November 4, 1789, on the occasion of a celebration of the anniversary of the Revolution of 1688. According to Price, Burke mistook a laudatory reference to the taking of the Bastille (July 14, 1789) for an enthusiastic reaction to the return of the king from Versailles to Paris.*

Far am I from denying in theory; full as far is my heart from withholding in practice (if I were of power to give or to withhold) the *real* rights of men. In denying their false claims of rights, I do not mean to injure those which are real, and are such as their pretended rights would totally destroy. If civil society be made for the advantage of man, all the advantages for which it is made become his right. It is an institution of beneficence; and law itself is only beneficence acting by a rule. Men have a right to live by that rule; they have a right to justice; as between their fellows, whether their fellows are in politic function or in ordinary occupation. They have a right to the fruits of their industry; and to the means of making their industry fruitful. They have a right to the acquisitions of their parents; to the nourishment and improvement of their offspring; to instruction in life, and to consolation in death. Whatever each man can separately do, without trespassing upon others, he has a right to do for himself; and he has a right to a fair portion of all which society, with all its combinations of skill and force, can do in his favour. In this partnership all men have equal rights; but not to equal things. He that has but five shillings in the partnership, has as good a right to it, as he that has five hundred pounds has to his larger proportion. But he has not a right to an equal dividend in the product of the joint stock; and as to the share of power, authority, and direction which each individual ought to have in the management of the state, that I must deny to be amongst the direct original rights of man in civil society; for I have in my contemplation the civil social man, and no other. It is a thing to be settled by convention.

If civil society be the offspring of convention, that convention must be its law. That convention must limit and modify all the descriptions of constitution which are formed under it. Every sort of legislative judicial, or executory power are its creatures. They can have no being in any other state of things; and how can any man claim, under the conventions of civil society, rights which do not so much as suppose its existence? Rights which are absolutely repugnant to it? One of the first motives to civil society, and which becomes one of its fundamental rules, is, *that no man should be judge in his own cause.* By this each person has at once divested himself of the first fundamental right of uncovenanted man, that is, to judge for himself, and to assert his own cause. He abdicates all right to be his own governor. He inclusively, in a great measure, abandons the right of self-defence, the first law of nature. Men cannot enjoy the rights of an uncivil and of a civil state together. That he may obtain justice he gives up his right of determining what it is in points the most essential to him. That he may secure some liberty, he makes a surrender in trust of the whole of it.

Government is not made in virtue of natural rights, which may and do exist in total independence of it; and exist in much greater clearness, and in a much greater degree of abstract perfection: but their abstract perfection is their practical defect. By having a right to every thing they want every thing. Government is a contrivance of human wisdom to provide for human *wants.* Men have a right that these wants should be provided for by this wisdom. Among these wants is to be reckoned the want, out of civil society, of a sufficient restraint upon their passions. Society requires not only that the passions of individuals should be subjected, but that even in the mass and body as well as in the individuals, the inclinations of men should frequently be thwarted, their will controlled, and their passions brought into subjection. This can only be done *by a power out of themselves;* and not, in the exercise of its function, subject to that will and to those passions which it is its office to bridle and subdue. In this sense the restraints on men, as well as their liberties, are to be reckoned among their rights. But as the liberties and the restrictions vary with times and circumstances, and admit of infinite modifications, they cannot be settled upon any abstract rule; and nothing is so foolish as to discuss them upon that principle.

The moment you abate any thing from the full rights of men, each to govern himself, and suffer any artificial positive limitation upon those rights, from that moment the whole organization of government becomes a consideration of convenience. This it is which makes the constitution of a state, and the due distribution of its powers, a matter of the most delicate and complicated skill. It requires a deep knowledge of human nature and human necessities, and of the things which facilitate or obstruct the various ends which are to be pursued by the mechanism of civil institutions. The state is to have recruits to its strength, and remedies to its distempers. What is the use of discussing a man's abstract right to food or to medicine? The question is upon the method of procuring and administering them. In that deliberation I shall always advise to call in the aid of the farmer and the physician, rather than the professor of metaphysics.

The science of constructing a commonwealth, or renovating it, or reforming it, is, like every other experimental science, not to be taught *a priori*. Nor is it a short experience that can instruct us in that practical science; because the real effects of moral causes are not always immediate; but that which in the first instance is prejudicial may be excellent in its remoter operation; and its excellence may arise even from the ill effects it produces in the beginning. The reverse also happens; and very plausible schemes, with very pleasing commencements, have often shameful and lamentable conclusions. In states there are often some obscure and almost latent causes, things which appear at first view of little moment, on which a very great part of its prosperity or adversity may most essentially depend. The science of government being therefore so practical in itself, and intended for such practical purposes, a matter which requires experience, and even more experience than any person can gain in his whole life, however sagacious and observing he may be, it is with infinite caution that any man ought to venture upon pulling down an edifice which has answered in any tolerable degree for ages the common purposes of society, or on building it up again, without having models and patterns of approved utility before his eyes.

These metaphysic rights entering into common life, like rays of light which pierce into a dense medium, are, by the laws of nature, refracted from their straight line. Indeed in the gross and complicated mass of human passions and concerns, the primitive rights of men undergo such a variety of refractions and reflections, that it becomes absurd to talk of them as if they continued in the simplicity of their original direction. The nature of man is intricate; the objects of society are of the greatest possible complexity; and therefore no simple disposition or direction of power can be suitable either to man's nature, or to the quality of his affairs. When I hear the simplicity of contrivance aimed at and boasted of in any new political constitutions, I am at no loss to decide that the artificers are grossly ignorant of their trade, or totally negligent of their duty. The simple governments are fundamentally defective, to say no worse of them. If you were to contemplate society in but one point of view, all these simple modes of polity are infinitely captivating. In effect each would answer its single end much more perfectly than the more complex is able to attain all its complex purposes. But it is better that the whole should be imperfectly and anomalously answered, than that, while some parts are provided for with great exactness, others might be totally neglected, or perhaps materially injured, by the over-care of a favourite member.

The pretended rights of these theorists are all extremes; and in proportion as they are metaphysically true, they are morally and politically false. The rights of men are in a sort of *middle*, incapable of definition, but not impossible to be discerned. The rights of men in governments are their advantages; and these are often in balances between differences of good; in compromises sometimes between good and evil, and sometimes, between evil and evil. Political reason is a computing principle; adding, subtracting, multiplying, and dividing, morally and not metaphysically or mathematically, true moral denominations.

By these theorists the right of the people is almost always sophistically confounded with their power. The body of the community, whenever it can come to act, can meet with no effectual resistance; but till power and right are the same, the whole body of them has no right inconsistent with virtue, and the first of all virtues, prudence. . . . I confess to you, Sir, I never liked this continual talk of resistance and revolution, or the practice of making the extreme medicine of the constitution its daily bread. It renders the habit of society dangerously valetudinary:[1] it is taking periodical doses of mercury sublimate, and swallowing down repeated provocatives of cantharides[2] to our love of liberty.

This distemper of remedy, grown habitual, relaxes and wears out, by a vulgar and prostituted use, the spring of that spirit which is to be exerted on great occasions. It was in the most patient period of Roman servitude that themes of tyrannicide made the ordinary exercise of boys at school. . . . In the ordinary state of things, it produces in a country like ours the worst effects, even on the cause of that liberty which it abuses with the dissoluteness of an extravagant speculation. Almost all the high-bred republicans of my time have, after a short space, become the most decided, thorough-paced courtiers; they soon left the business of a tedious, moderate, but practical resistance to those of us whom, in the pride and intoxication of their theories, they have slighted, as not much better than tories. Hypocrisy, of course, delights in the most sublime speculations; for, never intending to go beyond speculation, it costs nothing to have it magnificent. But even in cases where rather levity than fraud was to be suspected in these ranting speculations, the issue has been much the same. These professors, finding their extreme principles not applicable to cases which call only for a qualified, or, as I may say, civil and legal resistance, in such cases employ no resistance at all. It is with them a war or a revolution, or it is nothing. Finding their schemes of politics not adapted to the state of the world in which they live, they often come to think lightly of all public principle; and are ready, on their part, to abandon for a very trivial interest what they find of very trivial value. Some indeed are of more steady and persevering natures; but these are eager politicians out of parliament, who have little to tempt them to abandon their favourite projects. They have some change in the church or state, or both, constantly in their view. When that is the case, they are always bad citizens, and perfectly unsure connexions. For, considering their speculative designs as of infinite value, and the actual arrangement of the state as of no

---

[1] *valetudinary:* preoccupied with a state of invalidism.

[2] *mercury sublimate . . . cantharides:* two poisonous, irritant substances used respectively as a curative for venereal disease and an aphrodisiac. Both required sustained physical activity to counteract their powerful side effects.

estimation, they are at best indifferent about it. They see no merit in the good, and no fault in the vicious management of public affairs; they rather rejoice in the latter, as more propitious to revolution. They see no merit or demerit in any man, or any action, or any political principle, any further than as they may forward or retard their design of change: they therefore take up, one day, the most violent and stretched prerogative, and another time the wildest democratic ideas of freedom, and pass from the one to the other without any sort of regard to cause, to person, or to party.

In France you are now in the crisis of a revolution, and in the transit from one form of government to another—you cannot see that character of men exactly in the same situation in which we see it in this country. With us it is militant; with you it is triumphant; and you know how it can act when its power is commensurate to its will. I would not be supposed to confine those observations to any description of men, or to comprehend all men of any description within them—No! far from it. I am as incapable of that injustice, as I am of keeping terms with those who profess principles of extremes; and who under the name of religion teach little else than wild and dangerous politics. The worst of these politics of revolution is this; they temper and harden the breast, in order to prepare it for the desperate strokes which are sometimes used in extreme occasions. But as these occasions may never arrive, the mind receives a gratuitous taint; and the moral sentiments suffer not a little, when no political purpose is served by the depravation. This sort of people are so taken up with their theories about the rights of man, that they have totally forgot his nature. Without opening one new avenue to the understanding, they have succeeded in stopping up those that lead to the heart. They have perverted in themselves, and in those that attend to them, all the well-placed sympathies of the human breast.

This famous sermon of the Old Jewry breathes nothing but this spirit through all the political part. Plots, massacres, assassinations, seem to some people a trivial price for obtaining a revolution. A cheap, bloodless reformation, a guiltless liberty, appear flat and vapid to their taste. There must be a great change of scene; there must be a magnificent stage effect; there must be a grand spectacle to rouze the imagination, grown torpid with the lazy enjoyment of sixty years security, and the still unanimating repose of public prosperity. The Preacher found them all in the French revolution. This inspires a juvenile warmth through his whole frame. His enthusiasm kindles as he advances; and when he arrives at his peroration, it is in a full blaze. Then viewing, from the Pisgah of his pulpit, the free, moral, happy, flourishing, and glorious state of France, as in a bird-eye landscape of a promised land, he breaks out into the following rapture:

'What an eventful period is this! I am *thankful* that I have lived to it; I could almost say, *Lord, now lettest thou thy servant depart in peace, for mine eyes have seen thy salvation.*—I have lived to see a *diffusion* of knowledge which has undermined superstition and error.—I have lived to see the *rights of men* better understood than ever; and nations panting for liberty which seemed to have lost the idea of it.—I have lived to see *Thirty Millions of People,* indignant and resolute, spurning at slavery, and demanding liberty with an irresistible voice. *Their King led in triumph, and an arbitrary monarch surrendering himself to his subjects.'* . . .

I find a preacher of the gospel prophaning the beautiful and prophetic ejaculation, commonly called *'nunc dimitis,'* made on the first presentation of our Saviour in the Temple, and applying it, with an inhuman and unnatural rapture, to the most horrid, atrocious, and afflicting spectacle, that perhaps ever was exhibited to the pity and indignation of mankind. This *'leading in triumph,'* a thing in its best form unmanly and irreligious, which fills our Preacher with such unhallowed transports, must shock, I believe, the moral taste of every well-born mind. Several English were the stupified and indignant spectators of that triumph. It was (unless we have been strangely deceived) a spectacle more resembling a procession of American savages, entering into Onondaga, after some of their murders called victories, and leading into hovels hung round with scalps, their captives, overpowered with the scoffs and buffets of women as ferocious as themselves, much more than it resembled the triumphal pomp of a civilized martial nation;—if a civilized nation, or any men who had a sense of generosity, were capable of a personal triumph over the fallen and afflicted.

This, my dear Sir, was not the triumph of France. I must believe that, as a nation, it overwhelmed you with shame and horror. I must believe that the National Assembly find themselves in a state of the greatest humiliation, in not being able to punish the authors of this triumph, or the actors in it; and that they are in a situation in which any enquiry they may make upon the subject, must be destitute even of the appearance of liberty or impartiality. The apology of that Assembly is found in their situation; but when we approve what they *must* bear, it is in us the degenerate choice of a vitiated mind.

With a compelled appearance of deliberation, they vote under the dominion of a stern necessity. They sit in the heart, as it were, of a foreign republic: they have their residence in a city whose constitution has emanated neither from the charter of their king, nor from their legislative power. There they are surrounded by an army not raised either by the authority of their crown, or by their command; and which, if they should order to dissolve itself, would instantly dissolve them. There they sit, after a gang of assassins had driven away some hundreds of the members; whilst those who held the same moderate principles, with more patience or better hope, continued every day exposed to outrageous insults and murderous threats. There a majority, sometimes real, sometimes pretended, captive itself, compels a

---

* Another of these reverend gentlemen, who was witness to some of the spectacles which Paris has lately exhibited—expresses himself thus, 'A *King dragged in submissive triumph by his conquering subjects* is one of those appearances of grandeur which seldom rise in the prospect of human affairs, and which, during the remainder of my life, I shall think of with wonder and gratification.' These gentlemen agree marvellously in their feelings.

captive king to issue as royal edicts, at third hand, the polluted nonsense of their most licentious and giddy coffee-houses. It is notorious, that all their measures are decided before they are debated. It is beyond doubt, that under the terror of the bayonet, and the lamp-post, and the torch to their houses, they are obliged to adopt all the crude and desperate measures suggested by clubs composed of a monstrous medley of all conditions, tongues, and nations. Among these are found persons, in comparison of whom Catiline would be thought scrupulous, and Cethegus[3] a man of sobriety and moderation. Nor is it in these clubs alone that the publick measures are deformed into monsters. They undergo a previous distortion in academies, intended as so many seminaries for these clubs, which are set up in all the places of publick resort. In these meetings of all sorts, every counsel, in proportion as it is daring, and violent, and perfidious, is taken for the mark of superior genius. Humanity and compassion are ridiculed as the fruits of superstition and ignorance. Tenderness to individuals is considered as treason to the public. Liberty is always to be estimated perfect as property is rendered insecure. Amidst assassination, massacre, and confiscation, perpetrated or meditated, they are forming plans for the good order of future society. Embracing in their arms the carcases of base criminals, and promoting their relations on the title of their offences, they drive hundreds of virtuous persons to the same end, by forcing them to subsist by beggary or by crime.

The Assembly, their organ, acts before them the farce of deliberation with as little decency as liberty. They act like the comedians of a fair before a riotous audience; they act amidst the tumultuous cries of a mixed mob of ferocious men, and of women lost to shame, who, according to their insolent fancies, direct, control, applaud, explode them; and sometimes mix and take their seats amongst them; domineering over them with a strange mixture of servile petulance and proud presumptuous authority. As they have inverted order in all things, the gallery is in the place of the house. This Assembly, which overthrows kings and kingdoms, has not even the physiognomy and aspect of a grave legislative body. . . . They have a power given to them, like that of the evil principle, to subvert and destroy; but none to construct, except such machines as may be fitted for further subversion and further destruction.

Who is it that admires, and from the heart is attached to national representative assemblies, but must turn with horror and disgust from such a profane burlesque, and abominable perversion of that sacred institute? Lovers of monarchy, lovers of republicks, must alike abhor it. The members of your Assembly must themselves groan under the tyranny of which they have all the shame, none of the direction, and little of the profit. I am sure many of the members who compose even the majority of that body, must feel as I do, notwithstanding the applauses of the Revolution Society.— Miserable king! miserable Assembly! How must that assembly be silently

[3] *Catiline . . . Cethegus:* Roman conspirators.

scandalized with those of their members, who could call a day which seemed to blot the sun out of Heaven, 'un beau jour!'* How must they be inwardly indignant at hearing others, who thought fit to declare to them, 'that the vessel of the state would fly forward in her course towards regeneration with more speed than ever,' from the stiff gale of treason and murder, which preceded our Preacher's triumph! What must they have felt, whilst with outward patience and inward indignation they heard of the slaughter of innocent gentlemen in their houses, that 'the blood spilled was not the most pure?' What must they have felt, when they were besieged by complaints of disorders which shook their country to its foundations, at being compelled coolly to tell the complainants, that they were under the protection of the law, and that they would address the king (the captive king) to cause the laws to be enforced for their protection; when the enslaved ministers of that captive king had formally notified to them, that there were neither law, nor authority, nor power left to protect? What must they have felt at being obliged, as a felicitation on the present new year, to request their captive king to forget the stormy period of the last, on account of the great good which *he* was likely to produce to his people; to the complete attainment of which good they adjourned the practical demonstrations of their loyalty, assuring him of their obedience, when he should no longer possess any authority to command?

This address was made with much good-nature and affection, to be sure. But among the revolutions in France, must be reckoned a considerable revolution in their ideas of politeness. In England we are said to learn manners at second-hand from your side of the water, and that we dress our behaviour in the frippery of France. If so, we are still in the old cut; and have not so far conformed to the new Parisian mode of good-breeding, as to think it quite in the most refined strain of delicate compliment (whether in condolence or congratulation) to say, to the most humiliated creature that crawls upon the earth, that great publick benefits are derived from the murder of his servants, the attempted assassination of himself and of his wife, and the mortification, disgrace, and degradation, that he has personally suffered. It is a topic of consolation which our ordinary of Newgate would be too humane to use to a criminal at the foot of the gallows. I should have thought that the hangman of Paris, now that he is liberalized by the vote of the National Assembly, and is allowed his rank and arms in the Herald's College of the rights of men, would be too generous, too gallant a man, too full of the sense of his new dignity, to employ that cutting consolation to any of the persons whom the *leze nation*[4] might bring under the administration of his *executive powers*.

A man is fallen indeed, when he is thus flattered. The anodyne draught of oblivion, thus drugged, is well calculated to preserve a galling wakefulness,

---

* 6th of October, 1789.
[4] *leze nation:* violation of the national order.

and to feed the living ulcer of a corroding memory. Thus to administer the opiate potion of amnesty, powdered with all the ingredients of scorn and contempt, is to hold to his lips, instead of 'the balm of hurt minds,' the cup of human misery full to the brim, and to force him to drink it to the dregs.

Yielding to reasons, at least as forcible as those which were so delicately urged in the compliment on the new year, the king of France will probably endeavour to forget these events, and that compliment. But history, who keeps a durable record of all our acts, and exercises her awful censure over the proceedings of all sorts of sovereigns, will not forget, either those events, or the aera of this liberal refinement in the intercourse of mankind. History will record, that on the morning of the 6th of October 1789, the king and queen of France, after a day of confusion, alarm, dismay, and slaughter, lay down, under the pledged security of public faith, to indulge nature in a few hours of respite, and troubled melancholy repose. From this sleep the queen was first startled by the voice of the centinel at her door, who cried out to her, to save herself by flight—that this was the last proof of fidelity he could give—that they were upon him, and he was dead. Instantly he was cut down. A band of cruel ruffians and assassins, reeking with his blood, rushed into the chamber of the queen, and pierced with an hundred strokes of bayonets and poniards the bed, from whence this persecuted woman had but just time to fly almost naked, and through ways unknown to the murderers had escaped to seek refuge at the feet of a king and husband, not secure of his own life for a moment.

This king, to say no more of him, and this queen, and their infant children (who once would have been the pride and hope of a great and generous people) were then forced to abandon the sanctuary of the most splendid palace in the world, which they left swimming in blood, polluted by massacre, and strewed with scattered limbs and mutilated carcases. Thence they were conducted into the capital of their kingdom. Two had been selected from the unprovoked, unresisted, promiscuous slaughter, which was made of the gentlemen of birth and family who composed the king's body guard. These two gentlemen, with all the parade of an execution of justice, were cruelly and publickly dragged to the block, and beheaded in the great court of the palace. Their heads were stuck upon spears, and led the procession; whilst the royal captives who followed in the train were slowly moved along, amidst the horrid yells, and shrilling screams, and frantic dances, and infamous contumelies, and all the unutterable abominations of the furies of hell, in the abused shape of the vilest of women. After they had been made to taste, drop by drop, more than the bitterness of death, in the slow torture of a journey of twelve miles, protracted to six hours, they were, under a guard, composed of those very soldiers who had thus conducted them through this famous triumph, lodged in one of the old palaces of Paris, now converted into a Bastile for kings.

Is this a triumph to be consecrated at altars? to be commemorated with grateful thanksgiving? to be offered to the divine humanity with fervent prayer and enthusiastick ejaculation?—The Theban and Thracian Orgies, acted in France, and applauded only in the Old Jewry, I assure you, kindle prophetic enthusiasm in the minds but of very few people in this kingdom; although a saint and apostle, who may have revelations of his own, and who has so completely vanquished all the mean superstitions of the heart, may incline to think it pious and decorous to compare it with the entrance into the world of the Prince of Peace, proclaimed in an holy temple by a venerable sage, and not long before not worse announced by the voice of angels to the quiet innocence of shepherds. . . .

Although this work of our new light and knowledge, did not go to the length, that in all probability it was intended it should be carried; yet I must think, that such treatment of any human creatures must be shocking to any but those who are made for accomplishing Revolutions. But I cannot stop here. Influenced by the inborn feelings of my nature, and not being illuminated by a single ray of this new-sprung modern light, I confess to you, Sir, that the exalted rank of the persons suffering, and particularly the sex, the beauty, and the amiable qualities of the descendant of so many kings and emperors, with the tender age of royal infants, insensible only through infancy and innocence of the cruel outrages to which their parents were exposed, instead of being a subject of exultation, adds not a little to my sensibility on that most melancholy occasion.

I hear that the august person, who was the principle object of our preacher's triumph, though he supported himself, felt much on that shameful occasion. As a man, it became him to feel for his wife and his children, and the faithful guards of his person, that were massacred in cold blood about him; as a prince, it became him to feel for the strange and frightful transformation of his civilized subjects, and to be more grieved for them, than solicitous for himself. It derogates little from his fortitude, while it adds infinitely to the honour of his humanity. I am very sorry to say it, very sorry indeed, that such personages are in a situation in which it is not unbecoming in us to praise the virtues of the great.

I hear, and I rejoice to hear, that the great lady, the other object of the triumph, has borne that day (one is interested that beings made for suffering should suffer well) and that she bears all the succeeding days, that she bears the imprisonment of her husband, and her own captivity, and the exile of her friends, and the insulting adulation of addresses, and the whole weight of her accumulated wrongs, with a serene patience, in a manner suited to her rank and race, and becoming the offspring of a sovereign distinguished for her piety and her courage; that like her she has lofty sentiments; that she feels with the dignity of a Roman matron; that in the last extremity she will save herself from the last disgrace, and that if she must fall, she will fall by no ignoble hand.

It is now sixteen or seventeen years since I saw the queen of France, then the dauphiness, at Versailles; and surely never lighted on this orb, which she hardly seemed to touch, a more delightful vision. I saw her just above the horizon, decorating and cheering the elevated sphere she just began to move in,—glittering like the morning-star, full of life, and splendor, and joy. Oh! What a revolution! and what an heart must I have, to contemplate without emotion that elevation and that fall! Little did I dream when she added titles of veneration to those of enthusiastic, distant, respectful love, that she should ever be obliged to carry the sharp antidote against disgrace concealed in that bosom; little did I dream that I should have lived to see such disasters fallen upon her in a nation of gallant men, in a nation of men of honour and of cavaliers. I thought ten thousand swords must have leaped from their scabbards to avenge even a look that threatened her with insult.—But the age of chivalry is gone.—That of sophisters, oeconomists, and calculators, has succeeded; and the glory of Europe is extinguished for ever. Never, never more, shall we behold that generous loyalty to rank and sex, that proud submission, that dignified obedience, that subordination of the heart, which kept alive, even in servitude itself, the spirit of an exalted freedom. The unbought grace of life, the cheap defence of nations, the nurse of manly sentiment and heroic enterprize is gone! It is gone, that sensibility of principle, that chastity of honour, which felt a stain like a wound, which inspired courage whilst it mitigated ferocity, which ennobled whatever it touched, and under which vice itself lost half its evil, by losing all its grossness.

This mixed system of opinion and sentiment had its origin in the antient chivalry; and the principle, though varied in its appearance by the varying state of human affairs, subsisted and influenced through a long succession of generations, even to the time we live in. If it should ever be totally extinguished, the loss I fear will be great. It is this which has given its character to modern Europe. It is this which has distinguished it under all its forms of government, and distinguished it to its advantage, from the states of Asia, and possibly from those states which flourished in the most brilliant periods of the antique world. It was this, which, without confounding ranks, had produced a noble equality, and handed it down through all the gradations of social life. It was this opinion which mitigated kings into companions, and raised private men to be fellows with kings. Without force, or opposition, it subdued the fierceness of pride and power; it obliged sovereigns to submit to the soft collar of social esteem, compelled stern authority to submit to elegance, and gave a domination, vanquisher of laws, to be subdued by manners.

But now all is to be changed. All the pleasing illusions, which made power gentle, and obedience liberal, which harmonized the different shades of life, and which, by a bland assimilation, incorporated into politics the sentiments which beautify and soften private society, are to be dissolved by this new conquering empire of light and reason. All the decent drapery of life is to be rudely torn off. All the super-added ideas, furnished from the wardrobe of a moral imagination, which the heart owns, and the understanding ratifies, as necessary to cover the defects of our naked shivering nature, and to raise it to dignity in our own estimation, are to be exploded as a ridiculous, absurd, and antiquated fashion.

On this scheme of things, a king is but a man; a queen is but a woman; a woman is but an animal; and an animal not of the highest order. All homage paid to the sex in general as such, and without distinct views, is to be regarded as romance and folly. Regicide, and parricide, and sacrilege, are but fictions of superstition, corrupting jurisprudence by destroying its simplicity. The murder of a king, or a queen, or a bishop, or a father, are only common homicide; and if the people are by any chance, or in any way gainers by it, a sort of homicide much the most pardonable, and into which we ought not to make too severe a scrutiny.

On the scheme of this barbarous philosophy, which is the offspring of cold hearts and muddy understandings, and which is as void of solid wisdom, as it is destitute of all taste and elegance, laws are to be supported only by their own terrors, and by the concern, which each individual may find in them, from his own private speculations, or can spare to them from his own private interests. In the groves of *their* academy, at the end of every vista, you see nothing but the gallows. Nothing is left which engages the affections on the part of the commonwealth. On the principles of this mechanic philosophy, our institutions can never be embodied, if I may use the expression, in persons; so as to create in us love, veneration, admiration, or attachment. But that sort of reason which banishes the affections is incapable of filling their place. These public affections, combined with manners, are required sometimes as supplements, sometimes as correctives, always as aids to law. The precept given by a wise man, as well as a great critic, for the construction of poems, is equally true as to states. *Non satis est pulchra esse poemata, dulcia sunto.*[5] There ought to be a system of manners in every nation which a well-formed mind would be disposed to relish. To make us love our country, our country ought to be lovely.

But power, of some kind or other, will survive the shock in which manners and opinions perish; and it will find other and worse means for its support. The usurpation which, in order to subvert antient institutions, has destroyed antient principles, will hold power by arts similar to those by which it has acquired it. When the old feudal and chivalrous spirit of *Fealty*, which, by freeing kings from fear, freed both kings and subjects from the precautions of tyranny, shall be extinct in the minds of men, plots and assassinations will be anticipated by preventive murder and preventive confiscation, and that long roll of grim and bloody maxims, which form the political code of all power, not standing on its own honour, and the honour of those who are to obey it. Kings will be tyrants from policy when subjects are rebels from principle.

When antient opinions and rules of life are taken away, the loss cannot possibly be estimated. From that moment we have no compass to govern us;

---

[5] *Non satis est pulchra esse poemata, dulcia sunto:* it is not enough that poems be beautiful; let them be delightful. (The distinction that Burke is emphasizing in using this statement of Horace's *Ars Poetica* is that between an aesthetic evaluation and an emotional response on the part of the reader.)

nor can we know distinctly to what port we steer. Europe undoubtedly, taken in a mass, was in a flourishing condition the day on which your Revolution was compleated. How much of that prosperous state was owing to the spirit of our old manners and opinions is not easy to say; but as such causes cannot be indifferent in their operation, we must presume, that, on the whole, their operation was beneficial.

We are but too apt to consider things in the state in which we find them, without sufficiently adverting to the causes by which they have been produced, and possibly may be upheld. Nothing is more certain, than that our manners, our civilization, and all the good things which are connected with manners, and with civilization, have, in this European world of ours, depended for ages upon two principles; and were indeed the result of both combined; I mean the spirit of a gentleman, and the spirit of religion. The nobility and the clergy, the one by profession, the other by patronage, kept learning in existence, even in the midst of arms and confusions, and whilst governments were rather in their causes than formed. Learning paid back what it received to nobility and to priesthood; and paid it with usury, by enlarging their ideas, and by furnishing their minds. Happy if they had all continued to know their indissoluble union, and their proper place! Happy if learning, not debauched by ambition, had been satisfied to continue the instructor, and not aspired to be the master! Along with its natural protectors and guardians, learning will be cast into the mire, and trodden down under the hoofs of a swinish multitude.*

If, as I suspect, modern letters owe more than they are always willing to own to antient manners, so do other interests which we value full as much as they are worth. Even commerce, and trade, and manufacture, the gods of our oeconomical politicians, are themselves perhaps but creatures; are themselves but effects, which, as first causes, we choose to worship. They certainly grew under the same shade in which learning flourished. They too may decay with their natural protecting principles. With you, for the present at least, they all threaten to disappear together. Where trade and manufacturers are wanting to a people, and the spirit of nobility and religion remains, sentiment supplies, and not always ill supplies their place; but if commerce and the arts should be lost in an experiment to try how well a state may stand without these old fundamental principles, what sort of a thing must be a nation of gross, stupid, ferocious, and at the same time, poor and sordid barbarians, destitute of religion, honour, or manly pride, possessing nothing at present, and hoping for nothing hereafter?

I wish you may not be going fast, and by the shortest cut, to that horrible and disgustful situation. Already there appears a poverty of conception, a coarseness and vulgarity in all the proceedings of the assembly and of all their instructors. Their liberty is not liberal. Their science is presumptuous ignorance. Their humanity is savage and brutal.

* See the fate of Bailly and Condorcet, supposed to be here particularly alluded to. Compare the circumstances of the trial, and execution of the former with this prediction. (1803)

It is not clear, whether in England we learned those grand and decorous principles, and manners, of which considerable traces yet remain, from you, or whether you took them from us. But to you, I think, we trace them best. You seem to me to be—*gentis incunabula nostræ.*[6] France has always more or less influenced manners in England; and when your fountain is choaked up and polluted, the stream will not run long, or not run clear with us, or perhaps with any nation. This gives all Europe, in my opinion, but too close and connected a concern in what is done in France. Excuse me, therefore, if I have dwelt too long on the atrocious spectacle of the sixth of October 1789, or have given too much scope to the reflections which have arisen in my mind on occasion of the most important of all revolutions, which may be dated from that day, I mean a revolution in sentiments, manners, and moral opinions. As things now stand, with every thing respectable destroyed without us, and an attempt to destroy within us every principle of respect, one is almost forced to apologize for harbouring the common feelings of men.

Why do I feel so differently from the Reverend Dr. Price, and those of his lay flock, who will choose to adopt the sentiments of his discourse?—For this plain reason—because it is *natural* I should; because we are so made as to be affected at such spectacles with melancholy sentiments upon the unstable condition of mortal prosperity, and the tremendous uncertainty of human greatness; because in those natural feelings we learn great lessons; because in events like these our passions instruct our reason; because when kings are hurl'd from their thrones by the Supreme Director of this great drama, and become the objects of insult to the base, and of pity to the good, we behold such disasters in the moral, as we should behold a miracle in the physical order of things. We are alarmed into reflexion; our minds (as it has long since been observed) are purified by terror and pity; our weak unthinking pride is humbled, under the dispensations of a mysterious wisdom.— Some tears might be drawn from me, if such a spectacle were exhibited on the stage. I should be truly shamed of finding in myself that superficial, theatric sense of painted distress, whilst I could exult over it in real life. With such a perverted mind, I could never venture to shew my face at a tragedy. People would think the tears that Garrick formerly, or that Siddons not long since, have extorted from me, were the tears of hypocrisy; I should know them to be the tears of folly.

Indeed the theatre is a better school of moral sentiments than churches, where the feelings of humanity are thus outraged. Poets, who have to deal with an audience not yet graduated in the school of the rights of men, and who must apply themselves to the moral constitution of the heart, would not dare to produce such a triumph as a matter of exultation. There, where men follow their natural impulses, they would not bear the odious maxims of a Machiavelian policy, whether applied to the attainment of monarchical

---

[6] *gentis incunabula nostrae:* the cradle of our race (Vergil's *Aeneid*).

or democratic tyranny. They would reject them on the modern, as they once did on the antient stage, where they could not bear even the hypothetical proposition of such wickedness in the mouth of a personated tyrant, though suitable to the character he sustained. No theatric audience in Athens would bear what has been borne, in the midst of the real tragedy of this triumphal day; a principal actor weighing, as it were in scales hung in a shop of horrors, —so much actual crime against so much contingent advantage,—and after putting in and out weights, declaring that the balance was on the side of the advantages. They would not bear to see the crimes of new democracy posted as in a ledger against the crimes of old despotism, and the bookkeepers of politics finding democracy still in debt, but by no means unable or unwilling to pay the balance. In the theatre, the first intuitive glance, without any elaborate process of reasoning, would shew, that this method of political computation, would justify every extent of crime. They would see, that on these principles, even where the very worst acts were not perpetrated, it was owing rather to the fortune of the conspirators than to their parsimony in the expenditure of treachery and blood. They would soon see, that criminal means once tolerated are soon preferred. They present a shorter cut to the object than through the highway of the moral virtues. Justifying perfidy and murder for public benefit, public benefit would soon become the pretext, and perfidy and murder the end; until rapacity, malice, revenge, and fear more dreadful than revenge, could satiate their insatiable appetites. Such must be the consequences of losing in the splendour of these triumphs of the rights of men, all natural sense of wrong and right.

But the Reverend Pastor exults in this 'leading in triumph,' because truly Louis XVIth was 'an arbitrary monarch;' that is, in other words, neither more nor less, than because he was Louis the XVIth, and because he had the misfortune to be born king of France, with the prerogatives of which, a long line of ancestors, and a long acquiescence of the people, without any act of his, had put him in possession. A misfortune it has indeed turned out to him, that he was born king of France. But misfortune is not crime, nor is indiscretion always the greatest guilt. I shall never think that a prince, the acts of whose whole reign were a series of concessions to his subjects, who was willing to relax his authority, to remit his prerogatives, to call his people to a share of freedom, not known, perhaps not desired by their ancestors; such a prince, though he should be subject to the common frailties attached to men and to princes, though he should have once thought it necessary to provide force against the desperate designs manifestly carrying on against his person, and the remnants of his authority; though all this should be taken into consideration, I shall be led with great difficulty to think he deserves the cruel and insulting triumph of Paris, and of Dr. Price. I tremble for the cause of liberty, from such an example to kings. I tremble for the cause of humanity, in the unpunished outrages of the most wicked of mankind. But there are some people of that low and degenerate fashion of mind, that they look up with a sort of complacent awe and admiration to kings, who know to keep firm in their seat, to hold a strict hand over their subjects, to assert their prerogative, and by the awakened vigilance of a severe despotism, to guard against the very first approaches of freeedom. Against such as these they never elevate their voice. Deserters from principle, listed with fortune, they never see any good in suffering virtue, nor any crime in prosperous usurpation.

If it could have been made clear to me, that the king and queen of France (those I mean who were such before the triumph) were inexorable and cruel tyrants, that they had formed a deliberate scheme for massacring the National Assembly (I think I have seen something like the latter insinuated in certain publications) I should think their captivity just. If this be true, much more ought to have been done, but done, in my opinion, in another manner. The punishment of real tyrants is a noble and awful act of justice; and it has with truth been said to be consolatory to the human mind. But if I were to punish a wicked king, I should regard the dignity in avenging the crime. Justice is grave and decorous, and in its punishments rather seems to submit to a necessity, than to make a choice. . . .

If the French king, or King of the French, (or by whatever name he is known in the new vocabulary of your constitution) has in his own person, and that of his Queen, really deserved these unavowed but unavenged murderous attempts, and those subsequent indignities more cruel than murder, such a person would ill deserve even that subordinate executory trust, which I understand is to be placed in him; nor is he fit to be called chief in a nation which he has outraged and oppressed. A worse choice for such an office in a new commonwealth, than that of a deposed tyrant, could not possibly be made. But to degrade and insult a man as the worst of criminals, and afterwards to trust him in your highest concerns, as a faithful, honest, and zealous servant, is not consistent in reasoning, nor prudent in policy, nor safe in practice. Those who could make such an appointment must be guilty of a more flagrant breach of trust than any they have yet committed against the people. As this is the only crime in which your leading politicians could have acted inconsistently, I conclude that there is no sort of ground for these horrid insinuations. I think no better of all the other calumnies. . . .

To tell you the truth, my dear Sir, I think the honour of our nation to be somewhat concerned in the disclaimer of the proceedings of this society of the Old Jewry and the London Tavern. I have no man's proxy. I speak only from myself; when I disclaim, as I do with all possible earnestness, all communion with the actors in that triumph, or with the admirers of it. When I assert any thing else, as concerning the people of England, I speak from observation not from authority; but I speak from the experience I have had in a pretty extensive and mixed communication with the inhabitants of this kingdom, of all descriptions and ranks, and after a course of attentive observation, begun early in life, and continued for near forty years. I have often been astonished, considering that we are divided from you but by a slender dyke of about twenty-four miles, and that the mutual intercourse between the two countries has lately been very great, to find how little you seem to know of us. I suspect that this is owing to your forming a judgment of this nation from certain publications, which do, very erroneously, if they do at all, represent the opinions and dispositions generally prevalent in England. The vanity, restlessness, petulance, and spirit of intrigue of several petty cabals, who attempt to hide their total want of consequence in bustle and noise, and puffing, and mutual quotation of each other, makes you imagine that our contemptuous neglect of their abilities is a mark of general acquiescence in their opinions. No such thing, I assure you. Because half a dozen grasshoppers under a fern make the field ring with their importunate chink, whilst thousands of great cattle, reposed beneath the shadow of the British oak, chew the cud and are silent, pray do not imagine, that those who make the noise are the only inhabitants of the field; that of course, they are many in number; or that, after all, they are other than the little shrivelled, meagre, hopping, though loud and troublesome insects of the hour.

I almost venture to affirm, that not one in a hundred amongst us participates in the 'triumph' of the Revolution Society. If the king and queen of France, and their children, were to fall into our hands by the chance of war, in the most acrimonious of all hostilities (I deprecate such an event, I deprecate such hostility) they would be treated with another sort of triumphal entry into London. We formerly have had a king of France in that situation; you have read how he was treated by the victor in the field; and in what manner he was afterwards received in England. Four hundred years have gone over us; but I believe we are not materially changed since that period. Thanks to our sullen resistance to innovation, thanks to the cold sluggishness of our national character, we still bear the stamp of our forefathers. We have not (as I conceive) lost the generosity and dignity of thinking of the fourteenth century; nor as yet have we subtilized ourselves into savages. We are not the converts of Rousseau; we are not the disciples of Voltaire; Helvétius[7] has made no progress amongst us. Atheists are not our preachers; madmen are not our lawgivers. We know that *we* have made no discoveries; and we think that no discoveries are to be made, in morality; nor many in the great principles of government, nor in the ideas of liberty, which were understood long before we were born, altogether as well as they will be after the grave has heaped its mould upon our presumption, and the silent tomb shall have imposed its law on our pert loquacity. In England we have not yet been completely embowelled of our natural entrails; we still feel within us, and we cherish and cultivate, those inbred sentiments which are the faithful guardians, the active monitors of our duty, the true supporters of all liberal and manly morals. We have not been drawn and trussed, in order that we may be filled, like stuffed birds in a museum, with

---

[7] Claude Adrien Helvétius (1715–1771), French philosopher, author of *De l'esprit*, a work asserting the primal significance of sensation as the source of cognition. He conceived of man as basically motivated by self-interest.

chaff and rags, and paltry, blurred shreds of paper about the rights of man. We preserve the whole of our feelings still native and entire, unsophisticated by pedantry and infidelity. We have real hearts of flesh and blood beating in our bosoms. We fear God; we look up with awe to kings; with affection to parliaments; with duty to magistrates; with reverence to priests; and with respect to nobility.* Why? Because when such ideas are brought before our minds, it is *natural* to be affected; because all other feelings are false and spurious, and tend to corrupt our minds, to vitiate our primary morals, to render us unfit for rational liberty; and by teaching us a servile, licentious, and abandoned insolence, to be our low sport for a few holidays, to make us perfectly fit for, and justly deserving of slavery, through the whole course of our lives.

## Questions: *Burke, Reflections on the Revolution in France*

1. In speaking about those who are committed to revolutionary principles, Burke says: "This sort of people are so taken up with their theories about the rights of man, that they have totally forgot his nature." To what central failure in making distinctions is Burke alluding here? Would you associate it with the revolutionary temper as it is manifested today? If so, how?

2. In the above statement Burke *implies* his determination not to oversimplify; much of what he says elsewhere *demonstrates* his desire to draw meaningful distinctions. How does the following passage constitute such a demonstration? Why do Burke's arguments here have not only political but also philosophical and moral ramifications? Does he succeed in justifying the conservative tendency to caution? How does the light imagery support his viewpoint?

   > These *metaphysic* rights entering into *common* life, like rays of *light* which pierce into a *dense* medium, are by the laws of nature, refracted from their straight line. Indeed in the *gross* and *complicated* mass of human passions and concerns, the primitive rights of man undergo such a variety of *refractions* and *reflections*, that it becomes absurd to talk of them as if they continued in the *simplicity* of their original direction. The nature of man is *intricate*; the objects of society are of the greatest possible *complexity*: and therefore no simple disposition or direction of power can be suitable either to man's *nature*, or to the quality of his affairs.

   What specific instances can you find of the drawing of distinctions by Burke in presenting his ideas?

3. Still drawing distinctions, Burke says that "the rights of men in governments are their advantages." Speaking of the necessity, in determining these advantages, of balances and compromises between "differences of good ... good and evil ... evil and evil," he praises "political reason" as "a computing principle;

---

* The English are, I conceive, misrepresented in a Letter published in one of the papers, by a gentleman thought to be a dissenting minister.—When writing to Dr Price, of the spirit which prevails at Paris, he says, 'The spirit of the people in this place has abolished all the proud *distinctions* which the *king* and *nobles* had usurped in their minds; whether they talk of *the king, the noble,* or *the priest,* their whole language is that of the most *enlightened and liberal amongst the English.*' If this gentleman means to confine the terms *enlightened and liberal* to one set of men in England, it may be true. It is not generally so.

adding, subtracting, multiplying, and dividing, morally and not metaphysically or mathematically, true moral denominations." Why is the distinction between *moral* and *metaphysical* appropriate to the contrasting tempers dealt with in questions 1 and 2? Why is the term *mathematically* also opposed to *morally?* (Burke will later denounce his age as one "of sophisters, oeconomists, and calculators.") What connection does Burke make between metaphysical standards and moral laxity? Is that connection justifiable in your opinion? Take into account the applicability of the following clue to the politics of the left today. What terms might we use instead of *moral* and *metaphysical?*

Clue: • They [certain pro-revolutionaries] have some change in the church or state, or both, constantly in their view. When that is the case, they are always *bad citizens*, and perfectly unsure connexions. For, considering their *speculative* designs as of *infinite* value, and the *actual* arrangement of the state as of *no estimation*, they are at best *indifferent* about it. They see *no merit* in the *good*, and *no fault* in the *vicious* management of public affairs; they rather rejoice in the latter, as *more propitious* to revolution. They see no merit or demerit in any man, or any action, or any political principle, any further than as they may forward or retard their design of change. . . .

4. Burke contends that "Society requires not only that the passions of individuals should be subjected, but that . . . the inclinations of men should frequently be thwarted, their will controlled, and their passions brought into subjection." Is this conception of man as a fallible, erring being contradicted or supported by Burke's concern for the *human* aspects of the scenes of violence and humiliation to which he alludes? (Paine would later accuse him of involvement with "men" rather than "principles" in his concern for Louis XVI.) How is Burke's commitment to the ideals of chivalry relevant to his view of man's nature and role in society? Might this predilection for an ideal allow one to accuse *him* of *metaphysical* rather than *moral* inclinations? How might he defend himself against the charge?

Clue: • . . . now all is to be changed. All the pleasing illusions, which made power gentle, and obedience liberal . . . are to be dissolved by this new conquering empire of light and reason. All the decent drapery of life is to be rudely torn off. All the super-added ideas, furnished from the wardrobe of a moral imagination, which the heart owns, and the understanding ratifies, as necessary to cover the defects of our naked, shivering nature, and to raise it to dignity in our estimation, are to be exploded as a ridiculous, absurd, and antiquated fashion.

5. Paine was to accuse Burke of involvement not just with the passing of *chivalry* but with the demise of *aristocracy*, of respect for class and power rather than for principles. How just an accusation is Paine's in the light of Burke's comments on the treatment of the royal family in the incident of October 6? How could Burke's contention that it is desirable for the institutions of a commonwealth to "be embodied . . . in persons" serve as a defense against Paine's accusation?

6. How does *paradox* help Burke to suggest the moral upheaval which the revolution exemplifies?

Clue: • In . . . meetings of all sorts, every counsel, in proportion as it is daring, and violent, and *perfidious*, is taken for the mark of *superior* genius. *Humanity* and *compassion* are ridiculed as the fruits of superstition and ignorance. *Tenderness* to individuals is considered as *treason* to the public. Liberty is always to be estimated *perfect* as property is rendered *insecure*. Amidst *assassination, massacre,* and confiscation, perpetrated or meditated, they are forming plans for the *good order* of future society.

What other examples of such paradoxical treatment of ideas can you find?

7. Burke pessimistically suggests that "power, of some kind or other, will survive the shock in which manners and opinions perish; and it will find other and worse means for its support. The usurpation which, in order to subvert antient institutions, has destroyed antient principles, will hold power by arts similar to those by which it has acquired it." Writing in 1790, Burke is prophetically anticipating the ultimate tyrannical excesses of the French Revolution. Has he in this passage (and others) perhaps enunciated an inexorable law with regard to *revolutionary* action in general. Can you support or negate Burke's contention by examples from twentieth-century politics?

## *Thomas Paine (1737–1809)*
# Rights of Man

Among the incivilities by which nations or individuals provoke and irritate each other, Mr. Burke's pamphlet on the French Revolution is an extraordinary instance. Neither the people of France, nor the National Assembly, were troubling themselves about the affairs of England, or the English Parliament; and that Mr. Burke should commence an unprovoked attack upon them, both in parliament and in public, is a conduct that cannot be pardoned on the score of manners, nor justified on that of policy.

There is scarcely an epithet of abuse to be found in the English language, with which Mr. Burke has not loaded the French nation and the National Assembly. Everything which rancour, prejudice, ignorance or knowledge could suggest, is poured forth in the copious fury of near four hundred pages. In the strain and on the plan Mr. Burke was writing, he might have written on to as many thousands. When the tongue or the pen is let loose in a phrenzy of passion, it is the man, and not the subject, that becomes exhausted.

Hitherto Mr. Burke has been mistaken and disappointed in the opinions he had formed of the affairs of France; but such is the ingenuity of his hope, or the malignancy of his despair, that it furnishes him with new pretences to go on. There was a time when it was impossible to make Mr. Burke believe there would be any Revolution in France. His opinion then was, that the French had neither spirit to undertake it nor fortitude to support it; and now that there is one, he seeks an escape by condemning it.

Not sufficiently content with abusing the National Assembly, a great part of his work is taken up with abusing Dr. Price (one of the best-hearted men that lives) and the two societies in England known by the name of the Revolution Society and the Society for Constitutional Information.

Dr. Price had preached a sermon on the 4th of November, 1789, being the anniversary of what is called in England the Revolution, which took place 1688. Mr. Burke, speaking of this sermon, says, "The political Divine proceeds dogmatically to assert, that by the principles of the Revolution, the people of England have acquired three fundamental rights:

1. To choose our own governors.
2. To cashier them for misconduct.
3. To frame a government for ourselves."

Dr. Price does not say that the right to do these things exists in this or in that person, or in this or in that description of persons, but that it exists in the *whole*: that it is a right resident in the nation. Mr. Burke, on the contrary, denies that such a right exists in the nation, either in whole or in part, or that it exists anywhere; and, what is still more strange and marvellous, he says, "that the people of England utterly disclaim such a right, and that they will resist the practical assertion of it with their lives and fortunes." That men should take up arms and spend their lives and fortunes, *not to* maintain their rights, but to maintain they have *not* rights, is an entirely new species of discovery, and suited to the paradoxical genius of Mr. Burke.

The method which Mr. Burke takes to prove that the people of England have no such rights, and that such rights do not now exist in the nation, either in whole or in part, or anywhere at all, is of the same marvellous and monstrous kind with what he has already said; for his arguments are that the persons, or the generation of persons, in whom they did exist, are dead, and with them the right is dead also. To prove this, he quotes a declaration made by parliament about a hundred years ago, to William and Mary, in these words: "The Lords Spiritual and Temporal, and Commons, do, in the name of the people aforesaid [meaning the people of England then living], most humbly and faithfully *submit* themselves, their *heirs* and *posterities*, for EVER." He also quotes a clause of another act of parliament made in the same reign, the terms of which, he says, "bind us [meaning the people of that day], our *heirs* and our *posterity*, to *them*, their *heirs* and *posterity*, to the end of time."

Mr. Burke conceives his point sufficiently established by producing those clauses, which he enforces by saying that they exclude the right of the nation for *ever*. And not yet content with making such declarations, repeated over and over, he further says, "that if the people of England possessed such a right before the Revolution [which he acknowledges to have been the case, not only in England, but throughout Europe, at an early period], yet that the *English Nation* did, at the time of the Revolution, most solemnly renounce and abdicate it, for themselves, and for *all their posterity, for ever*."

As Mr. Burke occasionally applies the poison drawn from his horrid principles (if it is not prophanation to call them by the name of principles) not only to the English nation, but to the French Revolution and the National Assembly, and charges that august, illuminated and illuminating body of men with the epithet of *usurpers*, I shall, *sans cérémonie*, place another system of principles in opposition to his.

The English parliament of 1688 did a certain thing, which, for themselves and their constituents, they had a right to do, and which it appeared right should be done: but, in addition to this right, which they possessed by delegation, *they set up another right by assumption*, that of binding and controuling posterity to the end of time. The case, therefore, divides itself into two parts; the right which they possessed by delegation, and the right which they set up by assumption. The first is admitted; but with respect to the second, I reply—

There never did, there never will, and there never can, exist a parliament, or any description of men, or any generation of men, in any country, possessed of the right or the power of binding and controuling posterity to the *" end of time,"* or of commanding for ever how the world shall be governed, or who shall govern it; and therefore all such clauses, acts or declarations by which the makers of them attempt to do what they have neither the right nor the power to do, nor the power to execute, are in themselves null and void. Every age and generation must be as free to act for itself *in all cases* as the ages and generations which preceded it. The vanity and presumption of governing beyond the grave is the most ridiculous and insolent of all tyrannies. Man has no property in man; neither has any generation a property in the generations which are to follow. The parliament of the people of 1688, or of any other period, had no more right to dispose of the people of the present day, or to bind or to controul them *in any shape whatever*, than the parliament or the people of the present day have to dispose of, bind or controul those who are to live a hundred or a thousand years hence. Every generation is, and must be, competent to all the purposes which its occasions require. It is the living, and not the dead, that are to be accommodated. When man ceases to be, his power and his wants cease with him; and having no longer any participation in the concerns of this world, he has no longer any authority in directing who shall be its governors, or how its government shall be organized, or how administered.

I am not contending for nor against any form of government, nor for nor against any party, here or elsewhere. That which a whole nation chooses to do, it has a right to do. Mr. Burke says, No. Where, then, does the right exist? I am contending for the rights of the *living*, and against their being willed away, and controuled and contracted for, by the manuscript assumed authority of the dead; and Mr. Burke is contending for the authority of the dead over the rights and freedom of the living. There was a time when kings disposed of their crowns by will upon their death-beds, and consigned the people, like beasts of the field, to whatever successor they appointed. This is now so exploded as scarcely to be remembered, and so monstrous as hardly to be believed; but the parliamentary clauses upon which Mr. Burke builds his political church are of the same nature.

The laws of every country must be analogous to some common principle. In England no parent or master, nor all the authority of parliament, omnipotent as it has called itself, can bind or controul the personal freedom even of an individual beyond the age of twenty-one years. On what ground of right, then, could the parliament of 1688, or any other parliament, bind all posterity for ever?

Those who have quitted the world, and those who have not yet arrived at it, are as remote from each other as the utmost stretch of mortal imagination can conceive. What possible obligation, then, can exist between them; what rule or principle can be laid down that of two nonentities, the one out of existence and the other not in, and who never can meet in this world, the one should controul the other to the end of time?

In England it is said that money cannot be taken out of the pockets of the people without their consent. But who authorised, or who could authorise, the parliament of 1688 to controul and take away the freedom of posterity (who were not in existence to give or to withold their consent), and limit and confine their right of acting in certain cases for ever?

A greater absurdity cannot present itself to the understanding of man than what Mr. Burke offers to his readers. He tells them, and he tells the world to come, that a certain body of men who existed a hundred years ago, made a law, and that there does not now exist in the nation, nor ever will, nor ever can, a power to alter it. Under how many subtilties or absurdities has the divine right to govern been imposed on the credulity of mankind! Mr. Burke has discovered a new one, and he has shortened his journey to Rome by appealing to the power of this infallible parliament of former days; and he produces what it has done as of divine authority, for that power must certainly be more than human which no human power to the end of time can alter.

But Mr. Burke has done some service, not to his cause, but to his country, by bringing those clauses into public view. They serve to demonstrate how necessary it is at all times to watch against the attempted encroachment of power, and to prevent its running to excess. It is somewhat extraordinary that the offence for which James II. was expelled, that of setting up power by *assumption*, should be re-acted, under another shape and form, by the parliament that expelled him. It shews that the rights of man were but imperfectly understood at the Revolution; for certain it is that the right which that parliament set up by *assumption* (for by delegation it had not, and could not have it, because none could give it) over the persons and freedom of posterity for ever, was of the same tyrannical unfounded kind which James attempted to set up over the parliament and the nation, and for which he was expelled. The only difference is (for in principle they differ not) that the one was an usurper over the living, and the other over the unborn; and as the one had no better authority to stand upon than the other, both of them must be equally null and void, and of no effect.

From what, or from whence, does Mr. Burke prove the right of any human power to bind posterity for ever? He has produced his clauses, but he must produce also his proofs that such a right existed, and shew how it existed. If it ever existed it must now exist, for whatever appertains to the nature of man cannot be annihilated by man. It is the nature of man to die, and he will continue to die as long as he continues to be born. But Mr. Burke has set up a sort of political Adam, in whom all posterity are bound for ever; he must, therefore, prove that his Adam possessed such a power, or such a right.

The weaker any cord is the less will it bear to be stretched, and the worse is the policy to stretch it, unless it is intended to break it. Had anyone proposed the overthrow of Mr. Burke's positions, he would have proceeded as Mr. Burke has done. He would have magnified the authorities, on purpose to have called the *right* of them into question; and the instant the question of right was started the authorities must have been given up.

It requires but a very small glance of thought to perceive that altho' laws made in one generation often continue in force through succeeding generations, yet that they continue to derive their force from the consent of the living. A law not repealed continues in force, not because it *cannot* be repealed, but because it *is not* repealed; and the non-repealing passes for consent.

But Mr. Burke's clauses have not even this qualification in their favour. They become null, by attempting to become immortal. The nature of them precludes consent. They destroy the right which they *might* have, by grounding it on a right which they *cannot* have. Immortal power is not a human right, and therefore cannot be a right of parliament. The parliament of 1688 might as well have passed an act to have authorized themselves to live for ever, as to make their authority live for ever. All, therefore, that can be said of those clauses is that they are a formality of words, of as much import as if those who used them had addressed a congratulation to themselves, and in the oriental stile of antiquity had said: O Parliament, live for ever!

The circumstances of the world are continually changing, and the opinions of men change also; and as government is for the living, and not for the dead, it is the living only that has any right in it. That which may be thought right and found convenient in one age may be thought wrong and found inconvenient in another. In such cases, Who is to decide, the living or the dead?

As almost one hundred pages of Mr. Burke's book are employed upon these clauses, it will consequently follow that if the clauses themselves, so far as they set up an *assumed usurped* dominion over posterity for ever, are unauthoritative, and in their nature null and void; that all his voluminous inferences, and declamation drawn therefrom, or founded thereon, are null and void also; and on this ground I rest the matter.

We now come more particularly to the affairs of France. Mr. Burke's book has the appearance of being written as instruction to the French nation; but if I may permit myself the use of an extravagant metaphor, suited to the extravagance of the case, It is darkness attempting to illuminate light.

While I am writing this there are accidentally before me some proposals for a declaration of rights by the Marquis de la Fayette (I ask his pardon for using his former address, and do it only for distinction's sake) to the National Assembly, on the 11th of July, 1798, three days before the taking of the Bastille; and I cannot but remark with astonishment how opposite the sources are from which that gentleman and Mr. Burke draw their principles. Instead of referring to musty records and mouldy parchments to prove that the rights of the living are lost, "renounced and abdicated for ever," by those who are now no more, as Mr. Burke has done, M. de la Fayette applies to the living world, and emphatically says, "Call to mind the sentiments which Nature has engraved in the heart of every citizen, and which take a new force when they are solemnly recognized by all: For a nation to love liberty, it is sufficient that she knows it; and to be free, it is sufficient that she wills it." How dry, barren, and obscure is the source from which Mr. Burke labours; and how ineffectual, though gay with flowers, are all his declamation and his arguments compared with these clear, concise, and soul-animating sentiments! Few and short as they are, they lead on to a vast field of generous and manly thinking, and do not finish, like Mr. Burke's periods, with music in the ear, and nothing in the heart.

As I have introduced the mention of M. de la Fayette, I will take the liberty of adding an anecdote respecting his farewel address to the Congress of America in 1783, and which occurred fresh to my mind, when I saw Mr. Burke's thundering attack on the French revolution. M. de la Fayette went to America at an early period of the war, and continued a volunteer in her service to the end. His conduct through the whole of that enterprise is one of the most extraordinary that is to be found in the history of a young man, scarcely then twenty years of age. Situated in a country that was like the lap of sensual pleasure, and with the means of enjoying it, how few are there to be found who would exchange such a scene for the woods and wildernesses of America, and pass the flowery years of youth in unprofitable danger and hardship! But such is the fact. When the war ended, and he was on the point of taking his final departure, he presented himself to Congress, and contemplating, in his affectionate farewel, the revolution he had seen, expressed himself in these words: "May this great monument raised to Liberty, serve as a lesson to the oppressor, and an example to the oppressed!" When this address came to the hands of Dr. Franklin, who was then in France, he applied to Count Vergennes to have it inserted in the French Gazette, but never could obtain his consent. The fact was that Count Vergennes was an aristocratical despot at home, and dreaded the example of the American revolution in France, as certain other persons now dread the example of the French revolution in England; and Mr. Burke's tribute of fear (for in this light his book must be considered) runs parallel with Count Vergennes' refusal. But to return more particularly to his work—

"We have seen," says Mr. Burke, "the French rebel against a mild and lawful Monarch, with more fury, outrage, and insult, than any people has been known to rise against the most illegal usurper, or the most sanguinary tyrant." This is one among a thousand other instances, in which Mr. Burke shews that he is ignorant of the springs and principles of the French revolution.

It was not against Louis XVI., but against the despotic principles of the government, that the nation revolted. These principles had not their origin in him, but in the original establishment, many centuries back; and they were become too deeply rooted to be removed, and the Augean stable of parasites and plunderers too abominably filthy to be cleansed, by anything short of a complete and universal revolution. When it becomes necessary to do a thing, the whole heart and soul should go into the measure, or not attempt it. That crisis was then arrived, and there remained no choice but to act with determined vigour, or not to act at all. The King was known to be the friend of the nation, and this circumstance was favourable to the enterprise. Perhaps no man bred up in the stile of an absolute King, ever possessed a heart so little disposed to the exercise of that species of power as the present King of France. But the principles of the government itself remained the same. The Monarch and the Monarchy were distinct and separate things; and it was against the established despotism of the latter, and not against the person or principles of the former, that the revolt commenced, and the revolution has been carried.

Mr. Burke does not attend to the distinction between *men* and *principles*; and, therefore, he does not see that a revolt may take place against the despotism of the latter, while there lies no charge of despotism against the former.

The natural moderation of Louis XVI. contributed nothing to alter the hereditary despotism of the monarchy. All the tyrannies of former reigns, acted under that hereditary despotism, were still liable to be revived in the hands of a successor. It was not the respite of a reign that would satisfy France, enlightened as she was then become. A casual discontinuance of the *practice* of despotism, is not a discontinuance of its *principles*; the former depends on the virtue of the individual who is in immediate possession of the power; the latter, on the virtue and fortitude of the nation. In the case of Charles I. and James II. of England, the revolt was against the personal despotism of the men; whereas in France, it was against the hereditary despotism of the established government. But men who can consign over the rights of posterity for ever on the authority of a mouldy parchment, like Mr. Burke, are not qualified to judge of this revolution. It takes in a field too vast for their views to explore, and proceeds with a mightiness of reason they cannot keep pace with.

But there are many points of view in which this revolution may be considered. When despotism has established itself for ages in a country, as in France, it is not in the person of the King only that it resides. It has the appearance of being so in show, and in nominal authority; but it is not so in practice and in fact. It has its standard everywhere. Every office and department has its despotism, founded upon custom and usage. Every place has its Bastille, and every Bastille its despot. The original hereditary despotism resident in the person of the King, divides and sub-divides itself into a thousand shapes and forms, till at last the whole of it is acted by deputation. This was the case in France; and against this species of despotism, proceeding on through an endless labyrinth of office till the source of it is scarcely perceptible, there is no mode of redress. It strengthens itself by assuming the appearance of duty, and tyrannises under the pretence of obeying.

When a man reflects on the condition which France was in from the nature of her government, he will see other causes for revolt than those which immediately connect themselves with the person or character of Louis XVI. There were, if I may so express it, a thousand despotisms to be reformed in France, which had grown up under the hereditary despotism of the monarch, and became so rooted as to be in a great measure independent of it. Between the monarchy, the parliament, and the church there was a *rivalship* of despotism; besides the feudal despotism operating locally, and the ministerial despotism operating everywhere. But Mr. Burke, by considering the King as the only possible object of a revolt, speaks as if France was a village, in which everything that passed must be known to its commanding officer, and no oppression could be acted but what he could immediately controul. Mr. Burke might have been in the Bastille his whole life, as well under Louis XVI. as Louis XIV., and neither the one nor the other have known that such a man as Mr. Burke existed. The despotic principles of the government were the same in both reigns, though the dispositions of the men were as remote as tyranny and benevolence.

What Mr. Burke considers as a reproach to the French revolution (that of bringing it forward under a reign more mild than the preceding ones) is one of its highest honours. The revolutions that have taken place in other European countries, have been excited by personal hatred. The rage was against the man, and he became the victim. But, in the instance of France we see a revolution generated in the rational contemplation of the rights of man, and distinguishing from the beginning between persons and principles.

But Mr. Burke appears to have no idea of principles when he is contemplating governments. "Ten years ago," says he, "I could have felicitated France on her having a government, without inquiring what the nature of that government was, or how it was administered." Is this the language of a rational man? Is it the language of a heart feeling as it ought to feel for the rights and happiness of the human race? On this ground, Mr. Burke must compliment all the governments in the world, while the victims who suffer under them, whether sold into slavery, or tortured out of existence, are wholly forgotten. It is power, and not principles, that Mr. Burke venerates; and under this abominable depravity he is disqualified to judge between them. Thus much for his opinion as to the occasions of the French revolution. I now proceed to other considerations.

I know a place in America called Point-no-Point, because as you proceed along the shore, gay and flowery as Mr. Burke's language, it continually recedes and presents itself at a distance before you; but when you have got as far as you can go, there is no point at all. Just thus it is with Mr. Burke's three hundred and fifty-six pages. It is therefore difficult to reply to him. But as the points he wishes to establish may be inferred from what he abuses, it is in his paradoxes that we must look for his arguments.

As to the tragic paintings by which Mr. Burke has outraged his own imagination, and seeks to work upon that of his readers, they are very well calculated for theatrical representation, where facts are manufactured for the sake of show, and accommodated to produce, through the weakness of sympathy, a weeping effect. But Mr. Burke should recollect that he is writing History, and not *Plays*, and that his readers will expect truth, and not the spouting rant of high-toned declamation.

When we see a man dramatically lamenting in a publication intended to be believed that *"The age of chivalry is gone! that the glory of Europe is extinguished for ever! that the unbought grace of life* [if anyone knows what it is], *the cheap defence of nations, the nurse of manly sentiment and heroic enterprise is gone!"* and all this because the Quixote age of chivalry nonsense is gone, what opinion can we form of his judgment, or what regard can we pay to his facts? In the rhapsody of his imagination he has discovered a world of windmills, and his sorrows are that there are no Quixotes to attack them. But if the age of aristocracy, like that of chivalry, should fall (and they had originally some connection), Mr. Burke, the trumpeter of the Order, may continue his parody to the end, and finish with exclaiming; *"Othello's occupation's gone!"*

Notwithstanding Mr. Burke's horrid paintings, when the French revolution is compared with the revolutions of other countries, the astonishment will be that it is marked with so few sacrifices; but this astonishment will cease when we reflect that *principles*, and not *persons*, were the meditated objects of destruction. The mind of the nation was acted upon by a higher stimulus than what the consideration of persons could inspire, and sought a higher conquest than could be produced by the downfall of an enemy. Among the few who fell there do not appear to be any that were intentionally singled out. They all of them had their fate in the circumstances of the moment, and were not pursued with that long, coldblooded, unabated revenge which pursued the unfortunate Scotch in the affair of 1745.

Through the whole of Mr. Burke's book I do not observe that the Bastille is mentioned more than once, and that with a kind of implication as if he were sorry it was pulled down, and wished it were built up again. "We have rebuilt Newgate," says he, "and tenanted the mansion; and we have prisons almost as strong as the Bastille for those who dare to libel the queens of France." As to what a madman like the person called Lord George Gordon[1] might say, and to whom Newgate is rather a bedlam than a prison, it is unworthy a rational consideration. It was a madman that libelled, and that is sufficient apology; and it afforded an opportunity for confining him, which was the

---

[1] *Lord George Gordon:* Burke had referred to the imprisonment in Newgate (in 1788) of this leader of the "no popery" riots in London in 1780.

thing that was wished for. But certain it is that Mr. Burke, who does not call himself a madman (whatever other people may do), has libelled in the most unprovoked manner, and in the grossest stile of the most vulgar abuse, the whole representative authority of France, and yet Mr. Burke takes his seat in the British House of Commons! From his violence and his grief, his silence on some points and his excess on others, it is difficult not to believe that Mr. Burke is sorry, extremely sorry, that arbitrary power, the power of the Pope and the Bastille, are pulled down.

Not one glance of compassion, not one commiserating reflection that I can find throughout his book, has he bestowed on those who lingered out the most wretched of lives, a life without hope in the most miserable of prisons. It is painful to behold a man employing his talents to corrupt himself. Nature has been kinder to Mr. Burke than he is to her. He is not affected by the reality of distress touching his heart, but by the showy resemblance of it striking his imagination. He pities the plumage, but forgets the dying bird. Accustomed to kiss the aristocratical hand that hath purloined him from himself, he degenerates into a composition of art, and the genuine soul of nature forsakes him. His hero or his heroine must be a tragedy-victim expiring in show, and not the real prisoner of misery, sliding into death in the silence of a dungeon.

As Mr. Burke has passed over the whole transaction of the Bastille (and his silence is nothing in his favour), and has entertained his readers with reflections on supposed facts distorted into real falsehoods, I will give, since he has not, some account of the circumstances which preceded that transaction. They will serve to show that less mischief could scarcely have accompanied such an event when considered with the treacherous and hostile aggravations of the enemies of the revolution.

The mind can hardly picture to itself a more tremendous scene than what the city of Paris exhibited at the time of taking the Bastille and for two days before and after, nor perceive the possibility of its quieting so soon. At a distance this transaction has appeared only as an act of heroism standing on itself, and the close political connection it had with the revolution is lost in the brilliancy of the achievement. But we are to consider it as the strength of the parties brought man to man, and contending for the issue. The Bastille was to be either the prize or the prison of the assailants. The downfall of it included the idea of the downfall of despotism, and this compounded image was become as figuratively united as Bunyan's Doubting Castle and Giant Despair.

The National Assembly, before and at the time of taking the Bastille, was sitting at Versailles, twelve miles distant from Paris. About a week before the rising of the Parisians, and their taking the Bastille, it was discovered that a plot was forming, at the head of which was the Count d'Artois, the king's youngest brother, for demolishing the National Assembly, seizing its members, and thereby crushing, by a *coup de main*, all hopes and prospects of forming a free government. For the sake of humanity, as well as freedom, it is well this plan did not succeed. Examples are not wanting to show how dreadfully vindictive and cruel are all old governments, when they are successful against what they call a revolt.

This plan must have been some time in contemplation; because, in order to carry it into execution, it was necessary to collect a large military force round Paris, and cut off the communication between that city and the National Assembly at Versailles. The troops destined for this service were chiefly the foreign troops in the pay of France, and who, for this particular purpose, were drawn from the distant provinces where they were then stationed. When they were collected to the amount of between twenty-five and thirty thousand, it was judged time to put the plan into execution. The ministry who were then in office, and who were friendly to the revolution, were instantly dismissed and a new ministry formed of those who had concerted the project, among whom was Count de Broglio, and to his share was given the command of those troops. The character of this man as described to me in a letter which I communicated to Mr. Burke before he began to write his book, and from an authority which Mr. Burke well knows was good, was that of "a high-flying aristocrat, cool, and capable of every mischief."

While these matters were agitating, the National Assembly stood in the most perilous and critical situation that a body of men can be supposed to act in. They were the devoted victims, and they knew it. They had the hearts and wishes of their country on their side, but military authority they had none. The guards of Broglio surrounded the hall where the assembly sat, ready, at the word of command, to seize their persons, as had been done the year before to the parliament of Paris. Had the National Assembly deserted their trust, or had they exhibited signs of weakness or fear, their enemies had been encouraged and the country depressed. When the situation they stood in, the cause they were engaged in and the crisis then ready to burst, which should determine their personal and political fate and that of their country, and probably of Europe, are taken into one view, none but a heart callous with prejudice or corrupted by dependence can avoid interesting itself in their success.

The archbishop of Vienne was at this time president of the National Assembly—a person too old to undergo the scene that a few days or a few hours might bring forth. A man of more activity and bolder fortitude was necessary, and the National Assembly chose (under the form of a vice-president, for the presidency still resided in the archbishop) M. de la Fayette; and this is the only instance of a vice-president being chosen. It was at the moment that this storm was pending (July 11th) that a declaration of rights was brought forward by M. de la Fayette. . . . It was hastily drawn up, and makes only a part of the more extensive declaration of rights agreed upon and adopted afterwards by the National Assembly. The particular reason for bringing it forward at this moment (M. de la Fayette has since informed me) was that, if the National Assembly should fall in the threatened destruction that then surrounded it, some trace of its principles might have the chance of surviving the wreck.

Everything now was drawing to a crisis. The event was freedom or slavery. On one side, an army of nearly thirty thousand men; on the other, an unarmed body of citizens; for the citizens of Paris, on whom the National Assembly must then immediately depend, were as unarmed and as undisciplined as the citizens of London are now. The French guards had given strong symptoms of their being attached to the national cause; but their members were small, not a tenth part of the force that Broglio commanded, and their officers were in the interest of Broglio.

Matters being now ripe for execution, the new ministry made their appearance in office. The reader will carry in his mind that the Bastille was taken the 14th July; the point of time I am now speaking of is the 12th. Immediately on the news of the change of ministry reaching Paris, in the afternoon, all the playhouses and places of entertainment, shops and houses, were shut up. The change of ministry was considered as the prelude of hostilities, and the opinion was rightly founded.

The foreign troops began to advance towards the city. The Prince de Lambesc, who commanded a body of German cavalry, approached by the Place of Louis XV, which connects itself with some of the streets. In his march, he insulted and struck an old man with a sword. The French are remarkable for their respect to old age and the insolence with which it appeared to be done, uniting with the general fermentation they were in, produced a powerful effect, and a cry of "*To arms! To arms!*" spread itself in a moment over the city.

Arms they had none, nor scarcely any who knew the use of them; but desperate resolution, when every hope is at stake, supplies, for a while, the want of arms. Near where the Prince de Lambesc was drawn up, were large piles of stones collected for building the new bridge, and with these the people attacked the cavalry. A party of French guards, upon hearing the firing, rushed from their quarters and joined the people; and night coming on, the cavalry retreated.

The streets of Paris, being narrow, are favourable for defence, and the loftiness of the houses, consisting of many stories, from which great annoyance might be given, secured them against nocturnal enterprises; and the night was spent in providing themselves with every sort of weapon they could make or procure: guns, swords, blacksmiths' hammers, carpenters' axes, iron crows, pikes, halberts, pitchforks, spits, clubs, etc., etc. The incredible numbers with which they assembled the next morning, and the still more incredible resolution they exhibited, embarrassed and astonished their enemies. Little did the new ministry expect such a salute. Accustomed to slavery themselves, they had no idea that Liberty was capable of such inspiration, or that a body of unarmed citizens would dare to face the military force of thirty thousand men. Every moment of this day was employed in collecting arms, concerting plans, and arranging themselves into the best order which such an instantaneous movement could afford. Broglio continued lying round the city, but made no further advances this day, and the succeeding night passed with as much tranquillity as such a scene could possibly produce.

But defence only was not the object of the citizens. They had a cause at stake, on which depended their freedom or their slavery. They every moment expected an attack, or to hear of one made on the National Assembly; and in such a situation, the most prompt measures are sometimes the best. The object that now presented itself was the Bastille; and the *éclat* of carrying such a fortress in the face of such an army, could not fail to strike terror into the new ministry, who had scarcely yet had time to meet. By some intercepted correspondence this morning, it was discovered that the Mayor of Paris, M. Defflesselles, who appeared to be in their interest, was betraying them; and from this discovery, there remained no doubt that Broglio would rein-force the Bastille the ensuing evening. It was therefore necessary to attack it that day; but before this could be done, it was first necessary to procure a better supply of arms than they were then possessed of.

There was, adjoining to the city, a large magazine of arms deposited at the Hospital of the Invalids, which the citizens summoned to surrender; and as the place was neither defensible, nor attempted much defence, they soon succeeded. Thus supplied, they marched to attack the Bastille; a vast mixed multitude of all ages, and of all degrees, armed with all sorts of weapons. Imagination would fail in describing to itself the appearance of such a procession, and of the anxiety of the events which a few hours or a few minutes might produce. What plans the ministry were forming, were as unknown to the people within the city, as what the citizens were doing was unknown to the ministry; and what movements Broglio might make for the support or relief of the place, were to the citizens equally as unknown. All was mystery and hazard.

That the Bastille was attacked with an enthusiasm of heroism, such only as the highest animation of liberty could inspire, and carried in the space of a few hours, is an advent which the world is fully possessed of. I am not undertaking a detail of the attack, but bringing into view the conspiracy against the nation which provoked it, and which fell with the Bastille. The prison to which the new ministry were dooming the National Assembly, in addition to its being the high altar and castle of despotism, became the proper object to begin with. This enterprize broke up the new ministry, who began now to fly from the ruin they had prepared for others. The troops of Broglio dispersed, and himself fled also.

Mr. Burke has spoken a great deal about plots, but he has never once spoken of this plot against the National Assembly, and the liberties of the nation; and that he might not, he has passed over all the circumstances that might throw it in his way. The exiles who have fled from France, whose case he so much interests himself in, and from whom he has had his lesson, fled in consequence of the miscarriage of this plot. No plot was formed against them; they were plotting against others; and those who fell, met, not unjustly, the punishment they were preparing to execute. But will Mr. Burke say, that if this plot, contrived with the subtility of an ambuscade, had succeeded, the successful party would have restrained their wrath so soon? Let the history of all old governments answer the question.

Whom has the National Assembly brought to the scaffold? None. They were themselves the devoted victims of this plot, and they have not retaliated; why, then, are they charged with revenge they have not acted? In the tremendous breaking forth of a whole people, in which all degrees, tempers, and characters are confounded, delivering themselves by a miracle of exertion from the destruction meditated against them, is it to be expected that nothing will happen? When men are sore with the sense of oppressions, and menaced with the prospect of new ones, is the calmness of philosophy or the palsy of insensibility to be looked for? Mr. Burke exclaims against outrage; yet the greatest is that which himself has committed. His book is a volume of outrage, not apologized for by the impulse of a moment, but cherished through a space of ten months; yet Mr. Burke had no provocation, no life, no interest at stake.

More of the citizens fell in this struggle than of their opponents; but four or five persons were seized by the populace and instantly put to death; the Governor of the Bastille, and the Mayor of Paris, who was detected in the act of betraying them; and afterwards Foulon, one of the new ministry, and Berthier, his son-in-law, who had accepted the office of intendant of Paris. Their heads were stuck upon spikes, and carried about the city; and it is upon this mode of punishment that Mr. Burke builds a great part of his tragic scenes. Let us therefore examine how men came by the idea of punishing in this manner.

They learn it from the governments they live under, and retaliate the punishments they have been accustomed to behold. The heads stuck upon spikes, which remained for years upon Temple Bar, differed nothing in the horror of the scene from those carried about upon spikes at Paris; yet this was done by the English government. It may perhaps be said that it signifies nothing to a man what is done to him after he is dead; but it signifies much to the living; it either tortures their feelings or hardens their hearts, and in either case it instructs them how to punish when power falls into their hands.

Lay then the axe to the root, and teach governments humanity. It is their sanguinary punishments which corrupt mankind. In England the punishment in certain cases is by *hanging, drawing,* and *quartering*: the heart of the sufferer is cut out and held up to the view of the populace. In France, under the former government, the punishments were not less barbarous. Who does not remember the execution of Damien, torn to pieces by horses? The effect of those cruel spectacles exhibited to the populace is to destroy tenderness or excite revenge; and by the base and false idea of governing men by terror, instead of reason, they become precedents. It is over the lowest class of mankind that government by terror is intended to operate, and it is on them that it operates to the worst effect. They have sense enough to feel they are the objects aimed at; and they inflict in their turn the examples of terror they have been instructed to practise.

There is in all European countries a large class of people of that description, which in England is called the *"mob."* Of this class were those who committed the burnings and devastations in London in 1780, and of this class were those who carried the heads upon spikes in Paris. Foulon and Berthier were taken up in the country, and sent to Paris, to undergo their examination at the Hotel de Ville; for the National Assembly, immediately on the new ministry coming into office, passed a decree, which they communicated to the King and Cabinet, that they (the National Assembly) would hold the ministry, of which Foulon was one, responsible for the measures they were advising and pursuing; but the mob, incensed at the appearance of Foulon and Berthier, tore them from their conductors before they were carried to the Hotel de Ville, and executed them on the spot. Why then does Mr. Burke charge outrages of this kind on a whole people? As well may he charge the riots and outrages of 1780 on all the people of London, or those in Ireland on all his countrymen.

But everything we see or hear offensive to our feelings and derogatory to the human character should lead to other reflections than those of reproach. Even the beings who commit them have some claim to our consideration. How then is it that such vast classes of mankind as are distinguished by the appellation of the vulgar, or the ignorant mob, are so numerous in all old countries? The instant we ask ourselves this question, reflection feels an answer. They arise, as an unavoidable consequence, out of the ill construction of all old governments in Europe, England included with the rest. It is by distortedly exalting some men, that others are distortedly debased, till the whole is out of nature. A vast mass of mankind are degradedly thrown into the background of the human picture, to bring forward, with greater glare, the puppet-show of state and aristocracy. In the commencement of a revolution, those men are rather the followers of the *camp* than of the *standard* of liberty, and have yet to be instructed how to reverence it.

I give to Mr. Burke all his theatrical exaggerations for facts, and I then ask him if they do not establish the certainty of what I here lay down? Admitting them to be true, they show the necessity of the French revolution, as much as any one thing he could have asserted. These outrages were not the effect of the principles of the revolution, but of the degraded mind that existed before the revolution, and which the revolution is calculated to reform. Place them then to their proper cause, and take the reproach of them to your own side.

It is to the honour of the National Assembly and the city of Paris that, during such a tremendous scene of arms and confusion, beyond the controul of all authority, they have been able, by the influence of example and exhortation, to restrain so much. Never were more pains taken to instruct and enlighten mankind, and to make them see that their interest consisted in their virtue, and not in their revenge, than have been displayed in the revolution of France. I now proceed to make some remarks on Mr. Burke's account of the expedition to Versailles, October the 5th and 6th.

I can consider Mr. Burke's book in scarcely any other light than a dramatic performance; and he must, I think, have considered it in the same light himself, by the poetical liberties he has taken of omitting some facts, distorting others, and making the whole machinery bend to produce a stage effect. Of this kind is his account of the expedition to Versailles. He begins this account by omitting the only facts which as causes are known to be true; everything beyond these is conjecture even in Paris; and then he works up a tale accommodated to his own passions and prejudices.

It is to be observed throughout Mr. Burke's book that he never speaks of plots *against* the revolution; and it is from those plots that all the mischiefs have arisen. It suits his purpose to exhibit the consequences without their causes. It is one of the arts of the drama to do so. If the crimes of men were exhibited with their sufferings, the stage effect would sometimes be lost, and the audience would be inclined to approve where it was intended they should commiserate.

After all the investigations that have been made into this intricate affair (the expedition to Versailles), it still remains enveloped in all that kind of mystery which ever accompanies events produced more from a concurrence of awkward circumstances than from fixed design. While the characters of men are forming, as is always the case in revolutions, there is a reciprocal suspicion, and a disposition to misinterpret each other; and even parties directly opposite in principle will sometimes concur in pushing forward the same movement with very different views, and with the hopes of its producing very different consequences. A great deal of this may be discovered in this embarrassed affair, and yet the issue of the whole was what nobody had in view.

The only things certainly known are that considerable uneasiness was at this time excited at Paris by the delay of the King in not sanctioning and forwarding the decrees of the National Assembly, particularly that of the *Declaration of the Rights of Man*, and the decrees of the *fourth of August*, which contained the foundation principles on which the constitution was to be erected. The kindest, and perhaps the fairest conjecture upon this matter is, that some of the ministers intended to make remarks and observations upon certain parts of them before they were finally sanctioned and sent to the provinces; but be this as it may, the enemies of the revolution derived hope from the delay, and the friends of the revolution uneasiness.

During this state of suspense, the *Garde du Corps*, which was composed as such regiments generally are, of persons much connected with the Court, gave an entertainment at Versailles (October 1) to some foreign regiments then arrived; and when the entertainment was at the height, on a signal given the *Garde du Corps* tore the national cockade from their hats, trampled it under foot, and replaced it with a counter-cockade prepared for the purpose. An indignity of this kind amounted to defiance. It was like declaring war; and if men will give challenges they must expect consequences. But all this Mr. Burke has carefully kept out of sight. He begins his account by saying: "History will record that on the morning of the 6th October, 1789, the King and Queen of France, after a day of confusion, alarm, dismay, and slaughter, lay down under the pledged security of public faith to indulge nature in a few hours of respite, and troubled melancholy repose." This is neither the sober stile of history, nor the intention of it. It leaves everything to be guessed at and mistaken. One would at least think there had been a battle; and a battle there probably would have been had it not been for the moderating prudence of those whom Mr. Burke involves in his censures. By his keeping the *Garde du Corps* out of sight Mr. Burke has afforded himself the dramatic licence of putting the King and Queen in their places, as if the object of the expedition was against them. But to return to my account—

This conduct of the *Garde du Corps*, as might well be expected, alarmed and enraged the Parisians. The colours of the cause, and the cause itself, were become too united to mistake the intention of the insult, and the Parisians were determined to call the *Garde du Corps* to an account. There was certainly nothing of the cowardice of assassination in marching in the face of the day to demand satisfaction, if such a phrase may be used, of a body of armed men who had voluntarily given defiance. But the circumstance which serves to throw this affair into embarrassment is, that the enemies of the revolution appear to have encouraged it as well as its friends. The one hoped to prevent a civil war by checking it in time, and the other to make one. The hopes of those opposed to the revolution rested in making the King of their party, and getting him from Versailles to Metz, where they expected to collect a force and set up a standard. We have, therefore, two different objects presenting themselves at the same time, and to be accomplished by the same means; the one to chastise the *Garde du Corps*, which was the object of the Parisians; the other to render the conclusion of such a scene an inducement to the King to set off for Metz.

On the 5th of October a very numerous body of women, and men in the disguise of women, collected round the Hotel de Ville or town-hall of Paris, and set off for Versailles. Their professed object was the *Garde du Corps*; but prudent men readily recollect that mischief is more easily begun than ended; and this impressed itself with the more force from the suspicions already stated, and the irregularity of such a cavalcade. As soon, therefore, as a sufficient force could be collected, M. de la Fayette, by order from the civil authority of Paris, set off after them at the head of twenty thousand of the Paris militia. The revolution could derive no benefit from confusion, and its opposers might. By an amiable and spirited manner of address he had hitherto been fortunate in calming disquietudes, and in this he was extraordinarily successful; to frustrate, therefore, the hopes of those who might seek to improve this scene into a sort of justifiable necessity for the King's quitting

Versailles and withdrawing to Metz, and to prevent at the same time the consequences that might ensue between the *Garde du Corps* and this phalanx of men and women, he forwarded expresses to the King, that he was on his march to Versailles, by the orders of the civil authority of Paris, for the purpose of peace and protection, expressing at the same time the necessity of restraining the *Garde du Corps* from firing upon the people.[2]

He arrived at Versailles between ten and eleven at night. The *Garde du Corps* was drawn up, and the people had arrived some time before, but everything had remained suspended. Wisdom and policy now consisted in changing a scene of danger into a happy event. M. de la Fayette became the mediator between the enraged parties; and the King, to remove the uneasiness which had arisen from the delay already stated, sent for the President of the National Assembly, and signed the *Declaration of the Rights of Man*, and such other parts of the constitution as were in readiness.

It was now about one in the morning. Everything appeared to be composed, and a general congratulation took place. By the beat of the drum a proclamation was made that the citizens of Versailles would give the hospitality of their houses to their fellow-citizens of Paris. Those who could not be accommodated in this manner remained in the streets, or took up their quarters in the churches; and at two o'clock the King and Queen retired.

In this state matters passed till the break of day, when a fresh disturbance arose from the censurable conduct of some of both parties, for such characters there will be in all such scenes. One of the *Garde du Corps* appeared at one of the windows of the palace, and the people who had remained during the night in the streets accosted him with reviling and provocative language. Instead of retiring, as in such a case prudence would have dictated, he presented his musket, fired, and killed one of the Paris militia. The peace being thus broken, the people rushed into the palace in quest of the offender. They attacked the quarters of the *Garde du Corps* within the palace, and pursued them throughout the avenues of it, and to the apartments of the King. On this tumult, not the Queen only, as Mr. Burke has represented it, but every person in the palace was awakened and alarmed; and M. de la Fayette had a second time to interpose between the parties, the event of which was that the *Garde du Corps* put on the national cockade, and the matter ended as by oblivion, after the loss of two or three lives.

During the latter part of the time in which this confusion was acting, the King and Queen were in public at the balcony, and neither of them concealed for safety's sake, as Mr. Burke insinuates. Matters being thus appeased, and tranquility restored, a general acclamation broke forth of *Le Roi à Paris*— *Le Roi à Paris*—The King to Paris. It was the shout of peace, and immediately accepted on the part of the King. By this measure all future projects of trepanning the King to Metz, and setting up the standard of opposition

---

[2] I am warranted in asserting this, as I had it personally from M. de la Fayette, with whom I lived in habits of friendship for fourteen years.—*Author*.

to the constitution, were prevented, and the suspicions extinguished. The King and his family reached Paris in the evening, and were congratulated on their arrival by M. Bailly, the Mayor of Paris, in the name of the citizens. Mr. Burke, who throughout his book confounds things, persons, and principles, as in his remarks on M. Bailly's address, confounded time also. He censures M. Bailly for calling it *"un bon jour,"* a good day. Mr. Burke should have informed himself that this scene took up the space of two days, the day on which it began with every appearance of danger and mischief, and the day on which it terminated without the mischiefs that threatened; and that it is to this peaceful termination that M. Bailly alludes, and to the arrival of the King at Paris. Not less than three hundred thousand persons arranged themselves in the procession from Versailles to Paris, and not an act of molestation was committed during the whole march.

Mr. Burke, on the authority of M. Lally Tollendal, a deserter from the National Assembly, says, that on entering Paris, the people shouted *"Tous les évèques à la lanterne."* All Bishops to be hanged at the lanthorn or lampposts. It is surprising that nobody should hear this but Lally Tollendal, and that nobody should believe it but Mr. Burke. It has not the least connection with any part of the transaction, and is totally foreign to every circumstance of it. The bishops had never been introduced before into any scene of Mr. Burke's drama: why then are they, all at once, and altogether, *tout à coup, et tous ensemble,* introduced now? Mr. Burke brings forward his bishops and his lanthorn-like figures in a magic lanthorn, and raises his scenes by contrast instead of connection. But it serves to show, with the rest of his book, what little credit ought to be given where even probability is set at defiance, for the purpose of defaming; and with this reflection, instead of a soliloquy in praise of chivalry, as Mr. Burke has done, I close the account of the expedition to Versailles.

I have now to follow Mr. Burke through a pathless wilderness of rhapsodies, and a sort of descant upon governments, in which he asserts whatever he pleases, on the presumption of its being believed, without offering either evidence or reasons for so doing.

Before anything can be reasoned upon to a conclusion, certain facts, principles, or data, to reason from, must be established, admitted, or denied. Mr. Burke, with his usual outrage, abused the *Declaration of the Rights of Man,* published by the National Assembly of France as the basis on which the constitution of France is built. This he calls "paltry and blurred sheets of paper about the rights of man." Does Mr. Burke mean to deny that *man* has any rights? If he does, then he must mean that there are no such things as rights anywhere, and that he has none himself; for who is there in the world but man? But if Mr. Burke means to admit that man has rights, the question then will be: What are those rights, and how came man by them originally?

The error of those who reason by precedents drawn from antiquity, respecting the rights of man, is that they do not go far enough into antiquity.

They do not go the whole way. They stop in some of the intermediate stages of an hundred or a thousand years, and produce what was then done, as a rule for the present day. This is no authority at all. If we travel still farther into antiquity, we shall find a direct contrary opinion and practice prevailing; and if antiquity is to be authority, a thousand such authorities may be produced, successively contradicting each other; but if we proceed on, we shall at last come out right; we shall come to the time when man came from the hand of his Maker. What was he then? Man. Man was his high and only title, and a higher cannot be given him. But of titles I shall speak hereafter.

We are now got at the origin of man, and at the origin of his rights. As to the manner in which the world has been governed from that day to this, it is no farther any concern of ours than to make a proper use of the errors or the improvements which the history of it presents. Those who lived an hundred or a thousand years ago, were then moderns, as we are now. They had *their* ancients, and those ancients had others, and we also shall be ancients in our turn. If the mere name of antiquity is to govern in the affairs of life, the people who are to live an hundred or a thousand years hence, may as well take us for a precedent, as we make a precedent of those who lived an hundred or a thousand years ago. The fact is, that portions of antiquity, by proving everything, establish nothing. It is authority against authority all the way, till we come to the divine origin of the rights of man at the creation. Here our inquiries find a resting-place, and our reason finds a home. If a dispute about the rights of man had arisen at the distance of an hundred years from the creation, it is to this source of authority they must have referred, and it is to this same source of authority that we must now refer.

Though I mean not to touch upon any sectarian principle of religion, yet it may be worth observing, that the genealogy of Christ is traced to Adam. Why then not trace the rights of man to the creation of man? I will answer the question. Because there have been upstart governments, thrusting themselves between and presumptuously working to *un-make* man.

If any generation of men ever possessed the right of dictating the mode by which the world should be governed for ever, it was the first generation that existed; and if that generation did it not, no succeeding generation can show any authority for doing it, nor set any up. The illuminating and divine principle of the equal rights of man (for it has its origin from the Maker of man) relates, not only to the living individuals, but to generations of men succeeding each other. Every generation is equal in rights to the generations which preceded it, by the same rule that every individual is born equal in rights with his contemporary.

Every history of the creation, and every traditionary account, whether from the lettered or unlettered world, however they may vary in their opinion or belief of certain particulars, all agree in establishing one point, *the unity of men*; by which I mean that men are all of *one degree*, and consequently that all men are born equal, and with equal natural rights, in the same manner as if posterity had been continued by *creation* instead of *generation*, the latter being the only mode by which the former is carried forward; and consequently every child born into the world must be considered as deriving its existence from God. The world is as new to him as it was to the first man that existed, and his natural right in it is of the same kind.

The Mosaic account of the creation, whether taken as divine authority or merely historical, is fully up to this point, *the unity or equality of man.* The expressions admit of no controversy. "And God said, Let us make man in our own image. In the image of God created he him; male and female created he them." The distinction of sexes is pointed out, but no other distinction is even implied. If this be not divine authority, it is at least historical authority, and shows that the equality of man, so far from being a modern doctrine, is the oldest upon record.

It is also to be observed that all the religions known in the world are founded, so far as they relate to man, on the *unity of man,* as being all of one degree. Whether in heaven or in hell, or in whatever state man may be supposed to exist hereafter, the good and the bad are the only distinctions. Nay, even the laws of governments are obliged to slide into this principle, by making degrees to consist in crimes and not in persons.

It is one of the greatest of all truths, and of the highest advantage to cultivate. By considering man in this light, and by instructing him to consider himself in this light, it places him in a close connection with all his duties, whether to his Creator or to the creation, of which he is a part; and it is only when he forgets his origin, or, to use a more fashionable phrase, his *birth and family,* that he becomes dissolute. It is not among the least of the evils of the present existing governments in all parts of Europe that man, considered as man, is thrown back to a vast distance from his Maker, and the artificial chasm filled up with a succession of barriers, or sort of turnpike gates, through which he has to pass. I will quote Mr. Burke's catalogue of barriers that he has set up between Man and his Maker. Putting himself in the character of a herald, he says: "We fear God—we look with *awe* to kings—with affection to parliaments—with duty to magistrates—with reverence to priests, and with respect to nobility." Mr. Burke has forgotten to put in *"chivalry."* He has also forgotten to put in Peter.

The duty of man is not a wilderness of turnpike gates, through which he is to pass by tickets from one to the other. It is plain and simple, and consists but of two points. His duty to God, which every man must feel; and with respect to his neighbour, to do as he would be done by. If those to whom power is delegated do well, they will be respected; if not, they will be despised; and with regard to those to whom no power is delegated, but who assume it, the rational world can know nothing of them.

Hitherto we have spoken only (and that but in part) of the natural rights of man. We have now to consider the civil rights of man, and to show how the one originates from the other. Man did not enter into society to become *worse* than he was before, nor to have fewer rights than he had before, but to have those rights better secured. His natural rights are the foundation of all his civil rights. But in order to pursue this distinction with more precision, it will be necessary to mark the different qualities of natural and civil rights.

A few words will explain this. Natural rights are those which appertain to man in right of his existence. Of this kind are all the intellectual rights, or rights of the mind, and also all those rights of acting as an individual for his own comfort and happiness, which are not injurious to the natural rights of others. Civil rights are those which appertain to man in right of his being a member of society. Every civil right has for its foundation some natural right pre-existing in the individual, but to the enjoyment of which his individual power is not, in all cases, sufficiently competent. Of this kind are all those which relate to security and protection.

From this short review it will be easy to distinguish between that class of natural rights which man retains after entering into society and those which he throws into the common stock as a member of society.

The natural rights which he retains are all those in which the *power* to execute is as perfect in the individual as the right itself. Among this class, as is before mentioned, are all the intellectual rights, or rights of the mind; consequently religion is one of those rights. The natural rights which are not retained, are all those in which, though the right is perfect in the individual, the power to excute them is defective. They answer not his purpose. A man, by natural right, has a right to judge in his own cause; and so far as the right of the mind is concerned, he never surrenders it. But what availeth it him to judge, if he has not power to redress? He therefore deposits this right in the common stock of society, and takes the arm of society, of which he is a part, in preference and in addition to his own. Society *grants* him nothing. Every man is a proprietor in society, and draws on the capital as a matter of right.

## Questions: *Paine, Rights of Man*

1. Paine accuses Burke of an intemperate attack on "the French nation and the National Assembly." Does Paine himself, in the selection you have read, appear to be free from the vituperative tendencies he deplores in Burke? How does his rhetoric affect his power to persuade us of the weakness of Burke's judgment and of the justness of his own?

   *Clues:* • The method [by which Burke denies basic rights] is of the same *marvellous* and *monstrous* kind with what he has already said;

   • ... the poison drawn from his horrid principles. ...

   • It is power, and not principles, that Mr. Burke venerates; and under this *abominable depravity* he is disqualified to judge between them.

   In this present age of catchwords and slogans the rhetoric of the left and right has been much in evidence (for example, "Power to the People," "America, Love it or Leave it"). Can you detect any resemblances between political language as it is used today and as it was used by Burke and Paine?

2. Paine, opposing Burke's emphasis on the binding force of tradition and precedent, bases the right of each generation to determine its mode of existence on the fact that "The circumstances of the world are continually changing, and the opinions of men change also; and as government is for the living, and not for the dead, it is the living only that has any right in it." Why may such a viewpoint justly be characterized as *revolutionary?* What assumptions about progress, the validity of tradition, and the generational bond, and about the constancy of human nature are implicitly challenged?

3. Paine characterizes Lafayette's words "For a nation to love liberty, it is sufficient that she knows it; and to be free, it is sufficient that she wills it" as "clear, concise, and soul-animating sentiments" in contrast to the "ineffectual, though gay with flowers" contentions of Burke. Lafayette's statement is certainly concise. Is it, in fact, clear? Explain your answer. What sort of persons would be likely to find it "soul-animating"? Paine says of Burke's expressions that they leave one "with music in the ear, and nothing in the heart." Might this criticism be justifiably made of Lafayette's words? Why or why not?

4. In refuting Burke's criticism that the Revolution was unjustly directed against a relatively moderate king, Paine contends that "Mr. Burke does not attend to the distinction between *men* and *principles*; and therefore, he does not see that a revolt may take place against the despotism of the latter, while there lies no charge of despotism against the former." Burke is here indirectly accused of putting men before principles. What evidence is there that Paine is erring in the opposite direction?

   *Clues:* • These [despotic] principles had not their origin in him [Louis XVI] but in the original establishment, many centuries back; and they were become too deeply rooted to be removed, and the Augean stable of parasites and plunderers too abominably filthy to be cleansed, by anything short of a complete and universal revolution. When it becomes necessary to do a thing, the *whole heart and soul should go into the measure*, or not attempt it.

   • . . . M. de la Fayette had a second time to interpose between the parties, the event of which was that the *Garde du Corps* put on the national cockade, and the matter ended as by oblivion, *after the loss of two or three lives.*

5. Why could Burke's lament for the death of chivalry be expected to arouse Paine's antipathy? Although Paine uses the term *Quixote* in the pejorative sense— with the connotations of absurd, anachronistic, foolishly misguided if not demented idealism—what positive attributes in the term might Burke have used to defend his viewpoint? (Paine does not quote what immediately follows upon the mention that "the age of chivalry is gone": "That of sophisters, oeconomists, and calculators, has succeeded . . .")

6. How convincing are the following arguments of Paine with regard to the acts of bloodshed growing out of the expedition of the mob to Versailles and the ultimate return of the royal family to Paris?
   a. If the mob are cruel, it is because governments have set them a bad example: "It is their sanguinary punishments which corrupt mankind."
   b. Restraint is an inappropriate response when anger and fear prevail: "When men are sore with the sense of oppressions, and menaced with the prospect of new ones, is the calmness of philosophy or the palsy of insensibility to be looked for?"

What general questions about moral reponsibility in revolutionary action are raised by these arguments?

## EXERCISE

Discuss how the central difference in political viewpoints between Burke and Paine is clarified by their conceptions of the reasons why men abrogate some *natural rights* in *civil society*. Note the following statements:

Burke:    One of the first motives to civil society, and which becomes one of its fundamental rules, is, *that no man should be judge in his own cause.* By this each person has at once divested himself of the first fundamental right of un-covenanted man, that is, to judge for himself, and to assert his own cause. He abdicates all right to be his own governor. He inclusively, in a great measure, abandons the right of self-defence, the first law of nature. Man cannot enjoy the rights of an uncivil and of a civil state together. That he may obtain justice he gives up his right of determining what is in points the most essential to him. That he may secure some liberty, he makes a surrender in trust of the whole of it.

Paine:    The natural rights which are not retained, are all those in which, though the right is perfect in the individual, the power to execute them is defective. They answer not his purpose. A man, by natural right, has a right to judge in his own cause; and so far as the right of the mind is concerned, he never surrenders it. But what availeth him to judge, if he has not power to redress? He therefore deposits this right in the common stock of society, and takes the arm of society, of which he is a part, in preference and in addition to his own. Society *grants* him nothing. Every man is a proprietor in society, and draws on the capital as a matter of right.

## *William Wordsworth (1770–1850)*
# To Toussaint L'Ouverture

*This poem was published in the* Morning Post *of February 2, 1803, at a time when Pierre Dominique Toussaint (called "L'Ouverture"), a leader of the Black revolt against French rule in Haiti, was imprisoned in Paris. Originally a slave, Toussaint educated himself and became a central force in the emancipation movement, a leader in securing British withdrawal from Haiti, and ultimately the governor of Santo Domingo. After Napoleon in 1802 moved to curb his power, Toussaint was captured and imprisoned. He died in a dungeon in the Jura, in eastern France, the very year Wordsworth's poem appeared.*

> Toussaint, the most unhappy man of men!
> Whether the whistling Rustic tend his plough
> Within thy hearing, or thy head be now

Pillowed in some deep dungeon's earless den;—
O miserable Chieftain! where and when                    5
Wilt thou find patience? Yet die not; do thou
Wear rather in thy bonds a cheerful brow:
Though fallen thyself, never to rise again
Live, and take comfort. Thou hast left behind
Powers that will work for thee; air, earth, and skies;   10
There's not a breathing of the common wind
That will forget thee; thou hast great allies;
Thy friends are exultations, agonies,
And love, and man's unconquerable mind.

QUESTIONS: *Wordsworth, "To Toussaint L'Ouverture"*

1. How do *paradox, alliteration,* and *personification* in line 4 help to characterize
   Toussaint's plight? What is the effect of certain other paradoxes in suggesting
   the rebel's present condition and future fate?
   *Clues:*  • Toussaint [All Saints] . . . man of men!

             • O miserable Chieftain! . . .

             • Thy friends are exultations, agonies,

2. How does nature imagery function to suggest the quality and scope of Toussaint's
   achievements? Compare the handling here with that in Wordsworth's sonnet
   to Milton, "London, 1802," as, for example, in the lines:
   Thou hadst a voice whose sound was *like the sea:*
   Pure as the *naked heavens,* majestic, free,
   So didst thou travel on life's common way,
   In *cheerful godliness;* [Editor's italics]

3. What significance do you attach to the order in the last line? Does the reliance
   on the power of "man's unconquerable mind"—the ultimate consolation extended by Wordsworth—suggest a rejection of the revolutionary impulse or an
   affirmation of its ultimately most effective manifestation?

*Percy Bysshe Shelley (1792–1822)*

# Song to the Men of England and England in 1819

*Both of the following poems were written in the post-Napoleonic period of
economic depression and political repression. The reference in line 7 of "England in 1819" is to the "Peterloo" massacre of August 16 in which working
men and women peacefully assembled in St. Peter's Fields in Manchester to
petition for political reforms were fired upon by the militia, several being killed
and hundreds wounded.*

## Song to the Men of England

### I

Men of England, wherefore plough
For the lords who lay ye low?
Wherefore weave with toil and care
The rich robes your tyrants wear?

### II

Wherefore feed, and clothe, and save,                    5
From the cradle to the grave,
Those ungrateful drones who would
Drain your sweat—nay, drink your blood?

### III

Wherefore, Bees of England, forge
Many a weapon, chain, and scourge,                       10
That these stingless drones may spoil
The forced produce of your toil?

### IV

Have ye leisure, comfort, calm,
Shelter, food, love's gentle balm?
Or what is it ye buy so dear                             15
With your pain and with your fear?

### V

The seed ye sow, another reaps;
The wealth ye find, another keeps;
The robes ye weave, another wears;
The arms ye forge, another bears.                        20

### VI

Sow seed,—but let no tyrant reap;
Find wealth,—let no impostor heap;
Weave robes,—let not the idle wear;
Forge arms,—in your defence to bear.

## VII

Shrink to your cellars, holes, and cells;                    25
In halls ye deck another dwells.
Why shake the chains ye wrought? Ye see
The steel ye tempered glance on ye.

## VIII

With plough and spade, and hoe and loom
Trace your grave, and build your tomb,                    30
And weave your winding-sheet, till fair
England be your sepulchre.

*Shelley, "Song to the Men of England"*

QUESTIONS:

1. Why is the image that Shelley uses in stanzas II and III to convey the position of the English working class in 1819 an appropriate one for his purposes? In what sense are the drones "ungrateful," "stingless"? Do the expressions "drain your sweat" and "drink your blood" continue to develop the image?

2. Shelley is writing of a contemporary situation. What effect does he achieve by using a vocabulary that suggests earlier times ("robes," "tyrants," "halls ye deck," "shake the chains")?

3. How do repetition and the choice of verbs (mood and tense) emphasize the *para-doxical* situation that is central to the poem?

4. What is Shelley's initial suggestion to the working class in stanza VI? How would you characterize it? Can one reconcile the mood of the last two stanzas with that of stanza VI?

## ENGLAND IN 1819

An old, mad, blind, despised, and dying king,[1]—
Princes, the dregs of their dull race, who flow
Through public scorn,—mud from a muddy spring,—
Rulers who neither see, nor feel, nor know,
But leech-like to their fainting country cling,                    5
Till they drop, blind in blood, without a blow,—
A people starved and stabbed in the untilled field,—
An army, which liberticide and prey
Makes as a two-edged sword to all who wield,—
Golden[2] and sanguine laws which tempt and slay;                    10
Religion Christless, Godless—a book sealed;
A Senate,—Time's worst statute[3] unrepealed,—
Are graves, from which a glorious Phantom may
Burst, to illumine our tempestuous day.

[1] *king:* George III (1738–1820).    [2] *Golden:* the result of bribes.    [3] *Time's worst statute:* law discriminating against Catholics.

## QUESTIONS: *Shelley, "England in 1819"*

1. What is the central *subject* of the poem? What universal *theme* underlies the handling of this subject (as the final paradox makes clear)? What general view of revolution does such a handling suggest?
2. Why may the poem be called *one* extended metaphor? Explain.
3. What do the following *devices* contribute to the treatment of the theme?
   a. Enumeration (of persons, classes, institutions).
   b. References to sight and light (for example, "Rulers who neither see," "blind in blood," "illumine our tempestuous day").
   c. References to manifestations of disease and death (for example, "mad," "leech-like," "fainting," "liberticide").
   d. Ironic contrasts (for example, "despised . . . king," "Princes, the dregs," "muddy spring," "Rulers who . . . cling," "book sealed").
   e. Alliteration and repetition.
4. What in the handling of mood and theme in this poem might lead us to assume that its author also wrote "Song to the Men of England"? Might one make a case for a different authorship? On what evidence? Which of the two poems is the more directly appealing and why? Which is the greater work of art and why?

## *Thomas Carlyle (1795–1881)*
# The French Revolution

*The following two chapters deal with the same incident in the early days of the French Revolution that concerns Burke and Paine in the selections of their work included here. The reading of all three selections together would therefore be most appropriate.*

*Several factors (as Paine partly makes clear) contributed to the march mainly of Paris women and members of the National Guard to Versailles on October 5, 1789: Louis XVI's failure to ratify the August reform decrees and the Declaration of the Rights of Man passed by the National Assembly; a critical economic situation (unemployment was high, and a scarcity of bread demanded immediate action); the insulting behavior of royal officers during a regimental banquet, when they trampled on the national cockade. Despite the threat of violence on this day, no incident occurred, Lafayette's arrival in the evening being a good influence for order, along with the king's acceptance of the Assembly decrees. The next day, October 6, proved to be the tumultuous one.*

*The three following paragraphs, a modern account of the material Carlyle deals with here, are from Volume II, Chapter 7 of Georges Lefebvre's* The French Revolution, *translated by Elizabeth Moss Evanson (Columbia University Press, New York, 1962), and should serve as an interesting counterpoint to Carlyle's text:*

"*The next morning demonstrators entered the courtyard and were stopped by the bodyguard. A scuffle ensued. One worker and several guards were killed. The mob found its way to the queen's antechamber, but she escaped, fleeing to the king. The National Guards finally arrived and cleared out the palace. Lafayette appeared on the balcony with the royal family. They were hailed, but with cries of 'To Paris!' Louis gave in, and the Assembly declared it would follow him.*

"*At one o'clock the bizarre procession set out. The National Guards first, with bread stuck on their bayonets; then wagons of wheat and flour garnished with leaves, followed by market porters and the women, sometimes sitting on horses or cannons; next the disarmed bodyguard, the Swiss, and the Flanders Regiment; the carriages bearing the king and his family with Lafayette riding beside the doors; carriages of one hundred deputies representing the Assembly; more National Guards; and finally, the crowd bringing up the rear. They forged ahead willy-nilly through the mud. It was raining, and day gave way to night at an early hour. Insensitive to the gloom, the people, appeased and confident for the moment, rejoiced in their victory. They had brought back 'the baker, the baker's wife, and the baker's boy'.*

"*The king was welcomed by Bailly, who led him to the Hotel de Ville; then he retired to the Tuileries. The Assembly did not leave Versailles until October 19. After sitting first in the archbishop's residence, on November 9 it was installed in a hastily redecorated riding school adjoining the Tuileries.*"

# VOLUME I, BOOK VII, CHAPTER X

## THE GRAND ENTRIES

The dull dawn of a new morning, drizzly and chill, had but broken over Versailles, when it pleased Destiny that a Bodyguard should look out of a window, on the right wing of the Château, to see what prospect there was in Heaven and in Earth. Rascality male and female is prowling in view of him. His fasting stomach is, with good cause, sour; he perhaps can not forbear a passing malison[1] on them; least of all can he forbear answering such.

Ill words breed worse: till the worst word come; and then the ill deed. Did the maledicent Bodyguard, getting (as was too inevitable) better malediction than he gave, load his musketoon, and threaten to fire; nay actually fire? Were wise who wist! It stands asserted; to us not credibly. But be this as it may, menaced Rascality, in whinnying scorn, is shaking at all Grates: the fastening of one (some write, it was a chain merely) gives way; Rascality is in the Grand Court, whinnying louder still.

The maledicent Bodyguard, more Bodyguards than he do now give fire; a man's arm is shattered. Lecointre will depose that "the Sieur Cardine, a

---

[1] *malison:* curse.

National Guard without arms, was stabbed." But see, sure enough, poor Jérôme l'Héritier, an unarmed National Guard he too, "cabinet-maker, a saddler's son, of Paris," with the down of youthhood still on his chin—he reels death-stricken; rushes to the pavement, scattering it with his blood and brains!—Alleleu! Wilder than Irish wake rises the howl; of pity, of infinite revenge. In few moments, the Grate of the inner and inmost Court, which they name Court of Marble, this too is forced, or surprised, and bursts open: the Court of Marble too is overflowed: up the Grand Staircase, up all stairs and entrances rushes the living Deluge! Deshuttes and Varigny, the two sentry Bodyguards, are trodden down, are massacred with a hundred pikes. Women snatch their cutlasses, or any weapon, and storm-in Menadic[2] —other women lift the corpse of shot Jerome; lay it down on the Marble steps; there shall the livid face and smashed head, dumb forever, speak.

Wo now to all Bodyguards, mercy is none for them! Miomandre de Sainte-Marie pleads with soft words, on the Grand Staircase, "descending four steps"—to the roaring tornado. His comrades snatch him up, by the skirts and belts; literally, from the jaws of Destruction; and slam-to their Door. This also will stand few instants; the panels shivering in, like potsherds.[3] Barricading serves not: fly fast, ye Bodyguards: rabid Insurrection, like the Hellhound Chase, uproaring at your heels!

The terror-struck Bodyguards fly, bolting and barricading; it follows. Whitherward? Through hall on hall: wo, now! toward the Queen's Suite of Rooms, in the farthest room of which the Queen is now asleep. Five sentinels rush through that long Suite; they are in the Anteroom knocking loud: "Save the Queen!" Trembling women fall at their feet with tears: are answered: "Yes, we will die; save ye the Queen!"

Tremble not, women, but haste: for, lo, another voice shouts far through the outermost door, "Save the Queen!" and the door is shut. It is brave Miomandre's voice that shouts this second warning. He has stormed across imminent death to do it; fronts imminent death, having done it. Brave Tardivet du Repaire, bent on the same desperate service, was borne down with pikes; his comrades hardly snatched him in again alive. Miomandre and Tardivet: let the names of these two Bodyguards, as the names of brave men should, live long.

Trembling Maids-of-Honour, one of whom from afar caught glimpse of Miomandre as well as heard him, hastily wrap the Queen; not in robes of state. She flies for her life, across the Œil-de-Bœuf; against the main door of which too Insurrection batters. She is in the King's Apartment, in the King's arms; she clasps her children amid a faithful few. The Imperial-hearted bursts into mother's tears: "O my friends, save me and my children; O mes amis, sauvez-moi et mes enfans!" The battering of Insurrectionary axes clangs audible across the Œil-de-Bœuf. What an hour!

[2] *Menadic:* like the maenads, fierce women who participated in the Dionysian rites.
[3] *potsherds:* fragments of pottery.

Yes, Friends; a hideous fearful hour; shameful alike to Governed and Governor; wherein Governed and Governor ignominiously testify that their relation is at an end. Rage, which had brewed itself in twenty thousand hearts for the last four-and-twenty hours, has taken fire: Jérôme's brained corpse lies there as live-coal. It is, as we said, the infinite Element bursting in; wild-surging through all corridors and conduits.

Meanwhile the poor Bodyguards have got hunted mostly into the Œil-de-Bœuf. They may die there, at the King's threshold; they can do little to defend it. They are heaping tabourets (stools of honour), benches and all movables against the door; at which the axe of Insurrection thunders.—But did brave Miomandre perish, then, at the Queen's outer door? No, he was fractured, slashed, lacerated, left for dead; he has nevertheless crawled hither; and shall live, honoured of loyal France. Remark also, in flat contradiction to much which has been said and sung, that Insurrection did not burst that door he had defended; but hurried elsewhither, seeking new Bodyguards.

Poor Bodyguards, with their Thyestes Opera-Repast![4] Well for them that Insurrection has only pikes and axes; no right sieging-tools! It shakes and thunders. Must they all perish miserably, and Royalty with them? Deshuttes and Varigny, massacred at the first inbreak, have been beheaded in the Marble Court; a sacrifice to Jérôme's manes:[5] Jourdan with the tile-beard did that duty willingly; and asked, If there were no more? Another captive they are leading round the corpse, with howl-chantings: may not Jourdan again tuck-up his sleeves?

And louder and louder rages Insurrection within, plundering if it can not kill; louder and louder it thunders at the Œil-de-Bœuf: what can now hinder its bursting-in?—On a sudden it ceases; the battering has ceased! Wild-rushing; the cries grow fainter; there is silence, or the tramp of regular steps; then a friendly knocking: "We are the Centre Grenadiers, old Gardes Françaises: Open to us, Messieurs of the Garde-du-Corps; we have not forgotten how you saved us at Fontenoy!" The door is opened; enter Captain Gondran and the Centre Grenadiers: there are military embracings; there is sudden deliverance from death into life.

Strange Sons of Adam! It was to "exterminate" these Gardes-du-Corps that the Centre Grenadiers left home: and now they have rushed to save them from extermination. The memory of common peril, of old help, melts the rough heart; bosom is clasped to bosom, not in war. The King shows himself, one moment, through the door of his Apartment, with: "Do not hurt my Guards!"—"Soyons frères, Let us be brothers!" cries Captain Gondran; and again dashes off, with levelled bayonets, to sweep the Palace clear.

---

[4] *Thyestes Opera-Repast:* the gruesome revenge by which Thyestes was fed the flesh of his own children by his brother (whose wife he had seduced) begins the tragic history of the house of Atreus. The banquet alluded to here was given by the officers in the Opera Hall at Versailles five days before the events here described.

[5] *manes:* spirits of the dead.

Now too Lafayette, suddenly roused, not from sleep (for his eyes had not yet closed), arrives; with passionate popular eloquence, with prompt military word of command. National Guards, suddenly roused, by sound of trumpet and alarmdrum, are all arriving. The death-melly ceases: the first sky-lambent blaze of Insurrection is got damped down; it burns now, if unextinguished yet flameless, as charred coals do, and not inextinguishable. The King's Apartments are safe. Ministers, Officials, and even some loyal National Deputies are assembling round their Majesties. The consternation will, with sobs and confusion, settle down gradually, into plan and counsel, better or worse.

But glance now, for a moment, from the royal windows! A roaring sea of human heads, inundating both Courts; billowing against all passages: Menadic women; infuriated men, mad with revenge, with love of mischief, love of plunder! Rascality has slipped its muzzle; and now bays, three-throated, like the Dog of Erebus. Fourteen Bodyguards are wounded; two massacred, and as we saw, beheaded; Jourdan asking, "Was it worth while to come so far for two?" Hapless Deshuttes and Varigny! Their fate surely was sad. Whirled down so suddenly to the abyss; as men are suddenly, by the wide thunder of the Mountain Avalanche, awakened not by them, awakened far off by others! When the Château Clock last struck, they two were pacing languid, with poised musketoon; anxious mainly that the next hour would strike. It has struck; to them inaudible. Their trunks lie mangled: their heads parade, "on pikes twelve feet long," through the streets of Versailles; and shall, about noon, reach the Barriers of Paris—a too ghastly contradiction to the large comfortable Placards that have been posted there!

The other captive Bodyguard is still circling the corpse of Jérôme, amid Indian war-whooping; bloody Tilebeard, with tucked sleeves, brandishing his bloody axe; when Gondran and the Grenadiers come in sight. "Comrades, will you see a man massacred in cold blood?"—"Off, butchers!" answer they; and the poor Bodyguard is free. Busy runs Gondran, busy run Guards and Captains; scouring all corridors; dispersing Rascality and Robbery; sweeping the Palace clear. The mangled carnage is removed; Jérôme's body to the Town-hall, for inquest: the fire of Insurrection gets damped, more and more, into measurable, manageable heat.

Transcendent things of all sorts, as in the general outburst of multitudinous Passion, are huddled together; the ludicrous, nay the ridiculous, with the horrible. Far over the billowy sea of heads, may be seen Rascality, caprioling on horses from the Royal Stud. The Spoilers these; for Patriotism is always infected so, with a proportion of mere thieves and scoundrels. Gondran snatched their prey from them in the Château; whereupon they hurried to the Stables, and took horse there. But the generous Diomedes'[6]

----

[6] *Diomedes:* king of Thrace, slain by Hercules during the eighth labor to obtain his man-eating horses.

steeds, according to Weber, disdained such scoundrel-burden; and, flinging-up their royal heels, did soon project most of it, in parabolic curves, to a distance, amid peals of laughter; and were caught. Mounted National Guards secured the rest.

Now too is witnessed the touching last-flicker of Etiquette; which sinks not here, in the Cimmerian[7] World-wreckage, without a sign; as the house-cricket might still chirp in the pealing of a Trump of Doom. "Monsieur," said some Master of Ceremonies (one hopes it might be De Brézé), as Lafayette, in these fearful moments, was rushing toward the inner Royal Apartments, "Monsieur, le Roi vous accorde les grandes entrées, Monsieur, the King grants you the Grand Entries"—not finding it convenient to refuse them!

## FROM CHAPTER XI

### FROM VERSAILLES

However, the Paris National Guard, wholly under arms, has cleared the Palace, and even occupies the nearer external spaces; extruding miscellaneous Patriotism, for most part, into the Grand Court, or even into the Fore-court.

The Bodyguards, you can observe, have now of a verity "hoisted the National Cockade"; for they step forward to the windows or balconies, hat aloft in hand, on each hat a huge tricolor; and fling over their bandoleers in sign of surrender; and shout "Vive la Nation!" To which how can the generous heart respond but with, "Vive le Roi; vivent les Gardes-du-Corps"? His Majesty himself has appeared with Lafayette on the balcony, and again appears: "Vive le Roi!" greets him from all throats; but also from some one throat is heard "Le Roi à Paris, The King to Paris!"

Her Majesty too, on demand, shows herself, though there is peril in it: she steps out on the balcony, with her little boy and girl. "No children, Point d'enfans!" cry the voices. She gently pushes back her children; and stands alone, her hands serenely crossed on her breast: "Should I die," she had said, "I will do it." Such serenity of heroism has its effect. Lafayette, with ready wit, in his highflown chivalrous way, takes that fair queenly hand, and, reverently kneeling, kisses it: thereupon the people do shout "Vive la Reine!" Nevertheless, poor Weber "saw" (or even thought he saw; for hardly the third part of poor Weber's experiences, in such hysterical days, will stand scrutiny) "one of these brigands level his musket at her Majesty"—with or without intention to shoot; for another of the brigands "angrily struck it down."

So that all, and the Queen herself, nay the very Captain of the Bodyguards, have grown National! The very Captain of the Bodyguards steps out now with Lafayette. On the hat of the repentant man is an enormous tricolor;

[7] *Cimmerian:* dark and gloomy; a mythical people said by Homer to dwell in such a realm.

large as a soup-platter or sunflower; visible to the utmost Forecourt. He takes the National Oath with a loud voice, elevating his hat; at which sight all the army raise their bonnets on their bayonets; with shouts. Sweet is reconcilement to the heart of man. Lafayette has sworn Flandre; he swears the remaining Bodyguards, down in the Marble Court; the people clasp them in their arms: O my brothers, why would ye force us to slay you? Behold, there is joy over you, as over returning prodigal sons!—The poor Bodyguards, now National and tricolor, exchange bonnets, exchange arms; there shall be peace and fraternity. And still "Vive le Roi"; and also "Le Roi à Paris," not now from one throat, but from all throats as one, for it is the heart's wish of all mortals.

Yes, The King to Paris: what else? Ministers may consult, and National Deputies wag their heads: but there is now no other possibility. You have forced him to go willingly. "At one o'clock!" Lafayette gives audible assurance to that purpose; and universal Insurrection, with immeasurable shout, and a discharge of all the fire-arms, clear and rusty, great and small, that it has, returns him acceptance. What a sound; heard for leagues: a doom-peal!—That sound too rolls away; into the Silence of Ages. And the Château of Versailles stands ever since vacant, hushed-still; its spacious Courts grassgrown, responsive to the hoe of the weeder. Times and generations roll on, in their confused Gulf-current; and buildings, like builders, have their destiny.

Till one o'clock, then, there will be three parties, National Assembly, National Rascality, National Royalty, all busy enough. Rascality rejoices; women trim themselves with tricolor. Nay, motherly Paris has sent her Avengers sufficient "cartloads of loaves"; which are shouted over, which are gratefully consumed. The Avengers, in return, are searching for grainstores; loading them in fifty wagons; that so a National King, probable harbinger of all blessings, may be the evident bringer of plenty, for one.

And thus has Sansculottism[8] made prisoner its King; revoking his parole. The Monarchy has fallen; and not so much as honourably: no, ignominiously; with struggle, indeed, oft-repeated; but then with unwise struggle; wasting its strength in fits and paroxysms; at every new paroxysm foiled more pitifully than before. . . .

Now, however, the short hour has struck. His Majesty is in his carriage, with his Queen, sister Elizabeth and two royal children. Not for another hour can the infinite Procession get marshalled and under way. The weather is dim drizzling; the mind confused; the noise great.

Processional marches not a few our world has seen; Roman triumphs and

---

[8] *Sansculottism:* The term *sansculottes* was first applied to the revolutionaries by the aristocrats in reference to their exchanging of breeches for long pants and later adopted by the revolutionaries as a term designating patriotism.

ovations, Cabiric[9] cymbal-beatings, Royal progresses, Irish funerals; but this of the French Monarchy marching to its bed remained to be seen. Miles long, and of breadth losing itself in vagueness, for all the neighbouring country crowds to see. Slow; stagnating along, like shoreless Lake, yet with a noise like Niagara, like Babel and Bedlam. A splashing and a tramping; a hurrahing, uproaring, musket-volleying—the truest segment of Chaos seen in these latter Ages! Till slowly it disembogue itself, in the thickening dusk, into expectant Paris, through a double row of faces all the way from Passy to the Hôtel-de-Ville.

Consider this: Vanguard of National troops; with trains of artillery; of pikemen and pikewomen, mounted on cannons, on carts, hackney-coaches, or on foot—tripudiating, in tricolor ribbons from head to heel; loaves stuck on the points of bayonets, green boughs stuck in gun-barrels. Next, as main-march, "fifty cart-loads of corn," which have been lent, for peace, from the stores of Versailles. Behind which follow stragglers of the Garde-du-Corps; all humiliated, in Grenadier bonnets. Close on these comes the Royal Carriage; come Royal Carriages: for there are a Hundred National Deputies too, among whom sits Mirabeau—his remarks not given. Then finally, pellmell, as rear-guard, Flandre, Swiss, Hundred Swiss, other Bodyguards, Brigands, whosoever can not get before. Between and among all which masses flows without limit Saint-Antoine and the Menadic Cohort. Menadic especially about the Royal Carriage: tripudiating there, covered with tri-color; singing "allusive songs"; pointing with one hand to the Royal Carriage, which the allusions hit, and pointing to the Provision-wagons with the other hand, and these words: "Courage, Friends! We shall not want bread now; we are bringing you the Baker, the Bakeress and Baker's-boy (le Boulanger, la Boulangère et le petit Mitron)."

The wet day draggles the tricolor, but the joy is unextinguishable. Is not all well now? "Ah, Madame, notre bonne Reine," said some of these Strong-women some days hence, "Ah, Madame, our good Queen, don't be a traitor any more (ne soyez plus traître), and we will all love you!" Poor Weber went splashing along, close by the Royal Carriage, with the tear in his eye: "their Majesties did me the honour," or I thought they did it, "to testify, from time to time, by shrugging of the shoulders, by looks directed to Heaven, the emotions they felt." Thus, like frail cockle, floats the royal Lifeboat, helmless, on black deluges of Rascality.

Mercier, in his loose way, estimates the Procession and assistants at two hundred thousand. He says it was one boundless inarticulate Haha—transcendent World-Laughter; comparable to the Saturnalia of the Ancients. Why not? Here too, as we said, is Human Nature once more human; shudder at it whoso is of shuddering humour; yet, behold, it is human. It has "swallowed all formulas"; it tripudiates even so. For which reason they that collect Vases and Antiques, with figures of Dancing Bacchantes "in wild and all-but impossible positions," may look with some interest on it.

---

[9] *Cabiric:* pertaining to magical beings worshiped on the islands of Lemnos and Samothrace.

Thus, however, has the slow-moving Chaos, or modern Saturnalia of the Ancients, reached the Barrier; and must halt, to be harangued by Mayor Bailly. Thereafter it has to lumber along, between the double row of faces, in the transcendent heaven-lashing Haha: two hours longer, toward the Hôtel-de-Ville. Then again to be harangued there, by several persons; by Moreau de Saint-Méry among others; Moreau of the Three-thousand orders, now National Deputy for St. Domingo. To all which poor Louis, "who seemed to experience a slight emotion" on entering this Townhall, can answer only that he "comes with pleasure, with confidence among his people." Mayor Bailly, in reporting it, forgets "confidence"; and the poor Queen says eagerly: "Add, with confidence."—"Messieurs," rejoins Mayor Bailly, "you are happier than if I had not forgotten."

Finally, the King is shown on an upper balcony, by torchlight, with a huge tricolor in his hat: "and all the people," says Weber, "grasped one another's hand"—thinking now surely the New Era was born. Hardly till eleven at night can Royalty get to its vacant, long-deserted Palace of the Tuileries; to lodge there, somewhat in strolling-player fashion. It is Tuesday the 6th of October, 1789.

Poor Louis has Two other Paris Processions to make: one ludicrous-ignominious like this; the other not ludicrous nor ignominious, but serious, nay sublime.

## QUESTIONS: *Carlyle, The French Revolution*

1. Carlyle's account is obviously an attempt at *re-creating* events rather than presenting an objective historical narrative. What is he interested in doing besides generating the kind of excitement that gives a reader the sense of direct participation in tumultuous happenings at a particular time? Consider the effect he achieves by the use of the following devices:

   a. Abstractions (and capitalizations) in his treatment of events and human behavior.

   Clues:   • . . . rabid Insurrection, like the Hellhound Chase, uproaring at your heels!

   • It is, as we said, the infinite Element bursting in . . .

   • And thus has Sansculottism made prisoner its King; revoking his parole.

   • Thus, like frail cockle, floats the royal Lifeboat, helmless, on black deluges of Rascality.

   b. Mythological and Biblical references.

   Clues:   • . . . up the Grand Staircase, up all stairs and entrances rushes the living Deluge!

   • Women . . . storm-in Menadic. . . .

   • Poor Bodyguards, with their Thyestes Opera-Repast!

   • Strange Sons of Adam!

   • Rascality . . . now bays, three-throated, like the Dog of Erebus.

   • . . . with a noise like Niagara, like Babel and Bedlam.

   c. References to the past and future.
     *Clues:*  • And the Château of Versailles stands ever since vacant. . . .
            • Processional marches not a few our world has seen. . . .
   d. Imagery (especially of fire).

2. Where is Carlyle's sympathy for the victims of the onslaught tempered by a sense of irony suggesting the capacity for a wider vision? What is the attitude conveyed by the following sentences? "Far over the billowy sea of heads, may be seen Rascality, caprioling on horses from the Royal Stud. The Spoilers these; for Patriotism is always infected so, with a proportion of mere thieves and scoundrels."

3. Carlyle might well agree in many ways with Burke's treatment of this particular incident. What aspects of that treatment might he fail to sympathize with or find uncongenial? Explain.

*Ralph Waldo Emerson (1803–1882)*

# Speech at the Kansas Relief Meeting in Cambridge

## (Wednesday Evening, September 10, 1856)

*On January, 23, 1854, Stephen A. Douglas introduced in Congress an amendment to the bill organizing the territories of Kansas and Nebraska. It proposed to leave the question of slavery in these territories "and in the new States to be formed therefrom . . . to the decision of the people residing therein, through their appropriate representatives." Whereas the Compromise of 1850 had seemed to assure that these territories would remain "free," that is, that slavery would not be permitted within their borders, the entire question was thrown open again when the Kansas-Nebraska Act of 1854, incorporating Douglas' principle and repealing the antislavery provision of the Compromise, was passed on May 30.*

*Both the antislavery, or "free soil," North and the slave-owning South recognized that they had a vested interest in establishing a majority population in Kansas that would swing the plebiscite on slavery in the "right" direction. The abolitionist Eli Thayer organized the New England Emigrant Aid Company to assist free-soil immigration into Kansas. Proslavery Southern farmers moved in from Missouri. Violence between the two groups was the inevitable result.*

*Emerson, who in 1851 and 1854 had spoken out publicly against the Fugitive Slave Law provision of the Missouri Compromise, was again moved to take a public stand by the upheavals in Kansas.*

I regret, with all this company, the absence of Mr. Whitman of Kansas, whose narrative was to constitute the interest of this meeting. Mr. Whitman is not here; but knowing, as we all do, why he is not, what duties kept him at home, he is more than present. His vacant chair speaks for him. For quite other reasons, I had been wiser to have stayed at home, unskilled as I am to address a political meeting, but it is imposible for the most recluse to extricate himself from the questions of the times.

There is this peculiarity about the case of Kansas, that all the right is on one side. We hear the screams of hunted wives and children answered by the howl of the butchers. The testimony of the telegraphs from St. Louis and the border confirm the worst details. The printed letters of the border ruffians avow the facts. When pressed to look at the cause of the mischief in the Kansas laws, the President falters and declines the discussion; but his supporters in the Senate, Mr. Cass, Mr. Geyer, Mr. Hunter, speak out, and declare the intolerable atrocity of the code. It is a maxim that all party spirit produces the incapacity to receive natural impression from facts; and our recent political history has abundantly borne out the maxim. But these details that have come from Kansas are so horrible, that the hostile press have but one word in reply, namely, that it is all exaggeration, 't is an Abolition lie. Do the Committee of Investigation say that the outrages have been overstated? Does their dismal catalogue of private tragedies show it? Do the private letters? Is it an exaggeration, that Mr. Hopps of Somerville, Mr. Hoyt of Deerfield, Mr. Jennison of Groton, Mr. Phillips of Berkshire, have been murdered? That Mr. Robinson of Fitchburg has been imprisoned? Rev. Mr. Nute of Springfield seized, and up to this time we have no tidings of his fate?

In these calamities under which they suffer, and the worse which threaten them, the people of Kansas ask for bread, clothes, arms and men, to save them alive, and enable them to stand against these enemies of the human race. They have a right to be helped, for they have helped themselves.

This aid must be sent, and this is not to be doled out as an ordinary charity; but bestowed up to the magnitude of the want, and, as has been elsewhere said, "on the scale of a national action." I think we are to give largely, lavishly, to these men. And we must prepare to do it. We must learn to do with less, live in a smaller tenement, sell our apple-trees, our acres, our pleasant houses. I know people who are making haste to reduce their expenses and pay their debts, not with a view to new accumulations, but in preparation to save and earn for the benefit of the Kansas emigrants.

We must have aid from individuals,—we must also have aid from the State. I know that the last Legislature refused that aid. I know that lawyers hesitate on technical grounds, and wonder what method of relief the Legislature will apply. But I submit that, in a case like this, where citizens of Massachusetts, legal voters here, have emigrated to national territory under the sanction of every law, and are then set on by highwaymen, driven from their new homes, pillaged, and numbers of them killed and scalped, and the whole world knows that this is no accidental brawl, but a systematic war to the knife, and in defiance of all laws and liberties, I submit that the Governor and Legislature should neither slumber nor sleep till they have found out how to send effectual aid and comfort to these poor farmers, or else should resign their seats to those who can. But first let them hang the halls of the State House with black crape, and order funeral service to be said there for the citizens whom they were unable to defend.

We stick at the technical difficulties. I think there never was a people so choked and stultified by forms. We adore the forms of law, instead of making them vehicles of wisdom and justice. I like the primary assembly. I own I have little esteem for governments. I esteem them only good in the moment when they are established. I set the private man first. He only who is able to stand alone is qualified to be a citizen. Next to the private man, I value the primary assembly, met to watch the government and to correct it. That is the theory of the American State, that it exists to execute the will of the citizens, is always responsible to them, and is always to be changed when it does not. First, the private citizen, then the primary assembly, and the government last.

In this country for the last few years the government has been the chief obstruction to the common weal. Who doubts that Kansas would have been very well settled, if the United States had let it alone? The government armed and led the ruffians against the poor farmers. I do not know any story so gloomy as the politics of this country for the last twenty years, centralizing ever more manifestly round one spring, and that a vast crime, and ever more plainly, until it is notorious that all promotion, power and policy are dictated from one source,—illustrating the fatal effects of a false position to demoralize legislation and put the best people always at a disadvantage;—one crime always present, always to be varnished over, to find fine names for; and we free-statesmen, as accomplices to the guilt, ever in the power of the grand offender.

Language has lost its meaning in the universal cant. *Representative Government* is really misrepresentative; *Union* is a conspiracy against the Northern States which the Northern States are to have the privilege of paying for; the *adding of Cuba and Central America* to the slave marts is *enlarging the area of Freedom. Manifest Destiny, Democracy, Freedom,* fine names for an ugly thing. They call it otto of rose and lavender,—I call it bilge water. They call it Chivalry and Freedom; I call it the stealing all the earnings of a poor man and the earnings of his little girl and boy, and the earnings of all that shall come from him, his children's children forever.

But this is Union, and this is Democracy; and our poor people, led by the nose by these fine words, dance and sing, ring bells and fire cannon, with every new link of the chain which is forged for their limbs by the plotters in the Capitol.

What are the results of law and union? There is no Union. Can any citizen of Massachusetts travel in honor through Kentucky and Alabama and speak his mind? Or can any citizen of the Southern country who happens to think kidnapping a bad thing, say so? Let Mr. Underwood of Virginia answer. Is it to be supposed that there are no men in Carolina who dissent from the popular sentiment now reigning there? It must happen, in the variety of human opinions, that there are dissenters. They are silent as the grave. Are there no women in that country,—women, who always carry the conscience of a people? Yet we have not heard one discordant whisper.

In the free States, we give a snivelling support to slavery. The judges give cowardly interpretations to the law, in direct opposition to the known foundation of all law, that *every immoral statute is void.* And here of Kansas, the President says: "Let the complainants go to the courts;" though he knows that when the poor plundered farmer comes to the court, he finds the ringleader who has robbed him, dismounting from his own horse, and unbuckling his knife to sit as his judge.

The President told the Kansas Committee that the whole difficulty grew from "the factious spirit of the Kansas people, respecting institutions which they need not have concerned themselves about." A very remarkable speech from a Democratic President to his fellow citizens, that they are not to concern themselves with institutions which they alone are to create and determine. The President is a lawyer, and should know the statutes of the land. But I borrow the language of an eminent man, used long since, with far less occasion: "If that be law, let the ploughshare be run under the foundations of the Capitol";—and if that be Government, extirpation is the only cure.

I am glad to see that the terror at disunion and anarchy is disappearing. Massachusetts, in its heroic day, had no government—was an anarchy. Every man stood on his own feet, was his own governor; and there was no breach of peace from Cape Cod to Mount Hoosac. California, a few years ago, by the testimony of all people at that time in the country, had the best government that ever existed. Pans of gold lay drying outside of every man's tent, in perfect security. The land was measured into little strips of a few feet wide, all side by side. A bit of ground that your hand could cover was worth one or two hundred dollars, on the edge of your strip; and there was no dispute. Every man throughout the country was armed with knife and revolver, and it was known that instant justice would be administered to each offence, and perfect peace reigned. For the Saxon man, when he is well awake, is not a pirate but a citizen, all made of hooks and eyes, and links himself naturally to his brothers, as bees hook themselves to one another and to their queen in a loyal swarm.

But the hour is coming when the strongest will not be strong enough. A harder task will the new revolution of the nineteenth century be, than was the revolution of the eighteenth century. I think the American Revolution bought its glory cheap. If the problem was new, it was simple. If there were few people, they were united, and the enemy 3,000 miles off. But now, vast property, gigantic interests, family connections, webs of party, cover the land with a network that immensely multiplies the dangers of war.

Fellow Citizens, in these times full of the fate of the Republic, I think the towns should hold town meetings, and resolve themselves into Committees of Safety, go into permanent sessions, adjourning from week to week, from month to month. I wish we could send the Sergeant-at-arms to stop every American who is about to leave the country. Send home every one who is abroad, lest they should find no country to return to. Come home and stay at home, while there is a country to save. When it is lost it will be time enough then for any who are luckless enough to remain alive to gather up their clothes and depart to some land where freedom exists.

## QUESTIONS: *Emerson, "Speech at the Kansas Relief Meeting in Cambridge, Wednesday Evening, September 10, 1856"*

1. What resources of language does Emerson use to express feelings of sympathy and condemnation? How persuasive is this technique?

    Clues: • We hear the *screams* of hunted *wives* and *children* answered by the *howl* of the *butchers*.

    • . . . the people of Kansas ask for bread, clothes, arms and men, to save them alive, and enable them to stand against these *enemies of the human race*.

    • . . . our poor people, *led by the nose* by these fine words, dance and sing, ring bells and fire cannon, with every new link of the *chain* which is forged for their limbs by the *plotters in the Capitol*.

    • . . . the President says: "Let the complainants go to the courts;" though he knows that when the *poor plundered farmer* comes to the court, he finds the *ringleader* who has robbed him dismounting from *his own* horse, and *unbuckling his knife* to sit as his judge.

2. Emerson obviously has a profound faith in the capacity of men to regulate themselves without government interference. "Massachusetts, in its heroic day," he writes, "had no government—was an anarchy. Every man stood on his own feet, was his own governor; and there was no breach of peace. . . ." At the same time he concedes that the total repression of antislavery sentiment in the South is due to "the popular sentiment now reigning there," a view that might seem to call into question his belief in the spontaneous wisdom of the ungoverned masses. Does he provide any way of reconciling these positions?

    Clue: • If there were few people, they were united, and the enemy three thousand miles off. But now, vast property, gigantic interests, family connections, webs of party, cover the land with a network that immensely multiplies the dangers of war.

3. Emerson declares that "the new revolution of the nineteenth century" will be a "harder task" than the one which began in 1776. On the evidence of the speech, what might the nineteenth-century revolution be like and why would it be so difficult to achieve?

    Clues: • I own I have little esteem for governments. I esteem them only good *in the moment when they are established*.

    • In this country for *the last few years* the government has been the chief *obstruction* to the common weal.

- Language has lost its meaning in the universal cant. . . . the *adding of Cuba and Central America* to the slave marts is *enlarging the area of Freedom. Manifest Destiny, Democracy, Freedom,* fine names for an ugly thing. They call it otto of rose and lavender,—I call it bilge water.

- In the free States, we give a snivelling support to slavery.

- Massachusetts, in its heroic day, had no government—was an anarchy. Every man stood on his own feet, was his own governor; and there was no breach of peace from Cape Cod to Mount Hoosac.

4. Emerson writes: "For the Saxon man, when he is well awake, is not a pirate but a citizen, all made of hooks and eyes, and links himself naturally to his brothers, as bees hook themselves to one another and to their queen in a loyal swarm." Is the simile of the bees a good one? If so, why? If not, why not?

5. Emerson's concern over government, bureaucracy, and the debasement of official language, together with his forthright demand for decentralization, seem very modern. The statement "I am glad to see that the terror at disunion and anarchy is disappearing" could almost have been written by Abbie Hoffman or Jerry Rubin; the same is true of Emerson's declaration that "we adore the forms of law, instead of making them vehicles of wisdom and justice." Would you attribute this modernity (a) to the fact that figures like Hoffman and Rubin are finally moving to implement Emerson's "revolution" after a century of postponement or (b) to the fact that the American character before and after 1856 has consistently—and perhaps impractically—admired the values of individualism and self-rule, while distrusting all government as a form of "interference"?

6. Emerson passionately values liberty, distrusts all government, praises a Saxon anarchy in which every man is armed and capable of dispensing his own justice, and declares at one point: "He only who is able to stand alone is qualified to be a citizen." How do such views link him to a modern conservative or Minuteman-style militant? How can we resolve the contradiction suggested by the affinity of some of Emerson's views with the left (see question 5) and with the right?

## EXERCISES

1. Discuss the relevance at this time of Emerson's criticism of governmental use of language to attenuate or conceal its aims and activities.

2. Emerson and Thoreau were close friends. What evidence of affinity do you see in their writings and opinions?

## Henry David Thoreau (1817–1862)
# Civil Disobedience

I heartily accept the motto,—"That government is best which governs least;" and I should like to see it acted up to more rapidly and systematically. Carried out, it finally amounts to this, which also I believe,—"That government is best which governs not at all;" and when men are prepared for it, that will be the kind of government which they will have. Government is at best but an expedient; but most governments are usually, and all governments are sometimes, inexpedient. The objections which have been brought against a standing army, and they are many and weighty, and deserve to prevail, may also at last be brought against a standing government. The standing army is only an arm of the standing government. The government itself, which is only the mode which the people have chosen to execute their will, is equally liable to be abused and perverted before the people can act through it. Witness the present Mexican war, the work of comparatively a few individuals using the standing government as their tool; for, in the outset, the people would not have consented to this measure.

This American government,—what is it but a tradition, though a recent one, endeavoring to transmit itself unimpaired to posterity, but each instant losing some of its integrity? It has not the vitality and force of a single living man; for a single man can bend it to his will. It is a sort of wooden gun to the people themselves; and, if ever they should use it in earnest as a real one against each other, it will surely split. But it is not the less necessary for this; for the people must have some complicated machinery or other, and hear its din, to satisfy that idea of government which they have. Governments show thus how successfully men can be imposed on, even impose on themselves, for their own advantage. It is excellent, we must all allow; yet this government never of itself furthered any enterprise, but by the alacrity with which it got out of its way. *It* does not keep the country free. *It* does not settle the West. *It* does not educate. The character inherent in the American people has done all that has been accomplished; and it would have done somewhat more, if the government had not sometimes got in its way. For government is an expedient by which men would fain succeed in letting one another alone; and, as has been said, when it is most expedient, the governed are most let alone by it. Trade and commerce, if they were not made of India rubber, would never manage to bounce over the obstacles which legislators are continually putting in their way; and, if one were to judge these men wholly by the effects of their actions, and not partly by their intentions, they would deserve to be classed and punished with those mischievous persons who put obstructions on the railroads.

But, to speak practically and as a citizen, unlike those who call themselves no-government men, I ask for, not at once no government, but *at once* a better government. Let every man make known what kind of government would command his respect, and that will be one step toward obtaining it.

After all, the practical reason why, when the power is once in the hands of the people, a majority are permitted, and for a long period continue, to rule, is not because they are most likely to be in the right, nor because this seems fairest to the minority, but because they are physically the strongest. But a government in which the majority rule in all cases cannot be based on justice, even as far as men understand it. Can there not be a government in which majorities do not virtually decide right and wrong, but conscience?—in which majorities decide only those questions to which the rule of expediency is applicable? Must the citizen ever for a moment, or in the least degree, resign his conscience to the legislator? Why has every man a conscience, then? I think that we should be men first, and subjects afterward. It is not desirable to cultivate a respect for the law, so much as for the right. The only obligation which I have a right to assume, is to do at any time what I think right. It is truly enough said, that a corporation has no conscience; but a corporation of conscientious men is a corporation *with* a conscience. Law never made men a whit more just; and, by means of their respect for it, even the well-disposed are daily made the agents of injustice. A common and natural result of an undue respect for law is, that you may see a file of soldiers, colonel, captain, corporal, privates, powder-monkeys and all, marching in admirable order over hill and dale to the wars, against their wills, aye, against their common sense and consciences, which makes it very steep marching indeed, and produces a palpitation of the heart. They have no doubt that it is a damnable business in which they are concerned; they are all peaceably inclined. Now, what are they? Men at all? or small moveable forts and magazines, at the service of some unscrupulous man in power? Visit the Navy Yard, and behold a marine, such a man as an American government can make, or such as it can make a man with its black arts, a mere shadow and reminiscence of humanity, a man laid out alive and standing, and already, as one may say, buried under arms with funeral accompaniments, though it may be

> "Not a drum was heard, nor a funeral note,
>   As his corse to the ramparts we hurried;
> Not a soldier discharged his farewell shot
>   O'er the grave where our hero we buried."[1]

The mass of men serve the State thus, not as men mainly, but as machines, with their bodies. They are the standing army, and the militia, jailers, constables, *posse comitatus*, &c. In most cases there is no free exercise whatever of the judgment or of the moral sense; but they put themselves on a level with wood and earth and stones; and wooden men can perhaps be manufactured that will serve the purpose as well. Such command no more respect than men of straw, or a lump of dirt. They have the same sort of worth only as horses and dogs. Yet such as these even are commonly esteemed good citizens. Others, as most legislators, politicians, lawyers, ministers, and office-holders, serve the State chiefly with their heads; and, as they rarely make any moral distinctions, they are as likely to serve the devil, without intending it, as God. A very few, as heroes, patriots, martyrs, reformers in the great sense, and *men*, serve the State with their consciences also, and so necessarily resist it for the most part; and they are commonly treated by it as enemies. A wise man will only be useful as a man, and will not submit to

---

[1] The first lines of "Burial of Sir John Moore at Corunna," by Charles Wolfe (1791–1823).

be "clay," and "stop a hole to keep the wind away,"[2] but leave that office
to his dust at least:—

> "I am too high-born to be propertied,
> To be a secondary at control,
> Or useful serving-man and instrument
> To any sovereign state throughout the world."[3]

He who gives himself entirely to his fellow-men appears to them useless
and selfish; but he who gives himself partially to them is pronounced a
benefactor and philanthropist.

How does it become a man to behave toward this American government
to-day? I answer that he cannot without disgrace be associated with it. I
cannot for an instant recognize that political organization as *my* government
which is the *slave's* government also.

All men recognize the right of revolution; that is, the right to refuse
allegiance to and to resist the government, when its tyranny or its inefficiency
are great and unendurable. But almost all say that such is not the case now.
But such was the case, they think, in the Revolution of '75. If one were to
tell me that this was a bad government because it taxed certain foreign
commodities brought to its ports, it is most probable that I should not make
an ado about it, for I can do without them: all machines have their friction;
and possibly this does enough good to counterbalance the evil. At any rate,
it is a great evil to make a stir about it. But when the friction comes to have
its machine, and oppression and robbery are organized, I say, let us not
have such a machine any longer. In other words, when a sixth of the population of a nation which has undertaken to be the refuge of liberty are slaves,
and a whole country is unjustly overrun and conquered by a foreign army,
and subjected to military law, I think that it is not too soon for honest men
to rebel and revolutionize. What makes this duty the more urgent is the fact,
that the country so overrun is not our own, but ours is the invading army.

Paley, a common authority with many on moral questions, in his chapter
on the "Duty of Submission to Civil Government," resolves all civil obligation into expediency; and he proceeds to say, "that so long as the interest of
the whole society requires it, that is, so long as the established government
cannot be resisted or changed without public inconveniency, it is the will of
God that the established government be obeyed, and no longer."—"This
principle being admitted, the justice of every particular case of resistance is
reduced to a computation of the quantity of the danger and grievance on the
one side, and of the probability and expense of redressing it on the other."
Of this, he says, every man shall judge for himself. But Paley appears never
to have contemplated those cases to which the rule of expediency does not
apply, in which a people, as well as an individual, must do justice, cost what
it may. If I have unjustly wrested a plank from a drowning man, I must

[2] *Hamlet,* v, i, 236–37.  [3] *King John,* v, i, 79–82.

*334*

restore it to him though I drown myself. This, according to Paley, would be inconvenient. But he that would save his life, in such a case, shall lose it. This people must cease to hold slaves, and to make war on Mexico, though it cost them their existence as a people.

In their practice, nations agree with Paley; but does any one think that Massachusetts does exactly what is right at the present crisis?

> "A drab of state, a cloth-o'-silver slut,
> To have her train borne up, and her soul trail in the dirt."[4]

Practically speaking, the opponents to a reform in Massachusetts are not a hundred thousand politicians at the South, but a hundred thousand merchants and farmers here, who are more interested in commerce and agriculture than they are in humanity, and are not prepared to do justice to the slave and to Mexico, *cost what it may*. I quarrel not with far-off foes, but with those who, near at home, co-operate with, and do the bidding of those far away, and without whom the latter would be harmless. We are accustomed to say, that the mass of men are unprepared; but improvement is slow, because the few are not materially wiser or better than the many. It is not so important that many should be as good as you, as that there be some absolute goodness somewhere; for that will leaven the whole lump. There are thousands who are *in opinion* opposed to slavery and to the war, who yet in effect do nothing to put an end to them; who, esteeming themselves children of Washington and Franklin, sit down with their hands in their pockets, and say that they know not what to do, and do nothing; who even postpone the question of freedom to the question of free-trade, and quietly read the prices-current along with the latest advices from Mexico, after dinner, and, it may be, fall asleep over them both. What is the price-current of an honest man and patriot to-day? They hesitate, and they regret, and sometimes they petition; but they do nothing in earnest and with effect. They will wait, well disposed, for others to remedy the evil, that they may no longer have it to regret. At most, they give only a cheap vote, and a feeble countenance and God-speed, to the right, as it goes by them. There are nine hundred and ninety-nine patrons of virtue to one virtuous man; but it is easier to deal with the real possessor of a thing than with the temporary guardian of it.

All voting is a sort of gaming, like chequers or backgammon, with a slight moral tinge to it, a playing with right and wrong, with moral questions; and betting naturally accompanies it. The character of the voters is not staked. I cast my vote, perchance, as I think right; but I am not vitally concerned that that right should prevail. I am willing to leave it to the majority. Its obligation, therefore, never exceeds that of expediency. Even voting *for the right* is *doing* nothing for it. It is only expressing to men feebly your desire that it should prevail. A wise man will not leave the right to the mercy of chance, nor wish it to prevail through the power of the majority.

[4] Cyril Tourneur, *The Revenger's Tragedy,* iv, iv, 72–73.

There is but little virtue in the action of masses of men. When the majority shall at length vote for the abolition of slavery, it will be because they are indifferent to slavery, or because there is but little slavery left to be abolished by their vote. *They* will then be the only slaves. Only *his* vote can hasten the abolition of slavery who asserts his own freedom by his vote.

I hear of a convention to be held at Baltimore, or elsewhere, for the selection of a candidate for the Presidency, made up chiefly of editors, and men who are politicians by profession; but I think, what is it to any independent, intelligent, and respectable man what decision they may come to, shall we not have the advantage of his wisdom and honesty, nevertheless? Can we not count upon some independent votes? Are there not many individuals in the country who do not attend conventions? But no: I find that the respectable man, so called, has immediately drifted from his position, and despairs of his country, when his country has more reason to despair of him. He forthwith adopts one of the candidates thus selected as the only *available* one, thus proving that he is himself *available* for any purposes of the demagogue. His vote is of no more worth than that of any unprincipled foreigner or hireling native, who may have been bought. Oh for a man who is a *man*, and, as my neighbor says, has a bone in his back which you cannot pass your hand through! Our statistics are at fault: the population has been returned too large. How many *men* are there to a square thousand miles in this country? Hardly one. Does not America offer any inducement for men to settle here? The American has dwindled into an Odd Fellow,—one who may be known by the development of his organ of gregariousness, and a manifest lack of intellect and cheerful self-reliance; whose first and chief concern, on coming into the world, is to see that the alms-houses are in good repair; and, before yet he has lawfully donned the virile garb, to collect a fund for the support of the widows and orphans that may be; who, in short, ventures to live only by the aid of the mutual insurance company, which has promised to bury him decently.

It is not a man's duty, as a matter of course, to devote himself to the eradication of any, even the most enormous wrong; he may still properly have other concerns to engage him; but it is his duty, at least, to wash his hands of it, and, if he gives it no thought longer, not to give it practically his support. If I devote myself to other pursuits and contemplations, I must first see, at least, that I do not pursue them sitting upon another man's shoulders. I must get off him first, that he may pursue his contemplations too. See what gross inconsistency is tolerated. I have heard some of my townsmen say, "I should like to have them order me out to help put down an insurrection of the slaves, or to march to Mexico—see if I would go;" and yet these very men have each, directly by their allegiance, and so indirectly, at least by their money, furnished a substitute. The soldier is applauded who refuses to serve in an unjust war by those who do not refuse to sustain the unjust government which makes the war; is applauded by those whose own act and authority he disregards and sets at nought; as if the State were penitent to that degree that it hired one to scourge it while it sinned, but not to that degree that it left off sinning for a moment. Thus, under the name of order and civil government, we are all made at last to pay homage to and support our own meanness. After the first blush of sin, comes its indifference; and from immoral it becomes, as it were, *un*moral, and not quite unnecessary to that life which we have made.

The broadest and most prevalent error requires the most disinterested virtue to sustain it. The slight reproach to which the virtue of patriotism is commonly liable, the noble are most likely to incur. Those who, while they disapprove of the character and measures of a government, yield to it their allegiance and support, are undoubtedly its most conscientious supporters, and so frequently the most serious obstacles to reform. Some are petitioning the State to dissolve the Union, to disregard the requisitions of the President. Why do they not dissolve it themselves,—the union between themselves and the State,—and refuse to pay their quota into its treasury? Do not they stand in the same relation to the State, that the State does to the Union? And have not the same reasons prevented the State from resisting the Union, which have prevented them from resisting the State?

How can a man be satisfied to entertain an opinion merely, and enjoy *it?* Is there any enjoyment in it, if his opinion is that he is aggrieved? If you are cheated out of a single dollar by your neighbor, you do not rest satisfied with knowing that you are cheated, or with saying that you are cheated, or even with petitioning him to pay you your due; but you take effectual steps at once to obtain the full amount, and see that you are never cheated again. Action from principle,—the perception and the performance of right,— changes things and relations; it is essentially revolutionary, and does not consist wholly with any thing which was. It not only divides states and churches, it divides families; aye, it divides the *individual*, separating the diabolical in him from the divine.

Unjust laws exist: shall we be content to obey them, or shall we endeavour to amend them, and obey them until we have succeeded, or shall we transgress them at once? Men generally, under such a government as this, think they ought to wait until they have persuaded the majority to alter them. They think that, if they should resist, the remedy would be worse than the evil. But it is the fault of the government itself that the remedy *is* worse than the evil. *It* makes it worse. Why is it not more apt to anticipate and provide for reform? Why does it not cherish its wise minority? Why does it cry and resist before it is hurt? Why does it not encourage its citizens to be on the alert to point out its faults, and *do* better than it would have them? Why does it always crucify Christ, and excommunicate Copernicus and Luther, and pronounce Washington and Franklin rebels?

One would think, that a deliberate and practical denial of its authority was the only offence never contemplated by government; else, why has it not assigned its definite, its suitable and proportionate penalty? If a man who has no property refuses but once to earn nine shillings for the State, he is put in prison for a period unlimited by any law that I know, and determined only by the discretion of those who placed him there; but if he should steal ninety times nine shillings from the State, he is soon permitted to go at large again.

If the injustice is part of the necessary friction of the machine of government, let it go, let it go: perchance it will wear smooth,—certainly the machine will wear out. If the injustice has a spring, or a pulley, or a rope, or a crank, exclusively for itself, then perhaps you may consider whether the remedy will not be worse than the evil; but if it is of such a nature that it requires you to be the agent of injustice to another, then, I say, break the law. Let your life be a counter friction to stop the machine. What I have to do is to see, at any rate, that I do not lend myself to the wrong which I condemn.

As for adopting the way which the State has provided for remedying the evil, I know not of such ways. They take too much time and a man's life will be gone. I have other affairs to attend to. I came into this world, not chiefly to make this a good place to live in, but to live in it, be it good or bad. A man has not every thing to do, but something; and because he cannot do *every thing*, it is not necessary that he should do *something* wrong. It is not my business to be petitioning the governor or the legislature any more than it is theirs to petition me; and, if they should not hear my petition, what should I do then? But in this case the State has provided no way: its very Constitution is the evil. This may seem to be harsh and stubborn and unconciliatory; but it is to treat with the utmost kindness and consideration the only spirit that can appreciate or deserves it. So is all change for the better, like birth and death which convulse the body.

I do not hesitate to say, that those who call themselves abolitionists should at once effectually withdraw their support, both in person and property, from the government of Massachusetts, and not wait till they constitute a majority of one, before they suffer the right to prevail through them. I think that it is enough if they have God on their side, without waiting for that other one. Moreover, any man more right than his neighbors, constitutes a majority of one already.

I meet this American government, or its representative the State government, directly, and face to face, once a year, no more, in the person of its tax-gatherer; this is the only mode in which a man situated as I am necessarily meets it; and it then says distinctly, Recognize me; and the simplest, the most effectual, and, in the present posture of affairs, the indispensablest mode of treating with it on this head, of expressing your little satisfaction with and love for it, is to deny it then. My civil neighbor, the tax-gatherer, is the very man I have to deal with,—for it is, after all, with men and not with parchment that I quarrel,—and he has voluntarily chosen to be an agent of the government. How shall he ever know well what he is and does as an officer of the government, or as a man, until he is obliged to consider whether he shall treat me, his neighbor, for whom he has respect, as a neighbor and well-disposed man, or as a maniac and disturber of the peace, and see if he can get over this obstruction to his neighborliness without a ruder and more impetuous thought or speech corresponding with his action? I know this well, that if one thousand, if one hundred, if ten men whom I could name,—if ten *honest* men only,—aye, if *one* HONEST man, in this State of Massachusetts, *ceasing to hold slaves*, were actually to withdraw from this copartnership, and be locked up in the county jail therefor, it would be the abolition of slavery in America. For it matters not how small the beginning may seem to be: what is once well done is done for ever. But we love better to talk about it: that we say is our mission. Reform keeps many scores of newspapers in its service, but not one man. If my esteemed neighbor, the State's ambassador,[5] who will devote his days to the settlement of the question of human rights in the Council Chamber, instead of being threatened with the prisons of Carolina, were to sit down the prisoner of Massachusetts, that State which is so anxious to foist the sin of slavery upon her sister,—though at present she can discover only an act of inhospitality to be the ground of a quarrel with her,—the Legislature would not wholly waive the subject the following winter.

Under a government which imprisons any unjustly, the true place for a just man is also a prison. The proper place to-day, the only place which Massachusetts has provided for her freer and less desponding spirits, is in her own prisons, to be put out and locked out of the State by her own act, as they have already put themselves out by their principles. It is there that the fugitive slave, and the Mexican prisoner on parole, and the Indian come to plead the wrongs of his race, should find them; on that separate, but more free and honorable ground, where the State places those who are not *with* her but *against* her,—the only house in a slave-state in which a free man can abide with honor. If any think that their influence would be lost there, and their voices no longer afflict the ear of the State, that they would not be as an enemy within its walls, they do not know by how much truth is stronger than error, nor how much more eloquently and effectively he can combat injustice who has experienced a little in his own person. Cast your whole vote, not a strip of paper merely, but your whole influence. A minority is powerless while it conforms to the majority; it is not even a minority then; but it is irresistible when it clogs by its whole weight. If the alternative is to keep all just men in prison, or give up war and slavery, the State will not hesitate which to choose. If a thousand men were not to pay their tax-bills this year, that would not be a violent and bloody measure, as it would be to pay them, and enable the State to commit violence and shed innocent blood. This is, in fact, the definition of a peaceable revolution, if any such is possible. If the tax-gatherer, or any other public officer, asks me, as one has done, "But what shall I do?" my answer is, "If you really wish to do any thing, resign your office." When the subject has refused allegiance, and the officer

[5] *the State's ambassador:* Congressman Samuel Hoar (1778–1856) was expelled from Charleston, S.C., where he had gone to prevent the imprisonment and enslavement of Black seamen from Massachusetts.

has resigned his office, then the revolution is accomplished. But even suppose blood should flow. Is there not a sort of blood shed when the conscience is wounded? Through this wound a man's real manhood and immortality flow out, and he bleeds to an everlasting death. I see this blood flowing now.

I have contemplated the imprisonment of the offender, rather than the seizure of his goods,—though both will serve the same purpose,—because they who assert the purest right, and consequently are most dangerous to a corrupt State, commonly have not spent much time in accumulating property. To such the State renders comparatively small service, and a slight tax is wont to appear exorbitant, particularly if they are obliged to earn it by special labor with their hands. If there were one who lived wholly without the use of money, the State itself would hesitate to demand it of him. But the rich man—not to make any invidious comparison—is always sold to the institution which makes him rich. Absolutely speaking, the more money, the less virtue; for money comes between a man and his objects, and obtains them for him; and it was certainly no great virtue to obtain it. It puts to rest many questions which he would otherwise be taxed to answer; while the only new question which it puts is the hard but superfluous one, how to spend it. Thus his moral ground is taken from under his feet. The opportunities of living are diminished in proportion as what are called the "means" are increased. The best thing a man can do for his culture when he is rich is to endeavour to carry out those schemes which he entertained when he was poor. Christ answered the Herodians according to their condition. "Show me the tribute-money," said he;—and one took a penny out of his pocket;— If you use money which has the image of Cæsar on it, and which he has made current and valuable, that is, *if you are men of the State*, and gladly enjoy the advantages of Cæsar's government, then pay him back some of his own when he demands it; "Render therefore to Cæsar that which is Cæsar's, and to God those things which are God's,"—leaving them no wiser than before as to which was which; for they did not wish to know.

When I converse with the freest of my neighbors, I perceive that, whatever they may say about the magnitude and seriousness of the question, and their regard for the public tranquillity, the long and the short of the matter is, that they cannot spare the protection of the existing government, and they dread the consequences of disobedience to it to their property and families. For my own part, I should not like to think that I ever rely on the protection of the State. But, if I deny the authority of the State when it presents its tax-bill, it will soon take and waste all my property, and so harass me and my children without end. This is hard. This makes it impossible for a man to live honestly and at the same time comfortably in outward respects. It will not be worth the while to accumulate property; that would be sure to go again. You must hire or squat somewhere, and raise but a small crop, and eat that soon. You must live within yourself, and depend upon yourself, always tucked up and ready for a start, and not have many affairs. A man may grow rich in Turkey even, if he will be in all respects a good subject of the Turkish government. Confucius said,—"If a State is governed by the principles of reason, poverty and misery are subjects of shame; if a State is not governed by the principles of reason, riches and honors are the subjects of shame." No: until I want the protection of Massachusetts to be extended to me in some distant southern port, where my liberty is endangered, or until I am bent solely on building up an estate at home by peaceful enterprise, I can afford to refuse allegiance to Massachusetts, and her right to my property and life. It costs me less in every sense to incur the penalty of disobedience to the State, than it would to obey. I should feel as if I were worth less in that case.

Some years ago, the State met me in behalf of the church, and commanded me to pay a certain sum toward the support of a clergyman whose preaching my father attended, but never I myself. "Pay it," it said, "or be locked up in the jail." I declined to pay. But, unfortunately, another man saw fit to pay it. I did not see why the schoolmaster should be taxed to support the priest, and not the priest the schoolmaster; for I was not the State's schoolmaster, but I supported myself by voluntary subscription. I did not see why the lyceum should not present its tax-bill, and have the State to back its demand, as well as the church. However, at the request of the selectmen, I condescended to make some such statement as this in writing:—"Know all men by these presents, that I, Henry Thoreau, do not wish to be regarded as a member of any incorporated society which I have not joined." This I gave to the town-clerk; and he has it. The State, having thus learned that I did not wish to be regarded as a member of that church, has never made a like demand on me since; though it said that it must adhere to its original presumption that time. If I had known how to name them, I should then have signed off in detail from all the societies which I never signed on to; but I did not know where to find a complete list.

I have paid no poll-tax for six years. I was put into a jail once on this account, for one night; and, as I stood considering the walls of solid stone, two or three feet thick, the door of wood and iron, a foot thick, and the iron grating which strained the light, I could not help being struck with the foolishness of that institution which treated me as if I were mere flesh and blood and bones, to be locked up. I wondered that it should have concluded at length that this was the best use it could put me to, and had never thought to avail itself of my services in some way. I saw that, if there was a wall of stone between me and my townsmen, there was a still more difficult one to climb or break through, before they could get to be as free as I was. I did not for a moment feel confined, and the walls seemed a great waste of stone and mortar. I felt as if I alone of all my townsmen had paid my tax. They plainly did not know how to treat me, but behaved like persons who are underbred. In every threat and in every compliment there was a blunder; for they thought that my chief desire was to stand the other side of that stone wall. I could not but smile to see how industriously they locked the door on my meditations, which followed them out again without let or hindrance, and *they* were really all that was dangerous. As they could not reach me, they had resolved to punish my body; just as boys, if they cannot come at some person against whom they have a spite, will abuse his dog. I saw that the State was half-witted, that it was timid as a lone woman with her silver spoons, and that it did not know its friends from its foes, and I lost all my remaining respect for it, and pitied it.

Thus the State never intentionally confronts a man's sense, intellectual or moral, but only his body, his senses. It is not armed with superior wit or honesty, but with superior physical strength. I was not born to be forced. I will breathe after my own fashion. Let us see who is the strongest. What force has a multitude? They only can force me who obey a higher law than I. They force me to become like themselves. I do not hear of *men* being *forced* to live this way or that by masses of men. What sort of life were that to live? When I meet a government which says to me, "Your money or your life," why should I be in haste to give it my money? It may be in a great strait, and not know what to do: I cannot help that. It must help itself; do as I do. It is not worth the while to snivel about it. I am not responsible for the successful working of the machinery of society. I am not the son of the engineer. I perceive that, when an acorn and a chestnut fall side by side, the one does not remain inert to make way for the other, but both obey their own laws, and spring and grow and flourish as best they can, till one, perchance, overshadows and destroys the other. If a plant cannot live according to its nature, it dies; and so a man.

The night in prison was novel and interesting enough. The prisoners in their shirt-sleeves were enjoying a chat and the evening air in the door-way, when I entered. But the jailer said, "Come, boys, it is time to lock up;" and so they dispersed, and I heard the sound of their steps returning into the hollow apartments. My room-mate was introduced to me by the jailer, as "a first-rate fellow and a clever man." When the door was locked, he showed me where to hang my hat, and how he managed matters there. The rooms were whitewashed once a month; and this one, at least, was the whitest, most simply furnished, and probably the neatest apartment in the town. He naturally wanted to know where I came from, and what brought me there; and, when I had told him, I asked him in my turn how he came there, presuming him to be an honest man, of course; and, as the world goes, I believe he was. "Why," said he, "they accuse me of burning a barn; but I never did it." As near as I could discover, he had probably gone to bed in a barn when drunk, and smoked his pipe there; and so a barn was burnt. He had the reputation of being a clever man, had been there some three months waiting for his trial to come on, and would have to wait as much longer; but he was quite domesticated and contented, since he got his board for nothing, and thought that he was well treated.

He occupied one window, and I the other; and I saw, that if one stayed there long, his principal business would be to look out the window. I had soon read all the tracts that were left there, and examined where former prisoners had broken out, and where a grate had been sawed off, and heard the history of the various occupants of that room; for I found that even here there was a history and a gossip which never circulated beyond the walls of the jail. Probably this is the only house in the town where verses are composed, which are afterward printed in a circular form, but not published. I was shown quite a long list of verses which were composed by some young men who had been detected in an attempt to escape, who avenged themselves by singing them.

I pumped my fellow-prisoner as dry as I could, for fear I should never see him again; but at length he showed me which was my bed, and left me to blow out the lamp.

It was like travelling into a far country, such as I had never expected to behold, to lie there for one night. It seemed to me that I never had heard the town-clock strike before, nor the evening sounds of the village; for we slept with the windows open, which were inside the grating. It was to see my native village in the light of the middle ages, and our Concord was turned into a Rhine stream, and visions of knights and castles passed before me. They were the voices of old burghers that I heard in the streets. I was an involuntary spectator and auditor of whatever was done and said in the kitchen of the adjacent village-inn,—a wholly new and rare experience to me. It was a closer view of my native town. I was fairly inside of it. I never had seen its institutions before. This is one of its peculiar institutions; for it is a shire town. I began to comprehend what its inhabitants were about.

In the morning, our breakfasts were put through the hole in the door, in small oblong-square tin pans, made to fit, and holding a pint of chocolate, with brown bread, and an iron spoon. When they called for the vessels again, I was green enough to return what bread I had left; but my comrade seized it, and said that I should lay that up for lunch or dinner. Soon after, he was let out to work at haying in a neighboring field, whither he went every day, and would not be back till noon; so he bade me good-day, saying that he doubted if he should see me again.

When I came out of prison,—for some one interfered, and paid the tax,—I did not perceive that great changes had taken place on the common, such as he observed who went in a youth, and emerged a tottering and gray-headed man; and yet a change had to my eyes come over the scene,—the town, and State, and country,—greater than any that mere time could effect. I saw yet more distinctly the State in which I lived. I saw to what extent the people among whom I lived could be trusted as good neighbors and friends; that their friendship was for summer weather only; that they did not greatly purpose to do right; that they were a distinct race from me by their prejudices and superstitions, as the Chinamen and Malays are; that, in their sacrifices to humanity, they ran no risks, not even to their property; that, after all, they were not so noble but they treated the thief as he had treated them, and hoped, by a certain outward observance and a few prayers, and by walking in a particular straight though useless path from time to time, to save their souls. This may be to judge my neighbors harshly; for I believe that most of them are not aware that they have such an institution as the jail in their village.

It was formerly the custom in our village, when a poor debtor came out of jail, for his acquaintances to salute him, looking through their fingers, which were crossed to represent the grating of a jail window, "How do ye do?" My neighbors did not thus salute me, but first looked at me, and then at one another, as if I had returned from a long journey. I was put into jail as I was going to the shoemaker's to get a shoe which was mended. When I was let out the next morning, I proceeded to finish my errand, and, having put on my mended shoe, joined a huckleberry party, who were impatient to put themselves under my conduct; and in half an hour,—for the horse was soon tackled,—was in the midst of a huckleberry field, on one of our highest hills, two miles off; and then the State was nowhere to be seen.

This is the whole history of "My Prisons."[6]

I have never declined paying the highway tax, because I am as desirous of being a good neighbor as I am of being a bad subject; and, as for supporting schools, I am doing my part to educate my fellow-countrymen now. It is for no particular item in the tax-bill that I refuse to pay it. I simply wish to refuse allegiance to the State, to withdraw and stand aloof from it effectually. I do not care to trace the course of my dollar, if I could, till it buys a man, or a musket to shoot one with,—the dollar is innocent,—but I am concerned to trace the effects of my allegiance. In fact, I quietly declare war with the State, after my fashion, though I will still make what use and get what advantage of her I can, as is usual in such cases.

If others pay the tax which is demanded of me, from a sympathy with the State, they do but what they have already done in their own case, or rather they abet injustice to a greater extent than the State requires. If they pay the tax from a mistaken interest in the individual taxed, to save his property or prevent his going to jail, it is because they have not considered wisely how far they let their private feelings interfere with the public good.

This, then, is my position at present. But one cannot be too much on his guard in such a case, lest his action be biassed by obstinacy, or an undue regard for the opinions of men. Let him see that he does only what belongs to himself and to the hour.

I think sometimes, Why, this people mean well; they are only ignorant; they would do better if they knew how: why give your neighbors this pain to treat you as they are not inclined to? But I think, again, this is no reason why I should do as they do, or permit others to suffer much greater pain of a different kind. Again, I sometimes say to myself, When many millions of men, without heat, without ill-will, without personal feeling of any kind, demand of you a few shillings only, without the possibility, such is their constitution, of retracting or altering their present demand, and without the possibility, on your side, of appeal to any other millions, why expose yourself to this overwhelming brute force? You do not resist cold and hunger, the winds and the waves, thus obstinately; you quietly submit to a thousand similar necessities. You do not put your head into the fire. But just in proportion as I regard this as not wholly a brute force, but partly a human force, and consider that I have relations to those millions as to so many millions of men, and not of mere brute or inanimate things, I see that appeal is possible, first and instantaneously, from them to the Maker of them, and,

---

[6] "My Prisons": Le mie Prigioni, an account of the imprisonment by Austrian authorities of the Italian poet Silvio Pellico (1789–1854).

secondly, from them to themselves. But, if I put my head deliberately into the fire, there is no appeal to fire or to the Maker of fire, and I have only myself to blame. If I could convince myself that I have any right to be satisfied with men as they are, and to treat them accordingly, and not according, in some respects, to my requisitions and expectations of what they and I ought to be, then, like a good Mussulman and fatalist, I should endeavor to be satisfied with things as they are, and say it is the will of God. And, above all, there is this difference between resisting this and a purely brute or natural force, that I can resist this with some effect; but I cannot expect, like Orpheus, to change the nature of the rocks and trees and beasts.

I do not wish to quarrel with any man or nation. I do not wish to split hairs, to make fine distinctions, or set myself up as better than my neighbors. I seek rather, I may say, even an excuse for conforming to the laws of the land. I am but too ready to conform to them. Indeed I have reason to suspect myself on this head; and each year, as the tax-gatherer comes round, I find myself disposed to review the acts and position of the general and state governments, and the spirit of the people, to discover a pretext for conformity. I believe that the State will soon be able to take all my work of this sort out of my hands, and then I shall be no better a patriot than my fellow-country-men. Seen from a lower point of view, the Constitution, with all its faults, is very good; the law and the courts are very respectable; even this State and this American government are, in many respects, very admirable and rare things, to be thankful for, such as a great many have described them; but seen from a point of view a little higher, they are what I have described them; seen from a higher still, and the highest, who shall say what they are, or that they are worth looking at or thinking of at all?

However, the government does not concern me much, and I shall bestow the fewest possible thoughts on it. It is not many moments that I live under a government, even in this world. If a man is thought-free, fancy-free, imagination-free, that which *is not* never for a long time appearing *to be* to him, unwise rulers or reformers cannot fatally interrupt him.

I know that most men think differently from myself; but those whose lives are by profession devoted to the study of these or kindred subjects, content me as little as any. Statesmen and legislators, standing so completely within the institution, never distinctly and nakedly behold it. They speak of moving society, but have no resting-place without it. They may be men of a certain experience and discrimination, and have no doubt invented ingenious and even useful systems, for which we sincerely thank them; but all their wit and usefulness lie within certain not very wide limits. They are wont to forget that the world is not governed by policy and expediency. Webster never goes behind government, and so cannot speak with authority about it. His words are wisdom to those legislators who contemplate no essential reform in the existing government; but for thinkers, and those who legislate for all time, he never once glances at the subject. I know of those whose serene and wise speculations on this theme would soon reveal the limits of his mind's range and hospitality. Yet, compared with the cheap professions of most reformers, and the still cheaper wisdom and eloquence of politicians in general, his are almost the only sensible and valuable words, and we thank Heaven for him. Comparatively, he is always strong, original, and, above all, practical. Still his quality is not wisdom, but prudence. The lawyer's truth is not Truth, but consistency, or a consistent expediency. Truth is always in harmony with herself, and is not concerned chiefly to reveal the justice that may consist with wrong-doing. He well deserves to be called, as he has been called, the Defender of the Constitution. There are really no blows to be given by him but defensive ones. He is not a leader, but a follower. His leaders are the men of '87. "I have never made an effort," he says, "and never propose to make an effort; I have never countenanced an effort, and never mean to countenance an effort, to disturb the arrangement as originally made, by which the various States came into the Union." Still thinking of the sanction which the Constitution gives to slavery, he says, "Because it was a part of the original compact,—let it stand." Notwithstanding his special acuteness and ability, he is unable to take a fact out of its merely political relations, and behold it as it lies absolutely to be disposed of by the intellect, —what, for instance, it behoves a man to do here in America to-day with regard to slavery, but ventures, or is driven, to make some such desperate answer as the following, while professing to speak absolutely, and as a private man,—from which what new and singular code of social duties might be inferred?—"The manner," says he, "in which the government of those States where slavery exists are to regulate it, is for their own consideration, under their responsibility to their constituents, to the general laws of propriety, humanity, and justice, and to God. Associations formed elsewhere, springing from a feeling of humanity, or any other cause, have nothing whatever to do with it. They have never received any encouragement from me, and they never will."

They who know of no purer sources of truth, who have traced up its stream no higher, stand, and wisely stand, by the Bible and the Constitution, and drink at it there with reverence and humility; but they who behold where it comes trickling into this lake or that pool, gird up their loins once more, and continue their pilgrimage toward its fountain-head.

No man with a genius for legislation has appeared in America. They are rare in the history of the world. There are orators, politicians, and eloquent men, by the thousand; but the speaker has not yet opened his mouth to speak, who is capable of settling the much-vexed questions of the day. We love eloquence for its own sake, and not for any truth which it may utter, or any heroism it may inspire. Our legislators have not yet learned the comparative value of free-trade and of freedom, of union, and of rectitude, to a nation. They have no genius or talent for comparatively humble questions of taxation and finance, commerce and manufactures and agriculture. If we were left solely to the wordy wit of legislators in Congress for our guidance, uncorrected by the seasonable experience and the effectual complaints of the people, America would not long retain her rank among the nations. For eighteen hundred years, though perchance I have no right to say it, the New Testament has been written; yet where is the legislator who has wisdom and practical talent enough to avail himself of the light which it sheds on the science of legislation?

The authority of government, even such as I am willing to submit to,— for I will cheerfully obey those who know and can do better than I, and in many things even those who neither know nor can do so well,—is still an impure one: to be strictly just, it must have the sanction and consent of the governed. It can have no pure right over my person and property but what I concede to it. The progress from an absolute to a limited monarchy, from a limited monarchy to a democracy, is a progress toward a true respect for the individual. Is a democracy, such as we know it, the last improvement possible in government? Is it not possible to take a step further towards recognizing and organizing the rights of man? There will never be a really free and enlightened State, until the State comes to recognize the individual as a higher and independent power, from which all its own power and authority are derived, and treats him accordingly. I please myself with imagining a State at last which can afford to be just to all men, and to treat the individual with respect as a neighbor; which even would not think it inconsistent with its own repose, if a few were to live aloof from it, not meddling with it, nor embraced by it, who fulfilled all the duties of neighbors and fellow-men. A State which bore this kind of fruit, and suffered it to drop off as fast as it ripened, would prepare the way for a still more perfect and glorious State, which also I have imagined, but not yet anywhere seen.

## QUESTIONS: *Thoreau, Civil Disobedience*

1. Thoreau believes that the qualities of which an individual man is capable make it possible to have *anarchy* (literally "no rule") without *disorder*. What are some of these qualities?

    *Clues:* • Yet this government never of itself furthered any enterprise, but by the alacrity with which it got out of its way. *It* does not keep the country free. *It* does not settle the West. *It* does not educate.

    • Trade and commerce, if they were not made of India rubber, would never manage to bounce over the obstacles which legislators are continually putting in their way. . . .

    • Must the citizen even for a moment, or in the least degree, resign his conscience to a legislator? Why has every man a conscience, then?

    • It is not desirable to cultivate a respect for the law, so much as for the right.

2. Does Thoreau's apparent praise of "trade and commerce," energetically leaping the ridiculous barriers put up by government, contradict his distrust of money and property? If not, why not?

    *Clue:* • But the rich man . . . is always sold to the institution which makes him rich. Absolutely speaking, the more money, the less virtue. . . . The opportunities of living are diminished in proportion as what are called the "means" are increased.

3. Thoreau's ideal vision is of a commonwealth in which every man is his own ruler, a kind of perfect (rather than representative) democracy. Yet his vision of the present is so intensely pessimistic that it could be described as an ultimate form of *elitism*. "How many *men* are there to a square thousand miles in this country? Hardly one." Does Thoreau try to reconcile his optimism about the future and his pessimism about the present? If so, how? Does he succeed?

   *Clues:* • The mass of men serve the state ... not as men mainly, but as machines, with their bodies. . . . In most cases there is no free exercise whatever of the judgment or of the moral sense. . . . Others . . . serve the state chiefly with their heads. . . . A very few—as heroes, patriots, martyrs, reformers in the great sense, and *men*—serve the state with their consciences also; and so necessarily resist it for the most part. . . .

   • A *wise man* will not leave the right to the mercy of chance, nor wish it to prevail through the power of the majority. There is but little virtue in the action of masses of men.

   • Why does it [the government] not cherish its *wise minority*? ... Why does it always crucify Christ, and excommunicate Copernicus and Luther, and pronounce Washington and Franklin rebels?

4. Thoreau speaks of the *progress* that has taken place from absolute monarchy to democracy. Yet he suggests elsewhere that the history of America since the Revolution of 1776 has been a process of decline. "The American has dwindled into an Odd Fellow," he says, "who may be known by the development of his organ of gregariousness, and a manifest lack of intellect and cheerful self-reliance." Does this contradiction represent a serious tension in Thoreau's outlook? Is it in any way typical of the modern reformer or revolutionary?

5. How do Thoreau's attitudes toward government and the individual (as dealt with in the questions above) determine the quality of (a) his protest against *war* and *slavery* and (b) his view of imprisonment as an instrument of protest?

   *Clues:* • A common and natural result of an undue respect for law is, that you may see a file of soldiers, colonel, captain, corporal, privates, powder-monkeys, and all, marching in admirable order over hill and dale to the wars, against their wills, aye, against their common sense and consciences, which makes it very steep marching indeed, and produces a palpitation of the heart.

   • There is but little virtue in the action of masses of men. When the majority shall at length vote for the abolition of slavery, it will be because they are indifferent to slavery, or because there is but little slavery left to be abolished by their vote. *They* will then be the only slaves. Only *his* vote can hasten the abolition of slavery who asserts his own freedom by his vote.

   • [A minority] is irresistible when it clogs by its whole weight. If the alternative is to keep all just men in prison, or give up war and slavery, the State will not hesitate which to choose.

   What part do traditional Christian values play in Thoreau's views on war and slavery? Consider such a statement as "But he that would save his life, in such a case, shall lose it. This people must cease to hold slaves, and to make war on Mexico, though it cost them their existence as a people."

*Matthew Arnold (1822–1888)*

# Culture and Anarchy

## FROM CHAPTER II

### Doing as One Likes

I have been trying to show that culture is, or ought to be, the study and pursuit of perfection; and that of perfection as pursued by culture, beauty and intelligence, or, in other words, sweetness and light, are the main characters. But hitherto I have been insisting chiefly on beauty, or sweetness, as a character of perfection. To complete rightly my design, it evidently remains to speak also of intelligence, or light, as a character of perfection.

First, however, I ought perhaps to notice that, both here and on the other side of the Atlantic, all sorts of objections are raised against the 'religion of culture,' as the objectors mockingly call it, which I am supposed to be promulgating. It is said to be a religion proposing parmaceti, or some scented salve or other, as a cure for human miseries; a religion breathing a spirit of cultivated inaction, making its believer refuse to lend a hand at uprooting the definite evils on all sides of us, and filling him with antipathy against the reforms and reformers which try to extirpate them. In general, it is summed up as being not practical, or,—as some critics familiarly put it, —all moonshine. . . .

It is impossible that all these remonstrances and reproofs should not affect me, and I shall try my very best, in completing my design and in speaking of light as one of the characters of perfection, and of culture as giving us light, to profit by the objections I have heard and read, and to drive at practice as much as I can, by showing the communications and passages into practical life from the doctrine which I am inculcating.

It is said that a man with my theories of sweetness and light is full of antipathy against the rougher or coarser movements going on around him, that he will not lend a hand to the humble operation of uprooting evil by their means, and that therefore the believers in action grow impatient with him. But what if rough and coarse action, ill-calculated action, action with insufficient light, is, and has for a long time been, our bane? What if our urgent want now is, not to act at any price, but rather to lay in a stock of light for our difficulties? In that case, to refuse to lend a hand to the rougher and coarser movements going on round us, to make the primary need, both for oneself and others, to consist in enlightening ourselves and qualifying ourselves to act less at random, is surely the best and in real truth the most practical line our endeavours can take. So that if I can show what my opponents call rough or coarse action, but what I would rather call random and ill-regulated action,—action with insufficient light, action pursued because we like to be doing something and doing it as we please, and do not like the trouble of thinking and the severe constraint of any kind of rule,—if I can show this to be, at the present moment, a practical mischief and dangerous to us, then I have found a practical use for light in correcting this state of things, and have only to exemplify how, in cases which fall under everybody's observation, it may deal with it.

When I began to speak of culture, I insisted on our bondage to machinery, on our proneness to value machinery as an end in itself, without looking beyond it to the end for which alone, in truth, it is valuable. Freedom, I said, was one of those things we which thus worshipped in itself, without enough regarding the ends for which freedom is to be desired. In our common notions and talk about freedom, we eminently show our idolatry of machinery. Our prevalent notion is,—and I quoted a number of instances to prove it,—that it is a most happy and important thing for a man merely to be able to do as he likes. On what he is to do when he is thus free to do as he likes, we do not lay so much stress. Our familiar praise of the British Constitution under which we live, is that it is a system of checks,—a system which stops and paralyses any power in interfering with the free action of individuals. To this effect Mr. Bright, who loves to walk in the old ways of the Constitution, said forcibly in one of his great speeches, what many other people are every day saying less forcibly, that the central idea of English life and politics is *the assertion of personal liberty*. Evidently this is so; but evidently, also, as feudalism, which with its ideas, and habits of subordination was for many centuries silently behind the British Constitution, dies out, and we are left with nothing but our system of checks, and our notion of its being the great right and happiness of an Englishman to do as far as possible what he likes, we are in danger of drifting towards anarchy. We have not the notion, so familiar on the Continent and to antiquity, of *the State*,—the nation in its collective and corporate character, entrusted with stringent powers for the general advantage, and controlling individual wills in the name of an interest wider than that of individuals. We say, what is very true, that this notion is often made instrumental to tyranny; we say that a State is in reality made up of the individuals who compose it, and that every individual is the best judge of his own interests. Our leading class is an aristocracy, and no aristocracy likes the notion of a State-authority greater than itself, with a stringent administrative machinery superseding the decorative inutilities of lord-lieutenancy, deputy-lieutenancy, and the *posse comitatus*, which are all in its own hands. Our middle class, the great representative of trade and Dissent, with its maxims of every man for himself in business, every man for himself in religion, dreads a powerful administration which might somehow interfere with it; and besides, it has its own decorative inutilities of vestrymanship and guardianship, which are to this class what lord-lieutenancy and the county magistracy are to the aristocratic class, and a stringent administration might either take these functions out of its hands, or prevent its exercising them in its own comfortable, independent manner, as at present.

Then as to our working class. This class, pressed constantly by hard daily compulsion of material wants, is naturally the very centre and stronghold of our national idea, that it is man's ideal right and felicity to do as he likes. I think I have somewhere related how M. Michelet said to me of the people of France, that it was 'a nation of barbarians civilised by the conscription'. He meant that through their military service the idea of public duty and of discipline was brought to the mind of these masses, in other respects so raw and uncultivated. Our masses are quite as raw and uncultivated as the French; and so far from their having the idea of public duty and of discipline, superior to the individual's self-will, brought to their mind by a universal obligation of military service, such as that of the conscription,—so far from their having this, the very idea of a conscription is so at variance with our English notion of the prime right and blessedness of doing as one likes, that I remember the manager of the Clay Cross works in Derbyshire told me during the Crimean war, when our want of soldiers was much felt and some people were talking of a conscription, that sooner than submit to a conscription the population of that district would flee to the mines, and lead a sort of Robin Hood life under ground.

For a long time, as I have said, the strong feudal habits of subordination and deference continued to tell upon the working class. The modern spirit has now almost entirely dissolved those habits, and the anarchical tendency of our worship of freedom in and for itself, of our superstitious faith, as I say, in machinery, is becoming very manifest. More and more, because of this our blind faith in machinery, because of our want of light to enable us to look beyond machinery to the end for which machinery is valuable, this and that man, and this and that body of men, all over the country, are beginning to assert and put in practice an Englishman's right to do what he likes; his right to march where he likes, meet where he likes, enter where he likes, hoot as he likes, threaten as he likes, smash as he likes. All this, I say, tends to anarchy; and though a number of excellent people, and particularly my friends of the Liberal or progressive party, as they call themselves, are kind enough to reassure us by saying that these are trifles, that a few transient outbreaks of rowdyism signify nothing, that our system of liberty is one which itself cures all the evils which it works, that the educated and intelligent classes stand in overwhelming strength and majestic repose, ready, like our military force in riots, to act at a moment's notice,—yet one finds that one's Liberal friends generally say this because they have such faith in themselves and their nostrums, when they shall return, as the public welfare requires, to place and power. But this faith of theirs one cannot exactly share, when one has so long had them and their nostrums at work, and sees that they have not prevented our coming to our present embarrassed condition. And one finds, also, that the outbreaks of rowdyism tend to become less and less of trifles, to become more frequent rather than less frequent; and that meanwhile our educated and intelligent classes remain in their majestic repose, and somehow or other, whatever happens, their overwhelming strength, like our military force in riots, never does act.

How, indeed, *should* their overwhelming strength act, when the man who gives an inflammatory lecture, or breaks down the park railings, or invades a Secretary of State's office, is only following an Englishman's impulse to do as he likes; and our own conscience tells us that we ourselves have always regarded this impulse as something primary and sacred? Mr. Murphy lectures at Birmingham, and showers on the Catholic population of that town 'words,' says the Home Secretary, 'only fit to be addressed to thieves or murderers.' What then? Mr. Murphy has his own reasons of several kinds. He suspects the Roman Catholic Church of designs upon Mrs. Murphy; and he says if mayors and magistrates do not care for their wives and daughters, he does. But, above all, he is doing as he likes; or, in worthier language, asserting his personal liberty. 'I will carry out my lectures if they walk over my body as a dead corpse, and I say to the Mayor of Birmingham that he is my servant while I am in Birmingham, and as my servant he must do his duty and protect me.' Touching and beautiful words, which find a sympathetic chord in every British bosom! The moment it is plainly put before us that a man is asserting his personal liberty, we are half disarmed; because we are believers in freedom, and not in some dream of a right reason to which the assertion of our freedom is to be subordinated. Accordingly, the Secretary of State had to say that although the lecturer's language was 'only fit to be addressed to thieves or murderers,' yet, 'I do not think he is to be deprived, I do not think that anything I have said could justify the inference that he is to be deprived, of the right of protection in a place built by him for the purpose of these lectures; because the language was not language which afforded grounds for a criminal prosecution.' No, nor to be silenced by Mayor, or Home Secretary, or any administrative authority on earth, simply on their notion of what is discreet and reasonable! This is in perfect consonance with our public opinion, and with our national love for the assertion of personal liberty. . . .

There are many things to be said on behalf of this exclusive attention of ours to liberty, and of the relaxed habits of government which it has engendered. It is very easy to mistake or to exaggerate the sort of anarchy from which we are in danger through them. We are not in danger from Fenianism, fierce and turbulent as it may show itself; for against this our conscience is free enough to let us act resolutely and put forth our overwhelming strength the moment there is any real need for it. In the first place, it never was any part of our creed that the great right and blessedness of an Irishman, or, indeed, of anybody on earth except an Englishman, is to do as he likes; and we can have no scruple at all about abridging, if necessary, a non-Englishman's assertion of personal liberty. The British Constitution, its checks, and its prime virtues, are for Englishmen. We may extend them to others out of love and kindness; but we find no real divine law written on our hearts constraining us so to extend them. And then the difference between an Irish Fenian and an English rough is so immense, and the case, in dealing with the Fenian, so much more clear! He is so evidently desperate and dangerous, a man of a conquered race, a Papist, with centuries of ill-usage to inflame him against us, with an alien religion established in his country by us at his expense, with no admiration of our institutions, no love of our virtues, no talents for our business, no turn for our comfort! Show him our symbolical Truss Manufactory on the finest site in Europe, and tell him that British industrialism and individualism can bring a man to that, and he remains cold! Evidently, if we deal tenderly with a sentimentalist like this, it is out of pure philanthropy.

But with the Hyde Park rioter how different! He is our own flesh and blood; he is a Protestant; he is framed by nature to do as we do, hate what we hate, love what we love; he is capable of feeling the symbolical force of the Truss Manufactory; the question of questions, for him, is a wages question. That beautiful sentence Sir Daniel Gooch quoted to the Swindon workmen, and which I treasure as Mrs. Gooch's Golden Rule, or the Divine Injunction 'Be ye Perfect' done into British,—the sentence Sir Daniel Gooch's mother repeated to him every morning when he was a boy going to work:—'*Ever remember, my dear Dan, that you should look forward to being some day manager of that concern!*'—this truthful maxim is perfectly fitted to shine forth in the heart of the Hyde Park rough also, and to be his guiding-star through life. He has no visionary schemes of revolution and transformation, though of course he would like his class to rule, as the aristocratic class like their class to rule, and the middle class theirs. But meanwhile our social machine is a little out of order; there are a good many people in our paradisiacal centres of industrialism and individualism taking the bread out of one another's mouths. The rough has not yet quite found his groove and settled down to his work, and so he is just asserting his personal liberty a little, going where he likes, assembling where he likes, bawling as he likes, hustling as he likes. Just as the rest of us,—as the country squires in the aristocratic class, as the political dissenters in the middle class,—he has no idea of a *State*, of the nation in its collective and corporate character controlling, as government, the free swing of this or that one of its members in the name of the higher reason of all of them, his own as well as that of others. He sees the rich, the aristocratic class, in occupation of the executive government, and so if he is stopped from making Hyde Park a bear-garden or the streets impassable, he says he is being butchered by the aristocracy.

His apparition is somewhat embarrassing, because too many cooks spoil the broth; because, while the aristocratic and middle classes have long been doing as they like with great vigour, he has been too undeveloped and submissive hitherto to join in the game; and now, when he does come, he comes in immense numbers, and is rather raw and rough. But he does not break many laws, or not many at one time; and, as our laws were made for very different circumstances from our present (but always with an eye to Englishmen doing as they like), and as the clear letter of the law must be against our Englishman who does as he likes, and not only the spirit of the law and public policy, and as Government must neither have any discretionary power nor act resolutely on its own interpretation of the law if any one disputes it, it is evident our laws give our playful giant, in doing as he likes, considerable advantage. Besides, even if he can be clearly proved to commit an illegality in doing as he likes, there is always the resource of not putting the law in force, or of abolishing it. So he has his way, and if he has his way he is soon satisfied for the time. However, he falls into the habit of taking it oftener and oftener, and at last begins to create by his operations a confusion of which mischievous people can take advantage, and which, at any rate, by troubling the common course of business throughout the country, tends to cause distress, and so to increase the sort of anarchy and social disintegration which had previously commenced. And thus that profound sense of settled order and security, without which a society like ours cannot live and grow at all, sometimes seems to be beginning to threaten us with taking its departure.

Now, if culture, which simply means trying to perfect oneself, and one's mind as part of oneself, brings us light, and if light shows us that there is nothing so very blessed in merely doing as one likes, that the worship of the mere freedom to do as one likes is worship of machinery, that the really blessed thing is to like what right reason ordains, and to follow her authority, then we have got a practical benefit out of culture. We have got a much wanted principle, a principle of authority, to counteract the tendency to anarchy which seems to be threatening us.

## QUESTIONS: *Arnold, Culture and Anarchy*

1. Arnold says here that "enlightening ourselves and qualifying ourselves to act less at random" should be considered "the primary need." What direct connection do you see between that assertion and his criticism of the Englishman's conception of freedom? What central flaw in that conception does Arnold focus on? Why is his term *machinery* (even if you are not familiar with Arnold's previous use of it in *Culture and Anarchy*) so appropriate to his point?

2. Arnold sees the "danger of drifting towards anarchy" in the Englishman's reliance on the principles of checks and balances and "doing as one likes." Why, although he grants the dangers of tyranny in control by the State, does he not reject that conception? What different sort of tyranny inherent to anarchy does he complain of?

   *Clue:* • Our leading class is an aristocracy, and no aristocracy likes the notion of a State-authority *greater than itself*. . . . Our middle class . . . with its maxims of *every man for himself* in business, every man for himself in religion, dreads a powerful administration which might somehow *interfere* with it; and besides it has its own *decorative inutilities* of vestry-manship and guardianship, which are to this class what lord-lieutenancy and the country magistracy are to the aristocratic class . . .

3. How does Arnold's view of the advantages of military service in suggesting "the idea of public duty and of discipline, superior to the individual's self-will" strike our modern consciousness? What dangers does he seem to be ignoring here? Is there anything to be said for his contention that military service can function as a civilizing influence?

*354*

4. When Arnold asserts that, with the prevalence of "the modern spirit," the working class is no longer influenced by "the strong feudal habits of subordination and deference" is he merely expressing a nostalgia for the past? What *psychological* and *moral* aspects of subordination and deference (rather than *political* and *social* ones) now appear to interest him?

   *Clue:* • . . . we are believers in freedom, and not in some dream of a right reason to which the assertion of our freedom is to be subordinated.

5. The following two passages refer respectively to (a) the Hyde Park Riots, manifestations of lower-class violence that grew out of demonstrations against the defeat of the reform bill of 1866 (which would have extended voting rights to the poor); and (b) the anti-Catholic riots instigated by the inflammatory rhetoric of Mr. Murphy in Birmingham in 1867. Using these passages as clues, determine what connection Arnold establishes between riot (or incitement to riot) and the conviction of personal liberty. What central questions of responsibility does the actualizing of one's conviction, the *doing as one likes*, raise?

   *Clues:* • More and more, because of this our blind faith in machinery . . . this and that man, and this and that body of men, all over the country, are beginning to assert and put in practice an Englishman's right to do what he likes; his right to march where he likes, meet where he likes, enter where he likes, hoot as he likes, threaten as he likes, smash as he likes.

   • Mr. Murphy lectures at Birmingham, and showers on the Catholic population of that town 'words,' says the Home Secretary, 'only fit to be addressed to thieves or murderers.' Mr. Murphy has his own reasons of several kinds. He suspects the Roman Catholic Church of designs upon Mrs. Murphy; and he says if mayors and magistrates do not care for their wives and daughters, he does. But, above, all he is doing as he likes; or, in worthier language, asserting his personal liberty.

6. How does *irony* function to strengthen Arnold's attack against the Englishman's conception of freedom in the paragraph devoted to the dangers of Fenianism (the extreme Nationalist Irish movement, whose supporters committed many acts of violence against England in 1867)? What is, in fact, the symbolic effect here of the reference to the Truss Manufactory (a real factory housed in a very ugly building in Trafalgar Square)?

7. How does Arnold escape the accusation of narrow-minded conservatism in his treatment of the aims, reactions, and position of the working class in the last three paragraphs of this selection?

   *Clues:* • But meanwhile our social machine is a little out of order; there are a good many people in our paradisiacal centres of industrialism and individualism taking the bread out of one another's mouths.

   • . . . too many cooks spoil the broth,

## EXERCISE

From the vantage point of our present age, with its jaundiced view of "law and order" as a principle, its sympathy for the impulse toward "doing one's thing," its familiarity with the techniques of confrontation politics, sit-ins, marches, and picketing, write an essay assessing (or reacting to) Arnold's condemnation of "the man who gives an inflammatory lecture, or breaks down the park railings, or invades a Secretary of State's office." Consider in your treatment whether or not the prevalence of such behavior in our own time is the sign of our ultimate drift toward anarchy, the fate Arnold feared for his own generation.

## *George Bernard Shaw (1856–1950)*

# Maxims for Revolutionists

*These maxims, of which only a selection is presented here (some sections have been cut, some omitted), are part of* The Revolutionist's Handbook and Pocket Companion *appended to* Man and Superman.

### *The Golden Rule*

Do not do unto others as you would that they should do unto you. Their tastes may not be the same.

Never resist temptation: prove all things: hold fast that which is good.

Do not love your neighbor as yourself. If you are on good terms with yourself it is an impertinence: if on bad, an injury.

The golden rule is that there are no golden rules.

### *Idolatry*

The art of government is the organization of idolatry.

The bureaucracy consists of functionaries; the aristocracy, of idols; the democracy, of idolaters.

The populace cannot understand the bureaucracy: it can only worship the national idols.

The savage bows down to idols of wood and stone: the civilized man to idols of flesh and blood.

A limited monarchy is a device for combining the inertia of a wooden idol with the credibility of a flesh and blood one.

When the wooden idol does not answer the peasant's prayer, he beats it: when the flesh and blood idol does not satisfy the civilized man, he cuts its head off.

He who slays a king and he who dies for him are alike idolaters.

### *Democracy*

If the lesser mind could measure the greater as a footrule can measure a pyramid, there would be finality in universal suffrage. As it is, the political problem remains unsolved.

Democracy substitutes election by the incompetent many for appointment by the corrupt few.

Democratic republics can no more dispense with national idols than monarchies with public functionaries.

Government presents only one problem: the discovery of a trustworthy anthropometric method.

## Liberty and Equality

He who confuses political liberty with freedom and political equality with similarity has never thought for five minutes about either.

Nothing can be unconditional: consequently nothing can be free.

Liberty means responsibility. That is why most men dread it.

Where equality is undisputed, so also is subordination.

## Crime and Punishment

Imprisonment is as irrevocable as death.

Criminals do not die by the hands of the law. They die by the hands of other men.

Assassination on the scaffold is the worst form of assassination, because there it is invested with the approval of society.

Whilst we have prisons it matters little which of us occupy the cells.

## Property

Property, said Proudhon, is theft. This is the only perfect truism that has been uttered on the subject.

## Reason

The reasonable man adapts himself to the world: the unreasonable one persists in trying to adapt the world to himself. Therefore all progress depends on the unreasonable man.

The man who listens to Reason is lost: Reason enslaves all whose minds are not strong enough to master her.

## Decency

Decency is Indecency's Conspiracy of Silence.

## Good Intentions

Hell is paved with good intentions, not with bad ones.

All men mean well.

## Charity

Charity is the most mischievous sort of pruriency.

Those who minister to poverty and disease are accomplices in the two worst of all the crimes.

He who gives money he has not earned is generous with other people's labor.

Every genuinely benevolent person loathes almsgiving and mendicity.

## Women in the Home

Home is the girl's prison and the woman's workhouse.

## Civilization

Civilization is a disease produced by the practice of building societies with rotten material.

Those who admire modern civilization usually identify it with the steam engine and the electric telegraph.

Those who understand the steam engine and the electric telegraph spend their lives in trying to replace them with something better.

The imagination cannot conceive a viler criminal than he who should build another London like the present one, nor a greater benefactor than he who should destroy it.

## The Social Question

Do not waste your time on Social Questions. What is the matter with the poor is Poverty: what is the matter with the rich is Uselessness.

## Stray Sayings

The reformer for whom the world is not good enough finds himself shoulder to shoulder with him that is not good enough for the world.

Every man over forty is a scoundrel.

Youth, which is forgiven everything, forgives itself nothing: age, which forgives itself everything, is forgiven nothing.

When we learn to sing that Britons never will be masters we shall make an end of slavery.

## QUESTIONS: Shaw, "Maxims for Revolutionists"

1. To what kind of revolutionists do you think Shaw is addressing these maxims? Consider (a) the wide scope of his attack (even in these selections); (b) the aspects of the reader's nature to which he is appealing; (c) the prevalence of wit; (d) the absence of a concrete program.
2. Why do Shaw's pronouncements in "The Golden Rule" deserve to be called *revolutionary?* Why are the maxims here an appropriate introduction to what

follows? Are the injunction "never resist temptation" and the assertion "there are no golden rules" invitations to license? Does Shaw abide by the advice he gives here to "prove all things"?

3. In what other sections of the maxims does Shaw react to *traditional* spiritual, moral, and political dogmas? Why, in these cases, is he not merely being iconoclastic? What does his revolutionary challenge have to do with the *discrepancy between ideal and reality?*

   Clues: • The art of government is the organization of idolatry.

   • Liberty means responsibility. That is why most men dread it.

   • Decency is Indecency's Conspiracy of Silence.

   • Every genuinely benevolent person loathes almsgiving and mendicity.

4. We tend to associate the revolutionary temperament with idealism about the nature of man and the ultimate goals of society. What vision of man and of his fundamental institutions emerges from Shaw's maxims? Can it be reconciled with revolutionary optimism?

   Clues: • The populace cannot understand the bureaucracy: it can only worship the national idols.

   • All men mean well.

   • Home is the girl's prison and the woman's workhouse.

   • Civilization is a disease produced by the practice of building societies with rotten materials.

   • Every man over forty is a scoundrel.

## EXERCISE

Other sections of the "Maxims for Revolutionists" deal with such aspects of man's civilization as *Education, Marriage, Religion, Greatness, Experience, Fame,* and others. Demonstrate how some or all of the following—among the most famous of Shaw's maxims—are representative of the viewpoint you have already encountered above:

a. "Marriage is popular because it combines the maximum of temptation with the maximum of opportunity."

b. "He who can, does. He who cannot, teaches."

c. "If a great man could make us understand him, we should hang him."

## *William Butler Yeats (1865–1939)*
# Easter 1916 and The Second Coming

### EASTER 1916

*The short-lived revolt of Irish Nationalists at Easter in 1916 led to the execution by the English of a number of leaders, among them Patrick Pearse (lines 24–25), Thomas MacDonagh (lines 29–30), Major John MacBride —the husband of Maud Gonne, the woman Yeats had loved, admired, and*

*vainly wooed—and James Connolly (lines 76), who with Pearse had led
the rebellion. " That woman" refers to the Countess Markiewicz (Constance
Gore-Booth), also a participant in the rebellion, who received a sentence of
life imprisonment.*

I have met them at close of day
Coming with vivid faces
From counter or desk among grey
Eighteenth-century houses.
I have passed wth a nod of the head                                5
Or polite meaningless words,
Or have lingered awhile and said
Polite meaningless words,
And thought before I had done
Of a mocking tale or a gibe                                       10
To please a companion
Around the fire at the club,
Being certain that they and I
But lived where motley is worn:
All changed, changed utterly:                                     15
A terrible beauty is born.

That woman's days were spent
In ignorant good-will,
Her nights in argument
Until her voice grew shrill.                                      20
What voice more sweet than hers
When, young and beautiful,
She rode to harriers?
This man had kept a school
And rode our wingèd horse;                                        25
This other his helper and friend
Was coming into his force;
He might have won fame in the end,
So sensitive his nature seemed,
So daring and sweet his thought.                                 30
This other man I had dreamed
A drunken, vainglorious lout.
He had done most bitter wrong
To some who are near my heart,
Yet I number him in the song;                                     35
He, too, has resigned his part
In the casual comedy;
He, too, has been changed in his turn,

Transformed utterly:                                          40
A terrible beauty is born.

Hearts with one purpose alone
Through summer and winter seem
Enchanted to a stone
To trouble the living stream.
The horse that comes from the road,                           45
The rider, the birds that range
From cloud to tumbling cloud,
Minute by minute they change;
A shadow of cloud on the stream
Changes minute by minute;                                     50
A horse-hoof slides on the brim,
And a horse plashes within it;
The long-legged moor-hens dive,
And hens to moor-cocks call;
Minute by minute they live:                                   55
The stone's in the midst of all.

Too long a sacrifice
Can make a stone of the heart.
O when may it suffice?
That is Heaven's part, our part                               60
To murmur name upon name,
As a mother names her child
When sleep at last has come
On limbs that had run wild.
What is it but nightfall–                                     65
No, no, not night but death;
Was it needless death after all?
For England may keep faith
For all that is done and said.
We know their dream; enough                                   70
To know they dreamed and are dead ;
And what if excess of love
Bewildered them till they died?
I write it out in a verse—
MacDonagh and MacBride                                        75
And Connolly and Pearse
Now and in time to be,
Wherever green is worn,
Are changed, changed utterly:
A terrible beauty is born.                                    80

*September 25, 1916*

## QUESTIONS: *Yeats, "Easter 1916"*

1. What aspects of the first stanza anticipate *by contrast* the nature of the "terrible beauty" that has come into being?

   *Clues:* • From counter or desk among grey
   Eighteenth-century houses.

   • Or polite meaningless words,

   • But lived where motley is worn:

   What single word early in the stanza suggests the possibility of change?

2. Why is the significant revolutionary experience conceived in paradoxical terms? Consider what other momentous experience qualifies the poet's judgment.

   *Clues:* • A *terrible beauty* is *born.*

   • He, too, has *resigned* his part
   In the *casual comedy;*

   • Transformed *utterly:*

3. How does the poet's view of the various natures of those to whom he pays tribute enhance the meaningfulness of the transfiguration they have undergone?

   *Clues:* • In *ignorant* good-will,

   • Until her voice grew *shrill.*

   • So *daring* and *sweet* his thought.

   • A drunken, vainglorious lout.

4. What is the central significance of the image of the *stone* in stanza 3? Consider the following elements in the stanza:

   a. The paradoxical meanings of "with one purpose alone," "Enchanted," "To trouble the living stream."

   b. The actions of man, the animals, and nature (note "range," "tumbling," "change," "slides," "plashes," "dive," "call").

   c. The sense of time ("Through summer and winter" and "Minute by minute"). How does the treatment of the stone in this stanza prepare us for the reference to it in the last stanza?

5. What larger questions does the poet raise in the concluding stanza about the ultimate nature and value of revolutionary action?

   *Clues:* • What is it but nightfall?
   No, no, not night but death;

   • And what if excess of love
   Bewildered them till they died?

6. Has Yeats lived up to his conception of the "part" he must play? Consider his description of it:

   To *murmur* name upon name
   As a mother *names* her child
   When *sleep at last* has come
   On limbs that had *run wild.*

   In what sense can it be said that through the poem itself "a terrible beauty is born"?

## The Second Coming

*This poem, written in 1919, reflects a reaction to the recent cataclysms of World War I and the Russian Revolution (1917) and to the continuing unrest in Ireland itself (independence was not achieved until 1921). But the poem's implications transcend the immediate events as well as the moral and political climate of Yeats's age.*

Turning and turning in the widening gyre[1]
The falcon cannot hear the falconer;
Things fall apart; the centre cannot hold;
Mere anarchy is loosed upon the world,
The blood-dimmed tide is loosed, and everywhere          5
The ceremony of innocence is drowned;
The best lack all conviction, while the worst
Are full of passionate intensity.

Surely some revelation is at hand;
Surely the Second Coming[2] is at hand.          10
The Second Coming! Hardly are those words out
When a vast image out of *Spiritus Mundi*[3]
Troubles my sight: somewhere in sands of the desert
A shape with lion body and the head of a man,
A gaze blank and pitiless as the sun,          15
Is moving its slow thighs, while all about it
Reel shadows of the indignant desert birds.
The darkness drops again; but now I know
That twenty centuries of stony sleep
Were vexed to nightmare by a rocking cradle,          20
And what rough beast, its hour come round at last,
Slouches towards Bethlehem to be born?

## Questions: *Yeats, "The Second Coming"*

1. Why is the image of falcon and falconer an effective means of suggesting that chaos has become the central phenomenon of the world the poet is describing?
2. What figure of speech is implied in the repeated phrase "is loosed"? How does it continue to develop the central point of this stanza and prepare us for the animal images in the last stanza (for example, "Reel shadows of the indignant

---

[1] *gyre:* a spiraling or circular movement. The term is also associated in Yeats with a cyclical pattern of history, a cycle giving way to its opposite after two thousand years.

[2] *Second Coming:* a term applicable both to the prophecy of Christ's return (*Matthew* 24) and the vision of an anti-Christ (1 John 2:18–22; 4:3; 2 John 7).

[3] *Spiritus Mundi:* World Spirit and *Anima Mundi* (World Soul) suggest the collective memory or unconscious of the human race.

desert birds")? What connotations of an earlier cataclysm do we attach to the "blood-dimmed tide" and the reference to "drowned"? In what way is the title pertinent here?

3. How can we reconcile the seeming contradiction in associating "ceremony" with its connotation of artifice with "innocence" and its suggestion of spontaneity? How is the central meaning of the stanza heightened by this conjunction? How does one account for the paradoxical situation in the last two lines of stanza 1?

4. How are the basic characteristics of the figure in stanza 2 suggestive of an anti-Christ?

   *Clues:* • A shape with *lion* body and the head of a man,
   A gaze *blank* and *pitiless* as the sun,
   Is moving its *slow thighs* . . .

   • And what *rough* beast, its hour come round at last,
   *Slouches.* . . .

   Does the *shape* of the creature here described perhaps have some connection with Yeats's reference in stanza 1 to "passionate intensity" and the absence of "all conviction?" Why in "the head of a man" might the gaze be "blank and pitiless"?

5. How can one explain the paradox of being "vexed to nightmare by a rocking cradle"? What qualitative difference is suggested between the *nightmare* effect of that birth and that of the imminent birth in Bethlehem which concludes the poem? Would the term *vexed* be applicable as a possible reaction to this new phenomenon? Explain.

6. In stanza 1 destructive connotations are attached to water imagery. How does the nature imagery in stanza 2 manage to evoke a certain *quality* of chaos? Consider the effect of "sands," "desert," and "sun" leading up to "stony sleep."

7. Taking into account the preceding questions on details, suggest the final general impression the poem leaves of Yeats's evaluation of his own world and of the future.

## EXERCISE

Yeats's lines "The best lack all conviction, while the worst/ Are full of passionate intensity" have often been quoted in recent years. Discuss the applicability of these lines to such contemporary events as (a) the Democratic National Convention of 1968, (b) recent campus upheavals (consider their connection with the American involvement in the war in Southeast Asia), and (c) the handling of and reactions to racial problems in the United States.

## E. E. Cummings (1894–1962)
# i sing of Olaf

i sing of Olaf glad and big
whose warmest heart recoiled at war:
a conscientious object-or

his wellbelovéd colonel (trig[1]
westpointer most succinctly bred)                    5
took erring Olaf soon in hand;
but—though an host of overjoyed
noncoms (first knocking on the head
him) do through icy waters roll
that helplessness which others stroke            10
with brushes recently employed
anent[2] this muddy toiletbowl,
while kindred intellects evoke
allegiance per blunt instruments—
Olaf (being to all intents                          15
a corpse and wanting any rag
upon what God unto him gave)
responds without getting annoyed
"I will not kiss your f.ing flag"

straightway the silver bird looked grave        20
(departing hurriedly to shave)

but—though all kinds of officers
(a yearning nation's blueeyed pride)
their passive prey did kick and curse
until for wear their clarion                         25
voices and boots were much the worse,
and egged the firstclassprivates on
his rectum wickedly to tease
by means of skillfully applied
bayonets roasted hot with heat—                  30
Olaf (upon what were once knees)
does almost ceaselessly repeat
"there is some s. I will not eat"

[1] *trig:* trim, neat, tidy; also has connotations of firmness and strength.
[2] *anent:* with reference to.

our president, being of which
assertions duly notified                                        35
threw the yellowsonofabitch
into a dungeon, where he died

Christ (of His mercy infinite)
i pray to see; and Olaf, too

preponderatingly because                                        40
unless statistics lie he was
more brave than me: more blond than you.

## QUESTIONS: *Cummings, "i sing of Olaf"*

1. The language in this poem is clearly unusual. Would it be reasonable to argue that part of what makes it unusual is that it consists of two or more *levels of diction* (forms and patterns of English usage) that are being combined in the poem? How would you distinguish between these levels? Which words, phrases, sentences belong to which category? What is achieved by juxtaposing these different kinds of diction?

   *Clues:*  • (trig
   • him) do through icy waters roll
     that helplessness which others stroke
   • per
   • duly notified
   • preponderatingly
   • muddy toiletbowl
   • blunt instruments
   • rectum
   • dungeon
   • f.ing flag
   • s.
   • threw the yellowsonofabitch
   Cummings systematically disassociates *language* from the reality it conveys and describes. In what way is this technique a comment on institutions like the government and the Army?

2. Cummings gives his poem a traditional epic beginning, reminding the reader of the *Iliad* ("Sing, goddess, the anger of Peleus' son Achilleus . . .") and the *Aeneid* (I sing of arms and the man . . ."). What effect does he gain by placing Olaf in the tradition of Achilles, Aeneas, and other epic heroes? Does the epic framework jar or harmonize with the fact that Olaf is a Scandinavian-American?

3. Olaf speaks only twice in the poem, each time in a simple declarative sentence centered on an obscenity. A hostile reader might feel that Olaf's reactions confirm the stereotype of the "dumb Swede," especially when we note that Olaf is described as "glad and big," and that in our culture a warm heart is often associated with an empty head. Is Cummings *confirming* the stereotype or is he *working* with it? What is the relation between Olaf's speaking style and the polysyllabic jargon that studs the poem? What is here suggested about the connection between language and sincerity in the modern world?

4. Olaf is tortured not only by the Army power structure (the colonel, the noncoms, "all kinds of officers") but also by what are presumably his peers, "the first-classprivates." A hostile reader might say that Cummings is too easily attracting our sympathy toward Olaf by an exaggerated portrayal of individual innocence attacked by total collective evil. Is there some validity to this criticism?

5. Most readers would feel instinctively that the narrator of the poem sympathizes with Olaf and hates his torturers. Why then does he describe Olaf as "erring," and the worst part of the torture as teasing? In what sense does he use the adverb *wickedly* in this context?

6. How do the following curious usages serve as vehicles of criticism for the poet: "conscientious object-or," "wellbeloved," "westpointer," "the silver bird," "blueeyed," "firstclassprivates," "yellowsonofabitch"?

7. The verse paragraphs describing the torture are long; the others are very short. Why? Are all the short paragraphs short for the same reason?

8. Olaf is blond and presumably blue-eyed. The officers who torture him are blue-eyed and presumably blond. The narrator assures us in the closing line that Olaf was "more brave than me: more blond than you." Why all this fuss about eye- and hair-color, especially if these characteristics fail to distinguish the tortured from the torturers?

## EXERCISES

1. Write an essay on whether the experience of Cummings' poem encourages one to speech or to silence.

2. Compare Cummings' denunciation of the American system with that of Allen Ginsberg in "America." How does Ginsberg's *method* differ from that of Cummings? What are the similarities and differences in the use each writer makes of humor and irony? Consider which poem is more effective and why.

3. Comment on the possible reactions this poem might have evoked in Malcolm X (as he presents himself in Chapter 14 of his *Autobiography*).

*George Orwell (1903–1950)*

# Marrakech

As the corpse went past the flies left the restaurant table in a cloud and rushed after it, but they came back a few minutes later.

The little crowd of mourners—all men and boys, no women—threaded their way across the market-place between the piles of pomegranates and the taxis and the camels, wailing a short chant over and over again. What really appeals to the flies is that the corpses here are never put into coffins, they are merely wrapped in a piece of rag and carried on a rough wooden bier on the shoulders of four friends. When the friends get to the burying-ground they hack an oblong hole a foot or two deep, dump the body in it and fling over it a little of the dried-up, lumpy earth, which is like broken brick. No gravestone, no name, no identifying mark of any kind. The burying-ground is merely a huge waste of hummocky earth, like a derelict building-lot. After a month or two no one can even be certain where his own relatives are buried.

When you walk through a town like this—two hundred thousand inhabitants, of whom at least twenty thousand own literally nothing except the rags they stand up in—when you see how the people live, and still more how easily they die, it is always difficult to believe that you are walking among human beings. All colonial empires are in reality founded upon that fact. The people have brown faces—besides, there are so many of them! Are they really the same flesh as yourself? Do they even have names? Or are they merely a kind of undifferentiated brown stuff, about as individual as bees or coral insects? They rise out of the earth, they sweat and starve for a few years, and then they sink back into the nameless mounds of the graveyard and nobody notices that they are gone. And even the graves themselves soon fade back into the soil. Sometimes, out for a walk, as you break your way through the prickly pear, you notice that it is rather bumpy underfoot, and only a certain regularity in the bumps tells you that you are walking over skeletons.

I was feeding one of the gazelles in the public gardens.

Gazelles are almost the only animals that look good to eat when they are still alive, in fact, one can hardly look at their hindquarters without thinking of mint sauce. The gazelle I was feeding seemed to know that this thought was in my mind, for though it took the piece of bread I was holding out it obviously did not like me. It nibbled rapidly at the bread, then lowered its head and tried to butt me, then took another nibble and then butted again. Probably its idea was that if it could drive me away the bread would somehow remain hanging in mid-air.

An Arab navvy working on the path nearby lowered his heavy hoe and sidled slowly towards us. He looked from the gazelle to the bread and from the bread to the gazelle, with a sort of quiet amazement, as though he had never seen anything quite like this before. Finally he said shyly in French:

"*I* could eat some of that bread."

I tore off a piece and he stowed it gratefully in some secret place under his rags. This man is an employee of the Municipality.

When you go through the Jewish quarters you gather some idea of what the medieval ghettoes were probably like. Under their Moorish rulers the Jews were only allowed to own land in certain restricted areas, and after centuries of this kind of treatment they have ceased to bother about overcrowding. Many of the streets are a good deal less than six feet wide, the houses are completely windowless, and sore-eyed children cluster everywhere in unbelievable numbers, like clouds of flies. Down the centre of the street there is generally running a little river of urine.

In the bazaar huge families of Jews, all dressed in the long black robe and little black skull-cap, are working in dark fly-infested booths that look like caves. A carpenter sits crosslegged at a prehistoric lathe, turning chair-legs at lightning speed. He works the lathe with a bow in his right hand and guides the chisel with his left foot, and thanks to a lifetime of sitting in this position his left leg is warped out of shape. At his side his grandson, aged six, is already starting on the simpler parts of the job.

I was just passing the coppersmiths' booths when somebody noticed that I was lighting a cigarette. Instantly, from the dark holes all round, there was a frenzied rush of Jews, many of them old grandfathers with flowing grey beards, all clamouring for a cigarette. Even a blind man somewhere at the back of one of the booths heard a rumour of cigarettes and came crawling out, groping in the air with his hand. In about a minute I had used up the whole packet. None of these people, I suppose, works less than twelve hours a day, and every one of them looks on a cigarette as a more or less impossible luxury.

As the Jews live in self-contained communities they follow the same trades as the Arabs, except for agriculture. Fruit-sellers, potters, silversmiths, blacksmiths, butchers, leatherworkers, tailors, water-carriers, beggars, porters—whichever way you look you see nothing but Jews. As a matter of fact there are thirteen thousand of them, all living in the space of a few acres. A good job Hitler wasn't here. Perhaps he was on his way, however. You hear the usual dark rumours about the Jews, not only from the Arabs but from the poorer Europeans.

"Yes, mon vieux, they took my job away from me and gave it to a Jew. The Jews! They're the real rulers of this country, you know. They've got all the money. They control the banks, finance—everything."

"But," I said, "isn't it a fact that the average Jew is a labourer working for about a penny an hour?"

"Ah, that's only for show! They're all moneylenders really. They're cunning, the Jews."

In just the same way, a couple of hundred years ago, poor old women used to be burned for witchcraft when they could not even work enough magic to get themselves a square meal.

All people who work with their hands are partly invisible, and the more important the work they do, the less visible they are. Still, a white skin is always fairly conspicuous. In northern Europe, when you see a labourer ploughing a field, you probably give him a second glance. In a hot country, anywhere south of Gibraltar or east of Suez, the chances are that you don't even see him. I have noticed this again and again. In a tropical landscape one's eye takes in everything except the human beings. It takes in the dried-up soil, the prickly pear, the palm tree and the distant mountain, but it always misses the peasant hoeing at his patch. He is the same colour as the earth, and a great deal less interesting to look at.

It is only because of this that the starved countries of Asia and Africa are accepted as tourist resorts. No one would think of running cheap trips to the

Distressed Areas. But where the human beings have brown skins their poverty is simply not noticed. What does Morocco mean to a Frenchman? An orange-grove or a job in Government service. Or to an Englishman? Camels, castles, palm trees, Foreign Legionnaires, brass trays, and bandits. One could probably live there for years without noticing that for nine-tenths of the people the reality of life is an endless, back-breaking struggle to wring a little food out of an eroded soil.

Most of Morocco is so desolate that no wild animal bigger than a hare can live on it. Huge areas which were once covered with forest have turned into a treeless waste where the soil is exactly like broken-up brick. Nevertheless a good deal of it is cultivated, with frightful labour. Everything is done by hand. Long lines of women, bent double like inverted capital L's, work their way slowly across the fields, tearing up the prickly weeds with their hands, and the peasant gathering lucerne for fodder pulls it up stalk by stalk instead of reaping it, thus saving an inch or two on each stalk. The plough is a wretched wooden thing, so frail that one can easily carry it on one's shoulder, and fitted underneath with a rough iron spike which stirs the soil to a depth of about four inches. This is as much as the strength of the animals is equal to. It is usual to plough with a cow and a donkey yoked together. Two donkeys would not be quite strong enough, but on the other hand two cows would cost a little more to feed. The peasants possess no harrows, they merely plough the soil several times over in different directions, finally leaving it in rough furrows, after which the whole field has to be shaped with hoes into small oblong patches to conserve water. Except for a day or two after the rare rainstorms there is never enough water. Along the edges of the fields channels are hacked out to a depth of thirty or forty feet to get at the tiny trickles which run through the subsoil.

Every afternoon a file of very old women passes down the road outside my house, each carrying a load of firewood. All of them are mummified with age and the sun, and all of them are tiny. It seems to be generally the case in primitive communities that the women, when they get beyond a certain age, shrink to the size of children. One day a poor old creature who could not have been more than four feet tall crept past me under a vast load of wood. I stopped her and put a five-sou piece (a little more than a farthing) into her hand. She answered with a shrill wail, almost a scream, which was partly gratitude but mainly surprise. I suppose that from her point of view, by taking any notice of her, I seemed almost to be violating a law of nature. She accepted her status as an old woman, that is to say as a beast of burden. When a family is travelling it is quite usual to see a father and a grown-up son riding ahead on donkeys, and an old woman following on foot, carrying the baggage.

But what is strange about these people is their invisibility. For several weeks, always at about the same time of day, the file of old women had hobbled past the house with their firewood, and though they had registered themselves on my eyeballs I cannot truly say that I had seen them. Firewood was passing—that was how I saw it. It was only that one day I happened to be walking behind them, and the curious up-and-down motion of a load of wood drew my attention to the human being beneath it. Then for the first time I noticed the poor old earth-coloured bodies, bodies reduced to bones and leathery skin, bent double under the crushing weight. Yet I suppose I had not been five minutes on Moroccan soil before I noticed the overloading of the donkeys and was infuriated by it. There is no question that the donkeys are damnably treated. The Moroccan donkey is hardly bigger than a St. Bernard dog, it carries a load which in the British Army would be considered too much for a fifteen-hands mule, and very often its pack-saddle is not taken off its back for weeks together. But what is peculiarly pitiful is that it is the most willing creature on earth, it follows its master like a dog and does not need either bridle or halter. After a dozen years of devoted work it suddenly drops dead, whereupon its master tips it into the ditch and the village dogs have torn its guts out before it is cold.

This kind of thing makes one's blood boil, whereas—on the whole—the plight of the human beings does not. I am not commenting, merely pointing to a fact. People with brown skins are next door to invisible. Anyone can be sorry for the donkey with its galled back, but it is generally owing to some kind of accident if one even notices the old woman under her load of sticks.

As the storks flew northward the Negroes were marching southward— a long, dusty column, infantry, screwgun batteries, and then more infantry, four or five thousand men in all, winding up the road with a clumping of boots and a clatter of iron wheels.

They were Senegalese, the blackest Negroes in Africa, so black that sometimes it is difficult to see whereabouts on their necks the hair begins. Their splendid bodies were hidden in reach-me-down khaki uniforms, their feet squashed into boots that looked like blocks of wood, and every tin hat seemed to be a couple of sizes too small. It was very hot and the men had marched a long way. They slumped under the weight of their packs and the curiously sensitive black faces were glistening with sweat.

As they went past a tall, very young Negro turned and caught my eye. But the look he gave me was not in the least the kind of look you might expect. Not hostile, not contemptuous, not sullen, not even inquisitive. It was the shy, wide-eyed Negro look, which actually is a look of profound respect. I saw how it was. This wretched boy, who is a French citizen and has therefore been dragged from the forest to scrub floors and catch syphilis in garrison towns, actually has feelings of reverence before a white skin. He has been taught that the white race are his masters, and he still believes it.

But there is one thought which every white man (and in this connection it doesn't matter twopence if he calls himself a socialist) thinks when he sees a black army marching past. "How much longer can we go on kidding these people? How long before they turn their guns in the other direction?"

It was curious, really. Every white man there had this thought stowed somewhere or other in his mind. I had it, so had the other onlookers, so had the officers on their sweating chargers and the white N.C.O.'s marching in the ranks. It was a kind of secret which we all knew and were too clever to tell; only the Negroes didn't know it. And really it was like watching a flock of cattle to see the long column, a mile or two miles of armed men, flowing peacefully up the road, while the great white birds drifted over them in the opposite direction, glittering like scraps of paper.

*[1939]*

## QUESTIONS: *Orwell, "Marrakech"*

1. Often we think of fiction and essays as belonging to two different literary categories. Thus we may analyze a short story's images, episodes, narrative patterns, and development, while reading an essay only for its content, for the author's viewpoint, or his message. How does Orwell's "Marrakech" cut across the two categories?

   *Clues:* • As *the corpse* went past the flies left the restaurant table. . . . [Many people] own literally *nothing* except the rags they stand up in . . . you are walking over *skeletons* . . . .[One's eye] always *misses* the peasant hoeing at his patch . . . an *eroded* soil. Most of Morocco is so *desolate* that no wild animal bigger than a hare can live on it . . . there is *never enough water.* . . . All of them are mummified . . . bodies *reduced* to bones and leathery skin. . . .

   • As the corpse went past the *flies* left the restaurant table in a cloud and *rushed* after it. . . . [In the Jewish quarters] sore-eyed children *cluster* everywhere in unbelievable numbers, like *clouds of flies.* . . . In the bazaar huge families of Jews . . . are working in dark *fly-infested* booths that look like caves. . . . Instantly, from the dark holes all around, there was a frenzied *rush* of Jews . . .

   • As the corpse went past the flies left the *restaurant* table. . . . The little crowd of mourners . . . threaded their way across the market-place between the *piles of pomegranates* and the taxis and the camels. . . . I was *feeding* one of the gazelles in the public gardens. Gazelles are almost the only animals that look good to eat when they are still alive. . . . "*I* could eat some of that bread.". . . In just the same way, a couple of hundred years ago, poor old women used to be burned for witchcraft when they could not even work enough magic to get themselves *a square meal.*

2. Orwell's final point is that a colonial rebellion against the white rulers is inevitable. Yet much of the preceding material has not directly prepared us for this idea. What in this material suggests that Orwell is concerned with more than a political situation? In your judgment is the essay weakened or strengthened by its scope?

   *Clues:* • "Ah, that's only for show! They're all moneylenders really. They're cunning, the Jews."

   • Huge areas which were once covered with forest have turned into a treeless waste where the soil is exactly like broken-up brick.

- Except for a day or two after the rare rainstorms there is never enough water.
- [The inhabitants of Marrakech] rise out of the earth, they sweat and starve for a few years, and then they sink back into the nameless mounds of the graveyard. . . . [The peasant] is the same colour as the earth, and a great deal less interesting to look at. . . . Then for the first time I noticed the poor earth-coloured bodies, bodies reduced to bones and leathery skin, bent double under the crushing weight. . . . [The soldiers] were Senegalese, the blackest Negroes in Africa, so black that sometimes it is difficult to see whereabouts on their necks the hair begins. Their splendid bodies were hidden in reach-me-down khaki uniforms. . . . This wretched boy, who is a French citizen and has therefore been dragged from the forest. . . .

3. A repeated point in Orwell's essay is that human beings with "brown skins" are simply invisible to white colonialists, and count for less in the latter's eyes than animals. He gives several grim examples of this phenomenon, based on his own behavior and observations, yet we leave the essay with a sense that the brown-skinned people *are* human beings. How does Orwell convey this impression?

   *Clues:* • An Arab navvy . . . *sidled* slowly towards us. He looked from the gazelle to the bread and from the bread to the gazelle, with a sort of *quiet amazement*. . . . Finally he said *shyly* in French:
   "*I* could eat some of that bread."
   I tore off a piece and he stowed it *gratefully* in some *secret* place under his rags.
   • She answered with a shrill wail, almost a scream, which was partly *gratitude* but mainly *surprise*.
   • They slumped under the weight of their packs and the *curiously sensitive* black faces were glistening with sweat.

4. From the beginning to the end of the essay there is a consistent narrator who speaks in the first person. But are his *attitudes* and *feelings* consistent? Except in describing the mistreatment of Moroccan donkeys, he never seems to get angry or even annoyed, and his glance at the possibility of a German massacre of Moroccan Jews is noticeably detached: "A good job Hitler wasn't there. Perhaps he was on his way, however." Yet there are occasional touches that imply both sympathy and indignation—" his left leg is warped out of shape," "poor old women used to be burned for witchcraft," "then for the first time I noticed the poor old earth-coloured bodies"—and it is hard to leave the essay without sensing Orwell's genuine *humaneness*. Why might he tend to give so little direct expression to his emotional reactions? Consider the possibility that he achieves more than one goal by his restraint.

5. What is the significance of the storks in the closing section of the essay? What is achieved by comparing them to "scraps of paper"? Why does Orwell twice point out that they are flying northward, "in the opposite direction" to the Senegalese?

## EXERCISES

1. Compare "Marrakech" with Chapter 14 of *The Autobiography of Malcolm X.* Consider whether the Black Muslim repudiation of Christianity and the white man corresponds to the anticolonial rebellion envisioned at the end of Orwell's

essay. Comment on whether certain aspects of the Black Muslim movement might have surprised Orwell.

2. In the Introduction to Orwell's *Homage to Catalonia* Lionel Trilling says of him: "He made no effort to show that his heart was in the right place, or the left place. He was not interested in where his heart might be thought to be, since he knew where it was. He was interested only in telling the truth." Discuss the pertinence of this comment to Orwell's treatment of his subject in "Marrakech." Could it be applied to Mailer's handling of "The Siege of Chicago"? If not, why not?

# Cross Questions :

## *Shakespeare, Burke, Paine, Emerson, Thoreau, Arnold, Shaw, Orwell, Malcolm X*

1. These authors fall into two broad categories: those who support drastic, purposeful social change, and those who find social change abhorrent unless it makes its appearance in a gradual, evolutionary way. But there are more subtle bonds and differences between them. In order to discover what these are, identify the assumptions each writer makes about (a) the nature of man, (b) the *purpose* of society as it is actually constituted as well as its meaning for the individual, (c) what society *ought* to be.

*Clues:* *(a) The nature of man*

> Shakespeare: ... appetite, a universal wolf,

> Arnold: ... men, all over the country, are beginning to assert and put into practice an Englishman's right to do what he likes; his right to march where he likes, meet where he likes ... threaten as he likes, smash as he likes.

> Shaw: Criminals do not die by the hand of the law. They die by the hands of other men.

> Malcolm X: "The greatest miracle Christianity has achieved in America is that the black man in white Christian hands has not grown violent. It *is* a miracle that 22 million black people have not *risen up* against their oppressors. . . . It *is* a *miracle* that the American black people have remained a peaceful people. . . ."

> America had never seen such fantastic all-black meetings! . . .
> The white man was barred from attendance. . . .

*(b) The purpose of society*

> Burke: Government is a contrivance of human wisdom to provide for human *wants*. . . . Among these wants is to be reckoned the want . . . of a sufficient restraint upon their [men's] passions. Society requires . . . that . . . the inclinations of men should frequently be thwarted, their will controlled, and their passions brought into subjection.

Thoreau: Thus the State never intentionally confronts a man's sense, intellectual or moral, but only his body, his senses. It is not armed with superior wit or honesty, but with superior physical strength. I was not born to be forced.

Emerson: I set the private man first. He only who is able to stand alone is qualified to be a citizen.

Orwell: But there is one thought which every white man . . . thinks when he sees a black army marching past. "How much longer can we go on kidding these people?"

*(c) What society ought to be*

Thoreau: The authority of government . . . to be strictly just . . . must have the sanction and consent of the governed. . . . There will never be a really free and enlightened State, until the State comes to recognize the individual as a higher and independent power. . . .

Arnold: We have not the notion, so familiar on the Continent and to antiquity, of *the State*,—the nation in its collective and corporate character. . . .

Malcolm X: "My black brothers and sisters—of all religious beliefs, or of no religious beliefs—we all have in common the greatest binding tie we could have . . . we are all *black* people! . . . "Our *enemy* is the *white man*!"

2. What relation is there between the writers' opinions on these three questions and their attitudes toward revolution, protest, and anarchy?

## Burke, Arnold

Both of these writers imply that the man who is truly humane and civilized is one who has an understanding of, and a respect for, tradition and history. Does this view amount to a repudiation of all social change? Is social change something that Burke and Arnold, in any way, allow for? If so, how? If not, what means do they recommend for the handling of individual or social disorder?

Clues: Burke: If it could have been made clear to me, that the king and queen of France . . . were inexorable and cruel tyrants, that they had formed a deliberate scheme for massacring the National Assembly . . . I should think their captivity just.

Arnold: But what if rough and coarse action, ill-calculated action, action with insufficient light, is, and has for a long time been, our bane? . . . In that case, to refuse to lend a hand to the rougher and coarser movements going on round us, to make the primary need, both for oneself and others, to consist in enlightening ourselves . . . is surely the best and in real truth the most practical line our endeavours can take.

## Thoreau, Orwell, Malcolm X, Cummings, Mailer, Ginsberg

1. Identify the central institutions of power or authority criticized by each of these writers. Do these institutions have anything in common? Do the criticisms have anything in common? Do you think that most institutions, groups, and organizations are beset by such characteristic problems and dissatisfactions?

   *Clues:*    Thoreau:    This American government .... has not the vitality and force of a single living man. ... It is a sort of wooden gun. ... Governments show ... how successfully men can be imposed on. ...

           Orwell:   ... when you see how the people live, and still more how easily they die, it is always difficult to believe that you are walking among human beings. All colonial empires are in reality founded upon that fact.

           Mailer:   The nation divided was going to war with stinks; each side would inflict a stink upon the other. (Chapter 14).

                   On the greatest national issue any convention had ever faced since the second world war, debate would provide an hour of speech for each side. (Chapter 15).

                   Police cars rolled up, prisoners were beaten, shoved into wagons, driven away. (Chapter 16).

           Ginsberg:  I'm sick of your insane demands.

                   Are you going to let your emotional life be run by Time Magazine?

        Cummings:  straightway the silver bird looked grave
                     (departing hurriedly to shave)

                     but—though all kinds of officers
                     (a yearning nation's blueeyed pride)
                     their passive prey did kick and curse

2. Are any of the problems inherent in institutions and organizations *also* found in individual men?

   *Clue:*    Malcom X:    "Why *shouldn't* this white man who likes to think and call himself so good, and so generous . . . subsidize a separate state . . . for we black people who have been such good and faithful slaves and servants?"

## Shelley, Emerson, Orwell, Tolson, Malcolm X

1. Oppression is a theme in the works you have read by these authors. On the basis of these works would it be correct to say (a) that oppression is a universal fact inherent in the very existence of organized society or (b) that there are qualitative differences between one kind of oppression and another?

   *Clues:*    Shelley:  The seed ye sow, another reaps;
                       The wealth ye find, another keeps;

                     A people starved and stabbed in the untilled field,—

Emerson: ... citizens of Massachusetts, legal voters, have emigrated to national territory under the sanction of every law, and are then set on by highwaymen, driven from their new homes, pillaged, and numbers of them killed and scalped, and the whole world knows that this is no accidental brawl, but a systematic war to the knife, and in defiance of all laws and liberties. ...

Orwell: In a tropical landscape one's eye takes in everything except the human beings ... it always misses the peasant hoeing at his patch. He is the same colour as the earth, and a great deal less interesting to look at.

Tolson: Black slaves singing *Swing Low, Sweet Chariot*
In cabins of death,
Black slaves singing *Go Down Moses*
In the canebreaks of the Southern Pharaohs.

Malcolm X: ... if you study closely any conked ... Negro, you usually find he is an ignorant Negro. ... He will discover, just as I did, that he will be much-improved mentally whenever he discovers enough black self-pride to have that mess clipped off, and then wear the natural hair that God gives black men to wear.

2. Do any of these authors suggest that oppression, rather than being a *social condition* is in essence *a state of mind*? If so, explain which author gives this impression and why. Cite specific passages that support your view.

3. Neither Shelley (a member of the British upper class) nor Emerson (a Boston intellectual) nor Orwell (a white British journalist) were members of the oppressed groups they portray; Tolson and Malcolm X were. Do either *tone* or *imagery* in the works themselves show that the first group were writing out of sympathy and the second from direct personal experience? Cite specific passages.

## Burke, Paine, Shaw, Orwell, Malcolm X

The assertion that "all men are created equal" has been an axiom of social philosophy since its appearance in the Declaration of Independence. The assertion has been admired for its humanitarianism and criticized for denying biological reality. Where does each of these writers stand on the matter? Can they be divided into egalitarians and elitists, or are there significant differences even between those who share the same basic position?

*Clues:*

Burke: They [men] have a right to the acquisitions of their parents; to the nourishment and improvement of their offspring; to instruction in life, and to consolation in death. Whatever each man can separately do, without trespassing upon others, he has a right to do for himself. ... all men have equal rights; but not to equal things.

Paine: But everything we see or hear offensive to our feelings and derogatory to the human character should lead to other reflections than those of reproach. Even the beings who commit them have some claim to our consideration. . . . They arise, as an unavoidable consequence, out of the ill construction of all old governments. . . .

Shaw:    Do not do unto others as you would that they should do unto you. Their tastes may not be the same.

Liberty means responsibility. That is why most men dread it.

Where equality is undisputed, so also is subordination.

Orwell:    When you walk through a town like this . . . when you see how the people live, and still more how easily they die, it is always difficult to believe that you are walking among human beings.

Malcolm X:    "The white man so guilty of white supremacy can't hide *his* guilt by trying to accuse The Honorable Elijah Muhammad of teaching black supremacy and hate! All Mr. Muhammad is doing is trying to uplift the black man's mentality and the black man's social and economic condition in this country."

## Burke, Paine, Carlyle

Each of these writers takes the same body of basic fact—the events of the French Revolution—and interprets them according to his polemical and political inclinations. Does such a treatment of events show that Henry Ford was right when he declared "History is bunk"? If not, why not?

## Burke, Carlyle, Shaw, Cummings, Malcolm X, Lowell

1. In his novel *Animal Farm*, Orwell dramatizes one of the central contradictions of revolution: when it succeeds it creates a new "establishment" that often becomes as authoritarian and insensitive as the one that has been overthrown. Do any of these writers apply a comparable paradoxical insight to social change?

Clues:    Burke:    But power, of some kind or other, will survive the shock in which manners and opinions perish; and it will find other and worse means for its support.

Shaw:    He who slays a king and he who dies for him are alike idolaters.

Malcolm X:    The white man was barred from attendance. . . . In anterooms just inside the halls, more Fruit of Islam men and white-gowned veiled mature Muslim sisters thoroughly searched every man, woman, and child seeking to enter. Any alcohol and tobacco had to be checked, and any objects which could possibly be used to attempt to harm Mr. Muhammad.

Lowell:  And fenced their gardens with the Redman's bones;

Pilgrims unhoused by Geneva's night,

And candles gutter by an empty altar,

2. How is an awareness of the contradictions in man's nature and man's institutions likely to affect an author's attitude toward social change? Is it possible for such an awareness to leave the revolutionary drive *unaffected*?

## *Wordsworth, Thoreau, Arnold, Yeats, Cummings, Malcolm X*

1. Thoreau in *Civil Disobedience*, and Olaf in Cummings' poem act upon their convictions. What characteristics do they share? In what significant ways are they different? Does one of them command more of your respect than the other? Justify your answer.

   *Clues:*     Thoreau:    It is not a man's duty, as a matter of course, to devote himself to the eradication of any, even the most enormous wrong . . . but it is his duty . . . to wash his hands of it, and . . . not to give it practically his support. . . . If I devote myself to other pursuits and contemplations, I must first see . . . that I do not pursue them sitting upon another man's shoulders.

              Cummings: [Olaf] responds without getting annoyed

   "I will not kiss your f.ing flag."

   Olaf (upon what were once knees)

   does almost ceaselessly repeat

   "there is some s. I will not eat"

2. Leaders like Toussaint, the three Irish revolutionaries in Yeats' poem "Easter 1916," and Elijah Muhammad are all driven by powerful convictions. Do their convictions differ in any *fundamental* way from those of Olaf in Cummings' poem and of Thoreau in *Civil Disobedience*? Are they distinguished from Olaf and Thoreau by any *personal* characteristics? Does anything like a "leader type" emerge from these different portraits?

   *Clues:*     Yeats: He might have won fame in the end,

   So sensitive his nature seemed,

   So daring and sweet his thought.

   This other man . . .

   He too has been changed in his turn,

   Transformed utterly:

   A terrible beauty is born.

          Malcom X: I couldn't understand how Mr. Muhammad could maintain his calm and patience, hearing the things I told him.

3. What support (if any) do the works of these writers give to the idea that leadership is *entirely* the product of historical circumstances? What support (if any) do they give to Carlyle's assertion that "history is the biography of great men"? Or do they suggest that there is a viable intermediate position between these extremes?

4. Arnold, in *Culture and Anarchy*, points out the antisocial implications of "doing as one likes." Of the figures mentioned above (in questions 1 through 3) is any merely "doing as he likes"? Can any clear distinction be drawn between the kind of attitude Arnold deplores and the activities and attitudes you have read about in this section?

## Shakespeare, Yeats

1. Neither Shakespeare in *Troilus and Cressida* nor Yeats in "The Second Coming" is writing about specific events. Each seems to be reflecting imaginatively upon the implications of anarchy. Do they share any characteristic *imagery* or tone?

   *Clues:* Shakespeare:

   > But when the planets
   > In evil mixture to disorder wander,
   > What plagues, and what portents, what mutiny,
   > What raging of the sea, shaking of earth,
   > Commotion in the winds, frights, changes, horrors,
   > Divert and crack, rend and deracinate
   > The unity and married calm of states

   Yeats:

   > Things fall apart; the centre cannot hold;
   > The ceremony of innocence is drowned;

2. The effect of anarchy on politics, society, and even the cosmos is suggested in the imagery of these poems. Is there a parallel impact on the individual? If so, what is the imagery used by Shakespeare and Yeats to suggest this impact? Are there any significant differences between the imagery each poet chooses to convey this aspect of his analysis?

3. Here are some passages from "The Revelation of St. John" in the New Testament:

   > When he opened the fourth seal, I heard the voice . . . say, "Come!" And I saw, and behold, a pale horse, and its rider's name was Death, and Hades followed him; and they were given power over a fourth of the earth, to kill with sword and with famine and with pestilence and by wild beasts of the earth. . . .

   > When he opened the sixth seal, I looked, and behold, there was a great earthquake; and the sun became black as sackcloth, the full moon became like blood, and the stars of the sky fell to the earth. . . .

   > And I saw a beast rising out of the sea, with ten horns and seven heads. . . . And the beast that I saw was like a leopard, its feet were like a bear's, and its mouth was like a lion's mouth. . . . One of its heads seemed to have a mortal wound, but its mortal wound was healed, and the whole earth followed the beast with wonder. Men . . . worshipped the beast, saying, "Who is like the beast, and who can fight against it?"

   Compare the imagery of these passages with the selection from *Troilus and Cressida* and with Yeats's "The Second Coming." What does your comparison suggest about the originality of the viewpoints expressed by these two writers?

## Burke, Paine, Carlyle, Mailer

In his *Reflections* Burke describes the regicides as "a band of cruel ruffians and assassins" and their activities as "Theban and Thracian Orgies." His account exemplifies the fear of mob action that often characterizes conservative or antidemocratic sentiment. How do leaderless group actions—what Burke would call "the mob"— appear in the other authors listed? In each case, what is the characteristic *tone* and *imagery* with which such actions are described? How do they differ from and how do they resemble the tone and imagery of Burke? What, in each case, is the connection between the tone and imagery chosen by the writer and his general social, political, and moral views?

*Clues:* Paine: On one side, an army of nearly thirty thousand men; on the other, an unarmed body of citizens; for the citizens of Paris, on whom the National Assembly must then immediately depend, were as unarmed and as undisciplined as the citizens of London are now.

    Carlyle: A roaring sea of human heads, inundating both Courts; billowing against all passages: Menadic women; infuriated men, mad with revenge, with love of mischief, love of plunder!

    Mailer: The demonstrators were afterward delighted to have been man-handled before the public eye, delighted to have pushed and prodded, antagonized and provoked the cops over these days with rocks and bottles and cries of "Pig" to the point where police had charged in a blind rage. . . .

## General Questions

1. Drawing upon the readings in Section II, give *separate* definitions of *protest, revolution,* and *anarchy.* Do these three terms imply three different attitudes toward social change? Or do they describe three different means of bringing it about?

2. Of the works in this section, which (a) approach their subject sympathetically, (b) handle their subject critically, (c) incite the reader to undertake social action of some kind, (d) make the reader feel ambivalent about the meaningfulness or advisability of such action, or (e) do two or more of these things at the same time? (Specify which.)

3. Abbie Hoffman coined the phrase "Revolution for the hell of it!" Does the phrase indicate that the twentieth century has produced a new revolutionary theory which moves beyond the categories of the writers in this section? Might Hoffman's revolutionary vision stand a better chance of success than those of his predecessors? Would those young people of today who share this drastic view, in your opinion, regard the works in this section as outmoded? (Note: in answering this question, you may find it useful to refer back to Section I, "The Generation Gap.")

4. It has been suggested that the true revolutionary wave of the present time is cultural rather than political or social. In fact, it has been asserted that the "cultural revolution" will succeed where all previous revolutions have failed, and will bring about an egalitarian, or anti-elitist, or detechnologized world. Do you agree? Draw upon the works in this section in writing an essay on this question.

# Section III

## Dropping Out and Tuning In: Escape from the World and Transcendence of Self

## James Dickey (1923–    )

# In the Mountain Tent

I am hearing the shape of the rain
Take the shape of the tent and believe it,
Laying down all around where I lie
A profound, unspeakable law.
I obey, and am free-falling slowly                     5


Through the thought-out leaves of the wood
Into the minds of animals.
I am there in the shining of water
Like dark, like light, out of Heaven.


I am there like the dead, or the beast             10
Itself, which thinks of a poem—
Green, plausible, living, and holy—
And cannot speak, but hears,
Calling forth from the waiting of things,


A vast, proper, reinforced crying                      15
With the sifted, harmonious pause,
The sustained intake of all breath
Before the first word of the Bible.


At midnight water dawns
Upon the held skulls of the foxes                       20
And weasels and tousled hares
On the eastern side of the mountain.
Their light is the image I make


As I wait as if recently killed,
Receptive, fragile, half-smiling,                          25
My brow watermarked with the mark
On the wing of a moth


And the tent taking shape on my body
Like ill-fitting, Heavenly clothes.
From holes in the ground comes my voice          30
In the God-silenced tongue of the beasts.
"I shall rise from the dead," I am saying.

## QUESTIONS: *Dickey, "In the Mountain Tent"*

As in Marvell's "The Garden," the *transcendence of self*, which is the central subject of the poem, is intimately related to a *communion with nature.*

1. What aspects of the self are abnegated in this communion? Consider in what sense the transcendence is a retrogression to a more primitive state.

   *Clues:* • *Laying* down all around where I *lie*
   A profound, *unspeakable* law.

   • I obey, and am *free-falling* slowly

   • Through the thought-out leaves of the wood
   Into the minds of animals.

   • And cannot *speak*, but *hears*,

   • In the God-*silenced* tongue of the *beasts.*

   What is the appropriateness of the references to being "there like the dead" and "as if recently killed"?

2. What aspects of the self are raised to a more significant state?

   *Clues:* • I am there in the shining of water
   Like dark, like light, out of Heaven.

   • And the tent taking shape on my body
   Like ill-fitting, Heavenly clothes.

3. How do the references to *water* and *light* prepare for the idea in the last line?

4. How does the consistent use of religious imagery help to enforce the significance of the experience?

# *Jack Kerouac (1922–1969)*
# On the Road

### PART TWO, CHAPTER 6

It was drizzling and mysterious at the beginning of our journey. I could see that it was all going to be one big saga of the mist. "Whooee!" yelled Dean. "Here we go!" And he hunched over the wheel and gunned her; he was back in his element, everybody could see that. We were all delighted, we all realized we were leaving confusion and nonsense behind and performing our one and noble function of the time, *move.* And we moved! We flashed past the mysterious white signs in the night somewhere in New Jersey that say SOUTH (with an arrow) and WEST (with an arrow) and took the south one. New Orleans! It burned in our brains. From the dirty snows of "frosty fagtown New York," as Dean called it, all the way to the greeneries and river smells of old New Orleans at the washed-out bottom of America; then west. Ed was in the back seat; Marylou and Dean and I sat in front and had the warmest talk about the goodness and joy of life. Dean suddenly became tender. "Now dammit, look here, all of you, we all must admit that everything is fine and there's no need in the world to worry, and in fact we should realize what it would mean to us to UNDERSTAND that we're not REALLY worried about ANYTHING. Am I right?" We all agreed. "Here we go, we're all together . . . What did we do in New York? Let's forgive." We all had our spats back there. "That's behind us, merely by miles and inclinations. Now we're heading down to New Orleans to dig Old Bull Lee and ain't that going to be kicks and listen will you to this old tenorman blow his top"—he shot up the radio volume till the car shuddered—"and listen to him tell the story and put down true relaxation and knowledge."

We all jumped to the music and agreed. The purity of the road. The white line in the middle of the highway unrolled and hugged our left front tire as if glued to our groove. Dean hunched his muscular neck, T-shirted in the winter night, and blasted the car along. He insisted I drive through Baltimore for traffic practice; that was all right, except he and Marylou insisted on steering while they kissed and fooled around. It was crazy; the radio was on full blast. Dean beat drums on the dashboard till a great sag developed in it; I did too. The poor Hudson—the slow boat to China—was receiving her beating.

"Oh man, what kicks!" yelled Dean. "Now Marylou, listen really, honey, you know that I'm hotrock capable of everything at the same time and I have unlimited energy—now in San Francisco we must go on living together. I know just the place for you—at the end of the regular chain-gang run—I'll be home just a cut-hair less than every two days and for twelve hours at a stretch, and *man*, you know what we can do in twelve hours, darling. Meanwhile I'll go right on living at Camille's like nothin, see, she won't know. We can work it, we've done it before." It was all right with Marylou, she was really out for Camille's scalp. The understanding had been that Marylou would switch to me in Frisco, but I now began to see they were going to stick and I was going to be left alone on my butt at the other end of the continent. But why think about that when all the golden land's ahead of you and all kinds of unforeseen events wait lurking to surprise you and make you glad you're alive to see?

We arrived in Washington at dawn. It was the day of Harry Truman's inauguration for his second term. Great displays of war might were lined along Pennsylvania Avenue as we rolled by in our battered boat. There were B-29's, PT boats, artillery, all kinds of war material that looked murderous in the snowy grass; the last thing was a regular small ordinary lifeboat that looked pitiful and foolish. Dean slowed down to look at it. He kept shaking his head in awe. "What are these people up to? Harry's sleeping somewhere in this town. . . . Good old Harry. . . . Man from Missouri, as I am. . . . That must be his own boat."

Dean went to sleep in the back seat and Dunkel drove. We gave him specific instructions to take it easy. No sooner were we snoring than he gunned the car up to eighty, bad bearings and all, and not only that but he made a triple pass at a spot where a cop was arguing with a motorist—he was in the fourth lane of a four-lane highway, going the wrong way. Naturally the cop took after us with his siren whining. We were stopped. He told us to follow him to the station house. There was a mean cop in there who took an immediate dislike to Dean; he could smell jail all over him. He sent his cohort outdoors to question Marylou and me privately. They wanted to know how old Marylou was, they were trying to whip up a Mann Act idea. But she had her marriage certificate. Then they took me aside alone and wanted to know who was sleeping with Marylou. "Her husband," I said quite simply. They were curious. Something was fishy. They tried some amateur Sherlocking by asking the same questions twice, expecting us to make a slip. I said, "Those two fellows are going back to work on the railroad in California, this is the short one's wife, and I'm a friend on a two-week vacation from college."

The cop smiled and said, "Yeah? Is this really your own wallet?"

Finally the mean one inside fined Dean twenty-five dollars. We told them we only had forty to go all the way to the Coast; they said that made no difference to them. When Dean protested, the mean cop threatened to take him back to Pennsylvania and slap a special charge on him.

"What charge?"

"Never mind what charge. Don't worry about *that*, wise guy."

We had to give them the twenty-five. But first Ed Dunkel, that culprit, offered to go to jail. Dean considered it. The cop was infuriated; he said, "If you let your partner go to jail I'm taking you back to Pennsylvania right now. You hear that?" All we wanted to do was go. "Another speeding ticket in Virginia and you lose your car," said the mean cop as a parting volley. Dean was red in the face. We drove off silently. It was just like an invitation to steal to take our trip-money away from us. They knew we were broke and had no relatives on the road or to wire to for money. The American police are involved in psychological warfare against those Americans who don't frighten them with imposing papers and threats. It's a Victorian police force; it peers out of musty windows and wants to inquire about everything, and can make crimes if the crimes don't exist to its satisfaction. "Nine lines of crime, one of boredom." said Louis-Ferdinand Céline. Dean was so mad he wanted to come back to Virginia and shoot the cop as soon as he had a gun.

"Pennsylvania!" he scoffed. "I wish I knew what that charge was! Vag, probably; take all my money and charge me vag. Those guys have it so damn easy. They'll out and shoot you if you complain, too." There was nothing to do but get happy with ourselves again and forget about it. When we got through Richmond we began forgetting about it, and soon everything was okay.

Now we had fifteen dollars to go all the way. We'd have to pick up hitch-hikers and bum quarters off them for gas. In the Virginia wilderness suddenly we saw a man walking on the road. Dean zoomed to a stop. I looked back and said he was only a bum and probably didn't have a cent.

"We'll just pick him up for kicks!" Dean laughed. The man was a ragged, bespectacled mad type, walking along reading a paperbacked muddy book he'd found in a culvert by the road. He got in the car and went right on reading; he was incredibly filthy and covered with scabs. He said his name was Hyman Solomon and that he walked all over the USA, knocking and sometimes kicking at Jewish doors and demanding money: "Give me money to eat, I am a Jew."

He said it worked very well and that it was coming to him. We asked him what he was reading. He didn't know. He didn't bother to look at the title page. He was only looking at the words, as though he had found the real Torah where it belonged, in the wilderness.

"See? See? See?" cackled Dean, poking my ribs. "I told you it was kicks. Everybody's kicks, man!" We carried Solomon all the way to Testament. My brother by now was in his new house on the other side of town. Here we were back on the long, bleak street with the railroad track running down the middle and the sad, sullen Southerners loping in front of hardware stores and five-and-tens.

Solomon said, "I see you people need a little money to continue your journey. You wait for me and I'll go hustle up a few dollars at a Jewish home and I'll go along with you as far as Alabama." Dean was all beside himself with happiness; he and I rushed off to buy bread and cheese spread for a lunch in the car. Marylou and Ed waited in the car. We spent two hours in Testament waiting for Hyman Solomon to show up; he was hustling for his bread somewhere in town, but we couldn't see him. The sun began to grow red and late.

Solomon never showed up so we roared out of Testament. "Now you see, Sal, God does exist, because we keep getting hung-up with this town, no matter what we try to do, and you'll notice the strange Biblical name of it, and that strange Biblical character who made us stop here once more, and all things tied together all over like rain connecting everybody the world over by chain touch. . . ." Dean rattled on like this; he was overjoyed and exuberant. He and I suddenly saw the whole country like an oyster for us to open; and the pearl was there, the pearl was there. Off we roared south. We picked up another hitchhiker. This was a sad young kid who said he had an aunt who owned a grocery store in Dunn, North Carolina, right outside Fayetteville. "When we get there can you bum a buck off her? Right! Fine! Let's go!" We were in Dunn in an hour, at dusk. We drove to where the kid said his aunt had the grocery store. It was a sad little street that deadended at a factory wall. There was a grocery store but there was no aunt. We wondered what the kid was talking about. We asked him how far he was going; he didn't know. It was a big hoax; once upon a time, in some lost back-alley adventure, he had seen the grocery store in Dunn, and it was the first story that popped into his disordered, feverish mind. We bought him a hot dog, but Dean said we couldn't take him along because we needed room to sleep and room for hitchhikers who could buy a little gas. This was sad but true. We left him in Dunn at nightfall.

I drove through South Carolina and beyond Macon, Georgia as Dean, Marylou, and Ed slept. All alone in the night I had my own thoughts and held the car to the white line in the holy road. What was I doing? Where was I going? I'd soon find out. I got dog-tired beyond Macon and woke up Dean to resume. We got out of the car for air and suddenly both of us were stoned with joy to realize that in the darkness all around us was fragrant green grass and the smell of fresh manure and warm waters. "We're in the South! We've left the winter!" Faint daybreak illuminated green shoots by the side of the road. I took a deep breath; a locomotive howled across the darkness, Mobile-bound. So were we. I took off my shirt and exulted. Ten miles down the road Dean drove into a filling station with the motor off, noticed that the attendant was fast asleep at the desk, jumped out quietly, filled the gas tank, saw to it the bell didn't ring, and rolled off like an Arab with a five dollar tankful of gas for our pilgrimage.

I slept and woke up to the crazy exultant sounds of music and Dean and Marylou talking and the great green land rolling by. "Where are we?"

"Just passed the tip of Florida, man—Flomaton, it's called." Florida! We were rolling down to the coastal plain and Mobile; up ahead were great soaring clouds of the Gulf of Mexico. It was only thirty-two hours since we'd said good-by to everybody in the dirty snows of the North. We stopped at a gas station, and there Dean and Marylou played piggyback around the tanks and Dunkel went inside and stole three packs of cigarettes without trying. We were fresh out. Rolling into Mobile over the long tidal highway, we all took our winter clothes off and enjoyed the Southern temperature. This was when Dean started telling his life story and when, beyond Mobile, he came upon an obstruction of wrangling cars at a crossroads and instead of slipping around them just balled right through the driveway of a gas station and went right on without realizing his steady continental seventy. We left gaping faces behind us. He went right on with his tale. "I tell you it's true. I started at nine, with a girl called Milly Mayfair in back of Rod's garage on Grand Street—same street Carlo lived on in Denver. That's when my father was still working at the smithy's a bit. I remember my aunt yelling out the window, 'What are you doing down there in back of the garage?' Oh honey Marylou, if I'd only known you then! Wow! How sweet you musta been at nine." He tittered maniacally; he stuck his finger in her mouth and licked it; he took her hand and rubbed it over himself. She just sat there, smiling serenely.

Big long Ed Dunkel sat looking out the window, talking to himself. "Yes sir, I thought I was a ghost that night," He was also wondering what Galatea Dunkel would say to him in New Orleans.

Dean went on. "One time I rode a freight from New Mexico clear to LA—I was eleven years old, lost my father at a siding, we were all in a hobo jungle. I was with a man called Big Red, my father was out drunk in a boxcar—it started to roll—Big Red and I missed it—I didn't see my father for months. I rode a long freight all the way to California, really flying, firstclass freight, a desert Zipper. All the way I rode over the couplings—you can imagine how dangerous, I was only a kid, I didn't know—clutching a loaf of bread under one arm and the other hooked around the brake bar. This is no story, this is true. When I got to LA I was so starved for milk and cream I got a job in a dairy and the first thing I did I drank two quarts of heavy cream and puked."

"Poor Dean," said Marylou, and she kissed him. He stared ahead proudly. He loved her.

We were suddenly driving along the blue waters of the Gulf, and at the same time a momentous mad thing began on the radio; it was the Chicken Jazz'n Gumbo disk-jockey show from New Orleans, all mad jazz records, colored records, with the disk jockey saying, "Don't wory 'bout *nothing*!" We saw New Orleans in the night ahead of us with joy. Dean rubbed his hands over the wheel. "Now we're going to get our kicks!" At dusk we were coming into the humming streets of New Orleans. "Oh, smell the people!" yelled Dean with his face out the window, sniffing. "Ah! God! Life!" He swung around a trolley. "Yes!" He darted the car and looked in every direction for girls. "Look at *her*!" The air was so sweet in New Orleans it seemed to come in soft bandannas; and you could smell the river and really smell the people, and mud, and molasses, and every kind of tropical exhalation with your nose suddenly removed from the dry ices of a Northern winter. We bounced in our seats. "And dig her!" yelled Dean, pointing at another woman. "Oh, I love, love, love women! I think women are wonderful! I love women!" He spat out the window; he groaned; he clutched his head. Great beads of sweat fell from his forehead from pure excitement and exhaustion.

We bounced the car up on the Algiers ferry and found ourselves crossing the Mississippi River by boat. "Now we must all get out and dig the river and the people and smell the world," said Dean, bustling with his sunglasses and cigarettes and leaping out of the car like a jack-in-the-box. We followed. On rails we leaned and looked at the great brown father of waters rolling down from mid-America like the torrent of broken souls—bearing Montana logs and Dakota muds and Iowa vales and things that had drowned in Three Forks, where the secret began in ice. Smoky New Orleans receded on one side; old, sleepy Algiers with its warped woodsides bumped us on the other. Negroes were working in the hot afternoon, stoking the ferry furnaces that burned red and made our tires smell. Dean dug them, hopping up and down in the heat. He rushed around the deck and upstairs with his baggy pants hanging halfway down his belly. Suddenly I saw him eagering on the flying bridge. I expected him to take off on wings. I heard his mad laugh all over the boat—"Hee-hee-hee-hee-hee!" Marylou was with him. He covered everything in a jiffy, came back with the full story, jumped in the car just as everybody was tooting to go, and we slipped off, passing two or three cars in a narrow space, and found ourselves darting through Algiers.

"Where? Where?" Dean was yelling.

We decided first to clean up at a gas station and inquire for Bull's whereabouts. Little children were playing in the drowsy river sunset; girls were going by with bandannas and cotton blouses and bare legs. Dean ran up the street to see everything. He looked around; he nodded; he rubbed his belly. Big Ed sat back in the car with his hat over his eyes, smiling at Dean. I sat on the fender. Marylou was in the women's john. From bushy shores where infinitesimal men fished with sticks, and from delta sleeps that stretched up along the reddening land, the big humpbacked river with its mainstream leaping came coiling around Algiers like a snake, with a nameless rumble. Drowsy, peninsular Algiers with all her bees and shanties was like to be washed away someday. The sun slanted, bugs flip-flopped, the awful waters groaned.

We went to Old Bull Lee's house outside town near the river levee. It was on a road that ran across a swampy field. The house was a dilapidated old heap with sagging porches running around and weeping willows in the yard; the grass was a yard high, old fences leaned, old barns collapsed. There was no one in sight. We pulled right into the yard and saw washtubs on the back porch. I got out and went to the screen door. Jane Lee was standing in it with her eyes cupped toward the sun. "Jane," I said ."It's me. It's us."

She knew that. "Yes, I know. Bull isn't here now. Isn't that a fire or something over there?" We both looked toward the sun.

"You mean the sun?"

"Of course I don't mean the sun—I heard sirens that way. Don't you know a peculiar glow?" It was toward New Orleans; the clouds were strange.

"I don't see anything," I said.

Jane snuffed down her nose. "Same old Paradise."

That was the way we greeted each other after four years; Jane used to live with my wife and me in New York. "And is Galatea Dunkel here?" I asked. Jane was still looking for her fire; in those days she ate three tubes of benzedrine paper a day. Her face, once plump and Germanic and pretty, had become stony and red and gaunt. She had caught polio in New Orleans and limped a little. Sheepishly Dean and the gang came out of the car and more or less made themselves at home. Galatea Dunkel came out of her stately retirement in the back of the house to meet her tormentor. Galatea was a serious girl. She was pale and looked like tears all over. Big Ed passed his hand through his hair and said hello. She looked at him steadily.

"Where have you been? Why did you do this to me?" And she gave Dean a dirty look; she knew the score. Dean paid absolutely no attention; what he wanted now was food; he asked Jane if there was anything. The confusion began right there.

Poor Bull came home in his Texas Chevy and found his house invaded by maniacs; but he greeted me with a nice warmth I hadn't seen in him for a long time. He had bought this house in New Orleans with some money he had made growing black-eyed peas in Texas with an old college schoolmate whose father, a mad paretic, had died and left a fortune. Bull himself got fifty dollars a week from his own family, which wasn't too bad except that he spent almost that much per week on his drug habit—and his wife was also expensive, gobbling up about ten dollars worth of benny tubes a week. Their food bill was the lowest in the country; they hardly ever ate; nor did the children—they didn't seem to care. They had two wonderful children: Dodie, eight years old; and little Ray, one year. Ray ran around stark naked in the yard, a little blond child of the rainbow. Bull called him "the Little Beast," after W. C. Fields. Bull came driving into the yard and unrolled himself from the car bone by bone, and came over wearily, wearing glasses, felt hat, shabby suit, long, lean, strange, and laconic, saying, "Why, Sal, you finally got here; let's go in the house and have a drink."

It would take all night to tell about Old Bull Lee; let's just say now, he was a teacher, and it may be said that he had every right to teach because he spent all his time learning; and the things he learned were what he considered to be and called "the facts of life," which he learned not only out of necessity but because he wanted to. He dragged his long, thin body around the entire United States and most of Europe and North Africa in his time, only to see what was going on; he married a White Russian countess in Yugoslavia to get her away from the Nazis in the thirties; there are pictures of him with the international cocaine set of the thirties—gangs with wild hair, leaning on one another; there are other pictures of him in a Panama hat, surveying the streets of Algiers; he never saw the White Russian countess again. He was an exterminator in Chicago, a bartender in New York, a summons-server in Newark. In Paris he sat at café tables, watching the sullen French faces go by. In Athens he looked up from his *ouzo* at what he called the ugliest people in the world. In Istanbul he threaded his way through crowds of opium addicts and rug-sellers, looking for the facts. In English hotels he read Spengler and the Marquis de Sade. In Chicago he planned to hold up a Turkish bath, hesitated just for two minutes too long for a drink, and wound up with two dollars and had to make a run for it. He did all these things merely for the experience. Now the final study was the drug habit. He was now in New Orleans, slipping along the streets with shady characters and haunting connection bars.

There is a strange story about his college days that illustrates something else about him: he had friends for cocktails in his well-appointed rooms one afternoon when suddenly his pet ferret rushed out and bit an elegant teacup queer on the ankle and everybody hightailed it out the door, screaming. Old Bull leaped up and grabbed his shotgun and said, "He smells that old rat again," and shot a hole in that wall big enough for fifty rats. On the wall hung a picture of an ugly old Cape Cod house. His friends said, "Why do you have that ugly thing hanging there?" and Bull said, "I like it because it's ugly." All his life was in that line. Once I knocked on his door in the 60th Street slums of New York and he opened it wearing a derby hat, a vest with nothing underneath, and long striped sharpster pants; in his hands he had a cookpot, birdseed in the pot, and was trying to mash the seed to roll in cigarettes. He also experimented in boiling codeine cough syrup down to a black mash—that didn't work too well. He spent long hours with Shakespeare—the "Immortal Bard," he called him—on his lap. In New Orleans he had begun to spend long hours with the Mayan Codices on his lap, and, although he went on talking, the book lay open all the time. I said once, "What's going to happen to us when we die?" and he said, "When you die you're just dead, that's all." He had a set of chains in his room that he said he used with his psychoanalyst; they were experimenting with narcoanalysis and found that Old Bull had seven separate personalities, each growing worse and worse on the way down, till finally he was a raving idiot and had to be restrained with chains. The top personality was an English lord, the bottom the idiot. Halfway he was an old Negro, who stood in line, waiting with everyone else, and said, "Some's bastards, some's ain't, that the score."

Bull had a sentimental streak about the old days in America, especially 1910, when you could get morphine in a drugstore without prescription and Chinese smoked opium in their evening windows and the country was wild and brawling and free, with abundance and any kind of freedom for everyone. His chief hate was Washington bureaucracy; second to that, liberals; then cops. He spent all his time talking and teaching others. Jane sat at his feet; so did I; so did Dean, and so had Carlo Marx. We'd all learned from him. He was a gray, nondescript-looking fellow you wouldn't notice on the street, unless you looked closer and saw his mad, bony skull with its strange youthfulness—a Kansas minister with exotic, phenomenal fires and mysteries. He had studied medicine in Vienna; had studied anthropology, read everything; and now he was settling to his life's work, which was the study of things themselves in the streets of life and the night. He sat in his chair; Jane brought drinks, martinis. The shades by his chair were always drawn, day and night; it was his corner of the house. On his lap were the Mayan Codices and an air gun which he occasionally raised to pop benzedrine tubes across the room. I kept rushing around, putting up new ones. We all took shots and meanwhile we talked. Bull was curious to know the reason for this trip. He peered at us and snuffed down his nose, *thfump*, like a sound in a dry tank.

"Now, Dean, I want you to sit quiet a minute and tell me what you're doing crossing the country like this."

Dean could only blush and say, "Ah well, you know how it is."

"Sal, what are you going to the Coast for?"

"Only for a few days. I'm coming back to school."

"What's the score with this Ed Dunkel? What kind of character is he?"

At that moment Ed was making up to Galatea in the bedroom; it didn't take him long. We didn't know what to tell Bull about Ed Dunkel. Seeing that we didn't know anything about ourselves, he whipped out three sticks of tea and said to go ahead, supper'd be ready soon.

"Ain't nothing better in the world to give you an appetite. I once ate a horrible lunchcart hamburg on tea and it seemed like the most delicious thing in the world. I just got back from Houston last week, went to see Dale about our black-eyed peas. I was sleeping in a motel one morning when all of a sudden I was blasted out of bed. This damn fool had just shot his wife in the room next to mine. Everybody stood around confused, and the guy just got in his car and drove off, left the shotgun on the floor for the sheriff. They finally caught him in Houma, drunk as a lord. Man ain't safe going around this country any more without a gun." He pulled back his coat and showed us his revolver. Then he opened the drawer and showed us the rest of his arsenal. In New York he once had a sub-machine-gun under his bed. "I got something better than that now—a German Scheintoth gas gun; look at this beauty, only got one shell. I could knock out a hundred men with this gun and have plenty of time to make a getaway. Only thing wrong, I only got one shell."

"I hope I'm not around when you try it," said Jane from the kitchen. "How do *you* know it's a gas shell?" Bull snuffed; he never paid any attention to her sallies but he heard them. His relation with his wife was one of the strangest: they talked till late at night; Bull liked to hold the floor, he went right on in his dreary monotonous voice, she tried to break in, she never could; at dawn he got tired and then Jane talked and he listened, snuffing and going *thfump* down his nose. She loved that man madly, but in a delirious way of some kind; there was never any mooching and mincing around, just talk and a very deep companionship that none of us would ever be able to fathom. Something curiously unsympathetic and cold between them was really a form of humor by which they communicated their own set of subtle vibrations. Love is all; Jane was never more than ten feet away from Bull and never missed a word he said, and he spoke in a very low voice, too.

Dean and I were yelling about a big night in New Orleans and wanted Bull to show us around. He threw a damper on this. "New Orleans is a very dull town. It's against the law to go to the colored section. The bars are insufferably dreary."

I said, "There must be some ideal bars in town."

"The ideal bar doesn't exist in America. An ideal bar is something that's gone beyond our ken. In nineteen ten a bar was a place where men went to meet during or after work, and all there was was a long counter, brass rails, spittoons, player piano for music, a few mirrors, and barrels of whisky at ten cents a shot together with barrels of beer at five cents a mug. Now all you get is chromium, drunken women, fags, hostile bartenders, anxious owners who hover around the door, worried about their leather seats and the law; just a lot of screaming at the wrong time and deadly silence when a stranger walks in."

We argued about bars. "All right," he said, "I'll take you to New Orleans tonight and show you what I mean." And he deliberately took us to the dullest bars. We left Jane with the children, supper was over; she was reading the want ads of the New Orleans *Times-Picayune*. I asked her if she was looking for a job; she only said it was the most interesting part of the paper. Bull rode into town with us and went right on talking. "Take it easy, Dean, we'll get there, I hope; hup, there's the ferry, you don't have to drive us clear into the river." He held on. Dean had gotten worse, he confided in me. "He seems to me to be headed for his ideal fate which is compulsive psychosis dashed with a jigger of psychopathic irresponsibility and violence." He looked at Dean out of the corner of his eye. "If you go to California with this madman you'll never make it. Why don't you stay in New Orleans with me? We'll play the horses over to Gretna and relax in my yard. I've got a nice set of knives and I'm building a target. Some pretty juicy dolls downtown, too, if that's in your line these days." He snuffed. We were on the ferry and Dean had leaped out to lean over the rail. I followed, but Bull sat on in the car, snuffing, *thfump*. There was a mystic wraith of fog over the brown waters that night, together with dark driftwoods; and across the way New Orleans glowed orange-bright, with a few dark ships at her hem, ghostly fogbound Cereno ships with Spanish balconies and ornamental poops, till you got up close and saw they were just old freighters from Sweden and Panama. The ferry fires glowed in the night; the same Negroes plied the shovel and sang. Old Big Slim Hazard had once worked on the Algiers ferry as a deckhand; this made me think of Mississippi Gene too; and as the river poured down from mid-America by starlight, I knew, I knew like mad that everything I had ever known and would ever know was One. Strange to say, too, that night we crossed the ferry with Bull Lee a girl committed suicide off the deck; either just before or just after us; we saw it in the paper the next day.

We hit all the dull bars in the French Quarter with Old Bull and went back home at midnight. That night Marylou took everything in the books; she took tea, goofballs, benny, liquor, and even asked Old Bull for a shot of M, which of course he didn't give her; he did give her a martini. She was so saturated with elements of all kinds that she came to a standstill and stood goofy on the porch with me. It was a wonderful porch Bull had. It ran clear around the house; by moonlight with the willows it looked like an old Southern mansion that had seen better days. In the house Jane sat reading the want ads in the living room; Bull was in the bathroom taking his fix, clutching his old black necktie in his teeth for a tourniquet and jabbing with the needle into his woesome arm with the thousand holes; Ed Dunkel was sprawled out with Galatea in the massive master bed that Old Bull and Jane never used; Dean was rolling tea; and Marylou and I imitated Southern aristocracy.

"Why, Miss Lou, you look lovely and most fetching tonight."

"Why, thank you, Crawford, I sure do appreciate the nice things you do say."

Doors kept opening around the crooked porch, and members of our sad drama in the American night kept popping out to find out where everybody was. Finally I took a walk alone to the levee. I wanted to sit on the muddy bank and dig the Mississippi River; instead of that I had to look at it with my nose against a wire fence. When you start separating the people from their rivers what have you got? "Bureaucracy!" says Old Bull; he sits with Kafka on his lap, the lamp burns above him, he snuffs, *thfump*. His old house creaks. And the Montana log rolls by in the black river of the night. "'Tain't nothin' but bureaucracy. And unions! Especially unions!" But dark laughter would come again.

## QUESTIONS : *Kerouac, On the Road*

1. In keeping with the title of Kerouac's novel, this section of the work is concerned with a journey—one not merely in search of different places but of new experiences. What are some of the elements of the world from which directly or indirectly an escape is here being sought?

   *Clues:* • "frosty fagtown New York,"

   • "What did we do in New York? Let's forgive."

   • . . . all kinds of war material that looked murderous in the snowy grass;

   • It's a Victorian police force. . . .

2. What additional light is shed on the characters' impulse to escape into new experiences by their generally antisocial behavior (reckless driving, theft, drug addiction)?

3. How does the treatment of the journey suggest that the kind of experience sought here goes beyond the diversion wanted by the conventional traveler?

   *Clues:* • I could see that it was all going to be one big saga of the mist.

   • The poor Hudson—the slow boat to China . . . our battered boat. . . .

   • "Everybody's kicks, man!"

   • . . . the white line in the holy road.

   • He spat out the window; he groaned; he clutched his head. Great beads of sweat fell from his forehead from pure excitement and exhaustion.

4. How does Bull Lee serve to epitomize the rejection of worldy values and the yearnings of the other characters for certain kinds of experiences? Does he seem a convincingly realistic character? Why are the names of several literary figures (Spengler, De Sade, Kafka) associated with him?

5. The word *beat* attached to Kerouac's writings (and others in a similar vein) relates not only to "beaten" in the sense of morally and spiritually exhausted but has some connection with "beatific." An experience of transcendence is described here, culminating in the narrator's sense "that everything [he] had ever known was One." Do you find the author's handling of it convincing? Justify your view.

6. Though the narrator participates in the adventures, he is also at times an onlooker. What intermittent suggestions are there of his awareness that the buoyancy, zest, vitality of the life he describes has its seamy side, that "a sad drama in the American night" is being played out?

7. Kerouac's work has been impishly described as not being "writing" but "typing." How just do you think that comment is?

## EXERCISE

Discuss the relevance of the following passage to our present consciousness:

> Finally I took a walk alone to the levee. I wanted to sit on the muddy bank and dig the Mississippi River; instead of that I had to look at it with my nose against a wire fence. When you start separating the people from their rivers what have you got? "Bureaucracy!" says Old Bull; he sits with Kafka on his lap, the lamp burns above him, he snuffs, *thfump*. His old house creaks. And the Montana log rolls by in the black river of the night. "'Tain't nothin' but bureaucracy. And unions! Especially unions!"

In addition indicate what other aspects of Kerouac's novel (published in 1955) make us realize that the "beat" world of the fifties and earlier (the novel begins in 1947) anticipates assumptions and attitudes sometimes thought to be characteristic only of our own time.

## *Theodore Roethke (1908–1963)*
# In a Dark Time

*In his poem "Correspondences" in* Flowers of Evil, *Baudelaire asserts the symbolic power of Nature (it is a "temple" whose "pillars" are alive and vocal; its realms are "forests of symbols") and the subtle interconnections—or correspondences—between perfumes, colors, and sounds.*

In a dark time, the eye begins to see,
I meet my shadow in the deepening shade;
I hear my echo in the echoing wood—
A lord of nature weeping to a tree.
I live between the heron and the wren,          5
Beasts of the hill and serpents of the den.

What's madness but nobility of soul
At odds with circumstance? The day's on fire!
I know the purity of pure despair,
My shadow pinned against a sweating wall.       10
That place among the rocks—is it a cave,
Or winding path? The edge is what I have.

A steady storm of correspondences!
A night flowing with birds, a ragged moon,
And in broad day the midnight comes again!      15
A man goes far to find out what he is—
Death of the self in a long, tearless night,
All natural shapes blazing unnatural light.

Dark, dark my light, and darker my desire.
My soul, like some heat-maddened summer fly,     20
Keeps buzzing at the sill. Which I is *I*?
A fallen man. I climb out of my fear.
The mind enters itself, and God the mind,
And one is One, free in the tearing wind.

## QUESTIONS: *Roethke, "In a Dark Time"*

1. How do you explain the paradox in the first line? What connotations does the term *see* have?

2. How is the state of mind of the speaker illumined in the first stanza by instances of his identification with *nature*? Consider whether that identification is essentially affirmative or negative or partakes of both qualities. (Note the paradox of the fourth line and the animal references.)

3. What additional insight into the speaker's state are we given in the second stanza by (a) the reference to and definition of "madness"? (b) the recurring reference to "my shadow" (later the poet will ask "which I is *I*?")? (c) the references to "the day" being "on fire" and to the "sweating wall"? In the light of the statement "The edge [of some mental or spiritual abyss?] is what I have," what do the questions about the "cave" and "winding path" "among the rocks" suggest?

4. Consider how the third stanza represents both a repetition and amplification of the material in the preceding stanzas.
   *Clues:*   A steady storm of *correspondences*!
   A *night* flowing with birds, a ragged *moon*,
   And in broad *day* the midnight comes again!
   A man goes far to find out *what he is*—
   Death of the self in a long, tearless night.
   All *natural* shapes *blazing unnatural* light.

## Robert Lowell *(1917–     )*

# The Voyage

*(For T. S. Eliot)*

"*I have tried to write alive English and to do what my authors might have done if they were writing their poems now and in America.*" *(From Lowell's Introduction to his book* Imitations *in which this imitation of a poem by Baudelaire [1821–1867] appears.)*

### I

For the boy playing with globe and stamps,
the world is equal to his appetite—
how grand the world in the blaze of the lamps,
how petty in tomorrow's small dry light!

One morning we lift anchor, full of brave                    5
prejudices, prospects, ingenuity—
we swing with the velvet swell of the wave,
our infinite is rocked by the fixed sea.

Some wish to fly a cheapness they detest,
others, their cradles' terror—others stand          10
with their binoculars on a woman's breast,
reptilian Circe with her junk and wand.

Not to be turned to reptiles, such men daze
themselves with spaces, light, the burning sky;
cold toughens them, they bronze in the sun's blaze    15
and dry the sores of their debauchery.

But the true voyagers are those who move
simply to move—like lost balloons! Their heart
is some old motor thudding in one groove.
It says its single phrase, "Let us depart!"          20

They are like conscripts lusting for the guns;
our sciences have never learned to tag
their projects and designs—enormous, vague
hopes grease the wheels of these automatons!

## II

We imitate, oh horror! tops and bowls               25
in their eternal waltzing marathon;
even in sleep, our fever whips and rolls—
like a black angel flogging the brute sun.

Strange sport! where destination has no place
or name, and may be anywhere we choose—             30
where man, committed to his endless race,
runs like a madman diving for repose!

Our soul is a three-master[1] seeking port:
a voice from starboard shouts, "We're at the dock!"
Another, more elated, cries from port,              35
"Here's dancing, gin and girls!" Balls! it's a rock!

The islands sighted by the lookout seem
the El Dorados[2] promised us last night;
imagination wakes from its drugged dream,
sees only ledges in the morning light.              40

[1] *three-master:* a ship with three masts.
[2] *El Dorado:* mythical treasure city of South America.

What dragged these patients from their German spas?
Shall we throw them in chains, or in the sea?
Sailors discovering new Americas,
who drown in a mirage of agony!

The worn-out sponge, who scuffles through our slums     45
sees whiskey, paradise and liberty
wherever oil-lamps shine in furnished rooms—
we see Blue Grottoes, Caesar and Capri.[3]

### III

Stunningly simple Tourists, your pursuit
is written in the tear-drops in your eyes!     50
Spread out the packing cases of your loot,
your azure sapphires made of seas and skies!

We want to break the boredom of our jails
and cross the oceans without oars or steam—
give us visions to stretch our minds like sails,     55
the blue, exotic shoreline of your dream!

Tell us, what have you seen?

### IV

    "We've seen the stars,
a wave or two—we've also seen some sand;
although we peer through telescopes and spars,
we're often deadly bored as you on land.     60

The shine of sunlight on the violet sea,
the roar of cities when the sun goes down:
these stir our hearts with restless energy;
we worship the Indian Ocean where we drown!

No old chateau or shrine besieged by crowds     65
of crippled pilgrims sets our souls on fire,
as these chance countries gathered from the clouds.
Our hearts are always anxious with desire.

Desire, that great elm fertilized by lust,
gives its old body, when the heaven warms     70
its bark that winters and old age encrust;
green branches draw the sun into its arms.

[3] *Blue Grottoes, Caesar and Capri:* The Blue Grotto is an eerie cavern on Capri, reachable only by boat, and flooded with a blue underwater light. According to the Roman historian Suetonius, Capri was the site of the debaucheries and sexual perversions practiced by the emperor Tiberius Caesar.

Why are you always growing taller, Tree—
Oh longer-lived than cypress! Yet we took
one or two sketches for your picture-book,     75
Brothers who sell your souls for novelty!

We have salaamed to pagan gods with horns,
entered shrines peopled by a galaxy
of Buddhas, Slavic saints, and unicorns,
so rich Rothschild[4] must dream of bankruptcy!     80

Priests' robes that scattered solid golden flakes,
dancers with tatooed bellies and behinds,
charmers supported by braziers of snakes . . ."

### V

Yes, and what else?

### VI

Oh trivial, childish minds!

You've missed the more important things that we     85
were forced to learn against our will. We've been
from top to bottom of the ladder, and see
only the pageant of immortal sin:

there women, servile, peacock-tailed, and coarse,
marry for money, and love without disgust     90
horny, pot-bellied tyrants stuffed on lust,
slaves' slaves—the sewer in which their gutter pours!

old maids who weep, playboys who live each hour,
state banquets loaded with hot sauces, blood and trash,
ministers sterilized by dreams of power,     95
workers who love their brutalizing lash;

and everywhere religions like our own
all storming heaven, propped by saints who reign
like sybarites on beds of nails and frown—
all searching for some orgiastic pain!     100

Many, self-drunk, are lying in the mud—
mad now, as they have always been, they roll
in torment screaming to the throne of God:
"My image and my lord, I hate your soul!"

[4] *Rothschild:* a member of the banking house of Rothschild, founded in the eighteenth century.

And others, dedicated without hope,                    105
flee the dull herd—each locked in his own world
hides in his ivory-tower of art and dope—
this is the daily news from the whole world!

### VII

How sour the knowledge travellers bring away!
The world's monotonous and small; we see          110
ourselves today, tomorrow, yesterday,
an oasis of horror in sands of ennui!

Shall we move or rest? Rest, if you can rest;
move if you must. One runs, but others drop
and trick their vigilant antagonist.              115
Time is a runner who can never stop,

the Wandering Jew or Christ's Apostles. Yet
nothing's enough; no knife goes through the ribs
of this retarius throwing out his net;
others can kill and never leave their cribs.      120

And even when Time's heel is on our throat
we still can hope, still cry, "On, on, let's go!"
Just as we once took passage on the boat
for China, shivering as we felt the blow,

so we now set our sails for the Dead Sea,         125
light-hearted as the youngest voyager.
If you look seaward, Traveller, you will see
a spectre rise and hear it sing, "Stop, here,

and eat my lotus-flowers, here's where they're sold.
Here are the fabulous fruits; look, my boughs bend;   130
eat yourself sick on knowledge. Here we hold
time in our hands, it never has to end."

We know the accents of this ghost by heart;
Our comrade spreads his arms across the seas;
"On, on, Orestes. Sail and feast your heart—      135
Here's Clytemnestra." Once we kissed her knees.

### VIII

It's time. Old Captain, Death, lift anchor, sink!
The land rots; we shall sail into the night;
if now the sky and sea are black as ink,
our hearts, as you must know, are filled with light.   140

> Only when we drink poison are we well—
> we want, this fire so burns our brain tissue,
> to drown in the abyss—heaven or hell,
> who cares? Through the unknown, we'll find the *new*.

Baudelaire: Le voyage.

## QUESTIONS: *Lowell, "The Voyage"*

1. The poem begins with a reference to a child: "For the boy playing with his globe and stamps,/the world is equal to his appetite—" What other allusions does the poem contain to the chronology of human life?

   *Clues:*  • One morning we lift anchor, full of brave
   prejudices, prospects, ingenuity—

   • Our soul is a three-master seeking port:

   • And even when Time's heel is on our throat
   we still can hope . . .

2. The poem's references to the activities of human life (for example, "they are like conscripts lusting for the guns"; "what dragged these patients from their German spas") support a metaphor of the voyage as man's *progression* through life, a metaphor that is central to the poem. What suggestions does the poem contain that the voyage also functions as an image of an *escape* from life?

   *Clues:*  • Some wish *to fly* a cheapness they detest,

   • Stunningly simple *Tourists*, your pursuit is written
   *in the tear-drops* in your eyes!

   • We want to break the boredom of our jails

3. Examine the imagery of the supernatural, the mechanical, and the debauched in this poem. How does the imagery function in the poem to (a) justify the *desire* to "drop out"? (b) characterize the *hopes for release* which motivate the voyage of escape? (c) describe the *discoveries* made in the voyage of escape? (Notice the correspondence between the reactions to experience and stages in the chronology of human life.)

   *Clues:*

   *The supernatural*
   • others, their cradles' terror—others stand
   with their binoculars on a woman's breast,
   reptilian Circe with her junk and wand.

   • entered shrines peopled by a galaxy
   of Buddhas, Slavic saints, and unicorns,
   *The mechanical*
   •                              Their heart
   is some old motor thudding in one groove.

   • We imitate, oh horror! tops and bowls

   • although we peer through telescopes and spars,

   • slaves' slaves—the sewer in which their gutter pours!
   *The debauched*
   • Another, more elated, cries from port,
   "Here's dancing, gin and girls!" Balls! it's a rock!

*404*

> • Desire, that great elm fertilized by lust,
> • dancers with tatooed bellies and behinds,
> • horny, pot-bellied tyrants stuffed on lust,
> • Only when we drink poison are we well—

4. The concept of *ennui* (see part VII) is often identified with Baudelaire. Though he was hardly the first person to discover or describe this state of mind, his poetry gave it currency. What definition of ennui does the poem offer? What is its relation to the voyage? How do the images of the supernatural, the mechanical, and the debauched, examined in question 3, contribute to this definition?

   *Clues:* • We want to break the boredom of our jails
   • imagination wakes from its drugged dream,
     sees only ledges in the morning light.
   • The world's monotonous and small; we see
     ourselves today, tomorrow, yesterday,
     an oasis of horror. . . .

5. Examine closely the passage in part VI of the poem which begins with the words "and everywhere religions like our own" and ends with the line "this is the daily news from the whole world!" On what grounds does the poem here disparage religion, art, and drugs, three standard forms of escape from reality? What relation does the poem draw between these forms of escape and *ennui*?

6. What total view of human experience does the poem project? What connection do you see between that view and the yearning for the ultimate experience ("It's time. Old Captain, Death, lift anchor, sink!")? What connection is there between that yearning and the poem's diagnosis with regard to men that "Only when we drink poison are we well"?

## *Sir Walter Ralegh (1552?–1618)*
## The Passionate Man's Pilgrimage

Give me my scallop-shell[1] of quiet,
My staff of faith to walk upon,
My scrip[2] of joy, immortal diet,
My bottle of salvation,
My gown of glory, hope's true gage,[3]               5
And thus I'll take my pilgrimage.

Blood must be my body's balmer,
No other balm will there be given,
Whilst my soul like a white palmer
Travels to the land of heaven,                        10
Over the silver mountains,
Where spring the nectar fountains;
And there I'll kiss

---

[1] *scallop-shell:* emblem worn by pilgrims.  [2] *scrip:* wallet carried by traveler.  [3] *gage:* pawn.

The bowl of bliss,
And drink my eternal fill                                      15
On every milken hill.
My soul will be a-dry before,

But after it will ne'er thirst more;
And by the happy blissful way
More peaceful pilgrims I shall see,                            20
That have shook off their gowns of clay
And go appareled fresh like me.
I'll bring them first
To slake their thirst,
And then to taste those nectar suckets,[4]                    25
At the clear wells
Where sweetness dwells,
Drawn up by saints in crystal buckets.

And when our bottles and all we
Are filled with immortality,                                  30
Then the holy paths we'll travel,
Strewed with rubies thick as gravel,
Ceilings of diamonds, sapphire floors,
High walls of coral, and pearl bowers.

From thence to heaven's bribeless hall                        35
Where no corrupted voices brawl,
No conscience molten into gold,
Nor forged accusers bought and sold,
No cause deferred, nor vain-spent journey,
For there Christ is the king's attorney,                      40
Who pleads for all without degrees,
And he hath angels,[5] but no fees.
When the grand twelve million jury
Of our sins and sinful fury,
'Gainst our souls black verdicts give,                        45
Christ pleads his death, and then we live.
Be thou my speaker, taintless pleader,
Unblotted[6] lawyer, true proceeder,
Thou movest salvation even for alms,
Not with a bribèd lawyer's palms.                             50

And this is my eternal plea
To him that made heaven, earth, and sea,
Seeing my flesh must die so soon,

---

[4] *suckets:* candies.  [5] *angel:* gold coin; used here as a pun.  [6] *unblotted:* having an unblemished reputation.

And want a head to dine next noon,
Just at the stroke when my veins start and spread,    55
Set on my soul an everlasting head.
Then am I ready, like a palmer fit,
To tread those blest paths which before I writ.

## QUESTIONS: *Ralegh, "The Passionate Man's Pilgrimage"*

1.  In the first six lines the speaker is about to embark on a pilgrimage. How does the poet throughout this stanza suggest that the voyage is a far more momentous expedition than a journey to a place of religious worship?

2.  What is the significance for the poem as a whole of the distinction made in the second stanza between (a) man's body and its destiny; (b) man's soul and its destination?

3.  In the first stanza of the poem abstract and concrete are consistently yoked together (for example, "gown of glory"). The most dramatic instance of this paradoxical yoking later on in the poem occurs in line 56 in which the speaker entreats: "Set on my soul an everlasting head." How typical is this type of metaphor of the poem as a whole? What light does it shed on the conflict within the poem with regard to a conception of *heaven* as (a) an inner *state* of spiritual regeneration? (b) a *place* and a source of sensual satisfaction? (c) a tribunal which in its adjudications transcends earthly moral corruption?

    *Clues:*  • More peaceful pilgrims I shall see,

    • . . . and all we
      Are filled with immortality,

    • And drink my eternal fill
      On every milken hill.

    • Then the holy paths we'll travel,
      Strewed with rubies thick as gravel,

    • From thence to heaven's bribeless hall
      Where no corrupted voices brawl,

    • And he hath angels, but no fees.

    Evaluate the notion that the conflict stems from the speaker's reluctance to forego his physical state.

4.  Only in stanza 4 are we first given some explanation of the speaker's urge to transcend his state. Consider the extent to which the *journey to* transfiguration is also a *journey of escape from* the world.

5.  Although the vices here suggested are those which appear characteristically in moral indictments of the world (materialism, corruption, falsehood, injustice), what makes Raleigh's treatment of them effective?

    *Clues:*  • Use of the negative (for instance, "No cause deferred," "but no fees").

    • Use of qualifiers and modifiers (for instance, "the grand twelve million jury," "taintless pleader," "true proceeder").

6.  Even if we do not know that Raleigh was executed soon after he wrote this poem, the last stanza provides a more immediate justification for the poem than

the earlier stanzas do. How do the preceding stanzas justify the tone of lines 53–54? How does the concrete imagery give us the sense that we are participating in a very personal experience?

7. The word *passionate* means both "suffering" and "emotionally aroused." How appropriate then is the title of the poem to its content?

## *Sir Philip Sidney (1554–1586)*

# Leave Me, O Love

Leave me, O love which reachest but to dust;
And thou, my mind, aspire to higher things;
Grow rich in that which never taketh rust,
Whatever fades but fading pleasure brings.
Draw in thy beams, and humble all thy might      5
To that sweet yoke where lasting freedoms be;
Which breaks the clouds and opens forth the light,
That doth both shine and give us sight to see.
O take fast hold; let that light be thy guide
In this small course which birth draws out to death,      10
And think how evil becometh him to slide,
Who seeketh heav'n, and comes of heav'nly breath.
    Then farewell, world; thy uttermost I see;
    Eternal Love, maintain thy life in me.

QUESTIONS: *Sidney, "Leave Me, O Love"*

1. Two kinds of aspirations are contrasted in the first four lines. How and why is each to a certain extent defined in terms of the other?
    *Clues:* • Leave me, O love which *reachest* but to dust;

    • Grow rich in that which never taketh rust,

2. How do lines 5 and 6 provide an appropriate transition to the rest of the poem?
    a. Consider the paradoxical relation between (1) the command to "aspire to higher things" and to "Draw in thy beams"; (2) the "sweet yoke" and "lasting freedoms."
    b. Consider the function of the imagery of light in the rest of the poem.
3. How do the last two lines complement the first two?

## EXERCISE

Discuss Sidney's sonnet in conjunction with Shakespeare's "Sonnet 146," "Poor soul, the center of my sinful earth." What thematic similarities and contrasts do you note? Which use of imagery is more effective in conveying the poet's meaning and why? Which in your judgment is the more personal utterance? Explain.

## William Shakespeare (1564–1616)

# Sonnet 66

Tired with all these, for restful death I cry:
As, to behold desert[1] a beggar born,
And needy[2] nothing[3] trimmed in jollity,
And purest faith unhappily forsworn,
And gilded[4] honor shamefully misplaced,                    5
And maiden virtue rudely strumpeted,
And right perfection wrongfully disgraced,
And strength by limping sway disablèd,
And art made tongue-tied by authority,
And folly (doctor-like) controlling skill,                    10
And simple truth miscalled simplicity,[5]
And captive good attending captain ill—
    Tired with all these, from these would I be gone,
    Save that, to die, I leave my love alone.

QUESTIONS: *Shakespeare, "Sonnet 66"*

1. Consider the following nouns and modifiers: "faith . . . forsworn," "honor . . . misplaced," "virtue . . . strumpeted," "perfection . . . disgraced," "strength . . . disabled." What do they suggest about the fate of ideals in the world? In no instance does the speaker name an agent for the conditions he cites. How does this omission help to explain why the ills of the world induce in the speaker *tiredness* rather than indignation, surprise, anguish? What is the effect of the omission on the reader?

2. In what way does the expression of personal emotion in the last line not really introduce a new idea but amplify the point already made?
   *Clue:* • Save that, to die, I leave my love *alone*.

3. How do the following stylistic devices help us clarify the meaning of the poem?
   a. Repetition: the use of the initial "And."
   b. Prefixes: "mis."
   c. Alliteration: "needy nothing."
   d. Assonance: "And folly (doctor-like) controlling skill."
   e. Personification: "art made tongue-tied."
   f. Hyperbole: "maiden virtue rudely strumpeted."

## EXERCISE

Suggest the similarities and differences in theme, wording, and structure between this sonnet and the following seven lines of Hamlet's second soliloquy.

    For who would bear the whips and scorns of time,
    The oppressor's wrong, the proud man's contumely,
    The pangs of despised love, the law's delay,
    The insolence of office and the spurns

[1] *desert:* the quality of being deserving.  [2] *needy:* vacuous.  [3] *nothing:* worthlessness.
[4] *gilded:* resplendent.  [5] *simplicity:* ignorance.

That patient merit of the unworthy takes,
When he himself might his quietus make
With a bare bodkin?

## John Donne (1572-1631)
# Holy Sonnet XIV

Batter my heart, three-personed God[1]; for You
As yet but knock, breathe, shine, and seek to mend;
That I may rise and stand, o'erthrow me, and bend
Your force to break, blow, burn, and make me new.
I, like an usurped town, to another due,                              5
Labor to admit You, but O, to no end;
Reason, Your viceroy in me, me should defend,
But is captived, and proves weak or untrue.
Yet dearly I love You, and would be loved fain.
But am betrothed unto Your enemy.                                    10
Divorce me, untie or break that knot[2] again;
Take me to You, imprison me, for I,
Except You enthrall me, never shall be free,
Nor ever chaste, except You ravish me.

QUESTIONS: *Donne, "Holy Sonnet XIV"*

1.  What aspects of this poem tend to challenge our assumption that only (a) a
    certain language and (b) certain situations are suitable for a religious poem?
    How would you justify the presence of such language and such circumstances here?
    *Clues:*  • I, like an usurped town, to another due,
            Labor to admit You . . .
           • Divorce me, untie or break that knot again;
           • Nor ever chaste, except You ravish me.

2.  The language and situations are not only unconventional but highly paradoxical.
    a. How can you resolve the contradiction between "imprisonment" and "ravish-
       ing" *and* the speaker's statement "Yet dearly I love You, and would be loved
       fain"?
    b. Donne asks to be "overthrown" in order "That I may rise and stand." What
       spiritual truth is he trying to convey in this paradox? How does it relate to the core
       of Christian belief, the Crucifixion and Resurrection? In what sense can the
       desire to be "overthrown" be equated with the impulse to *escape from the world?*

3.  Donne is dissatisfied with God's present efforts toward him: "for You/As yet
    but knock, breathe, shine, and seek to mend." What do each of these terms
    suggest? Is there any sense of progression in them? A remarkable number of the
    verbs in the first four lines begin with the letter *b*. What shape or structure does
    the manner in which the *b*-verbs are disposed over the first four lines give them?
    How might it enhance the poem? Who is the "enemy" in line 10? What is
    effective about his never being named?

[1] *three-personed God:* the Holy Trinity.
[2] *knot:* the marriage bond; also a woman's maidenhead.

## EXERCISES

1.  Martin Luther's most famous hymn begins

    > A mighty Fortress is our God,
    >   A Bulwark never failing;
    > Our Helper he amid the flood
    >   Of mortal ills prevailing:
    > For still our ancient foe
    > Doth seek to work us woe;
    > His craft and power are great,
    > And, armed with cruel hate,
    >   On earth is not his equal.

    Compare Luther's hymn and Donne's sonnet. What are the similarities and differences in their central ideas and their imagery? Which, in your opinion, is the more effective work, and why?

2.  Discuss the ways in which the experience described in Donne's poem resembles modern attempts at "transcendence of self." In what ways might it be different?

## George Herbert (1593–1633)

# Easter Wings and The Collar

### EASTER WINGS

> Lord, who createdst man in wealth and store,
>   Though foolishly he lost the same,
>     Decaying more and more,
>       Till   he   became
>         Most poore:      5
>       With   thee
>     O   let   me   rise
>   As   larks,   harmoniously,
> And sing this day thy victories:
> Then shall the fall further the flight in me.    10
>
> My tender age in sorrow did beginne:
>   And still with sicknesses and shame
>     Thou didst so punish sinne,
>       That   I   became
>         Most thinne.      15
>       With   thee
>     Let me combine
>   And feel this day thy victorie:
> For, if I imp[1] my wing on thine,
> Affliction shall advance the flight in me.    20

[1] *imp:* a way of mending a bird's wing by the grafting on of feathers; more generally a process of implanting, particularly by grafting.

## QUESTIONS: *Herbert, "Easter Wings"*

1. Traditional Christian symbolism represents the Holy Ghost (the spirit of God) as a dove. What use does this poem make of this convention in (a) the title and theme, (b) the actual *appearance* of the poem on the page?
   *Clues:* •⠀⠀⠀⠀⠀O let me rise
   ⠀⠀⠀⠀⠀As larks, harmoniously
   ⠀⠀And sing this day thy victories;
   ⠀⠀• For if I imp my wing on thine,
2. Easter is the annual Christian celebration of redemption. How does the poet's diction dramatize (a) the condition of human life and man's responsibility for it? (b) man's desire to transcend that condition and his capacity for doing so?
   *Clues:* • Though foolishly he lost the same,
   ⠀⠀⠀• My tender age in sorrow did beginne:
   ⠀⠀⠀• And feel this day thy victorie:

## EXERCISE

In view of the various meanings of *fall* (the literal act of falling; man's fall from grace; the speaker's own spiritual humility) and of *flight* (the literal act of soaring; escape; aspiration), what is the nature of the paradox contained in the line "Then shall the fall further the flight in me"? How is it given a more complex treatment in the poem's climactic conclusion:

⠀⠀⠀⠀For, if I imp my wing on thine,
⠀⠀⠀⠀Affliction shall advance the flight in me.

## THE COLLAR

I struck the board[1] and cried, No more!
⠀⠀I will abroad.
What? Shall I ever sigh and pine?
My lines[2] and life are free, free as the road,
⠀⠀Loose as the wind, as large as store.⠀⠀⠀⠀⠀5
⠀⠀⠀Shall I be still in suit[3]?
Have I no harvest but a thorn
⠀⠀To let me blood, and not restore
What I have lost with cordial[4] fruit?
⠀⠀⠀Sure there was wine⠀⠀⠀⠀⠀10
Before my sighs did dry it; there was corn
⠀⠀Before my tears did drown it.
Is the year only lost to me?
⠀⠀Have I no bays[5] to crown it?

[1] *board:* literally a table where meals are served.
[2] *lines:* options, directions, destiny (as in *Psalms* XVI:6, "The lines are fallen unto me in pleasant places . . .").
[3] *suit:* legal process of demanding reforms (possibly also livery?).
[4] *cordial:* restorative.
[5] *bays:* laurel, traditionally woven in wreaths and worn as a sign of wordly triumph.

No flowers, no garlands gay? All blasted?      15
      All wasted?
Not so, my heart! But there is fruit,
      And thou hast hands.
       Recover all thy sigh-blown age
On double pleasures. Leave thy cold dispute      20
Of what is fit and not. Forsake thy cage,
      Thy rope of sands,
Which petty[6] thoughts have made, and made to thee
     Good cable, to enforce and draw,
       And be thy law,      25
    While thou didst wink and wouldst not see.
      Away! Take heed!
      I will abroad.
Call in thy death's head there. Tie up thy fears.
      He that forbears      30
    To suit and serve his need
     Deserves his load.
But as I raved and grew more fierce and wild
      At every word,
Me thoughts I heard one calling, Child!      35
     And I replied, My Lord.

## QUESTIONS: *Herbert, "The Collar"*

1. "I will abroad" spoken twice sounds the note of escape. What elements in the poem might lead one to believe that what the speaker desired to escape from is an enslavement by worldly cares and responsibilities? What suggests that it is a very different kind of burden under which he chafes? Note the function of contrasting types of nature imagery—"garlands," "thorn," and so on—and of images of anger, suffering, and incarceration.

2. Question and answer is the *dramatic* essence of the poem. What function do the questions perform in the poem? Are they addressed to someone in particular, or are they mainly rhetorical? Would the contention that they have never been raised in the speaker's mind be valid?
   *Clues:*   • Shall I ever sigh and pine?
           • Shall I be still in suit?
           • Is the year only lost to me?

3. How does the speaker characterize the processes of his mind?
   *Clue:*   •             Leave thy cold dispute
      Of what is fit and not. Forsake thy cage,
         Thy rope of sands,
    Which petty thoughts have made . . .
What bearing do these processes have on the ultimate resolution of the poem?

---

[6] *petty:* casuistical.

4. The title of the poem and the line "My lines and life are free" indicate that the poem deals with a central paradox of human experience. How is the nature of that paradox clarified by the *ambiguous* use of the following?
   a. References to food ("Sure there was wine/Before my sighs did dry it").
   b. Images of bondage and release ("Forsake thy cage,/Thy rope of sands").
   c. Images of natural processes ("Recover all thy sigh-blown age").
5. Why, if they were joined, could the first and last two lines of the poem constitute in telescoped form the psychological and spiritual essence of the poem? What would be lost in such a compression that illumines the conflict in this poem?

## Andrew Marvell (1621–1678)

# The Garden

How vainly men themselves amaze[1]
To win the palm, the oak, or bays,[2]
And their uncessant labors see
Crowned from some single herb or tree,
Whose short and narrow vergèd shade     5
Does prudently their toils upbraid;
While all flowers and all trees do close
To weave the garlands of repose.

Fair quiet, have I found thee here,
And innocence, thy sister dear!       10
Mistaken long, I sought you then
In busy[3] companies of men;
Your sacred plants, if here below,
Only among the plants will grow.
Society is all but rude,         15
To this delicious solitude.

No white nor red was ever seen
So am'rous as this lovely green.
Fond lovers, cruel as their flame,
Cut in these trees their mistress' name;    20
Little, alas, they know or heed

---

[1] *amaze:* perplex, harass.
[2] *palm ... oak ... bays:* leaves woven into wreaths or garlands to crown or adorn victors: (1) in physical combat, (2) in civic achievements, and (3) in contests of rhetoric.
[3] *busy:* frenetic.

How far these beauties hers exceed!
Fair trees! wheres'e'er your barks I wound,
No name shall but your own be found.
When we have run our passion's heat,                    25
Love hither makes his best retreat.
The gods that mortal beauty chase,
Still in a tree did end their race:
Apollo hunted Daphne so,
Only that she might laurel grow;                        30
And Pan did after Syrinx speed,
Not as a nymph, but for a reed.

What wond'rous life in this I lead!
Ripe apples drop about my head;
The luscious clusters of the vine                       35
Upon my mouth do crush their wine;
The nectarine and curious peach
Into my hands themselves do reach;
Stumbling on melons as I pass,
Ensnared with flowers, I fall on grass.                 40

Meanwhile the mind from pleasure less
Withdraws into its happiness;
The mind, that ocean where each kind
Does straight its own resemblance find,
Yet it creates, transcending these,                     45
Far other worlds and other seas,
Annihilating all that's made
To a green thought in a green shade.

Here at the fountain's sliding foot,
Or at some fruit tree's mossy root,                     50
Casting the body's vest aside,
My soul into the boughs does glide;
There like a bird it sits and sings,
Then whets,[4] then combs its silver wings;
And till prepared for longer flight,                    55
Waves in its plumes the various light.

Such was that happy garden-state,
While man there walked without a mate;
After a place so pure and sweet,
What other help could yet be meet!                      60

[4] *whets:* sharpens.

But 'twas beyond a mortal's share
To wander solitary there;
Two paradises 'twere, in one,
To live in paradise alone.
How well the skillful gard'ner drew                    65
Of flowers and herbs this dial new,
Where, from above, the milder sun
Does through a fragrant zodiac run;
And as it works, th' industrious bee
Computes its time as well as we.                       70
How could such sweet and wholesome hours
Be reckoned but with herbs and flowers?

## QUESTIONS: *Marvell, "The Garden"*

This poem is not only the description of a place; it also explores the complex ways in which nature acts as an aesthetic and moral ideal for man.

1.  How is *nature* imagery used in the first two stanzas to contrast two modes of existence (in the world and in the garden)?
    *Clues:*  • Contrast of "some single herb or tree" to "all flowers and all trees."
    
    • The unstated contrast to "the garlands of repose."
    
    • The figurative and literal use of the word *plants* in lines 13–14.

2.  What difference does the speaker draw, through nature imagery and mythological references, between *emotional* experiences in the world and in the garden? Consider the opposition of (a) "white" and "red" with "green"; (b) "mortal beauty" with "a tree"; (c) "run," "chase," "hunted," "speed" with "retreat," "end their race," "grow," "a reed." What similarities are implied? Examine the ways in which the use of the *pathetic fallacy* (attributing to natural phenomena human characteristics) in stanza 5 suggests that within the garden the new emotional pleasures still offer gratifications similar to those in the world. Can it be said that the experience of contact with nature involves a process of *sublimation* (the substitution of an emotion for another that one cannot allow oneself to express)?
    *Clue:*  • Upon my mouth do crush their wine;

3.  Stanzas 3, 4, and 5 deal with the impact of the garden upon the *life of the senses;* the next two stanzas deal with the impact of the garden upon the *life of the mind.* In so doing they suggest a transcending experience in contact with nature that can truly be called *mind-expanding.* In attempting to determine its quality and essence take the following into account:
    a.  The comparison of the mind to an *ocean.* (The latter, being the source of life, subsumes all phenomena under itself. Moreover, in popular belief each land animal had a counterpart in the sea. Since the mind could contain representations of all earthly things, it too could be considered an ocean.)
    b.  The fact that the *expansion* of the mind in fusion with nature involves a *reduction,* a telescoping of all other experiences as well as a transcending of them. Note that "green" suggests creativity, freshness, and "shade" protectiveness from

external elements, coolness, insubstantiality. What connection do you see between the birth of "other worlds and other seas" here mentioned and the artistic process? What light do the paradoxes of "green thought" and "green shade" throw on the process projected here?

    c. The fact that the experience of *ascent* involves a separation of body from soul. Why is the bird image particularly appropriate here? Note "whets, then combs," "sits and sings." In what sense is this present experience a preparation for a "longer flight"?

4. What elements in the poem prepare us for its climactic praise of paradise before the creation of Eve, and the crowning tribute to the pleasures of solitude?

5. The last stanza describes a decorative clock sometimes found in formal gardens. Flowers and plants are grown in beds which themselves rest on the face and hands of a clock. This stanza is thought by some readers to have no meaningful connection with the rest of the poem, What justice is there to this view?

6. What psychological explanation could be given for the relative formality of the last stanza? How would the poem be affected by the removal of the last two stanzas? Consider both the positive and negative aspects of such a change.

7. What do the coexistence of sensual, mental, and spiritual pleasures suggest is the identity of the garden? Is it a real place, a vision of paradise before the fall of man, a conception of heaven, a view of man's highest realm of experience?

## EXERCISE

Discuss the aptness of the following comment: "Marvell's 'The Garden' is not only an insult to women, it is a rejection of all human beings."

## Henry Vaughan (1622–1695)
# The World

> I saw eternity the other night
> Like a great ring of pure and endless light,
>     All calm as it was bright;
> And round beneath it, time in hours, days, years,
>     Driv'n by the spheres,[1]       5
> Like a vast shadow moved, in which the world
>     And all her train were hurled:
> The doting lover in his quaintest strain
>     Did there complain;
> Near him his lute, his fancy, and his flights,    10
>     Wit's sour delights,

[1] *spheres:* technical term used in ancient, medieval, and Renaissance descriptions of the universe. Refers to the supposedly fixed paths in the heavens followed by the planets, the sun, and the moon in their supposed movement around the earth.

With gloves and knots, the silly snares of pleasure,
     Yet his dear treasure,
All scattered lay, while he his eyes did pore
     Upon a flower.            15
The darksome statesman, hung with weights and woe,
Like a thick midnight fog moved there so slow
     He did not stay, nor go;
Condemning thoughts, like sad eclipses, scowl
     Upon his soul,            20
And clouds of crying witnesses without
     Pursued him with one shout;
Yet digged the mole, and lest his ways be found
     Worked underground,
Where he did clutch his prey, but One did see       25
     That policy;
Churches and altars fed him; perjuries
     Were gnats and flies;

It rained about him blood and tears, but he
     Drank them as free.           30

The fearful miser on a heap of rust
Sat pining all his life there, did scarce trust
     His own hands with the dust,
Yet would not place one piece above, but lives
     In fear of thieves.           35
Thousands there were as frantic as himself,
     And hugged each one his pelf:
The downright epicure[2] placed heav'n in sense,
     And scorned pretense;
While others, slipped into a wide excess,          40
     Said little less;
The weaker sort slight trivial wares enslave,
     Who think them brave;
And poor despisèd truth sat counting by
     Their victory.            45

Yet some, who all this while did weep and sing,
And sing and weep, soared up into the ring;
     But most would use no wing.
O fools, said I, thus to prefer dark night
     Before true light.           50

---

[2] *epicure*: a form of the word *Epicurean*. Used here to mean a self-indulgent or excessively sensual person.

To live in grots and caves, and hate the day
    Because it shows the way,
The way which from this dead and dark abode
    Leads up to God,
A way where you might tread the sun, and be        55
    More bright than he.
But as I did their madness so discuss,
    One whispered thus:
This ring the bridegroom did for none provide
    But for his bride.[3]       60

## QUESTIONS: *Vaughan, "The World"*

1. The opening line of the poem states, "I saw eternity the other night." But the speaker then proceeds to describe the world. Does this shift really constitute a change of subject? What qualitative contrast is established between the "great ring of pure and endless light" and the rest of the universe in the first stanza? Note the use of "Driv'n," "hurled," "scattered."

2. The speaker sees eternity as *light* "the other *night*."
   a. What significant effect do images of light and dark have in the poem?
   *Clues:* • Like a vast shadow moved,

       • The darksome statesman, hung with weights and woe,
       Like a thick midnight fog moved there so slow

       • O fools, said I, thus to prefer dark night
          Before true light,

   b. What characteristics of the world are conveyed through animal imagery in stanza 2? Note "Yet digged the mole," "perjuries / Were gnats and flies."

3. The world is largely portrayed in this poem by means of capsule portraits of human types: the lover, the statesman, the "epicure," and the miser. What negative values do their experiences exemplify? Are these figures sufficiently representative for the poem to make an effective comment on human experience?

4. By what *means* does the speaker give the impression that he is viewing the world as an outsider? Note the use of *allegory* (a narrative that implies through dramatic form a psychological state or an idea) in the portraits above and in the treatment of institutions and qualities.
   *Clues:* • Churches and altars fed him;

       • The fearful miser on a heap of rust
       Sat pining all his life there,

       • And poor despisèd truth sat counting by
          Their victory.

5. The word *ring* appears only twice in the entire poem. How does its use clarify the poet's conception of eternity? Compare the function of the word in each of the stanzas in which it appears.

[3] *bride:* Christian symbolism traditionally describes the bond between believer and God (and between God and the church) as a marriage.

*William Blake (1757–1827)*

# Ah, Sun-flower

Ah, Sun-flower! weary of time,
Who countest the steps of the sun;
Seeking after that sweet golden clime,
Where the traveller's journey is done;

Where the Youth pined away with desire,
And the pale Virgin shrouded in snow,
Arise from their graves, and aspire
Where my Sun-flower wishes to go.

## QUESTIONS: *Blake, "Ah, Sun-flower"*

1. Why is the sunflower a particularly appropriate image for conveying the poet's concern with a transcendent state? What connotations of transcendent power does the sun itself evoke?
2. Explain the identity of the traveler and the implied connection between him and the sunflower.
3. We are given some direct suggestions as to the state from which escape is sought in the poem. In what sense is it a moral and psychological state rather than the condition of earthly existence that is condemned?
   *Clues:* • . . . pined away with *desire,*

   • . . . pale *Virgin shrouded* in *snow,*

   What can we deduce about the state aspired to?
   *Clues:* • Where the . . . journey is done;

   • Arise from their graves . . .

## EXERCISE

Blake speaks of the sunflower as "weary of time." In a paragraph suggest the appropriateness to Blake's poem of Vaughan's vision in "The World" of eternity as "a great ring of pure and endless light" and his conception that "round beneath it, time in hours, days, years, / Driv'n by the spheres, / Like a vast shadow moved."


*William Wordsworth (1770–1850)*

# The World Is Too Much with Us

The world is too much with us; late and soon,
Getting and spending, we lay waste our powers:
Little we see in Nature that is ours;
We have given our hearts away, a sordid boon!

This Sea that bares her bosom to the moon;                          5
The winds that will be howling at all hours,
And are up-gathered now like sleeping flowers;
For this, for everything, we are out of tune;
It moves us not.—Great God! I'd rather be
A Pagan suckled in a creed outworn;                                10
So might I, standing on this pleasant lea,
Have glimpses that would make me less forlorn;
Have sight of Proteus rising from the sea;
Or hear old Triton blow his wreathèd horn.

## QUESTIONS: *Wordsworth, "The World Is Too Much with Us"*

1. What does the metaphor of "getting and spending" suggest has become the central concern of man? Throughout the first four lines the poet's language reflects the values he is attacking in its use of *quantitative* terms. Explain how this usage heightens the poet's description of the modern predicament.

   Clues:   • The world is *too much* with us; *late* and *soon*,

   • *Getting* and *spending*, we lay waste our powers:

   • *Little* we see in Nature that is *ours*;

   • We have *given* our hearts *away*, a sordid boon!

2. How do the next four lines suggest the circumstances of the poem? To what extent do the descriptions of Nature in these lines *not support* the climactic statement "It moves us not?"

   Clues:   •• . . . bares her bosom to the moon;

   • . . . up-gathered now like sleeping flowers;

3. The poet moves from a metaphorical to a mythic view of nature. How does this movement dramatize the contrast between the speaker's consciousness and that of the "pagan suckled in a creed outworn"? In what sense does "forlorn" represent not only a *social* but a *cosmic* condition for the speaker? Consider the implied alternative to "creed outworn" and the possible identity of "Great God!"

4. How does the pagan perception of the universe presented in the last three lines of the poem constitute a corrective for the plight of man described in line 3, "Little we see in Nature that is ours"?

   Clues:   • Have sight of Proteus

   • *old Triton* blow

5. What is "the world" in this poem? Can the mode of escape which the speaker yearns for be termed *transcendence?* Note that the speaker's longings lead him to look *back*, not *up*, and that the central image is the *sea*, not the *sky*.

## Samuel Taylor Coleridge (1772–1834)

# The Rime of the Ancient Mariner

### In Seven Parts

### PART I

An ancient
Mariner
meeteth three
gallants bid-
den to a wed-
ding-feast,
and detaineth
one.

It is an ancient Mariner,
And he stoppeth one of three.
'By thy long grey beard and glittering eye,
Now wherefore stopp'st thou me?

'The Bridegroom's doors are opened wide,                    5
And I am next of kin;
The guests are met, the feast is set;
May'st hear the merry din.'

The wedding
guest is spell-
bound by the
eye of the old
sea-faring
man, and
constrained
to hear his
tale.

He holds him with his skinny hand,
'There was a ship,' quoth he.                               10
'Hold off! unhand me, grey-beard loon!'
Eftsoons his hand dropt he.

He holds him with his glittering eye—
The wedding-guest stood still,
And listens like a three years' child:                     15
The Mariner hath his will.

The wedding-guest sat on a stone:
He cannot choose but hear;
And thus spake on that ancient man,
The bright-eyed Mariner.                                    20

The ship was cheered, the harbour cleared,
Merrily did we drop
Below the kirk, below the hill,
Below the light house top.

The Mariner
tells how the
ship sailed
southward
with a good
wind and fair
weather, till
it reached the
Line.

The sun came up upon the left,                              25
Out of the sea came he!
And he shone bright, and on the right
Went down into the sea.

Higher and higher every day,
Till over the mast at noon—
The Wedding-Guest here beat his breast,
For he heard the loud bassoon.

The wedding
guest heareth
the bridal
music; but
the Mariner
continueth
his tale.

The bride hath paced into the hall,
Red as a rose is she;
Nodding their heads before her goes
The merry minstrelsy.

35

The Wedding-Guest he beat his breast,
Yet he cannot choose but hear;
And thus spake on that ancient man,
The bright-eyed Mariner.

40

And now the storm-blast came, and he
Was tyrannous and strong:
He struck with his o'ertaking wings,
And chased us south along.

With sloping masts and dipping prow,
As who pursued with yell and blow
Still treads the shadow of his foe,
And forward bends his head,
The ship drove fast, loud roared the blast,
And southward aye we fled.

45

50

And now there came both mist and snow,
And it grew wondrous cold:
And ice, mast-high, came floating by,
As green as emerald.

The land of
ice, and of
fearful
sounds where
no living
thing was to
be seen.

And through the drifts the snowy clifts
Did send a dismal sheen:
Nor shapes of men nor beasts we ken—
The ice was all between.

55

The ice was here, the ice was there,
The ice was all around:
It cracked and growled, and roared and howled,
Like noises in a swound!

60

At length did cross an Albatross,
Thorough the fog it came;
As if it had been a Christian soul, 65
We hailed it in God's name.

It ate the food it ne'er had eat,
And round and round it flew.
The ice did split with a thunder-fit;
The helmsman steered us through! 70

And a good south wind sprung up behind;
The Albatross did follow,
And every day, for food or play,
Came to the mariners' hollo!

In mist or cloud, on mast or shroud, 75
It perched for vespers nine;
Whiles all the night, through fog-smoke white,
Glimmered the white moon-shine.

'God save thee, ancient Mariner!
From the fiends, that plague thee thus!— 80
Why look'st thou so?'—With my cross-bow
I shot the Albatross.

## PART II

The Sun now rose upon the right:
Out of the sea came he,
Still hid in mist, and on the left 85
Went down into the sea.

And the good south wind still blew behind,
But no sweet bird did follow,
Nor any day for food or play
Came to the mariners' hollo! 90

And I had done a hellish thing,
And it would work 'em woe:
For all averred, I had killed the bird
That made the breeze to blow.
Ah wretch! said they, the bird to slay, 95
That made the breeze to blow!

But when the
fog cleared off,
they justify the
same, and thus
make them-
selves accom-
plices in the
crime.

Nor dim nor red, like God's own head,
The glorious Sun uprist:
Then all averred, I had killed the bird
That brought the fog and mist.          100
T'was right, said they, such birds to slay,
That bring the fog and mist.

The fair breeze
continues; the
ship enters the
Pacific Ocean,
and sails north-
ward, even till
it reaches the
Line.

The fair breeze blew, the white foam flew,
The furrow followed free;
We were the first that ever burst          105
Into that silent sea.

The ship hath
been suddenly
becalmed.

Down dropt the breeze, the sails dropt down,
'Twas sad as sad could be;
And we did speak only to break
The silence of the sea!          110

All in a hot and copper sky,
The bloody Sun, at noon,
Right up above the mast did stand,
No bigger than the Moon.

Day after day, day after day,          115
We stuck, nor breath nor motion;
As idle as a painted ship
Upon a painted ocean.

And the
Albatross begins
to be avenged.

Water, water, every where,
And all the boards did shrink;          120
Water, water, every where,
Nor any drop to drink.

The very deep did rot: O Christ!
That ever this should be!
Yea, slimy thing did crawl with legs          125
Upon the slimy sea.

About, about, in reel and rout
The death-fires danced at night;
The water, like a witch's oils,
Burnt green, and blue and white.          130

A spirit had
followed them;
one of the
invisible in-
habitants of
this planet,
neither de-

And some in dreams assured were
Of the spirit that plagued us so;
Nine fathom deep he had followed us
From the land of mist and snow.

parted souls nor angels; concerning whom the learned Jew, Josephus, and the Platonic Constantino-
politan, Michael Psellus, may be consulted. They are very numerous, and there is no climate or element
without one or more.

And every tongue, through utter drought,                135
Was withered at the root;
We could not speak, no more than if
We had been choked with soot.

Ah! well a-day! what evil looks

The shipmates,
in their sore
distress, would
fain throw the
whole guilt on

Had I from old and young!                               140
Instead of the cross, the Albatross
About my neck was hung.

the ancient Mariner: in sign whereof they hang the dead sea-bird round his neck.

## PART III

There passed a weary time. Each throat
Was parched, and glazed each eye.
A weary time! a weary time,                             145
How glazed each weary eye,

The ancient
Mariner be-
holdeth a sign
in the element
afar off.

When looking westward, I beheld
A something in the sky.

At first it seemed a little speck,
And then it seemed a mist;                              150
It moved and moved, and took at last
A certain shape, I wist.

A speck, a mist, a shape, I wist!
And still it neared and neared:
As if it dodged a water-sprite,                         155
It plunged and tacked and veered.

At its nearer
approach, it
seemeth him to
be a ship; and
at a dear ran-
som he freeth
his speech from
the bonds of
thirst.

With throats unslaked, with black lips baked,
We could nor laugh nor wail;
Through utter drought all dumb we stood!
I bit my arm, I sucked the blood,                       160
And cried, A sail! a sail!

With throats unslaked, with black lips baked,
Agape they heard me call:

A flash of joy;

Gramercy! they for joy did grin,
And all at once their breath drew in,                   165
As they were drinking all.

And horror
follows. For can
it be a ship that
comes onward
without wind or
tide?

See! see! (I cried) she tacks no more!
Hither to work us weal;
Without a breeze, without a tide,
She steadies with upright keel!                    170

The western wave was all a-flame.
The day was well nigh done!
Almost upon the western wave
Rested the broad bright Sun;
When that strange shape drove suddenly              175
Betwixt us and the Sun.

It seemeth him
but the skeleton
of a ship.

And straight the Sun was flecked with bars,
(Heaven's Mother send us grace!)
As if through a dungeon-grate he peered
With broad and burning face.                        180

Alas! (thought I, and my heart beat loud)
How fast she nears and nears!
Are those her sails that glance in the Sun,
Like restless gossameres?

And its ribs are
seen as bars on
the face of the
setting Sun.
The spectre-
woman and her
deathmate, and
no other on
board the
skeleton-ship.

Are those her ribs through which the Sun            185
Did peer, as through a grate?
And is that Woman all her crew?
Is that a Death? and are there two?
Is Death that woman's mate?

Like vessel,
like crew!

Her lips were red, her looks were free,             190
Her locks were yellow as gold:
Her skin was as white as leprosy,
The Night-mare Life-in-Death was she,
Who thicks man's blood with cold.

Death and
Life-in-death
have diced for
the ship's crew,
and she (the
latter) winneth
the ancient
Mariner.

The naked hulk alongside came,                      195
And the twain were casting dice;
'The game is done! I've won, I've won!'
Quoth she, and whistles thrice.

No twilight
within the courts
of the sun.

The Sun's rim dips; the stars rush out:
At one stride comes the dark;                       200
With far-heard whisper, o'er the sea,
Off shot the spectre-bark.

At the rising of
the Moon.

We listened and looked sideways up!
Fear at my heart, as at a cup,
My life-blood seemed to sip!          205
The stars were dim, and thick the night,
The steersman's face by his lamp gleamed white;
From the sails the dew did drip—
Till clomb above the eastern bar
The horned Moon, with one bright star      210
Within the nether tip.

One after
another.

One after one, by the star-dogged Moon,
Too quick for groan or sigh,
Each turned his face with a ghastly pang,
And cursed me with his eye.         215

His shipmates
drop down
dead.

Four times fifty living men,
(And I heard nor sigh nor groan)
With heavy thump, a lifeless lump,
They dropped down one by one.

But Life-in-
Death begins
her work on the
ancient
Mariner.

The souls did from their bodies fly,—    220
They fled to bliss or woe!
And every soul, it passed me by,
Like the whizz of my cross-bow!

## PART IV

The wedding
guest feareth
that a spirit is
talking to him.

'I fear thee, ancient Mariner!
I fear thy skinny hand!
And thou art long, and lank, and brown,    225
As is the ribbed sea-sand.[1]

I fear thee and thy glittering eye,
And thy skinny hand, so brown.'—

But the ancient
Mariner as-
sureth him of
his bodily life,
and proceedeth
to relate his
horrible
penance.

Fear not, fear not, thou wedding-guest!    230
This body dropt not down.

Alone, alone, all, all alone,
Alone on a wide wide sea!
And never a saint took pity on
My soul in agony.         235

[1] For the last two lines of this stanza, I am indebted to Mr. Wordsworth. It was on a delightful walk from Nether Stowey to Dulverton, with him and his sister, in the autumn of 1797, that this poem was planned, and in part composed.

He despiseth
the creatures of
the calm.

The many men, so beautiful!
And they all dead did lie:
And a thousand thousand slimy things
Lived on; and so did I.

And envieth
that they should
live, and so
many lie dead.

I looked upon the rotting sea,                                        240
And drew my eyes away;
I looked upon the rotting deck,
And there the dead men lay.

I looked to heaven, and tried to pray;
But or ever a prayer had gusht,                                        245
A wicked whisper came, and made
My heart as dry as dust.

I closed my lids, and kept them close,
And the balls like pulses beat;
For the sky and the sea, and the sea and the sky                       250
Lay like a load on my weary eye,
And the dead were at my feet.

But the curse
liveth for him
in the eye of the
dead men.

The cold sweat melted from their limbs,
Nor rot nor reek did they:
The look with which they looked on me                                  255
Had never passed away.

An orphan's curse would drag to hell
A spirit from on high;
But oh! more horrible than that
Is the curse in a dead man's eye!                                      260
Seven days, seven nights, I saw that curse,
And yet I could not die.

The moving Moon went up the sky,

In his loneliness
and fixedness he
yearneth to-
wards the
journeying
Moon, and the

And no where did abide:
Softly she was going up,                                               265
And a star or two beside—
stars that still sojourn, yet still move onward; and every where the blue sky belongs to them, and
is their appointed rest, and their native country and their own natural homes, which they enter
unannounced, as lords that are certainly expected and yet there is a silent joy at their arrival.

Her beams bemocked the sultry main,
Like April hoar-frost spread;
But where the ship's huge shadow lay,
The charmed water burnt alway                                          270
A still and awful red.

Beyond the shadow of the ship,
I watched the water-snakes:
They moved in tracks of shining white,
And when they reared, the elfish light                    275
Fell off in hoary flakes.

Within the shadow of the ship
I watched their rich attire:
Blue, glossy green, and velvet black,
They coiled and swam; and every track                   280
Was a flash of golden fire.

O happy living things! no tongue
Their beauty might declare:
A spring of love gushed from my heart,
And I blessed them unaware:                              285

Sure my kind saint took pity on me,
And I blessed them unaware.

The selfsame moment I could pray;
And from my neck so free
The Albatross fell off, and sank                         290
Like lead into the sea.

## PART V

Oh sleep! it is a gentle thing,
Beloved from pole to pole!
To Mary Queen the praise by given!
She sent the gentle sleep from Heaven,                   295
That slid into my soul.

The silly buckets on the deck,
That had so long remained,
I dreamt that they were filled with dew;
And when I awoke, it rained.                             300

My lips were wet, my throat was cold,
My garments all were dank;
Sure I had drunken in my dreams,
And still my body drank.

I moved, and could not feel my limbs:                   305
I was so light—almost
I thought that I had died in sleep,
And was a blessed ghost.

He heareth
sounds and
seeth strange
sights and
commotions in
the sky and the
element.

And soon I heard a roaring wind:
It did not come anear;                                     310
But with its sound it shook the sails,
That were so thin and sere.

The upper air burst into life!
And a hundred fire-flags sheen,
To and fro they were hurried about!                        315
And to and fro, and in and out,
The wan stars danced between.

And the coming wind did roar more loud,
And the sails did sigh like sedge;
And the rain poured down from one black cloud;             320
The Moon was at its edge.

The thick black cloud was cleft, and still
The Moon was at its side:
Like waters shot from some high crag,
The lightning fell with never a jag,                       325
A river steep and wide.

The bodies of
the ship's crew
are inspired,
and the ship
moves on.

The loud wind never reached the ship,
Yet now the ship moved on!
Beneath the lightning and the moon
The dead men gave a groan.                                  330

They groaned, they stirred, they all uprose,
Nor spake, nor moved their eyes;
It had been strange, even in a dream,
To have seen those dead men rise.

The helmsman steered, the ship moved on;                   335
Yet never a breeze up blew;
The mariners all 'gan work the ropes,
Where they were wont to do;
They raised their limbs like lifeless tools—
We were a ghastly crew.                                    340

The body of my brother's son
Stood by me, knee to knee:
The body and I pulled at one rope,
But he said nought to me.

But not by the souls of the men, nor by demons of earth or middle air, but by a blessed troop of angelic spirits, sent down by the invocation of the guardian saint.

'I fear thee, ancient Mariner!'  345
Be calm, thou Wedding-Guest!
'Twas not those souls that fled in pain,
Which to their corses came again,
But a troop of spirits blest:

For when it dawned—they dropped their arms,  350
And clustered round the mast;
Sweet sounds rose slowly through their mouths,
And from their bodies passed.

Around, around, flew each sweet sound,
Then darted to the Sun;  355
Slowly the sounds came back again,
Now mixed, now one by one.

Sometimes a-dropping from the sky
I heard the sky-lark sing;
Sometimes all little birds that are,  360
How they seemed to fill the sea and air
With their sweet jargoning!

And now 'twas like all instruments,
Now like a lonely flute;
And now it is an angel's song,  365
That makes the heavens be mute.

It ceased; yet still the sails made on
A pleasant noise till noon,
A noise like of a hidden brook
In the leafy month of June,  370
That to the sleeping woods all night
Singeth a quiet tune.

Till noon we quietly sailed on,
Yet never a breeze did breathe:
Slowly and smoothly went the ship,  375
Moved onward from beneath.

The lonesome spirit from the south pole carries on the ship as far as the Line, in obedience to the angelic troop, but still requireth vengeance.

Under the keel nine fathom deep,
From the land of mist and snow,
The spirit slid: and it was he
That made the ship to go.  380
The sails at noon left off their tune,
And the ship stood still also.

*432*

The Sun, right up above the mast,
Had fixed her to the ocean:
But in a minute she 'gan stir,                385
With a short uneasy motion—
Backwards and forwards half her length
With a short uneasy motion.

Then like a pawing horse let go,
She made a sudden bound:                      390
It flung the blood into my head,
And I fell down in a swound.

The Polar Spirit's fellow demons, the invisible inhabitants of the element, take part in his wrong; and two of them relate, one to the other, that penance long and heavy for the ancient Mariner hath been accorded to the Polar Spirit, who returneth southward.

How long in that same fit I lay,
I have not to declare;
But ere my living life returned,              395
I heard, and in my soul discerned
Two voices in the air.

'Is it he?' quoth one, 'Is this the man?
By him who died on cross,
With his cruel bow he laid full low           400
The harmless Albatross.

'The spirit who bideth by himself
In the land of mist and snow,
He loved the bird that loved the man
Who shot him with his bow.'                   405

The other was a softer voice,
As soft as honey-dew:
Quoth he, 'The man hath penance done,
And penance more will do.'

## PART VI

### First Voice

But tell me, tell me! speak again,            410
Thy soft response renewing—
What makes that ship drive on so fast?
What is the ocean doing?

### Second Voice

Still as a slave before his lord,
The ocean hath no blast;                      415
His great bright eye most silently
Up to the Moon is cast—

If he may know which way to go;
For she guides him smooth or grim.
See, brother, see! how graciously                              420
She looketh down on him.

### First Voice

The Mariner
hath been cast
into a trance;
for the angelic
power causeth
the vessel to
drive north-
ward faster
than human life
could endure.

But why drives on that ship so fast,
Without or wave or wind?

### Second Voice

The air is cut away before,
And closes from behind.                                        425

Fly, brother, fly! more high, more high!
Or we shall be belated:
For slow and slow that ship will go,
When the Mariner's trance is abated.

The super-
natural motion
is retarded; the
Mariner awakes,
and his penance
begins anew.

I woke, and we were sailing on                                 430
As in a gentle weather:
'Twas night, calm night, the moon was high;
The dead men stood together.

All stood together on the deck,
For a charnel-dungeon fitter:
All fixed on me their stony eyes,                              435
That in the Moon did glitter.

The pang, the curse, with which they died,
Had never passed away:
I could not draw my eyes from theirs,
Nor turn them up to pray.                                      440

The curse is
finally expiated.

And now this spell was snapt: once more
I viewed the ocean green,
And looked far forth, yet little saw
Of what had else been seen—                                    445

Like one, that on a lonesome road
Doth walk in fear and dread,
And having once turned round walks on,
And turns no more his head;
Because he knows, a frightful fiend                            450
Doth close behind him tread.

But soon there breathed a wind on me,
Nor sound nor motion made:
Its path was not upon the sea,
In ripple or in shade.           455

It raised my hair, it fanned my cheek
Like a meadow-gale of spring—
It mingled strangely with my fears,
Yet it felt like a welcoming.

Swiftly, swiftly flew the ship,           460
Yet she sailed softly too:
Sweetly, sweetly blew the breeze—
On me alone it blew.

*And the ancient Mariner beholdeth his native country.*

Oh! dream of joy! is this indeed
The light-house top I see?           465
Is this the hill? is this the kirk?
Is this mine own countree?

We drifted o'er the harbour-bar,
And I with sobs did pray—
O let me be awake, my God!           470
Or let me sleep alway.

The harbour-bay was clear as glass,
So smoothly it was strewn!
And on the bay the moonlight lay,
And the shadow of the moon.           475

The rock shone bright, the kirk no less,
That stands above the rock:
The moonlight steeped in silentness
The steady weathercock.

*The angelic spirits leave the dead bodies.*

And the bay was white with silent light,           480
Till rising from the same,
Full many shapes, that shadows were,
In crimson colours came.

*And appear in their own forms of light.*

A little distance from the prow
Those crimson shadows were:           485
I turned my eyes upon the deck—
Oh, Christ! what saw I there!

Each corse lay flat, lifeless and flat,
And, by the holy rood!
A man all light, a seraph-man,                          490
On every corse there stood.

This seraph-band, each waved his hand:
It was a heavenly sight!
They stood as signals to the land,
Each one a lovely light;                                495

This seraph-band, each waved his hand,
No voice did they impart—
No voice; but oh! the silence sank
Like music on my heart.

But soon I heard the dash of oars,                      500
I heard the Pilot's cheer;
My head was turned perforce away,
And I saw a boat appear.

The Pilot and the Pilot's boy,
I heard them coming fast:                               505
Dear Lord in Heaven! it was a joy
The dead men could not blast.

I saw a third—I heard his voice:
It is the Hermit good!
He singeth loud his godly hymns                         510
That he makes in the wood.
He'll shrieve my soul, he'll wash away
The Albatross's blood.

## PART VII

The Hermit of
the wood.

This Hermit good lives in that wood
Which slopes down to the sea.                           515
How loudly his sweet voice he rears!
He loves to talk with marineres
That come from a far countree.

He kneels at morn, and noon, and eve—
He hath a cushion plump:                                520
It is the moss that wholly hides
The rotted old oak-stump.

The skiff-boat neared: I heard them talk,
'Why, this is strange, I trow!
Where are those lights so many and fair,      525
That signal made but now?'

'Strange, by my faith!' the Hermit said—
'And they answered not our cheer!
The planks looked warped! and see those sails,
How thin they are and sere!      530
I never saw aught like to them,
Unless perchance it were

Brown skeletons of leaves that lag
My forest-brook along;
When the ivy-tod is heavy with snow,      535
And the owlet whoops to the wolf below,
That eats the she-wolf's young.'

'Dear Lord! it hath a fiendish look—
(The Pilot made reply)
I am a-feared'—'Push on, push on!'      540
Said the Hermit cheerily.

The boat came closer to the ship,
But I nor spake nor stirred;
The boat came close beneath the ship,
And straight a sound was heard.      545

Under the water it rumbled on,
Still louder and more dread:

It reached the ship, it split the bay;
The ship went down like lead.

Stunned by that loud and dreadful sound,      550
Which sky and ocean smote,
Like one that hath been seven days drowned
My body lay afloat;
But swift as dreams, myself I found
Within the Pilot's boat.      555

Upon the whirl, where sank the ship,
The boat spun round and round;
And all was still, save that the hill
Was telling of the sound.

I moved my lips—the Pilot shrieked      560
And fell down in a fit;
The holy Hermit raised his eyes,
And prayed where he did sit.

I took the oars: the Pilot's boy,
Who now doth crazy go,      565
Laughed loud and long, and all the while
His eyes went to and fro.
'Ha! ha!' quoth he, 'full plain I see,
The Devil knows how to row.'

And now, all in my own countree,      570
I stood on the firm land!
The Hermit stepped forth from the boat,
And scarcely he could stand.

*The ancient Mariner earnestly entreateth the Hermit to shrieve him; and the penance of life falls on him.*

'O shrieve me, shrieve me, holy man!'
The Hermit crossed his brow.      575
'Say quick,' quoth he, 'I bid thee say—
What manner of man art thou?'

Forthwith this frame of mine was wrenched
With a woful agony,
Which forced me to begin my tale;      580
And then it left me free.

*And ever and anon throughout his future life an agony constraineth him to travel from land to land.*

Since then, at an uncertain hour,
That agony returns:
And till my ghastly tale is told,
This heart within me burns.      585

I pass, like night, from land to land;
I have strange power of speech;
That moment that his face I see,
I know the man that must hear me:
To him my tale I teach.      590

What loud uproar bursts from that door
The wedding-guests are there:
But in the garden-bower the bride
And bride-maids singing are:
And hark the little vesper bell,      595
Which biddeth me to prayer!

O Wedding-Guest! this soul hath been
Alone on a wide wide sea:
So lonely 'twas, that God himself
Scarce seemed there to be. 600

O sweeter than the marriage-feast,
'Tis sweeter far to me,
To walk together to the kirk
With a goodly company!—

To walk together to the kirk, 605
And all together pray,
While each to his great Father bends,
Old men, and babes, and loving friends,
And youths and maidens gay!

And to teach, by his own example, love and reverence to all things that God made and loveth.

Farewell, farewell! but this I tell 610
To thee, thou Wedding-Guest!
He prayeth well, who loveth well
Both man and bird and beast.

He prayeth best, who loveth best
All things both great and small; 615
For the dear God who loveth us,
He made and loveth all.

The Mariner, whose eye is bright,
Whose beard with age is hoar,
Is gone: and now the Wedding-Guest 620
Turned from the bridegroom's door.

He went like one that hath been stunned,
And is of sense forlorn:
A sadder and a wiser man,
He rose the morrow morn. 625

## QUESTIONS: *Coleridge, "The Rime of the Ancient Mariner"*

1. Much less is said in detail here about the ways of *the world*—its problems, its physical properties, its psychic impact—than in some of the other works in Section III. (See, for example, the men who "amaze" themselves in Marvell, the "darksome statesman" in Vaughan, and the references to "getting and spending" in Wordsworth.) But the world is nevertheless part of this poem. Explain what worldly pursuits are implied or characterized in the poem and how the position of the Ancient Mariner in the universe is clarified by the following contacts with other human beings:

a. The Wedding Guest.

> *Clue:* • 'The Bridegroom's doors are opened wide,
>    And I am next of kin;
>    The guests are met, the feast is set:
>    May'st hear the merry din.'
>
>    He holds him with his skinny hand,
>    'There was a ship,' quoth he.
>    'Hold off! Unhand me, grey-beard loon!'
>    Eftsoons his hand dropt he.

b. The members of his crew.

> *Clue:* • Ah wretch! said they, the bird to slay,
>    That made the breeze to blow!
>
>    'Twas right, said they, such birds to slay,
>    That bring the fog and mist.

c. The Pilot and the Hermit.

> *Clues:* • . . . the Pilot's boy,
>    Who now doth crazy go, . . .
>
>    'Ha! ha!' quoth he, 'full plain I see
>    The Devil knows how to row.'
>
>    • 'O shrieve me, shrieve me, holy man!'
>    The Hermit crossed his brow.
>    'Say quick,' quoth he, 'I bid thee say—
>    What manner of man art thou?'

2. As in Lowell's "The Voyage," a sea voyage functions here to suggest a spiritual experience of *self-discovery* and *self-transcendence*, the water itself being associated with regenerative powers. As in Marvell's "The Garden" and Blake's "Ah! Sun-flower," natural settings and creatures in nature function to suggest mental and emotional states. Explain what each of the following reveals about the Mariner's voyage:

a. References to ice, fog, mist, snow, cold.

> *Clue:* • And through the drifts the snowy clifts
>    Did send a dismal sheen:
>    Nor shapes of men nor beasts we ken—
>    The ice was all between.  (Part I)

b. References to heat, bloodiness, drought and dust, windlessness.

> *Clues:* • All in a hot and copper sky,
>    The bloody Sun, at noon,
>    Right up above the mast did stand,
>    No bigger than the Moon.  (Part II)
>
>    • Water, water, ever ywhere,
>    And all the boards did shrink;
>    Water, water, every where,
>    Nor any drop to drink.  (Part II)

c. References to sea creatures.

> *Clues:* • The very deep did rot: O Christ!

That ever this should be!
Yea, slimy things did crawl with legs
Upon the slimy sea.   (Part II)

• Within the shadow of the ship
I watched their rich attire:
Blue, glossy green, and velvet black,
They coiled and swam; and every track
Was a flash of golden fire.   (Part IV)

d. References to water, wind.
   *Clues:*   • And a good south wind sprung up behind;
The albatross did follow,   (Part I)

• My lips were wet, my throat was cold,
My garments all were dank;
Sure I had drunken in my dreams,
And still my body drank.   (Part V)

• And soon I heard a roaring wind:
It did not come anear;
But with its sound it shook the sails,
That were so thin and sere.   (Part V)

• It raised my hair, it fanned my cheek
Like a meadow-gale of spring—
It mingled strangely with my fears,
Yet it felt like a welcoming.   (Part VI)

3. Read closely the last five stanzas in Part I. Explain what they reveal about the nature of the Albatross and its function in the poem. Note references to "the fog," the "good south wind," the "vespers nine," "the white moonshine." Why is the reference to "the fiends" significant here?

4. The Ancient Mariner kills the Albatross. He may also be responsible for the death of his crewmates. The poem suggests that he may, at the same time, have destroyed himself. Considering his temporary loss of speech, mental and perceptual imbalance, anxiety, and hysteria, discuss the possible nature of the psychological and spiritual sickness of which the above are symptoms. How is his relation to God, Nature, and Man implicated in his crime?
   *Clues:*   • And every tongue, through utter drought,
Was *withered* at the root;
We could not speak, no more than if
We had been *choked with soot*.

• Ah! well-a-day! what evil looks
Had I from *old* and *young*!
Instead of the *cross*, the *Albatross*
About my neck was hung.

5. What aspects of the Mariner's psychic state are further suggested by the "Life-in-Death" sequence through *description* (of the bark, the sun, the figure) and through *action*? Consider why it is appropriate that the "Night-mare Life-in-Death" rather than Death should win the Mariner.

6. What symbolic relationship is there between the ultimate forbidding appearance of the Mariner's ship and the appearance of the "spectre bark?" How central to the theme of the poem is the eventual fate of the ship and the fact that the Mariner alone is rescued?

7. The dramatic climax of the poem occurs in Part IV. The Mariner is "alone, alone, all, all alone," "in agony," and under a "curse." But Part IV also reveals a turning point in the Mariner's psychic state from the desire for death to the affirmation of life.

   a. Why is it appropriate that the atonement for the sin should dramatically be ushered in not by a conscious act of penitence but by a spontaneous, *unconscious* reaction which is expressed in *religious* terms? ("And I blessed them unaware" is said twice).

   b. Why is it appropriate that the creatures as the Mariner perceives them are endowed with the distinction of being "happy living things"?

   c. Why is it appropriate that their "beauty" is felt to be one "no tongue . . . might declare"? Consider the Mariner's previous sense of revulsion at the sea and its creatures.

   d. Why is it appropriate that other forces and sounds in *Nature* (wind, water, songs of birds), described in Part V, participate in the Mariner's recovery?

8. Does the lesson the Ancient Mariner has learned and which he teaches the Wedding Guest—the need to love "man and bird and beast" as part of the divine and loving creation—seem fully to encompass the experience he has undergone? Consider the following as you assess the value of the lesson:

   a. The unprovoked and unpremeditated nature of the initial deed ("the bird that loved the man").

   b. The spontaneous nature of the liberating action.

   c. The recurring agony that demands the retelling of the story.

   d. The choice of the Wedding Guest as audience ("he stoppeth one of three") and the reaction of the latter (who "went like one that hath been stunned").

## EXERCISE

Consider the possible influence on Coleridge's conception of the Ancient Mariner of other figures in stories of guilt and expiation, such as the Wandering Jew or the Flying Dutchman.

*Alfred, Lord Tennyson (1809–1892)*
# The Lotos-Eaters and Ulysses

## THE LOTOS-EATERS

*The poem is based on a passage in the* Odyssey *relating the brief but tempting visit of Odysseus (Ulysses) and his companions in the land of the lotus-eaters; those members of the crew who ate the lotus lost all desire to return home and had to be forcibly removed.*

"Courage!" he said, and pointed toward the land,
"This mounting wave will roll us shoreward soon."
In the afternoon they came unto a land,
In which it seemèd always afternoon.
All round the coast the languid air did swoon,                        5
Breathing like one that hath a weary dream.
Full-faced above the valley stood the moon;
And like a downward smoke, the slender stream
Along the cliff to fall and pause and fall did seem.

A land of streams! some, like a downward smoke,                       10
Slow-dropping veils of thinnest lawn, did go;
And some through wavering lights and shadows broke,
Rolling a slumbrous sheet of foam below.
They saw the gleaming river seaward flow
From the inner land: far off, three mountain-tops,                    15
Three silent pinnacles of agèd snow,
Stood sunset-flushed: and, dewed with showery drops,
Up-clomb the shadowy pine above the woven copse.

The charmèd sunset lingered low adown
In the red West: through mountain clefts the dale                     20
Was seen far inland, and the yellow down
Bordered with palm, and many a winding vale
And meadow, set with slender galingale;
A land where all things always seemed the same!
And round about the keel with faces pale,                             25
Dark faces pale against that rosy flame,
The mild-eyed melancholy Lotos-eaters came.

Branches they bore of that enchanted stem,
Laden with flower and fruit, whereof they gave
To each, but whoso did receive of them,                              30
And taste, to him the gushing of the wave
Far, far away did seem to mourn and rave
On alien shores; and if his fellow spake,
His voice was thin, as voices from the grave;
And deep-asleep he seemed, yet all awake,                            35
And music in his ears his beating heart did make.

They sat them down upon the yellow sand,
Between the sun and moon upon the shore;
And sweet it was to dream of Fatherland,
Of child, and wife, and slave; but evermore                          40
Most weary seemed the sea, weary the oar,

Weary the wandering fields of barren foam.
Then some one said, "We will return no more";
And all at once they sang, "Our island home
Is far beyond the wave; we will no longer roam."          45

### Choric Song

#### I

There is sweet music here that softer falls
Than petals from blown rose on the grass,
Or night-dews on still waters between walls
Of shadowy granite, in a gleaming pass;
Music that gentlier on the spirit lies,                    50
Than tired eyelids upon tired eyes;
Music that brings sweet sleep down from the blissful skies.
Here are cool mosses deep,
And through the moss the ivies creep,
And in the stream the long-leaved flowers weep,           55
And from the craggy ledge the poppy hangs in sleep.

#### II

Why are we weighed upon with heaviness,
And utterly consumed with sharp distress,
While all things else have rest from weariness?
All things have rest: why should we toil alone,           60
We only toil, who are the first of things,
And make perpetual moan,
Still from one sorrow to another thrown:
Nor ever fold our wings,
And cease from wanderings,                                 65
Nor steep our brows in slumber's holy balm;
Nor harken what the inner spirit sings,
'There is no joy but calm!'—
Why should we only toil, the roof and crown of things?

#### III

Lo! in the middle of the wood,                            70
The folded leaf is wooed from out the bud
With winds upon the branch, and there
Grows green and broad, and takes no care,
Sun-steeped at noon, and in the moon
Nightly dew-fed; and turning yellow                       75
Falls, and floats adown the air.
Lo! sweetened with the summer light,
The full-joiced apple, waxing over-mellow,

*444*

Drops in a silent autumn night.
All its allotted length of days,                                    80
The flower ripens in its place,
Ripens and fades, and falls, and hath no toil,
Fast-rooted in the fruitful soil.

### IV

Hateful is the dark-blue sky,
Vaulted o'er the dark-blue sea.                                    85
Death is the end of life; ah, why
Should life all labour be?
Let us alone. Time driveth onward fast,
And in a little while our lips are dumb.
Let us alone. What is it that will last?                          90
All things are taken from us, and become
Portions and parcels of the dreadful Past.
Let us alone. What pleasure can we have
To war with evil? Is there any peace
In ever climbing up the climbing wave?                            95
All things have rest, and ripen toward the grave
In silence; ripen, fall and cease:
Give us long rest or death, dark death, or dreamful ease.

### V

How sweet it were, hearing the downward stream,
With half-shut eyes ever to seem                                  100
Falling asleep in a half-dream!
To dream and dream, like yonder amber light,
Which will not leave the myrrh-bush on the height;
To hear each other's whispered speech;
Eating the Lotos day by day,                                      105
To watch the crisping ripples on the beach,
And tender curving lines of creamy spray;
To lend our hearts and spirits wholly
To the influence of mild-minded melancholy;
To muse and brood and live again in memory,                      110
With those old faces of our infancy
Heaped over with a mound of grass,
Two handfuls of white dust, shut in an urn of brass!

### VI

Dear is the memory of our wedded lives,
And dear the last embraces of our wives                          115
And their warm tears: but all hath suffered change;
For surely now our household hearths are cold:

Our sons inherit us: our looks are strange:
And we should come like ghosts to trouble joy.
Or else the island princes over-bold                    120
Have eat our substance, and the minstrel sings
Before them of the ten years' war in Troy,
And our great deeds, as half-forgotten things.
Is there confusion in the little isle?
Let what is broken so remain.                           125
The Gods are hard to reconcile:
'Tis hard to settle order once again.
There *is* confusion worse than death,
Trouble on trouble, pain on pain,
Long labour unto agèd breath,                           130
Sore task to hearts worn out with many wars
And eyes grown dim with gazing on the pilot-stars

VII

But, propt on beds of amaranth and moly,
How sweet (while warm airs lull us, blowing lowly)
With half-dropt eyelids still,                          135
Beneath a heaven dark and holy,
To watch the long bright river drawing slowly
His waters from the purple hill—
To hear the dewy echoes calling
From cave to cave through the thick-twinèd vine—        140
To watch the emerald-coloured water falling
Through many a woven acanthus-wreath divine!
Only to hear and see the far-off sparkling brine,
Only to hear were sweet, stretched out beneath the pine.

The Lotos blooms below the barren peak:                 145
The Lotos blows by every winding creek:
All day the wind breathes low with mellower tone:
Through every hollow cave and alley lone
Round and round the spicy downs the yellow Lotos-dust is blown.
We have had enough of action, and of motion we,        150
Rolled to starboard, rolled to larboard, when the surge was seething free,
Where the wallowing monster spouted his foam-fountains in the sea.
Let us swear an oath, and keep it with an equal mind,
In the hollow Lotos-land to live and lie reclined
On the hills like gods together, careless of mankind.   155
For they lie beside their nectar, and the bolts are hurled
Far below them in the valleys, and the clouds are lightly curled
Round their golden houses, girdled with the gleaming world;
Where they smile in secret, looking over wasted lands,

*446*

Blight and famine, plague and earthquake, roaring deeps and fiery sands, 160
Clanging fights, and flaming towns, and sinking ships, and praying hands.
But they smile, they find a music centred in a doleful song
Steaming up, a lamentation and an ancient tale of wrong,
Like a tale of little meaning though the words are strong;
Chanted from an ill-used race of men that cleave the soil,    165
Sow the seed, and reap the harvest with enduring toil,
Storing yearly little dues of wheat, and wine and oil;
Till they perish and they suffer—some, 'tis whispered—down in hell
Suffer endless anguish, others in Elysian valleys dwell,
Resting weary limbs at last on beds of asphodel.    170
Surely, surely, slumber is more sweet than toil, the shore
Than labour in the deep mid-ocean, wind and wave and oar;
O rest ye, brother mariners, we will not wander more.

## QUESTIONS: *Tennyson, "The Lotos-Eaters"*

1.  Shakespeare prefaces his moral indictment of the world's ills in "Sonnet 66" with the statement: "Tired with all these, for restful death I cry." The mariners ask here, "Give us long rest or death, dark death, or dreamful ease." What is the qualitative singularity of their weariness? Is it essentially a state of *moral* despair, or a *psychological* and *aesthetic* revulsion from the psychic demands and losses of earthly life? What difference is there between the mariners' weariness and the "mild-minded melancholy" state of the lotus-eaters?

    Clues: • All things have rest: why should we *toil* alone,
    *We only toil*, who are the first of things,

    • All things are *taken from us*, and become
    Portions and parcels of the *dreadful Past*.
    Let us alone. What *pleasure* can we have
    To *war* with *evil?* Is there any peace
    In ever *climbing up* the climbing wave?

    • Let what is *broken* so remain.
    The Gods are *hard* to reconcile:
    'Tis hard to settle order once again.

    • Blight and famine, plague and earthquake, *roaring* deeps and *fiery* sands,

2.  Given the state of the mariners, what kind of withdrawal from the world does the lotus provide? What creative elements are in the state which is achieved? What part do *music* and *dreams* play in that creativity?

    Clues: • And deep-*asleep* he seemed, yet all *awake*,
    And music in his ears his beating heart did make.

    • Nor steep our brows in *slumber's holy balm;*
    Nor harken what the inner spirit *sings*,
    'There is no joy but calm!'—

3.  In the concluding lines the mariners state
    Surely, surely, slumber is more sweet than toil, the shore
    Than labour in the deep mid-ocean, wind and wave and oar;

How does the ocean serve as a representative of the life of action imposed upon man in the world? What other water imagery effectively contrasts with it to suggest a different mode of existence and apprehension?

Clues: Note the contrasts between these lines:

· "This mounting wave will roll us shoreward soon."

and

And like a downward smoke, the slender stream
Along the cliff to fall and pause and fall did seem.

· Weary the wandering fields of barren foam.

and

And in the stream the long-leaved flowers weep,

4. Through the eating of the lotus the mariners attempt to transcend their human condition and to approximate a state resembling that of *Nature* or of *the Gods*. Consider carefully the way in which Nature and the Gods are characterized. What in each of their states is particularly attractive to man in contrast with his own state?

Clues: · The *full-juiced* apple, waxing over-mellow,
*Drops* in a *silent* autumn night.

· But they *smile*, they find a music centred in a doleful song
Steaming up, a lamentation and an ancient tale of wrong,
Like a tale of *little meaning* though the *words* are *strong*;

## ULYSSES

*Tennyson said about this poem that it "was written under the sense of loss [of his university friend Arthur Hallam whose premature death deeply affected the poet] and all that had gone by, but that still life must be fought out to the end." It is also inspired by Ulysses' harangue to "that small company, which had not deserted [him]" in Dante's* Inferno, Canto XXVI:

'O brothers!' I said, 'who through a hundred
thousand dangers have reached the West, deny
not, to this the brief vigil

of your senses that remains, experience of the
unpeopled world behind the Sun.

Consider your origin: ye were not formed to
live like brutes, but to follow virtue and knowledge.'

It little profits that an idle king,
By this still hearth, among these barren crags,
Matched with an agèd wife, I mete and dole
Unequal laws unto a savage race,
That hoard, and sleep, and feed, and know not me. 5
I cannot rest from travel: I will drink
Life to the lees. All time I have enjoyed

Greatly, have suffered greatly, both with those
That loved me, and alone; on shore, and when
Through scudding drifts the rainy Hyades                    10
Vext the dim sea. I am become a name;
For always roaming with a hungry heart
Much have I seen and known,—cities of men
And manners, climates, councils, governments,
Myself not least, but honoured of them all,—                15
And drunk delight of battle with my peers,
Far on the ringing plains of windy Troy.
I am a part of all that I have met;
Yet all experience is an arch where-through
Gleams that untravelled world whose margin fades            20
Forever and forever when I move.
How dull it is to pause, to make an end,
To rust unburnished, not to shine in use!
As though to breathe were life! Life piled on life
Were all too little, and of one to me                       25
Little remains; but every hour is saved
From that eternal silence, something more,
A bringer of new things; and vile it were
For some three suns to store and hoard myself,
And this gray spirit yearning in desire                     30
To follow knowledge like a sinking star,
Beyond the utmost bound of human thought.
　　This is my son, mine own Telemachus,
To whom I leave the sceptre and the isle—
Well-loved of me, discerning to fulfil                      35
This labor, by slow prudence to make mild
A rugged people, and through soft degrees
Subdue them to the useful and the good.
Most blameless is he, centred in the sphere
Of common duties, decent not to fail                        40
In offices of tenderness, and pay
Meet adoration to my household gods,
When I am gone. He works his work, I mine.
　　There lies the port; the vessel puffs her sail;
There gloom the dark, broad seas. My mariners,              45
Souls that have toiled, and wrought, and thought with me,—
That ever with a frolic welcome took
The thunder and the sunshine, and opposed
Free hearts, free foreheads,—you and I are old;
Old age hath yet his honor and his toil.                    50
Death closes all; but something ere the end,
Some work of noble note, may yet be done,

Not unbecoming men that strove with gods.
The lights begin to twinkle from the rocks;
The long day wanes; the slow moon climbs; the deep          55
Moans round with many voices. Come, my friends.
'Tis not too late to seek a newer world.
Push off, and sitting well in order smite
The sounding furrows; for my purpose holds
To sail beyond the sunset, and the baths          60
Of all the western stars, until I die.
It may be that the gulfs will wash us down;
It may be we shall touch the Happy Isles,
And see the great Achilles, whom we knew.
Though much is taken, much abides; and though          65
We are not now that strength which in old days
Moved earth and heaven, that which we are, we are,—
One equal temper of heroic hearts,
Made weak by time and fate, but strong in will
To strive, to seek, to find, and not to yield.          70

## QUESTIONS

1.  In the first twenty-one lines what significant contrast is established between the world which Ulysses now seeks to escape and the world of warfare and voyaging which makes up his former experience? Note that the experiences in both worlds are measured by *quantitative* standards and that images of *acquisition* and *appetite* function in both worlds to convey values.

    Clues:  • It *little profits* that an idle king,
         By this still hearth, among these barren crags,
         Matched with an agèd wife, I *mete* and *dole*
         *Unequal* laws unto a savage race,
         That *hoard*, and *sleep*, and *feed*, and *know not* me.

        • For always roaming with a *hungry* heart
         *Much* have I seen and known,—cities of men
         And manners, climates, councils, governments,
         Myself *not least*, but honored of them *all*,—
         And *drunk* delight of battle with my peers,

        •        Life *piled* on life
        Were all *too little* . . .
                  and vile it were
        For some *three* suns to *store* and *hoard* myself,

2.  Ulysses says of Telemachus: "He works his work, I mine." How does the description of Telemachus' work, coming after the reference to Ulysses' "gray spirit yearning in desire/To follow knowledge like a sinking star,/Beyond the utmost bound of human thought" further amplify the contrast between two worlds—or two modes of experience?

*Clue:* • Well-loved of me, discerning to fulfil
   This labor, by *slow prudence* to *make mild*
   A rugged people, and through *soft* degrees
   Subdue them to the *useful* and the *good.*

In what sense can it be said that Ulysses rejects authority but not leadership?

3.  In Homer's poem Odysseus is desperately trying to return to his home, his family, and his social and personal responsibilities. Tennyson's Ulysses, as we have suggested, rejects these commitments and does so in order "to follow knowledge" and perhaps perform "some work of noble note." What are the complexities and ambiguities of this aspiration?

*Clues:* • Yet all experience is an arch where-through
   Gleams that untravelled world whose margin *fades*
   *Forever* and *forever when* I *move.*

   • To follow knowledge like a *sinking star,*
   Beyond the *utmost bound* of human thought.

   • 'Tis not too late to seek a newer world.

   • To sail *beyond the sunset,* and the baths
   Of all the western stars, until I die.

   • It may be we shall *touch* the *Happy Isles,*
   And see the great Achilles, whom we knew.

Ulysses refers to himself and his companions as "men that strove with gods." How is his present aspiration another form of strife? Consider the several possible interpretations of his final resolve "not to yield."

4.  How does the imagery of boat, sea, and voyage function to suggest the twofold possibilities of a new intellectual experience or a new spiritual state achieved through struggle and suffering?

*Clues:* • There *gloom* the *dark, broad* seas.

   • The long day wanes; the slow moon climbs; the deep
   *Moans* round with *many voices.*

   • *Push* off, and sitting well in order *smite*
   The sounding furrows; for my purpose holds
   To *sail beyond* the sunset, and the baths
   Of all the western stars, until I die.

## EXERCISES

1.  In Homer Odysseus dissuades the mariners from staying in the land of the lotus-eaters. Discuss how the sources of pleasure for Ulysses in Tennyson's "Ulysses" differ from those to which the mariners are drawn in his poem "The Lotos-Eaters." Suggest also how the different views of repose in these poems are a clue to Tennyson's conception of the meaning and purpose of life.

2.  In the light of both Tennyson poems, comment on the lines in Lowell's "The Voyage" (stanza vii): "Here are the fabulous fruits; look, my boughs bend; / eat yourself sick on knowledge."

*Henry David Thoreau (1817–1862)*

# Walden

## Chapter II

### Where I Lived, and What I Lived for

At a certain season of our life we are accustomed to consider every spot as the possible site of a house. I have thus surveyed the country on every side within a dozen miles of where I live. In imagination I have bought all the farms in succession, for all were to be bought, and I knew their price. I walked over each farmer's premises, tasted his wild apples, discoursed on husbandry with him, took his farm at his price, at any price, mortgaging it to him in my mind; even put a higher price on it,—took every thing but a deed of it,—took his word for his deed, for I dearly love to talk,—cultivated it, and him too to some extent, I trust, and withdrew when I had enjoyed it long enough, leaving him to carry it on. This experience entitled me to be regarded as a sort of real-estate broker by my friends. Wherever I sat, there I might live, and the landscape radiated from me accordingly. What is a house but a *sedes*, a seat?—better if a country seat. I discovered many a site for a house not likely to be soon improved, which some might have thought too far from the village, but to my eyes the village was too far from it. Well, there I might live, I said; and there I did live, for an hour, a summer and a winter life; saw how I could let the years run off, buffet the winter through, and see the spring come in. The future inhabitants of this region, wherever they may place their houses, may be sure that they have been anticipated. An afternoon sufficed to lay out the land into orchard, woodlot, and pasture, and to decide what fine oaks or pines should be left to stand before the door, and whence each blasted tree could be seen to the best advantage; and then I let it lie, fallow perchance, for a man is rich in proportion to the number of things which he can afford to let alone.

My imagination carried me so far that I even had the refusal of several farms,—the refusal was all I wanted,—but I never got my fingers burned by actual possession. The nearest that I came to actual possession was when I bought the Hollowell place, and had begun to sort my seeds, and collected materials with which to make a wheelbarrow to carry it on or off with; but before the owner gave me a deed of it, his wife—every man has such a wife—changed her mind and wished to keep it, and he offered me ten dollars to release him. Now, to speak the truth, I had but ten cents in the world, and it surpassed my arithmetic to tell, if I was that man who had ten cents, or who had a farm, or ten dollars, or all together. However, I let him keep the ten dollars and the farm too, for I had carried it far enough; or rather, to be generous, I sold him the farm for what I gave for it, and, as he was not a rich man, made him a present of ten dollars, and still had my ten cents, and seeds, and materials for a wheelbarrow left. I found thus that I had been a rich man without any damage to my poverty. But I retained the landscape, and I have since annually carried off what it yielded without a wheelbarrow. With respect to landscapes,—

> "I am monarch of all I *survey*,
> My right there is none to dispute."[1]

I have frequently seen a poet withdraw, having enjoyed the most valuable part of a farm, while the crusty farmer supposed that he had got a few wild apples only. Why, the owner does not know it for many years when a poet has put his farm in rhyme, the most admirable kind of invisible fence, has fairly impounded it, milked it, skimmed it, and got all the cream, and left the farmer only the skimmed milk.

The real attractions of the Hollowell farm, to me, were; its complete retirement, being about two miles from the village, half a mile from the nearest neighbor, and separated from the highway by a broad field; its bounding on the river, which the owner said protected it by its fogs from frosts in the spring, though that was nothing to me; the gray color and ruinous state of the house and barn, and the dilapidated fences, which put such an interval between me and the last occupant; the hollow and lichen-covered apple trees, gnawed by rabbits, showing what kind of neighbors I should have; but above all, the recollection I had of it from my earliest voyages up the river, when the house was concealed behind a dense grove of red maples, through which I heard the house-dog bark. I was in haste to buy it, before the proprietor finished getting out some rocks, cutting down the hollow apple trees, and grubbing up some young birches which had sprung up in the pasture, or, in short, had made any more of his improvements. To enjoy these advantages I was ready to carry it on; like Atlas, to take the world on my shoulders,—I never heard what compensation he received for that,—and do all those things which had no other motive or excuse but that I might pay for it and be unmolested in my possession of it; for I knew all the while that it would yield the most abundant crop of the kind I wanted if I could only afford to let it alone. But it turned out as I have said.

All that I could say, then, with respect to farming on a large scale, (I have always cultivated a garden,) was, that I had had my seeds ready. Many think that seeds improve with age. I have no doubt that time discriminates between the good and the bad; and when at last I shall plant, I shall be less likely to be disappointed. But I would say to my fellows, once for all, As long as possible live free and uncommitted. It makes but little difference whether you are committed to a farm or the county jail.

Old Cato, whose "De Re Rusticâ" is my "Cultivator," says, and the

---

[1] From "Verses Supposed to Be Written by Alexander Selkirk," by William Cowper (1731–1800).

only translation I have seen makes sheer nonsense of the passage, "When you think of getting a farm, turn it thus in your mind, not to buy greedily; nor spare your pains to look at it, and do not think it enough to go round it once. The oftener you go there the more it will please you, if it is good." I think I shall not buy greedily, but go round and round it as long as I live, and be buried in it first, that it may please me the more at last.

The present was my next experiment of this kind, which I purpose to describe more at length; for convenience, putting the experience of two years into one. As I have said, I do not propose to write an ode to dejection, but to brag as lustily as chanticleer in the morning, standing on his roost, if only to waken my neighbors up.

When first I took up my abode in the woods, that is, began to spend my nights as well as days there, which, by accident, was on Independence day, or the fourth of July, 1845, my house was not finished for winter, but was merely a defence against the rain, without plastering or chimney, the walls being of rough weather-stained boards, with wide chinks, which made it cool at night. The upright white hewn studs and freshly planed door and window casings gave it a clean and airy look, especially in the morning, when its timbers were saturated with dew, so that I fancied that by noon some sweet gum would exude from them. To my imagination it retained throughout the day more or less of this auroral character, reminding me of a certain house on a mountain which I had visited the year before. This was an airy and unplastered cabin, fit to entertain a travelling god, and where a goddess might trail her garments. The winds which passed over my dwelling were such as sweep over the ridges of mountains, bearing the broken strains, or celestial parts only, of terrestrial music. The morning wind forever blows, the poem of creation is uninterrupted; but few are the ears that hear it. Olympus is but the outside of the earth every where.

The only house I had been the owner of before, if I except a boat, was a tent, which I used occasionally when making excursions in the summer, and this is still rolled up in my garret; but the boat, after passing from hand to hand, has gone down the stream of time. With this more substantial shelter about me, I had made some progress toward settling in the world. This frame, so slightly clad, was a sort of crystallization around me, and reacted on the builder. It was suggestive somewhat as a picture in outlines. I did not need to go out doors to take the air, for the atmosphere within had lost none of its freshness. It was not so much within doors as behind a door where I sat, even in the rainiest weather. The Harivansa says, "An abode without birds is like a meat without seasoning." Such was not my abode, for I found myself suddenly neighbor to the birds; not by having imprisoned one, but having caged myself near them. I was not only nearer to some of those which commonly frequent the garden and the orchard, but to those wilder and more thrilling songsters of the forest which never, or rarely, serenade a villager,—the wood-thrush, the veery, the scarlet tanager, the field-sparrow, the whippoorwill, and many others.

I was seated by the shore of a small pond, about a mile and a half south of the village of Concord and somewhat higher than it, in the midst of an extensive wood between that town and Lincoln, and about two miles south of that our only field known to fame, Concord Battle Ground; but I was so low in the woods that the opposite shore, half a mile off, like the rest, covered with wood, was my most distant horizon. For the first week, whenever I looked out on the pond it impressed me like a tarn high up on the side of a mountain, its bottom far above the surface of other lakes, and, as the sun arose, I saw it throwing off its nightly clothing of mist, and here and there, by degrees, its soft ripples or its smooth reflecting surface was revealed, while the mists, like ghosts, were stealthily withdrawing in every direction into the woods, as at the breaking up of some nocturnal conventicle. The very dew seemed to hang upon the trees later into the day than usual, as on the sides of mountains.

This small lake was of most value as a neighbor in the intervals of a gentle rain storm in August, when, both air and water being perfectly still, but the sky overcast, mid-afternoon had all the serenity of evening, and the wood-thrush sang around, and was heard from shore to shore. A lake like this is never smoother than at such a time; and the clear portion of the air above it being shallow and darkened by clouds, the water, full of light and reflections, becomes a lower heaven itself so much the more important. From a hill top near by, where the wood had been recently cut off, there was a pleasing vista southward across the pond, through a wide indentation in the hills which form the shore there, where their opposite sides sloping toward each other suggested a stream flowing out in that direction through a wooded valley, but stream there was none. That way I looked between and over the near green hills to some distant and higher ones in the horizon, tinged with blue. Indeed, by standing on tiptoe I could catch a glimpse of some of the peaks of the still bluer and more distant mountain ranges in the north-west, those true-blue coins from heaven's own mint, and also of some portion of the village. But in other directions, even from this point, I could not see over or beyond the woods which surrounded me. It is well to have some water in your neighborhood, to give buoyancy to and float the earth. One value even of the smallest well is, that when you look into it you see that earth is not continent but insular. This is as important as that it keeps butter cool. When I looked across the pond from this peak toward the Sudbury meadows, which in time of flood I distinguished elevated perhaps by a mirage in their seething valley, like a coin in a basin, all the earth beyond the pond appeared like a thin crust insulated and floated even by this small sheet of intervening water, and I was reminded that this on which I dwelt was but *dry land*.

Though the view from my door was still more contracted, I did not feel crowded or confined in the least. There was pasture enough for my imagination. The low shrub-oak plateau to which the opposite shore arose, stretched away toward the prairies of the West and the steppes of Tartary, affording ample room for all the roving families of men. "There are none happy in the world but beings who enjoy freely a vast horizon,"—said Damodara, when his herds required new and larger pastures.

Both place and time were changed, and I dwelt nearer to those parts of the universe and to those eras in history which had most attracted me. Where I lived was as far off as many a region viewed nightly by astronomers. We are wont to imagine rare and delectable places in some remote and more celestial corner of the system, behind the constellation of Cassiopeia's Chair, far from noise and disturbance. I discovered that my house actually had its site in such a withdrawn, but forever new and unprofaned, part of the universe. If it were worth the while to settle in those parts near to the Pleiades or the Hyades, to Aldebaran or Altair, then I was really there, or at an equal remoteness from the life which I had left behind, dwindled and twinkling with as fine a ray to my nearest neighbor, and to be seen only in moonless nights by him. Such was that part of creation where I had squatted;—

> "There was a shepherd that did live,
>   And held his thoughts as high
> As were the mounts whereon his flocks
>   Did hourly feed him by."[2]

What should we think of the shepherd's life if his flocks always wandered to higher pastures than his thoughts?

Every morning was a cheerful invitation to make my life of equal simplicity, and I may say innocence, with Nature herself. I have been as sincere a worshipper of Aurora as the Greeks. I got up early and bathed in the pond; that was a religious exercise, and one of the best things which I did. They say that characters were engraven on the bathing tub of king Tching-thang to this effect: "Renew thyself completely each day; do it again, and again, and forever again." I can understand that. Morning brings back the heroic ages. I was as much affected by the faint hum of a mosquito making its invisible and unimaginable tour through my apartment at earliest dawn, when I was sitting with door and windows open, as I could be by any trumpet that ever sang of fame. It was Homer's requiem; itself an Iliad and Odyssey in the air, singing its own wrath and wanderings. There was something cosmical about it; a standing advertisement, till forbidden, of the everlasting vigor and fertility of the world. The morning, which is the most memorable season of the day, is the awakening hour. Then there is least somnolence in us; and for an hour, at least, some part of us awakes which slumbers all the rest of the day and night. Little is to be expected of that day, if it can be called a day, to which we are not awakened by our Genius, but by the mechanical nudgings of some servitor, are not awakened by our own newly-acquired

---

[2] First quatrain of "The Shepherd's Love for Philliday," an anonymous Jacobean poem, probably known to Thoreau from an 1810 volume, *Old Ballads* (collected by Thomas Evans).

force and aspirations from within, accompanied by the undulations of celestial music, instead of factory bells, and a fragrance filling the air—to a higher life than we fell asleep from; and thus the darkness bear its fruit, and prove itself to be good, no less than the light. That man who does not believe that each day contains an earlier, more sacred, and auroral hour than he has yet profaned, has despaired of life, and is pursuing a descending and darkening way. After a partial cessation of his sensuous life, the soul of man, or its organs rather, are reinvigorated each day, and his Genius tries again what noble life it can make. All memorable events, I should say, transpire in morning time and in a morning atmosphere. The Vedas say, "All intelligences awake with the morning." Poetry and art, and the fairest and most memorable of the actions of men, date from such an hour. All poets and heroes, like Memnon, are the children of Aurora, and emit their music at sunrise. To him whose elastic and vigorous thought keeps pace with the sun, the day is a perpetual morning. It matters not what the clocks say or the attitudes and labors of men. Morning is when I am awake and there is a dawn in me. Moral reform is the effort to throw off sleep. Why is it that men give so poor an account of their day if they have not been slumbering? They are not such poor calculators. If they had not been overcome with drowsiness they would have performed something. The millions are awake enough for physical labor; but only one in a million is awake enough for effective intellectual exertion, only one in a hundred millions to a poetic or divine life. To be awake is to be alive. I have never yet met a man who was quite awake. How could I have looked him in the face?

We must learn to reawaken and keep ourselves awake, not by mechanical aids, but by an infinite expectation of the dawn, which does not forsake us in our soundest sleep. I know of no more encouraging fact than the unquestionable ability of man to elevate his life by a conscious endeavor. It is something to be able to paint a particular picture, or to carve a statue, and so to make a few objects beautiful; but it is far more glorious to carve and paint the very atmosphere and medium through which we look, which morally we can do. To affect the quality of the day, that is the highest of arts. Every man is tasked to make his life, even in its details, worthy of the contemplation of his most elevated and critical hour. If we refused, or rather used up, such paltry information as we get, the oracles would distinctly inform us how this might be done.

I went to the woods because I wished to live deliberately, to front only the essential facts of life, and see if I could not learn what it had to teach, and not, when I came to die, discover that I had not lived. I did not wish to live what was not life, living is so dear; nor did I wish to practise resignation, unless it was quite necessary. I wanted to live deep and suck out all the marrow of life, to live so sturdily and Spartan-like as to put to rout all that was not life, to cut a broad swath and shave close, to drive life into a corner, and reduce it to its lowest terms, and, if it proved to be mean, why then to get the whole and genuine meanness of it, and publish its meanness to the world; or if it were sublime, to know it by experience, and be able to give a true account of it in my next excursion. For most men, it appears to me, are in a strange uncertainty about it, whether it is of the devil or of God, and have *somewhat hastily* concluded that it is the chief end of man here to "glorify God and enjoy him forever."

Still we live meanly, like ants; though the fable tells us that we were long ago changed into men; like pygmies we fight with cranes; it is error upon error, and clout upon clout, and our best virtue has for its occasion a superfluous and evitable wretchedness. Our life is frittered away by detail. An honest man has hardly need to count more than his ten fingers, or in extreme cases he may add his ten toes, and lump the rest. Simplicity, simplicity, simplicity! I say, let your affairs be as two or three, and not a hundred or a thousand; instead of a million count half a dozen, and keep your accounts on your thumb nail. In the midst of this chopping sea of civilized life, such are the clouds and storms and quicksands and thousand-and-one items to be allowed for, that a man has to live, if he would not founder and go to the bottom and not make his port at all, by dead reckoning, and he must be a great calculator indeed who succeeds. Simplify, simplify. Instead of three meals a day, if it be necessary eat but one; instead of a hundred dishes, five; and reduce other things in proportion. Our life is like a German Confederacy made up of petty states, with its boundary forever fluctuating, so that even a German cannot tell you how it is bounded at any moment. The nation itself, with all its so called internal improvements, which, by the way, are all external and superficial, is just such an unwieldy and overgrown establishment, cluttered with furniture and tripped up by its own traps, ruined by luxury and needless expense, by want of calculation and a worthy aim, as the million households in the land; and the only cure for it as for them is in a rigid economy, a stern and more than Spartan simplicity of life and elevation of purpose. It lives too fast. Men think that it is essential that the *Nation* have commerce, and export ice, and talk through a telegraph, and ride thirty miles an hour, without a doubt, whether *they* do or not; but whether we should live like baboons or like men, is a little uncertain. If we do not get out sleepers, and forge rails, and devote days and nights to the work, but go to tinkering upon our *lives* to improve *them*, who will build railroads? And if railroads are not built, how shall we get to heaven in season? But if we stay at home and mind our business, who will want railroads? We do not ride on the railroad; it rides upon us. Did you ever think what those sleepers are that underlie the railroad? Each one is a man, an Irishman, or a Yankee man. The rails are laid on them, and they are covered with sand, and the cars run smoothly over them. They are sound sleepers, I assure you. And every few years a new lot is laid down and run over; so that, if some have the pleasure of riding on a rail, others have the misfortune to be ridden upon. And when they run over a man that is walking in his sleep, a supernumerary sleeper in the wrong position, and wake him up, they suddenly stop the cars, and make a hue and cry about it, as if this were an exception. I am glad to know that it takes a gang of men for every five miles to keep the sleepers down and level in their beds as it is, for this is a sign that they may sometime get up again.

Why should we live with such hurry and waste of life? We are determined to be starved before we are hungry. Men say that a stitch in time saves nine, and so they take a thousand stitches today to save nine to-morrow. As for *work*, we haven't any of any consequence. We have the Saint Vitus' dance, and cannot possibly keep our heads still. If I should only give a few pulls at the parish bell-rope, as for a fire, that is, without setting the bell, there is hardly a man on his farm in the outskirts of Concord, notwithstanding that press of engagements which was his excuse so many times this morning, nor a boy, not a woman, I might almost say, but would forsake all and follow that sound, not mainly to save property from the flames, but, if we will confess the truth, much more to see it burn, since burn it must, and we, be it known, did nor set it on fire,—or to see it put out, and have a hand in it, if that is done as handsomely; yes, even if it were the parish church itself. Hardly a man takes a half hour's nap after dinner, but when he wakes he holds up his head and asks, "What's the news?" as if the rest of mankind had stood his sentinels. Some give directions to be waked every half hour, doubtless for no other purpose; and then, to pay for it, they tell what they have dreamed. After a night's sleep the news is as indispensable as the breakfast. "Pray tell me any thing new that has happened to a man any where on this globe,"—and he reads it over his coffee and rolls, that a man has had his eyes gouged out this morning on the Wachito River; never dreaming the while that he lives in the dark unfathomed mammoth cave of this world, and has but the rudiment of an eye himself.

For my part, I could easily do without the post-office. I think that there are very few important communications made through it. To speak critically, I never missed more than one or two letters in my life—I wrote this some years ago—that were worth the postage. The penny-post is, commonly, an institution through which you seriously offer a man that penny for his thoughts which is so often safely offered in jest. And I am sure that I never read any memorable news in a newspaper. If we read of one man robbed, or murdered, or killed by accident, or one house burned, or one vessel wrecked, or one steamboat blown up, or one cow run over on the Western Railroad, or one mad dog killed, or one lot of grasshoppers in the winter,—we never read of another. One is enough. If you are acquainted with the principle, what do you care for a myriad instances and applications? To a philosopher all *news*, as it is called, is gossip, and they who edit and read it are old women over their tea. Yet not a few are greedy after this gossip. There was such a rush, as I hear, the other day at one of the offices to learn the foreign news by the last arrival, that several large squares of plate glass belonging to the establishment were broken by the pressure,—news which I seriously think a ready wit might write a twelvemonth or twelve years beforehand with sufficient accuracy. As for Spain, for instance, if you know how to throw in Don Carlos and the Infanta, and Don Pedro and Seville and Granada, from time to time in the right proportions,—they may have have changed the names a little since I saw the papers,—and serve up a bull-fight when other entertainments fail, it will be true to the letter, and give us as good an idea of the exact state or ruin of things in Spain as the most succinct and lucid reports under this head in the newspapers: and as for England, almost the last significant scrap of news from that quarter was the revolution of 1649; and if you have learned the history of her crops for an average year, you never need attend to that thing again, unless your speculations are of a merely pecuniary character. If one may judge who rarely looks into the newspapers, nothing new does ever happen in foreign parts, a French revolution not excepted.

What news! how much more important to know what that is which was never old! "Kieou-he-yu (great dignitary of the state of Wei) sent a man to Khoung-tseu to know his news. Khoung-tseu caused the messenger to be seated near him, and questioned him in these terms: What is your master doing? The messenger answered with respect: My master desires to diminish the number of his faults, but he cannot accomplish it. The messenger being gone, the philosopher remarked: What a worthy messenger! What a worthy messenger!" The preacher, instead of vexing the ears of drowsy farmers on their day of rest at the end of the week,—for Sunday is the fit conclusion of an ill-spent week, and not the fresh and brave beginning of a new one,—with this one other draggletail of a sermon, should shout with thundering voice,—"Pause! Avast! Why so seeming fast, but deadly slow?"

Shams and delusions are esteemed for soundest truths, while reality is fabulous. If men would steadly observe realities only, and not allow themselves to be deluded, life, to compare it with such things as we know, would be like a fairy tale and the Arabian Nights' Entertainments. If we respected only what is inevitable and has a right to be, music and poetry would resound along the streets. When we are unhurried and wise, we perceive that only great and worthy things have any permanent and absolute existence,—that petty fears and petty pleasures are but the shadow of the reality. This is always exhilarating and sublime. By closing the eyes and slumbering, and consenting to be deceived by shows, men establish and confirm their daily life of routine and habit every where, which still is built on purely illusory foundations. Children, who play life, discern its true law and relations more clearly than men, who fail to live it worthily, but who think that they are wiser by experience, that is, by failure. I have read in a Hindoo book, that "there was a king's son, who, being expelled in infancy from his native city, was brought up by a forester, and, growing up to maturity in that state, imagined himself to belong to the barbarous race with which he lived. One of his father's ministers having discovered him, revealed to him what he was, and the misconception of his character was removed, and he knew himself to be a prince. So soul," continues the Hindoo philosopher, "from the circumstances in which it is placed, mistakes its own character, until the truth is revealed to it by some holy teacher, and then it knows itself to be

*Brahme.*" I perceive that we inhabitants of New England live this mean life that we do because our vision does not penetrate the surface of things. We think that that *is* which *appears* to be. If a man should walk through this town and see only the reality, where, think you, would the "Milldam" go to? If he should give us an account of the realities he beheld there, we should not recognize the place in his description. Look at a meeting-house, or a court-house, or a jail, or a shop, or a dwelling-house, and say what that thing really is before a true gaze, and they would all go to pieces in your account of them. Men esteem truth remote, in the outskirts of the system, behind the farthest star, before Adam and after the last man. In eternity there is indeed something true and sublime. But all these times and places and occasions are now and here. God himself culminates in the present moment, and will never be more divine in the lapse of all the ages. And we are enabled to apprehend at all what is sublime and noble only by the perpetual instilling and drenching of the reality that surrounds us. The universe constantly and obediently answers to our conceptions; whether we travel fast or slow, the track is laid for us. Let us spend our lives in conceiving then. The poet or the artist never yet had so fair and noble a design but some of his posterity at least could accomplish it.

Let us spend one day as deliberately as Nature, and not be thrown off the track by every nutshell and mosquito's wing that falls on the rails. Let us rise early and fast, or break fast, gently and without perturbation; let company come and let company go, let the bells ring and the children cry,— determined to make a day of it. Why should we knock under and go with the stream? Let us not be upset and overwhelmed in that terrible rapid and whirlpool called a dinner, situated in the meridian shallows. Weather this danger and you are safe, for the rest of the way is down hill. With unrelaxed nerves, with morning vigor, sail by it, looking another way, tied to the mast like Ulysses. If the engine whistles, let it whistle till it is hoarse for its pains. If the bell rings, why should we run? We will consider what kind of music they are like. Let us settle ourselves, and work and wedge our feet down- ward through the mud and slush of opinion, and prejudice, and tradition, and delusion, and appearance, that alluvion which covers the globe, through Paris and London, through New York and Boston and Concord, through church and state, through poetry and philosophy and religion, till we come to a hard bottom and rocks in place, which we can call *reality*, and say, This is, and no mistake; and then begin, having a *point d'appui*, below freshet and frost and fire, a place where you might found a wall or a state, or set a lamp- post safely, or perhaps a gauge, not a Nilometer, but a Realometer, that future ages might know how deep a freshet of shams and appearances had gathered from time to time. If you stand right fronting and face to face to a fact, you will see the sun glimmer on both its surfaces, as if it were a cimeter, and feel its sweet edge dividing you through the heart and marrow, and so you will happily conclude your mortal career. Be it life or death, we crave only reality. If we are really dying, let us hear the rattle in our throats and feel cold in the extremities: if we are alive, let us go about our business.

Time is but the stream I go a-fishing in. I drink at it; but while I drink I see the sandy bottom and detect how shallow it is. Its thin current slides away, but eternity remains. I would drink deeper; fish in the sky, whose bottom is pebbly with stars. I cannot count one. I know not the first letter of the alphabet. I have always been regretting that I was not as wise as the day I was born. The intellect is a cleaver; it discerns and rifts its way into the secret of things. I do not wish to be any more busy with my hands than is necessary. My head is hands and feet. I feel all my best faculties concentrated in it. My instinct tells me that my head is an organ for burrowing, as some creatures use their snout and fore-paws, and with it I would mine and burrow my way through these hills. I think that the richest vein is somewhere hereabouts; so by the divining rod and thin rising vapors I judge; and here I will begin to mine.

## QUESTIONS: *Thoreau, Walden*

1. Thoreau describes his physical location at Walden as being one and a half miles from Concord (about forty minutes' walk) and writes in another chapter of receiving visitors. Yet his remarks are punctuated with disparagements of human contact. How does Thoreau reveal that neither his decision to reside at Walden nor his general attitude toward human beings is merely the manifestation of misanthropy? What are the specific tendencies of *men* from which he seeks escape?

    *Clues:* • The morning wind forever blows, the poem of creation is uninterrupted; but few are the ears that hear it.

    • The millions are awake enough for physical labor; but only one in a million is awake enough for effective intellectual exertion, only one in a hundred millions to a poetic or divine life.

    • Shams and delusions are esteemed for soundest truths . . .

2. Thoreau praises a life of "simplicity" and yet can dwell (at times here and in another section of *Walden*) on agricultural and household details. If his view of simplicity is not that of a complete renunciation of material values, how might it be characterized? What connection can we establish between that goal and Thoreau's view of man's *institutions?*

    *Clues:* • We do not ride on the railroad: it rides upon us.

    • For my part, I could easily do without the post-office.

3. Examine closely the paragraph beginning "Still we live meanly, like ants" and comment on the effectiveness of the following:

    a. The pun on *sleeper* as a word for railway ties and for a person who is resting or stupefied. Does it sustain or confuse the metaphor of sleeping used three paragraphs earlier (as in the statement: "I have never yet met a man who was quite awake")?

    b. The elaborate metaphor of the *sea voyage* (so frequently used to suggest the vicissitudes of life) in itself and in conjunction with such later references as "Let us not be upset and overwhelmed in that terrible rapid and whirlpool called a dinner, situated in the meridian shallows."

    c. Similes and numbers.

4. Taking into account the preceding questions and the following clues, try to determine as clearly as possible the *quality* of the transcending experience Thoreau is trying to achieve. Why do the references to it so often take the form of a *paradox?*

Clues: • I found myself suddenly neighbor to the birds; not by having imprisoned one, but having *caged myself* near them.

• When I looked across the pond . . . all the earth beyond [it] appeared like a thin crust insulated and floated even by this small sheet of intervening water, and I was reminded that this on which I dwelt was but *dry land.*

• If men would steadily observe *realities* only . . . life, to compare it with such things as we know, would be like a *fairy tale* and the Arabian Nights' Entertainments.

• Time is but the stream I go a-fishing in. I drink at it; but while I drink I see the sandy bottom and detect how shallow it is. Its thin current slides away, but eternity remains. I would drink deeper; fish in the sky, whose bottom is pebbly with stars. I *cannot count one.* I know not the first letter of the alphabet. I have always been regretting that I was *not as wise as the day I was born.*

## Walt Whitman (1819–1892)

# Song of Myself

### XXXI

I believe a leaf of grass is no less than the journeywork of the stars,
And the pismire[1] is equally perfect, and a grain of sand, and the egg of the
    wren,
And the tree-toad is a chef-d'œuvre for the highest,
And the running blackberry would adorn the parlors of heaven,
And the narrowest hinge in my hand puts to scorn all machinery,     5
And the cow crunching with depress'd head surpasses any statue,
And a mouse is miracle enough to stagger sextillions of infidels.

I find I incorporate gneiss,[2] coal, long-threaded moss, fruits, grains, esculent[3]
    roots,
And am stucco'd with quadrupeds and birds all over,
And have distanced what is behind me for good reasons,     10
But call any thing back again when I desire it.

In vain the speeding or shyness,
In vain the plutonic rocks[4] send their old heat against my approach,

---

[1] *pismire:* ant. [2] *gneiss:* granite-like layered rock. [3] *esculent:* edible. [4] *plutonic rocks:* produced by the hardening of molten rock under the earth.

In vain the mastodon[5] retreats beneath its own powder'd bones,
In vain objects stand leagues off and assume manifold shapes,                     15
In vain the ocean settling in hollows and the great monsters lying low,
In vain the buzzard houses herself with the sky,
In vain the snake slides through the creepers and logs,
In vain the elk takes to the inner passes of the woods,
In vain the razor-bill'd auk sails far north to Labrador,                         20
I follow quickly, I ascend to the nest in the fissure of the cliff.

## QUESTIONS: *Whitman, "Song of Myself"*

1.  What double assertion about the *creativity* of *Nature* is made in the first stanza?
    What limitation in the human world is thereby emphasized?
    *Clues:*   • I believe a leaf of grass is not less than the journeywork of the stars,
             • And the cow crunching with depress'd head surpasses any statue,

2.  What capacities of *man* do the next two stanzas suggest? In what way are these
    *creative?* Consider the relationship to Nature that these entail and the transcen-
    dence that they imply. Consider also the following elements:
    a.  The significance of these lines:
        And have distanced what is behind me for good reasons,
        But call any thing back again when I desire it.
    b.  The references to the geological and zoological past (for instance, "plutonic
        rocks," "mastodon").
    c.  The repetition of "In vain." Why does the poet depict Nature as resisting
        human penetration of its mysteries? What characteristics of human aspiration
        are indirectly suggested by the actions of "buzzard," "snake," "elk," and
        "auk"?
    d.  The metaphorical force of "I follow quickly, I ascend to the nest in the
        fissure of the cliff."

## EXERCISE

Compare and contrast this poem with James Dickey's "In the Mountain Tent,"
particularly  with regard to the references to *animal life* and *time past* in suggesting
man's interaction with Nature. In conclusion suggest which poem in your judgment
has a wider scope, is more moving, is the greater work of art.

---

[5] *mastodon:* prehistoric animal resembling the elephant.

## Matthew Arnold (1822–1888)
# Dover Beach

*In his reference to Sophocles, Arnold has in mind the lines in* Antigone *in which the metaphor of sea and wind is used to convey the pervasiveness of the suffering that a doomed house (here that of Oedipus) endures.*

The sea is calm to-night,
The tide is full, the moon lies fair
Upon the Straits;—on the French coast, the light
Gleams, and is gone; the cliffs of England stand,
Glimmering and vast, out in the tranquil bay.          5
Come to the window, sweet is the night air!
Only, from the long line of spray
Where the ebb meets the moon-blanch'd sand,
Listen! you hear the grating roar
Of pebbles which the waves suck back, and fling,          10
At their return, up the high strand,
Begin, and cease, and then again begin,
With tremulous cadence slow, and bring
The eternal note of sadness in.

   Sophocles long ago          15
Heard it on the Aegaean, and it brought
Into his mind the turbid ebb and flow
Of human misery; we
Find also in the sound a thought,
Hearing it by this distant northern sea.          20

The sea of faith
Was once, too, at the full, and round earth's shore
Lay like the folds of a bright girdle furl'd;
But now I only hear
Its melancholy, long, withdrawing roar,          25
Retreating to the breath
Of the night-wind down the vast edges drear
And naked shingles of the world.

Ah, love, let us be true
To one another! for the world, which seems          30
To lie before us like a land of dreams,
So various, so beautiful, so new,

Hath really neither joy, nor love, nor light,
Nor certitude, nor peace, nor help for pain;
And we are here as on a darkling plain                    35
Swept with confused alarms of struggle and flight,
Where ignorant armies clash by night.

## QUESTIONS: *Arnold, "Dover Beach"*

1. What mood and tone are established in the introductory five lines? What function
   do these lines therefore have in the poem as a whole
   *Clues:* • The sea is *calm* to-night
   The tide is *full*, the moon lies *fair*
   Upon the straits . . .
   . . . the cliffs of England *stand*,
   Glimmering and *vast*, out in the *tranquil* bay.
   Come to the window . . .

2. How do the lines "Listen! you hear the grating roar/Of pebbles which the waves
   suck back, and fling" mark a certain transition in the poem? What element do
   they first introduce into the poem that becomes central to it?

3. How are both comparisons induced by the sound of the sea (that made by
   Sophocles and that by the speaker) relevant to the ultimate assessment of the
   world in the last stanza?

4. In the elaborate metaphor in stanza 4, through which the poet conveys the crisis
   of doubt of his generation, how does imagery suggest the qualities of a *former* and
   *present* spiritual state?
   *Clues:* • Lay like the *folds* of a *bright girdle* furl'd.

   • Of the night-wind down the vast edges drear
   And *naked* shingles of the world.

5. How is the conviction that the central flaw of the world the poet observes is a
   *deceiving appearance* validated by elements dealt with earlier in the poem? How
   is the injunction to the beloved related to the basic flaw in the universe? Consider
   that the "alarms" are "confused," the "armies" "ignorant."

## Emily Dickinson (1830–1886)

# No rack can torture me

No rack can torture me,
My soul's at liberty,
Behind this mortal bone
There knits a bolder one

You cannot prick with saw                    5
Nor rend with scimitar.
Two bodies therefore be;
Bind one, and one will flee.

The eagle of his nest
No easier divest                                       10
And gain the sky,
Than mayest thou,

Except thyself may be
Thine enemy;
Captivity is consciousness,                            15
So's liberty.

## QUESTIONS: *Dickinson, "No rack can torture me"*

1.  The title sometimes provided for this poem is "Emancipation." *From what* has emancipation been achieved according to the first two stanzas?

    *Clues:* • No *rack* can *torture* me,

    • You cannot *prick* with *saw*,
      Nor rend with *scimitar*.

    How is the concept of emancipation strengthened in these first eight lines (a) by the variety of synonyms: "rack," "saw," and "scimitar"? (b) by the reference to two kinds of bones and bodies?
2.  How does the image of the eagle in stanza 3 amplify the central statement made in the earlier stanzas? What is conventional in its use? What is original?
3.  What paradox about the nature of liberty does the poem imply in these lines?
    a. Bind one, and one will flee.
    b. Captivity is consciousness,
       So's liberty.
4.  In what does the affirmation of the last stanza reside?

    *Clue:* Except thyself may be
       Thine enemy;

## *William Butler Yeats (1865–1939)*

# The Lake Isle of Innisfree and Sailing to Byzantium

### THE LAKE ISLE OF INNISFREE

I will arise and go now, and go to Innisfree,
And a small cabin build there, of clay and wattles made:
Nine bean-rows will I have there, a hive for the honey-bee,
And live alone in the bee-loud glade.

And I shall have some peace there, for peace comes dropping slow,    5
Dropping from the veils of the morning to where the cricket sings;
There midnight's all a glimmer, and noon a purple glow,
And evening full of the linnet's wings.

I will arise and go now, for always night and day
I hear lake water lapping with low sounds by the shore;          10
While I stand on the roadway, or on the pavements gray,
I hear it in the deep heart's core.


QUESTIONS: *Yeats, "The Lake Isle of Innisfree"*

1. What do the plans of the speaker in the first stanza indirectly tell us about the attributes of the life he wants to leave behind?

   *Clue:*   • And a *small* cabin *build* there, of clay and *wattles* made:
   *Nine* bean-rows will I have there, a hive for the *honey-bee*,
   And live *alone* in the *bee-loud* glade.

2. In the light of the first stanza, why is it appropriate that the state yearned for should be described in the next stanza as one of peace? How is the achievement of that state suggested by the following?

   a. The combination of *auditory* and *visual* effects (for example, "And evening full of the linnet's wings").

   b. The treatment of *time* (what is the function of color? why is chronology ignored?)

3. How does the last stanza amplify the impression of the world from which the speaker seeks to escape? How does it affirm the yearning for transcendence? Does the last line rob the stanza of some of its power? If so, why?


EXERCISE

Suggest what Yeats and Thoreau have in common in their treatment of the life of nature (comparing with this poem the excerpt from *Walden* in this section).


SAILING TO BYZANTIUM

*Two statements by Yeats concerning Byzantium[1] are helpful to an understanding of the poem:*

*"I think that in early Byzantium, maybe never before or since in recorded history, religious, aesthetic and practical life were one, that architect and artificers—though not, it may be, poets, for language had been the instrument of controversy and must have grown abstract—spoke to the multitude and the few alike. The painter, the mosaic worker, the worker in gold and silver, the illuminator of sacred books, were almost impersonal, almost perhaps without the consciousness of individual design, absorbed in their subject matter and that the vision of a whole people. They could copy out of old Gospel books these pictures that seemed as sacred as the text, and yet weave all into a vast design, the work of many that seemed the work of one. . . .*

[1] *Byzantium:* capital of the Eastern Roman Empire, "holy city" of the Greek Orthodox Church; modern Istanbul (also formerly Constantinople).

*"I have read somewhere that in the Emperor's palace at Byzantium was a tree made of gold and silver, and artificial birds that sang."*

That is no country for old men. The young
In one another's arms, birds in the trees
—Those dying generations—at their song,
The salmon-falls, the mackerel-crowded seas,
Fish, flesh, or fowl, commend all summer long          5
Whatever is begotten, born, and dies.
Caught in that sensual music all neglect
Monuments of unaging intellect.

An aged man is but a paltry thing,
A tattered coat upon a stick, unless                   10
Soul clap its hands and sing, and louder sing
For every tatter in its mortal dress,
Nor is there singing school but studying
Monuments of its own magnificence;
And therefore I have sailed the seas and come          15
To the holy city of Byzantium.

O sages standing in God's holy fire
As in the gold mosaic of a wall,[2]
Come from the holy fire, perne[3] in a gyre,[4]
And be the singing-masters of my soul.                 20
Consume my heart away; sick with desire
And fastened to a dying animal
It knows not what it is; and gather me
Into the artifice of eternity.

Once out of nature I shall never take                  25
My bodily form from any natural thing,
But such a form as Grecian goldsmiths make
Of hammered gold and gold enamelling
To keep a drowsy emperor awake;
Or set upon a golden bough to sing                     30
To lords and ladies of Byzantium
Or what is past, or passing, or to come.    *1928*

## QUESTIONS: *Yeats, "Sailing to Byzantium"*

1.  What is the nature of the "sensual music" which makes "That" (the country
    the speaker wishes to escape from) inimical to "old men"? The music is created

---

[2] *the gold mosaic of a wall:* a reference to the mosaics in the church of Hagia Sophia in
Byzantium.   [3] *perne:* spin round.   [4] *gyre:* a spiraling motion.

by those least likely to feel its full impact. What limitations does this paradox suggest in the capacity of old and young to deal with experience? Why is the indifference of the young to "Monuments of unaging intellect" predictable?

Clues:  • —Those *dying generations*—at their song,
     The salmon-*falls*, the mackerel-crowded seas,

  • Whatever is *begotten, born,* and *dies.*

2. What elements in the second stanza reinforce the need to reject or *escape from* the "sensual music"? Consider the following questions: What *kind* of music will replace it? How does the *clothes* imagery emphasize the significance of the new music? What is the importance of the term *studying* in the light of the preceding stanza? What is the relevance of the term *holy* (as applied to Byzantium) here?

3. How are the suggestions of "singing" and "studying" amplified in stanza 3 to convey the idea of *transcending* a "sensual" state?

Clues:  • O *sages* standing in God's holy *fire*
     As in the gold *mosaic* of a *wall,*

  • And be the *singing*-masters of my soul.

Why does the triumph of the *soul* involve the consumption of the *heart*? How can "studying/Monuments of its own magnificence" lead to the vision of eternity as an "artifice"?

4. Is the poet's art or the poet himself refined in the last stanza? Are both? Explain. In the light of all that precedes, why is the escape from *nature* so significant? What is the importance of the references to gold both here and in the stanza above? What connection do you see between the last line of the poem and the line in the first stanza, "Whatever is begotten, born, and dies"?

5. As in many other works dealing with this theme of escape and transcendence, the image of a *voyage* is central to the poem. What significant stages and levels of voyaging are there in the poem?


*John Millington Synge (1871–1909)*

# In the Shadow of the Glen

SCENE.  *The last cottage at the head of a long glen in County Wicklow.*
*(Cottage kitchen; turf fire on the right; a bed near it against the wall with a body lying on it covered with a sheet. A door is at the other end of the room, with a low table near it, and stools, or wooden chairs. There are a couple of glasses on the table, and a bottle of whisky, as if for a wake, with two cups, a teapot, and a home-made cake. There is another small door near the bed. Nora Burke is moving about the room, settling a few things, and lighting candles on the table, looking now and then at the bed with an uneasy look. Some one knocks softly at the door. She takes up a stocking with money from the table and puts it in her pocket. Then she opens the door.)*

TRAMP.  *(outside).* Good evening to you, lady of the house.

NORA.  Good evening, kindly stranger, it's a wild night, God help you, to be out in the rain falling.

TRAMP. It is, surely, and I walking to Brittas from the Aughrim fair.

NORA. Is it walking on your feet, stranger?

TRAMP. On my two feet, lady of the house, and when I saw the light below I thought maybe if you'd a sup of new milk and a quiet decent corner where a man could sleep. *(He looks in past her and sees the dead man.)* The Lord have mercy on us all!

NORA. It doesn't matter anyway, stranger, come in out of the rain.

TRAMP. *(coming in slowly and going towards the bed).* Is it departed he is?

NORA. It is, stranger. He's after dying on me, God forgive him, and there I am now with a hundred sheep beyond on the hills, and no turf drawn for the winter.

TRAMP. *(looking closely at the dead man).* It's a queer look is on him for a man that's dead.

NORA. *(half-humorously).* He was always queer, stranger, and I suppose them that's queer and they living men will be queer bodies after.

TRAMP. Isn't it a great wonder you're letting him lie there, and he is not tidied, or laid out itself?

NORA. *(coming to the bed).* I was afeard, stranger, for he put a black curse on me this morning if I'ld touch his body the time he'ld die sudden, or let any one touch it except his sister only, and it's ten miles away she lives in the big glen over the hill.

TRAMP. *(looking at her and nodding slowly).* It's a queer story he wouldn't let his own wife touch him, and he dying quiet in his bed.

NORA. He was an old man, and an odd man, stranger, and it's always up on the hills he was thinking thoughts in the dark mist. *(She pulls back a bit of the sheet.)* Lay your hand on him now, and tell me if it's cold he is surely.

TRAMP. Is it getting the curse on me you'ld be, woman of the house? I wouldn't lay my hand on him for the Lough Nahanagan and it filled with gold.

NORA. *(looking uneasily at the body).* Maybe cold would be no sign of death with the like of him, for he was always cold, every day since I knew him, —and every night, stranger,—*(she covers up his face and comes away from the bed)*; but I'm thinking it's dead he is surely, for he's complaining a while back of a pain in his heart, and this morning, the time he was going off to Brittas for three days or four, he was taken with a sharp turn. Then he went into his bed and he was saying it was destroyed he was, the time the shadow was going up through the glen, and when the sun set on the bog beyond he made a great lep, and let a great cry out of him, and stiffened himself out the like of a dead sheep.

TRAMP. *(crosses himself).* God rest his soul.

NORA. *(pouring him out a glass of whisky).* Maybe that would do you better than the milk of the sweetest cow in County Wicklow.

TRAMP. The Almighty God reward you, and may it be to your good health.

*(He drinks).*

NORA. *(giving him a pipe and tobacco)*. I've no pipes saving his own, stranger, but they're sweet pipes to smoke.

TRAMP. Thank you kindly, lady of the house.

NORA. Sit down now, stranger, and be taking your rest.

TRAMP. *(filling a pipe and looking about the room)*. I've walked a great way through the world, lady of the house, and seen great wonders, but I never seen a wake till this day with fine spirits, and good tobacco, and the best of pipes, and no one to taste them but a woman only.

NORA. Didn't you hear me say it was only after dying on me he was when the sun went down, and how would I go out into the glen and tell the neighbours, and I a lone woman with no house near me?

TRAMP. *(drinking)*. There's no offence, lady of the house?

NORA. No offence in life, stranger. How would the like of you, passing in the dark night, know the lonesome way I was with no house near me at all?

TRAMP. *(sitting down)*. I knew rightly. *(He lights his pipe so that there is a sharp light beneath his haggard face)*. And I was thinking, and I coming in through the door, that it's many a lone woman would be afeard of the like of me in the dark night, in a place wouldn't be as lonesome as this place, where there aren't two living souls would see the little light you have shining from the glass.

NORA. *(slowly)*. I'm thinking many would be afeard, but I never knew what way I'd be afeard of beggar or bishop or any man of you at all. *(She looks towards the window and lowers her voice.)* It's other things than the like of you, stranger, would make a person afeard.

TRAMP. *(looking round with a half-shudder)*. It is surely, God help us all!

NORA. *(looking at him for a moment with curiosity)*. You're saying that, stranger, as if you were easy afeard.

TRAMP. *(speaking mournfully)*. Is it myself, lady of the house, that does be walking round in the long nights, and crossing the hills when the fog is on them, the time a little stick would seem as big as your arm, and a rabbit as big as a bay horse, and a stack of turf as big as a towering church in the city of Dublin? If myself was easily afeard, I'm telling you, it's long ago I'ld have been locked into the Richmond Asylum, or maybe have run up into the back hills with nothing on me but an old shirt, and been eaten with crows the like of Patch Darcy—the Lord have mercy on him—in the year that's gone.

NORA. *(with interest)*. You knew Darcy?

TRAMP. Wasn't I the last one heard his living voice in the whole world?

NORA. There were great stories of what was heard at that time, but would any one believe the things they do be saying in the glen?

TRAMP. It was no lie, lady of the house. . . . I was passing below on a dark night the like of this night, and the sheep were lying under the ditch and every one of them coughing, and choking, like an old man, with the great rain and the fog. Then I heard a thing talking—queer talk, you wouldn't believe at all, and you out of your dreams,—and "Merciful God," says I, "if I begin hearing the like of that voice out of the thick mist, I'm destroyed surely." Then I run, and I run, and I run, till I was below in Rathvanna. I got drunk that night, I got drunk in the morning, and drunk the day after,—I was coming from the races beyond—and the third day they found Darcy. . . . Then I knew it was himself I was after hearing, and I wasn't afeard any more.

NORA. *(speaking sorrowfully and slowly).* God spare Darcy, he'ld always look in here and he passing up or passing down, and it's very lonesome I was after him a long while *(she looks over at the bed and lowers her voice, speaking very clearly),* and then I got happy again—if it's ever happy we are, stranger,—for I got used to being lonesome.

*(A short pause, then she stands up.)*

NORA. Was there any one on the last bit of the road, stranger, and you coming from Aughrim?

TRAMP. There was a young man with a drift of mountain ewes, and he running after them this way and that.

NORA. *(with a half-smile).* Far down, stranger?

TRAMP. A piece only.

*(She fills the kettle and puts it on the fire.)*

NORA. Maybe, if you're not easy afeard, you'ld stay here a short while alone with himself.

TRAMP. I would surely. A man that's dead can do no hurt.

NORA. *(speaking with a sort of constraint).* I'm going a little back to the west, stranger, for himself would go there one night and another and whistle at that place, and then the young man you're after seeing—a kind of a farmer has come up from the sea to live in a cottage beyond—would walk round to see if there was a thing we'ld have to be done, and I'm wanting him this night, the way he can go down into the glen when the sun goes up and tell the people that himself is dead.

TRAMP. *(looking at the body in the sheet).* It's myself will go for him, lady of the house, and let you not be destroying yourself with the great rain.

NORA. You wouldn't find your way, stranger, for there's a small path only, and it running up between two sluigs where an ass and cart would be drowned. *(She puts a shawl over her head).* Let you be making yourself easy, and saying a prayer for his soul, and it's not long I'll be coming again.

TRAMP. *(moving uneasily).* Maybe if you'd a piece of a grey thread and a sharp needle—there's great safety in a needle, lady of the house—I'ld be putting a little stitch here and there in my old coat, the time I'll be praying for his soul, and it going up naked to the saints of God.

NORA. *(takes a needle and thread from the front of her dress and gives it to him).* There's the needle, stranger, and I'm thinking you won't be lonesome, and you used to the back hills, for isn't a dead man itself more company than

473

to be sitting alone, and hearing the winds crying, and you not knowing on what thing your mind would stay?

TRAMP. *(slowly).* It's true, surely, and the Lord have mercy on us all!

*(Nora goes out. The Tramp begins stitching one of the tags in his coat, saying the " De Profundis" under his breath. In an instant the sheet is drawn slowly down, and Dan Burke looks out. The Tramp moves uneasily, then looks up and springs to his feet with a movement of terror.)*

DAN. *(with a hoarse voice).* Don't be afeard, stranger; a man that's dead can do no hurt.

TRAMP. *(trembling).* I meant no harm, your honour; and won't you leave me easy to be saying a little prayer for your soul?

*(A long whistle is heard outside.)*

DAN. *(sitting up in his bed and speaking fiercely).* Ah, the devil mend her. . . . Do you hear that, stranger? Did ever you hear another woman could whistle the like of that with two fingers in her mouth–? *(He looks at the table hurriedly.)* I'm destroyed with the drouth, and let you bring me a drop quickly before herself will come back.

TRAMP. *(doubtfully).* Is it not dead you are?

DAN. How would I be dead, and I as dry as a baked bone, stranger?

TRAMP. *(pouring out the whisky).* What will herself say if she smells the stuff on you, for I'm thinking it's not for nothing you're letting on to be dead?

DAN. It is not, stranger, but she won't be coming near me at all, and it's not long now I'll be letting on, for I've a cramp in my back, and my hip's asleep on me, and there's been the devil's own fly itching my nose. It's near dead I was wanting to sneeze, and you blathering about the rain, and Darcy *(bitterly)*—the devil choke him—and the towering church. *(Crying out impatiently.)* Give me that whisky. Would you have herself come back before I taste a drop at all?

*(Tramp gives him the glass.)*

DAN. *(after drinking).* Go over now to that cupboard, and bring me a black stick you'll see in the west corner by the wall.

TRAMP. *(taking a stick from the cupboard).* Is it that?

DAN. It is, stranger; it's a long time I'm keeping that stick for I've a bad wife in the house.

TRAMP. *(with a queer look).* Is it herself, master of the house, and she a grand woman to talk?

DAN. It's herself, surely, it's a bad wife she is—a bad wife for an old man, and I'm getting old, God help me, though I've an arm to me still. *(He takes the stick in his hand).* Let you wait now a short while, and it's a great sight you'll see in this room in two hours or three. *(He stops to listen.)* Is that somebody above?

TRAMP. *(listening).* There's a voice speaking on the path.

DAN. Put that stick here in the bed and smooth the sheet the way it was lying. *(He covers himself up hastily.)* Be falling to sleep now and don't let on you know anything, or I'll be having your life. I wouldn't have told you at all but it's destroyed with the drouth I was.

TRAMP. *(covering his head)*. Have no fear, master of the house. What is it I know of the like of you that I'ld be saying a word or putting out my hand to stay you at all?

*(He goes back to the fire, sits down on a stool with his back to the bed and goes on stitching his coat.)*

DAN. *(under the sheet, querulously)*. Stranger.

TRAMP. *(quickly)*. Whisht, whisht. Be quiet I'm telling you, they're coming now at the door.

*(Nora comes in with Micheal Dara, a tall, innocent young man behind her.)*

NORA. I wasn't long at all, stranger, for I met himself on the path.

TRAMP. You were middling long, lady of the house.

NORA. There was no sign from himself?

TRAMP. No sign at all, lady of the house.

NORA. *(to Micheal)*. Go over now and pull down the sheet, and look on himself, Micheal Dara, and you'll see it's the truth I'm telling you.

MICHEAL. I will not, Nora, I do be afeard of the dead.

*(He sits down on a stool next the table facing the Tramp. Nora puts the kettle on a lower hook of the pothooks, and piles turf under it.)*

NORA. *(turning to Tramp)*. Will you drink a sup of tea with myself and the young man, stranger, or *(speaking more persuasively)* will you go into the little room and stretch yourself a short while on the bed, I'm thinking it's destroyed you are walking the length of that way in the great rain.

TRAMP. Is it to go away and leave you, and you having a wake, lady of the house? I will not surely. *(He takes a drink from his glass which he has beside him.)* And it's none of your tea I'm asking either.

*(He goes on stitching. Nora makes the tea.)*

MICHEAL. *(after looking at the Tramp rather scornfully for a moment)*. That's a poor coat you have, God help you, and I'm thinking it's a poor tailor you are with it.

TRAMP. If it's a poor tailor I am, I'm thinking it's a poor herd does be running back and forward after a little handful of ewes the way I seen yourself running this day, young fellow, and you coming from the fair.

*(Nora comes back to the table.)*

NORA. *(to Micheal in a low voice)*. Let you not mind him at all, Micheal Dara, he has a drop taken and it's soon he'll be falling asleep.

MICHEAL. It's no lie he's telling, I was destroyed surely. They were that wilful they were running off into one man's bit of oats, and another man's bit of hay, and tumbling into the red bogs till it's more like a pack of old goats than sheep they were. Mountain ewes is a queer breed, Nora Burke, and I'm not used to them at all.

NORA. *(settling the tea things)*. There's no one can drive a mountain ewe but the men do be reared in the Glen Malure, I've heard them say, and above by Rathvanna, and the Glen Imaal, men the like of Patch Darcy, God spare his soul, who would walk through five hundred sheep and miss one of them, and he not reckoning them at all.

MICHEAL. *(uneasily)*. Is it the man went queer in his head the year that's gone?

NORA. It is surely.

TRAMP. *(plaintively)*. That was a great man, young fellow, a great man I'm telling you. There was never a lamb from his own ewes he wouldn't know before it was marked, and he'd run from this to the city of Dublin and never catch for his breath.

NORA. *(turning round quickly)*. He was a great man surely, stranger, and isn't it a grand thing when you hear a living man saying a good word of a dead man, and he mad dying?

TRAMP. It's the truth I'm saying, God spare his soul.

*(He puts the needle under the collar of his coat, and settles himself to sleep in the chimney-corner. Nora sits down at the table; their backs are turned to the bed.)*

MICHEAL. *(looking at her with a queer look)*. I heard tell this day, Nora Burke, that it was on the path below Patch Darcy would be passing up and passing down, and I heard them say he'd never pass it night or morning without speaking with yourself.

NORA. *(in a low voice)*. It was no lie you heard, Micheal Dara.

MICHEAL. I'm thinking it's a power of men you're after knowing if it's in a lonesome place you live itself.

NORA. *(giving him his tea)*. It's in a lonesome place you do have to be talking with some one, and looking for some one, in the evening of the day, and if it's a power of men I'm after knowing they were fine men, for I was a hard child to please, and a hard girl to please *(she looks at him a little sternly)*, and it's a hard woman I am to please this day, Micheal Dara, and it's no lie I'm telling you.

MICHEAL. *(looking over to see that the Tramp is asleep, and then pointing to the dead man)*. Was it a hard woman to please you were when you took himself for your man?

NORA. What way would I live and I an old woman if I didn't marry a man with a bit of a farm, and cows on it, and sheep on the back hills?

MICHEAL. *(considering)*. That's true, Nora, and maybe it's no fool you were, for there's good grazing on it, if it is a lonesome place, and I'm thinking it's a good sum he's left behind.

NORA. *(taking the stocking with money from her pocket, and putting it on the table)*. I do be thinking in the long nights it was a big fool I was that time, Micheal Dara, for what good is a bit of a farm with cows on it, and sheep on the back hills, when you do be sitting looking out from a door the like of that door, and seeing nothing but the mists rolling down the bog, and the mists again, and they rolling up the bog, and hearing nothing but the wind crying out in the bits of broken trees were left from the great storm, and the streams roaring with the rain.

MICHEAL. *(looking at her uneasily).* What is it ails you, this night, Nora Burke? I've heard tell it's the like of that talk you do hear from men, and they after being a great while on the back hills.

NORA. *(putting out the money on the table).* It's a bad night, and a wild night, Micheal Dara, and isn't it a great while I am at the foot of the back hills, sitting up here boiling food for himself, and food for the brood sow, and baking a cake when the night falls? *(She puts up the money, listlessly, in little piles on the table.)* Isn't it a long while I am sitting here in the winter and the summer, and the fine spring, with the young growing behind me and the old passing, saying to myself one time, to look on Mary Brien who wasn't that height *(holding out her hand),* and I a fine girl growing up, and there she is now with two children, and another coming on her in three months or four.

*(She pauses.)*

MICHEAL. *(moving over three of the piles).* That's three pounds we have now, Nora Burke.

NORA. *(continuing in the same voice).* And saying to myself another time, to look on Peggy Cavanagh, who had the lightest hand at milking a cow that wouldn't be easy, or turning a cake, and there she is now walking round on the roads, or sitting in a dirty old house, with no teeth in her mouth, and no sense and no more hair than you'ld see on a bit of a hill and they after burning the furze from it.

MICHEAL. That's five pounds and ten notes, a good sum, surely! . . . It's not that way you'll be talking when you marry a young man, Nora Burke, and they were saying in the fair my lambs were the best lambs, and I got a grand price, for I'm no fool now at making a bargain when my lambs are good.

NORA. What was it you got?

MICHEAL. Twenty pound for the lot, Nora Burke. . . . We'ld do right to wait now till himself will be quiet awhile in the Seven Churches, and then you'll marry me in the chapel of Rathvanna, and I'll bring the sheep up on the bit of a hill you have on the back mountain, and we won't have anything we'ld be afeard to let our minds on when the mist is down.

NORA. *(pouring him out some whisky).* Why would I marry you, Mike Dara? You'll be getting old and I'll be getting old, and in a little while I'm telling you, you'll be sitting up in your bed—the way himself was sitting—with a shake in your face, and your teeth falling, and the white hair sticking out round you like an old bush where sheep do be leaping a gap.

*(Dan Burke sits up noiselessly from under the sheet, with his hand to his face. His white hair is sticking out round his head.)*

NORA. *(goes on slowly without hearing him).* It's a pitiful thing to be getting old, but it's a queer thing surely. It's a queer thing to see an old man sitting up there in his bed with no teeth in him, and a rough word in his mouth, and his chin the way it would take the bark from the edge of an oak board you'ld have building a door. . . . God forgive me, Micheal Dara, we'll all be getting old, but it's a queer thing surely.

MICHEAL. It's too lonesome you are from living a long time with an old man, Nora, and you're talking again like a herd that would be coming down from the thick mist *(he puts his arm around her)*, but it's a fine life you'll have now with a young man, a fine life surely. . . .

*(Dan sneezes violently. Micheal tries to get to the door, but before he can do so, Dan jumps out of the bed in queer white clothes, with his stick in his hand, and goes over and puts his back against it.)*

MICHEAL. Son of God deliver us.

*(Crosses himself, and goes backward across the room.)*

DAN. *(holding up his hand at him)*. Now you'll not marry her the time I'm rotting in the Seven Churches, and you'll see the thing I'll give you will follow you on the back mountains when the wind is high.

MICHEAL. *(to Nora)*. Get me out of it, Nora, for the love of God. He always did what you bid him, and I'm thinking he would do it now.

NORA. *(looking at the Tramp)*. Is it dead he is or living?

DAN. *(turning towards her)*. It's little you care if it's dead or living I am, but there'll be an end now of your fine times, and all the talk you have of young men and old men, and of the mist coming up or going down. *(He opens the door.)* You'll walk out now from that door, Nora Burke, and it's not to-morrow, or the next day, or any day of your life, that you'll put in your foot through it again.

TRAMP. *(standing up)*. It's a hard thing you're saying for an old man, master of the house, and what would the like of her do if you put her out on the roads?

DAN. Let her walk round the like of Peggy Cavanagh below, and be begging money at the cross-road, or selling songs to the men. *(To Nora.)* Walk out now, Nora Burke, and it's soon you'll be getting old with that life, I'm telling you; it's soon your teeth'll be falling and your head'll be the like of a bush where sheep do be leaping a gap.

*(He pauses: she looks round at Micheal.)*

MICHEAL. *(timidly)*. There's a fine Union below in Rathdrum.

DAN. The like of her would never go there. . . . It's lonesome roads she'll be going and hiding herself away till the end will come, and they find her stretched like a dead sheep with the frost on her, or the big spiders, maybe, and they putting their webs on her, in the butt of a ditch.

NORA. *(angrily)*. What way will yourself be that day, Daniel Burke? What way will you be that day and you lying down a long while in your grave? For it's bad you are living, and it's bad you'll be when you're dead. *(She looks at him a moment fiercely, then turns away and speaks plaintively again.)* Yet, if it is itself, Daniel Burke, who can help it at all, and let you be getting up into your bed, and not be taking your death with the wind blowing on you, and the rain with it, and you half in your skin.

DAN. It's proud and happy you'ld be if I was getting my death the day I was shut of yourself. (*Pointing to the door.*) Let you walk out through that door, I'm telling you, and let you not be passing this way if it's hungry you are, or wanting a bed.

TRAMP. (*pointing to Micheal*). Maybe himself would take her.

NORA. What would he do with me now?

TRAMP. Give you the half of a dry bed, and good food in your mouth.

DAN. Is it a fool you think him, stranger, or is it a fool you were born yourself? Let her walk out of that door, and let you go along with her, stranger—if it's raining itself—for it's too much talk you have surely.

TRAMP. (*going over to Nora*). We'll be going now, lady of the house—the rain is falling, but the air is kind and maybe it'll be a grand morning by the grace of God.

NORA. What good is a grand morning when I'm destroyed surely, and I going out to get my death walking the roads?

TRAMP. You'll not be getting your death with myself, lady of the house, and I knowing all the ways a man can put food in his mouth. . . . We'll be going now, I'm telling you, and the time you'll be feeling the cold, and the frost, and the great rain, and the sun again, and the south wind blowing in the glens, you'll not be sitting up on a wet ditch, the way you're after sitting in the place, making yourself old with looking on each day, and it passing you by. You'll be saying one time, "It's a grand evening, by the grace of God," and another time, "It's a wild night, God help us, but it'll pass surely." You'll be saying—

DAN. (*goes over to them crying out impatiently*). Go out of that door, I'm telling you, and do your blathering below in the glen.

(*Nora gathers a few things into her shawl.*)

TRAMP. (*at the door*). Come along with me now, lady of the house, and it's not my blather you'll be hearing only, but you'll be hearing the herons crying out over the black lakes, and you'll be hearing the grouse and the owls with them, and the larks and the big thrushes when the days are warm, and it's not from the like of them you'll be hearing a talk of getting old like Peggy Cavanagh, and losing the hair off you, and the light of your eyes, but it's fine songs you'll be hearing when the sun goes up, and there'll be no old fellow wheezing, the like of a sick sheep, close to your ear.

NORA. I'm thinking it's myself will be wheezing that time with lying down under the Heavens when the night is cold; but you've a fine bit of talk, stranger, and it's with yourself I'll go. (*She goes towards the door, then turns to Dan*). You think it's a grand thing you're after doing with your letting on to be dead, but what is it at all? What way would a woman live in a lonesome place the like of this place, and she not making a talk with the men passing? And what way will yourself live from this day, with none to care for you? What is it you'll have now but a black life, Daniel Burke, and it's not long I'm telling you, till you'll be lying again under that sheet, and you dead surely.

(*She goes out with the Tramp. Micheal is slinking after them, but Dan stops him.*)

DAN.  Sit down now and take a little taste of the stuff, Micheal Dara. There's a great drouth on me, and the night is young.

MICHEAL.  *(coming back to the table.)* And it's very dry I am, surely, with the fear of death you put on me, and I after driving mountain ewes since the turn of the day.

DAN.  *(throwing away his stick).* I was thinking to strike you, Micheal Dara, but you're a quiet man, God help you, and I don't mind you at all.
*(He pours out two glasses of whisky, and gives one to Micheal.)*

DAN.  Your good health, Micheal Dara.

MICHEAL.  God reward you, Daniel Burke, and may you have a long life, and a quiet life, and good health with it.
*( They drink.)*

CURTAIN

## QUESTIONS: *Synge, In the Shadow of the Glen*

1. Early in the play Nora disclaims fear of the Tramp, telling him that "It's other things than the like of you, stranger, would make a person afeard." What are the things Nora has been afraid of? Which does she seem to fear most? What do her apprehensions reveal about her nature?

    *Clues:*  • . . . for he was always cold, every day since I knew him,—and every night, stranger,—

    • . . . isn't a dead man itself more company than to be sitting alone, and hearing the winds crying, and you not knowing on what thing your mind would stay?

    • . . . and there she is now walking round on the roads, or sitting in a dirty old house, with no teeth in her mouth, and no sense . . .

2. Even though Nora gives practical reasons for marrying Dan, asking how she would subsist in old age if she were not married to "a man with a bit of a farm, and cows on it, and sheep on the back hills," what evidence is there that material possessions and the pedestrian tasks of daily life are not congenial to her nature? How do her tastes and interest run counter to those of a conventional housewife?

    *Clues:*  • There were great stories of what was heard at that time . . .

    • There's no one can drive a mountain ewe but the men do be reared in the Glen Malure, I've heard them say, and above by Rathvanna, and the Glen Imaal, men the like of Patch Darcy . . . who would walk through five hundred sheep and miss one of them, and he not reckoning them at all."

3. Although Nora is more realistic than the Tramp and sees herself on the road "wheezing that time with lying down under the Heavens when the night is cold," she accepts the Tramp's company because he has "a fine bit of talk." The Tramp earlier referred to Nora as "a grand woman to talk." Dan throws Nora out to "do [her] blathering below in the glen" and praises Micheal Dara for being "a quiet man." What do these reactions to *the power of words* suggest not only about the characters but also about the author's conception of what kind of meaningful experiences allow one an escape from the cares and fears of human existence? What part does Nature play in these experiences?

*Clue:* • TRAMP (*at the door*). Come along with me now, lady of the house, and it's not *my blather* you'll be *hearing* only, but you'll be hearing the *herons crying out* over the black lakes, and you'll be hearing the *grouse* and the *owls* with them, and the *larks* and the big *thrushes* when the days are warm, and it's not from the like of them you'll be hearing a talk of getting old like Peggy Cavanagh, and losing the hair off you, and the light of your eyes, but it's *fine songs* you'll be hearing when the sun goes up, and there'll be *no old* fellow *wheezing*, the like of a sick sheep, close to your ear.

4. Examine the language of the play. In what sense may it be said that the playwright himself throughout has "a fine bit of talk"? Note particularly the use of similes (for example, "and the white hair sticking round you like an old bush where sheep do be leaping a gap").

## EXERCISE

W. B. Yeats has said in his preface to Synge's *The Well of the Saints*:
> Every writer, even every small writer, who has belonged to the great tradition, has had his dream of an impossibly noble life, and the greater he is, the more does it seem to plunge him into some beautiful or bitter reveries. . . . Mr. Synge . . . sets before us ugly, deformed or sinful people, but his people, moved by no practical ambition, are driven by a dream of that impossible life.

Comment on the appropriateness of that statement to *In the Shadow of the Glen*.

## *James Joyce (1882–1941)*
# A Portrait of the Artist as a Young Man

*At the beginning of the previous chapter, Stephen Dedalus is absorbed in coldly tormenting realizations of guilt for sexual incontinence. Prodded by the terrifying vision of damnation that a graphically detailed sermon has evoked, he finally goes to confession, is absolved of his sin, and, at the very conclusion of that chapter, receives communion.*

### CHAPTER IV

Sunday was dedicated to the mystery of the Holy Trinity, Monday to the Holy Ghost, Tuesday to the Guardian Angels, Wednesday to Saint Joseph, Thursday to the Most Blessed Sacrament of the Altar, Friday to the Suffering Jesus, Saturday to the Blessed Virgin Mary.

Every morning he hallowed himself anew in the presence of some holy image or mystery. His day began with an heroic offering of its every moment of thought or action for the intentions of the sovereign pontiff and with an early mass. The raw morning air whetted his resolute piety; and often as he knelt among the few worshippers at the sidealtar, following with his interleaved prayerbook the murmur of the priest, he glanced up for an instant towards the vested figure standing in the gloom between the two candles which were the old and the new testaments and imagined that he was kneeling at mass in the catacombs.

His daily life was laid out in devotional areas. By means of ejaculations[1] and prayers he stored up ungrudgingly for the souls in purgatory centuries of days and quarantines[2] and years; yet the spiritual triumph which he felt in achieving with ease so many fabulous ages of canonical penances[3] did not wholly reward his zeal of prayer since he could never know how much temporal punishment he had remitted by way of suffrage for the agonising souls: and, fearful lest in the midst of the purgatorial fire, which differed from the infernal only in that it was not everlasting, his penance might avail no more than a drop of moisture, he drove his soul daily through an increasing circle of works of supererogation.

Every part of his day, divided by what he regarded now as the duties of his station in life, circled about its own centre of spiritual energy. His life seemed to have drawn near to eternity; every thought, word and deed, every instance of consciousness could be made to revibrate radiantly in heaven: and at times his sense of such immediate repercussion was so lively that he seemed to feel his soul in devotion pressing like fingers the keyboard of a great cash register and to see the amount of his purchase start forth immediately in heaven, not as a number but as a frail column of incense or as a slender flower.

The rosaries too which he said constantly—for he carried his beads loose in his trousers' pockets, that he might tell them as he walked the streets—transformed themselves into coronals of flowers of such vague unearthly texture that they seemed to him as hueless and odourless as they were nameless. He offered up each of his three daily chaplets[4] that his soul might grow strong in each of the three theological virtues, in faith in the Father, Who had created him, in hope in the Son Who had redeemed him, and in love of the Holy Ghost Who had sanctified him, and this thrice triple prayer he offered to the Three persons through Mary in the name of her joyful and sorrowful and glorious mysteries.

On each of the seven days of the week he further prayed that one of the seven gifts of the Holy Ghost[5] might descend upon his soul and drive out of it day by day the seven deadly sins which had defiled it in the past; and he prayed for each gift on its appointed day, confident that it would descend

---

[1] *ejaculations:* short prayers.
[2] *quarantines:* forty-day fasts remitting that length of penance.
[3] *canonical penances:* acts of atonement for forgiven sins.
[4] *chaplets:* one third of a rosary.
[5] *seven gifts of the Holy Ghost:* wisdom, understanding, counsel, fortitude, knowledge, piety, fear of the Lord.

upon him, though it seemed strange to him at times that wisdom and understanding and knowledge were so distinct in their nature that each should be prayed for apart from the others. Yet he believed that at some future stage of his spiritual progress this difficulty would be removed when his sinful soul had been raised up from its weakness and enlightened by the Third Person of the Most Blessed Trinity. He believed this all the more, and with trepidation, because of the divine gloom and silence wherein dwelt the unseen Paraclete,[6] Whose symbols were a dove and a mighty wind, to sin against Whom was a sin beyond forgiveness, the eternal, mysterious secret Being to Whom, as God, the priests offered up mass once a year, robed in the scarlet of the tongues of fire.

The imagery through which the nature and kinship of the Three Persons of the Trinity were darkly shadowed forth in the books of devotion which he read—the Father contemplating from all eternity as in a mirror His Divine Perfections and thereby begetting eternally the Eternal Son and the Holy Spirit proceeding out of Father and Son from all eternity—were easier of acceptance by his mind by reason of their august incomprehensibility than was the simple fact that God had loved his soul from all eternity, for ages before he had been born into the world, for ages before the world itself had existed.

He had heard the names of the passions of love and hate pronounced solemnly on the stage and in the pulpit, had found them set forth solemnly in books, and had wondered why his soul was unable to harbour them for any time or to force his lips to utter their names with conviction. A brief anger had often invested him but he had never been able to make it an abiding passion and had always felt himself passing out of it as if his very body were being divested with ease of some outer skin or peel. He had felt a subtle, dark and murmurous presence penetrate his being and fire him with a brief iniquitous lust: it too had slipped beyond his grasp leaving his mind lucid and indifferent. This, it seemed, was the only love and that the only hate his soul would harbour.

But he could no longer disbelieve in the reality of love since God Himself had loved his individual soul with divine love from all eternity. Gradually, as his soul was enriched with spiritual knowledge, he saw the whole world forming one vast symmetrical expression of God's power and love. Life became a divine gift for every moment and sensation of which, were it even the sight of a single leaf hanging on the twig of a tree, his soul should praise and thank the Giver. The world for all its solid substance and complexity no longer existed for his soul save as a theorem of divine power and love and universality. So entire and unquestionable was this sense of the divine meaning in all nature granted to his soul that he could scarcely understand why it was in any way necessary that he should continue to live. Yet that was part of the divine purpose and he dared not question its

[6] *Paraclete*: Holy Spirit.

use, he above all others who had sinned so deeply and so foully against the divine purpose. Meek and abased by this consciousness of the one eternal omnipresent perfect reality his soul took up again her burden of pieties, masses and prayers and sacraments and mortifications, and only then for the first time since he had brooded on the great mystery of love did he feel within him a warm movement like that of some newly born life or virtue of the soul itself. The attitude of rapture in sacred art, the raised and parted hands, the parted lips and eyes as of one about to swoon, became for him an image of the soul in prayer, humiliated and faint before her Creator.

But he had been forewarned of the dangers of spiritual exaltation and did not allow himself to desist from even the least or lowliest devotion, striving also by constant mortification to undo the sinful past rather than to achieve a saintliness fraught with peril. Each of his senses was brought under a rigorous discipline. In order to mortify the sense of sight he made it his rule to walk in the street with downcast eyes, glancing neither to right nor left and never behind him. His eyes shunned every encounter with the eyes of women. From time to time also he balked them by a sudden effort of the will, as by lifting them suddenly in the middle of an unfinished sentence and closing the book. To mortify his hearing he exerted no control over his voice which was then breaking, neither sang nor whistled and made no attempt to flee from noises which caused him painful nervous irritation such as the sharpening of knives on the knifeboard, the gathering of cinders on the fire-shovel and the twigging of the carpet. To mortify his smell was more difficult as he found in himself no instinctive repugnance to bad odours, whether they were the odours of the outdoor world such as those of dung and tar or the odours of his own person among which he had made many curious comparisons and experiments. He found in the end that the only odour against which his sense of smell revolted was a certain stale fishy stink like that of longstanding urine: and whenever it was possible he subjected himself to this unpleasant odour. To mortify the taste he practised strict habits at table, observed to the letter all the fasts of the church and sought by distraction to divert his mind from the savours of different foods. But it was to the mortification of touch that he brought the most assiduous ingenuity of inventiveness. He never consciously changed his position in bed, sat in the most uncomfortable positions, suffered patiently every itch and pain, kept away from the fire, remained on his knees all through the mass except at the gospels, left parts of his neck and face undried so that air might sting them and, whenever he was not saying his beads, carried his arms stiffly at his sides like a runner and never in his pockets or clasped behind him.

He had no temptations to sin mortally. It surprised him however to find that at the end of his course of intricate piety and selfrestraint he was so easily at the mercy of childish and unworthy imperfections. His prayers and fasts availed him little for the suppression of anger at hearing his mother sneeze or at being disturbed in his devotions. It needed an immense effort of his will to master the impulse which urged him to give outlet to such irritation. Images of the outbursts of trivial anger which he had often noted among his masters, their twitching mouths, closeshut lips and flushed cheeks, recurred to his memory, discouraging him, for all his practice of humility, by the comparison. To merge his life in the common tide of other lives was harder for him than any fasting or prayer, and it was his constant failure to do this to his own satisfaction which caused in his soul at last a sensation of spiritual dryness together with a growth of doubts and scruples. His soul traversed a period of desolation in which the sacraments themselves seemed to have turned into dried up sources. His confession became a channel for the escape of scrupulous and unrepented imperfections. His actual reception of the eucharist did not bring him the same dissolving moments of virginal selfsurrender as did those spiritual communions made by him sometimes at the close of some visit to the Blessed Sacrament. The book which he used for these visits was an old neglected book written by saint Alphonsus Liguori, with fading characters and sere foxpapered leaves. A faded world of fervent love and virginal responses seemed to be evoked for his soul by the reading of its pages in which the imagery of the canticles[7] was interwoven with the communicant's prayers. An inaudible voice seemed to caress the soul, telling her names and glories, bidding her arise as for espousal and come away, bidding her look forth, a spouse, from Amana[8] and from the mountains of the leopards; and the soul seemed to answer with the same inaudible voice, surrendering herself: *Inter ubera mea commorabitur.*[9]

This idea of surrender had a perilous attraction for his mind now that he felt his soul beset once again by the insistent voices of the flesh which began to murmur to him again during his prayers and meditations. It gave him an intense sense of power to know that he could by a single act of consent, in a moment of thought, undo all that he had done. He seemed to feel a flood slowly advancing towards his naked feet and to be waiting for the first timid noiseless wavelet to touch his fevered skin. Then, almost at the instant of that touch, almost at the verge of sinful consent, he found himself standing far away from the flood upon a dry shore, saved by a sudden act of the will or a sudden ejaculation: and, seeing the silver line of the flood far away and beginning again its slow advance towards his feet, a new thrill of power and satisfaction shook his soul to know that he had not yielded nor undone all.

When he had eluded the flood of temptation many times in this way he grew troubled and wondered whether the grace which he had refused to lose was not being filched from him little by little. The clear certitude of his own immunity grew dim and to it succeeded a vague fear that his soul had really fallen unawares. It was with difficulty that he won back his old consciousness of his state of grace by telling himself that he had prayed to God at every

[7] *canticles:* sacred songs taken from the Bible.

[8] *Amana:* mountain in Lebanon mentioned in The Song of Solomon in conjunction with an injunction to "a spouse" and "the mountains of the leopards." (See 4:8).

[9] *Inter ubera mea commorabitur:* "He shall lie betwixt my breasts" (The Song of Solomon, 1:13).

temptation and that the grace which he had prayed for must have been given to him inasmuch as God was obliged to give it. The very frequency and violence of temptations showed him at last the truth of what he had heard about the trials of the saints. Frequent and violent temptations were a proof that the citadel of the soul had not fallen and that the devil raged to make it fall.

Often when he had confessed his doubts and scruples, some momentary inattention at prayer, a movement of trivial anger in his soul or a subtle wilfulness in speech or act, he was bidden by his confessor to name some sin of his past life before absolution was given him. He named it with humility and shame and repented of it once more. It humiliated and shamed him to think that he would never be freed from it wholly, however holily he might live or whatever virtues or perfections he might attain. A restless feeling of guilt would always be present with him: he would confess and repent and be absolved, confess and repent again and be absolved again, fruitlessly. Perhaps that first hasty confession wrung from him by the fear of hell had not been good? Perhaps, concerned only for his imminent doom, he had not had sincere sorrow for his sin? But the surest sign that his confession had been good and that he had had sincere sorrow for his sin was, he knew, the amendment of his life.

—I have amended my life, have I not? he asked himself.

*　　*　　*

The director stood in the embrasure of the window, his back to the light, leaning an elbow on the brown crossblind and, as he spoke and smiled, slowly dangling and looping the cord of the other blind. Stephen stood before him, following for a moment with his eyes the waning of the long summer daylight above the roofs or the slow deft movements of the priestly fingers. The priest's face was in total shadow but the waning daylight from behind him touched the deeply grooved temples and the curves of the skull. Stephen followed also with his ears the accents and intervals of the priest's voice as he spoke gravely and cordially of indifferent themes, the vacation which had just ended, the colleges of the order abroad, the transference of masters. The grave and cordial voice went on easily with its tale, and in the pauses Stephen felt bound to set it on again with respectful questions. He knew that the tale was a prelude and his mind waited for the sequel. Ever since the message of summons had come for him from the director his mind had struggled to find the meaning of the message; and during the long restless time he had sat in the college parlour waiting for the director to come in his eyes had wandered from one sober picture to another around the walls and his mind wandered from one guess to another until the meaning of the summons had almost become clear. Then, just as he was wishing that some unforeseen cause might prevent the director from coming, he had heard the handle of the door turning and the swish of a soutane.

The director had begun to speak of the dominican and franciscan orders and of the friendship between saint Thomas and saint Bonaventure.[10] The capuchin dress,[11] he thought, was rather too . . .

Stephen's face gave back the priest's indulgent smile and, not being anxious to give an opinion, he made a slight dubitative movement with his lips.

—I believe, continued the director, that there is some talk now among the capuchins themselves of doing away with it and following the example of the other franciscans.

—I suppose they would retain it in the cloister, said Stephen.

—O, certainly, said the director. For the cloister it is all right but for the street I really think it would be better to do away with, don't you?

—It must be troublesome, I imagine?

—Of course it is, of course. Just imagine when I was in Belgium I used to see them out cycling in all kinds of weather with this thing up about their knees! It was really ridiculous. *Les jupes,*[12] they call them in Belgium.

The vowel was so modified as to be indistinct.

—What do they call them?

—*Les jupes.*

—O.

Stephen smiled again in answer to the smile which he could not see on the priest's shadowed face, its image or spectre only passing rapidly across his mind as the low discreet accent fell upon his ear. He gazed calmly before him at the waning sky, glad of the cool of the evening and the faint yellow glow which hid the tiny flame kindling upon his cheek.

The names of articles of dress worn by women or of certain soft and delicate stuffs used in their making brought always to his mind a delicate and sinful perfume. As a boy he had imagined the reins by which horses are driven as slender silken bands and it shocked him to feel at Stradbrook the greasy leather of harness. It had shocked him too when he had felt for the first time beneath his tremulous fingers the brittle texture of a woman's stocking for, retaining nothing of all he read save that which seemed to him an echo or a prophecy of his own state, it was only amid softworded phrases or within rosesoft stuffs that he dared to conceive of the soul or body of a woman moving with tender life.

But the phrase on the priest's lips was disingenuous for he knew that a priest should not speak lightly on that theme. The phrase had been spoken lightly with design and he felt that his face was being searched by the eyes in the shadow. Whatever he had heard or read of the craft of jesuits he had put aside frankly as not borne out by his own experience. His masters, even when they had not attracted him, had seemed to him always intelligent and

---

[10] *Saint Thomas [Aquinas] and saint Bonaventure:* thirteenth-century philosophers and theologians, respectively members of the Dominican and Franciscan Orders.

[11] *capuchin dress:* brown robe belted with a cord, and sandals. The Capuchins were a suborder of Franciscans.

[12] *Les jupes:* the skirts.

serious priests, athletic and highspirited prefects. He thought of them as men who washed their bodies briskly with cold water and wore clean cold linen. During all the years he had lived among them in Clongowes and in Belvedere[13] he had received only two pandies and, though these had been dealt him in the wrong, he knew that he had often escaped punishment. During all those years he had never heard from any of his masters a flippant word: it was they who had taught him christian doctrine and urged him to live a good life and, when he had fallen into grievous sin, it was they who had led him back to grace. Their presence had made him diffident of himself when he was a muff in Clongowes and it had made him diffident of himself also while he had held his equivocal position in Belvedere. A constant sense of this had remained with him up to the last year of his school life. He had never once disobeyed or allowed turbulent companions to seduce him from his habit of quiet obedience: and, even when he doubted some statement of a master, he had never presumed to doubt openly. Lately some of their judgements had sounded a little childish in his ears and had made him feel a regret and pity as though he were slowly passing out of an accustomed world and were hearing its language for the last time. One day when some boys had gathered round a priest under the shed near the chapel, he had heard the priest say:

—I believe that Lord Macaulay was a man who probably never committed a mortal sin in his life, that is to say, a deliberate mortal sin.

Some of the boys had then asked the priest if Victor Hugo were not the greatest French writer. The priest had answered that Victor Hugo had never written half so well when he had turned against the church as he had written when he was a catholic.

—But there are many eminent French critics, said the priest, who consider that even Victor Hugo, great as he certainly was, had not so pure a French style as Louis Veuillot.[14]

The tiny flame which the priest's allusion had kindled upon Stephen's cheek had sunk down again and his eyes were still fixed calmly on the colorless sky. But an unresting doubt flew hither and thither before his mind. Masked memories passed quickly before him: he recognised scenes and persons yet he was conscious that he had failed to perceive some vital circumstance in them. He saw himself walking about the grounds watching the sports in Clongowes and eating slim jim out of his cricketcap. Some jesuits were walking round the cycletrack in the company of ladies. The echoes of certain expressions used in Clongowes sounded in remote caves of his mind.

His ears were listening to these distant echoes amid the silence of the parlour when he became aware that the priest was addressing him in a different voice.

---

[13] *Clongowes and . . . Belvedere:* the two schools Stephen had attended earlier.
[14] *Louis Veuillot:* nineteenth-century pro-Catholic French journalist.

—I sent for you today, Stephen, because I wished to speak to you on a very important subject.

—Yes, sir.

—Have you ever felt that you had a vocation?

Stephen parted his lips to answer yes and then withheld the word suddenly. The priest waited for the answer and added:

—I mean have you ever felt within yourself, in your soul, a desire to join the order. Think.

—I have sometimes thought of it, said Stephen.

The priest let the blindcord fall to one side and, uniting his hands, leaned his chin gravely upon them, communing with himself.

—In a college like this, he said at length, there is one boy or perhaps two or three boys whom God calls to the religious life. Such a boy is marked off from his companions by his piety, by the good example he shows to others. He is looked up to by them; he is chosen perhaps as prefect by his fellow sodalists. And you, Stephen, have been such a boy in this college, prefect of Our Blessed Lady's sodality. Perhaps you are the boy in this college whom God designs to call to Himself.

A strong note of pride reinforcing the gravity of the priest's voice made Stephen's heart quicken in response.

—To receive that call, Stephen, said the priest, is the greatest honour that the Almighty God can bestow upon a man. No king or emperor on this earth has the power of the priest of God. No angel or archangel in heaven, no saint, not even the Blessed Virgin herself has the power of a priest of God: the power of the keys, the power to bind and to loose from sin, the power of exorcism, the power to cast out from the creatures of God the evil spirits that have power over them, the power, the authority, to make the great God of Heaven come down upon the altar and take the form of bread and wine. What an awful power, Stephen!

A flame began to flutter again on Stephen's cheek as he heard in this proud address an echo of his own proud musings. How often had he seen himself as a priest wielding calmly and humbly the awful power of which angels and saints stood in reverence! His soul had loved to muse in secret on this desire. He had seen himself, a young and silentmannered priest, entering a confessional swiftly, ascending the altarsteps, incensing, genuflecting, accomplishing the vague acts of the priesthood which pleased him by reason of their semblance of reality and of their distance from it. In that dim life which he had lived through in his musings he had assumed the voices and gestures which he had noted with various priests. He had bent his knee sideways like such a one, he had shaken the thurible only slightly like such a one, his chasuble had swung open like that of such another as he had turned to the altar again after having blessed the people. And above all it had pleased him to fill the second place in those dim scenes of his imagining. He shrank from the dignity of celebrant because it displeased him to imagine that all the vague pomp should end in his own person or that the ritual should assign to him so clear and final an office. He longed for the minor sacred offices, to be vested with the tunicle of subdeacon at high mass, to stand aloof from the altar, forgotten by the people, his shoulders covered with a humeral veil, holding the paten within its folds, or, when the sacrifice had been accomplished, to stand as deacon in a dalmatic of cloth of gold on the step below the celebrant, his hands joined and his face towards the people, and sing the chant *Ite, missa est.*[15] If ever he had seen himself celebrant it was as in the pictures of the mass in his child's massbook, in a church without worshippers, save for the angel of the sacrifice, at a bare altar and served by an acolyte scarcely more boyish than himself. In vague sacrificial or sacramental acts alone his will seemed drawn to go forth to encounter reality: and it was partly the absence of an appointed rite which had always constrained him to inaction whether he had allowed silence to cover his anger or pride or had suffered only an embrace he longed to give.

He listened in reverent silence now to the priest's appeal and through the words he heard even more distinctly a voice bidding him approach, offering him secret knowledge and secret power. He would know then what was the sin of Simon Magus[16] and what the sin against the Holy Ghost for which there was no forgiveness. He would know obscure things, hidden from others, from those who were conceived and born children of wrath. He would know the sins, the sinful longings and sinful thoughts and sinful acts, of others, hearing them murmured into his ears in the confessional under the shame of a darkened chapel by the slips of women and of girls: but rendered immune mysteriously at his ordination by the imposition of hands his soul would pass again uncontaminated to the white peace of the altar. No touch of sin would linger upon the hands with which he would elevate and break the host; no touch of sin would linger on his lips in prayer to make him eat and drink damnation to himself, not discerning the body of the Lord. He would hold his secret knowledge and secret power, being as sinless as the innocent: and he would be a priest for ever according to the order of Melchisedec.[17]

—I will offer up my mass tomorrow morning, said the director, that Almighty God may reveal to you His holy will. And let you, Stephen, make a novena to your holy patron saint, the first martyr, who is very powerful with God, that God may enlighten your mind. But you must be quite sure, Stephen, that you have a vocation because it would be terrible if you found afterwards that you had none. Once a priest always a priest, remember. Your catechism tells you that the sacrament of Holy Orders is one of those which can be received only once because it imprints on the soul an indelible

---

[15] *Ite, missa est:* "Go, it is sent forth"—words dismissing the congregation after Mass is ended.

[16] *Simon Magus:* his sin is that of presumption, desiring to purchase a power granted to the Apostles (Acts 8:9).

[17] *Melchisedec:* first priest referred to in the Old Testament.

spiritual mark which can never be effaced. It is before you must weigh well not after. It is a solemn question, Stephen, because on it may depend the salvation of your eternal soul. But we will pray to God together.

He held open the heavy hall door and gave his hand as if already to a companion in the spiritual life. Stephen passed out on to the wide platform above the steps and was conscious of the caress of mild evening air. Towards Findlater's church a quartet of young men were striding along with linked arms, swaying their heads and stepping to the agile melody of their leader's concertina. The music passed in an instant, as the first bars of sudden music always did, over the fantastic fabrics of his mind, dissolving them painlessly and noiselessly as a sudden wave dissolves the sandbuilt turrets of children. Smiling at the trivial air he raised his eyes to the priest's face and, seeing in it a mirthless reflection of the sunken day, detached his hand slowly which had acquiesced faintly in that companionship.

As he descended the steps the impression which effaced his troubled self-communion was that of a mirthless mask reflecting a sunken day from the threshold of the college. The shadow, then, of the life of the college passed gravely over his consciousness. It was a grave and ordered and passionless life that awaited him, a life without material cares. He wondered how he would pass the first night in the novitiate and with what dismay he would wake the first morning in the dormitory. The troubling odour of the long corridors of Clongowes came back to him and he heard the discreet murmur of the burning gasflames. At once from every part of his being unrest began to irradiate. A feverish quickening of his pulses followed and a din of meaningless words drove his reasoned thoughts hither and thither confusedly. His lungs dilated and sank as if he were inhaling a warm moist unsustaining air and he smelt again the warm moist air which hung in the bath in Clongowes above the sluggish turfcoloured water.

Some instinct, waking at these memories, stronger than education or piety, quickened within him at every near approach to that life, an instinct subtle and hostile, and armed him against acquiescence. The chill and order of the life repelled him. He saw himself rising in the cold of the morning and filing down with the others to early mass and trying vainly to struggle with his prayers against the fainting sickness of his stomach. He saw himself sitting at dinner with the community of a college. What, then, had become of that deeprooted shyness of his which had made him loth to eat or drink under a strange roof? What had come of the pride of his spirit which had always made him conceive himself as a being apart in every order?

The Reverend Stephen Dedalus, S. J.

His name in that new life leaped into characters before his eyes and to it there followed a mental sensation of an undefined face or colour of a face. The colour faded and became strong like a changing glow of pallid brick red. Was it the raw reddish glow he had so often seen on wintry mornings on the shaven gills of the priests? The face was eyeless and sourfavoured and devout, shot with pink tinges of suffocated anger. Was it not a mental spectre of the face of one of the jesuits whom some of the boys called Lantern Jaws and others Foxy Campbell?

He was passing at that moment before the jesuit house in Gardiner Street, and wondered vaguely which window would be his if he ever joined the order. Then he wondered at the vagueness of his wonder, at the remoteness of his soul from what he had hitherto imagined her sanctuary, at the frail hold which so many years of order and obedience had of him when once a definite and irrevocable act of his threatened to end for ever, in time and in eternity, his freedom. The voice of the director urging upon him the proud claims of the church and the mystery and power of the priestly office repeated itself idly in his memory. His soul was not there to hear and greet it and he knew now that the exhortation he had listened to had already fallen into an idle formal tale. He would never swing the thurible before the tabernacle as priest. His destiny was to be elusive of social or religious orders. The wisdom of the priest's appeal did not touch him to the quick. He was destined to learn his own wisdom apart from others or to learn the wisdom of others himself wandering among the snares of the world.

The snares of the world were its ways of sin. He would fall. He had not yet fallen but he would fall silently, in an instant. Not to fall was too hard, too hard: and he felt the silent lapse of his soul, as it would be at some instant to come, falling, falling but not yet fallen, still unfallen but about to fall.

He crossed the bridge over the stream of the Tolka and turned his eyes coldly for an instant towards the faded blue shrine of the Blessed Virgin which stood fowlwise on a pole in the middle of a hamshaped encampment of poor cottages. Then, bending to the left, he followed the lane which led up to his house. The faint sour stink of rotted cabbages came towards him from the kitchengardens on the rising ground above the river. He smiled to think that it was this disorder, the misrule and confusion of his father's house and the stagnation of vegetable life, which was to win the day in his soul. Then a short laugh broke from his lips as he thought of that solitary farmhand in the kitchengardens behind their house whom they had nicknamed the man with the hat. A second laugh, taking rise from the first after a pause, broke from him involuntarily as he thought of how the man with the hat worked, considering in turn the four points of the sky and then regretfully plunging his spade in the earth.

He pushed open the latchless door of the porch and passed through the naked hallway into the kitchen. A group of his brothers and sisters was sitting round the table. Tea was nearly over and only the last of the second watered tea remained in the bottoms of the small glassjars and jampots which did service for teacups. Discarded crusts and lumps of sugared bread, turned brown by the tea which had been poured over them, lay scattered on the table. Little wells of tea lay here and there on the board and a knife with a broken ivory handle was stuck through the pith of a ravaged turnover.

The sad quiet greyblue glow of the dying day came through the window and the open door, covering over and allaying quietly a sudden instinct of remorse in Stephen's heart. All that had been denied them had been freely given to him, the eldest: but the quiet glow of evening showed him in their faces no sign of rancour.

He sat near them at the table and asked where his father and mother were. One answered:

—Goneboro toboro lookboro atboro aboro houseboro.

Still another removal! A boy named Fallon in Belvedere had often asked him with a silly laugh why they moved so often. A frown of scorn darkened quickly his forehead as he heard again the silly laugh of the questioner.

He asked:

—Why are we on the move again, if it's a fair question?

The same sister answered:

—Becauseboro theboro landboro lordboro willboro putboro usboro outboro.

The voice of his youngest brother from the farther side of the fireplace began to sing the air *Oft in the Stilly Night*. One by one the others took up the air until a full choir of voices was singing. They would sing so for hours, melody after melody, glee after glee, till the last pale light died down on the horizon, till the first dark nightclouds came forth and night fell.

He waited for some moments, listening, before he too took up the air with them. He was listening with pain of spirit to the overtone of weariness behind their frail fresh innocent voices. Even before they set out on life's journey they seemed weary already of the way.

He heard the choir of voices in the kitchen echoed and multiplied through an endless reverberation of the choirs of endless generations of children: and heard in all the echoes an echo also of the recurring note of weariness and pain. All seemed weary of life even before entering upon it. And he remembered that Newman[18] had heard this note also in the broken lines of Virgil *giving utterance, like the voice of Nature herself, to that pain and weariness yet hope of better things which has been the experience of her children in every time.*

\* \* \*

He could wait no longer.

From the door of Byron's publichouse to the gate of Clontarf Chapel, from the gate of Clontarf Chapel to the door of Byron's publichouse and then back again to the chapel and then back again to the publichouse he had paced slowly at first, planting his steps scrupulously in the spaces of the patchwork of the footpath, then timing their fall to the fall of verses. A full hour had passed since his father had gone in with Dan Crosby, the tutor, to find out for him something about the university. For a full hour he had paced up and down, waiting: but he could wait no longer.

He set off abruptly for the Bull, walking rapidly lest his father's shrill whistle might call him back; and in a few moments he had rounded the curve at the police barrack and was safe.

[18] *Newman:* John Henry, writer and cardinal (1801–1890).

Yes, his mother was hostile to the idea, as he had read from her listless silence. Yet her mistrust pricked him more keenly than his father's pride and he thought coldly how he had watched the faith which was fading down in his soul aging and strengthening in her eyes. A dim antagonism gathered force within him and darkened his mind as a cloud against her disloyalty: and when it passed, cloudlike, leaving his mind serene and dutiful towards her again, he was made aware dimly and without regret of a first noiseless sundering of their lives.

The university! So he had passed beyond the challenge of the sentries who had stood as guardians of his boyhood and had sought to keep him among them that he might be subject to them and serve their ends. Pride after satisfaction uplifted him like long slow waves. The end he had been born to serve yet did not see had led him to escape by an unseen path: and now it beckoned to him once more and a new adventure was about to be opened to him. It seemed to him that he heard notes of fitful music leaping upwards a tone and downwards a diminished fourth, upwards a tone and downwards a major third, like triplebranching flames leaping fitfully, flame after flame, out of a midnight wood. It was an elfin prelude, endless and formless; and, as it grew wilder and faster, the flames leaping out of time, he seemed to hear from under the boughs and grasses wild creatures racing, their feet pattering like rain upon the leaves. Their feet passed in pattering tumult over his mind, the feet of hares and rabbits, the feet of harts and hinds and antelopes, until he heard them no more and remembered only a proud cadence from Newman: *Whose feet are as the feet of harts and underneath the everlasting arms.*

The pride of that dim image brought back to his mind the dignity of the office he had refused. All through his boyhood he had mused upon that which he had so often thought to be his destiny and when the moment had come for him to obey the call he had turned aside, obeying a wayward instinct. Now time lay between: the oils of ordination would never anoint his body. He had refused. Why?

He turned seaward from the road at Dollymount and as he passed on to the thin wooden bridge he felt the planks shaking with the tramp of heavily shod feet. A squad of christian brothers was on its way back from the Bull and had begun to pass, two by two, across the bridge. Soon the whole bridge was trembling and resounding. The uncouth faces passed him two by two, stained yellow or red or livid by the sea, and as he strove to look at them with ease and indifference, a faint stain of personal shame and commiseration rose to his own face. Angry with himself he tried to hide his face from their eyes by gazing down sideways into the shallow swirling water under the bridge but he still saw a reflection therein of their topheavy silk hats, and humble tapelike collars and loosely hanging clerical clothes.

—Brother Hickey.

Brother Quaid.

Brother MacArdle.

Brother Keogh.

Their piety would be like their names, like their faces, like their clothes, and it was idle for him to tell himself that their humble and contrite hearts, it might be, paid a far richer tribute of devotion than his had ever been, a gift tenfold more acceptable than his elaborate adoration. It was idle for him to move himself to be generous towards them, to tell himself that if he ever came to their gates, stripped of his pride, beaten and in beggar's weeds, that they would be generous towards him, loving him as themselves. Idle and embittering, finally, to argue, against his own dispassionate certitude, that the commandment of love bade us not to love our neighbour as ourselves with the same amount and intensity of love but to love him as ourselves with the same kind of love.

He drew forth a phrase from his treasure and spoke it softly to himself:

—A day of dappled seaborne clouds.

The phrase and the day and the scene harmonised in a chord. Words. Was it their colours? He allowed them to glow and fade, hue after hue: sunrise gold, the russet and green of apple orchards, azure of waves, the greyfringed fleece of clouds. No, it was not their colours: it was the poise and balance of the period itself. Did he then love the rhythmic rise and fall of words better than their associations of legend and colour? Or was it that, being as weak of sight as he was shy of mind, he drew less pleasure from the reflection of the glowing sensible world through the prism of a language manycoloured and richly storied than from the contemplation of an inner world of individual emotions mirrored perfectly in a lucid supple periodic prose?

He passed from the trembling bridge on to firm land again. At that instant, as it seemed to him, the air was chilled and looking askance towards the water he saw a flying squall darkening and crisping suddenly the tide. A faint click at his heart, a faint throb in his throat told him once more of how his flesh dreaded the cold infrahuman odour of the sea: yet he did not strike across the downs on his left but held straight on along the spine of rocks that pointed against the river's mouth.

A veiled sunlight lit up faintly the grey sheet of water where the river was embayed. In the distance along the course of the slowflowing Liffey slender masts flecked the sky and, more distant still, the dim fabric of the city lay prone in haze. Like a scene on some vague arras, old as man's weariness, the image of the seventh city of christendom was visible to him across the timeless air, no older nor more weary nor less patient of subjection than in the days of the thingmote.[19]

Disheartened, he raised his eyes towards the slowdrifting clouds, dappled and seaborne. They were voyaging across the deserts of the sky, a host of nomads on the march, voyaging high over Ireland, westward bound. The Europe they had come from lay out there beyond the Irish Sea, Europe of

---

[19] *thingmote*: legislative and judicial assembly during Viking rule of Ireland in ninth and tenth centuries.

strange tongues and valleyed and woodbegirt and citadelled and of entrenched and marshalled races. He heard a confused music within him as of
memories and names which he was almost conscious of but could not capture
even for an instant; then the music seemed to recede, to recede, to recede:
and from each receding trail of nebulous music there fell always one long-
drawn calling note, piercing like a star the dusk of silence. Again! Again!
Again! A voice from beyond the world was calling.

—Hello, Stephanos![20]

—Here comes The Dedalus!

—Ao! . . . Eh, give it over, Dwyer, I'm telling you or I'll give you a stuff
in the kisser for yourself. . . . Ao!

—Good man, Towser! Duck him!

—Come along, Dedalus! Bous Stephanoumenos![21] Bous Stephaneforos![22]

—Duck him! Guzzle him now, Towser!

—Help! Help! . . . Ao!

He recognised their speech collectively before he distinguished their faces.
The mere sight of that medley of wet nakedness chilled him to the bone.
Their bodies, corpsewhite or suffused with a pallid golden light or rawly
tanned by the suns, gleamed with the wet of the sea. Their divingstone,
poised on its rude supports and rocking under their plunges, and the rough-
hewn stones of the sloping breakwater over which they scrambled in their
horseplay, gleamed with cold wet lustre. The towels with which they smacked
their bodies were heavy with cold seawater: and drenched with cold brine
was their matted hair.

He stood still in deference to their calls and parried their banter with easy
words. How characterless they looked: Shuley without his deep unbuttoned
collar, Ennis without his scarlet belt with the snaky clasp, and Connolly
without his Norfolk coat with the flapless sidepockets! It was a pain to see
them and a swordlike pain to see the signs of adolescence that made repellent
their pitiable nakedness. Perhaps they had taken refuge in number and
noise from the secret dread in their souls. But he, apart from them and in
silence, remembered in what dread he stood of the mystery of his own
body.

—Stephanos Dedalos! Bous Stephanoumenos! Bous Stephaneforos!

Their banter was not new to him and now it flattered his mild proud
sovereignty. Now, as never before, his strange name seemed to him a
prophecy. So timeless seemed the grey warm air, so fluid and impersonal
his own mood, that all ages were as one to him. A moment before the ghost
of the ancient kingdom of the Danes[23] had looked forth through the vesture

[20] *Stephanos:* crown or garland (in Greek).

[21] *Bous Stephanoumenos:* ox garlanded.

[22] *Bous Stephaneforos:* ox garland bearing (the sacrificial ox was so adorned).

[23] *ancient kingdom of the Danes:* From 852 A.D. to 1066 A.D. (the Norman Conquest), Ireland
was under Danish rule.

of the hazewrapped city. Now, at the name of the fabulous artificer,[24] he seemed to hear the noise of dim waves and to see a winged form flying above the waves and slowly climbing the air. What did it mean? Was it a quaint device opening a page of some medieval book of prophecies and symbols, a hawklike man flying sunward above the sea, a prophecy of the end he had been born to serve and had been following through the mists of childhood and boyhood, a symbol of the artist forging anew in his workshop out of the sluggish matter of the earth a new soaring impalpable imperishable being?

His heart trembled; his breath came faster and a wild spirit passed over his limbs as though he were soaring sunward. His heart trembled in an ecstasy of fear and his soul was in flight. His soul was soaring in an air beyond the world and the body he knew was purified in a breath and delivered of incertitude and made radiant and commingled with the element of the spirit. An ecstasy of flight made radiant his eyes and wild his breath and tremulous and wild and radiant his windswept limbs.

—One! Two! . . . Look out!

—O, cripes, I'm drownded!

—One! Two! Three and away!

—Me next! Me next!

—One! . . . Uk!

—Stephaneforos!

His throat ached with a desire to cry aloud, the cry of a hawk or eagle on high, to cry piercingly of his deliverance to the winds. This was the call of life to his soul not the dull gross voice of the world of duties and despair, not the inhuman voice that had called him to the pale service of the altar. An instant of wild flight had delivered him and the cry of triumph which his lips withheld cleft his brain.

—Stephaneforos!

What were they now but cerements shaken from the body of death—the fear he had walked in night and day, the incertitude that had ringed him round, the shame that had abased him within and without—cerements, the linens of the grave?

His soul had arisen from the grave of boyhood, spurning her graveclothes. Yes! Yes! Yes! He would create proudly out of the freedom and power of his soul, as the great artificer whose name he bore, a living thing, new and soaring and beautiful, impalpable, imperishable.

He started up nervously from the stoneblock for he could no longer quench the flame in his blood. He felt his cheeks aflame and his throat throbbing with song. There was a lust of wandering in his feet that burned

---

[24] *the fabulous artificer:* Daedalus, the mythical craftsman who constructed the labyrinth for Minos, king of Crete; fallen into disfavor, he fashioned wings of feather and wax to escape in flight over the sea with his son Icarus (the latter drowned after flying too close to the sun).

to set out for the ends of the earth. On! On! his heart seemed to cry. Evening would deepen above the sea, night fall upon the plains, dawn glimmer before the wanderer and show him strange fields and hills and faces. Where?

He looked northward towards Howth. The sea had fallen below the line of seawrack on the shallow side of the breakwater and already the tide was running out fast along the foreshore. Already one long oval bank of sand lay warm and dry amid the wavelets. Here and there warm isles of sand gleamed above the shallow tide, and about the isles and around the long bank and amid the shallow currents of the beach were lightclad gayclad figures, wading and delving.

In a few moments he was barefoot, his stockings folded in his pockets and his canvas shoes dangling by their knotted laces over his shoulders: and, picking a pointed salteaten stick out of the jetsam among the rocks, he clambered down the slope of the breakwater.

There was a long rivulet in the strand: and, as he waded slowly up its course, he wondered at the endless drift of seaweed. Emerald and black and russet and olive, it moved beneath the current, swaying and turning. The water of the rivulet was dark with endless drift and mirrored the high-drifting clouds. The clouds were drifting above him silently and silently the seatangle was drifting below him; and the grey warm air was still: and a new wild life was singing in his veins.

Where was his boyhood now? Where was the soul that had hung back from her destiny, to brood alone upon the shame of her wounds and in her house of squalor and subterfuge to queen it in faded cerements and in wreaths that withered at the touch? Or where was he?

He was alone. He was unheeded, happy and near to the wild heart of life. He was alone and young and wilful and wildhearted, alone amid a waste of wild air and brackish waters and the seaharvest of shells and tangle and veiled grey sunlight and gayclad lightclad figures, of children and girls and voices childish and girlish in the air.

A girl stood before him in midstream, alone and still, gazing out to sea. She seemed like one whom magic had changed into the likeness of a strange and beautiful seabird. Her long slender bare legs were delicate as a crane's and pure save where an emerald trail of seaweed had fashioned itself as a sign upon the flesh. Her thighs, fuller and softhued as ivory, were bared almost to the hips where the white fringes of her drawers were like featherings of soft white down. Her slateblue skirts were kilted boldly about her waist and dovetailed behind her. Her bosom was as a bird's soft and slight, slight and soft as the breast of some darkplumaged dove. But her long fair hair was girlish: and girlish, and touched with the wonder of mortal beauty, her face.

She was alone and still, gazing out to sea; and when she felt his presence and the worship of his eyes her eyes turned to him in quiet sufferance of his gaze, without shame or wantonness. Long, long she suffered his gaze and then quietly withdrew her eyes from his and bent them towards the stream, gently stirring the water with her foot hither and thither. The first faint noise of gently moving water broke the silence, low and faint and whispering, faint as the bells of sleep; hither and thither, hither and thither: and a faint flame trembled on her cheek.

—Heavenly God! cried Stephen's soul, in an outburst of profane joy.

He turned away from her suddenly and set off across the strand. His cheeks were aflame; his body was aglow; his limbs were trembling. On and on and on and on he strode, far out over the sands, singing wildly to the sea, crying to greet the advent of the life that had cried to him.

Her image had passed into his soul for ever and no word had broken the holy silence of his ecstasy. Her eyes had called him and his soul had leaped at the call. To live, to err, to fall, to triumph, to recreate life out of life! A wild angel had appeared to him, the angel of mortal youth and beauty, an envoy from the fair courts of life, to throw open before him in an instant of ecstasy the gates of all the ways of error and glory. On and on and on and on!

He halted suddenly and heard his heart in the silence. How far had he walked? What hour was it?

There was no human figure near him nor any sound borne to him over the air. But the tide was near the turn and already the day was on the wane. He turned landward and ran towards the shore and, running up the sloping beach, reckless of the sharp shingle, found a sandy nook amid a ring of tufted sandknolls and lay down there that the peace and silence of the evening might still the riot of his blood.

He felt above him the vast indifferent dome and the calm processes of the heavenly bodies; and the earth beneath him, the earth that had borne him, had taken him to her breast.

He closed his eyes in the languor of sleep. His eyelids trembled as if they felt the cyclic movement of the earth and her watchers, trembled as if they felt the strange light of some new world. His soul was swooning into some new world, fantastic, dim, uncertain as under sea, traversed by cloudy shapes and beings. A world, a glimmer, or a flower? Glimmering and trembling, trembling and unfolding, a breaking light, an opening flower, it spread in endless succession to itself, breaking in full crimson and unfolding and fading to palest rose, leaf by leaf and wave of light by wave of light, flooding all the heavens with its soft flushes, every flush deeper than other.

Evening had fallen when he woke and the sand and arid grasses of his bed glowed no longer. He rose, slowly and, recalling the rapture of his sleep, sighed at its joy.

He climbed to the crest of the sandhill and gazed about him. Evening had fallen. A rim of the young moon cleft the pale waste of sky like the rim of a silver hoop embedded in grey sand; and the tide was flowing in fast to the land with a low whisper of her waves, islanding a few last figures in distant pools.

## Questions: *Joyce, A Portrait of the Artist as a Young Man*

1. At the beginning of Chapter IV the efforts of Stephen Dedalus to maintain a transcendent state of piety are described. What significant role do *quantitative* conceptions (especially numerical ones like adding, multiplying, and dividing) play in conveying the *qualities* of the life Stephen is attempting to follow? Note the divisions of the week, the day, the rosaries; the references to the Trinity, the gifts of the Holy Ghost, the deadly sins. How do quantitative standards affect his own reactions to that life and his capacity to embrace it?

   *Clues:* • . . . yet the spiritual triumph . . . did not wholly reward his zeal of prayer since he could never know how much temporal punishment he had remitted . . .

   • . . . he seemed to feel his soul in devotion pressing like fingers the keyboard of a great cash register . . .

   • . . . it seemed strange to him at times that wisdom and understanding and knowledge were so distinct in their nature that each should be prayed for apart from the others.

2. Stephen's discovery of the paradoxical situation that it is easier for him to fast and pray than "to merge his life in the common tide of other lives" initiates the failure of his attempt to achieve holiness. How do his reactions to *love* and *hate* (mentioned early in the chapter) document this sense of *apartness* with regard to the life of the world? Why is it significant that (concerning these two emotions) he had found "his soul . . . unable to harbour them for any time or to force his lips to utter their names with conviction," but that he can conceive of "the whole world forming one vast symmetrical expression of God's power and love"? Although the inability to blend his existence with that of others would seem to mark him for the priesthood, why does it ultimately play an important part in his decision not to become a priest?

3. Stephen's experiment in transcendence involves the mortification of all his *senses* by "a rigorous discipline." What *ironic* effect does the author achieve by detailing the means Stephen uses and by referring to his exercise in one instance as "the most assiduous ingenuity of inventiveness"? In view of Stephen's ultimate vocation, how can we reconcile his attitude toward human love and hate with his involvement in the life of the senses?

4. When doubts and temptations return to Stephen, both the sense that he can negate his achievements by "a single act of consent" and the awareness of not doing so give him a feeling of *power*. How central to Stephen's failure genuinely to transfigure his life up to this point has this desire for power and control been? Take into account earlier questions.

5. What aspects of Stephen's interview with the priest not only prepare us for Stephen's rejection of the call to the priesthood but for his ultimate choice of a vocation? Note Stephen's reaction to these:

   a. The discussion of the Capuchin mode of dressing (for instance, the reference to his "retaining nothing of all he read save that which seemed to him an echo or a prophecy of his own state. . . .")

   b. The past influence and present judgments of his teachers (for instance, the comment on Victor Hugo).

    c. The vision of "awful power" the priest presents to him (the word "power" appears nine times in the paragraph).

      *Clues:*  • In *vague* sacrificial or sacramental acts alone his will seemed drawn to go forth to encounter reality . . .

                • He would *know* the *sins*, the sinful longings and sinful thoughts and sinful acts, of *others* . . .

6. After leaving the priest Stephen considers the possibility of the "grave and ordered and passionless life . . . without material cares." Why is it appropriate that his reactions to that kind of life should not only be those of *restlessness* but also of *fastidiousness* with regard to privacy? ("What had come of the pride of his spirit which had always made him conceive himself as a being apart in every order?") What might the "instinct . . . stronger than education or piety" be? Why is the face of the imaginary "Reverend Stephen Dedalus, S. J." an "eyeless" one and "shot with pink tinges of suffocated anger"?

7. Stephen may be said at this point to be *escaping* from the priestly world *into the world* whose "snares" he sees "himself wandering among" in search of "wisdom" (his own or that of others). How does the scene with his family illustrate the contrast between the special world he has renounced and the one he has for now committed himself to?

8. Why is Stephen's reaction to his forthcoming entrance into the university (conveyed in paragraph five of the last part) an effective way of illuminating the past and looking ahead to the end of the chapter? Note particularly the references to *music* ("an elfin prelude"), to the *life of nature* ("he seemed to hear from under the boughs and grasses wild creatures racing, their feet pattering like rain upon the leaves"), and to the *written word* ("a proud cadence from Newman").

9. Why does the encounter with the Christian brothers on the bridge mark the ultimate rejection by Stephen of the world of the priesthood? What part is played in that rejection by the element of *pride?* How is that quality redeemed from being merely haughtiness or petty snobbery? Why is the immediate reaction of absorption in the "phrase from his treasure" a plausible one? What final understanding of the gap between him and the brothers is given us in his realization that perhaps his greatest pleasure lies in "the contemplation of an inner world of individual emotions mirrored perfectly in a lucid supple periodic prose"?

10. Why is it appropriate that the theme of a *call* or *calling* should first be introduced as Stephen looks at "the slowdrifting clouds, dappled and seaborne," and thinks of "the Europe they had come from"? What different kinds of *calls* are there in this concluding section of the chapter? What is the meaning they have in common for Stephen with regard to *his* calling?

      *Clues:*  • Again! Again! Again! A voice from beyond the world was calling.

                • —Stephanos Dedalos! Bous Stephanoumenos! Bous Stephaneforos! Their banter was not new to him and now it flattered his mild proud sovereignty.

                • . . . voices childish and girlish in the air.

                • Her eyes had called him and his soul had leaped at the call.

11. Although Stephen speaks of the girl he envisions as "an envoy from the fair courts of life," how are both this call and the calling they suggest made to seem

*otherworldly,* and Stephen's odyssey in this chapter ultimately an escape from one mode of transcendence into another? Note that not only the brothers on the bridge but the friends at the water hole are left behind. Take into account the function of the imagery of *water, flight,* and *birds* in suggesting an experience that transcends worldly commitments. Note also images of resurrection from the grave.

Clues:  • Now, at the *name* of the fabulous artificer, he *seemed to hear* the noise of dim waves and *to see* a winged form flying above the waves and slowly *climbing* the air. What did it mean? Was it a quaint device opening a page of some medieval book of prophecies and symbols, a *hawklike* man flying *sunward* above the sea, a prophecy of the end he had been born to serve . . .?

• She seemed like one whom *magic* had changed into the likeness of a strange and beautiful *seabird.* Her long slender bare legs were delicate as a *crane's* and pure save where an emerald trail of seaweed had fashioned itself as a sign upon the flesh. Her thighs, fuller and softhued as ivory, were bared almost to the hips where the white fringes of her drawers were like featherings of *soft white down.* Her slateblue skirts were kilted boldly about her waist and *dovetailed* behind. Her bosom was as a *bird's* soft and slight, slight and soft as the breast of some *darkplumaged dove.*

12.  Why is it fitting that Stephen's final experience of "tuning in" should not be one of communion with the world but of an exit from one world into another? Why is *the rose* (setting aside the evocation of the vision in Dante's *Paradiso*) an appropriate image for the universe as conceived by an artist? Is its significance here spiritual as well as aesthetic? Note that earlier Stephen has imagined "a slender flower" rising to heaven as his soul pressed the "great cash register" and envisaged his rosaries transformed "into coronals of flowers."

# D. H. Lawrence (1885–1930)
# The Man Who Loved Islands

## I

There was a man who loved islands. He was born on one, but it didn't suit him, as there were too many other people on it, besides himself. He wanted an island all of his own: not necessarily to be alone on it, but to make it a world of his own.

An island, if it is big enough, is no better than a continent. It has to be really quite small, before it *feels* like an island; and this story will show how tiny it has to be, before you can presume to fill it with your own personality.

Now circumstances so worked out that this lover of islands, by the time he was thirty-five, actually acquired an island of his own. He didn't own it as freehold property, but he had a ninety-nine years' lease of it, which, as far as a man and an island are concerned, is as good as everlasting. Since, if you are like Abraham, and want your offspring to be numberless as the sands of the sea-shore, you don't choose an island to start breeding on. Too soon there would be over-population, overcrowding, and slum conditions. Which is a horrid thought, for one who loves an island for its insulation. No, an island is a nest which holds one egg, and one only. This egg is the islander himself.

The island acquired by our potential islander was not in the remote oceans. It was quite near at home, no palm trees nor boom of surf on the reef, nor any of that kind of thing; but a good solid dwelling-house, rather gloomy, above the landing-place, and beyond, a small farmhouse with sheds, and a few outlying fields. Down on the little landing-bay, were three cottages in a row, like coastguards' cottages, all neat and whitewashed.

What could be more cosy and home-like? It was four miles if you walked all round your island, through the gorse and the blackthorn bushes, above the steep rocks of the sea and down in the little glades where the primroses grew. If you walked straight over the two humps of hills, the length of it, through the rocky fields where the cows lay chewing, and through the rather sparse oats, on into the gorse again, and so to the low cliffs' edge, it took you only twenty minutes. And when you came to the edge, you could see another, bigger island lying beyond. But the sea was between you and it. And as you returned over the turf where the short, downland cowslips nodded, you saw to the east still another island, a tiny one this time, like the calf of the cow. This tiny island also belonged to the islander.

Thus it seems that even islands like to keep each other company.

Our islander loved his island very much. In early spring, the little ways and glades were a snow of blackthorn, a vivid white among the Celtic still-ness of close green and grey rock, blackbirds calling out in the whiteness their first long, triumphant calls. After the blackthorn and the nestling primroses came the blue apparition of hyacinths, like elfin lakes and slipping sheets of blue, among the bushes and under the glade of trees. And many birds with nests you could peep into, on the island all your own. Wonderful what a great world it was!

Followed summer, and the cowslips gone, the wild roses faintly fragrant through the haze. There was a field of hay, the foxgloves stood looking down. In a little cove, the sun was on the pale granite where you bathed, and the shadow was in the rocks. Before the mist came stealing, you went home through the ripening oats, the glare of the sea fading from the high air as the fog-horn started to moo on the other island. And then the sea-fog went, it was autumn, the oatsheaves lying prone, the great moon, another island, rose golden out of the sea, and rising higher, the world of the sea was white.

So autumn ended with rain, and winter came, dark skies and dampness and rain, but rarely frost. The island, your island, cowered dark, holding away from you. You could feel, down in the wet, sombre hollows, the resent-ful spirit coiled upon itself, like a wet dog coiled in gloom, or a snake that is neither asleep nor awake. Then in the night, when the wind left off blowing in great gusts and volleys, as at sea, you felt that your island was a universe, infinite and old as the darkness; not an island at all, but an infinite dark world where all the souls from all the other bygone nights lived on, and the infinite distance was near.

Strangely, from your little island in space, you were gone forth into the dark, great realms of time, where all the souls that never die veer and swoop on their vast, strange errands. The little earthly island has dwindled, like a jumping-off place, into nothingness, for you have jumped off, you know not how, into the dark wide mystery of time, where the past is vastly alive, and the future is not separated off.

This is the danger of becoming an islander. When, in the city, you wear your white spats and dodge the traffic with the fear of death down your spine, then you are quite safe from the terrors of infinite time. The moment is your little islet in time, it is the spatial universe that careers round you.

But once isolate yourself on a little island in the sea of space, and the moment begins to heave and expand in great circles, the solid earth is gone, and your slippery, naked dark soul finds herself out in the timeless world, where the chariots of the so-called dead dash down the old streets of centuries, and souls crowd on the footways that we, in the moment, call bygone years. The souls of all the dead are alive again, and pulsating actively around you. You are out in the other infinity.

Something of this happened to our islander. Mysterious 'feelings' came upon him that he wasn't used to; strange awarenesses of old, far-gone men, and other influences; men of Gaul, with big moustaches, who had been on his island, and had vanished from the face of it, but not out of the air of night. They were there still, hurtling their big, violent, unseen bodies through the night. And there were priests, with golden knives and mistletoe; then other priests with a crucifix; then pirates with murder on the sea.

Our islander was uneasy. He didn't believe, in the day-time, in any of this nonsense. But at night it just was so. He had reduced himself to a single point in space, and, a point being that which has neither length nor breadth, he had to step off it into somewhere else. Just as you must step into the sea, if the waters wash your foothold away, so he had, at night, to step off into the other worlds of undying time.

He was uncannily aware, as he lay in the dark, that the blackthorn grove that seemed a bit uncanny even in the realm of space and day, at night was crying with old men of an invisible race, around the altar stone. What was a ruin under the hornbeam trees by day, was a moaning of blood-stained priests with crucifixes, on the ineffable night. What was a cave and a hidden beach between coarse rocks, became in the invisible dark the purple-lipped imprecation of pirates.

To escape any more of this sort of awareness, our islander daily concentrated upon his material island. Why should it not be the Happy Isle at last? Why not the last small isle of the Hesperides, the perfect place, all filled with his own gracious, blossom-like spirit? A minute world of pure perfection, made by man himself.

He began, as we begin all our attempts to regain Paradise, by spending money. The old, semi-feudal dwelling-house he restored, let in more light, put clear lovely carpets on the floor, clear, flower-petal curtains at the sullen windows, and wines in the cellars of rock. He brought over a buxom housekeeper from the world, and a soft-spoken, much-experienced butler. These two were to be islanders.

In the farmhouse he put a bailiff, with two farm-hands. There were Jersey cows, tinkling a slow bell, among the gorse. There was a call to meals at midday, and the peaceful smoking of chimneys at evening, when rest descended.

A jaunty sailing-boat with a motor accessory rode in the shelter in the bay, just below the row of three white cottages. There was also a little yawl, and two row-boats drawn up on the sand. A fishing-net was drying on its supports, a boatload of new white planks stood criss-cross, a woman was going to the well with a bucket.

In the end cottage lived the skipper of the yacht, and his wife and son. He was a man from the other, large island, at home on this sea. Every fine day he went out fishing, with his son, every fair day there was fresh fish in the island.

In the middle cottage lived an old man and wife, a very faithful couple. The old man was a carpenter, and man of many jobs. He was always working, always the sound of his plane or his saw; lost in his work, he was another kind of islander.

In the third cottage was a mason, a widower with a son and two daughters. With the help of his boy, this man dug ditches and built fences, raised buttresses and erected a new outbuilding, and hewed stone from the little quarry. One daughter worked at the big house.

It was a quiet, busy little world. When the islander brought you over as his guest, you met first the dark-bearded, thin, smiling skipper, Arnold, then his boy Charles. At the house, the smooth-lipped butler who had lived all over the world valeted you, and created that curious creamy-smooth, disarming sense of luxury around you which only a perfect and rather untrustworthy servant can create. He disarmed you and had you at his mercy. The buxom housekeeper smiled and treated you with the subtly respectful familiarity that is only dealt out to the true gentry. And the rosy maid threw a glance at you, as if you were very wonderful, coming from the great outer world. Then you met the smiling but watchful bailiff, who came from Cornwall, and the shy farm-hand from Berkshire, with his clean wife and two little children: then the rather sulky farm-hand from Suffolk. The mason, a Kent man, would talk to you by the yard if you let him. Only the old carpenter was gruff and elsewhere absorbed.

Well then, it was a little world to itself, and everybody feeling very safe, and being very nice to you, as if you were really something special. But it was the islander's world, not yours. He was the Master. The special smile, the special attention was to the Master. They all knew how well off they were. So the islander was no longer Mr. So-and-so. To everyone on the island, even to you yourself, he was 'the Master'.

Well, it was ideal. The Master was no tyrant. Ah, no! He was a delicate, sensitive, handsome Master, who wanted everything perfect and everybody happy. Himself, of course, to be the fount of this happiness and perfection.

But in his way, he was a poet. He treated his guests royally, his servants liberally. Yet he was shrewd, and very wise. He never came the boss over his people. Yet he kept his eye on everything, like a shrewd, blue-eyed young Hermes. And it was amazing what a lot of knowledge he had at hand. Amazing what he knew about Jersey cows, and cheese-making, ditching and fencing, flowers and gardening, ships and the sailing of ships. He was a fount of knowledge about everything, and this knowledge he imparted to his people in an odd, half-ironical, half-portentous fashion, as if he really belonged to the quaint, half-real world of the gods.

They listened to him with their hats in their hands. He loved white clothes; or creamy white; and cloaks, and broad hats. So, in fine weather, the bailiff would see the elegant tall figure in creamy-white serge coming like some bird over the fallow, to look at the weeding of the turnips. Then there would be a doffing of hats, and a few minutes of whimsical, shrewd, wise talk, to which the bailiff answered admiringly, and the farm-hands listened in silent wonder, leaning on their hoes. The bailiff was almost tender, to the Master.

Or, on a windy morning, he would stand with his cloak blowing in the sticky sea-wind, on the edge of the ditch that was being dug to drain a little swamp, talking in the teeth of the wind to the man below, who looked up at him with steady and inscrutable eyes.

Or at evening in the rain he would be seen hurrying across the yard, the broad hat turned against the rain. And the farmwife would hurriedly exclaim: "The Master! Get up, John, and clear him a place on the sofa." And then the door opened, and it was a cry of: "Why of all things, if it isn't the Master! Why, have ye turned out then, of a night like this, to come across to the like of we?" And the bailiff took his cloak, and the farm-wife his hat, the two farm-hands drew their chairs to the back, he sat on the sofa and took a child up near him. He was wonderful with children, talked to them simply wonderful, made you think of Our Saviour Himself, said the woman.

He was always greeted with smiles, and the same peculiar deference, as if he were a higher, but also frailer being. They handled him almost tenderly, and almost with adulation. But when he left, or when they spoke of him, they had often a subtle, mocking smile on their faces. There was no need to be afraid of 'the Master'. Just let him have his own way. Only the old carpenter was sometimes sincerely rude to him; so he didn't care for the old man.

It is doubtful whether any of them really liked him, man to man, or even woman to man. But then, it is doubtful if he really liked any of them, as man to man, or man to woman. He wanted them to be happy, and the little world to be perfect. But anyone who wants the world to be perfect must be careful not to have real likes or dislikes. A general goodwill is all you can afford.

The sad fact is, alas, that general goodwill is always felt as something of an insult, by the mere object of it; and so it breeds a quite special brand of malice. Surely general good-will is a form of egoism, that it should have such a result!

Our islander, however, had his own resources. He spent long hours in his library, for he was compiling a book of references to all the flowers mentioned in the Greek and Latin authors. He was not a great classical scholar; the usual public-school equipment. But there are such excellent translations nowadays. And it was so lovely, tracing flower after flower as it blossomed in the ancient world.

So the first year on the island passed by. A great deal had been done. Now the bills flooded in, and the Master, conscientious in all things, began to study them. The study left him pale and breathless. He was not a rich man. He knew he had been making a hole in his capital to get the island into running order. When he came to look, however, there was hardly anything left but hole. Thousands and thousands of pounds had the island swallowed into nothingness.

But surely the bulk of the spending was over! Surely the island would now begin to be self-supporting, even if it made no profit! Surely he was safe. He paid a good many of the bills, and took a little heart. But he had had a shock, and the next year, the coming year, there must be economy, frugality. He told his people so in simple and touching language. And they said: "Why, surely! Surely!"

So, while the wind blew and the rain lashed outside, he would sit in his library with the bailiff over a pipe and pot of beer, discussing farm projects. He lifted his narrow, handsome face, and his blue eyes became dreamy. "*What* a wind!" It blew like cannon-shots. He thought of his island, lashed with foam, and inaccessible, and he exulted. . . . No, he must not lose it. He turned back to the farm projects with the zest of genius, and his hands flicked white emphasis, while the bailiff intoned: "Yes, sir! Yes, sir! You're right, Master!"

But the man was hardly listening. He was looking at the Master's blue lawn shirt and curious pink tie with the fiery red stone, at the enamel sleeve-links, and at the ring with the peculiar scarab. The brown searching eyes of the man of the soil glanced repeatedly over the fine, immaculate figure of the Master, with a sort of slow, calculating wonder. But if he happened to catch the Master's bright, exalted glance, his own eye lit up with a careful cordiality and deference, as he bowed his head slightly.

Thus between them they decided what crops should be sown, what fertilizers should be used in different places, which breed of pigs should be imported, and which line of turkeys. That is to say, the bailiff, by continually cautiously agreeing with the Master, kept out of it, and let the young man have his own way.

The Master knew what he was talking about. He was brilliant at grasping the gist of a book, and knowing how to apply his knowledge. On the whole, his ideas were sound. The bailiff even knew it. But in the man of the soil there was no answering enthusiasm. The brown eyes smiled their cordial deference, but the thin lips never changed. The Master pursed his own flexible mouth in a boyish versatility, as he cleverly sketched in his ideas to the other man, and the bailiff made eyes of admiration, but in his heart he was not attending, he was only watching the Master as he would have watched a queer, caged animal, quite without sympathy, not implicated.

So, it was settled, and the Master rang for Elvery, the butler, to bring a sandwich. He, the Master, was pleased. The butler saw it, and came back with anchovy and ham sandwiches, and a newly opened bottle of vermouth. There was always a newly opened bottle of something.

It was the same with the mason. The Master and he discussed the drainage of a bit of land, and more pipes were ordered, more special bricks, more this, more that.

Fine weather came at last; there was a little lull in the hard work on the island. The Master went for a short cruise in his yacht. It was not really a yacht, just a little bit of a thing. They sailed along the coast of the mainland, and put in at the ports. At every port some friend turned up, the butler made elegant little meals in the cabin. Then the Master was invited to villas and hotels, his people disembarked him as if he were a prince.

And oh, how expensive it turned out! He had to telegraph to the bank for money. And he went home again to economise.

The marsh-marigolds were blazing in the little swamp where the ditches were being dug for drainage. He almost regretted, now, the work in hand. The yellow beauties would not blaze again.

Harvest came, and a bumper crop. There must be a harvest-home supper. The long barn was now completely restored and added to. The carpenter had made long tables. Lanterns hung from the beams of the high-pitched roof. All the people of the island were assembled. The bailiff presided. It was a gay scene.

Towards the end of the supper the Master, in a velvet jacket, appeared with his guests. Then the bailiff rose and proposed "The Master! Long life and health to the Master!" All the people drank the health with great enthusiasm and cheering. The Master replied with a little speech: They were on an island in a little world of their own. It depended on them all to make this world a world of true happiness and content. Each must do his part. He hoped he himself did what he could, for his heart was in his island, and with the people of his island.

The butler responded: As long as the island had such a Master, it could not help but be a little heaven for all the people on it. This was seconded with virile warmth by the bailiff and the mason, the skipper was beside himself. Then there was dancing, the old carpenter was fiddler.

But under all this, things were not well. The very next morning came the farm-boy to say that a cow had fallen over the cliff. The Master went to look. He peered over the not very high declivity, and saw her lying dead on a green ledge under a bit of late-flowering broom. A beautiful, expensive creature, already looking swollen. But what a fool, to fall so unnecessarily!

It was a question of getting several men to haul her up the bank, and then of skinning and burying her. No one would eat the meat. How repulsive it all was!

This was symbolic of the island. As sure as the spirits rose in the human breast, with a movement of joy, an invisible hand struck malevolently out of the silence. There must not be any joy, nor even any quiet peace. A man broke a leg, another was crippled with rheumatic fever. The pigs had some strange disease. A storm drove the yacht on a rock. The mason hated the butler, and refused to let his daughter serve at the house.

Out of the very air came a stony, heavy malevolence. The island itself seemed malicious. It would go on being hurtful and evil for weeks at a time. Then suddenly again one morning it would be fair, lovely as a morning in Paradise, everything beautiful and flowing. And everybody would begin to feel a great relief, and a hope for happiness.

Then as soon as the Master was opened out in spirit like an open flower, some ugly blow would fall. Somebody would send him an anonymous note, accusing some other person on the island. Somebody else would come hinting things against one of his servants.

"Some folks think they've got an easy job out here, with all the pickings they make!" the mason's daughter screamed at the suave butler, in the Master's hearing. He pretended not to hear.

"My man says this island is surely one of the lean kine of Egypt, it would swallow a sight of money, and you'd never get anything back out of it," confided the farm-hand's wife to one of the Master's visitors.

The people were not contented. They were not islanders. "We feel we're not doing right by the children," said those who had children. "We feel we're not doing right by ourselves," said those who had no children. And the various families fairly came to hate one another.

Yet the island was so lovely. When there was a scent of honeysuckle and the moon brightly flickering down on the sea, then even the grumblers felt a strange nostalgia for it. It set you yearning, with a wild yearning; perhaps for the past, to be far back in the mysterious past of the island, when the blood had a different throb. Strange floods of passion came over you, strange violent lusts and imaginations of cruelty. The blood and the passion and the lust which the island had known. Uncanny dreams, half-dreams, half-evocated yearnings.

The Master himself began to be a little afraid of his island. He felt here strange, violent feelings he had never felt before, and lustful desires that he had been quite free from. He knew quite well now that his people didn't love him at all. He knew that their spirits were secretly against him, malicious, jeering, envious, and lurking to down him. He became just as wary and secretive with regard to them.

But it was too much. At the end of the second year, several departures took place. The housekeeper went. The Master always blamed self-important women most. The mason said he wasn't going to be monkeyed about any more, so he took his departure, with his family. The rheumatic farm-hand left.

And then the year's bills came in, the Master made up his accounts. In spite of good crops, the assets were ridiculous, against the spending. The island had again lost, not hundreds but thousands of pounds. It was incredible. But you simply couldn't believe it! Where had it all gone?

The Master spent gloomy nights and days going through accounts in the library. He was thorough. It became evident, now the housekeeper had gone, that she had swindled him. Probably everybody was swindling him. But he hated to think it, so he put the thought away.

He emerged, however, pale and hollow-eyed from his balancing of unbalanceable accounts, looking as if something had kicked him in the stomach. It was pitiable. But the money had gone, and there was an end of it. Another great hole in his capital. How could people be so heartless?

It couldn't go on, that was evident. He would soon be bankrupt. He had to give regretful notice to his butler. He was afraid to find out how much his butler had swindled him. Because the man was such a wonderful butler, after all. And the farm bailiff had to go. The Master had no regrets in that quarter. The losses on the farm had almost embittered him.

The third year was spent in rigid cutting down of expenses. The island was still mysterious and fascinating. But it was also treacherous and cruel, secretly, fathomlessly malevolent. In spite of all its fair show of white blossom and bluebells, and the lovely dignity of foxgloves bending their rose-red bells, it was your implacable enemy.

With reduced staff, reduced wages, reduced splendour, the third year went by. But it was fighting against hope. The farm still lost a good deal. And once more there was a hole in that remnant of capital. Another hole in that which was already a mere remnant round the old holes. The island was mysterious in this also: it seemed to pick the very money out of your pocket, as if it were an octopus with invisible arms stealing from you in every direction.

Yet the Master still loved it. But with a touch of rancour now.

He spent, however, the second half of the fourth year intensely working on the mainland, to be rid of it. And it was amazing how difficult he found it, to dispose of an island. He had thought that everybody was pining for such an island as his; but not at all. Nobody would pay any price for it. And he wanted now to get rid of it, as a man who wants a divorce at any cost.

It was not till the middle of the fifth year that he transferred it, at a considerable loss to himself, to an hotel company who were willing to speculate in it. They were to turn it into a handy honeymoon-and-golf island.

There, take that, island which didn't know when it was well off. Now be a honeymoon-and-golf island!

## II

### THE SECOND ISLAND

The islander had to move. But he was not going to the mainland. Oh, no! He moved to the smaller island, which still belonged to him. And he took with him the faithful old carpenter and wife, the couple he never really cared for; also a widow and daughter, who had kept house for him the last year; also an orphan lad, to help the old man.

The small island was very small; but being a hump of rock in the sea, it was bigger than it looked. There was a little track among the rocks and bushes, winding and scrambling up and down around the islet, so that it took you twenty minutes to do the circuit. It was more than you would have expected.

Still, it was an island. The islander moved himself, with all his books, into the commonplace six-roomed house up to which you had to scramble from the rocky landing-place. There were also two joined-together cottages. The old carpenter lived in one, with his wife and the lad, the widow and daughter lived in the other.

At last all was in order. The Master's books filled two rooms. It was already autumn. Orion lifting out of the sea. And in the dark nights, the Master could see the lights on his late island, where the hotel company were entertaining guests who would advertise the new resort for honeymoon-golfers.

On his lump of rock, however, the Master was still master. He explored the crannies, the odd hand-breadths of grassy level, the steep little cliffs where the last harebells hung and the seeds of summer were brown above the sea, lonely and untouched. He peered down the old well. He examined the stone pen where the pig had been kept. Himself, he had a goat.

Yes, it was an island. Always, always underneath among the rocks the Celtic sea sucked and washed and smote its feathery greyness. How many different noises of the sea! Deep explosions, rumblings, strange long sighs and whistling noises; then voices, real voices of people clamouring as if they were in a market, under the waters: and again, the far-off ringing of a bell, surely an actual bell! Then a tremendous trilling noise, very long and alarming, and an undertone of hoarse gasping.

On this island there were no human ghosts, no ghosts of any ancient race. The sea, and the spume and the weather, had washed them all out, washed them out so there was only the sound of the sea itself, its own ghost, myriad-voiced, communing and plotting and shouting all winter long. And only the smell of the sea, with a few bristly bushes of gorse and coarse tufts of heather, among the grey, pellucid rocks, in the grey, more-pellucid air.

The coldness, the greyness, even the soft, creeping fog of the sea, and the islet of rock humped up in it all, like the last point in space.

Green star Sirius stood over the sea's rim. The island was a shadow. Out at sea a ship showed small lights. Below, in the rocky cove, the row-boat and the motor-boat were safe. A light shone in the carpenter's kitchen. That was all.

Save, of course, that the lamp was lit in the house, where the widow was preparing supper, her daughter helping. The islander went in to his meal. Here he was no longer the Master, he was an islander again and he had peace. The old carpenter, the widow and daughter were all faithfulness itself. The old man worked while ever there was light to see, because he had a passion for work. The widow and her quiet, rather delicate daughter of thirty-three worked for the Master, because they loved looking after him, and they were infinitely grateful for the haven he provided them. But they didn't call him 'the Master'. They gave him his name: 'Mr. Cathcart, sir!' softly and reverently. And he spoke back to them also softly, gently, like people far from the world, afraid to make a noise.

The island was no longer a 'world'. It was a sort of refuge. The islander no longer struggled for anything. He had no need. It was as if he and his few dependents were a small flock of sea-birds alighted on this rock, as they travelled through space, and keeping together without a word. The silent mystery of travelling birds.

He spent most of his day in his study. His book was coming along. The widow's daughter could type out his manuscript for him, she was not uneducated. It was the one strange sound on the island, the typewriter. But soon even its spattering fitted in with the sea's noises, and the wind's.

The months went by. The islander worked away in his study, the people of the island went quietly about their concerns. The goat had a little black kid with yellow eyes. There were mackerel in the sea. The old man went fishing in the row-boat with the lad, when the weather was calm enough; they went off in the motor-boat to the biggest island for the post. And they brought supplies, never a penny wasted. And the days went by, and the nights, without desire, without ennui.

The strange stillness from all desire was a kind of wonder to the islander. He didn't want anything. His soul at last was still in him, his spirit was like a dim-lit cave under water, where strange sea-foliage expands upon the watery atmosphere, and scarcely sways, and a mute fish shadowily slips in and slips away again. All still and soft and uncrying, yet alive as rooted seaweed is alive.

The islander said to himself: "Is this happiness?" He said to himself: "I am turned into a dream. I feel nothing, or I don't know what I feel. Yet it seems to me I am happy."

Only he had to have something upon which his mental activity could work. So he spent long, silent hours in his study, working not very fast, nor very importantly, letting the writing spin from him as if it were drowsy gossamer. He no longer fretted whether it were good or not, what he produced. He slowly, softly spun it like gossamer, and if it were to melt away as gossamer in autumn melts, he would not mind. It was only the soft evanescence of gossamy things which now seemed to him permanent. The very mist of eternity was in them. Whereas stone buildings, cathedrals for example, seemed to him to howl with temporary resistance, knowing they must fall at last; the tension of their long endurance seemed to howl forth from them all the time.

Sometimes he went to the mainland and to the city. Then he went elegantly, dressed in the latest style, to his club. He sat in a stall at the theatre, he shopped in Bond Street. He discussed terms for publishing his book. But over his face was that gossamy look of having dropped out of the race of progress, which made the vulgar city people feel they had won it over him, and made him glad to go back to his island.

He didn't mind if he never published his book. The years were blending into a soft mist, from which nothing obtruded. Spring came. There was never a primrose on his island, but he found a winter-aconite. There were two little sprayed bushes of blackthorn, and some wind-flowers. He began to make a list of the flowers of his islet, and that was absorbing. He noted a wild currant bush and watched for the elder flowers on a stunted little tree, then for the first yellow rags of the broom, and wild roses. Bladder campion, orchids, stitchwort, celandine, he was prouder of them than if they had been people on his island. When he came across the golden saxifrage, so inconspicuous in a damp corner, he crouched over it in a trance, he knew not for how long, looking at it. Yet it was nothing to look at. As the widow's daughter found, when he showed it her.

He had said to her in real triumph:

"I found the golden saxifrage this morning."

The name sounded splendid. She looked at him with fascinated brown eyes, in which was a hollow ache that frightened him a little.

"Did you, sir? Is it a nice flower?"

He pursed his lips and tilted his brows.

"Well—not showy exactly. I'll show it you if you like."

"I should like to see it."

She was so quiet, so wistful. But he sensed in her a persistency which made him uneasy. She said she was so happy: really happy. She followed him quietly, like a shadow, on the rocky track where there was never room for two people to walk side by side. He went first, and could feel her there, immediately behind him, following so submissively, gloating on him from behind.

It was a kind of pity for her which made him become her lover: though he never realised the extent of the power she had gained over him, and how *she* willed it. But the moment he had fallen, a jangling feeling came upon him, that it was all wrong. He felt a nervous dislike of her. He had not wanted it. And it seemed to him, as far as her physical self went, she had not wanted it

*513*

either. It was just her will. He went away, and climbed at the risk of his neck down to a ledge near the sea. There he sat for hours, gazing all jangled at the sea, and saying miserably to himself: "We didn't want it. We didn't really want it."

It was the automatism of sex that had caught him again. Not that he hated sex. He deemed it, as the Chinese do, one of the great life-mysteries. But it had become mechanical, automatic, and he wanted to escape that. Automatic sex shattered him, and filled him with a sort of death. He thought he had come through, to a new stillness of desirelessness. Perhaps beyond that there was a new fresh delicacy of desire, an unentered frail communion of two people meeting on untrodden ground.

Be that as it might, this was not it. This was nothing new or fresh. It was automatic, and driven from the will. Even she, in her true self, hadn't wanted it. It was automatic in her.

When he came home, very late, and saw her face white with fear and apprehension of his feeling against her, he pitied her, and spoke to her delicately, reassuringly. But he kept himself remote from her.

She gave no sign. She served him with the same silence, the same hidden hunger to serve him, to be near where he was. He felt her love following him with strange, awful persistency. She claimed nothing. Yet now, when he met her bright, brown, curiously vacant eyes, he saw in them the mute question. The question came direct at him, with a force and a power of will he never realised.

So he succumbed, and asked her again.

"Not," she said, "if it will make you hate me."

"Why should it?" he replied, nettled. "Of course not."

"You know I would do anything on earth for you."

It was only afterwards, in his exasperation, he remembered what she said, and was more exasperated. Why should she pretend to do this *for him?* Why not herself? But in his exasperation, he drove himself deeper in. In order to achieve some sort of satisfaction, which he never did achieve, he abandoned himself to her. Everybody on the island knew. But he did not care.

Then even what desire he had left him, and he felt only shattered. He felt that only with her will had she wanted him. Now he was shattered and full of self-contempt. His island was smirched and spoiled. He had lost his place in the rare, desireless levels of Time to which he had at last arrived, and he had fallen right back. If only it had been true, delicate desire between them, and a delicate meeting on the third rare place where a man might meet a woman, when they were both true to the frail, sensitive, crocus-flame of desire in them. But it had been no such thing: automatic, an act of will, not of true desire, it left him feeling humiliated.

He went away from the islet, in spite of her mute reproach. And he wandered about the continent, vainly seeking a place where he could stay. He was out of key; he did not fit in the world any more.

There came a letter from Flora—her name was Flora—to say she was afraid she was going to have a child. He sat down as if he were shot, and he remained sitting. But he replied to her: "Why be afraid? If it is so, it is so, and we should rather be pleased than afraid."

At this very moment, it happened there was an auction of islands. He got the maps, and studied them. And at the auction he bought, for very little money, another island. It was just a few acres of rock away in the north, on the outer fringe of the isles. It was low, it rose low out of the great ocean. There was not a building, not even a tree on it. Only northern sea-turf, a pool of rain-water, a bit of sedge, rock, and sea-birds. Nothing else. Under the weeping wet western sky.

He made a trip to visit his new possession. For several days, owing to the seas, he could not approach it. Then, in a light sea-mist, he landed, and saw it hazy, low, stretching apparently a long way. But it was illusion. He walked over the wet, springy turf, and dark-grey sheep tossed away from him, spectral, bleating hoarsely. And he came to the dark pool, with the sedge. Then on in the dampness, to the grey sea sucking angrily among the rocks.

This was indeed an island.

So he went home to Flora. She looked at him with guilty fear, but also with a triumphant brightness in her uncanny eyes. And again he was gentle, he reasured her, even he wanted her again, with that curious desire that was almost like toothache. So he took her to the mainland, and they were married, since she was going to have his child.

They returned to the island. She still brought in his meals, her own along with them. She sat and ate with him. He would have it so. The widowed mother preferred to stay in the kitchen. And Flora slept in the guest-room of his house, mistress of his house.

His desire, whatever it was, died in him with nauseous finality. The child would still be months coming. His island was hateful to him, vulgar, a suburb. He himself had lost all his finer distinction. The weeks passed in a sort of prison, in humiliation. Yet he stuck it out, till the child was born. But he was meditating escape. Flora did not even know.

A nurse appeared, and ate at table with them. The doctor came sometimes and, if the sea were rough, he too had to stay. He was cheery over his whisky.

They might have been a young couple in Golders Green.

The daughter was born at last. The father looked at the baby, and felt depressed, almost more than he could bear. The millstone was tied round his neck. But he tried not to show what he felt. And Flora did not know. She still smiled with a kind of half-witted triumph in her joy, as she got well again. Then she began again to look at him with those aching, suggestive, somehow impudent eyes. She adored him so.

This he could not stand. He told her that he had to go away for a time. She wept, but she thought she had got him. He told her he had settled the best part of his property on her, and wrote down for her what income it would produce. She hardly listened, only looked at him with those heavy, adoring, impudent eyes. He gave her a cheque-book, with the amount of her credit duly entered. This did arouse her interest. And he told her, if she got tired of the island, she could choose her home wherever she wished.

She followed him with those aching, persistent brown eyes, when he left, and he never even saw her weep.

He went straight north, to prepare his third island.

## III

### The Third Island

The third island was soon made habitable. With cement and the big pebbles from the shingle beach, two men built him a hut, and roofed it with corrugated iron. A boat brought over a bed and table, and three chairs, with a good cupboard, and a few books. He laid in a supply of coal and paraffin and food—he wanted so little.

The house stood near the flat shingle bay where he landed, and where he pulled up his light boat. On a sunny day in August the men sailed away and left him. The sea was still and pale blue. On the horizon he saw the small mail-steamer slowly passing northwards, as if she were walking. She served the outer isles twice a week. He could row out to her if need be, in calm weather, and he could signal her from a flagstaff behind his cottage.

Half a dozen sheep still remained on the island, as company; and he had a cat to rub against his legs. While the sweet, sunny days of the northern autumn lasted, he would walk among the rocks, and over the springy turf of his small domain, always coming to the ceaseless, restless sea. He looked at every leaf, that might be different from another, and he watched the endless expansion and contraction of the water-tossed seaweed. He had never a tree, not even a bit of heather to guard. Only the turf, and tiny turf-plants, and the sedge by the pool, the seaweed in the ocean. He was glad. He didn't want trees or bushes. They stood up like people, too assertive. His bare, low-pitched island in the pale blue sea was all he wanted.

He no longer worked at his book. The interest had gone. He liked to sit on the low elevation of his island, and see the sea; nothing but the pale, quiet sea. And to feel his mind turn soft and hazy, like the hazy ocean. Sometimes, like a mirage, he would see the shadow of land rise hovering to northwards. It was a big island beyond. But quite without substance.

He was soon almost startled when he perceived the steamer on the near horizon, and his heart contracted with fear, lest it were going to pause and molest him. Anxiously he watched it go, and not till it was out of sight did he feel truly relieved, himself again. The tension of waiting for human approach was cruel. He did not want to be approached. He did not want to hear voices. He was shocked by the sound of his own voice, if he inadvertently spoke to his cat. He rebuked himself for having broken the great silence. And he was irritated when his cat would look up at him and mew faintly, plaintively.

He frowned at her. And she knew. She was becoming wild, lurking in the rocks, perhaps fishing.

But what he disliked most was when one of the lumps of sheep opened its mouth and baa-ed its hoarse, raucous baa. He watched it, and it looked to him hideous and gross. He came to dislike the sheep very much.

He wanted only to hear the whispering sound of the sea, and the sharp cries of the gulls, cries that came out of another world to him. And best of all, the great silence.

He decided to get rid of the sheep when the boat came. They were accustomed to him now, and stood and stared at him with yellow or colourless eyes, in an insolence that was almost cold ridicule. There was a suggestion of cold indecency about them. He disliked them very much. And when they jumped with staccato jumps off the rocks, and their hoofs made the dry, sharp hit, and the fleece flopped on their square backs, he found them repulsive, degrading.

The fine weather passed, and it rained all day. He lay a great deal on his bed, listening to the water trickling from his roof into the zinc water-butt, looking through the open door at the rain, the dark rocks, the hidden sea. Many gulls were on the island now: many sea-birds of all sorts. It was another world of life. Many of the birds he had never seen before. His old impulse came over him, to send for a book, to know their names. In a flicker of the old passion, to know the name of everything he saw, he even decided to row out to the steamer. The names of these birds! He must know their names, otherwise he had not got them, they were not quite alive to him.

But the desire left him, and he merely watched the birds as they wheeled or walked around him, watched them vaguely, without discrimination. All interest had left him. Only there was one gull, a big, handsome fellow, who would walk back and forth, back and forth in front of the open door of the cabin as if he had some mission there. He was big, and pearlgrey, and his roundnesses were as smooth and lovely as a pearl. Only the folded wings had shut black pinions, and on the closed black feathers were three very distinct white dots, making a pattern. The islander wondered very much, why this bit of trimming on the bird out of the far, cold seas. And as the gull walked back and forth, back and forth in front of the cabin, strutting on pale-dusky gold feet, holding up his pale yellow beak, that was curved at the tip, with curious alien importance, the man wondered over him. He was portentous, he had a meaning.

Then the bird came no more. The island, which had been full of sea-birds, the flash of wings, the sound and cut of wings and sharp eerie cries in the air, began to be deserted again. No longer they sat like living eggs on the rocks and turf, moving their heads, but scarcely rising into flight round his feet. No longer they ran across the turf among the sheep, and lifted themselves upon low wings. The host had gone. But some remained, always.

The days shortened, and the world grew eerie. One day the boat came: as if suddenly, swooping down. The islander found it a violation. It was torture to talk to those two men, in their homely clumsy clothes. The air of familiarity around them was very repugnant to him. Himself, he was neatly dressed, his cabin was neat and tidy. He resented any intrusion, the clumsy homeliness, the heavy-footedness of the two fishermen was really repulsive to him.

The letters they had brought he left lying unopened in a little box. In one of them was his money. But he could not bear to open even that one. Any kind of contact was repulsive to him. Even to read his name on an envelope. He hid the letters away.

And the hustle and horror of getting the sheep caught and tied and put in the ship made him loathe with profound repulsion the whole of the animal creation. What repulsive god invented animals and evil-smelling men? To his nostrils, the fishermen and the sheep alike smelled foul; an uncleanness on the fresh earth.

He was still nerve-racked and tortured when the ship at last lifted sail and was drawing away, over the still sea. And sometimes, days after, he would start with repulsion, thinking he heard the munching of sheep.

The dark days of winter drew on. Sometimes there was no real day at all. He felt ill, as if he were dissolving, as if dissolution had already set in inside him. Everything was twilight, outside, and in his mind and soul. Once, when he went to the door, he saw black heads of men swimming in his bay. For some moments he swooned unconscious. It was the shock, the horror of unexpected human approach. The horror in the twilight! And not till the shock had undermined him and left him disembodied, did he realise that the black heads were the heads of seals swimming in. A sick relief came over him. But he was barely conscious, after the shock. Later on, he sat and wept with gratitude, because they were not men. But he never realised that he wept. He was too dim. Like some strange, ethereal animal, he no longer realised what he was doing.

Only he still derived his single satisfaction from being alone, absolutely alone, with the space soaking into him. The grey sea alone, and the footing of his sea-washed island. No other contact. Nothing human to bring its horror into contact with him. Only space, damp, twilit, sea-washed space! This was the bread of his soul.

For this reason, he was most glad when there was a storm, or when the sea was high. Then nothing could get at him. Nothing could come through to him from the outer world. True, the terrific violence of the wind made him suffer badly. At the same time, it swept the world utterly out of existence for him. He always liked the sea to be heavily rolling and tearing. Then no boat could get at him. It was like eternal ramparts round his island.

He kept no track of time, and no longer thought of opening a book. The print, the printed letters, so like the depravity of speech, looked obscene. He tore the brass label from his paraffin stove. He obliterated any bit of lettering in his cabin.

His cat had disappeared. He was rather glad. He shivered at her thin, obtrusive call. She had lived in the coal-shed. And each morning he had put her a dish of porridge, the same as he ate. He washed her saucer with repulsion. He did not like her writhing about. But he fed her scrupulously. Then one day she did not come for her porridge; she always mewed for it. She did not come again.

He prowled about his island in the rain, in a big oilskin coat, not knowing what he was looking at, nor what he went out to see. Time had ceased to pass. He stood for long spaces, gazing from a white, sharp face, with those keen, far-off blue eyes of his, gazing fiercely and almost cruelly at the dark sea under the dark sky. And if he saw the labouring sail of a fishing-boat away on the cold waters, a strange malevolent anger passed over his features.

Sometimes he was ill. He knew he was ill, because he staggered as he walked, and easily fell down. Then he paused to think what it was. And he went to his stores and took out dried milk and malt, and ate that. Then he forgot again. He ceased to register his own feelings.

The days were beginning to lengthen. All winter the weather had been comparatively mild, but with much rain, much rain. He had forgotten the sun. Suddenly, however, the air was very cold, and he began to shiver. A fear came over him. The sky was level and grey, and never a star appeared at night. It was very cold. More birds began to arrive. The island was freezing. With trembling hands he made a fire in his grate. The cold frightened him.

And now it continued, day after day, a dull, deathly cold. Occasional crumblings of snow were in the air. The days were greyly longer, but no change in the cold. Frozen grey daylight. The birds passed away, flying away. Some he saw lying frozen. It was as if all life were drawing away, contracting away from the north, contracting southwards. "Soon," he said to himself, "it will all be gone, and in all these regions nothing will be alive." He felt a cruel satisfaction in the thought.

Then one night there seemed to be a relief; he slept better, did not tremble half-awake, and writhe so much, half-conscious. He had become so used to the quaking and writhing of his body, he hardly noticed it. But when for once it slept deep, he noticed that.

He woke in the morning to a curious whiteness. His window was muffled. It had snowed. He got up and opened his door, and shuddered. Ugh! How cold! All white, with a dark leaden sea, and black rocks curiously speckled with white. The foam was no longer pure. It seemed dirty. And the sea ate at the whiteness of the corpse-like land. Crumbles of snow were silting down the dead air.

On the ground the snow was a foot deep, white and smooth and soft, windless. He took a shovel to clear round his house and shed. The pallor of morning darkened. There was a strange rumbling of far-off thunder in the frozen air, and through the newly-falling snow, a dim flash of lightning. Snow now fell steadily down in the motionless obscurity.

He went out for a few minutes. But it was difficult. He stumbled and fell in the snow, which burned his face. Weak, faint, he toiled home. And when he recovered, took the trouble to make hot milk.

It snowed all the time. In the afternoon again there was a muffled rumbling of thunder, and flashes of lightning blinking reddish through the falling snow. Uneasy, he went to bed and lay staring fixedly at nothingness.

Morning seemed never to come. An eternity long he lay and waited for one alleviating pallor on the night. And at last it seemed the air was paler. His house was a cell faintly illuminated with white light. He realised the snow was walled outside his window. He got up, in the dead cold. When he opened his door, the motionless snow stopped him in a wall as high as his breast. Looking over the top of it, he felt the dead wind slowly driving, saw the snow-powder lift and travel like a funeral train. The blackish sea churned and champed, seeming to bite at the snow, impotent. The sky was grey, but luminous.

He began to work in a frenzy, to get at his boat. If he was to be shut in, it must be by his own choice, not by the mechanical power of the elements. He must get to the sea. He must be able to get at his boat.

But he was weak, and at times the snow overcame him. It fell on him, and he lay buried and lifeless. Yet every time he struggled alive before it was too late, and fell upon the snow with the energy of fever. Exhausted, he would not give in. He crept indoors and made coffee and bacon. Long since he had cooked so much. Then he went at the snow once more. He must conquer the snow, this new, white brute force which had accumulated against him.

He worked in the awful, dead wind, pushing the snow aside, pressing it with his shovel. It was cold, freezing hard in the wind, even when the sun came out for a while, and showed him his white, lifeless surroundings, the black sea rolling sullen, flecked with dull spume, away to the horizons. Yet the sun had power on his face. It was March.

He reached the boat. He pushed the snow away, then sat down under the lee of the boat, looking at the sea, which swirled nearly to his feet, in the high tide. Curiously natural the pebbles looked, in a world gone all uncanny. The sun shone no more. Snow was falling in hard crumbs, that vanished as if by a miracle as they touched the hard blackness of the sea. Hoarse waves rang in the shingle, rushing up at the snow. The wet rocks were brutally black. And all the time the myriad swooping crumbs of snow, demonish, touched the dark sea and disappeared.

During the night there was a great storm. It seemed to him he could hear the vast mass of snow striking all the world with a ceaseless thud; and over it all, the wind roared in strange hollow volleys, in between which came a jump of blindfold lightning, then the low roll of thunder heavier than the wind. When at last the dawn faintly discoloured the dark, the storm had more or less subsided, but a steady wind drove on. The snow was up to the top of his door.

Sullenly, he worked to dig himself out. And he managed through sheer persistency to get out. He was in the tail of a great drift, many feet high. When he got through, the frozen snow was not more than two feet deep. But his island was gone. Its shape was all changed, great heaping white hills rose where no hills had been, inaccessible, and they fumed like volcanoes, but with snow powder. He was sickened and overcome.

His boat was in another, smaller drift. But he had not the strength to clear it. He looked at it helplessly. The shovel slipped from his hands, and he sank in the snow, to forget. In the snow itself, the sea resounded.

Something brought him to. He crept to his house. He was almost without feeling. Yet he managed to warm himself, just that part of him which leaned in snow-sleep over the coal fire. Then again he made hot milk. After which, carefully, he built up the fire.

The wind dropped. Was it night again? In the silence, it seemed he could hear the panther-like dropping of infinite snow. Thunder rumbled nearer, crackled quick after the bleared reddened lightning. He lay in bed in a kind of stupor. The elements! The elements! His mind repeated the word dumbly. You can't win against the elements.

How long it went on, he never knew. Once, like a wraith, he got out and climbed to the top of a white hill on his unrecognisable island. The sun was hot. "It is summer," he said to himself, "and the time of leaves." He looked stupidly over the whiteness of his foreign island, over the waste of the life-less sea. He pretended to imagine he saw the wink of a sail. Because he knew too well there would never again be a sail on that stark sea.

As he looked, the sky mysteriously darkened and chilled. From far off came the mutter of the unsatisfied thunder, and he knew it was the signal of the snow rolling over the sea. He turned, and felt its breath on him.

## QUESTIONS: *Lawrence, " The Man Who Loved Islands"*

1. Here are five interpretations of "The Man Who Loved Islands." Which of them is most fully convincing? Which is the least plausible? Is it possible to construct a better interpretation by using elements of the ones listed, or by including something from the story that they have omitted?

   a. The problem with the man who loved islands lies in his ridiculous and un-natural desire for isolation. Lawrence feels that this desire always leads to destruction. He notes ironically here that "even islands like to keep each other company." The more the man who loved islands tries to pull away from others, the more they crowd in on him. The first island turns out to be crammed with ghosts; it also turns out to be *alive*. In pulling away from the souls of his fellow human beings, the man never imagined that the island would turn out to have a soul too, a soul that insists "there must not be any joy, nor even any quiet peace." Still pulling away from humanity, the man finds on the second island that human biology comes back at him in the form of sex, an inescapable force as soon as even two human beings are near each other.

And on the third island the man learns too late how the human need for company is so powerful that, when frustrated, it reemerges as a killing (paralyzing) psychosis.

b. What is wrong with the man who loved islands is his *materialism*. He lacks spiritual values to sustain him. He wants to *own* things—islands, fine clothes, the "curious pink tie with the fiery stone"—and when he starts to "improve" his first island, the author notes that "he began, as we begin all our attempts to regain Paradise, by spending money." This materialism is the man's tragic flaw.

c. The fatal problem of the man who loved islands is his fundamental egotism. As Lawrence ironically notes in the second paragraph of his work, "this story will show how tiny it [an island] has to be, before you can presume to fill it with your own personality. The man's immense ego makes him love the idea of being "Master" to the other islanders and makes him blind to the activities of his untrustworthy butler. Lawrence notes: "He was a fount of knowledge about everything, and this knowledge he imparted to his people in an odd, half-ironical, half-portentous fashion, as if he really belonged to the quaint, half-real world of the gods." The man who loved islands also bolsters his tremendous ego by pretending to be a great scholar of Greek and Latin (though he actually has to depend on translations) and by condescending to everyone, including the woman who loves him on the second island and who would bear his child. "The child would still be months in coming. His island was hateful to him, vulgar, a suburb. He himself had lost all his finer distinction." An egotist and a snob, the man who loved islands is doomed to destruction like the hero of a Greek tragedy, brought down by his own pride.

d. The trouble with Lawrence's protagonist is that he is a coward and lacks the courage of his convictions. He wants to be noble, superior, and above the herd; but when the ghosts appear, instead of rejoicing in this opportunity to encounter the eternal, he becomes "uneasy" and tries to escape by concentrating "upon his material island." The islanders, despite the fact that they compare him to Christ, never really accept his pretensions; they see through him and realize that his assumed superiority is not supported by the real thing. The islander pretends that he is trying to escape other people; in fact, he is fleeing from the gnawing awareness of his own hypocrisy and failure to live up to his ideals.

e. "The Man Who Loved Islands" is an allegory of the human spirit, eternally torn between the contrary drives of self-realization and the demands of society. This struggle, which afflicts every human being, can never be resolved; the only escape from it is death.

2. "And out of the ground the Lord God formed every beast of the field, and every fowl of the air; and brought them unto Adam to see what he would call them: and whatsoever Adam called every living creature, that was the name thereof. . . . And the man said, The woman whom thou gavest to be with me, she gave me of the tree, and I did eat" (Genesis 2:19, 3:12). In what respects

is "The Man Who Loved Islands" a reworking of the story of Adam? What purpose is served by the allusions to the events in the Garden of Eden?

Clues : • Why should it not be the *Happy Isle* at last? Why not the last small isle of the *Hesperides*, the *perfect place* . . .?

• He began, as we begin all our attempts to regain *Paradise*, by spending money.

• He was the Master.

• He was wonderful with children, talked to them simply wonderful, made you think of *Our Saviour Himself*, said the woman.

• He felt here strange, violent feelings he had never felt before, and lustful desires that he had been quite free from.

• He began to make *a list* of the flowers of his islet . . .

• It was a kind of pity for her which made him become her lover: though he never realised the extent of the power she had gained over him, and how *she* willed it. But the moment he had *fallen,* a jangling feeling came upon him, that it was all wrong. He felt a nervous dislike of her. He had not wanted it. . . . It was just her will.

• She looked at him with *guilty fear*, but also with a triumphant brightness in her uncanny eyes.

• His old impulse came over him, to send for a book, *to know their names.* In a flicker of the old passion, *to know the name of everything he saw,* he even decided to row out to the steamer. The names of these birds! he must know their names, otherwise *he had not got them, they were not quite alive to him.*

• He kept no track of time, and no longer thought of opening a book. The print, the printed letters so like the *depravity of speech,* looked obscene. He tore the brass label from his paraffin stove. He obliterated any bit of lettering in his cabin.

3. The closing section of the story makes effective use of the *whiteness* with which the islander is surrounded. Do the story's earlier references to whiteness anticipate the later function of this color? How is the color used to convey the state of mind of the protagonist in the latter part of the story?

Clues : • In early spring, the little ways and glades were a *snow* of blackthorn, a vivid *white* among the Celtic stillness of close green and grey rock, blackbirds calling out in the whiteness their first long, triumphant calls.

• And then the sea-fog went, it was autumn, and oat-sheaves lying prone; the great moon, another island, rose golden out of the sea, and rising higher, the world of the sea was *white.*

• He loved *white* clothes; or *creamy white*; and cloaks, and broad hats. So, in fine weather, the bailiff would see the elegant tall figure in creamy-white serge coming *like some bird* over the fallow . . .

• He was big, and pearl-grey . . . and on the closed black feathers were three very distinct *white* dots, making a pattern. The islander wondered very much, why this bit of trimming on the bird out of the far, cold seas. And as the gull walked back and forth . . . the man wondered over him. He was portentous, he had a meaning.

• Ugh! How cold! *All white,* with a dark leaden sea, and black rocks *curiously speckled with white.* The foam was no longer pure. It seemed dirty. And the sea ate at the *whiteness* of the corpse-like land.

## EXERCISES

1. Compare the experiences of the man who loved islands with those of Coleridge's Ancient Mariner, noting the similarities and differences between Coleridge's and Lawrence's use of mythical and Biblical motifs. Explore the possible significance of the resemblance between the gulls in the closing part of Lawrence's story and the Mariner's albatross.

2. Compare Lawrence's use of the Garden motif with that of Andrew Marvell. Discuss what the difference between the two works suggests about the difference between the seventeenth and twentieth century view of man and of his relation to nature and society. Indicate those elements of similarity which assert the timeless nature of Marvell's and Lawrence's preoccupations.

## Cross Questions

### *Shakespeare, Marvell, Vaughan, Wordsworth, Tennyson, Thoreau*

1. In all of these authors' works, the desire to *escape* from the world is partly motivated by the rejection of *materialistic* values. What do the treatments of this subject have in common? How do they differ?

   *Clues:*          Vaughan: The fearful miser on a heap of rust

             Wordsworth: Getting and spending, we lay waste our powers;

             Thoreau: Men think that it is essential that the *Nation* have commerce, and export ice, and talk through a telegraph, and ride thirty miles an hour. . . .

             Tennyson: That hoard, and sleep, and feed, and know not me.

   a. What other specific aspects of the world are rejected along with materialism? Consider Shakespeare's, Vaughan's, and Marvell's references to statesmanship and Thoreau's contempt for governmental institutions. How can we account for the nostalgic reminiscences of war in Tennyson's "Ulysses" and the negative allusions to "Clanging fights, and flaming towns, and sinking ships" in "The Lotos-Eaters"?

   b. What part in some of these works does *Time* play in the impulse to escape?

2. Compare and contrast the roles *Nature* plays in the search for *transcendence* in the works of Marvell, Wordsworth, Tennyson, and Thoreau. Which of these four authors seem most generally akin? Why? In what ways may Vaughan's treatment be said to differ from theirs?

3. What differences and similarities are to be found in the depiction of the actual *state* of transcendence in each work (Shakespeare's excepted)? What part does *wakefulness* (or lack of it) play in achieving that state? Why is the distinction between wakefulness and *restlessness* important in some of these works? In which work is their *conjunction* significant? Explain why.

How are the *sense of the past* in general and *mythology* in particular used in some of these works to make more meaningful the condemnation of the world and the assertion of transcendence?

Clues:         Marvell: Apollo hunted Daphne so,
Only that she might laurel grow;

         Wordsworth: Have sight of Proteus rising from the sea;

         Thoreau: It was Homer's requiem; itself an Iliad and Odyssey in the air. . . .

         Tennyson: And see the great Achilles, whom we knew.

## Donne, Marvell, Coleridge, Yeats, Roethke, Dickey

1. All of these authors are concerned with the actual process of achieving a state of transcendence, with the kind of *transformation* (sometimes involving a loss) that must take place to make way for a new state. What similarities and differences do you see in the conception of what must be *abnegated* or *changed* in the process?

Clues:         Donne: . . . to break, blow, burn, and make me new.

         Marvell: Casting the body's vest aside,

         Yeats: Consume my heart away;

         Roethke: Death of the self in a long, tearless night,

         Dickey: I obey, and am free-falling slowly

2. How is the stage of transformation (or the ultimate process of transcendence) illumined by the imagery of the following?
   a. *Birds*: for example, the lark, the albatross and skylark, the "golden bird." In what two authors is the use of this imagery most similar? most different?
   b. Other *animals*: for example, the "water snakes," the "Beasts of the hill and serpents of the den" in Roethke.
   c. *Water*: for example, the use of rain by Coleridge and Dickey.
   d. *Imprisonment*: for example, "Reason . . . captived" in Donne; "the sun . . . flecked with bars" in Coleridge; "My shadow pinned against a sweating wall" in Roethke.
   e. *Clothes*: for example, "For every tatter in its mortal dress" in Yeats.

## Blake, Wordsworth, Tennyson, Arnold, Yeats, Joyce, Lowell, Kerouac

1. Earlier writers such as Ralegh, Shakespeare, Herbert, and Vaughan base the desire to escape from the world to a large extent on the rejection of corrupt *institutions* and of *universal* human failings—failings in which the authors often participate (for instance, desires for power, wealth, sensual love). How do the works of the later writers listed above suggest that although the desire to escape from the world is an abiding human impulse, the motivations for it have undergone a *qualitative* change—from the universal to the personal, from the moral to the psychological? What reactions have tended to replace the traditional moral and spiritual revulsion?

*Clues:*  Blake: And the pale Virgin *shrouded* in *snow,*

Wordsworth: Have glimpses that would make me *less forlorn;*

Tennyson: ... What *pleasure* can we have
To war with evil?

Arnold: Swept with *confused* alarms of struggle and flight,

Kerouac: ... frosty *fagtown* New York ...

Lowell: an oasis of horror in sands of *ennui!*

2. What changes can you detect in the aspirations to a new state (for instance, "To live, to err, to fall, to triumph, to recreate life out of life")? What contrasts between modern and traditional assumptions about man's nature and destiny do these changes suggest? What essential similarities in the striving toward transcendence remain?

## Herbert, Marvell, Coleridge, Whitman, Joyce, Roethke, Dickey

Examine the significance for these authors of the experiences of (1) climbing, (2) falling, (3) flying, (4) sleeping.

## Tennyson, Yeats, Synge, Joyce

Discuss the manner in which the above writers, in exploring the theme of escape and transcendence, have directly or indirectly dealt with the problem and destiny of the *artist* in society. Suggest the part *music* plays in that treatment.

## Sydney, Donne, Herbert, Coleridge, Arnold

Discuss the treatment by these authors of the theme of *love* and its role in the achievement of escape from the world and transcendence.

## Coleridge, Tennyson, Yeats, Lawrence, Lowell, Kerouac

In the works of all these authors the image of the *voyage* occurs. Indicate the ways in which that image functions as an emblem of (1) *contact with* the vicissitudes of life and *flight from* the human condition; (2) an *inner* process of discovery—spiritual, moral, or psychological; (3) *acceptance* of and *movement* toward ultimate *death.*
*Clues:*  Coleridge: ... this soul hath been
Alone on a wide wide sea:

Tennyson: There gloom the dark broad seas.

Lowell: so we now set our sails for the Dead Sea,

## Tennyson, Whitman, Synge, Yeats, Lowell

Discuss the manner in which these authors have treated transcendence as the triumph over *time.*

## *Yeats, Synge, Joyce, Lawrence, Kerouac*

Thoreau writes: "We have the Saint Vitus' dance, and cannot possibly keep our heads still." Show how the element of *restlessness* dealt with by earlier writers (as we have noted above) is central to the works of these modern writers (and to Baudelaire in Lowell's adaptation). What elements might account for the pervasiveness of this phenomenon in the nineteenth and twentieth centuries?

## *Ralegh, Shakespeare, Vaughan, Lowell*

Discuss the significant differences and similarities between the vision of the world projected by Ralegh, Shakespeare, and Vaughan and that in Lowell's adaptation of Baudelaire. Focus on the following excerpt from "The Voyage":

### VI
#### Oh trivial, childish minds!

You've missed the more important things that we
were forced to learn against our will. We've been
from top to bottom of the ladder, and see
only the pageant of immortal sin:

there women, servile, peacock-tailed, and coarse,
marry for money, and love without disgust
horny, pot-bellied tyrants stuffed on lust,
slaves' slaves—the sewer in which their gutter pours!

old maids who weep, playboys who live each hour,
state banquets loaded with hot sauces, blood and trash,
ministers sterilized by dreams of power,
workers who love their brutalizing lash;

and everywhere religions like our own
all storming heaven, propped by saints who reign
like sybarites on beds of nails and frown—
all searching for some orgiastic pain!

Many, self-drunk, are lying in the mud—
mad now, as they have always been, they roll
in torment screaming to the throne of God:
"My image and my lord, I hate your soul!"

And others, dedicated without hope,
flee the dull herd—each locked in his own world
hides in his ivory-tower of art and dope—
this is the daily news from the whole world!

# Section IV

## Parents and Children; Revolution and Transcendence

### A Gathering of Themes

George Bernard Shaw *(1856–1950)*

# Major Barbara

## ACT I

*It is after dinner in January 1906, in the library in Lady Britomart Undershaft's house in Wilton Crescent. A large and comfortable settee is in the middle of the room, upholstered in dark leather. A person sitting on it (it is vacant at present) would have, on his right, Lady Britomart's writing table, with the lady herself busy at it; a smaller writing table behind him on his left; the door behind him on Lady Britomart's side; and a window with a window seat directly on his left. Near the window is an armchair.*

*Lady Britomart is a woman of fifty or thereabouts, well dressed and yet careless of her dress, well bred and quite reckless of her breeding, well mannered and yet appallingly outspoken and indifferent to the opinion of her interlocutors, amiable and yet peremptory, arbitrary, and high-tempered to the last bearable degree, and withal a very typical managing matron of the upper class, treated as a naughty child until she grew into a scolding mother, and finally settling down with plenty of practical ability and worldly experience, limited in the oddest way with domestic and class limitations, conceiving the universe exactly as if it were a large house in Wilton Crescent, though handling her corner of it very effectively on that assumption, and being quite enlightened and liberal as to the books in the library, the pictures on the walls, the music in the portfolios, and the articles in the papers.*

*Her son, Stephen, comes in. He is a gravely correct young man under 25, taking himself very seriously, but still in some awe of his mother, from childish habit and bachelor shyness rather than from any weakness of character.*

STEPHEN.   Whats the matter?

LADY BRITOMART.   Presently, Stephen.

*[Stephen submissively walks to the settee and sits down. He takes up a Liberal weekly called The Speaker.]*

LADY BRITOMART.   Dont begin to read, Stephen. I shall require all your attention.

STEPHEN.   It was only while I was waiting –

LADY BRITOMART.   Dont make excuses, Stephen. *[He puts down The Speaker]*. Now! *[She finishes her writing; rises; and comes to the settee]*. I have not kept you waiting very long, I think.

STEPHEN.   Not at all, mother.

LADY BRITOMART.   Bring me my cushion. *[He takes the cushion from the chair at the desk and arranges it for her as she sits down on the settee]*. Sit down. *[He sits down and fingers his tie nervously]*. Dont fiddle with your tie, Stephen: there is nothing the matter with it.

STEPHEN.   I beg your pardon. *[He fiddles with his watch chain instead]*.

LADY BRITOMART.   Now are you attending to me, Stephen?

*531*

STEPHEN.  Of course, mother.

LADY BRITOMART.  No: it's not of course. I want something much more than your everyday matter-of-course attention. I am going to speak to you very seriously, Stephen. I wish you would let that chain alone.

STEPHEN *[hastily relinquishing the chain]*.  Have I done anything to annoy you, mother? If so, it was quite unintentional.

LADY BRITOMART *[astonished]*.  Nonsense! *[With some remorse]* My poor boy, did you think I was angry with you?

STEPHEN.  What is it, then, mother? You are making me very uneasy.

LADY BRITOMART *[squaring herself at him rather aggressively]*.  Stephen: may I ask how soon you intend to realize that you are a grown-up man, and that I am only a woman?

STEPHEN *[amazed]*.  Only a –

LADY BRITOMART.  Dont repeat my words, please: it is a most aggravating habit. You must learn to face life seriously, Stephen. I really cannot bear the whole burden of our family affairs any longer. You must advise me: you must assume the responsibility.

STEPHEN.  I!

LADY BRITOMART.  Yes, you, of course. You were 24 last June. Youve been at Harrow and Cambridge. Youve been to India and Japan. You must know a lot of things, now; unless you have wasted your time most scandalously. Well, advise me.

STEPHEN *[much perplexed]*.  You know I have never interfered in the household –

LADY BRITOMART.  No.: I should think not. I dont want you to order the dinner.

STEPHEN.  I mean in our family affairs.

LADY BRITOMART.  Well, you must interfere now; for they are getting quite beyond me.

STEPHEN *[troubled]*.  I have thought sometimes that perhaps I ought; but really, mother, I know so little about them; and what I do know is so painful! it is so impossible to mention some things to you – *[he stops, ashamed]*.

LADY BRITOMART.  I suppose you mean your father.

STEPHEN *[almost inaudibly]*.  Yes.

LADY BRITOMART.  My dear: we cant go on all our lives not mentioning him. Of course you were quite right not to open the subject until I asked you to; but you are old enough now to be taken into my confidence, and to help me to deal with him about the girls.

STEPHEN.  But the girls are all right. They are engaged.

LADY BRITOMART *[complacently]*.  Yes: I have made a very good match for Sarah. Charles Lomax will be a millionaire at 35. But that is ten years ahead; and in the meantime his trustees cannot under the terms of his father's will allow him more than £800 a year.

STEPHEN. But the will says also that if he increases his income by his own exertions, they may double the increase.

LADY BRITOMART. Charles Lomax's exertions are much more likely to decrease his income than to increase it. Sarah will have to find at least another £800 a year for the next ten years; and even then they will be as poor as church mice. And what about Barbara? I thought Barbara was going to make the most brilliant career of all of you. And what does she do? Joins the Salvation Army; discharges her maid; lives on a pound a week; and walks in one evening with a professor of Greek whom she has picked up in the street, and who pretends to be Salvationist, and actually plays the big drum for her in public because he has fallen head over ears in love with her.

STEPHEN. I was certainly rather taken aback when I heard they were engaged. Cusins is a very nice fellow, certainly: nobody would ever guess that he was born in Australia; but –

LADY BRITOMART. Oh, Adolphus Cusins will make a very good husband. After all, nobody can say a word against Greek: it stamps a man at once as an educated gentleman. And my family, thank Heaven, is not a pig-headed Tory one. We are Whigs, and believe in liberty. Let snobbish people say what they please: Barbara shall marry, not the man they like, but the man *I* like.

STEPHEN. Of course I was thinking only of his income. However, he is not likely to be extravagant.

LADY BRITOMART. Dont be too sure of that, Stephen. I know your quiet, simple, refined, poetic people like Adolphus: quite content with the best of everything! They cost more than your extravagant people, who are always as mean as they are second rate. No: Barbara will need at least £2000 a year. You see it means two additional households. Besides, my dear, you must marry soon. I dont approve of the present fashion of philandering bachelors and late marriages; and I am trying to arrange something for you.

STEPHEN. It's very good of you, mother; but perhaps I had better arrange that for myself.

LADY BRITOMART. Nonsense! you are much too young to begin match-making: you would be taken in by some pretty little nobody. Of course I dont mean that you are not to be consulted: you know that as well as I do. *[Stephen closes his lips and is silent]*. Now dont sulk, Stephen.

STEPHEN. I am not sulking, mother. What has all this got to do with – with – with my father?

LADY BRITOMART. My dear Stephen: where is the money to come from? It is easy enough for you and the other children to live on my income as long as we are in the same house; but I cant keep four families in four separate houses. You know how poor my father is: he has barely seven thousand a year now; and really, if he were not the Earl of Stevenage, he would have to give up society. He can do nothing for us. He says, naturally enough, that it is absurd that he should be asked to provide for the children of a man who is rolling in money. You see, Stephen, your father must be fabulously wealthy, because there is always a war going on somewhere.

STEPHEN. You need not remind me of that, mother. I have hardly ever opened a newspaper in my life without seeing our name in it. The Undershaft torpedo! The Undershaft quick firers! The Undershaft ten inch! the Undershaft disappearing rampart gun! the Undershaft submarine! and now the Undershaft aerial battleship! At Harrow they called me the Woolwich Infant. At Cambridge it was the same. A little brute at King's who was always trying to get up revivals, spoilt my Bible – your first birthday present to me – by writing under my name, 'Son and heir to Undershaft and Lazarus, Death and Destruction Dealers: address Christendom and Judea.' But that was not so bad as the way I was kowtowed to everywhere because my father was making millions by selling cannons.

LADY BRITOMART. It is not only the cannons, but the war loans that Lazarus arranges under cover of giving credit for the cannons. You know, Stephen, it's perfectly scandalous. Those two men, Andrew Undershaft and Lazarus, positively have Europe under their thumbs. That is why your father is able to behave as he does. He is above the law. Do you think Bismarck or Gladstone or Disraeli could have openly defied every social and moral obligation all their lives as your father has? They simply wouldnt have dared. I asked Gladstone to take it up. I asked The Times to take it up. I asked the Lord Chamberlain to take it up. But it was just like asking them to declare war on the Sultan. They wouldnt. They said they couldnt touch him. I believe they were afraid.

STEPHEN. What could they do? He does not actually break the law.

LADY BRITOMART. Not break the law! He is always breaking the law. He broke the law when he was born: his parents were not married.

STEPHEN. Mother! Is that true?

LADY BRITOMART. Of course it's true: that was why we separated.

STEPHEN. He married without letting you know this!

LADY BRITOMART [rather taken aback by this inference]. Oh no. To do Andrew justice, that was not the sort of thing he did. Besides, you know the Undershaft motto: Unashamed. Everybody knew.

STEPHEN. But you said that was why you separated.

LADY BRITOMART. Yes, because he was not content with being a foundling himself: he wanted to disinherit you for another foundling. That was what I couldnt stand.

STEPHEN [ashamed]. Do you mean for – for – for –

LADY BRITOMART. Dont stammer, Stephen. Speak distinctly.

STEPHEN. But this is so frightful to me, mother. To have to speak to you about such things!

LADY BRITOMART. It's not pleasant for me, either, especially if you are still so childish that you must make it worse by a display of embarrassment. It is only in the middle classes, Stephen, that people get into a state of dumb helpless horror when they find that there are wicked people in the world. In our class, we have to decide what is to be done with wicked people; and nothing should disturb our self-possession. Now ask your question properly.

STEPHEN. Mother: have you no consideration for me? For Heaven's sake either treat me as a child, as you always do, and tell me nothing at all; or tell me everything and let me take it as best I can.

LADY BRITOMART. Treat you as a child! What do you mean? It is most unkind and ungrateful of you to say such a thing. You know I have never treated any of you as children. I have always made you my companions and friends, and allowed you perfect freedom to do and say whatever you liked, so long as you liked what I could approve of.

STEPHEN [*desperately*]. I daresay we have been the very imperfect children of a very perfect mother; but I do beg you to let me alone for once, and tell me about this horrible business of my father wanting to set me aside for another son.

LADY BRITOMART [*amazed*]. Another son! I never said anything of the kind. I never dreamt of such a thing. This is what comes of interrupting me.

STEPHEN. But you said –

LADY BRITOMART [*cutting him short*]. Now be a good boy, Stephen, and listen to me patiently. The Undershafts are descended from a foundling in the parish of St Andrew Undershaft in the city. That was long ago, in the reign of James the First. Well, this foundling was adopted by an armorer and gun-maker. In the course of time the foundling succeeded to the business; and from some notion of gratitude, or some vow or something, he adopted another foundling, and left the business to him. And that foundling did the same. Ever since that, the cannon business has always been left to an adopted foundling named Andrew Undershaft.

STEPHEN. But did they never marry? Were there no legitimate sons?

LADY BRITOMART. Oh yes: they married just as your father did; and they were rich enough to buy land for their own children and leave them well provided for. But they always adopted and trained some foundling to succeed them in the business; and of course they always quarrelled with their wives furiously over it. Your father was adopted in that way; and he pretends to consider himself bound to keep up the tradition and adopt somebody to leave the business to. Of course I was not going to stand that. There may have been some reason for it when the Undershafts could only marry women in their own class, whose sons were not fit to govern great estates. But there could be no excuse for passing over my son.

STEPHEN [*dubiously*]. I am afraid I should make a poor hand of managing a cannon foundry.

LADY BRITOMART. Nonsense! you could easily get a manager and pay him a salary.

STEPHEN. My father evidently had no great opinion of my capacity.

LADY BRITOMART. Stuff, child! you were only a baby: it had nothing to do with your capacity. Andrew did it on principle, just as he did every perverse and wicked thing on principle. When my father remonstrated, Andrew actually told him to his face that history tells us of only two successful institutions: one the Undershaft firm, and the other the Roman Empire under the Antonines. That was because the Antonine emperors all adopted their successors. Such rubbish! The Stevenages are as good as the Antonines, I hope; and you are a Stevenage. But that was Andrew all over. There you have the man! Always clever and unanswerable when he was defending nonsense and wickedness: always awkward and sullen when he had to behave sensibly and decently!

STEPHEN. Then it was on my account that your home life was broken up, mother. I am sorry.

LADY BRITOMART. Well, dear, there were other differences. I really cannot bear an immoral man. I am not a Pharisee, I hope; and I should not have minded his merely doing wrong things: we are none of us perfect. But your father didnt exactly do wrong things: he said them and thought them: that was what was so dreadful. He really had a sort of religion of wrongness. Just as one doesnt mind men practising immorality so long as they own that they are in the wrong by preaching morality; so I couldnt forgive Andrew for preaching immorality while he practised morality. You would all have grown up without principles, without any knowledge of right and wrong, if he had been in the house. You know, my dear, your father was a very attractive man in some ways. Children did not dislike him; and he took advantage of it to put the wickedest ideas into their heads, and make them quite unmanageable. I did not dislike him myself: very far from it; but nothing can bridge over moral disagreement.

STEPHEN. All this simply bewilders me, mother. People may differ about matters of opinion, or even about religion; but how can they differ about right and wrong? Right is right; and wrong is wrong; and if a man cannot distinguish them properly, he is either a fool or a rascal: thats all.

LADY BRITOMART [touched]. Thats my own boy [she pats his cheek]! Your father never could answer that: he used to laugh and get out of it under cover of some affectionate nonsense. And now that you understand the situation, what do you advise me to do?

STEPHEN. Well, what can you do?

LADY BRITOMART. I must get the money somehow.

STEPHEN. We cannot take money from him. I had rather go and live in some cheap place like Bedford Square or even Hampstead than take a farthing of his money.

LADY BRITOMART. But after all, Stephen, our present income comes from Andrew.

STEPHEN [*shocked*].  I never knew that.

LADY BRITOMART.  Well, you surely didnt suppose your grandfather had anything to give me. The Stevenages could not do everything for you. We gave you social position. Andrew had to contribute something. He had a very good bargain, I think.

STEPHEN [*bitterly*].  We are utterly dependent on him and his cannons, then?

LADY BRITOMART.  Certainly not: the money is settled. But he provided it. So you see it is not a question of taking money from him or not: it is simply a question of how much. I dont want any more for myself.

STEPHEN.  Nor do I.

LADY BRITOMART.  But Sarah does; and Barbara does. That is, Charles Lomax and Adolphus Cusins will cost them more. So I must put my pride in my pocket and ask for it, I suppose. That is your advice, Stephen, is it not?

STEPHEN.  No.

LADY BRITOMART [*sharply*].  Stephen!

STEPHEN.  Of course if you are determined –

LADY BRITOMART.  I am not determined: I ask your advice; and I am waiting for it. I will not have all the responsibility thrown on my shoulders.

STEPHEN [*obstinately*].  I would die sooner than ask him for another penny.

LADY BRITOMART [*resignedly*].  You mean that *I* must ask him. Very well, Stephen: it shall be as you wish. You will be glad to know that your grandfather concurs. But he thinks I ought to ask Andrew to come here and see the girls. After all, he must have some natural affection for them.

STEPHEN.  Ask him here!!!

LADY BRITOMART.  Do not repeat my words, Stephen. Where else can I ask him?

STEPHEN.  I never expected you to ask him at all.

LADY BRITOMART.  Now dont tease, Stephen. Come! you see that it is necessary that he should pay us a visit, dont you?

STEPHEN [*reluctantly*].  I suppose so, if the girls cannot do without his money.

LADY BRITOMART.  Thank you, Stephen: I knew you would give me the right advice when it was properly explained to you. I have asked your father to come this evening. [*Stephen bounds from his seat*]. Dont jump, Stephen: it fidgets me.

STEPHEN [*in utter consternation*].  Do you mean to say that my father is coming here tonight – that he may be here at any moment?

LADY BRITOMART [*looking at her watch*].  I said nine. [*He gasps. She rises*]. Ring the bell, please. [*Stephen goes to the smaller writing table; presses a button on it; and sits at it with his elbows on the table and his head in his hands, outwitted and overwhelmed*]. It is ten minutes to nine yet; and I have to prepare the girls. I asked Charles Lomax and Adolphus to dinner on purpose that they might be here. Andrew had better see them in case he should cherish any delusions as to their being capable of supporting their wives. *[The butler enters: Lady Britomart goes behind the settee to speak to him].* Morrison: go up to the drawing room and tell everybody to come down here at once. *[Morrison withdraws. Lady Britomart turns to Stephen].* Now remember, Stephen: I shall need all your countenance and authority. *[He rises and tries to recover some vestige of these attributes].* Give me a chair, dear. *[He pushes a chair forward from the wall to where she stands, near the smaller writing table. She sits down; and he goes to the armchair, into which he throws himself].* I dont know how Barbara will take it. Ever since they made her a major in the Salvation Army she has developed a propensity to have her own way and order people about which quite cows me sometimes. It's not ladylike: I'm sure I dont know where she picked it up. Anyhow, Barbara shant bully me; but still it's just as well that your father should be here before she has time to refuse to meet him or make a fuss. Dont look nervous, Stephen: it will only encourage Barbara to make difficulties. *I* am nervous enough, goodness knows; but I dont shew it.

*Sarah and Barbara come in with their respective young men, Charles Lomax and Adolphus Cusins. Sarah is slender, bored, and mundane. Barbara is robuster, jollier, much more energetic. Sarah is fashionably dressed: Barbara is in Salvation Army uniform. Lomax, a young man about town, is like many other young men about town. He is afflicted with a frivolous sense of humor which plunges him at the most inopportune moments into paroxysms of imperfectly suppressed laughter. Cusins is a spectacled student, slight, thin haired, and sweet voiced, with a more complex form of Lomax's complaint. His sense of humor is intellectual and subtle, and is complicated by an appalling temper. The lifelong struggle of a benevolent temperament and a high conscience against impulses of inhuman ridicule and fierce impatience has set up a chronic strain which has visibly wrecked his constitution. He is a most implacable, determined, tenacious, intolerant person who by mere force of character presents himself as – and indeed actually is – considerate, gentle, explanatory, even mild and apologetic, capable possibly of murder, but not of cruelty or coarseness. By the operation of some instinct which is not merciful enough to blind him with the illusions of love, he is obstinately bent on marrying Barbara. Lomax likes Sarah and thinks it will be rather a lark to marry her. Consequently he has not attempted to resist Lady Britomart's arrangements to that end.*

*All four look as if they had been having a good deal of fun in the drawing room. The girls enter first, leaving the swains outside. Sarah comes to the settee. Barbara comes in after her and stops at the door.*

BARBARA. Are Cholly and Dolly to come in?

LADY BRITOMART *[forcibly]*. Barbara: I will not have Charles called Cholly: the vulgarity of it positively makes me ill.

BARBARA. It's all right, mother: Cholly is quite correct nowadays. Are they to come in?

LADY BRITOMART. Yes, if they will behave themselves.

BARBARA *[through the door]*. Come in, Dolly; and behave yourself.

*Barbara comes to her mother's writing table. Cusins enters smiling, and wanders
towards Lady Britomart.*

SARAH *[calling]*.   Come in, Cholly. *[Lomax enters, controlling his features very
imperfectly, and places himself vaguely between Sarah and Barbara].*

LADY BRITOMART *[peremptorily]*.   Sit down, all of you. *[They sit. Cusins
crosses to the window and seats himself there. Lomax takes a chair. Barbara sits
at the writing table and Sarah on the settee].* I dont in the least know what you
are laughing at, Adolphus. I am surprised at you, though I expected
nothing better from Charles Lomax.

CUSINS *[in a remarkably gentle voice]*.   Barbara has been trying to teach me
the West Ham Salvation March.

LADY BRITOMART.   I see nothing to laugh at in that; nor should you if you
are really converted.

CUSINS *[sweetly]*.   You were not present. It was really funny, I believe.

LOMAX.   Ripping.

LADY BRITOMART.   Be quiet, Charles. Now listen to me, children. Your
father is coming here this evening.

*General stupefaction. Lomax, Sarah, and Barbara rise: Sarah scared, and
Barbara amused and expectant.*

LOMAX *[remonstrating]*.   Oh I say!

LADY BRITOMART.   You are not called on to say anything, Charles.

SARAH.   Are you serious, mother?

LADY BRITOMART.   Of course I am serious. It is on your account, Sarah,
and also on Charles's. *[Silence. Sarah sits, with a shrug. Charles looks painfully
unworthy].* I hope you are not going to object, Barbara.

BARBARA.   I! why should I? My father has a soul to be saved like anybody
else. He's quite welcome as far as I am concerned. *[She sits on the table,
and softly whistles ' Onward, Christian Soldiers '].*

LOMAX *[still remonstrant]*.   But really, dont you know! Oh I say!

LADY BRITOMART *[frigidly]*.   What do you wish to convey, Charles?

LOMAX.   Well, you must admit that this is a bit thick.

LADY BRITOMART *[turning with ominous suavity to Cusins]*.   Adolphus: you are
a professor of Greek. Can you translate Charles Lomax's remarks into
reputable English for us?

CUSINS *[cautiously]*.   If I may say so, Lady Brit, I think Charles has rather
happily expressed what we all feel. Homer, speaking of Autolycus, uses
the same phrase. πυκινὸν δόμον ἐλθεῖν means a bit thick.

LOMAX *[handsomely]*.   Not that I mind, you know, if Sarah dont. *[He sits].*

LADY BRITOMART *[crushingly]*.   Thank you. Have I your permission,
Adolphus, to invite my own husband to my own house?

CUSINS *[gallantly]*.   You have my unhesitating support in everything you do.

LADY BRITOMART.   Tush! Sarah: have you nothing to say?

SARAH.   Do you mean that he is coming regularly to live here?

LADY BRITOMART.   Certainly not. The spare room is ready for him if he likes to stay for a day or two and see a little more of you; but there are limits.

SARAH.   Well, he cant eat us, I suppose. *I* dont mind.

LOMAX *[chuckling]*.   I wonder how the old man will take it.

LADY BRITOMART.   Much as the old woman will, no doubt, Charles.

LOMAX *[abashed]*.   I didnt mean – at least –

LADY BRITOMART.   You didnt think, Charles. You never do; and the result is, you never mean anything. And now please attend to me, children. Your father will be quite a stranger to us.

LOMAX.   I suppose he hasnt seen Sarah since she was a little kid.

LADY BRITOMART.   Not since she was a little kid, Charles, as you express it with that elegance of diction and refinement of thought that seem never to desert you. Accordingly – er – *[impatiently]*. Now I have forgotten what I was going to say. That comes of your provoking me to be sarcastic, Charles. Adolphus: will you kindly tell me where I was.

CUSINS *[sweetly]*.   You were saying that as Mr Undershaft has not seen his children since they were babies, he will form his opinion of the way you have brought them up from their behavior tonight, and that therefore you wish us all to be particularly careful to conduct ourselves well, especially Charles.

LADY BRITOMART *[with emphatic approval]*.   Precisely.

LOMAX.   Look here, Dolly: Lady Brit didnt say that.

LADY BRITOMART *[vehemently]*.   I did, Charles. Adolphus's recollection is perfectly correct. It is most important that you should be good; and I do beg you for once not to pair off into opposite corners and giggle and whisper while I am speaking to your father.

BARBARA.   All right, mother. We'll do you credit. *[She comes off the table, and sits in her chair with ladylike elegance]*.

LADY BRITOMART.   Remember, Charles, that Sarah will want to feel proud of you instead of ashamed of you.

LOMAX.   Oh I say! theres nothing to be exactly proud of, dont you know.

LADY BRITOMART.   Well, try and look as if there was.

*Morrison, pale and dismayed, breaks into the room in unconcealed disorder.*

MORRISON.   Might I speak a word to you, my lady?

LADY BRITOMART.   Nonsense! Shew him up.

MORRISON. Yes, my lady. *[He goes]*.

LOMAX.   Does Morrison know who it is?

LADY BRITOMART.   Of course. Morrison has always been with us.

LOMAX.   It must be a regular corker for him, dont you know.

LADY BRITOMART.   Is this a moment to get on my nerves, Charles, with your outrageous expressions?

LOMAX.   But this is something out of the ordinary, really –

MORRISON *[at the door]*.   The – er – Mr Undershaft. *[He retreats in confusion]*.

*Andrew Undershaft comes in. All rise. Lady Britomart meets him in the middle of the room behind the settee.*

*Andrew, is, on the surface, a stoutish, easygoing elderly man, with kindly patient manners, and an engaging simplicity of character. But he has a watchful, deliberate, waiting, listening face, and formidable reserves of power, both bodily and mental, in his capacious chest and long head. His gentleness is partly that of a strong man who has learnt by experience that his natural grip hurts ordinary people unless he handles them very carefully, and partly the mellowness of age and success. He is also a little shy in his present very delicate situation.*

LADY BRITOMART. Good evening, Andrew.

UNDERSHAFT. How d'ye do, my dear.

LADY BRITOMART. You look a good deal older.

UNDERSHAFT *[apologetically]*. I am somewhat older. *[Taking her hand with a touch of courtship]* Time has stood still with you.

LADY BRITOMART *[throwing away his hand]*. Rubbish! This is your family.

UNDERSHAFT *[surprised]*. Is it so large? I am sorry to say my memory is failing very badly in some things. *[He offers his hand with paternal kindness to Lomax]*.

LOMAX *[jerkily shaking his hand]*. Ahdedoo.

UNDERSHAFT. I can see you are my eldest. I am very glad to meet you again, my boy.

LOMAX *[remonstrating]*. No, but look here dont you know – *[Overcome]*. Oh I say!

LADY BRITOMART *[recovering from momentary speechlessness]*. Andrew: do you mean to say that you dont remember how many children you have?

UNDERSHAFT. Well, I am afraid I – . They have grown so much – er. Am I making any ridiculous mistake? I may as well confess: I recollect only one son. But so many things have happened since, of course – er –

LADY BRITOMART *[decisively]*. Andrew: you are talking nonsense. Of course you have only one son.

UNDERSHAFT. Perhaps you will be good enough to introduce me, my dear.

LADY BRITOMART. That is Charles Lomax, who is engaged to Sarah.

UNDERSHAFT. My dear sir, I beg your pardon.

LOMAX. Notatall. Delighted, I assure you.

LADY BRITOMART. This is Stephen.

UNDERSHAFT *[bowing]*. Happy to make your acquaintance, Mr. Stephen. Then *[going to Cusins]* you must be my son. *[Taking Cusins' hands in his]*. How are you, my young friend? *[To Lady Britomart]*. He is very like you, my love.

CUSINS. You flatter me, Mr Undershaft. My name is Cusins: engaged to Barbara. *[Very explicitly]*. That is Major Barbara Undershaft, of the Salvation Army. That is Sarah, your second daughter. This is Stephen Undershaft, your son.

UNDERSHAFT. My dear Stephen, I beg your pardon.

STEPHEN. Not at all.

UNDERSHAFT. Mr Cusins: I am much indebted to you for explaining so precisely. *[Turning to Sarah]*. Barbara, my dear –

SARAH [*prompting him*]. Sarah.

UNDERSHAFT. Sarah, of course. [*They shake hands. He goes over to Barbara*] Barbara – I am right this time, I hope?

BARBARA. Quite right. [*They shake hands*].

LADY BRITOMART [*resuming command*]. Sit down, all of you. Sit down, Andrew. [*She comes forward and sits on the settee. Cusins also brings his chair forward on her left. Barbara and Stephen resume their seats. Lomax gives his chair to Sarah and goes for another*].

UNDERSHAFT. Thank you, my love.

LOMAX [*conversationally, as he brings a chair forward between the writing table and the settee, and offers it to Undershaft*]. Takes you some time to find out exactly where you are, dont it?

UNDERSHAFT [*accepting the chair, but remaining standing*]. That is not what embarrasses me, Mr Lomax. My difficulty is that if I play the part of a father, I shall produce the effect of an intrusive stranger; and if I play the part of a discreet stranger, I may appear a callous father.

LADY BRITOMART. There is no need for you to play any part at all, Andrew. You had much better be sincere and natural.

UNDERSHAFT [*submissively*]. Yes, my dear: I daresay that will be best. [*He sits down comfortably*]. Well, here I am. Now what can I do for you all?

LADY BRITOMART. You need not do anything, Andrew. You are one of the family. You can sit with us and enjoy yourself.

*A painfully conscious pause. Barbara makes a face at Lomax, whose too long suppressed mirth immediately explodes in agonized neighings.*

LADY BRITOMART [*outraged*]. Charles Lomax: if you can behave yourself, behave yourself. If not, leave the room.

LOMAX. I'm awfully sorry, Lady Brit; but really you know, upon my soul! [*He sits on the settee between Lady Britomart and Undershaft, quite overcome*].

BARBARA. Why dont you laugh if you want to, Cholly? It's good for your inside.

LADY BRITOMART. Barbara: you have had the education of a lady. Please let your father see that; and dont talk like a street girl.

UNDERSHAFT. Never mind me, my dear. As you know, I am not a gentleman; and I was never educated.

LOMAX [*encouragingly*]. Nobody'd know it, I assure you. You look all right, you know.

CUSINS. Let me advise you to study Greek, Mr Undershaft. Greek scholars are privileged men. Few of them know Greek; and none of them know anything else; but their position is unchallengeable. Other languages are the qualifications of waiters and commercial travellers: Greek is to a man of position what the hallmark is to silver.

BARBARA. Dolly: dont be insincere. Cholly: fetch your concertina and play something for us.

LOMAX [*jumps up eagerly, but checks himself to remark doubtfully to Undershaft*]. Perhaps that sort of thing isnt in your line, eh?

UNDERSHAFT. I am particularly fond of music.

LOMAX [*delighted*]. Are you? Then I'll get it. [*He goes upstairs for the instrument*].

UNDERSHAFT. Do you play, Barbara?

BARBARA. Only the tambourine. But Cholly's teaching me the concertina.

UNDERSHAFT. Is Cholly also a member of the Salvation Army?

BARBARA. No: he says it's bad form to be a dissenter. But I dont despair of Cholly. I made him come yesterday to a meeting at the dock gates, and take the collection in his hat.

UNDERSHAFT [*looks whimsically at his wife*]!!

LADY BRITOMART. It is not my doing, Andrew. Barbara is old enough to take her own way. She has no father to advise her.

BARBARA. Oh yes she has. There are no orphans in the Salvation Army.

UNDERSHAFT. Your father there has a great many children and plenty of experience, eh?

BARBARA [*looking at him with quick interest and nodding*]. Just so. How did you come to understand that? [*Lomax is heard at the door trying the concertina*].

LADY BRITOMART. Come in, Charles. Play us something at once.

LOMAX. Righto! [*He sits down in his former place, and preludes*].

UNDERSHAFT. One moment, Mr Lomax. I am rather interested in the Salvation Army. Its motto might be my own: Blood and Fire.

LOMAX [*shocked*]. But not your sort of blood and fire, you know.

UNDERSHAFT. My sort of blood cleanses: my sort of fire purifies.

BARBARA. So do ours. Come down tomorrow to my shelter – the West Ham shelter – and see what we're doing. We're going to march to a great meeting in the Assembly Hall at Mile End. Come and see the shelter and then march with us: it will do you a lot of good. Can you play anything?

UNDERSHAFT. In my youth I earned pennies, and even shillings occasionally, in the streets and in public house parlors by my natural talent for step-dancing. Later on, I became a member of the Undershaft orchestral society, and performed passably on the tenor trombone.

LOMAX [*scandalized – putting down the concertina*]. Oh I say!

BARBARA. Many a sinner has played himself into heaven on the trombone, thanks to the Army.

LOMAX [*to Barbara, still rather shocked*]. Yes; but what about the cannon business, dont you know? [*To Undershaft*]. Getting into heaven is not exactly in your line, is it?

LADY BRITOMART. Charles!!!

LOMAX. Well; but it stands to reason, dont it? The cannon business may be necessary and all that: we cant get on without cannons; but it isnt right, you know. On the other hand, there may be a certain amount of tosh about the Salvation Army – I belong to the Established Church myself – but still you cant deny that it's religion; and you cant go against religion, can you? At least unless youre downright immoral, dont you know.

UNDERSHAFT.  You hardly appreciate my position, Mr Lomax –

LOMAX [hastily].  I'm not saying anything against you personally –

UNDERSHAFT.  Quite so, quite so. But consider for a moment. Here I am, a profiteer in mutilation and murder. I find myself in a specially amiable humor just now because, this morning, down at the foundry, we blew twenty-seven dummy soldiers into fragments with a gun which formerly destroyed only thirteen.

LOMAX [leniently].  Well, the more destructive war becomes, the sooner it will be abolished, eh?

UNDERSHAFT.  Not at all. The more destructive war becomes the more fascinating we find it. No, Mr Lomax: I am obliged to you for making the usual excuse for my trade; but I am not ashamed of it. I am not one of those men who keep their morals and their business in watertight compartments. All the spare money my trade rivals spend on hospitals, cathedrals, and other receptacles for conscience money, I devote to experiments and researches in improved methods of destroying life and property. I have always done so; and I always shall. Therefore your Christmas card moralities of peace on earth and goodwill among men are of no use to me. Your Christianity, which enjoins you to resist not evil, and to turn the other cheek, would make me a bankrupt. My morality – my religion – must have a place for cannons and torpedoes in it.

STEPHEN [coldly – almost sullenly].  You speak as if there were half a dozen moralities and religions to choose from, instead of one true morality and one true religion.

UNDERSHAFT.  For me there is only one true morality; but it might not fit you, as you do not manufacture aerial battleships. There is only one true morality for every man; but every man has not the same true morality.

LOMAX [overtaxed].  Would you mind saying that again? I didnt quite follow it.

CUSINS.  It's quite simple. As Euripides says, one man's meat is another man's poison morally as well as physically.

UNDERSHAFT.  Precisely.

LOMAX.  Oh, that! Yes, yes, yes. True. True.

STEPHEN.  In other words, some men are honest and some are scoundrels.

BARBARA.  Bosh! There are no scoundrels.

UNDERSHAFT.  Indeed? Are there any good men?

BARBARA.  No. Not one. There are neither good men nor scoundrels: there are just children of one Father; and the sooner they stop calling one another names the better. You neednt talk to me: I know them. Ive had scores of them through my hands: scoundrels, criminals, infidels, philanthropists, missionaries, county councillors, all sorts. Theyre all just the same sort of sinner; and theres the same salvation ready for them all.

UNDERSHAFT. May I ask have you ever saved a maker of cannons?

BARBARA. No. Will you let me try?

UNDERSHAFT. Well, I will make a bargain with you. If I go to see you tomorrow in your Salvation Shelter, will you come the day after to see me in my cannon works?

BARBARA. Take care. It may end in your giving up the cannons for the sake of the Salvation Army.

UNDERSHAFT. Are you sure it will not end in your giving up the Salvation Army for the sake of the cannons?

BARBARA. I will take my chance of that.

UNDERSHAFT. And I will take my chance of the other. *[They shake hands on it]*. Where is your shelter?

BARBARA. In West Ham. At the sign of the cross. Ask anybody in Canning Town. Where are your works?

UNDERSHAFT. In Perivale St Andrews. At the sign of the sword. Ask anybody in Europe.

LOMAX. Hadnt I better play something?

BARBARA. Yes. Give us Onward, Christian Soldiers.

LOMAX. Well, thats rather a strong order to begin with, dont you know. Suppose I sing Thou't passing hence, my brother. It's much the same tune.

BARBARA. It's too melancholy. You get saved, Cholly; and youll pass hence, my brother, without making such a fuss about it.

LADY BRITOMART. Really, Barbara, you go on as if religion were a pleasant subject. Do have some sense of propriety.

UNDERSHAFT. I do not find it an unpleasant subject, my dear. It is the only one that capable people really care for.

LADY BRITOMART *[looking at her watch]*. Well, if you are determined to have it, I insist on having it in a proper and respectable way. Charles: ring for prayers.

*General amazement. Stephen rises in dismay.*

LOMAX *[rising]*. Oh I say!

UNDERSHAFT *[rising]*. I am afraid I must be going.

LADY BRITOMART. You cannot go now, Andrew: it would be most improper. Sit down. What will the servants think?

UNDERSHAFT. My dear: I have conscientious scruples. May I suggest a compromise? If Barbara will conduct a little service in the drawing room, with Mr Lomax as organist, I will attend it willingly. I will even take part, if a trombone can be procured.

LADY BRITOMART. Dont mock, Andrew.

UNDERSHAFT *[shocked – to Barbara]*. You dont think I am mocking, my love, I hope.

BARBARA. No, of course not; and it wouldnt matter if you were: half the Army came to their first meeting for a lark. *[Rising]*. Come along. *[She throws her arms around her father and sweeps him out, calling to the others from the threshold].* Come, Dolly. Come, Cholly.

*[Cusins rises].*

LADY BRITOMART. I will not be disobeyed by everybody. Adolphus: sit down. *[He does not].* Charles: you may go. You are not fit for prayers: you cannot keep your countenance.

LOMAX. Oh I say! *[He goes out].*

LADY BRITOMART *[continuing].* But you, Adolphus, can behave yourself if you choose to. I insist on your staying.

CUSINS. My dear Lady Brit: there are things in the family prayer book that I couldnt bear to hear you say.

LADY BRITOMART. What things, pray?

CUSINS. Well, you would have to say before all the servants that we have done things we ought not to have done, and left undone things we ought to have done, and that there is no health in us. I cannot bear to hear you doing yourself such an injustice, and Barbara such an injustice. As for myself, I flatly deny it: I have done my best. I shouldnt dare to marry Barbara – I couldnt look you in the face – if it were true. So I must go to the drawing room.

LADY BRITOMART *[offended].* Well, go. *[He starts for the door].* And remember this, Adolphus *[he turns to listen]:* I have a very strong suspicion that you went to the Salvation Army to worship Barbara and nothing else. And I quite appreciate the very clever way in which you systematically humbug me. I have found you out. Take care Barbara doesnt. Thats all.

CUSINS *[with unruffled sweetness].* Dont tell on me. *[He steals out].*

LADY BRITOMART. Sarah: if you want to go, go. Anything's better than to sit there as if you wished you were a thousand miles away.

SARAH *[languidly].* Very well, mamma. *[She goes].*

*Lady Britomart, with a sudden flounce, gives way to a little gust of tears.*

STEPHEN *[going to her].* Mother: whats the matter?

LADY BRITOMART *[swishing away her tears with her handkerchief].* Nothing. Foolishness. You can go with him, too, if you like, and leave me with the servants.

STEPHEN. Oh, you mustnt think that, mother. I – I dont like him.

LADY BRITOMART. The others do. That is the injustice of a woman's lot. A woman has to bring up her children; and that means to restrain them, to deny them things they want, to set them tasks, to punish them when they do wrong, to do all the unpleasant things. And then the father, who has nothing to do but pet them and spoil them, comes in when all her work is done and steals their affection from her.

STEPHEN. He has not stolen our affection from you. It is only curiosity.

LADY BRITOMART *[violently].* I wont be consoled, Stephen. There is nothing the matter with me. *[She rises and goes towards the door].*

STEPHEN. Where are you going, mother?

LADY BRITOMART. To the drawing room, of course. *[She goes out. Onward,*

*Christian Soldiers, on the concertina, with tambourine accompaniment, is heard when the door opens]*. Are you coming, Stephen?

STEPHEN.   No. Certainly not. *[She goes. He sits down on the settee, with compressed lips and an expression of strong dislike]*.


# ACT II

*The yard of the West Ham shelter of the Salvation Army is a cold place on a January morning. The building itself, an old warehouse, is newly whitewashed. Its gabled end projects into the yard in the middle, with a door on the ground floor, and another in the loft above it without any balcony or ladder, but with a pulley rigged over it for hoisting sacks. Those who come from this central gable end into the yard have the gateway leading to the street on their left, with a stone horse-trough just beyond it, and, on the right, a penthouse shielding a table from the weather. There are forms at the table; and on them are seated a man and a woman, both much down on their luck, finishing a meal of bread (one thick slice each, with margarine and golden syrup) and diluted milk.*

*The man, a workman out of employment, is young, agile, a talker, a poser, sharp enough to be capable of anything in reason except honesty or altruistic considerations of any kind. The woman is a commonplace old bundle of poverty and hard-worn humanity. She looks sixty and probably is forty-five. If they were rich people, gloved and muffed and well wrapped up in furs and overcoats, they would be numbed and miserable; for it is a grindingly cold raw January day; and a glance at the background of grimy warehouses and leaden sky visible over the whitewashed walls of the yard would drive any idle rich person straight to the Mediterranean. But these two, being no more troubled with visions of the Mediterranean than of the moon, and being compelled to keep more of their clothes in the pawnshop, and less on their persons, in winter than in summer, are not depressed by the cold: rather are they stung into vivacity, to which their meal has just now given an almost jolly turn. The man takes a pull at his mug, and then gets up and moves about the yard with his hands deep in his pockets, occasionally breaking into a stepdance.*

THE WOMAN.   Feel better arter your meal, sir?

THE MAN.   No. Call that a meal! Good enough for you, praps; but wot is it to me, an intelligent workin man.

THE WOMAN.   Workin man! Wot are you?

THE MAN.   Painter.

THE WOMAN *[sceptically]*.   Yus, I dessay.

THE MAN.   Yus, you dessay! I know. Every loafer that cant do nothink calls isself a painter. Well, I'm a real painter: grainer, finisher, thirty-eight bob a week when I can get it.

THE WOMAN.   Then why dont you go and get it?

THE MAN.   I'll tell you why. Fust: I'm intelligent – fffff! it's rotten cold here *[he dances a step or two]* – yes: intelligent beyond the station o life into which it has pleased the capitalists to call me; and they dont like a man that sees through em. Second, an intelligent bein needs a doo share of appiness; so I drink somethink cruel when I get the chawnce. Third, I stand by my class and do as little as I can so's to leave arf the job for me fellow workers. Fourth, I'm fly enough to know wots inside the law and wots outside it; and inside it I do as the capitalists do: pinch wot I can lay me ands on. In a proper state of society I am sober, industrious and honest: in Rome, so to speak, I do as the Romans do. Wots the consequence? When trade is bad – and it's rotten bad just now – and the employers az to sack arf their men, they generally start on me.

THE WOMAN. What's your name?

THE MAN. Price. Bronterre O'Brien Price. Usually called Snobby Price, for short.

THE WOMAN. Snobby's a carpenter, aint it? You said you was a painter.

PRICE. Not that kind of snob, but the genteel sort. I'm too uppish, owing to my intelligence, and my father being a Chartist and a reading, thinking man: a stationer, too. I'm none of your common hewers of wood and drawers of water; and dont you forget it. [He returns to his seat at the table, and takes up his mug]. Wots your name?

THE WOMAN. Rummy Mitchens, sir.

PRICE [quaffing the remains of his milk to her]. Your elth, Miss Mitchens.

RUMMY [correcting him]. Missis Mitchens.

PRICE. Wot! Oh Rummy, Rummy! Respectable married woman, Rummy, gittin rescued by the Salvation Army by pretendin to be a bad un. Same old game!

RUMMY. What am I to do? I cant starve. Them Salvation lasses is dear good girls; but the better you are, the worse they likes to think you were before they rescued you. Why shouldnt they av a bit o credit, poor loves? theyre worn to rags by their work. And where would they get the money to rescue us if we was to let on we're no worse than other people? You know what ladies and gentlemen are.

PRICE. Thievin swine! Wish I ad their job, Rummy, all the same. Wot does Rummy stand for? Pet name praps?

RUMMY. Short for Romola.

PRICE. For wot!?

RUMMY. Romola. It was out of a new book. Somebody me mother wanted me to grow up like.

PRICE. We're companions in misfortune, Rummy. Both on us got names that nobody cawnt pronounce. Consequently I'm Snobby and youre Rummy because Bill and Sally wasnt good enough for our parents. Such is life!

RUMMY. Who saved you, Mr Price? Was it Major Barbara?

PRICE. No: I come here on my own. I'm going to be Bronterre O'Brien Price, the converted painter. I know wot they like. I'll tell em how I blasphemed and gambled and wopped my poor old mother –

RUMMY [shocked]. Used you to beat your mother?

PRICE. Not likely. She used to beat me. No matter: you come and listen
to the converted painter, and youll hear how she was a pious woman that
taught me me prayers at er knee, an how I used to come home drunk and
drag her out o bed be er snow white airs, an lam into er with the poker.

RUMMY. Thats whats so unfair to us women. Your confessions is just as
big lies as ours: you dont tell what you really done no more than us; but
you men can tell your lies right out at the meetins and be made much of
for it; while the sort o confessions we az to make az to be wispered to one
lady at a time. It aint right, spite of all their piety.

PRICE. Right! Do you spose the Army'd be allowed if it went and did right?
Not much. It combs our air and makes us good little blokes to be robbed
and put upon. But I'll play the game as good as any of em. I'll see
somebody struck by lightnin, or hear a voice sayin 'Snobby Price: where
will you spend eternity?' I'll av a time of it, I tell you.

RUMMY. You wont be let drink, though.

PRICE. I'll take it out in gorspellin, then. I dont want to drink if I can get
fun enough any other way.

> *Jenny Hill, a pale, overwrought, pretty Salvation lass of 18, comes in through
> the yard gate, leading Peter Shirley, a half hardened, half worn-out elderly man,
> weak with hunger.*

JENNY [*supporting him*]. Come! pluck up. I'll get you something to eat.
Youll be all right then.

PRICE [*rising and hurrying officiously to take the old man off Jenny's hands*]. Poor
old man! Cheer up, brother: youll find rest and peace and appiness ere.
Hurry up with the food, miss: e's fair done. [*Jenny hurries into the shelter*].
Ere, buck up, daddy! she's fetchin y'a thick slice o breadn treacle, an a
mug of skyblue. [*He seats him at the corner of the table*].

RUMMY [*gaily*]. Keep up your old art! Never say die!

SHIRLEY. I'm not an old man. I'm only 46. I'm as good as ever I was.
The grey patch come in my hair before I was thirty. All it wants is three
pennorth o hair dye: am I to be turned on the streets to starve for it?
Holy God! Ive worked ten to twelve hours a day since I was thirteen,
and paid my way all through; and now am I to be thrown into the gutter
and my job given to a young man that can do it no better than me because Ive black hair that goes white at the first change?

PRICE [*cheerfully*]. No good jawrin about it. Youre ony a jumped-up,
jerked-off, orspittle-turned-out incurable of an ole workin man: who
cares about you? Eh? Make the thievin swine give you a meal: theyve stole
many a one from you. Get a bit o your own back. [*Jenny returns with the
usual meal*]. There you are, brother. Awsk a blessin an tuck that into you.

SHIRLEY [*looking at it ravenously but not touching it, and crying like a child*]. I
never took anything before.

JENNY [*petting him*]. Come, come! the Lord sends it to you: he wasnt above
taking bread from his friends; and why should you be? Besides, when we
find you a job you can pay us for it if you like.

SHIRLEY [*eagerly*].   Yes, yes: thats true. I can pay you back: it's only a loan. [*Shivering*] Oh Lord! oh Lord! [*He turns to the table and attacks the meal ravenously*].

JENNY.   Well, Rummy, are you more comfortable now?

RUMMY.   God bless you, lovey! youve fed my body and saved my soul, havnt you? [*Jenny, touched, kisses her*]. Sit down and rest a bit: you must be ready to drop.

JENNY.   Ive been going hard since morning. But theres more work than we can do. I mustnt stop.

RUMMY.   Try a prayer for just two minutes. Youll work all the better after.

JENNY [*her eyes lighting up*].   Oh isnt it wonderful how a few minutes prayer revives you! I was quite lightheaded at twelve o'clock, I was so tired; but Major Barbara just sent me to pray for five minutes; and I was able to go on as if I had only just begun. [*To Price*] Did you have a piece of bread?

PRICE [*with unction*].   Yes, miss; but Ive got the piece that I value more; and thats the peace that passeth hall hannerstennin.

RUMMY [*fervently*].   Glory Hallelujah!

    *Bill Walker, a rough customer of about 25, appears at the yard gate and looks malevolently at Jenny.*

JENNY.   That makes me so happy. When you say that, I feel wicked for loitering here. I must get to work again.

    *She is hurrying to the shelter, when the new-comer moves quickly up to the door and intercepts her. His manner is so threatening that she retreats as he comes at her truculently, driving her down the yard.*

BILL.   Aw knaow you. Youre the one that took awy maw girl. Youre the one that set er agen me. Well, I'm gowin to eve er aht. Not that Aw care a carse for er or you: see? Bat Aw'll let er knaow; and Aw'll let you knaow. Aw'm gowin to give her a doin thatll teach er to cat awy from me. Nah in wiv you and tell er to cam aht afore Aw cam in and kick er aht. Tell er Bill Walker wants er. She'll knaow wot thet means; and if she keeps me witin itll be worse. You stop to jawr beck at me; and Aw'll stawt on you: d'ye eah? Theres your wy. In you gow. [*He takes her by the arm and slings her towards the door of the shelter. She falls on her hand and knee. Rummy helps her up again*].

PRICE [*rising, and venturing irresolutely towards Bill*].   Easy there, mate. She aint doin you no arm.

BILL.   Oo are you callin mite? [*Standing over him threateningly*].   Youre gowin to stend ap for er, aw yer? Put ap your ends.

RUMMY [*running indignantly to him to scold him*].   Oh, you great brute – [*He instantly swings his left hand back against her face. She screams and reels back to the trough, where she sits down, covering her bruised face with her hands and rocking herself and moaning with pain*].

JENNY [*going to her*].   Oh, God forgive you! How could you strike an old woman like that?

BILL [*seizing her by the hair so violently that she also screams, and tearing her away from the old woman*]. You Gawd forgimme again and Aw'll Gawd forgive you one on the jawr thetll stop you pryin for a week. [*Holding her and turning fiercely on Price*]. Ev you ennything to sy agen it?

PRICE [*intimidated*]. No, matey: she aint anything to do with me.

BILL. Good job for you! Aw'd pat two meals into you and fawt you with one finger arter, you stawved cur. [*To Jenny*]. Nah are you gowin to fetch aht Mog Ebbijem; or em Aw to knock your fice off you and fetch her meself?

JENNY [*writhing in his grasp*]. Oh please someone go in and tell Major Barbara – [*she screams again as he wrenches her head down; and Price and Rummy flee into the shelter*].

BILL. You want to gow in and tell your Mijor of me, do you?

JENNY. Oh please dont drag my hair. Let me go.

BILL. Do you or downt you? [*She stifles a scream*]. Yus or nao?

JENNY. God give me strength –

BILL [*striking her with his fist in the face*]. Gow and shaow her thet, and tell her if she wants one lawk it to cam and interfere with me. [*Jenny, crying with pain, goes into the shed. He goes to the form and addresses the old man*]. Eah: finish your mess; an git aht o maw wy.

SHIRLEY [*springing up and facing him fiercely, with the mug in his hand*]. You take a liberty with me, and I'll smash you over the face with the mug and cut your eye out. Aint you satisfied – young whelps like you – with takin the bread out o the mouths of your elders that have brought you up and slaved for you, but you must come shovin and cheekin and bullyin in here, where the bread o charity is sickenin in our stummicks?

BILL [*contemptuously, but backing a little*]. Wot good are you, you aold palsy mag? Wot good are you?

SHIRLEY. As good as you and better. I'll do a day's work agen you or any fat young soaker of your age. Go and take my job at Horrockses, where I worked for ten year. They want young men there: they cant afford to keep men over forty-five. Theyre very sorry – give you a character and happy to help you to get anything suited to your years – sure a steady man wont be long out of a job. Well, let em try you. Theyll find the differ. What do you know? Not as much as how to beeyave yourself – layin your dirty fist across the mouth of a respectable woman!

BILL. Downt provowk me to ly it acrost yours: d'ye eah?

SHIRLEY [*with blighting contempt*]. Yes: you like an old man to hit, dont you, when youve finished with the women. I aint seen you hit a young one yet.

BILL [*stung*]. You loy, you aold soupkitchener, you. There was a yang menn eah. Did Aw offer to itt him or did Aw not?

SHIRLEY. Was he starvin or was he not? Was he a man or only a crosseyed thief an a loafer? Would you hit my son-in-law's brother?

BILL. Oo's ee?

SHIRLEY. Todger Fairmile o Balls Pond. Him that won £20 off the

Japanese wrastler at the music hall by standin out 17 minutes 4 seconds agen him.

BILL *[sullenly]*. Aw'm nao music awl wrastler. Ken he box?

SHIRLEY. Yes: an you cant.

BILL. Wot! Aw cawnt, cawnt Aw? Wots thet you sy *[threatening him]*?

SHIRLEY *[not budging an inch]*. Will you box Todger Fairmile if I put him on to you? Say the word.

BILL *[subsiding with a slouch]*. Aw'll stend ap to enny menn alawv, if he was ten Todger Fairmawls. But Aw dont set ap to be a perfeshnal.

SHIRLEY *[looking down on him with unfathomable disdain]*. You box! Slap an old woman with the back o your hand! You hadnt even the sense to hit her where a magistrate couldnt see the mark of it, you silly young lump of conceit and ignorance. Hit a girl in the jaw and ony make her cry! If Todger Fairmile'd done it, she wouldnt a got up inside o ten minutes, no more than you would if he got on to you. Yah! I'd set about you myself if I had a week's feedin in me instead o two months' starvation. *[He turns his back on him and sits down moodily at the table]*.

BILL *[following him and stooping over him to drive the taunt in]*. You loy! youve the bread and treacle in you that you cam eah to beg.

SHIRLEY *[bursting into tears]*. Oh God! it's true: I'm only an old pauper on the scrap heap. *[Furiously]*. But youll come to it yourself; and then youll know. Youll come to it sooner than a teetotaller like me, fillin yourself with gin at this hour o the mornin!

BILL. Aw'm nao gin drinker, you oald lawr; bat wen Aw want to give my girl a bloomin good awdin Aw lawk to ev a bit o devil in me: see? An eah Aw emm, talkin to a rotten aold blawter like you sted o givin her wot for. *[Working himself into a rage]*. Aw'm gowin in there to fetch her aht. *[He makes vengefully for the shelter door]*.

SHIRLEY. Youre going to the station on a stretcher, more likely; and theyll take the gin and the devil out of you there when they get you inside. You mind what youre about: the major here is the Earl o Stevenage's granddaughter.

BILL *[checked]*. Garn!

SHIRLEY. Youll see.

BILL *[his resolution oozing]*. Well, Aw aint dan nathin to er.

SHIRLEY. Spose she said you did! who'd believe you?

BILL *[very uneasy, skulking back to the corner of the penthouse]*. Gawd! theres no jastice in this cantry. To think wot them people can do! Aw'm as good as er.

SHIRLEY. Tell her so. It's just what a fool like you would do.

*Barbara, brisk and businesslike, comes from the shelter with a note book, and addresses herself to Shirley. Bill, cowed, sits down in the corner on a form, and turns his back on them.*

BARBARA. Good morning.

SHIRLEY *[standing up and taking off his hat]*. Good morning, miss.

BARBARA. Sit down: make yourself at home. *[He hesitates; but she puts a friendly hand on his shoulder and makes him obey].* Now then! since youve made friends with us, we want to know all about you. Names and addresses and trades.

SHIRLEY. Peter Shirley. Fitter. Chucked out two months ago because I was too old.

BARBARA *[not at all surprised].* Youd pass still. Why didnt you dye your hair?

SHIRLEY. I did. Me age come out at a coroner's inquest on me daughter.

BARBARA. Steady?

SHIRLEY. Teetotaller. Never out of a job before. Good worker. And sent to the knackers like an old horse!

BARBARA. No matter: if you did your part God will do his.

SHIRLEY *[suddenly stubborn].* My religion's no concern of anybody but myself.

BARBARA *[guessing].* I know. Secularist?

SHIRLEY *[hotly].* Did I offer to deny it?

BARBARA. Why should you? My own father's a Secularist, I think. Our Father – yours and mine – fulfils himself in many ways; and I daresay he knew what he was about when he made a Secularist of you. So buck up, Peter! we can always find a job for a steady man like you. *[Shirley, disarmed and a little bewildered, touches his hat. She turns from him to Bill].* Whats your name?

BILL *[insolently].* Wots thet to you?

BARBARA *[calmly making a note].* Afraid to give his name. Any trade?

BILL. Oo's afride to give is nime? *[Doggedly, with a sense of heroically defying the House of Lords in the person of Lord Stevenage].* If you want to bring a chawge agen me, bring it. *[She waits, unruffled].* Moy nime's Bill Walker.

BARBARA *[as if the name were familiar: trying to remember how].* Bill Walker? *[Recollecting].* Oh, I know: youre the man that Jenny Hill was praying for inside just now. *[She enters his name in her note book].*

BILL. Oo's Jenny Ill? And wot call as she to pry for me?

BARBARA. I dont know. Perhaps it was you that cut her lip.

BILL *[defiantly].* Yus, it was me that cat her lip. Aw aint afride o you.

BARBARA. How could you be, since youre not afraid of God? Youre a brave man, Mr Walker. It takes some pluck to do our work here; but none of us dare lift our hand against a girl like that, for fear of her father in heaven.

BILL *[sullenly].* I want nan o your kentin jawr. I spowse you think Aw cam eah to beg from you, like this demmiged lot eah. Not me. Aw downt want your bread and scripe and ketlep. Aw dont blieve in your Gawd, no more than you do yourself.

BARBARA *[sunnily apologetic and ladylike, as on a new footing with him].* Oh, I beg your pardon for putting your name down, Mr Walker. I didnt understand. I'll strike it out.

BILL [*taking this as a slight, and deeply wounded by it*].  Eah! you let maw nime alown. Aint it good enaff to be in your book?

BARBARA [*considering*].  Well, you see, theres no use putting down your name unless I can do something for you, is there? Whats your trade?

BILL [*still smarting*].  Thets nao concern o yours.

BARBARA.  Just so. [*Very businesslike*]. I'll put you down as [*writing*] the man who – struck – poor little Jenny Hill – in the mouth.

BILL [*rising threateningly*].  See eah. Awve ed enaff o this.

BARBARA [*quite sunny and fearless*].  What did you come to us for?

BILL.  Aw cam for maw gel, see? Aw cam to tike her aht o this and to brike er jawr for er.

BARBARA [*complacently*].  You see I was right about your trade. [*Bill, on the point of retorting furiously, finds himself, to his great shame and terror, in danger of crying instead. He sits down again suddenly*]. Whats her name?

BILL [*dogged*].  Er nime's Mog Ebbijem: thets wot her nime is.

BARBARA.  Mog Habbijam! Oh, she's gone to Canning Town, to our barracks there.

BILL [*fortified by his resentment of Mog's perfidy*].  Is she? [*Vindictively*]. Then Aw'm gowin to Kennintahn arter her. [*He crosses to the gate; hesitates; finally comes back at Barbara*]. Are you loyin to me to git shat o me?

BARBARA.  I dont want to get shut of you. I want to keep you here and save your soul. Youd better stay: youre going to have a bad time today, Bill.

BILL.  Oo's gowin to give it to me? You, preps?

BARBARA.  Someone you dont believe in. But youll be glad afterwards.

BILL [*slinking off*].  Aw'll gow to Kennintahn to be aht o reach o your tangue. [*Suddenly turning on her with intense malice*]. And if Aw downt fawnd Mog there, Aw'll cam beck and do two˙years for you, selp me Gawd if Aw downt!

BARBARA [*a shade kindlier, if possible*].  It's no use, Bill. She's got another bloke.

BILL.  Wot!

BARBARA.  One of her own converts. He fell in love with her when he saw her with her soul saved, and her face clean, and her hair washed.

BILL [*surprised*].  Wottud she wash it for, the carroty slat? It's red.

BARBARA.  It's quite lovely now, because she wears a new look in her eyes with it. It's a pity youre too late. The new bloke has put your nose out of joint, Bill.

BILL.  Aw'll put his nowse aht o joint for him. Not that Aw care a carse for her, mawnd thet. But Aw'll teach her to drop me as if Aw was dirt. And Aw'll teach him to meddle with maw judy. Wots iz bleedin nime?

BARBARA.  Sergeant Todger Fairmile.

SHIRLEY [*rising with grim joy*].  I'll go with him, miss. I want to see them two meet. I'll take him to the infirmary when it's over.

BILL [*to Shirley, with undissembled misgiving*].  Is thet im you was speakin on?

SHIRLEY. Thats him.

BILL. Im that wrastled in the music awl?

SHIRLEY. The competitions at the National Sportin Club was worth nigh a hundred a year to him. He's gev em up now for religion; so he's a bit fresh for want of the exercise he was accustomed to. He'll be glad to see you. Come along.

BILL. Wots is wight?

SHIRLEY. Thirteen four. *[Bill's last hope expires].*

BARBARA. Go and talk to him, Bill. He'll convert you.

SHIRLEY. He'll convert your head into a mashed potato.

BILL *[sullenly]*. Aw aint afride of im. Aw aint afride of ennybody. Bat e can lick me. She's dan me. *[He sits down moodily on the edge of the horse trough].*

SHIRLEY. You aint going. I thought not. *[He resumes his seat].*

BARBARA *[calling]*. Jenny!

JENNY *[appearing at the shelter door with a plaster on the corner of her mouth]*. Yes, Major.

BARBARA. Send Rummy Mitchens out to clear away here.

JENNY. I think she's afraid.

BARBARA *[her resemblance to her mother flashing out for a moment]*. Nonsense! she must do as she's told.

JENNY *[calling into the shelter]*. Rummy: the Major says you must come.

*Jenny comes to Barbara, purposely keeping on the side next Bill, lest he should suppose that she shrank from him or bore malice.*

BARBARA. Poor little Jenny! Are you tired? *[Looking at the wounded cheek]*. Does it hurt?

JENNY. No: it's all right now. It was nothing.

BARBARA *[critically]*. It was as hard as he could hit, I expect. Poor Bill! You dont feel angry with him, do you?

JENNY. Oh no, no, no: indeed I dont, Major, bless his poor heart! *[Barbara kisses her; and she runs away merrily into the shelter. Bill writhes with an agonizing return of his new and alarming symptoms, but says nothing. Rummy Mitchens comes from the shelter].*

BARBARA *[going to meet Rummy]*. Now Rummy, bustle. Take in those mugs and plates to be washed; and throw the crumbs about for the birds.

*[Rummy takes the three plates and mugs; but Shirley takes back his mug from her, as there is still some milk left in it.]*

RUMMY. There aint any crumbs. This aint a time to waste good bread on birds.

PRICE *[appearing at the shelter door]*. Gentleman come to see the shelter, Major. Says he's your father.

BARBARA. All right. Coming. *[Snobby goes back into the shelter, followed by Barbara].*

RUMMY *[stealing across to Bill and addressing him in a subdued voice, but with intense conviction]*. I'd av the lor of you, you flat eared pignosed potwalloper, if she'd let me. Youre no gentleman, to hit a lady in the face.

*[Bill, with greater things moving in him, takes no notice].*

SHIRLEY *[following her].* Here! in with you and dont get yourself into more trouble by talking.

RUMMY *[with hauteur].* I aint ad the pleasure o being hintroduced to you, as I can remember. *[She goes into the shelter with the plates].*

SHIRLEY. Thats the –

BILL *[savagely].* Downt you talk to me, d'ye eah? You lea me alown, or Aw'll do you a mischief. Aw'm not dirt under your feet, ennywy.

SHIRLEY *[calmly].* Dont you be afeerd. You aint such prime company that you need expect to be sought after. *[He is about to go into the shelter when Barbara comes out, with Undershaft on her right].*

BARBARA. Oh, there you are, Mr Shirley! *[Between them].* This is my father: I told you he was a Secularist, didnt I? Perhaps youll be able to comfort one another.

UNDERSHAFT *[startled].* A Secularist! Not the least in the world: on the contrary, a confirmed mystic.

BARBARA. Sorry, I'm sure. By the way, papa, what is your religion? in case I have to introduce you again.

UNDERSHAFT. My religion? Well, my dear, I am a Millionaire. That is my religion.

BARBARA. Then I'm afraid you and Mr Shirley wont be able to comfort one another after all. Youre not a Millionaire, are you, Peter?

SHIRLEY. No; and proud of it.

UNDERSHAFT *[gravely].* Poverty, my friend, is not a thing to be proud of.

SHIRLEY *[angrily].* Who made your millions for you? Me and my like. Whats kep us poor? Keepin you rich. I wouldnt have your conscience, not for all your income.

UNDERSHAFT. I wouldnt have your income, not for all your conscience, Mr Shirley. *[He goes to the penthouse and sits down on a form].*

BARBARA *[stopping Shirley adroitly as he is about to retort].* You wouldnt think he was my father, would you, Peter? Will you go into the shelter and lend the lasses a hand for a while: we're worked off our feet.

SHIRLEY *[bitterly].* Yes: I'm in their debt for a meal, aint I?

BARBARA. Oh, not because youre in their debt, but for love of them, Peter, for love of them. *[He cannot understand, and is rather scandalized].* There! dont stare at me. In with you; and give that conscience of yours a holiday *[bustling him into the shelter].*

SHIRLEY *[as he goes in].* Ah! it's a pity you never was trained to use your reason, miss. Youd have been a very taking lecturer on Secularism.

*Barbara turns to her father.*

UNDERSHAFT. Never mind me, my dear. Go about your work; and let me watch it for a while.

BARBARA. All right.

UNDERSHAFT. For instance, whats the matter with that outpatient over there?

*556*

BARBARA [*looking at Bill, whose attitude has never changed, and whose expression of brooding wrath has deepened*]. Oh, we shall cure him in no time. Just watch. [*She goes over to Bill and waits. He glances up at her and casts his eyes down again, uneasy, but grimmer than ever*]. It would be nice to just stamp on Mog Habbijam's face, wouldnt it, Bill?

BILL [*starting up from the trough in consternation*]. It's a loy: Aw never said so. [*She shakes her head*]. Oo taold you wot was in moy mawnd?

BARBARA. Only your new friend.

BILL. Wot new friend?

BARBARA. The devil, Bill. When he gets round people they get miserable, just like you.

BILL [*with a heartbreaking attempt at devil-may-care cheerfulness*]. Aw aint miserable. [*He sits down again, and stretches his legs in an attempt to seem indifferent*].

BARBARA. Well, if youre happy, why dont you look happy, as we do?

BILL [*his legs curling back in spite of him*]. Aw'm eppy enaff, Aw tell you. Woy cawnt you lea me alown? Wot ev I dan to you? Aw aint smashed your fice, ev Aw?

BARBARA [*softly: wooing his soul*]. It's not me thats getting at you, Bill.

BILL. Oo else is it?

BARBARA. Somebody that doesnt intend you to smash women's faces, I suppose. Somebody or something that wants to make a man of you.

BILL [*blustering*]. Mike a menn o m e! Aint Aw a menn? eh? Oo sez Aw'm not a menn?

BARBARA. Theres a man in you somewhere, I suppose. But why did he let you hit poor little Jenny Hill? That wasnt very manly of him, was it?

BILL [*tormented*]. Ev dan wiv it, Aw tell you. Chack it. Aw'm sick o your Jenny Ill and er silly little fice.

BARBARA. Then why do you keep thinking about it? Why does it keep coming up against you in your mind? Youre not getting converted, are you?

BILL [*with conviction*]. Not M E. Not lawkly.

BARBARA. Thats right, Bill. Hold out against it. Put out your strength. Dont lets get you cheap. Todger Fairmile said he wrestled for three nights against his salvation harder than he ever wrestled with the Jap at the music hall. He gave in to the Jap when his arm was going to break. But he didnt give in to his salvation until his heart was going to break. Perhaps youll escape that. You havent any heart, have you?

BILL. Wot d'ye mean? Woy aint Aw got a awt the sime as ennybody else?

BARBARA. A man with a heart wouldnt have bashed poor little Jenny's face, would he?

BILL [*almost crying*]. Ow, will you lea me alown? Ev Aw ever offered to meddle with you, that you cam neggin and provowkin me lawk this? [*He writhes convulsively from his eyes to his toes*].

BARBARA [*with a steady soothing hand on his arm and a gentle voice that never lets *him go]*. It's your soul thats hurting you, Bill, and not me. Weve been through it all ourselves. Come with us, Bill. *[He looks wildly round]*. To brave manhood on earth and eternal glory in heaven. *[He is on the point of breaking down]*. Come. *[A drum is heard in the shelter; and Bill, with a gasp, escapes from the spell as Barbara turns quickly. Adolphus enters from the shelter with a big drum]*. Oh! there you are, Dolly. Let me introduce a new friend of mine, Mr. Bill Walker. This is my bloke, Bill: Mr. Cusins *[Cusins salutes with his drumstick]*.

BILL.   Gowin to merry im?

BARBARA.   Yes.

BILL *[fervently]*.   Gawd elp im! Gaw-aw-aw-awd elp im!

BARBARA.   Why? Do you think he wont be happy with me?

BILL.   Awve aony ed to stend it for a mawnin: e'll ev to stend it for a lawftawm.

CUSINS.   That is a frightful reflection, Mr Walker. But I cant tear myself away from her.

BILL.   Well, Aw ken. *[To Barbara]*. Eah! do you knaow where Aw'm gowin to, and wot Aw'm gowin to do?

BARBARA.   Yes: youre going to heaven; and youre coming back here before the week's out to tell me so.

BILL.   You loy. Aw'm gowin to Kennintahn, to spit in Todger Fairmawl's eye. Aw beshed Jenny Ill's fice; an nar Aw'll git me aown fice beshed and cam beck and shaow it to er. Ee'll itt me ardern Aw itt her. Thatll mike us square. *[To Adolphus]*. Is thet fair or is it not? Youre a genlmn: you oughter knaow.

BARBARA.   Two black eyes wont make one white one, Bill.

BILL.   Aw didnt awst you. Cawnt you never keep your mahth shat? Oy awst the genlmn.

CUSINS *[reflectively]*.   Yes: I think youre right, Mr Walker. Yes: I should do it. It's curious: it's exactly what an ancient Greek would have done.

BARBARA.   But what good will it do?

CUSINS.   Well, it will give Mr Fairmile some exercise; and it will satisfy Mr Walker's soul.

BILL.   Rot! there aint nao such a thing as a saoul. Ah kin you tell wevver Awve a saoul or not? You never seen it.

BARBARA.   Ive seen it hurting you when you went against it.

BILL *[with compressed aggravation]*.   If you was maw gel and took the word aht o me mahth lawk thet, Aw'd give you sathink youd feel urtin, Aw would. *[To Adolphus]*. You tike maw tip, mite. Stop er jawr; or youll doy afoah your tawm *[With intense expression]*. Wore aht: thets wot youll be: wore aht. *[He goes away through the gate]*.

CUSINS *[looking after him]*.   I wonder!

BARBARA.   Dolly! *[indignant, in her mother's manner]*.

CUSINS.   Yes, my dear, it's very wearing to be in love with you. If it lasts, I quite think I shall die young.

BARBARA. Should you mind?

CUSINS. Not at all. *[He is suddenly softened, and kisses her over the drum, evidently not for the first time, as people cannot kiss over a big drum without practice. Undershaft coughs].*

BARBARA. It's all right, papa, weve not forgotten you. Dolly: explain the place to papa: I havnt time. *[She goes busily into the shelter].*

*Undershaft and Adolphus now have the yard to themselves. Undershaft, seated on a form, and still keenly attentive, looks hard at Adolphus. Adolphus looks hard at him.*

UNDERSHAFT. I fancy you guess something of what is in my mind, Mr Cusins. *[Cusins flourishes his drumsticks as if in the act of beating a lively rataplan, but makes no sound].* Exactly so. But suppose Barbara finds you out!

CUSINS. You know, I do not admit that I am imposing on Barbara. I am quite genuinely interested in the views of the Salvation Army. The fact is, I am a sort of collector of religions; and the curious thing is that I find I can believe them all. By the way, have you any religion?

UNDERSHAFT. Yes.

CUSINS. Anything out of the common?

UNDERSHAFT. Only that there are two things necessary to Salvation.

CUSINS *[disappointed, but polite].* Ah, the Church Catechism. Charles Lomax also belongs to the Established Church.

UNDERSHAFT. The two things are –

CUSINS. Baptism and –

UNDERSHAFT. No. Money and gunpowder.

CUSINS *[surprised, but interested].* That is the general opinion of our governing classes. The novelty is in hearing any man confess it.

UNDERSHAFT. Just so.

CUSINS. Excuse me: is there any place in your religion for honor, justice, truth, love, mercy and so forth?

UNDERSHAFT. Yes: they are the graces and luxuries of a rich, strong, and safe life.

CUSINS. Suppose one is forced to choose between them and money or gunpowder?

UNDERSHAFT. Choose money and gunpowder; for without enough of both you cannot afford the others.

CUSINS. That is your religion?

UNDERSHAFT. Yes.

*The cadence of this reply makes a full close in the conversation, Cusins twists his face dubiously and contemplates Undershaft. Undershaft contemplates him.*

CUSINS. Barbara wont stand that. You will have to choose between your religion and Barbara.

UNDERSHAFT. So will you, my friend. She will find out that that drum of yours is hollow.

CUSINS. Father Undershaft: you are mistaken: I am a sincere Salvationist. You do not understand the Salvation Army. It is the army of joy, of love, of courage: it has banished the fear and remorse and despair of the old hell-ridden evangelical sects: it marches to fight the devil with trumpet and drum, with music and dancing, with banner and palm, as becomes a sally from heaven by its happy garrison. It picks the waster out of the public house and makes a man of him: it finds a worm wriggling in a back kitchen, and lo! a woman! Men and women of rank too, sons and daughters of the Highest. It takes the poor professor of Greek, the most artificial and self-suppressed of human creatures, from his meal of roots, and lets loose the rhapsodist in him; reveals the true worship of Dionysos to him; sends him down the public street drumming dithyrambs *[he plays a thundering flourish on the drum]*.

UNDERSHAFT.   You will alarm the shelter.

CUSINS.   Oh, they are accustomed to these sudden ecstasies. However, if the drum worries you – *[he pockets the drumsticks; unhooks the drum; and stands it on the ground opposite the gateway]*.

UNDERSHAFT.   Thank you.

CUSINS.   You remember what Euripides says about your money and gunpowder?

UNDERSHAFT.   No.

CUSINS *[declaiming]*.

> One and another
> In money and guns may outpass his brother;
> And men in their millions float and flow
> And seethe with a million hopes as leaven;
> And they win their will; or they miss their will;
> And their hopes are dead or are pined for still;
> But who'er can know
> As the long days go
> That to live is happy, has found his heaven.

My translation: what do you think of it?

UNDERSHAFT.   I think, my friend, that if you wish to know, as the long days go, that to live is happy, you must first acquire money enough for a decent life, and power enough to be your own master.

CUSINS.   You are damnably discouraging. *[He resumes his declamation]*.

> Is it so hard a thing to see
> That the spirit of God – whate'er it be –
> The law that abides and changes not, ages long,
> The Eternal and Nature-born: these things be strong?
> What else is Wisdom? What of Man's endeavor,
> Or God's high grace so lovely and so great?
> To stand from fear set free? to breath and wait?
> To hold a hand uplifted over Fate?
> And shall not Barbara be loved for ever?

UNDERSHAFT.   Euripides mentions Barbara, does he?

CUSINS. It is a fair translation. The word means Loveliness.

UNDERSHAFT. May I ask – as Barbara's father – how much a year she is to be loved for ever on?

CUSINS. As for Barbara's father, that is more your affair than mine. I can feed her by teaching Greek: that is about all.

UNDERSHAFT. Do you consider it a good match for her?

CUSINS [*with polite obstinacy*]. Mr Undershaft: I am in many ways a weak, timid, ineffectual person; and my health is far from satisfactory. But whenever I feel that I must have anything, I get it, sooner or later. I feel that way about Barbara. I dont like marriage: I feel intensely afraid of it; and I dont know what I shall do with Barbara or what she will do with me. But I feel that I and nobody else must marry her. Please regard that as settled. – Not that I wish to be arbitrary; but why should I waste your time in discussing what is inevitable?

UNDERSHAFT. You mean that you will stick at nothing: not even the conversion of the Salvation Army to the worship of Dionysos.

CUSINS. The business of the Salvation Army is to save, not to wrangle about the name of the pathfinder. Dionysos or another: what does it matter?

UNDERSHAFT [*rising and approaching him*]. Professor Cusins: you are a young man after my own heart.

CUSINS. Mr Undershaft: you are, as far as I am able to gather, a most infernal old rascal; but you appeal very strongly to my sense of ironic humor.

*Undershaft mutely offers his hand. They shake.*

UNDERSHAFT [*suddenly concentrating himself*]. And now to business.

CUSINS. Pardon me. We are discussing religion. Why go back to such an uninteresting and unimportant subject as business?

UNDERSHAFT. Religion is our business at present, because it is through religion alone that we can win Barbara.

CUSINS. Have you, too, fallen in love with Barbara?

UNDERSHAFT. Yes, with a father's love.

CUSINS. A father's love for a grown-up daughter is the most dangerous of all infatuations. I apologize for mentioning my own pale, coy, mistrustful fancy in the same breath with it.

UNDERSHAFT. Keep to the point. We have to win her; and we are neither of us Methodists.

CUSINS. That doesnt matter. The power Barbara wields here – the power that wields Barbara herself – is not Calvinism, not Presbyterianism, not Methodism –

UNDERSHAFT. Not Greek Paganism either, eh?

CUSINS. I admit that. Barbara is quite original in her religion.

UNDERSHAFT [*triumphantly*]. Aha! Barbara Undershaft would be. Her inspiration comes from within herself.

CUSINS. How do you suppose it got there?

UNDERSHAFT [*in towering excitement*]. It is the Undershaft inheritance. I shall hand on my torch to my daughter. She shall make my converts and preach my gospel –

CUSINS. What! Money and gunpowder!

UNDERSHAFT. Yes, money and gunpowder. Freedom and power. Command of life and command of death.

CUSINS [*urbanely: trying to bring him down to earth*]. This is extremely interesting, Mr Undershaft. Of course you know that you are mad.

UNDERSHAFT [*with redoubled force*]. And you?

CUSINS. Oh, mad as a hatter. You are welcome to my secret since I have discovered yours. But I am astonished. Can a madman make cannons?

UNDERSHAFT. Would anyone else than a madman make them? And now [*with surging energy*] question for question. Can a sane man translate Euripides?

CUSINS. No.

UNDERSHAFT [*seizing him by the shoulder*]. Can a sane woman make a man of a waster or a woman of a worm?

CUSINS [*reeling before the storm*]. Father Colossus – Mammoth Millionaire–

UNDERSHAFT [*pressing him*]. Are there two mad people or three in this Salvation shelter today?

CUSINS. You mean Barbara is as mad as we are?

UNDERSHAFT [*pushing him lightly off and resuming his equanimity suddenly and completely*]. Pooh, Professor! let us call things by their proper names. I am a millionaire; you are a poet: Barbara is a savior of souls. What have we three to do with the common mob of slaves and idolators? [*He sits down again with a shrug of contempt for the mob*].

CUSINS. Take care! Barbara is in love with the common people. So am I. Have you never felt the romance of that love?

UNDERSHAFT [*cold and sardonic*]. Have you ever been in love with Poverty, like St Francis? Have you ever been in love with Dirt, like St Simeon! Have you ever been in love with disease and suffering, like our nurses and philanthropists? Such passions are not virtues, but the most unnatural of all the vices. This love of the common people may please an earl's granddaughter and a university professor; but I have been a common man and a poor man; and it has no romance for me. Leave it to the poor to pretend that poverty is a blessing: leave it to the coward to make a religion of his cowardice by preaching humility: we know better than that. We three must stand together above the common people: how else can we help their children to climb up beside us? Barbara must belong to us, not to the Salvation Army.

CUSINS. Well, I can only say that if you think you will get her away from the Salvation Army by talking to her as you have been talking to me, you dont know Barbara.

UNDERSHAFT. My friend: I never ask for what I can buy.

CUSINS [*in a white fury*].   Do I understand you to imply that you can buy
  Barbara?
UNDERSHAFT.   No; but I can buy the Salvation Army.
CUSINS.   Quite impossible.
UNDERSHAFT.   You shall see. All religious organizations exist by selling
  themselves to the rich.
CUSINS.   Not the Army. That is the Church of the poor.
UNDERSHAFT.   All the more reason for buying it.
CUSINS.   I dont think you quite know what the Army does for the poor.
UNDERSHAFT.   Oh yes I do. It draws their teeth: that is enough for me as
  a man of business.
CUSINS.   Nonsense! It makes them sober –
UNDERSHAFT.   I prefer sober workmen. The profits are larger.
CUSINS.   – honest –
UNDERSHAFT.   Honest workmen are the most economical.
CUSINS.   – attached to their homes –
UNDERSHAFT.   So much the better: they will put up with anything sooner
  than change their shop.
CUSINS.   – happy –
UNDERSHAFT.   An invaluable safeguard against revolution.
CUSINS.   – unselfish –
UNDERSHAFT.   Indifferent to their own interests, which suits me exactly.
CUSINS.   – with their thoughts on heavenly things –
UNDERSHAFT [*rising*].   And not on Trade Unionism nor Socialism. Excellent.
CUSINS [*revolted*].   You really are an infernal old rascal.
UNDERSHAFT [*indicating Peter Shirley, who has just come from the shelter and
  strolled dejectedly down the yard between them*].   And this is an honest man!
SHIRLEY.   Yes; and what av I got by it? [*he passes on bitterly and sits on the
  form, in the corner of the penthouse*].
    *Snobby Price, beaming sanctimoniously, and Jenny Hill, with a tambourine
  full of coppers, come from the shelter and go to the drum, on which Jenny begins to
  count the money.*
UNDERSHAFT [*replying to Shirley*].   Oh, your employers must have got a good
  deal by it from first to last. [*He sits on the table, with one foot on the side form,
  Cusins, overwhelmed, sits down on the same form nearer the shelter. Barbara comes
  from the shelter to the middle of the yard. She is excited and a little overwrought*].
BARBARA.   Weve just had a splendid experience meeting at the other gate
  in Cripps's lane. Ive hardly ever seen them so much moved as they were
  by your confession, Mr Price.
PRICE.   I could almost be glad of my past wickedness if I could believe
  that it would elp to keep hathers stright.
BARBARA.   So it will, Snobby. How much, Jenny?
JENNY.   Four and tenpence, Major.
BARBARA.   Oh Snobby, if you had given your poor mother just one more
  kick, we should have got the whole five shillings!

PRICE.   If she heard you say that, miss, she'd be sorry I didnt. But I'm glad. Oh what a joy it will be to her when she hears I'm saved!

UNDERSHAFT.   Shall I contribute the odd twopence, Barbara? The millionaire's mite, eh? [He takes a couple of pennies from his pocket].

BARBARA.   How did you make that twopence?

UNDERSHAFT.   As usual. By selling cannons, torpedoes, submarines, and my new patent Grand Duke hand grenade.

BARBARA.   Put it back in your pocket. You cant buy your salvation here for twopence: you must work it out.

UNDERSHAFT.   Is twopence not enough? I can afford a little more, if you press me.

BARBARA.   Two million millions would not be enough. There is bad blood on your hands; and nothing but good blood can cleanse them. Money is no use. Take it away. [She turns to Cusins].   Dolly: you must write another letter for me to the papers. [He makes a wry face]. Yes: I know you dont like it; but it must be done. The starvation this winter is beating us: everybody is unemployed. The General says we must close this shelter if we cant get more money. I force the collections at the meetings until I am ashamed: dont I, Snobby?

PRICE.   It's a fair treat to see you work it, miss. The way you got them up from three-and-six to four-and-ten with that hymn, penny by penny and verse by verse, was a caution. Not a Cheap Jack on Mile End Waste could touch you at it.

BARBARA.   Yes; but I wish we could do without it. I am getting at last to think more of the collection than of the people's souls. And what are those hatfuls of pence and halfpence? We want thousands! tens of thousands! hundreds of thousands! I want to convert people, not to be always begging for the Army in a way I'd die sooner than beg for myself.

UNDERSHAFT [in profound irony].   Genuine unselfishness is capable of anything, my dear.

BARBARA [unsuspectingly, as she turns away to take the money from the drum and put it in a cash bag she carries].   Yes, isnt it? [Undershaft looks sardonically at Cusins].

CUSINS [aside to Undershaft].   Mephistopheles! Machiavelli!

BARBARA [tears coming into her eyes as she ties the bag and pockets it].   How are we to feed them? I cant talk religion to a man with bodily hunger in his eyes. [Almost breaking down]. It's frightful.

JENNY [running to her].   Major, dear –

BARBARA [rebounding].   No: dont comfort me. It will be all right. We shall get the money.

UNDERSHAFT.   How?

JENNY.   By praying for it, of course. Mrs Baines says she prayed for it last night; and she has never prayed for it in vain: never once. [She goes to the gate and looks out into the street].

BARBARA [*who has dried her eyes and regained her composure*]. By the way, dad, Mrs Baines has come to march with us to our big meeting this afternoon; and she is very anxious to meet you, for some reason or other. Perhaps she'll convert you.

UNDERSHAFT. I shall be delighted, my dear.

JENNY [*at the gate: excitedly*]. Major! Major! heres that man back again.

BARBARA. What man?

JENNY. The man that hit me. Oh, I hope he's coming back to join us.

*Bill Walker, with frost on his jacket, comes through the gate, his hands deep in his pockets and his chin sunk between his shoulders, like a cleaned-out gambler. He halts between Barbara and the drum.*

BARBARA. Hullo, Bill! Back already!

BILL [*nagging at her*]. Bin talkin ever sence, ev you?

BARBARA. Pretty nearly. Well, has Todger paid you out for poor Jenny's jaw?

BILL. Nao e aint.

BARBARA. I thought your jacket looked a bit snowy.

BILL. Sao it is snaowy. You want to knaow where the snaow cam from, downt you?

BARBARA. Yes.

BILL. Well, it cam from orf the grahnd in Pawkinses Corner in Kennintahn. It got rabbed orf be maw shaoulders: see?

BARBARA. Pity you didnt rub some off with your knees, Bill! That would have done you a lot of good.

BILL [*with sour mirthless humor*]. Aw was sivin anather menn's knees at the tawm. E was kneelin on moy ed, e was.

JENNY. Who was kneeling on your head?

BILL. Todger was. E was pryin for me: pryin camfortable wiv me as a cawpet. Sow was Mog. Sao was the aol bloomin meetin. Mog she sez 'Ow Lawd brike is stabborn sperrit; bat downt urt is dear art.' Thet was wot she said. 'Downt urt is dear art'! An er blowk – thirteen stun four! – kneelin wiv all is wight on me. Fanny, aint it?

JENNY. Oh no. We're so sorry, Mr Walker.

BARBARA [*enjoying it frankly*]. Nonsense! of course it's funny. Served you right, Bill! You must have done something to him first.

BILL [*doggedly*]. Aw did wot Aw said Aw'd do. Aw spit in is eye. E looks ap at the skoy and sez, 'Ow that Aw should be fahnd worthy to be spit upon for the gospel's sike!' e sez; an Mog sez 'Glaory Allelloolier!'; an then e called me Braddher, an dahned me as if Aw was a kid and e was me mather worshin me a Setterda nawt. Aw ednt jast nao shaow wiv im at all. Arf the street pryed; and the tather arf larfed fit to split theirselves. [*To Barbara*]. There! you are settisfawd nah?

BARBARA [*her eyes dancing*]. Wish I'd been there, Bill.

BILL. Yus: youd a got in a hextra bit o talk on me, wouldnt you?

JENNY. I'm so sorry, Mr Walker.

BILL [*fiercely*]. Downt you gow being sorry for me: youve no call. Listen eah. Aw browk your jawr.

JENNY. No, it didnt hurt me: indeed it didnt, except for a moment. It was only that I was frightened.

BILL. Aw downt want to be forgive be you, or be ennybody. Wot Aw did Aw'll py for. Aw trawd to gat me aown jawr browk to settisfaw you –

JENNY [*distressed*]. Oh no –

BILL [*impatiently*]. Tell y' Aw did: cawnt you listen to wots bein taold you? All Aw got be it was bein mide a sawt of in the pablic street for me pines. Well, if Aw cawnt settisfaw you one wy, Aw ken anather. Listen eah! Aw ed two quid sived agen the frost; an Awve a pahnd of it left. A mite o mawn last week ed words with the judy e's gowing to merry. E give er wot-for; an e's bin fawnd fifteen bob. E ed a rawt to itt er cause they was gowin to be merrid; but Ad ednt nao rawt to itt you; sao put anather fawv bob on an call it a pahnd's worth. [*He produces a sovereign*]. Eahs the manney. Tike it; and lets ev no more o your forgivin an prying and your Mijor jawrin me. Let wot Aw dan be dan an pide for; and let there be a end of it.

JENNY. Oh, I couldnt take it, Mr Walker. But if you would give a shilling or two to poor Rummy Mitchens! you really did hurt her; and she's old.

BILL [*contemptuously*]. Not lawkly. Aw'd give her anather as soon as look at er. Let her ev the lawr o me as she threatened! She aint forgiven me: not mach. Wot Aw dan to er is not on my mawnd – wot she [*indicating Barbara*] mawt call on me conscience – no more than stickin a pig. It's this Christian gime o yours that Aw wownt ev plyed agen me: this bloomin forgivin an neggin an jawrin that mikes a menn thet sore that iz lawf's a burdn to im. Aw wownt ev it, Aw tell you; sao tike your manney and stop thraowin your silly beshed fice hap agen me.

JENNY. Major: may I take a little of it for the Army?

BARBARA. No: the Army is not to be bought. We want your soul, Bill; and we'll take nothing less.

BILL [*bitterly*]. Aw knaow. Me an maw few shillins is not good enaff for you. Youre a earl's grendorter, you are. Nathink less than a andered pahnd for you.

UNDERSHAFT. Come, Barbara! you could do a great deal of good with a hundred pounds. If you will set this gentleman's mind at ease by taking his pound, I will give the other ninety-nine.

*Bill, dazed by such opulence, instinctively touches his cap.*

BARBARA. Oh, youre too extravagant, papa. Bill offers twenty pieces of silver. All you need offer is the other ten. That will make the standard price to buy anybody who's for sale. I'm not; and the Army's not. [*To Bill*] Youll never have another quiet moment, Bill, until you come round to us. You cant stand out against your salvation.

BILL [*sullenly*]. Aw cawnt stend aht agen music awl wrastlers and awtful tangued women. Awve offered to py. Aw can do no more. Tike it or leave it. There it is. *[He throws the sovereign on the drum, and sits down on the horse-trough. The coin fascinates Snobby Price, who takes an early opportunity of dropping his cap on it].*

*Mrs Baines comes from the shelter. She is dressed as a Salvation Army Commissioner. She is an earnest looking woman of about 40, with a caressing, urgent voice, and an appealing manner.*

BARBARA. This is my father, Mrs Baines *[Undershaft comes from the table, taking his hat off with marked civility].* Try what you can do with him. He wont listen to me, because he remembers what a fool I was when I was a baby. *[She leaves them together and chats with Jenny].*

MRS BAINES. Have you been shewn over the shelter, Mr Undershaft? You know the work we're doing, of course.

UNDERSHAFT *[very civilly].* The whole nation knows it, Mrs Baines.

MRS BAINES. No, sir: the whole nation does not know it, or we should not be crippled as we are for want of money to carry our work through the length and breadth of the land. Let me tell you that there would have been rioting this winter in London but for us.

UNDERSHAFT. You really think so?

MRS BAINES. I know it. I remember 1886, when you rich gentlemen hardened your hearts against the cry of the poor. They broke the windows of your clubs in Pall Mall.

UNDERSHAFT *[gleaming with approval of their method].* And the Mansion House Fund went up next day from thirty thousand pounds to seventy-nine thousand! I remember quite well.

MRS BAINES. Well, wont you help me to get at the people? They wont break windows then. Come here, Price. Let me shew you to this gentleman *[Price comes to be inspected].* Do you remember the window breaking?

PRICE. My ole father thought it was the revolution, maam.

MRS BAINES. Would you break windows now?

PRICE. Oh no, maam. The windows of eaven av bin opened to me. I know now that the rich man is a sinner like myself.

RUMMY *[appearing above at the loft door].* Snobby Price!

SNOBBY. Wot is it?

RUMMY. Your mother's askin for you at the other gate in Cripps's Lane. She's heard about your confession *[Price turns pale].*

MRS BAINES. Go, Mr Price; and pray with her.

JENNY. You can go through the shelter, Snobby.

PRICE *[to Mrs Baines].* I couldnt face her now, maam, with all the weight of my sins fresh on me. Tell her she'll find her son at ome, waitin for her in prayer. *[He skulks off through the gate, incidentally stealing the sovereign on his way out by picking up his cap from the drum].*

MRS BAINES *[with swimming eyes].* You see how we take the anger and the bitterness against you out of their hearts, Mr Undershaft.

UNDERSHAFT. It is certainly most convenient and gratifying to all large employers of labor, Mrs Baines.

MRS BAINES. Barbara: Jenny: I have good news: most wonderful news.

*[Jenny runs to her]*. My prayers have been answered. I told you they would, Jenny, didnt I?

JENNY. Yes, yes.

BARBARA *[moving nearer to the drum]*. Have we got money enough to keep the shelter open?

MRS BAINES. I hope we shall have enough to keep all the shelters open. Lord Saxmundham has promised us five thousand pounds –

BARBARA. Hooray!

JENNY. Glory!

MRS BAINES. – if –

BARBARA. 'If!' If what?

MRS BAINES. – if five other gentlemen will give a thousand each to make it up to ten thousand.

BARBARA. Who is Lord Saxmundham? I never heard of him.

UNDERSHAFT *[who has pricked up his ears at the peer's name, and is now watching Barbara curiously]*. A new creation, my dear. You have heard of Sir Horace Bodger?

BARBARA. Bodger! Do you mean the distiller? Bodger's whisky!

UNDERSHAFT. That is the man. He is one of the greatest of our public benefactors. He restored the cathedral at Hakington. They made him a baronet for that. He gave half a million to the funds of his party: they made him a baron for that.

SHIRLEY. What will they give him for the five thousand?

UNDERSHAFT. There is nothing left to give him. So the five thousand, I should think, is to save his soul.

MRS BAINES. Heaven grant it may! Oh Mr Undershaft, you have some very rich friends. Cant you help us towards the other five thousand? We are going to hold a great meeting this afternoon at the Assembly Hall in the Mile End Road. If I could only announce that one gentleman had come forward to support Lord Saxmundham, others would follow. Dont you know somebody? couldnt you? wouldnt you? *[her eyes fill with tears]* oh, think of those poor people, Mr Undershaft: think of how much it means to them, and how little to a great man like you.

UNDERSHAFT *[sardonically gallant]*. Mrs Baines: you are irresistible. I cant disappoint you; and I cant deny myself the satisfaction of making Bodger pay up. You shall have your five thousand pounds.

MRS BAINES. Thank God!

UNDERSHAFT. You dont thank me?

MRS BAINES. Oh sir, dont try to be cynical: dont be ashamed of being a good man. The Lord will bless you abundantly; and our prayers will be like a strong fortification round you all the days of your life. *[With a touch of caution]*. You will let me have the cheque to shew at the meeting, won't you? Jenny: go in and fetch a pen and ink. *[Jenny runs to the shelter door]*.

UNDERSHAFT. Do not disturb Miss Hill: I have a fountain pen *[Jenny halts.*

*He sits at the table and writes the cheque. Cusins rises to make room for him. They all watch him silently].*

BILL *[cynically, aside to Barbara, his voice and accent horribly debased].* Wot prawce selvytion nah?

BARBARA. Stop. *[Undershaft stops writing: they all turn to her in surprise].* Mrs Baines: are you really going to take this money?

MRS BAINES *[astonished].* Why not, dear?

BARBARA. Why not! Do you know what my father is? Have you forgotten that Lord Saxmundham is Bodger the whisky man? Do you remember how we implored the County Council to stop him from writing Bodger's Whisky in letters of fire against the sky; so that the poor drink-ruined creatures on the Embankment could not wake up from their snatches of sleep without being reminded of their deadly thirst by that wicked sky sign? Do you know that the worst thing I have had to fight here is not the devil, but Bodger, Bodger, Bodger, with his whisky, his distilleries, and his tied houses? Are you going to make our shelter another tied house for him, and ask me to keep it?

BILL. Rotten dranken whisky it is too.

MRS BAINES. Dear Barbara: Lord Saxmundham has a soul to be saved like any of us. If heaven has found the way to make a good use of his money, are we to set ourselves up against the answer to our prayers?

BARBARA. I know he has a soul to be saved. Let him come down here; and I'll do my best to help him to his salvation. But he wants to send his cheque down to buy us, and go on being as wicked as ever.

UNDERSHAFT *[with a reasonableness which Cusins alone perceives to be ironical].* My dear Barbara: alcohol is a very necessary article. It heals the sick –

BARBARA. It does nothing of the sort.

UNDERSHAFT. Well, it assists the doctor: that is perhaps a less questionable way of putting it. It makes life bearable to millions of people who could not endure their existence if they were quite sober. It enables Parliament to do things at eleven at night that no sane person would do at eleven in the morning. Is it Bodger's fault that this inestimable gift is deplorably abused by less than one per cent of the poor? *[He turns again to the table; signs the cheque; and crosses it].*

MRS BAINES. Barbara: will there be less drinking or more if all those poor souls we are saving come tomorrow and find the doors of our shelters shut in their faces? Lord Saxmundham gives us the money to stop drinking – to take his own business from him.

CUSINS *[impishly].* Pure self-sacrifice on Bodger's part, clearly! Bless dear Bodger! *[Barbara almost breaks down as Adolphus, too, fails her].*

UNDERSHAFT *[tearing out the cheque and pocketing the book as he rises and goes past Cusins to Mrs Baines].* I also, Mrs Baines, may claim a little disinterestedness. Think of my business! think of the widows and orphans! the men and lads torn to pieces with shrapnel and poisoned with lyddite! *[Mrs Baines shrinks; but he goes on remorselessly]* the oceans of blood, not one drop of which is shed in a really just cause! the ravaged crops! the peaceful peasants forced, women and men, to till their fields under the fire of opposing armies on pain of starvation! the bad blood of the fierce little cowards at home who egg on others to fight for the gratification of their national vanity! All this makes money for me: I am never richer, never busier than when the papers are full of it. Well, it is your work to preach peace on earth and good will to men. [*Mrs Baines's face lights up again*]. Every convert you make is a vote against war. [*Her lips move in prayer*]. Yet I give you this money to help you to hasten my own commercial ruin. [*He gives her the cheque*].

CUSINS [*mounting the form in an ecstasy of mischief*]. The millennium will be inaugurated by the unselfishness of Undershaft and Bodger. Oh be joyful! [*He takes the drum-sticks from his pocket and flourishes them*].

MRS BAINES [*taking the cheque*]. The longer I live the more proof I see that there is an Infinite Goodness that turns everything to the work of salvation sooner or later. Who would have thought that any good could have come out of war and drink? And yet their profits are brought today to the feet of salvation to do its blessed work. [*She is affected to tears*].

JENNY [*running to Mrs Baines and throwing her arms round her*]. Oh dear! how blessed, how glorious it all is!

CUSINS [*in a convulsion of irony*]. Let us seize this unspeakable moment. Let us march to the great meeting at once. Excuse me just an instant. [*He rushes into the shelter. Jenny takes her tambourine from the drum head*].

MRS BAINES. Mr Undershaft: have you ever seen a thousand people fall on their knees with one impulse and pray? Come with us to the meeting. Barbara shall tell them that the Army is saved, and saved through you.

CUSINS [*returning impetuously from the shelter with a flag and a trombone, and coming between Mrs Baines and Undershaft*]. You shall carry the flag down the first street, Mrs Baines [*he gives her the flag*]. Mr Undershaft is a gifted trombonist: he shall intone an Olympian diapason to the West Ham Salvation March. [*Aside to Undershaft, as he forces the trombone on him*]. Blow, Machiavelli, blow.

UNDERSHAFT [*aside to him, as he takes the trombone*]. The trumpet in Zion! [*Cusins rushes to the drum, which he takes up and puts on. Undershaft continues, aloud*]. I will do my best. I could vamp a bass if I knew the tune.

CUSINS. It is a wedding chorus from one of Donizetti's operas; but we have converted it. We convert everything to good here, including Bodger. You remember the chorus. 'For thee immense rejoicing – immenso giubilo – immenso giubilo.' [*With drum obbligato*]. Rum tum ti tum tum, tum tum ti ta –

BARBARA. Dolly: you are breaking my heart.

CUSINS. What is a broken heart more or less here? Dionysos Undershaft has descended. I am possessed.

MRS BAINES. Come, Barbara: I must have my dear Major to carry the flag with me.

JENNY. Yes, yes, Major darling.

CUSINS *[snatches the tambourine out of Jenny's hand and mutely offers it to Barbara]*.

BARBARA *[coming forward a little as she puts the offer behind her with a shudder, whilst Cusins recklessly tosses the tambourine back to Jenny and goes to the gate]*. I cant come.

JENNY. Not come!

MRS BAINES *[with tears in her eyes]*. Barbara: do you think I am wrong to take the money?

BARBARA *[impulsively going to her and kissing her]*. No, no: God help you, dear, you must: you are saving the Army. Go; and may you have a great meeting!

JENNY. But arnt you coming?

BARBARA. No. *[She begins taking off the silver S brooch from her collar]*.

MRS BAINES. Barbara: what are you doing?

JENNY. Why are you taking your badge off? You cant be going to leave us, Major.

BARBARA *[quietly]*. Father: come here.

UNDERSHAFT *[coming to her]*. My dear! *[Seeing that she is going to pin the badge on his collar, he retreats to the penthouse in some alarm]*.

BARBARA *[following him]*. Dont be frightened. *[She pins the badge on and steps back towards the table, shewing him to the others]*. There! It's not much for £5000, is it?

MRS BAINES. Barbara: if you wont come and pray with us, promise me you will pray for us.

BARBARA. I cant pray now. Perhaps I shall never pray again.

MRS BAINES. Barbara!

JENNY. Major!

BARBARA *[almost delirious]*. I cant bear any more. Quick march!

CUSINS *[calling to the procession in the street outside]*. Off we go. Play up, there! Immenso giubilo. *[He gives the time with his drum; and the band strikes up the march, which rapidly becomes more distant as the procession moves briskly away]*.

MRS BAINES. I must go, dear. Youre overworked: you will be all right tomorrow. We'll never lose you. Now Jenny: step out with the old flag. Blood and Fire! *[She marches out through the gate with her flag]*.

JENNY. Glory Hallelujah! *[flourishing her tambourine and marching]*.

UNDERSHAFT *[to Cusins, as he marches out past him easing the slide of his trombone]*. 'My ducats and my daughter'!

CUSINS *[following him out]*. Money and gunpowder!

BARBARA. Drunkenness and Murder! My God: why hast thou forsaken me?

    *She sinks on the form with her face buried in her hands. The march passes away into silence. Bill Walker steals across to her.*

BILL *[taunting]*. Wot prawce selvytion nah?

SHIRLEY. Dont you hit her when she's down.

BILL. She itt me wen aw wiz dahn. Waw shouldnt Aw git a bit o me aown beck?

BARBARA [raising her head]. I didnt take your money, Bill. [She crosses the yard to the gate and turns her back on the two men to hide her face from them].

BILL [sneering after her]. Naow, it warnt enaff for you. [Turning to the drum, he misses the money]. Ellow! If you aint took it sammun else ez. Weres it gorn? Bly me if Jenny Ill didnt tike it arter all!

RUMMY [screaming at him from the loft]. You lie, you dirty blackguard! Snobby Price pinched it off the drum when he took up his cap. I was up here all the time an see im do it.

BILL. Wot! Stowl maw manney! Waw didnt you call thief on him, you silly aold macker you?

RUMMY. To serve you aht for ittin me acrost the fice. It's cost y'pahnd, that az. [Raising a pæan of squalid triumph]. I done you. I'm even with you.

Uve ad it aht o y – [Bill snatches up Shirley's mug and hurls it at her. She slams the loft door and vanishes. The mug smashes against the door and falls in fragments].

BILL [beginning to chuckle]. Tell us, aol menn, wot o'clock this mawnin was it wen im as they call Snobby Prawce was sived?

BARBARA [turning to him more composedly, and with unspoiled sweetness]. About half past twelve, Bill. And he pinched your pound at a quarter to two. I know. Well, you cant afford to lose it. I'll send it to you.

BILL [his voice and accent suddenly improving]. Not if Aw wiz to stawve for it. Aw aint to be bought.

SHIRLEY. Aint you? Youd sell yourself to the devil for a pint o beer; only there aint no devil to make the offer.

BILL [unashamed]. Sao Aw would, mite, and often ev, cheerful. But she cawnt baw me. [Approaching Barbara]. You wanted maw saoul, did you? Well, you aint got it.

BARBARA. I nearly got it, Bill. But weve sold it back to you for ten thousand pounds.

SHIRLEY. And dear at the money!

BARBARA. No, Peter: it was worth more than money.

BILL [salvationproof]. It's nao good: you cawnt get rahnd me nah. Aw downt blieve in it; and Awve seen tody that Aw was rawt. [Going]. Sao long, aol soupkitchener! Ta, ta, Mijor Earl's Grendorter! [Turning at the gate]. Wot prawce selvytion nah? Snobby Prawce! Ha! Ha!

BARBARA [offering her hand]. Goodbye, Bill.

BILL [taken aback, half plucks his cap off; then shoves it on again defiantly]. Git aht. [Barbara drops her hand, discouraged. He has a twinge of remorse]. But thets aw rawt, you knaow. Nathink pasnl. Naow mallice. Sao long, Judy. [He goes].

BARBARA. No malice. So long, Bill.

SHIRLEY [*shaking his head*]. You make too much of him, miss, in your innocence.

BARBARA [*going to him*]. Peter: I'm like you now. Cleaned out, and lost my job.

SHIRLEY. Youve youth an hope. Thats two better than me.

BARBARA. I'll get you a job, Peter. Thats hope for you: the youth will have to be enough for me. [*She counts her money*]. I have just enough left for two teas at Lockharts, a Rowton doss for you, and my tram and bus home. [*He frowns and rises with offended pride. She takes his arm*]. Don't be proud, Peter: it's sharing between friends. And promise me youll talk to me and not let me cry. [*She draws him towards the gate*].

SHIRLEY. Well, I'm not accustomed to talk to the like of you –

BARBARA [*urgently*]. Yes, yes: you must talk to me. Tell me about Tom Paine's books and Bradlaugh's lectures. Come along.

SHIRLEY. Ah, if you would only read Tom Paine in the proper spirit, miss! [*They go out through the gate together*].

## ACT III

*Next day after lunch Lady Britomart is writing in the library in Wilton Crescent. Sarah is reading in the armchair near the window. Barbara, in ordinary fashionable dress, pale and brooding, is on the settee. Charles Lomax enters. He starts on seeing Barbara fashionably attired and in low spirits.*

LOMAX. Youve left off your uniform!

    *Barbara says nothing; but an expression of pain passes over her face.*

LADY BRITOMART [*warning him in low tones to be careful*]. Charles!

LOMAX [*much concerned, coming behind the settee and bending sympathetically over Barbara*]. I'm awfully sorry, Barbara. You know I helped you all I could with the concertina and so forth. [*Momentously*]. Still, I have never shut my eyes to the fact that there is a certain amount of tosh about the Salvation Army. Now the claims of the Church of England –

LADY BRITOMART. Thats enough, Charles. Speak of something suited to your mental capacity.

LOMAX. But surely the Church of England is suited to all our capacities.

BARBARA *pressing his hand*. Thank you for your sympathy, Cholly. Now go and spoon with Sarah.

LOMAX [*dragging a chair from the writing table and seating himself affectionately by Sarah's side*]. How is my ownest today?

SARAH. I wish you wouldnt tell Cholly to do things, Barbara. He always comes straight and does them. Cholly: we're going to the works this afternoon.

LOMAX. What works?

SARAH. The cannon works.

LOMAX. What? your governor's shop!

SARAH. Yes.

LOMAX. Oh I say!

*Cusins enters in poor condition. He also starts visibly when he sees Barbara without her uniform.*

BARBARA. I expected you this morning, Dolly. Didnt you guess that?

CUSINS *[sitting down beside her]*. I'm sorry. I have only just breakfasted.

SARAH. But weve just finished lunch.

BARBARA. Have you had one of your bad nights?

CUSINS. No: I had rather a good night: in fact, one of the most remarkable nights I have ever passed.

BARBARA. The meeting?

CUSINS. No: after the meeting.

LADY BRITOMART. You should have gone to bed after the meeting. What were you doing?

CUSINS. Drinking.

| LADY BRITOMART. | ⎫ | ⎧ Adolphus! |
|---|---|---|
| SARAH. | ⎬ | ⎨ Dolly! |
| BARBARA. | | Dolly! |
| LOMAX. | ⎭ | ⎩ Oh I say! |

LADY BRITOMART. What were you drinking, may I ask?

CUSINS. A most devilish kind of Spanish burgundy, warranted free from added alcohol: a Temperance burgundy in fact. Its richness in natural alcohol made any addition superfluous.

BARBARA. Are you joking, Dolly?

CUSINS *[patiently]*. No. I have been making a night of it with the nominal head of this household: that is all.

LADY BRITOMART. Andrew made you drunk!

CUSINS. No: he only provided the wine. I think it was Dionysos who made me drunk. *[To Barbara]*. I told you I was possessed.

LADY BRITOMART. Youre not sober yet. Go home to bed at once.

CUSINS. I have never before ventured to reproach you, Lady Brit; but how could you marry the Prince of Darkness?

LADY BRITOMART. It was much more excusable to marry him than to get drunk with him. That is a new accomplishment of Andrew's, by the way. He usent to drink.

CUSINS. He doesnt now. He only sat there and completed the wreck of my moral basis, the rout of my convictions, the purchase of my soul. He cares for you, Barbara. That is what makes him so dangerous to me.

BARBARA. That has nothing to do with it, Dolly. There are larger loves and diviner dreams than the fireside ones. You know that, dont you?

CUSINS. Yes: that is our understanding. I know it. I hold to it. Unless he can win me on that holier ground he may amuse me for a while; but he can get no deeper hold, strong as he is.

BARBARA. Keep to that; and the end will be right. Now tell me what happened at the meeting?

*574*

CUSINS. It was an amazing meeting. Mrs Baines almost died of emotion. Jenny Hill simply gibbered with hysteria. The Prince of Darkness played his trombone like a madman: its brazen roarings were like the laughter of the damned. 117 conversions took place then and there. They prayed with the most touching sincerity and gratitude for Bodger, and for the anonymous donor of the £5000. Your father would not let his name be given.

LOMAX. That was rather fine of the old man, you know. Most chaps would have wanted the advertisement.

CUSINS. He said all the charitable institutions would be down on him like kites on a battle-field if he gave his name.

LADY BRITOMART. Thats Andrew all over. He never does a proper thing without giving an improper reason for it.

CUSINS. He convinced me that I have all my life been doing improper things for proper reasons.

LADY BRITOMART. Adolphus: now that Barbara has left the Salvation Army, you had better leave it too. I will not have you playing that drum in the streets.

CUSINS. Your orders are already obeyed, Lady Brit.

BARBARA. Dolly: were you ever really in earnest about it? Would you have joined if you had never seen me?

CUSINS [*disingenuously*]. Well – er – well, possibly, as a collector of religions –

LOMAX [*cunningly*]. Not as a drummer, though, you know. You are a very clearheaded brainy chap, Dolly; and it must have been apparent to you that there is a certain amount of tosh about –

LADY BRITOMART. Charles: if you must drivel, drivel like a grown-up man and not like a schoolboy.

LOMAX [*out of countenance*]. Well, drivel is drivel, dont you know, whatever a man's age.

LADY BRITOMART. In good society in England, Charles, men drivel at all ages by repeating silly formulas with an air of wisdom. Schoolboys make their own formulas out of slang, like you. When they reach your age, and get political private secretaryships and things of that sort, they drop slang and get their formulas out of the Spectator or The Times. You had better confine yourself to The Times. You will find that there is a certain amount of tosh about The Times; but at least its language is reputable.

LOMAX [*overwhelmed*]. You are so awfully strong-minded, Lady Brit –

LADY BRITOMART. Rubbish! [*Morrison comes in*]. What is it?

MORRISON. If you please, my lady, Mr Undershaft has just drove up to the door.

LADY BRITOMART. Well, let him in. [*Morrison hesitates*]. Whats the matter with you?

MORRISON. Shall I announce him, my lady; or is he at home here, so to speak, my lady?

LADY BRITOMART. Announce him.

MORRISON. Thank you, my lady. You wont mind my asking, I hope. The occasion is in a manner of speaking new to me.

LADY BRITOMART. Quite right. Go and let him in.

MORRISON. Thank you, my lady. *[He withdraws]*.

LADY BRITOMART. Children: go and get ready. *[Sarah and Barbara go upstairs for their out-of-door wraps]*. Charles: go and tell Stephen to come down here in five minutes: you will find him in the drawing room. *[Charles goes]*. Adolphus: tell them to send round the carriage in about fifteen minutes. *[Adolphus goes]*.

MORRISON *[at the door]*. Mr Undershaft.

*Undershaft comes in. Morrison goes out.*

UNDERSHAFT. Alone! How fortunate!

LADY BRITOMART *[rising]*. Dont be sentimental, Andrew. Sit down. *[She sits on the settee: he sits beside her, on her left. She comes to the point before he has time to breathe]*. Sarah must have £800 a year until Charles Lomax comes into his property. Barbara will need more, and need it permanently, because Adolphus hasnt any property.

UNDERSHAFT *[resignedly]*. Yes, my dear: I will see to it. Anything else? for yourself, for instance?

LADY BRITOMART. I want to talk to you about Stephen.

UNDERSHAFT *[rather wearily]*. Dont, my dear. Stephen doesnt interest me.

LADY BRITOMART. He does interest me. He is our son.

UNDERSHAFT. Do you really think so? He has induced us to bring him into the world; but he chose his parents very incongruously, I think. I see nothing of myself in him, and less of you.

LADY BRITOMART. Andrew: Stephen is an excellent son, and a most steady, capable, highminded young man. You are simply trying to find an excuse for disinheriting him.

UNDERSHAFT. My dear Biddy: the Undershaft tradition disinherits him. It would be dishonest of me to leave the cannon foundry to my son.

LADY BRITOMART. It would be most unnatural and improper of you to leave it to anyone else, Andrew. Do you suppose this wicked and immoral tradition can be kept up for ever? Do you pretend that Stephen could not carry on the foundry just as well as all the other sons of the big business houses?

UNDERSHAFT. Yes: he could learn the office routine without understanding the business, like all the other sons; and the firm would go on by its own momentum until the real Undershaft – probably an Italian or a German – would invent a new method and cut him out.

LADY BRITOMART. There is nothing that any Italian or German could do that Stephen could not do. And Stephen at least has breeding.

UNDERSHAFT. The son of a foundling! Nonsense!

LADY BRITOMART. My son, Andrew! And even you may have good blood in your veins for all you know.

UNDERSHAFT. True. Probably I have. That is another argument in favour of a foundling.

LADY BRITOMART. Andrew: dont be aggravating. And dont be wicked. At present you are both.

UNDERSHAFT. This conversation is part of the Undershaft tradition, Biddy. Every Undershaft's wife has treated him to it ever since the house was founded. It is mere waste of breath. If the tradition be ever broken it will be for an abler man than Stephen.

LADY BRITOMART *[pouting]*. Then go away.

UNDERSHAFT *[deprecatory]*. Go away!

LADY BRITOMART. Yes: go away. If you will do nothing for Stephen, you are not wanted here. Go to your foundling, whoever he is; and look after him.

UNDERSHAFT. The fact is, Biddy –

LADY BRITOMART. Dont call me Biddy. I dont call you Andy.

UNDERSHAFT. I will not call my wife Britomart: it is not good sense. Seriously, my love, the Undershaft tradition has landed me in a difficulty. I am getting on in years; and my partner Lazarus has at last made a stand and insisted that the succession must be settled one way or the other; and of course he is quite right. You see, I havent found a fit successor yet.

LADY BRITOMART *[obstinately]*. There is Stephen.

UNDERSHAFT. Thats just it: all the foundlings I can find are exactly like Stephen.

LADY BRITOMART. Andrew!!

UNDERSHAFT. I want a man with no relations and no schooling: that is, a man who would be out of the running altogether if he were not a strong man. And I cant find him. Every blessed foundling nowadays is snapped up in his infancy by Barnardo homes, or School Board officers, or Boards of Guardians; and if he shews the least ability he is fastened on by schoolmasters; trained to win scholarships like a racehorse; crammed with secondhand ideas; drilled and disciplined in docility and what they call good taste; and lamed for life so that he is fit for nothing but teaching. If you want to keep the foundry in the family, you had better find an eligible foundling and marry him to Barbara.

LADY BRITOMART. Ah! Barbara! Your pet! You would sacrifice Stephen to Barbara.

UNDERSHAFT. Cheerfully. And you, my dear, would boil Barbara to make soup for Stephen.

LADY BRITOMART. Andrew: this is not a question of our likings and dislikings: it is a question of duty. It is your duty to make Stephen your successor.

UNDERSHAFT. Just as much as it is your duty to submit to your husband. Come, Biddy! these tricks of the governing class are of no use with me. I am one of the governing class myself; and it is a waste of time giving tracts to a missionary. I have the power in this matter; and I am not to be humbugged into using it for your purposes.

LADY BRITOMART.   Andrew: you can talk my head off; but you cant change wrong into right. And your tie is all on one side. Put it straight.

UNDERSHAFT [*disconcerted*].   It wont stay unless it's pinned [*he fumbles at it with childish grimaces*] –
   *Stephen comes in.*

STEPHEN [*at the door*].   I beg your pardon [*about to retire*].

LADY BRITOMART.   No: come in, Stephen. [*Stephen comes forward to his mother's writing table*].

UNDERSHAFT [*not very cordially*].   Good afternoon.

STEPHEN [*coldly*].   Good afternoon.

UNDERSHAFT [*to Lady Britomart*].   He knows all about the tradition, I suppose.

LADY BRITOMART.   Yes. [*To Stephen*].   It is what I told you last night, Stephen.

UNDERSHAFT [*sulkily*].   I understand you want to come into the cannon business.

STEPHEN.   *I* go into trade! Certainly not.

UNDERSHAFT [*opening his eyes, greatly eased in mind and manner*].   Oh! in that case –

LADY BRITOMART.   Cannons are not trade, Stephen. They are enterprise.

STEPHEN.   I have no intention of becoming a man of business in any sense. I have no capacity for business and no taste for it. I intend to devote myself to politics.

UNDERSHAFT [*rising*].   My dear boy: this is an immense relief to me. And I trust it may prove an equally good thing for the country. I was afraid you would consider yourself disparaged and slighted. [*He moves towards Stephen as if to shake hands with him*].

LADY BRITOMART [*rising and interposing*].   Stephen: I cannot allow you to throw away an enormous property like this.

STEPHEN [*stiffly*].   Mother: there must be an end of treating me as a child, if you please. [*Lady Britomart recoils, deeply wounded by his tone*]. Until last night I did not take your attitude seriously, because I did not think you meant it seriously. But I find now that you left me in the dark as to matters which you should have explained to me years ago. I am extremely hurt and offended. Any further discussion of my intentions had better take place with my father, as between one man and another.

LADY BRITOMART.   Stephen! [*She sits down again, her eyes filling with tears*].

UNDERSHAFT [*with grave compassion*].   You see, my dear, it is only the big men who can be treated as children.

STEPHEN.   I am sorry, mother, that you have forced me –

UNDERSHAFT [*stopping him*].   Yes, yes, yes, yes: thats all right, Stephen. She wont interfere with you any more: your independence is achieved: you have won your latchkey. Dont rub it in; and above all, dont apologize. [*He resumes his seat*]. Now what about your future, as between one man and another – I beg your pardon, Biddy: as between two men and a woman.

LADY BRITOMART [*who has pulled herself together strongly*]. I quite understand, Stephen. By all means go your own way if you feel strong enough. [*Stephen sits down magisterially in the chair at the writing table with an air of affirming his majority*].

UNDERSHAFT. It is settled that you do not ask for the succession to the cannon business.

STEPHEN. I hope it is settled that I repudiate the cannon business.

UNDERSHAFT. Come, come! dont be so devilishly sulky: it's boyish. Freedom should be generous. Besides, I owe you a fair start in life in exchange for disinheriting you. You cant become prime minister all at once. Havnt you a turn for something? What about literature, art, and so forth?

STEPHEN. I have nothing of the artist about me, either in faculty or character, thank Heaven!

UNDERSHAFT. A philosopher, perhaps? Eh?

STEPHEN. I make no such ridiculous pretension.

UNDERSHAFT. Just so. Well, there is the army, the navy, the Church, the Bar. The Bar requires some ability. What about the Bar?

STEPHEN. I have not studied law. And I am afraid I have not the necessary push – I believe that is the name barristers give to their vulgarity – for success in pleading.

UNDERSHAFT. Rather a difficult case, Stephen. Hardly anything left but the stage, is there? [*Stephen makes an impatient movement*]. Well, come! is there anything you know or care for?

STEPHEN [*rising and looking at him steadily*]. I know the difference between right and wrong.

UNDERSHAFT [*hugely tickled*]. You dont say so! What! no capacity for business, no knowledge of law, no sympathy with art, no pretension to philosophy; only a simple knowledge of the secret that has puzzled all the philosophers, baffled all the lawyers, muddled all the men of business, and ruined most of the artists: the secret of right and wrong. Why, man, youre a genius, a master of masters, a god! At twentyfour, too!

STEPHEN [*keeping his temper with difficulty*]. You are pleased to be facetious. I pretend to nothing more than any honorable English gentleman claims as his birthright [*he sits down angrily*].

UNDERSHAFT. Oh, thats everybody's birthright. Look at poor little Jenny Hill, the Salvation lassie! she would think you were laughing at her if you asked her to stand up in the street and teach grammar or geography or mathematics or even drawing room dancing; but it never occurs to her to doubt that she can teach morals and religion. You are all alike, you respectable people. You cant tell me the bursting strain of a ten-inch gun, which is a very simple matter; but you all think you can tell me the bursting strain of a man under temptation. You darent handle high explosives; but youre all ready to handle honesty and truth and justice and the whole duty of man, and kill one another at that game. What a country! What a world!

LADY BRITOMART [*uneasily*]. What do you think he had better do, Andrew?

UNDERSHAFT. Oh, just what he wants to do. He knows nothing and he thinks he knows everything. That points clearly to a political career. Get him a private secretaryship to someone who can get him an Under Secretaryship; and then leave him alone. He will find his natural and proper place in the end on the Treasury Bench.

STEPHEN [springing up again]. I am sorry, sir, that you force me to forget the respect due to you as my father. I am an Englishman and I will not hear the Government of my country insulted. [He thrusts his hands in his pockets, and walks angrily across to the window].

UNDERSHAFT [with a touch of brutality]. The government of your country! I am the government of your country: I, and Lazarus. Do you suppose that you and half a dozen amateurs like you, sitting in a row in that foolish gabble shop, can govern Undershaft and Lazarus? No, my friend: you will do what pays us. You will make war when it suits us, and keep peace when it doesnt. You will find out that trade requires certain measures when we have decided on those measures. When I want anything to keep my dividends up, you will discover that my want is a national need. When other people want something to keep my dividends down, you will call out the police and military. And in return you shall have the support and applause of my newspapers, and the delight of imagining that you are a great statesman. Government of your country! Be off with you, my boy, and play with your caucuses and leading articles and historic parties and great leaders and burning questions and the rest of your toys. I am going back to my counting-house to pay the piper and call the tune.

STEPHEN [actually smiling, and putting his hand on his father's shoulder with indulgent patronage]. Really, my dear father, it is impossible to be angry with you. You dont know how absurd all this sounds to me. You are very properly proud of having been industrious enough to make money; and it is greatly to your credit that you have made so much of it. But it has kept you in circles where you are valued for your money and deferred to for it, instead of in the doubtless very old-fashioned and behind-the-times public school and university where I formed my habits of mind. It is natural for you to think that money governs England; but you must allow me to think I know better.

UNDERSHAFT. And what does govern England, pray?

STEPHEN. Character, father, character.

UNDERSHAFT. Whose character? Yours or mine?

STEPHEN. Neither yours nor mine, father, but the best elements in the English national character.

UNDERSHAFT. Stephen: Ive found your profession for you. Youre a born journalist. I'll start you with a high-toned weekly review. There!

Before Stephen can reply Sarah, Barbara, Lomax, and Cusins come in ready for walking. Barbara crosses the room to the window and looks out. Cusins drifts amiably to the armchair. Lomax remains near the door, whilst Sarah comes to her mother.

*Stephen goes to the smaller writing table and busies himself with his letters.*

SARAH.    Go and get ready, mamma: the carriage is waiting.

*[Lady Britomart leaves the room].*

UNDERSHAFT *[to Sarah]*.    Good day, my dear. Good afternoon, Mr Lomax.

LOMAX *[vaguely]*.    Ahdedoo.

UNDERSHAFT *[to Cusins]*.    Quite well after last night, Euripides, eh?

CUSINS.    As well as can be expected.

UNDERSHAFT.    Thats right. *[To Barbara]*.    So you are coming to see my death and devastation factory, Barbara?

BARBARA *[at the window]*.    You came yesterday to see my salvation factory. I promised you a return visit.

LOMAX *[coming forward between Sarah and Undershaft]*.    Youll find it awfully interesting. Ive been through the Woolwich Arsenal, and it gives you a ripping feeling of security, you know, to think of the lot of beggars we could kill if it came to fighting. *[To Undershaft, with sudden solemnity]*. Still, it must be rather an awful reflection for you, from the religious point of view as it were. Youre getting on, you know, and all that.

SARAH.    You dont mind Cholly's imbecility, papa, do you?

LOMAX *[much taken aback]*.    Oh I say!

UNDERSHAFT.    Mr Lomax looks at the matter in a very proper spirit, my dear.

LOMAX.    Just so. Thats all I meant, I assure you.

SARAH.    Are you coming, Stephen?

STEPHEN.    Well, I am rather busy – er – *[Magnanimously]*. Oh well, yes: I'll come. That is, if there is room for me.

UNDERSHAFT.    I can take two with me in a little motor I am experimenting with for field use. You wont mind its being rather unfashionable. It's not painted yet; but it's bullet proof.

LOMAX *[appalled at the prospect of confronting Wilton Crescent in an unpainted motor]*.    Oh I say!

SARAH.    The carriage for me, thank you. Barbara doesnt mind what she's seen in.

LOMAX.    I say, Dolly, old chap: do you really mind the car being a guy? Because of course if you do I'll go in it. Still –

CUSINS.    I prefer it.

LOMAX.    Thanks awfully, old man. Come, my ownest. *[He hurries out to secure his seat in the carriage. Sarah follows him].*

CUSINS *[moodily walking across to Lady Britomart's writing table]*.    Why are we two coming to this Works Department of Hell? that is what I ask myself.

BARBARA.    I have always thought of it as a sort of pit where lost creatures with blackened faces stirred up smoky fires and were driven and tormented by my father. Is it like that, dad?

UNDERSHAFT *[scandalized]*.    My dear! It is a spotlessly clean and beautiful hillside town.

CUSINS.    With a Methodist chapel? Oh do say theres a Methodist chapel.

UNDERSHAFT. There are two: a Primitive one and a sophisticated one. There is even an Ethical Society; but it is not much patronized, as my men are all strongly religious. In the High Explosives Sheds they object to the presence of Agnostics as unsafe.

CUSINS. And yet they dont object to you!

BARBARA. Do they obey all your orders?

UNDERSHAFT. I never give them any orders. When I speak to one of them it is 'Well, Jones, is the baby doing well? and has Mrs Jones made a good recovery?' 'Nicely, thank you, sir.' And thats all.

CUSINS. But Jones has to be kept in order. How do you maintain discipline among your men?

UNDERSHAFT. I dont. They do. You see, the one thing Jones wont stand is any rebellion from the man under him, or any assertion of social equality between the wife of the man with 4 shillings a week less than himself, and Mrs Jones! Of course they all rebel against me, theoretically. Practically, every man of them keeps the man just below him in his place. I never meddle with them. I never bully them. I dont even bully Lazarus. I say that certain things are to be done; but I dont order anybody to do them. I dont say, mind you, that there is no ordering about and snubbing and even bullying. The men snub the boys and order them about; the carmen snub the sweepers; the artisans snub the unskilled laborers; the foremen drive and bully both the laborers and artisans; the assistant engineers find fault with the foremen; the chief engineers drop on the assistants; the departmental managers worry the chiefs; and the clerks have tall hats and hymnbooks and keep up the social tone by refusing to associate on equal terms with anybody. The result is a colossal profit, which comes to me.

CUSINS [*revolted*]. You really are a – well, what I was saying yesterday.

BARBARA. What was he saying yesterday?

UNDERSHAFT. Never mind, my dear. He thinks I have made you unhappy. Have I?

BARBARA. Do you think I can be happy in this vulgar silly dress? I! who have worn the uniform. Do you understand what you have done to me? Yesterday I had a man's soul in my hand. I set him in the way of life with his face to salvation. But when we took your money he turned back to drunkenness and derision. [*With intense conviction*]. I will never forgive you for that. If I had a child, and you destroyed its body with your explosives – if you murdered Dolly with your horrible guns – I could forgive you if my forgiveness would open the gates of heaven to you. But to take a human soul from me, and turn it into the soul of a wolf! that is worse than any murder.

UNDERSHAFT. Does my daughter despair so easily? Can you strike a man to the heart and leave no mark on him?

BARBARA [*her face lighting up*]. Oh, you are right: he can never be lost now: where was my faith?

CUSINS. Oh, clever clever devil!

BARBARA. You may be a devil; but God speaks through you sometimes.

*[She takes her father's hands and kisses them].* You have given me back my happiness: I feel it deep down now, though my spirit is troubled.

UNDERSHAFT. You have learnt something. That always feels at first as if you had lost something.

BARBARA. Well, take me to the factory of death; and let me learn something more. There must be some truth or other behind all this frightful irony. Come, Dolly. *[She goes out].*

CUSINS. My guardian angel! *[To Undershaft].* Avaunt! *[He follows Barbara].*

STEPHEN *[quietly, at the writing table].* You must not mind Cusins, father. He is a very amiable good fellow; but he is a Greek scholar and naturally a little eccentric.

UNDERSHAFT. Ah, quite so, Thank you, Stephen. Thank you. *[He goes out].*

*Stephen smiles patronizingly; buttons his coat responsibly; and crosses the room to the door. Lady Britomart, dressed for out-of-doors, opens it before he reaches it. She looks round for others; looks at Stephen; and turns to go without a word.*

STEPHEN *[embarrassed].* Mother –

LADY BRITOMART. Dont be apologetic, Stephen. And dont forget that you have outgrown your mother. *[She goes out].*

*Perivale St Andrews lies between two Middlesex hills, half climbing the northern one. It is an almost smokeless town of white walls, roofs of narrow green slates or red tiles, tall trees, domes, campaniles, and slender chimney shafts, beautifully situated and beautiful in itself. The best view of it is obtained from the crest of a slope about half a mile to the east, where the high explosives are dealt with. The foundry lies hidden in the depths between, the tops of its chimneys sprouting like huge skittles into the middle distance. Across the crest runs an emplacement of concrete, with a firestep, and a parapet which suggests a fortification, because there is a huge cannon of the obsolete Woolwich Infant pattern peering across it at the town. The cannon is mounted on an experimental gun carriage: possibly the original model of the Undershaft disappearing rampart gun alluded to by Stephen. The firestep, being a convenient place to sit, is furnished here and there with straw disc cushions; and at one place there is the additional luxury of a fur rug.*

*Barbara is standing on the firestep, looking over the parapet towards the town. On her right is the cannon; on her left the end of a shed raised on piles, with a ladder of three or four steps up to the door, which opens outwards and has a little wooden landing at the threshold, with a fire bucket in the corner of the landing. Several dummy soldiers more or less mutilated, with straw protruding from their gashes, have been shoved out of the way under the landing. A few others are nearly upright against the shed; and one has fallen forward and lies, like a grotesque corpse, on the emplacement. The parapet stops short of the shed, leaving a gap which is the beginning of the path down the hill through the foundry to the town. The rug is on the firestep near this gap. Down on the emplacement behind the cannon is a trolley carrying a huge conical bombshell with a red band painted on it. Further to the right is the door of an office, which, like the sheds, is of the lightest possible construction.*

*Cusins arrives by the path from the town.*

BARBARA. Well?

CUSINS. Not a ray of hope. Everything perfect! wonderful! real! It only needs a cathedral to be a heavenly city instead of a hellish one.

BARBARA. Have you found out whether they have done anything for old Peter Shirley?

CUSINS. They have found him a job as gatekeeper and timekeeper. He's frightfully miserable. He calls the time-keeping brainwork, and says he isnt used to it; and his gate lodge is so splendid that he's ashamed to use the rooms, and skulks in the scullery.

BARBARA. Poor Peter!

*Stephen arrives from the town. He carries a fieldglass.*

STEPHEN [*enthusiastically*]. Have you two seen the place? Why did you leave us?

CUSINS. I wanted to see everything I was not intended to see; and Barbara wanted to make the men talk.

STEPHEN. Have you found anything discreditable?

CUSINS. No. They call him Dandy Andy and are proud of his being a cunning old rascal; but it's all horribly, frightfully, immorally, unanswerably perfect.

*[Sarah arrives.]*

SARAH. Heavens! what a place! [*She crosses to the trolley*]. Did you see the nursing home!? [*She sits down on the shell*].

STEPHEN. Did you see the libraries and schools!?

SARAH. Did you see the ball room and the banqueting chamber in the Town Hall!?

STEPHEN. Have you gone into the insurance fund, the pension fund, the building society, the various applications of cooperation!?

*Undershaft comes from the office, with a sheaf of telegrams in his hand.*

UNDERSHAFT. Well, have you seen everything? I'm sorry I was called away. [*Indicating the telegrams*]. Good news from Manchuria.

STEPHEN. Another Japanese victory?

UNDERSHAFT. Oh, I dont know. Which side wins does not concern us here. No: the good news is that the aerial battleship is a tremendous success. At the first trial it has wiped out a fort with three hundred soldiers in it.

CUSINS [*from the platform*]. Dummy soldiers?

UNDERSHAFT [*striding across to Stephen and kicking the prostrate dummy brutally out of his way*]. No: the real thing.

*Cusins and Barbara exchange glances. Then Cusins sits on the step and buries his face in his hands. Barbara gravely lays her hand on his shoulder. He looks up at her in whimsical desperation.*

UNDERSHAFT. Well, Stephen, what do you think of the place?

STEPHEN. Oh, magnificent. A perfect triumph of modern industry. Frankly, my dear father, I have been a fool: I had no idea of what it all meant: of the wonderful forethought, the power of organization, the administrative capacity, the financial genius, the colossal capital it represents. I have been repeating to myself as I came through your streets 'Peace hath her victories no less renowned than War.' I have only one misgiving about it all.

UNDERSHAFT. Out with it.

STEPHEN. Well, I cannot help thinking that all this provision for every want of your workmen may sap their independence and weaken their sense of responsibility. And greatly as we enjoyed our tea at that splendid restaurant – how they gave us all that luxury and cake and jam and cream for threepence I really cannot imagine! – still you must remember that restaurants break up home life. Look at the continent, for instance! Are you sure so much pampering is really good for the men's characters?

UNDERSHAFT. Well you see, my dear boy, when you are organizing civilization you have to make up your mind whether trouble and anxiety are good things or not. If you decide that they are, then, I take it, you simply dont organize civilization, and there you are, with trouble and anxiety enough to make us all angels! But if you decide the other way, you may as well go through with it. However, Stephen, our characters are safe here. A sufficient dose of anxiety is always provided by the fact that we may be blown to smithereens at any moment.

SARAH. By the way, papa, where do you make the explosives?

UNDERSHAFT. In separate little sheds, like that one. When one of them blows up, it costs very little; and only the people quite close to it are killed.

*Stephen, who is quite close to it, looks at it rather scaredly, and moves away quickly to the cannon. At the same moment the door of the shed is thrown abruptly open; and a foreman in overalls and list slippers comes out on the little landing and holds the door for Lomax, who appears in the doorway.*

LOMAX *[with studied coolness]*. My good fellow: you neednt get into a state of nerves. Nothing's going to happen to you; and I suppose it wouldnt be the end of the world if anything did. A little bit of British pluck is what you want, old chap. *[He descends and strolls across to Sarah]*.

UNDERSHAFT *[to the foreman]*. Anything wrong, Bilton?

BILTON *[with ironic calm]*. Gentleman walked into the high explosives shed and lit a cigaret, sir: thats all.

UNDERSHAFT. Ah, quite so. *[Going over to Lomax]*. Do you happen to remember what you did with the match?

LOMAX. Oh come! I'm not a fool. I took jolly good care to blow it out before I chucked it away.

BILTON. The top of it was red hot inside, sir.

LOMAX. Well, suppose it was! I didn't chuck it into any of your messes.

UNDERSHAFT. Think no more of it, Mr Lomax. By the way, would you mind lending me your matches.

LOMAX *[offering his box]*. Certainly.

UNDERSHAFT. Thanks. *[He pockets the matches]*.

LOMAX *[lecturing to the company generally]*. You know, these high explosives dont go off like gunpowder, except when theyre in a gun. When theyre spread loose, you can put a match to them without the least risk: they just burn quietly like a bit of paper *[Warming to the scientific interest of the subject]*. Did you know that, Undershaft? Have you ever tried?

UNDERSHAFT. Not on a large scale, Mr Lomax. Bilton will give you a sample of gun cotton when you are leaving if you ask him. You can experiment with it at home. *[Bilton looks puzzled]*.

SARAH. Bilton will do nothing of the sort, papa. I suppose it's your business to blow up the Russians and Japs; but you might really stop short of blowing up poor Cholly. *[Bilton gives it up and retires into the shed]*.

LOMAX. My ownest, there is no danger. *[He sits beside her on the shell]*.
*Lady Britomart arrives from the town with a bouquet.*

LADY BRITOMART *[impetuously]*. Andrew: you shouldnt have let me see this place.

UNDERSHAFT. Why, my dear?

LADY BRITOMART. Never mind why: you shouldnt have: thats all. To think of all that *[indicating the town]* being yours! and that you have kept it to yourself all these years!

UNDERSHAFT. It does not belong to me. I belong to it. It is the Undershaft inheritance.

LADY BRITOMART. It is not. Your ridiculous cannons and that noisy banging foundry may be the Undershaft inheritance; but all that plate and linen, all that furniture and those houses and orchards and gardens belong to us. They belong to me: they are not a man's business. I wont give them up. You must be out of your senses to throw them all away; and if you persist in such folly, I will call in a doctor.

UNDERSHAFT *[stooping to smell the bouquet]*. Where did you get the flowers, my dear?

LADY BRITOMART. Your men presented them to me in your William Morris Labor Church.

CUSINS. Oh! It needed only that. A Labor Church! *[he mounts the firestep distractedly, and leans with his elbows on the parapet, turning his back to them]*.

LADY BRITOMART. Yes, with Morris's words in mosaic letters ten feet high round the dome. NO MAN IS GOOD ENOUGH TO BE ANOTHER MAN'S MASTER. The cynicism of it!

UNDERSHAFT. It shocked the men at first, I am afraid. But now they take no more notice of it than of the ten commandments in church.

LADY BRITOMART. Andrew: you are trying to put me off the subject of the inheritance by profane jokes. Well, you shant. I dont ask it any longer for Stephen: he has inherited far too much of your perversity to be fit for it. But Barbara has rights as well as Stephen. Why should not Adolphus succeed to the inheritance? I could manage the town for him; and he can look after the cannons, if they are really necessary.

UNDERSHAFT. I should ask nothing better if Adolphus were a foundling. He is exactly the sort of new blood that is wanted in English business. But he's not a foundling; and theres an end of it. *[He makes for the office door]*.

CUSINS [*turning to them*]. Not quite. [*They all turn and stare at him*]. I think – Mind! I am not committing myself in any way as to my future course – but I think the foundling difficulty can be got over. [*He jumps down to the emplacement*].

UNDERSHAFT [*coming back to him*]. What do you mean?

CUSINS. Well, I have something to say which is in the nature of a confession.

SARAH.
LADY BRITOMART. } Confession!
BARBARA.
STEPHEN.

LOMAX. Oh I say!

CUSINS. Yes, a confession. Listen, all. Until I met Barbara I thought myself in the main an honorable, truthful man, because I wanted the approval of my conscience more than I wanted anything else. But the moment I saw Barbara, I wanted her far more than the approval of my conscience.

LADY BRITOMART. Adolphus!

CUSINS. It is true. You accused me yourself, Lady Brit, of joining the Army to worship Barbara; and so I did. She bought my soul like a flower at a street corner: but she bought it for herself.

UNDERSHAFT. What! Not for Dionysos or another?

CUSINS. Dionysos and all the others are in herself. I adored what was divine in her, and was therefore a true worshipper. But I was romantic about her too. I thought she was a woman of the people, and that a marriage with a professor of Greek would be far beyond the wildest social ambitions of her rank.

LADY BRITOMART. Adolphus!!

LOMAX. Oh I say!!!

CUSINS. When I learnt the horrible truth –

LADY BRITOMART. What do you mean by the horrible truth, pray?

CUSINS. That she was enormously rich; that her grandfather was an earl; that her father was the Prince of Darkness –

UNDERSHAFT. Chut!

CUSINS. – and that I was only an adventurer trying to catch a rich wife, then I stooped to deceive her about my birth.

BARBARA [*rising*]. Dolly!

LADY BRITOMART. Your birth! Now Adolphus, dont dare to make up a wicked story for the sake of these wretched cannons. Remember: I have seen photographs of your parents; and the Agent General for South Western Australia knows them personally and has assured me that they are most respectable married people.

CUSINS. So they are in Australia; but here they are outcasts. Their marriage is legal in Australia, but not in England. My mother is my father's deceased wife's sister; and in this island I am consequently a foundling. [*Sensation*].

BARBARA. Silly! [*She climbs to the cannon, and leans, listening, in the angle it makes with the parapet*].

CUSINS.   Is the subterfuge good enough, Machiavelli?

UNDERSHAFT [*thoughtfully*].   Biddy: this may be a way out of the difficulty.

LADY BRITOMART.   Stuff! A man cant make cannons any the better for being his own cousin instead of his proper self [*she sits down on the rug with a bounce that expresses her downright contempt for their casuistry*].

UNDERSHAFT [*to Cusins*].   You are an educated man. That is against the tradition.

CUSINS.   Once in ten thousand times it happens that the schoolboy is a born master of what they try to teach him. Greek has not destroyed my mind: it has nourished it. Besides, I did not learn it at an English public school.

UNDERSHAFT.   Hm! Well, I cannot afford to be too particular: you have cornered the foundling market. Let it pass. You are eligible, Euripides: you are eligible.

BARBARA.   Dolly: yesterday morning, when Stephen told us all about the tradition, you became very silent; and you have been strange and excited ever since. Were you thinking of your birth then?

CUSINS.   When the finger of Destiny suddenly points at a man in the middle of his breakfast, it makes him thoughtful.

UNDERSHAFT.   Aha! You have had your eye on the business, my young friend, have you?

CUSINS.   Take care! There is an abyss of moral horror between me and your accursed aerial battleships.

UNDERSHAFT.   Never mind the abyss for the present. Let us settle the practical details and leave your final decision open. You know that you will have to change your name. Do you object to that?

CUSINS.   Would any man named Adolphus – any man called Dolly! – object to be called something else?

UNDERSHAFT.   Good. Now, as to money! I propose to treat you handsomely from the beginning. You shall start at a thousand a year.

CUSINS [*with sudden heat, his spectacles twinkling with mischief*].   A thousand! You dare offer a miserable thousand to the son-in-law of a millionaire! No, by Heavens, Machiavelli! you shall not cheat me. You cannot do without me; and I can do without you. I must have two thousand five hundred a year for two years. At the end of that time, if I am a failure, I go. But if I am a success, and stay on, you must give me the other five thousand?

UNDERSHAFT.   What other five thousand?

CUSINS.   To make the two years up to five thousand a year. The two thousand five hundred is only half pay in case I should turn out a failure. The third year I must have ten per cent on the profits.

UNDERSHAFT [*taken aback*].   Ten per cent! Why, man, do you know what my profits are?

CUSINS.   Enormous, I hope: otherwise I shall require twenty-five per cent.

UNDERSHAFT.   But, Mr Cusins, this is a serious matter of business. You are not bringing any capital into the concern.

CUSINS. What! no capital! Is my mastery of Greek no capital? Is my access to the subtlest thought, the loftiest poetry yet attained by humanity, no capital? My character! my intellect! my life! my career! what Barbara calls my soul! are these no capital? Say another word; and I double my salary.

UNDERSHAFT. Be reasonable –

CUSINS [*peremptorily*]. Mr Undershaft: you have my terms. Take them or leave them.

UNDERSHAFT [*recovering himself*]. Very well. I note your terms; and I offer you half.

CUSINS [*disgusted*]. Half!

UNDERSHAFT [*firmly*]. Half.

CUSINS. You call yourself a gentleman; and you offer me half!!

UNDERSHAFT. I do not call myself a gentleman; but I offer you half.

CUSINS. This to your future partner! your successor! your son-in-law!

BARBARA. You are selling your own soul, Dolly, not mine. Leave me out of the bargain, please.

UNDERSHAFT. Come! I will go a step further for Barbara's sake. I will give you three fifths; but that is my last word.

CUSINS. Done!

LOMAX. Done in the eye! Why, *I* get only eight hundred, you know.

CUSINS. By the way, Mac, I am a classical scholar, not an arithmetical one. Is three fifths more than half or less?

UNDERSHAFT. More, of course.

CUSINS. I would have taken two hundred and fifty. How you can succeed in business when you are willing to pay all that money to a University don who is obviously not worth a junior clerk's wages! – well! What will Lazarus say?

UNDERSHAFT. Lazarus is a gentle romantic Jew who cares for nothing but string quartets and stalls at fashionable theatres. He will be blamed for your rapacity in money matters, poor fellow! as he has hitherto been blamed for mine. You are a shark of the first order, Euripides. So much the better for the firm!

BARBARA. Is the bargain closed, Dolly? Does your soul belong to him now?

CUSINS. No: the price is settled: that is all. The real tug of war is still to come. What about the moral question?

LADY BRITOMART. There is no moral question in the matter at all, Adolphus. You must simply sell cannons and weapons to people whose cause is right and just, and refuse them to foreigners and criminals.

UNDERSHAFT [*determinedly*]. No: none of that. You must keep the true faith of an Armorer, or you dont come in here.

CUSINS. What on earth is the true faith of an Armorer?

UNDERSHAFT. To give arms to all men who offer an honest price for them, without respect of persons or principles: to aristocrat and republican, to Nihilist and Tsar, to Capitalist and Socialist, to Protestant and Catholic, to burglar and policeman, to black man, white man and yellow man to, all sorts and conditions, all nationalities, all faiths, all follies, all causes and all crimes. The first Undershaft wrote up in his shop IF GOD GAVE THE HAND, LET NOT MAN WITHHOLD THE SWORD. The second wrote up ALL HAVE THE RIGHT TO FIGHT: NONE HAVE THE RIGHT TO JUDGE. The third wrote up TO MAN THE WEAPON: TO HEAVEN THE VICTORY. The fourth had no literary turn; so he did not write up anything; but he sold cannons to Napoleon under the nose of George the Third. The fifth wrote up PEACE SHALL NOT PREVAIL SAVE WITH A SWORD IN HER HAND. The sixth, my master, was the best of all. He wrote up NOTHING IS EVER DONE IN THIS WORLD UNTIL MEN ARE PREPARED TO KILL ONE ANOTHER IF IT IS NOT DONE. After that, there was nothing left for the seventh to say. So he wrote up, simply, UNASHAMED.

CUSINS. My good Machiavelli, I shall certainly write something up on the wall; only, as I shall write it in Greek, you wont be able to read it. But as to your Armorer's faith, if I take my neck out of the noose of my own morality I am not going to put it into the noose of yours. I shall sell cannons to whom I please and refuse them to whom I please. So there!

UNDERSHAFT. From the moment when you become Andrew Undershaft, you will never do as you please again. Dont come here lusting for power, young man.

CUSINS. If power were my aim I should not come here for it. You have no power.

UNDERSHAFT. None of my own, certainly.

CUSINS. I have more power than you, more will. You do not drive this place: it drives you. And what drives the place?

UNDERSHAFT [enigmatically]. A will of which I am a part.

BARBARA [startled]. Father! Do you know what you are saying; or are you laying a snare for my soul?

CUSINS. Dont listen to his metaphysics, Barbara. The place is driven by the most rascally part of society, the money hunters, the pleasure hunters, the military promotion hunters; and he is their slave.

UNDERSHAFT. Not necessarily. Remember the Armorer's Faith. I will take an order from a good man as cheerfully as from a bad one. If you good people prefer preaching and shirking to buying my weapons and fighting the rascals, dont blame me. I can make cannons: I cannot make courage and conviction. Bah! you tire me, Euripides, with your morality mongering. Ask Barbara: s h e understands. [He suddenly reaches up and takes Barbara's hands, looking powerfully into her eyes]. Tell him, my love, what power really means.

BARBARA [hypnotized]. Before I joined the Salvation Army, I was in my own power; and the consequence was that I never knew what to do with myself. When I joined it, I had not time enough for all the things I had to do.

UNDERSHAFT [approvingly]. Just so. And why was that, do you suppose?

BARBARA. Yesterday I should have said, because I was in the power of God. *[She resumes her self-possession, withdrawing her hands from his with a power equal to his own]*. But you came and shewed me that I was in the power of Bodger and Undershaft. Today I feel – oh! how can I put it into words? Sarah: do you remember the earthquake at Cannes, when we were little children? – how little the surprise of the first shock mattered compared to the dread and horror of waiting for the second? That is how I feel in this place today. I stood on the rock I thought eternal; and without a word of warning it reeled and crumbled under me. I was safe with an infinite wisdom watching me, an army marching to Salvation with me; and in a moment, at a stroke of your pen in a cheque book, I stood alone; and the heavens were empty. That was the first shock of the earthquake: I am waiting for the second.

UNDERSHAFT. Come, come, my daughter! dont make too much of your little tinpot tragedy. What do we do here when we spend years of work and thought and thousands of pounds of solid cash on a new gun or an aerial battleship that turns out just a hairsbreadth wrong after all? Scrap it. Scrap it without wasting another hour or another pound on it. Well, you have made for yourself something that you call a morality or a religion or what not. It doesnt fit the facts. Well, scrap it. Scrap it and get one that does fit. That is what is wrong with the world at present. It scraps its obsolete steam engines and dynamos; but it wont scrap its old prejudices and its old moralities and its old religions and its old political constitutions. Whats the result? In machinery it does very well; but in morals and religion and politics it is working at a loss that brings it nearer bankruptcy every year. Dont persist in that folly. If your old religion broke down yesterday, get a newer and a better one for tomorrow.

BARBARA. Oh how gladly I would take a better one to my soul! But you offer me a worse one. *[Turning on him with sudden vehemence]*. Justify yourself: shew me some light through the darkness of this dreadful place, with its beautifully clean workshops, and respectable workmen, and model homes.

UNDERSHAFT. Cleanliness and respectability do not need justification, Barbara: they justify themselves. I see no darkness here, no dreadfulness. In your Salvation shelter I saw poverty, misery, cold and hunger. You gave them bread and treacle and dreams of heaven. I give from thirty shillings a week to twelve thousand a year. They find their own dreams; but I look after the drainage.

BARBARA. And their souls?

UNDERSHAFT. I save their souls just as I saved yours.

BARBARA *[revolted]*. You saved my soul! What do you mean?

UNDERSHAFT. I fed you and clothed you and housed you. I took care that you should have money enough to live handsomely – more than enough; so that you could be wasteful, careless, generous. That saved your soul from the seven deadly sins.

BARBARA *[bewildered]*. The seven deadly sins!

UNDERSHAFT. Yes, the deadly seven. *[Counting on his fingers]*. Food, clothing, firing, rent, taxes, respectability and children. Nothing can lift those seven millstones from Man's neck but money; and the spirit cannot soar until the millstones are lifted. I lifted them from your spirit. I enabled Barbara to become Major Barbara; and I saved her from the crime of poverty.

CUSINS. Do you call poverty a crime?

UNDERSHAFT. The worst of crimes. All the other crimes are virtues beside it: all the other dishonors are chivalry itself by comparison. Poverty blights whole cities; spreads horrible pestilences; strikes dead the very souls of all who come within sight, sound, or smell of it. What you call crime is nothing: a murder here and a theft there, a blow now and a curse then: what do they matter? they are only the accidents and illnesses of life: there are not fifty genuine professional criminals in London. But there are millions of poor people, abject people, dirty people, ill fed, ill clothed people. They poison us morally and physically: they kill the happiness of society: they force us to do away with our own liberties and to organize unnatural cruelties for fear they should rise against us and drag us down into their abyss. Only fools fear crime: we all fear poverty. Pah! *[turning on Barbara]* you talk of your half-saved ruffian in West Ham: you accuse me of dragging his soul back to perdition. Well, bring him to me here; and I will drag his soul back again to salvation for you. Not by words and dreams; but by thirtyeight shillings a week, a sound house in a handsome street, and a permanent job. In three weeks he will have a fancy waistcoat; in three months a tall hat and a chapel sitting; before the end of the year he will shake hands with a duchess at a Primrose League meeting, and join the Conservative Party.

BARBARA. And will he be the better for that?

UNDERSHAFT. You know he will. Dont be a hypocrite, Barbara. He will be better fed, better housed, better clothed, better behaved; and his children will be pounds heavier and bigger. That will be better than an American cloth mattress in a shelter, chopping firewood, eating bread and treacle, and being forced to kneel down from time to time to thank heaven for it: knee drill, I think you call it. It is cheap work converting starving men with a Bible in one hand and a slice of bread in the other. I will undertake to convert West Ham to Mahometanism on the same terms. Try your hand on my men: their souls are hungry because their bodies are full.

BARBARA. And leave the east end to starve?

UNDERSHAFT *[his energetic tone dropping into one of bitter and brooding remembrance]*. I was an east ender. I moralized and starved until one day I swore that I would be a full-fed free man at all costs; that nothing should stop me except a bullet, neither reason nor morals nor the lives of other men. I said 'Thou shalt starve ere I starve'; and with that word I become free and great. I was a dangerous man until I had my will: now I am a useful, beneficent, kindly person. That is the history of most self-made

*592*

millionaires, I fancy. When it is the history of every Englishman we shall have an England worth living in.

LADY BRITOMART.   Stop making speeches, Andrew. This is not the place for them.

UNDERSHAFT [*punctured*].   My dear: I have no other means of conveying my ideas.

LADY BRITOMART.   Your ideas are nonsense. You got on because you were selfish and unscrupulous.

UNDERSHAFT.   Not at all. I had the strongest scruples about poverty and starvation. Your moralists are quite unscrupulous about both: they make virtues of them. I had rather be a thief than a pauper. I had rather be a murderer than a slave. I dont want to be either; but if you force the alternative on me, then, by Heaven, I'll choose the braver and more moral one. I hate poverty and slavery worse than any other crimes whatsoever. And let me tell you this. Poverty and slavery have stood up for centuries to your sermons and leading articles: they will not stand up to my machine guns. Dont preach at them: dont reason with them. Kill them.

BARBARA.   Killing. Is that your remedy for everything?

UNDERSHAFT.   It is the final test of conviction, the only lever strong enough to overturn a social system, the only way of saying Must. Let six hundred and seventy fools loose in the streets; and three policemen can scatter them. But huddle them together in a certain house in Westminster; and let them go through certain ceremonies and call themselves certain names until at last they get the courage to kill; and your six hundred and seventy fools become a government. Your pious mob fills up ballot papers and imagines it is governing its masters; but the ballot paper that really governs is the paper that has a bullet wrapped up in it.

CUSINS.   That is perhaps why, like most intelligent people, I never vote.

UNDERSHAFT.   Vote! Bah! When you vote, you only change the names of the cabinet. When you shoot, you pull down governments, inaugurate new epochs, abolish old orders and set up new. Is that historically true, Mr Learned Man, or is it not?

CUSINS.   It is historically true. I loathe having to admit it. I repudiate your sentiments. I abhor your nature. I defy you in every possible way. Still, it is true. But it ought not to be true.

UNDERSHAFT.   Ought! ought! ought! ought! ought! Are you going to spend your life saying ought, like the rest of our moralists? Turn your oughts into shalls, man. Come and make explosives with me. Whatever can blow men up can blow society up. The history of the world is the history of those who had courage enough to embrace its truth. Have you the courage to embrace it, Barbara?

LADY BRITOMART.   Barbara: I positively forbid you to listen to your father's abominable wickedness. And you, Adolphus, ought to know better than to go about saying that wrong things are true. What does it matter whether they are true if they are wrong?

UNDERSHAFT. What does it matter whether they are wrong if they are true?

LADY BRITOMART [rising]. Children: come home instantly. Andrew: I am exceedingly sorry I allowed you to call on us. You are wickeder than ever. Come at once.

BARBARA [shaking her head]. It's no use running away from wicked people, mamma.

LADY BRITOMART. It is every use. It shews your disapprobation of them.

BARBARA. It does not save them.

LADY BRITOMART. I can see that you are going to disobey me. Sarah: are you coming home or are you not?

SARAH. I daresay it's very wicked of papa to make cannons; but I dont think I shall cut him on that account.

LOMAX [pouring oil on the troubled waters]. The fact is, you know, there is a certain amount of tosh about this notion of wickedness. It doesnt work. You must look at facts. Not that I would say a word in favor of anything wrong; but then, you see, all sorts of chaps are always doing all sorts of things; and we have to fit them in somehow, dont you know. What I mean is that you cant go cutting everybody; and thats about what it comes to. [Their rapt attention to his eloquence makes him nervous]. Perhaps I dont make myself clear.

LADY BRITOMART. You are lucidity itself, Charles. Because Andrew is successful and has plenty of money to give to Sarah, you will flatter him and encourage him in his wickedness.

LOMAX [unruffled]. Well, where the carcase is, there will the eagles be gathered, dont you know. [To Undershaft]. Eh? What?

UNDERSHAFT. Precisely. By the way, may I call you Charles?

LOMAX. Delighted. Cholly is the usual ticket.

UNDERSHAFT [to Lady Britomart]. Biddy –

LADY BRITOMART [violently]. Dont dare call me Biddy. Charles Lomax: you are a fool. Adolphus Cusins: you are a Jesuit. Stephen: you are a prig. Barbara: you are a lunatic. Andrew: you are a vulgar tradesman. Now you all know my opinion; and my conscience is clear, at all events [she sits down with a vehemence that the rug fortunately softens].

UNDERSHAFT. My dear: you are the incarnation of morality. [She snorts]. Your conscience is clear and your duty done when you have called everybody names. Come, Euripides! it is getting late; and we all want to go home. Make up your mind.

CUSINS. Understand this, you old demon –

LADY BRITOMART. Adolphus!

UNDERSHAFT. Let him alone, Biddy. Proceed, Euripides.

CUSINS. You have me in a horrible dilemma. I want Barbara.

UNDERSHAFT. Like all young men, you greatly exaggerate the difference between one young woman and another.

BARBARA. Quite true, Dolly.

CUSINS.  I also want to avoid being a rascal.

UNDERSHAFT [*with biting contempt*].  You lust for personal righteousness, for self-approval, for what you call a good conscience, for what Barbara calls salvation, for what I call patronizing people who are not so lucky as yourself.

CUSINS.  I do not: all the poet in me recoils from being a good man. But there are things in me that I must reckon with. Pity –

UNDERSHAFT.  Pity! The scavenger of misery.

CUSINS.  Well, love.

UNDERSHAFT.  I know. You love the needy and the outcast: you love the oppressed races, the negro, the Indian ryot, the underdog everywhere. Do you love the Japanese? Do you love the French? Do you love the English?

CUSINS.  No. Every true Englishman detests the English. We are the wickedest nation on earth; and our success is a moral horror.

UNDERSHAFT.  That is what comes of your gospel of love, is it?

CUSINS.  May I not love even my father-in-law?

UNDERSHAFT.  Who wants your love, man? By what right do you take the liberty of offering it to me? I will have your due heed and respect, or I will kill you. But your love! Damn your impertinence!

CUSINS [*grinning*].  I may not be able to control my affections, Mac.

UNDERSHAFT.  You are fencing, Euripides. You are weakening: your grip is slipping. Come! try your last weapon. Pity and love have broken in your hand: forgiveness is still left.

CUSINS.  No: forgiveness is a beggar's refuge. I am with you there: we must pay our debts.

UNDERSHAFT.  Well said. Come! you will suit me. Remember the words of Plato.

CUSINS [*starting*].  Plato! You dare quote Plato to me!

UNDERSHAFT.  Plato says, my friend, that society cannot be saved until either the Professors of Greek take to making gunpowder, or else the makers of gunpowder become Professors of Greek.

CUSINS.  Oh, tempter, cunning tempter!

UNDERSHAFT.  Come! choose, man, choose.

CUSINS.  But perhaps Barbara will not marry me if I make the wrong choice.

BARBARA.  Perhaps not.

CUSINS [*desperately perplexed*].  You hear!

BARBARA.  Father: do you love nobody?

UNDERSHAFT.  I love my best friend.

LADY BRITOMART.  And who is that pray,?

UNDERSHAFT.  My bravest enemy. That is the man who keeps me up to the mark.

CUSINS.  You know, the creature is really a sort of poet in his way. Suppose he is a great man, after all!

UNDERSHAFT. Suppose you stop talking and make up your mind, my young friend.

CUSINS. But you are driving me against my nature. I hate war.

UNDERSHAFT. Hatred is the coward's revenge for being intimidated. Dare you make war on war? Here are the means: my friend Mr Lomax is sitting on them.

LOMAX *[springing up]*. Oh I say! You dont mean that this thing is loaded, do you? My ownest: come off it.

SARAH *[sitting placidly on the shell]*. If I am to be blown up, the more thoroughly it is done the better. Dont fuss, Cholly.

LOMAX *[to Undershaft, strongly remonstrant]*. Your own daughter, you know!

UNDERSHAFT. So I see. *[To Cusins]*. Well, my friend, may we expect you here at six tomorrow morning?

CUSINS *[firmly]*. Not on any account. I will see the whole establishment blown up with its own dynamite before I will get up at five. My hours are healthy, rational hours: eleven to five.

UNDERSHAFT. Come when you please: before a week you will come at six and stay until I turn you out for the sake of your health. *[Calling]*. Bilton! *[He turns to Lady Britomart, who rises]*. My dear: let us leave these two young people to themselves for a moment. *[Bilton comes from the shed]*. I am going to take you through the gun cotton shed.

BILTON *[barring the way]*. You cant take anything explosive in here, sir.

LADY BRITOMART. What do you mean? Are you alluding to me?

BILTON *[unmoved]*. No, maam. Mr Undershaft has the other gentleman's matches in his pocket.

LADY BRITOMART *[abruptly]*. Oh! I beg your pardon. *[She goes into the shed]*.

UNDERSHAFT. Quite right, Bilton, quite right: here you are. *[He gives Bilton the box of matches]*. Come, Stephen. Come, Charles. Bring Sarah. *[He passes into the shed]*.

*Bilton opens the box and deliberately drops the matches into the fire-bucket.*

LOMAX. Oh! I say *[Bilton stolidly hands him the empty box]*. Infernal nonsense! Pure scientific ignorance! *[He goes in]*.

SARAH. Am I all right, Bilton?

BILTON. Youll have to put on list slippers, miss: thats all. Weve got em inside. *[She goes in]*.

STEPHEN *[very seriously to Cusins]*. Dolly, old fellow, think. Think before you decide. Do you feel that you are a sufficiently practical man? It is a huge undertaking, an enormous responsibility. All this mass of business will be Greek to you.

CUSINS. Oh, I think it will be much less difficult than Greek.

STEPHEN. Well, I just want to say this before I leave you to yourselves. Dont let anything I have said about right and wrong prejudice you against this great chance in life. I have satisfied myself that the business is one of the highest character and a credit to our country. *[Emotionally]*.

I am very proud of my father. I – *[Unable to proceed, he presses Cusins' hand and goes hastily into the shed, followed by Bilton].*

*Barbara and Cusins, left alone together, look at one another silently.*

CUSINS.  Barbara: I am going to accept this offer.

BARBARA.  I thought you would.

CUSINS.  You understand, dont you, that I had to decide without consulting you. If I had thrown the burden of the choice on you, you would sooner or later have despised me for it.

BARBARA.  Yes: I did not want you to sell your soul for me any more than for this inheritance.

CUSINS.  It is not the sale of my soul that troubles me: I have sold it too often to care about that. I have sold it for a professorship. I have sold it for an income. I have sold it to escape being imprisoned for refusing to pay taxes for hangmen's ropes and unjust wars and things that I abhor. What is all human conduct but the daily and hourly sale of our souls for trifles? What I am now selling it for is neither money nor position nor comfort, but for reality and for power.

BARBARA.  You know that you will have no power, and that he has none.

CUSINS.  I know. It is not for myself alone. I want to make power for the world.

BARBARA.  I want to make power for the world too; but it must be spiritual power.

CUSINS.  I think all power is spiritual: these cannons will not go off by themselves. I have tried to make spiritual power by teaching Greek. But the world can never be really touched by a dead language and a dead civilization. The people must have power; and the people cannot have Greek. Now the power that is made here can be wielded by all men.

BARBARA.  Power to burn women's houses down and kill their sons and tear their husbands to pieces.

CUSINS.  You cannot have power for good without having power for evil too. Even mother's milk nourishes murderers as well as heroes. This power which only tears men's bodies to pieces has never been so horribly abused as the intellectual power, the imaginative power, the poetic, religious power that can enslave men's souls. As a teacher of Greek I gave the intellectual man weapons against the common man. I now want to give the common man weapons against the intellectual man. I love the common people. I want to arm them against the lawyers, the doctors, the priests, the literary men, the professors, the artists, and the politicians, who, once in authority, are more disastrous and tyrannical than all the fools, rascals, and imposters. I want a power simple enough for common men to use, yet strong enough to force the intellectual oligarchy to use its genius for the general good.

BARBARA.  Is there no higher power than that *[pointing to the shell]*?

CUSINS.  Yes; but that power can destroy the higher powers just as a tiger can destroy a man: therefore Man must master that power first. I admitted

this when the Turks and Greeks were last at war. My best pupil went out
to fight for Hellas. My parting gift to him was not a copy of Plato's
Republic, but a revolver and a hundred Undershaft cartridges. The blood
of every Turk he shot – if he shot any – is on my head as well as on
Undershaft's. That act committed me to this place for ever. Your father's
challenge has beaten me. Dare I make war on war? I must. I will. And
now, is it all over between us?

BARBARA [touched by his evident dread of her answer].  Silly baby Dolly! How
could it be!

CUSINS [overjoyed].  Then you – you – you – Oh for my drum! [He flourishes
imaginary drumsticks].

BARBARA [angered by his levity].  Take care, Dolly, take care. Oh, if only I
could get away from you and from father and from it all! if I could have
the wings of a dove and fly away to heaven!

CUSINS.  And leave me!

BARBARA.  Yes, you, and all the other naughty mischievous children of
men. But I cant. I was happy in the Salvation Army for a moment. I
escaped from the world into a paradise of enthusiasm and prayer and
soul saving; but the moment our money ran short, it all came back to
Bodger: it was he who saved our people: he, and the Prince of Darkness,
my papa. Undershaft and Bodger: their hands stretch everywhere: when
we feed a starving fellow creature, it is with their bread, because there is
no other bread; when we tend the sick, it is in the hospitals they endow;
if we turn from the churches they build, we must kneel on the stones of the
streets they pave. As long as that lasts, there is no getting away from them.
Turning our backs on Bodger and Undershaft is turning our backs on life.

CUSINS.  I thought you were determined to turn your back on the wicked
side of life.

BARBARA.  There is no wicked side: life is all one. And I never wanted to
shirk my share in whatever evil must be endured, whether it be sin or
suffering. I wish I could cure you of middle-class ideas, Dolly.

CUSINS [gasping].  Middle cl – ! A snub! A social snub to me! from the
daughter of a foundling!

BARBARA.  That is why I have no class, Dolly: I come straight out of the
heart of the whole people. If I were middle-class I should turn my
back on my father's business; and we should both live in an artistic
drawing room, with you reading the reviews in one corner, and I in the
other at the piano, playing Schumann: both very superior persons, and
neither of us a bit of use. Sooner than that, I would sweep out the gun-
cotton shed, or be one of Bodger's barmaids. Do you know what would
have happened if you had refused papa's offer?

CUSINS.  I wonder!

BARBARA.  I should have given you up and married the man who accepted
it. After all, my dear old mother has more sense than any of you. I felt
like her when I saw this place – felt that I must have it – that never, never,

never could I let it go; only she thought it was the houses and the kitchen ranges and the linen and china, when it was really all the human souls to be saved: not weak souls in starved bodies, sobbing with gratitude for a scrap of bread and treacle, but fullfed, quarrelsome, snobbish, uppish creatures, all standing on their little rights and dignities, and thinking that my father ought to be greatly obliged to them for making so much money for him – and so he ought. That is where salvation is really wanted. My father shall never throw it in my teeth again that my converts were bribed with bread. [*She is transfigured*]. I have got rid of the bribe of bread. I have got rid of the bribe of heaven. Let God's work be done for its own sake: the work he had to create us to do because it cannot be done except by living men and women. When I die, let him be in my debt, not I in his; and let me forgive him as becomes a woman of my rank.

CUSINS. Then the way of life lies through the factory of death?

BARBARA. Yes, through the raising of hell to heaven and of man to God, through the unveiling of an eternal light in the Valley of The Shadow. [*Seizing him with both hands*]. Oh, did you think my courage would never come back? did you believe that I was a deserter? that I, who have stood in the streets, and taken my people to my heart, and talked of the holiest and greatest things with them, could ever turn back and chatter foolishly to fashionable people about nothing in a drawing room? Never, never, never, never: Major Barbara will die with the colors. Oh! and I have my dear little Dolly boy still; and he has found me my place and my work. Glory Hallelujah! [*She kisses him*].

CUSINS. My dearest: consider my delicate health. I cannot stand as much happiness as you can.

BARBARA. Yes: it is not easy work being in love with me, is it? But it's good for you. [*She runs to the shed, and calls, childlike*]. Mamma! Mamma! [*Bilton comes out of the shed, followed by Undershaft*]. I want Mamma.

UNDERSHAFT. She is taking off her list slippers, dear. [*He passes on to Cusins*]. Well? What does she say?

CUSINS. She has gone right up into the skies.

LADY BRITOMART [*coming from the shed and stopping on the steps, obstructing Sarah, who follows with Lomax. Barbara clutches like a baby at her mother's skirt*]. Barbara: when will you learn to be independent and to act and think for yourself? I know as well as possible what that cry of 'Mamma, Mamma,' means. Always running to me!

SARAH [*touching Lady Britomart's ribs with her finger tips and imitating a bicycle horn*]. Pip! pip!

LADY BRITOMART [*highly indignant*]. How dare you say Pip! pip! to me, Sarah? You are both very naughty children. What do you want, Barbara?

BARBARA. I want a house in the village to live in with Dolly. [*Dragging at the skirt*]. Come and tell me which one to take.

UNDERSHAFT [*to Cusins*]. Six o'clock tomorrow morning, Euripides.

THE END

# Shaw, Major Barbara

## The Generation Gap

### GENERAL CONSIDERATIONS

1. In viewing *Major Barbara* as in part a play about the conflict between *parents and children* in the family, consider that directly or indirectly questions are being raised about
   a. the respective roles of mother, father, and child in the family.
   b. the need of the child for a father who *represents* meaningful values and the need of the father for a child who can *transmit* them.
   c. the rebellion of children against parents.
   d. the rebellion of parents against their conventional responsibilities in marriage.
   e. the assertion of parental authority over the child.
   Try to answer the following questions:
   a. Aside from the unorthodox situation, does the division of parental roles here represent a characteristic family pattern? Support your view.
   b. With regard to Stephen and Barbara, what questions are being raised about a child's right to take part in decisions affecting him generally (family welfare) and specifically (his education, profession, and marriage)?
   c. What factors lead to Barbara's search for a *substitute* (superhuman) father and Undershaft's search for a *substitute* (illegitimate) child?
   d. What features in the behavior of Barbara and Stephen are generally characteristic of the rebellion of children against parents? Why are the connotations attached to Undershaft's abrogation of his parental responsibility (especially to his son) *not* negative?
   e. How characteristic of any assertion of parental authority is the need for the *conversion* of the child and the *destruction* of certain of his values exemplified in this play? How characteristic of children's reactions is the desire for a genuine *confrontation* of values and a possible conversion of the parent (here seen in Barbara)?

2. In viewing *Major Barbara* as in part a play about the conflict between *youth and age*, consider how the contrasting attributes so often associated with each state (for example, altruism vs. selfishness, intransigence vs. capacity to compromise, naïveté vs. cynicism) are exemplified in the play, especially in the confrontations between Undershaft and Cusins in Act II and Undershaft, Cusins, and Barbara in Act III. Consider also whether *Major Barbara* is in fact a play about *growing up* and the renunciations it involves.

### QUESTIONS

1. What initial behavior and attitudes of Lady Britomart make her seem the traditional authoritarian parent? How does she soon manage to contradict that assumption? Why are these contradictions often comic, as in "I have always made you my companions and friends, and allowed you perfect freedom to do and say whatever you liked, so long as you liked what I could approve"?

Consider her relation to *two* views of parental authority—the traditional and the modern one.

2. Not only does Lady Britomart aim at being more than the traditional parent but she often succeeds. What dimensions of character and feeling displayed in Act I make her seem a worthy opponent of Andrew Undershaft?

   *Clues:* • LADY BRITOMART. . . . I know your quiet, simple, refined, poetic people like Adolphus: quite content with the best of everything! They cost more than your extravagant people, who are always as mean as they are second rate. No: Barbara will need at least 2000 a year.

   • LADY BRITOMART. . . . he wanted to disinherit you for another foundling. That was what I couldnt stand.
   STEPHEN [*ashamed*]. Do you mean for — for — for —
   LADY BRITOMART. Dont stammer, Stephen. Speak distinctly.

   • LADY BRITOMART. . . . So you see it is not a question of taking money from him or not: it is simply a question of how much. I dont want any more for myself.

   • LADY BRITOMART. . . . And remember this, Adolphus . . . I have a very strong suspicion that you went to the Salvation Army to worship Barbara and nothing else. . . . I have found you out. Take care Barbara doesnt. Thats all.

3. How is the complex character of Lady Britomart sustained in the last act? Note her reactions to Stephen's betrayal, to Undershaft's achievements at Perivale St. Andrews, and to the choices made by Cusins and Barbara.

4. How do Stephen's values and his reactions to his parents challenge standard assumptions about the generation gap? Consider that in part a *reversal* of generational roles is involved. Why is the confrontation between Stephen and his father at the beginning of Act III appropriately placed between Barbara's lesson of discovery at the end of Act II and Cusins' in the second part of Act III? Consider the following:

   (a) What effect do Stephen's oversimplifications about moral problems and his self-satisfaction have on Undershaft? How do you account for Undershaft's disinclination to *teach* Stephen (a task already undertaken with Barbara)? Is a reversal of roles a factor here? If so, how?

   (b) What significant qualities distinguish the instruction of Cusins and Barbara from the discussion with Stephen?

   (c) What connection do you find between Undershaft's rejection of Stephen and Stephen's rejection of Lady Britomart?

5. Lady Britomart comments on Undershaft in Act I: "Children did not dislike him; and he took advantage of it to put the wickedest ideas into their heads, and make them quite unmanageable." How does this comment anticipate Undershaft's behavior toward Barbara and Cusins? In what *double* sense could we read "wickedest" and "unmanageable"? Would (in addition to epithets Cusins applies to him) the term *Pied Piper* be appropriate for Undershaft? Explain.

6. What do the following aspects of Undershaft's behavior tell us about his nature, his values, his aims? Which of these make him an unconventional member of the older generation? Which a traditional one?

   a. He is initially summoned and willingly appears as a generous *giver of money*.

    b. He is easygoing with regard to Barbara's *manners* but ruthlessly challenges her *morals* (or ideals).

    c. He is fastidious in his choice of *students* (Sarah and Charles Lomax are like Stephen unworthy of his attention) but a dedicated *teacher* to the receptive.

    d. He acknowledges the scope and powers of Barbara's adoptive Father and yet proceeds relentlessly to suggest how limited their exercise on earth inevitably is. Is this behavior in part a reclaiming of *his* paternity with regard to Barbara? Is it an expression of skepticism about the *power of paternity* (considering his own illegitimacy and his separation from wife and children, whether spiritual or actual)?

7. In what ways is Barbara her mother's child? In what ways is she her father's? Might she be said to owe her integrity to both? What early signs are there of rebellion against both parents?

8. What elements make the brief confrontation between father and daughter in Act I realistic? How does the mutual challenge transcend realism? How much may confrontations between parents and children in general be said to be ritualistic challenges—the throwing down of gauntlets? Are *confrontations* often essentially efforts at mutual *conversion*?

9. What evidence is there that Barbara has entered the Salvation Army to find a father who will not only offer *guidance* but *power*? How does this dual aim make her extremely susceptible to the teachings of Undershaft in Acts II and III? Is such an aim characteristic of the younger generation? How could it lead to conflict with the older one?

# Protest and Revolution

## GENERAL CONSIDERATIONS

In viewing *Major Barbara* as in part a play concerned with *protest and revolution*, consider that directly or indirectly questions are being raised about the *viability* of (1) The institution of *capitalism*; (2) *Charitable* religious institutions; (3) The position of the *working class*; (4) The institutions of *government* (for instance, Parliament) and of political life itself; (5) Official *honors*; (6) A national prosperity based on *warfare*; (7) An economy in which *poverty* is a basic reality.

Try to answer the following questions:

1. What importance does Shaw want us to attach to Snobby Price's pronouncement, "inside of it [the law] I do as the capitalists do: pinch wot I can lay me ands on"? Are we asked to view capitalism merely as organized theft? Justify your answer.

2. Is the charitable organization here depicted to be viewed merely as a defuser of revolution for the benefit of the capitalist state? (Is Snobby Price justified in saying of the Salvation Army, "It combs our air and makes us good little blokes to be robbed and put upon"?) Is Undershaft's assertion that "All religious organizations exist by selling themselves to the rich" to be taken at face value?

3. How representative is the plight of Snobby Price and Shirley, whose jobs depend respectively on prosperity and youthfulness? What significance are we to see in Shirley's commitment to secularism and his admiration for Tom Paine?

4. What are the wider repercussions of Undershaft's ironic advice to Stephen to "Be off with you . . . and play with your caucuses and leading articles and

historic parties and great leaders and burning questions and the rest of your toys"?

5. How does the bestowing of official honors (here upon Bodger) suggest national dishonor?

6. What are the larger implications of Undershaft's comments on war, particularly to Lomax, "The more destructive war becomes the more fascinating we find it," and to Mrs. Baines, "I am never richer, never busier than when the papers are full of it. . . . Every convert you make is a vote against war. . . . Yet I give you this money to hasten my own commercial ruin"?

7. How encompassing a criticism of society is Undershaft's denunciation of poverty as "the worst of crimes" and of the poor as those who "poison us morally and physically"? How is life at Perivale St. Andrews the answer to this socioeconomic blight?

## Questions

1. Does Shaw present us in Undershaft with the portrait of a *revolutionist?* Consider whether the following paradoxes with regard to Undershaft's attitudes, aims, and actions can be resolved:

   a. Why does Undershaft seek to *undermine* his society and its corrupt institutions while deriving power and profit from the *permanence* of the evils he denounces?

   b. Why is Undershaft committed to *positive* values (the elimination of poverty, the maintenance of high standards for his workers) yet asserts the validity of such *negative* values as the amassing of wealth—*money*—and the use of force—*gunpowder?*

   c. Why does Undershaft feel he fulfills a higher will "of which I am a part" yet gives no indication of conventional *self-effacement* before a transcending power?

   d. Why is Undershaft convinced he can only transcend the petty aims of men by selling weapons *equally to all* yet indirectly encourages Cusins and Barbara to use arms for noble purposes—therefore discriminatingly?

   e. Why does Undershaft comment feelingly on the *brutality* of war (see above) yet take pride in the *refinement* of his armaments?

   f. Why does Undershaft, who is termed by Cusins "the Prince of Darkness," "Mephistopheles," "Machiavelli," choose as his successor the very man who sees him as the enemy of conventional goodness?

   g. Why does Undershaft, for whom the "love of the common people" holds "no romance," choose a successor whose main aim is "to give the common man weapons against the intellectual man"?

   h. Why has Undershaft, who attributes his success as a businessman to his use of profits for "experiments and researches in improved methods of destroying life and property," created the kind of welfare state Perivale St. Andrews obviously is: a state which must absorb a far larger amount of profits than his rivals expend on expiating their guilts, indeed should ruin him in short order?

2. Why did Shaw the *socialist* make his central character a *capitalist?* Why is Undershaft the *loather* of war a *munitions maker?* Why is the "confirmed mystic" a Millionaire by *conviction?* When only can one be a *bringer of light* by becoming the *Prince of Darkness?* Take into account the comparatively unsophisticated and

optimistic views of those whom Undershaft is trying to educate. What do these *ironies* tell us about the *symbolic* aspects of Undershaft?

3. In the light of the preceding question, how do you account for the fact that "Money and Gunpowder" are praised by Undershaft more for producing *intangible* benefits (freedom, dignity, self-respect) than *tangible* ones? What kinds of social and political action might the manufacture, accumulation, and employment of weapons *represent?*

   *Clues:* • UNDERSHAFT. . . . The fifth [Armorer] wrote PEACE SHALL NOT PREVAIL SAVE WITH A SWORD IN HER HAND. The sixth, my master, was the best of all. He wrote up NOTHING IS EVER DONE IN THIS WORLD UNTIL MEN ARE PREPARED TO KILL ONE ANOTHER IF IT IS NOT DONE. After that, there was nothing left for the seventh to say. So he wrote up, simply, UNASHAMED.

   • CUSINS. . . . The place is driven by the most rascally part of society, the money hunters, the pleasure hunters, the military promotion hunters; and he is their slave.

   UNDERSHAFT. Not necessarily. Remember the Armorer's Faith. . . . If you good people prefer preaching and shirking to buying my weapons and fighting the rascals, dont blame me. I can make cannons: I cannot make courage and conviction.

   • UNDERSHAFT. . . . I hate poverty and slavery worse than any other crimes whatsoever. And let me tell you this. Poverty and slavery have stood up for centuries to your sermons and leading articles: they will not stand up to my machine guns. Dont preach at them: dont reason with them. Kill them.

   • UNDERSHAFT. . . . Turn your oughts into shalls, man. Come and make explosives with me. Whatever can blow man up can blow society up. The history of the world is the history of those who had the courage to embrace this truth.

4. What connection does Shaw, through the image of the making and handling of explosives, establish between the *moral values* of a nation and its *political* and *social* life?

   *Clues:* • UNDERSHAFT. . . . You are all alike, you respectable people. You cant tell me the bursting strain of a ten-inch gun, which is a very simple matter; but you all think you can tell me the bursting strain of a man under temptation. You darent handle high explosive; but youre all ready to handle honesty and truth and justice and the whole duty of man, and kill one another at that game. What a country! What a world!

   • UNDERSHAFT. Come, come, my daughter! dont make too much of your little tinpot tragedy. What do we do here when we spend years of work and thought and thousands of pounds of solid cash on a new gun or an aerial battleship that turns out just a hairsbreadth wrong after all? Scrap it. . . . Well, you have made for yourself something that you call a morality or a religion or what not. It doesnt fit the facts. Well, scrap it. Scrap it and get one that does fit.

   • UNDERSHAFT. Plato says, my friend, that society cannot be saved until either the Professors of Greek take to making gunpowder, or else the makers of gunpowder become Professors of Greek.

# Escape from the World and Transcendence of Self

## General Considerations

In viewing *Major Barbara* as in part a play about *escape from the world* and *transcendence of self*, consider that directly and indirectly questions are raised about the respective merits of *worldly* concerns and *spiritual* strivings and the connections between them. At the heart of the play is the question of the *viability* of escape from the world as a mode of or prelude to transcendence.

## Questions

1. Certain significant similarities and differences between Barbara and Undershaft suggest the interconnection between the *worldly* and the *spiritual* in the universe and their ultimate reconciliation. In this regard consider the following questions:

    a. If both are eager to harness power—*material* power in Undershaft's case, *spiritual* power in Barbara's (Cusins too asserts that he has "tried to make spiritual power by teaching Greek")—if both are in the business of *conversion,* are buyers of souls, how is the intimate connection between the two kinds of power finally asserted in Act III? How does Barbara's final conception of conversion encompass Undershaft's?

    b. If both are involved in the *waging of warfare*—Undershaft as a munitions maker, Barbara as a member of the Salvation Army—how does Undershaft's challenge to Cusins (and indirectly to Barbara) to "wage war on war" and Cusins' acceptance of it in Act III represent a reconciliation between earthly and spiritual warfare?

    c. If both feel the need to serve a higher force—Barbara a heavenly Father, Undershaft a transcending will—and both believe that their work has a transfiguring effect (Undershaft says, commenting on "Blood and Fire," "My sort of blood cleanses: my sort of fire purifies"), what connection between the two processes of cleansing and transfiguration is ultimately suggested in Act III?

2. Many elements contribute to the precise nature of the lesson Barbara learns in Act I concerning the possibility of escaping from the world in the pursuit of transcendent experiences. Try to answer the following questions:

    a. What weaknesses in the Salvation Army, of which Barbara is early aware, anticipate the central flaw Undershaft will reveal to her (for instance, "I cant talk religion to a man with bodily hunger in his eyes")?

    b. Despite the above awareness, what confident assumption Barbara makes about salvation ("Bill offers twenty pieces of silver. All you need offer is the other ten") prepares us for her ironic defeat? What part does her attitude to Bodger play in that defeat?

    c. What significance should we attach to Barbara's seemingly contradictory behavior to Mrs. Baines in assuring the latter that she must take the money in order to save the Salvation Army and yet asserting soon after that "I cant pray now. Perhaps I shall never pray again"? What does Barbara's reaction to Bill's taunts with regard to Snobby Price's theft tell us about her capacity to learn from experience?

3. What is the nature of the lesson Cusins is taught by Undershaft in Act II with

regard to the viability of the Salvation Army and of a moral life transcending worldly concerns?

*Clues:* • CUSINS. I dont think you quite know what the Army does for the poor.

UNDERSHAFT. Oh yes I do. It draws their teeth: that is enough for me as a man of business.

• CUSINS. Excuse me: is there any place in your religion for honor, justice, truth, love, mercy, and so forth?

UNDERSHAFT. Yes: they are the graces and luxuries of a rich, strong, and safe life.

4. Why is it particularly appropriate that in Act III Barbara should express her experience of disillusionment in terms of the relation between the *self* and *power*? (She has moved from being "in my own power" to being "in the power of God" when she was in the Salvation Army to being shown that she "was in the power of Bodger and Undershaft.") How does this realization that the purchase of the Salvation Army has negated her experience of *transcendence* and asserted her *bondage* to earthly institutions and values prepare for us her ultimate choice? Will that choice produce a new relationship between her self and power? Does this new relationship involve a different kind of fulfillment?

*Clue:* • UNDERSHAFT. From the moment when you become Andrew Undershaft, you will never do as you please again. Dont come here lusting for power, young man.

CUSINS. If power were my aim I should not come here for it. You have no power.

UNDERSHAFT. None of my own, certainly.

CUSINS. I have more power than you, more will. You do not drive this place: it drives you. And what drives this place?

UNDERSHAFT [*enigmatically*]. A will of which I am a part.

BARBARA [*startled*]. Father! Do you know what you are saying; or are you laying a snare for my soul?

5. In Barbara's discussion with Undershaft concerning the merits of Perivale St. Andrews, why does Undershaft assert that he performs the function of saving the workers' *souls* "just as I saved yours"? Why does he continue to use the terminology of *spiritual* salvation for *physical* sustenance? of spiritual transgression for physical weaknesses and obstacles and social failings ("the seven deadly sins" of "food, clothing, firing, rent, taxes, respectability and children")? How does the following statement by Undershaft prepare us for Barbara's mission? "Nothing can lift those seven millstones from Man's neck but money; and the spirit cannot soar until the mill stones are lifted." How does Barbara's reaction to her mother in the following interchange also move us toward her final resolve?

BARBARA [*shaking her head*]. It's no use running away from wicked people, mamma.

LADY BRITOMART. It is every use. It shews your disapprobation of them.

BARBARA. It does not save them.

6. Can we fully reconcile Barbara's continuing desire to escape from the world of men ("if only I could get away from you and from father and from it all! if I could have the wings of a dove and fly away to heaven!") and her conviction that "Turning our backs on Bodger and Undershaft is turning our backs on life"?

What kind of a compromise does the work she is planning to do—saving the souls of her father's workmen—represent? Does her statement of a renewed commitment to her work represent an evolution of her striving toward transcendence? an alteration in her conception of divine power?

> BARBARA. . . . I have got rid of the bribe of bread. I have got rid of the bribe of heaven. Let God's work be done for its own sake: the work he had to create us to do because it cannot be done except by living men and women. When I die, let him be in my debt, not I in his; and let me forgive him as becomes a woman of my rank.